mce 0033

$40.00

D0140646

THREE SOUTH ETRURIAN CHURCHES:
SANTA CORNELIA, SANTA RUFINA AND SAN LIBERATO

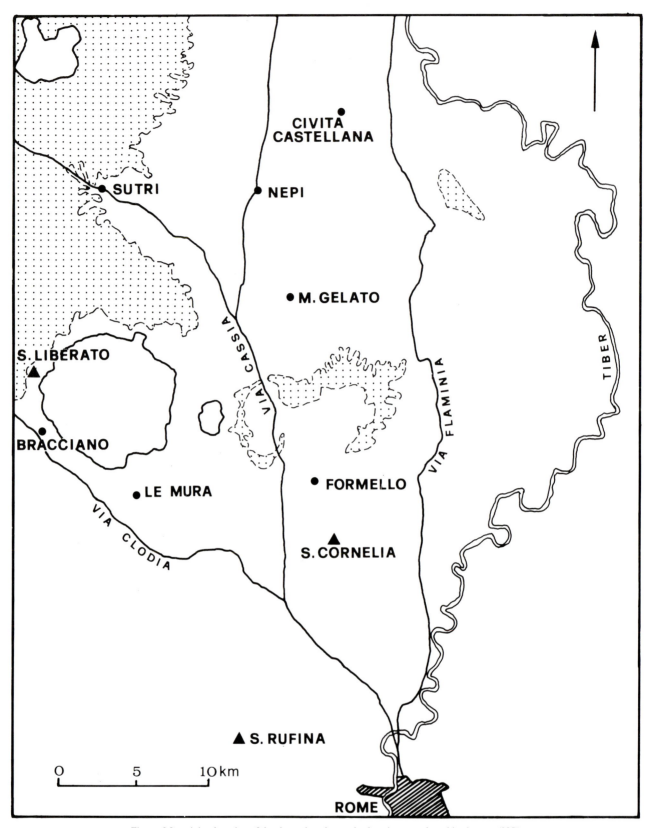

Fig. 1. Map giving location of the three churches and other sites mentioned in the text (NC)

THREE SOUTH ETRURIAN CHURCHES: SANTA CORNELIA, SANTA RUFINA AND SAN LIBERATO

EDITED BY

NEIL CHRISTIE

ARCHAEOLOGICAL MONOGRAPHS OF THE
BRITISH SCHOOL AT ROME
No. 4

BRITISH SCHOOL AT ROME, LONDON
1991

© The British School at Rome, Regent's College, Inner Circle, Regent's Park, London NW1 4NS

ISBN 0 904152 17 0

Cover illustration: Axonometric reconstruction of the second church and monastery at Santa Cornelia, *c.*1050.
(Drawn by Sheila Gibson)

Typeset by Method Limited, Epping, Essex
Printed by Whitstable Litho, Kent

Cover design: Three's Company, The Old School Hall, Perrin St., Headington, Oxford

Contents

Preface and Acknowledgements

The excavation and investigation of the three sites studied in this volume were integral elements in the detailed archaeological survey of the region of south Etruria carried out by the British School at Rome between 1950 and 1975. The survey sought to identify and classify sites of all periods, to collate surface evidence and, through selected excavations, to provide a dated sequence of pottery types. A huge body of data emerged. The results of the survey have been largely published and synthesized. These allowed a digestible, comprehensive overview of human settlement patterns and exploitation in a distinct, fertile region in close proximity to Rome, and in one go wholly altered earlier conceptions regarding the processes of settlement change. Yet while the basic pattern of settlement for the Etruscan, Roman and medieval periods became relatively clear, elements for understanding the period c. 500–1000 remained largely elusive.

The excavations at Santa Cornelia, Santa Rufina and certain medieval hilltop sites like Mazzano Romano and Castel Porciano were aimed at elucidating this gap between Roman and medieval and at giving a first material grasp of early medieval human activity in the Italian countryside. At Santa Cornelia, in fact, this result was somewhat accidental: its open location amongst the traces of a number of Roman sites, its apparent wealth of Roman architectural and decorative elements, and its basic outline, were intially thought to represent a luxurious villa. Closer analysis of the surface finds and a rapid identification of the site with a documented medieval monastic seat soon led to the realization that this instead represented an open early medieval and medieval site incorporating abundant Roman elements.

This volume offers detailed reports on the excavations at Santa Cornelia and Santa Rufina, and on the structural survey at San Liberato. Santa Cornelia was the most fully investigated of the three churches and therefore provides the focus of the volume as a whole. Excavations at Santa Rufina were less comprehensive but no less significant, providing a similar mixture of Roman and early medieval, and likewise supported by good documentation. San Liberato, by contrast, was an instance of architectural archaeology, whereby analysis of the fabric of a standing church provides a fascinating insight into church evolution, and helps flesh out the bare bones of the structures examined at Santa Cornelia and Santa Rufina.

Each of these studies was carried out in the 1960s; the preparation of their reports for publication has had a protracted history. The wait has been long but, I hope, worthwhile. I must thank all the various contributors for their patience and perseverance. In particular I extend my thanks to Prof. Graeme Barker, who first encouraged me to take on the task of writing up Santa Cornelia and then editing the volume as a whole, and to Dr Richard Hodges (present director of the British School at Rome), Dr John Lloyd (present editor of the *Papers of the British School at Rome*), and Dr Gillian Clark for helping see the volume through its last stages. Nicholas Purcell, former editor of the *Papers of the British School at Rome*, has been of great assistance throughout.

Neil Christie (Rome, 1990)

List of Figures

The following abbreviations have been used to indicate the draughtsperson: SC (Sally Cann); NC (Neil Christie); SG (Sheila Gibson); AH (Andrew Hanasz); SM (Sally Martin); VW (Vanessa Wills).

List of Plates

All plates are British School at Rome unless otherwise stated.

PART I

Santa Cornelia
The excavation of an early medieval
papal estate and a medieval monastery

by
Neil Christie and Charles Daniels

with contributions by
Dorothy Charlesworth, Amanda Claridge, Janet DeLaine, Valerie Higgins, Lidia Paroli,
Helen Patterson, Phil Perkins, Joyce Reynolds and Lucia Travaini

INTRODUCTION

The site of Santa Cornelia (863583) lies two long kilometres to the south of Monte Aguzzo, in the rolling countryside of the Roman *Ager Veientanus*, that is within the comune of Formello, some seventeen kilometres north-north-west of Rome and approximately four kilometres south-south-west of Formello itself (Fig. 1). It occupies a low, rounded ridge-top *c.* 200 m south of the two kilometre stone on the modern Via di Santa Cornelia, overlooking the confluence of two small tributaries of the Fosso di Pantanicci. A kilometre and a half to the east-south-east lies the Casale di Santa Cornelia, where a number of inscribed and sculptured stones have been collected from casual robbing of the site, and half that distance away, in the same general direction, is the Casale Muracciole, whose name probably once referred to the site's ruins. The conventional name of the site, Santa Cornelia, is that of the nearest *casale*.

In the days of the south Etruria survey and during the excavation, the site lay in what was still comparatively unspoiled countryside. Today, the whole area has been transformed by modern road-building and housing development: a rural residence abuts the site on the east and the modern Via Cassia autostrada, linking Rome and Viterbo, passes only a short distance to the south. However, the slight eminence on which the ruins lie is still locally called *Poggio della Chiesa* ('church mound').

The territory to the north of the Via di Santa Cornelia had already been sherded in the course of the south Etruria survey, and was known to be rich in

Plate 1. Santa Cornelia: view across church after identification in survey

the remains of Roman villas when, in the spring of 1960, it was reported that deep ploughing had turned up what on inspection proved to be the bases of a church colonnade, together with other major architectural elements and medieval pottery (Pl. 1). The site of this discovery, in a vicinity still bearing the name Santa Cornelia, was identified by John Ward-Perkins, then director of the British School at Rome, with two documentary references. The later of these recorded a *monasterium sancti Cornelii in Capracorio*, which was founded between 1026 and 1035 and was certainly in ruins by the sixteenth-seventeenth century, by which time the replacement toponym Santa Cornelia had emerged. The other reference, however, dating two and a half centuries earlier, referred to a papal estate founded by Pope Hadrian I in *c.* 776, at a site fifteen miles from Rome. The clue here lay in the monastery's designation '*in Capracorio*', which can be linked with the eighth century site's title *domusculta Capracorum* (cf. Chapter 1, below).

Once the true nature of the site had been realized, it was clear that this chance discovery presented a totally unexpected opportunity for the detailed examination of a well-documented early medieval papal estate centre which had later been replaced by an eleventh to fourteenth century rural monastery. Furthermore, as these successive buildings lay within an area which in antiquity had featured many Roman villas, some luxurious and some clearly surviving into the fourth and fifth centuries, there also existed the possibility of establishing direct continuity between villa structure and *domusculta* and the potential of establishing a vital ceramic bridge between the two periods.

As will be seen, unfortunately some of these hopes were not realized or were realized only in part, as deep ploughing had destroyed a large amount of the site's stratigraphy. At the same time the site's very nature, a religious complex, meant that only a limited number of artifacts, other than classical spoil, were found; for instance, just five small coins were recovered, and only two of these were stratified.

A trial excavation was organized to test how much of the actual structure had survived the ploughing. Permission to dig was granted by the *Soprintendenza Archeologica dell'Etruria Meridionale*, who gave continual support during the operation; in particular thanks are due to Professors R. Bartoccini and Mario Moretti and Dr Alfredo de Agostino, and members of their staff. The trial work was carried out in October 1960 under the supervision of Mr (now Professor) Barri Jones, when trenches I-III were dug, primarily to take a north–south section across the church, but also to pick up the perimeter wall and look at the campanile. It was then decided to embark upon a full-scale research excavation and Charles Daniels was invited to be field director of the project. The excavation comprised five seasons' work between

Plate 2. Santa Cornelia: helicopter view of excavations from south, 1964 (*Centro Elicotteri Rolei*)

1961 and 1964, for the most part carried out over periods from six to twelve weeks in the spring, but with the addition that in 1962 a second spell of work was undertaken in September.

All surviving structures which could be located within the area of the perimeter wall were excavated, down to the bedrock tufa (no detailed search was attempted outside the perimeter wall). The first two seasons were concerned principally with the church buildings (sectors A, B, D-S) and part of the south-east corner complex (area W) (cf. Fig. 2). In 1963 sector W was completed and the area east of the church was examined (sectors P and X). In the final season attention was turned to the monastic complex south of the church (sectors T, U, Y, Z), and trenching was completed in area X (Pl. 2). As it was clear that the plough had removed almost all trace of everything in the central and south-west areas, the decision was taken to leave them (cf. sector T); also parts of the area east of the church porch were left, as little survived in position there.

The basic labour force consisted of a team of *operai* from Formello, under the leadership of Signor Antonio Fantini of Isola Farnese, the British School at Rome's foreman excavator. They were assisted by a large number of volunteers from the British School at Rome and the expatriate community in Rome, amongst whom Mrs Betty Eastwood, Mrs Margaret

Ward-Perkins, Signorina Luciana Valentini, Tony Birley, George Finlayson, Joanna Close-Brooks, Gilly Jones, Claire Kahane and Miriam Medd (as they then were) are especially to be thanked. A particular debt of gratitude is due to Mrs Anne Kahane for her continual assistance in the excavation, in the transport of volunteers, and in many other ways. Site planning was carried out in the first season by Mr Alistair Merry, and subsequently by Miss Vanessa Wills (Mrs P. Winchester). Advice and assistance were given by Mr Michael Ballance, sometime Assistant Director of the School, and much was learned in discussion with Dr G.U.S. Corbett. Many other people could be mentioned individually, but it is hoped that a communal thank-you to them all will suffice: none who took part in the excavation will forget the violence of the Easter storms, the juke-box and bar at Prima Porta and those late spring days digging in a countryside of cypresses and pines, young corn and Etrurian poppies.

After the completion of the excavation, differences of opinion between Charles Daniels and John Ward-Perkins, difficulties in processing the material from the site (especially the marble fragments), and contemporary ignorance of the pottery chronology all combined to prevent an early publication. Short interims did appear but of a very abbreviated character ('St. Adrian's estate at Capracorum',

Illustrated London News, 1961, Archaeological section n.2069, 622-623; Ward-Perkins 1962, 1963, 1964, 1965, 1966), and by people who had not taken part in the excavation (Potter 1979a and Whitehouse 1980a). These temporarily filled a gap by providing summaries of the site sequence and its principal characteristics, but each concerned itself primarily with the eighth century *domusculta* complex (reflecting the focus of interest at that time, as during the excavation – cf. for instance, Llewellyn 1971). There things rested, in spite of attempts to revive interest in the site, until 1986 when Graeme Barker, then director of the British School, approached Charles Daniels with the offer of School assistance in the production of a comprehensive report. In response Daniels spent a total of three spells at the School reassembling the excavation records and producing the basic structural and stratigraphic sequence for the site. It was also agreed that Neil Christie, who was at the time a Rome Scholar, would spend a further year at the School to write the excavation report. This he did, and continued to work on it while holding a Sir James Knott Fellowship at Newcastle University.

Since the completion of the south Etruria survey and the publication of its main findings, one of the results has been a relative boom in early medieval archaeology in Italy, making it a particularly fashionable field of enquiry. This has made the publication of Santa Cornelia even more significant as there is now a far greater body of data in which to insert the excavation results. The site remains unique, however, in that no other contemporary *domusculta* has been archaeologically studied to anything like the same degree; therefore, Santa Cornelia offers the only (almost) complete site plan. Likewise, so very little is still known about the workings of rural monasteries in medieval Italy that the compact establishment which replaced the papal estate centre presents a fascinating challenge for wider research. The long delay in publication is regretted; but it is only honest to state that had this report appeared in the 1960s the

monastery would have received scant treatment by contrast with the *domusculta*, and the pottery and other reports would have been sparse at best.

Any piece of scholarly research carried out during the post-War decades owes an enormous debt to the late John Ward-Perkins, so long the School's director. Like much else, the Santa Cornelia excavation grew out of the south Etruria survey. The appreciation of the importance of the site of Santa Cornelia and the raising of funds to enable its excavation to be undertaken, were very typical of John Ward-Perkins, and to him must go the full credit for both. Unfortunately, it has not proved possible to recover the record of which institutions so generously contributed funds to the excavation. In the absence of this information it is hoped that a sincere and most grateful thank-you to them all will be acceptable in place of individual naming.

In the preparation of this report, first and foremost we gratefully acknowledge the support of the British School at Rome, extending to all the academic, library and other staff, but particularly we wish to thank Professor Graeme Barker, the previous director, for his fundamental help and support. The various contributors to the report are also warmly thanked, especially Sheila Gibson, whose line drawings and architectural know-how greatly illuminated the conclusions. Thanks also go to the staff of the *Museo dell'Alto Medioevo*, where the bulk of the excavated material is now stored and where there is a permanent exhibition of certain of its sculptural and ceramic elements; Dott.ssa Lidia Paroli has greatly aided us throughout our studies. Many others, including Dr Tim Potter of the British Museum and Dr David Whitehouse of the Corning Museum of Glass, have been of very great assistance. Errors and omissions no doubt remain, but hopefully they are few.

Charles Daniels
Neil Christie

CHAPTER ONE. HISTORICAL INTRODUCTION

THE *DOMUSCULTA CAPRACORUM*

In what is most probably a contemporary account, the *Liber Pontificalis* records the foundation by Pope Hadrian I (772-795) of the *domusculta* of *Capracorum* at a site fifteen miles from Rome in the territory of ancient Veii. The *domusculta* was composed of the farm (*fundus*) of *Capracorum* and a series of additional farms (*aliis plurimis fundis ei coherentibus*) which he had inherited from his kin (*ex hereditaria parentum suorum*) and to which he added various other farmsteads (*alios plures fundos seu casales et massas*); these additional properties were bought from neighbouring land-owners 'at a fair price' (*iusta reconpensatione*) [1]. According to the *Liber Pontificalis* the *domusculta* was designed to help alleviate the growing food problem at Rome by providing enough food to feed one hundred poor people every day from the steps of the Lateran palace, whereby each was given a portion of bread, wine and relish out of a daily overall ration of fifty 2lb bread loaves, two 60lb *decimatas* of wine, and a cauldron of relish. The produce grown on the lands of the *domusculta*, consisting of wheat, barley, vegetables, wine and also one hundred pigs per year, was kept for distribution in the papal storehouses (*horrea, paracellarium*) in Rome [2].

Not long after the foundation of the *domusculta* in *c.* 774-776, Pope Hadrian invited the whole of the Roman clergy and 'senate' (*cuncto clero suo senatuique Romano*) to attend the dedication of a church at *Capracorum*. This church, which Hadrian dedicated to Saint Peter, prince of the Apostles (*beato Petro apostolorum principi nutritori*), was decorated lavishly (*speciose*) and endowed not only with a rich array of relics, but also with the bodies of four previous popes, namely Saint Cornelius (251-253), Saint Lucius I (253-254), Saint Felix I (269-274) and Saint Innocent I (401-417) [3].

The *Liber Pontificalis* further records that Hadrian I founded another five *domuscultae* in the proximity of the city of Rome [4]. In this Hadrian was following the policy of Pope Zacharias I (741-752), who had created five such estates, extending from a location fourteen miles north of Rome to Anzio, and perhaps even Gaeta, in the south [5].

The function of these *domuscultae* has been much debated [6]. Ostensibly they were designed to help feed Rome's poor and to farm lands around Rome more efficiently: in the case of Zacharias' foundations the *domuscultae* have been seen as an attempt to counter the economic losses caused by the confiscation of all the papacy's holdings in southern Italy and Sicily by the emperor Leo in *c.* 730 [7].

As Wickham has shown, however, there is no need to see these papal estates as agricultural foundations in expanses of unoccupied land: the account in the *Liber Pontificalis* makes it clear that *Capracorum* was composed of existing farms, both inherited and bought; the only new construction recorded is in fact the church. Nor can we argue that those additional farms bought by Hadrian were unoccupied or unused units: Hadrian, as Zacharias before him, undoubtedly had to haggle about the purchase price before the owners accepted a just compensation (*digna* or *iusta reconpensatione*); in one instance Pope Hadrian even traded the office of deputy clerk (*secundicerius*) in order to obtain a certain area of land for the *domusculta* of San Leuco [8]. That some owners preferred not to sell may be shown in the fact that much of the territory owned by or linked to a certain *domusculta* was not contiguous. At the same time force may have been exerted to obtain desired properties: when in 816 several newly-founded *domuscultae* were attacked and burnt down, the main grievance voiced 'by the Romans' was that their lands 'had been taken from them contrary to the law' [9].

While we cannot therefore claim that the *domuscultae* marked a notable resettlement campaign [10], it is more difficult to argue against the idea that the *domuscultae* formed a more reliable network of farming units around Rome – or at least a more efficient system of farming of the papal lands. The task of feeding Rome's poor, long having become a customary burden upon the papal authorities, was undoubtedly made harder by the loss of the church's possessions in the south in *c.* 730. In addition, Longobard encroachments upon the Duchy of Rome, in particular under King Liutprand (712-744) who captured the *territorium* of Sutri (728-729) and in 738-739 the *castra* of Amelia, Orte, Bomarzo and Bieda (these restored to Rome in 741), consistently restricted the area that the popes could call upon. At the same time, in the countryside of the Duchy itself the popes faced the threat of semi-independent military commanders, the commanders of the Duchy's fortresses.

The origin of these military strongmen has recently been clarified by Brown, who has shown that the maintenance of an almost permanent war-footing in most of the reduced imperial provinces of Italy after 568 (this of course subsequent to the devastations suffered in the Gothic War of 535-553) naturally brought to the fore the military administration, to the detriment of the civilian authorities, whose roles were progressively absorbed by the leading military officials. The military, receiving fairly regular pay, was one of the few groups which was able to purchase land on the open market, in particular from the church, which had amassed vast amounts of property. Although some 'senior officers could exploit their political authority to obtain land by corruption, extortion and expropriation', most land was in fact 'purchased or rented by soldiers through legitimate transactions, a process understandable in the conditions of the period' [11]. As such, the emerging military aristocracy was at times able to accumulate substantial landed wealth, thus giving an even greater extension to their control in areas in which they resided or were stationed. In the eighth century, the decentralization of military power and the breakdown of the official military hierarchy saw the rise of a series of local military commanders who were able to exploit to the full their accumulated resources – personal followings, economic wealth and control of local communities. Militarization and insecurity had also combined to provoke in many rural areas a concentration of settlement on fortified or defensive sites, a process which itself greatly strengthened the power of the 'local strongmen'. The cumulative effect of this is witnessed in the coup of 768 when Duke Toto of Nepi, supported by Gracilis, the tribune of Alatri, gathered both troops and farmers (*rustici*), and entered Rome to install Toto's brother Constantine as anti-pope. Through force Toto was in fact able to maintain his position for more than a year [12].

It was against this background that the *domuscultae* were founded. To stem this breakdown in control and to counter the threatening breakup of the territorial and political organization of the Rome Duchy, the papacy sought to re-establish domination in the countryside through the amalgamation of sizeable farms into coherent papal-run estates, thus going against earlier 'large scale leases to the Roman aristocracy of papal lands' [13]. These estates were built up from units already belonging to the pope or bequeathed to the church, and then extended through purchase of additional farms or lands. The frequency of the use of the phrase '*iusta reconpensatione . . . emere*' in the *Liber Pontificalis* probably covers the fact that some property owners were unwillingly bought out. As noted above, the attack of 816 may indicate that Leo III had overstepped himself in ousting farmers in order to create new *domuscultae* [14].

The actual extent of the lands of the *domuscultae* has been much disputed. Since Tomassetti, it has always been claimed that these properties comprised wide expanses of territory – in the case of *Capracorum* an area of 8-9 × 24 km [15]. As Wickham has clearly shown, however, the data given in the *Liber Pontificalis* itself would suggest that the *domuscultae* were often made up of unconnected fragments of farms and lands, a pattern which indeed fits with what is known of landowning in the medieval Campagna. Likewise the combination of a series of farms (*fundi*) need not represent extensive properties, since the actual farm unit was relatively small in this period and in no way comparable to the large villas of the Roman imperial period [16].

Capracorum need be no exception to this picture.

Tomassetti misleadingly cited numerous farms and habitats as belonging to the *domusculta* on the basis of the erroneous assumption that the *domusculta* owned all the land between Santa Cornelia itself and the site of *castrum Capracorum*, the present Mola di Monte Gelato, recorded in documents of the eleventh and twelfth century at a distance twenty-seven miles from Rome [17]. While we should not reject the hypothesis that Monte Gelato at one time formed a part of the property of the *domusculta* – hence the adoption of the estate centre's name – there is no evidence whatsoever to show an unbroken block of land between the two sites [18]. Certainly eleventh and twelfth century documents show that sites such as nearby Formello were independent of, or rather lay outside, the territorial boundaries of the *domusculta Capracorum*. While it is possible that the medieval documentation post-dates the splintering and dispersal of the *domusculta*'s lands, the mid-eighth century inscription recording the gift of farms such as *Trea*, *Scrofanum*, *Agelli* and *Antiquum* to the church and *diaconia* (deaconry) of Santa Maria in Cosmedin, – 'a *diaconia* in its own right and so a separate institution from anything directly under the control of the popes' –, is contemporary 'proof that other proprietors owned in the area claimed for the *domusculta*' [19].

While we may assume that the *domusculta*'s properties were extensive, we are nowhere told of the physical relationship of these farms to the core of the estate. Accordingly we do not fully understand the mechanics of its organization: was the produce of each unit transported directly to Rome, or was it first accumulated in stores at *Capracorum*? How much co-ordination existed between the various parts of the whole, and how was each of the farms managed and organized? From the description given in the *Liber Pontificalis*, it seems clear that produce from the estate's lands was sent regularly to the papal storehouses in Rome. This regularity of supply 'is characteristic of any bi-partite (demesne/tenant) estate with rents in fixed quantities of produce' [20]. It is unnecessary to envisage preliminary storage at the estate centre if we assume that each farm had its own appointed manager who oversaw the business of collecting the stipulated quantities of grain or vegetables.

That the various tenant-farmers and other workers could be collectively organized for projects relating to the estate is not to be doubted. In 846, following the Arab assault of Rome and the sack of Saint Peter's, Pope Leo IV ordered the construction of a defensive wall around the Vatican (the Leonine Wall). As well as invoking the public duty of the citizens of Rome, the pope also called on the peasantry of the papal estates (the *massae publicae*) to help build the circuit wall: a surviving inscription here attests to the *militia* or work-crew of the estate of *Capracorum* which, under the supervisor (*corrector*) Agatho, built a tower and a stretch of wall. The *militia* of the otherwise unknown estate of *Saltasina* (perhaps one of Leo III's foundations) is mentioned in an additional inscription as building two towers and a length of wall [21]. Presumably such a work-crew was responsible for erecting Hadrian's church and other structures at *Capracorum* in *c.* 774-780.

The peasantry employed on the papal estates is elsewhere collectively termed *familia sancti Petri* as an indication of its loyal subjection to the church of Rome. Their mobilization as a work-force reveals the possibility that they could also be utilized in a military role to counter the threat of the lay aristocracy of Rome: this indeed was the case in 824 when Pope Paschal I used a part of the *familia* in his *coup d'état* against the chief clerk (*primicerius*) Theodore and his son-in-law Leo [22]. The quasi-military potential of the papal labour force may in fact have prevented any repetition of Duke Toto of Nepi's *coup* during the strong rule of Hadrian I. However, it was unsuccessful, it seems, in 816 in preventing the Romans from burning down some of the *domuscultae* [23].

The detailed account offered by the *Liber Pontificalis* must reflect the political importance that Pope Hadrian I attached to his foundation of the *domusculta Capracorum*. His pontificate was one of relative peace and prosperity, with the threat of the Longobards finally dispersed, and a strong relationship formed with the Frankish kingdom. As a reflection of this prosperity, Hadrian actively restored, rebuilt and constructed many churches and monasteries inside and indeed outside Rome, and also repaired the aqueducts and the city walls. His institution of the *domuscultae*, on the model of those created by Zacharias, was a further sign of papal strength: the *domuscultae* were designed both to increase the food supply to Rome and simultaneously to re-establish papal control in church lands, thereby countering the growing landed power and wealth of the lay aristocracy [24]. *Capracorum* was thus a showpiece of papal propaganda. Founded under apostolic privilege and dedicated to feeding Rome's poor, the *domusculta* was composed of properties inherited, bequeathed or 'fairly bought'; the lavishly-decorated, new church was embellished with numerous relics and the bodies of no less than four pope-saints were translated there. Understandably, therefore, did Hadrian invite not just the whole Roman clergy but also the nobility to attend the dedication of his foundation.

In 846 the *domusculta Capracorum* clearly remained one of a number of active papal estates, still available to give labour service. Subsequent documentation relating to the *domusculta* is lacking. Immediately after the Arab assault on Rome the estate of *Galeria* was destroyed, along with the adjacent basilica of Santa Rufina; it is possible that many other sites were attacked at this same time [25]. Although repulsed, after *c.* 870 the Muslims were able to gain footholds in Campania, raiding Latium, the Sabine Hills, and southern Tuscany, and occupying the territories of Nepi, Sutri, Narni and Orte; in the 890s the basilica of *Silva Candida*, the seat of a cardinal-bishop and the site of an earlier *domusculta*, was plundered. Only by *c.* 900 was the Arab threat finally dispersed [26]. Normal agricultural activity around Rome will have been difficult in this period, and it is unlikely that the collective labour forces of any surviving *domuscultae* would have been strong enough to repel the Arab threat. Whilst one cannot claim that the countryside became deserted, it is probable that the *domusculta* network was seriously, if not fatally, disrupted by these events, as well as by the decay in papal power and the rise in aristocratic control [27].

THE MONASTERY OF SAINT CORNELIUS

Although it is likely that the estate as a whole did not survive and that its various components became dispersed into the hands of alternative landowners, when our documentation resumes in the early eleventh century it is clear that there was at least religious continuity on the site. In 1026 a papal bull confirmed to the bishop of *Silva Candida* a series of parish churches (*plebes*) and their subordinate churches (*tituli*): among these is listed the *plebem S. Cornelii in Capracozio* (or *Craporio*) with its lands, vineyards and olive groves (*terris, vineis et ulivetis*) and its eight *tituli* of San Pancrazio, Santa Maria, San Valentino, San Donato, Santa Maria, San Lorenzo, Sant'Anastasio in Cannetolo, and San Vito. Here the qualifying name *Capracozio* represents a survival of the official name of the earlier papal *domusculta*, while the church dedication should signify the local preference for the earliest of the martyr-popes deposited at *Capracorum* by Hadrian I, or else mark a simplification of the full dedication. We should remember, however, that Pope Paschal I re-translated the bodies or relics of Saint Lucius and Saint Felix back to Rome in 817, and it is possible that that of Innocent may also have been returned. The fact that all four saints are renamed in the monastery foundation charter of 1041 (see below) may be an indication of the continued presence of their relics in the church, unless it marks merely a revival of the original dedication. In general, however, subsequent dedications refer solely to Cornelius: the exceptions are in 1035 when we hear of the *monasterio sancti Cornelii et Petri apostoli*, and in 1159 when Cornelius is recorded along with Saint Ciprianus [28].

The appurtenance of the *plebs Sancti Cornelii* to the diocese of *Silva Candida* is not surprising: as Llewellyn has shown, after the basilica of Santa Rufina and Secunda was restored by Hadrian I, *Silva Candida* appears as one of the principal bishop seats and may well have played an important role in the administration of Hadrian's *domuscultae* [29]. The bishopric came to real prominence, however, from the mid-tenth century, with three of its bishops holding the office of *bibliothecarius* (in 939-944,

966-975 and 1012-1013), thus marking a period of close co-operation with the papacy, which was slowly regaining control of its own affairs. Bishop Peter (1023-1048), nephew to Pope John XIX (1024-1032) and cousin to Pope Benedict IX (1032-1048), consolidated this position, and in 1026 and 1037 major confirmations of the lands and rights of the bishopric were issued by the popes. Those churches listed, among them the parish church of Saint Cornelius, will have been under the direct ecclesiastical jurisdiction of *Silva Candida*. Later, in the early twelfth century, *Silva Candida* was amalgamated with the diocese of Porto, and subsequently, after 1119, 'cardinalitial authority north of the Tiber was centred on Porto alone' [30].

Between 1026 and 1035 the site and the church of Saint Cornelius appears to have been transformed into a monastery: in 1035 Abbot Leo of the *venerabili monasterio sancti Cornelii et Petri apostoli* received the donation of a house in the *castello* of Pietra Pertusa [31]. The foundation of the monastery was only formally documented, however, in 1041, when Abbot Leo '*de venerabili monasterio sanctorum Christi martirum Cornelii, Felis, Luci atque Innocentii*' received the donation of lands around the monastery from Stephanus, son of Leo *de Nomiculatorem*. As Wickham has pointed out, 'Such belated foundation-charters are not uncommon, however; we need not doubt Stephanus' ownership of the monastery; and he may well have controlled the *pieve* even in 1026, as the bulls are here only concerned with ecclesiastical jurisdiction' [32]. Quite probably, the project of construction of the monasterial buildings required much time, and the complex as a whole may only have been completed or have been suitably near-completed in 1041.

Despite the detailed boundary-clause, the physical outlines of this donation are obscure, and we can only state with certainty that part of Monte Aguzzo to the north of the site was included in the property. The monastery is later recorded as adjoining the *terra* of the *fundum* or *curtem de Macerano*, which itself is listed as '*positam ad Petram Pertusam*' [33]. Significantly, the foundation charter of 1041 shows that the major part of the land around the church had, since the breakup of the *domusculta*, fallen into the hands of the Roman noble families: the background of Stephanus, *nobilis vir*, son of Leo *de Nomiculatorem*, is unclear, but the owners of an adjoining property are recorded as heirs of Crescenzo. The Crescenzo family had held sway in Rome between *c.* 970 and 1012, in which time they had accumulated much former papal land. Stephanus, however, makes no claim to belong to the Crescenzi, nor indeed to the Tusculan dynasty, whose family effectively controlled Rome until *c.* 1046. Stephanus should rather be seen as a member of a wealthy Roman aristocratic family which perhaps had close ties with the Tusculani.

Although nowhere stated in the documentation, the monastery of Santa Cornelia should be viewed as Benedictine. Its foundation came in the wake of a great monastic revival in Rome, as indeed in most of Europe, in the tenth century, and by *c.* 1000 the vast majority of these establishments observed the Benedictine Rule [35]. Following Saint Odo's reform of the Rome monasteries in 936, many of these followed Cluniac observance. Certainly the monastery of Santa Maria di Farneta, into whose possession Santa Cornelia was later transferred, was Benedictine in its order [36].

Leo was still abbot of the monastery in 1050 when he received, in donation, nine-twelfths (*nobe uncie*) of the inheritance of a married couple from the nearby *castello* of Formello [37]. Formello formed the nearest township and probably provided many specialist services for the monastery. The fact that the monastery did not actually own the *castellum* should demonstrate the pre-existence of Formello as a nucleated centre before the establishment of Santa Cornelia, and argue against its growth as a satellite to the monastic house [38].

The monastery appears to have received only one subsequent direct donation, namely that of two-thirds of a vineyard in the Cesana area in 1221; otherwise we see it engaged in relatively small-scale transactions of variously distributed properties. For example, in 1062 Peter, who had succeeded Leo as abbot, made a permanent exchange of a vineyard for one held at *Gripanula* in the territory of Nepi to the north. A further transaction regarding a vineyard occurred in 1079 under Abbot Dominicus, with the stipulation that it be returned to the monastery at the buyer's death. Additional land in the Nepi zone was purchased in 1124 by Abbot Guido, and a further property gain near Cesana is recorded in 1160 [39]. All these instances demonstrate that Santa Cornelia accumulated a number of scattered, though not necessarily extensive, properties, particularly in the territories of Nepi and Cesana.

The ownership of the monastery between *c.* 1050 and 1150 is uncertain. In 1158, however, a bull of Hadrian IV confirmed it in the possession of one of the four monasteries of San Pietro in Vaticano; this apparently repeated an earlier papal confirmation. This was re-confirmed by Urban III in 1186 (recording the '*monasterium Sancti Cornelii quod est positum in territorio Vegetano cum omnibus suis pertinenciis*') [40]. In 1188, Santa Cornelia is recorded among the properties of the wealthy abbey of Santa Maria di Farneta in the province of Arezzo, then being placed under apostolic protection. The properties of this abbey were in fact extensive, covering the territories of Arezzo, Città di Castello, Perugia, Assisi, Chiusi and even Rome, where it held the monastery of *Sancti Cosmatis in Transtiberium*, and the churches of *Sancta Maria Abunde*, San Cesario all'Arenula, Sant'Andrea '*in strata*', Santa Maria *Insulae Pontis Venerii*, and San Salvatore in Onda [41].

Santa Maria di Farneta retained possession of the monastery of Saint Cornelius until 1238, at which

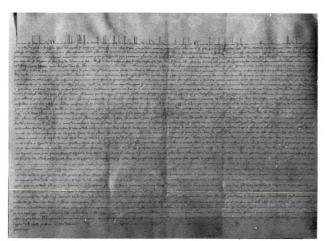

Plate 3. Santa Cornelia: bull of Innocent IV of 14 July 1248 (Christie, reproduced by kind permission of the *Archivio dello Stato*, Rome)

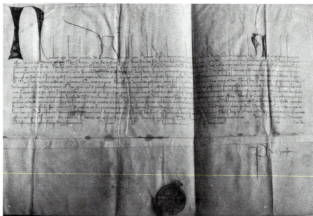

Plate 4. Santa Cornelia: charter of Nicholas V of 1448 (Christie, reproduced by kind permission of the *Archivio dello Stato*, Rome)

date it transferred rights over it to another of its former possessions, the *monasterio Sancti Cosme in Transtyberium* (the present San Cosimato or Santi Cosma e Damiano). In exchange San Cosimato gave the more closely sited monastery of San Crispolto at Bettona in the diocese of Assisi, a monastery described as 'spiritually badly-run' [42].

Documentation subsequent to this transfer is brief, limited to just four charters. In December of the same year two loans were repaid by Saint Cornelius. In 1247 Pope Innocent IV charged his vicar, the Cardinal Stefano, to maintain the monastery of Saint Cornelius [43] (Pl. 3). It is disputable whether the wording can be used to signify that the monastery had become run-down, but the possibility is strong. We receive our last reference to an active site in 1273, when Alberto, canon of San Pietro in Vaticano, was called upon to defend the monastery of San Cosimato and its possessions, among which is enumerated the church of Saint Cornelius in the diocese of Porto [44].

The thirteenth century was a time of great changes in the religious sphere, in response to new social conditions, prompted in particular by a flourishing of urban life. One of the most notable aspects of these changes was the growth of the various orders of preachers, at the expense of the monasteries. 'The Mendicant Orders broke free from one of the most basic principles of traditional monasticism by abandoning the seclusion and enclosure of the cloister in order to engage in an active pastoral mission to the society of their time'. They preached that salvation need not be attained through 'flight from the human hive or by attachment to the shirt-tails of a spiritual elite . . . all that was needed was that they should receive the Gospel' [45]. The appeal of this was enormous and it is apparent that these new orders, especially the friars, drained away some of the principal sources of recruits for the monasteries. As a result of this shrinkage in support, the ranks of most of the larger abbeys dwindled, and many lesser monasteries fell into irreversible decline. This general pattern appears closely reflected in the case of Saint

Cornelius. In 1247 the indications are of a somewhat run-down condition, while in 1273 the church alone, and not the monastery, is mentioned; it may be the case, therefore, that life still flickered in the church, but in the monastery itself this had been extinguished.

For how much longer Saint Cornelius remained a parish church is uncertain. Between 1271 and 1448 we find no reference to the site, though it is clear that it remained in the possession of the Clarisse (a female religious order) of Santi Cosma e Damiano. In 1448, however, Pope Nicholas V asked the bishop of Volterra to help, on behalf of the Clarisse, to sell the *Casali Sancto Cornelio* (Pl. 4). Two subsequent documents, both of 1449, record the actual sale of the property – an area of 194 *rubbia*, listed *in territorio Castri Formelli* – to Orsino degli Orsini, chancellor (*cancelliere*) of the Kingdom of Sicily, who was buying the land on behalf of the convent of Santa Maria Novella di Bracciano, a foundation of Augustinian monks. The land had clearly become somewhat unmanageable for the Clarisse of San Cosimato, who desired to sell the *casale* in order to purchase 'more convenient property within the city (Rome)' [46]. The fact that the site is referred to as *casale* (farmstead), and no longer as a parish church or mere church, must be significant.

The land remained in the hands of the Augustinian friars of Bracciano: we possess quite detailed maps of both 1637 and 1835 which show the division of the *casale* first into four main zones, and secondly into twelve sectors. In the 1835 plan, in fact, we have a detailed listing of the crops grown in each of the fields, with trees, in particular oak, dominant. Even the land on which the monastery had stood by now was under cultivation, since one entry notes: 'ploughed land with traces of the church of Santa Cornelia, banks and ditches with a spring, commonly known as Le Muraccie' (*Terra lavorativa con vestigie della Chiesa di S. Cornelio, e ripe de fossi sodive con fonte in vocabolo le Muraccie . . .*) [47].

Additional confirmation of the long-ruinous state of the church comes in 1647 when Nardini specifically relates: '*S. Cornelio chiesa diruta di quella campagna detta da molti corrottamente S. Cornelia; di cui e ancor in piedi gran parte delle mura, e del campanile*' (the ruined church of Saint Cornelius, in that place called by many, incorrectly, Santa Cornelia; there still remain standing most of the walls and of the campanile). Nardini further records the tradition that the head of Saint Cornelius was transferred to the church of San Lorenzo at Formello, presumably at the time the church of Saint Cornelius had fallen into ruins and been deconsecrated; to this we can add the local tradition of the removal to Formello of the bells of the monastery [48]. The abandoned church and monastery subsequently will have been stripped of their internal furnishings and used as a quarry for building material, hence their reduced state by 1647. The robbing was clearly such that the land on which they stood could eventually be extensively ploughed, adding further to the destruction of the former *domusculta Capracorum*.

NOTES

1. *Liber Pontificalis*, i, 501-502. See Appendix 1.
2. See note 1 above. The text is translated in Llewellyn 1971, 243-244, and Wickham 1978a, 174.
3. *Liber Pontificalis*, i, 506-507; see Appendix 1. Of the pope-saints, all but Innocent I were translated from the cemetery or catacombs of San Callisto; Innocent I had been buried along the *Via Portuensis*: Reekmans 1964; Llewellyn 1971, 244; Kelly 1986, 17-20, 23, 37-38.
4. *Liber Pontificalis*, i, 502, 505, 509: the *domuscultae* of *Galeria, alia Galeria, Calvisianus*, San Edisto, and San Leuco.
5. *Liber Pontificalis*, i, 434-435; Llewellyn 1971, 207.
6. On the *domuscultae* see Bertolini 1952; Jones 1965, 237-241; Gasbarri 1978; Wickham 1978a, 173-177; and more recently Marazzi 1985.
7. Cf. Llewellyn 1971, 168-169, 206-207; Bertolini 1952.
8. Wickham 1978a, 174-176; Llewellyn 1971, 244.
9. *Vita Hludowici Imperatoris, Monumenta Germaniae Historica, Scriptores* II, c. 25, 620: *Eadem etiam tempestate Romani, cum apostolicus Leo gravaretur adverso incommodo, praedia omnia, quae illi domocultas appellant, et novi ab eodem apostolico instituta erant, sed et ea quae sibi contra ius querebantur direpta, nullo iudice exspectato, diripere et sibi conati sunt restituere.*
10. Bertolini 1952, however, argued that the estates founded on the *Via Appia* were aimed at reviving the depopulated Maremma.
11. Brown 1984, 105. On military landholding, Brown 1984, 101-108, *contra* Hartmann 1889, 58; Schneider 1924, 15-37.
12. Duke Toto's *coup*: *Liber Pontificalis*, i, 468-472; Llewellyn 1971, 221-224; Brown 1984, 46-50, 217-218; Christie 1987, 463.
13. Wickham 1978a, 175.
14. Wickham 1978a, 175.
15. Tomassetti 1913, 109-112. Cf. Partner 1966, 68; Kahane *et al.* 1968, 163. *Contra*: Wickham 1978a, 174, as Luttrell 1976, 125 (note), who states that Tomassetti 'was prone to label wide ranges of places as being former *domusculta fundi*, on no evidence whatsoever'.
16. Wickham 1978a, 142-143 on the *fundus*; fragmentary nature of the *domusculta* property, 174-176, noting in

particular the scattered components of that of San Leuco, and Pope Hadrian's failure to include in this the adjoining *massa Acutiana*: *Liber Pontificalis*, i, 509.
17. See Tomassetti 1913, 111-112, followed in Potter 1979a, 166.
18. Monte Gelato: The *castrum Capracorum* is first recorded in 1053 '*cum terris, vineis . . . et molaria sua cum ecclesia sancti Iohannis que dicitur Latregia . . . positam territorio Vegetano miliario ab urbe Rome plus minus vicesimo septimo*': Schiaparelli 1901 number 18. This is confirmed in 1128 (noting *terris, fundis et casalibus suis*) but with the church of San Giovanni recorded as *diruta* (ruined): Schiaparelli 1902 number 47. This is repeated in papal bulls of 1186, 1205 and 1228: Schiaparelli 1902 number 70, *Collectionis bullarum sacro sanctae basilicae Vaticanae* I, 85 and 114. In 1211 the lands of the monastery of San Benedetto di Pentoma (Nepi) were ceded to San Paolo fuori le mura; these included the *fundus Linianus* which bordered up to '*ante portam castelli de Capracorio*': Margarini 1670, 234. A final reference occurs in an out-of-date entry in a census book of Saint Peters of 1535, noting a debt ('*tre libbre di cera lavorata*' (three pounds of processed wax)) by the ruined church of San Giovanni at *castrum Capracoro*: *Collectionis bullarum sacro sanctae basilicae Vaticanae* I, 33, note. We should perhaps argue for an adoption of *Capracorum*'s name during the lifetime of the *domusculta*, though this is unlikely to have involved the transfer of the actual estate centre northwards after the decline of *Capracorum* itself. The very role of the *domusculta* will have been lost by the time such a transfer could have taken place. Excavations here have revealed a fascinating sequence of Roman farmstead (with paved *diverticulum* and bathhouse), fifth-sixth century church, eighth century (*domusculta* period) church with adjoining baptistery, extending into the eleventh century: Potter and King 1988. Site is described in general in Potter 1979a, 166-167, and first noted by Tomassetti 1882, 146-148; Tomassetti 1913, 112.
19. Wickham 1978a, 175; Bertolini 1947, 127-130, 143-144.
20. Wickham 1978a, 176.
21. Construction of the Leonine wall: *Liber Pontificalis*, ii, 123-125; Gibson and Ward-Perkins 1979, especially 31-33; Gibson and Ward-Perkins 1983, 237. Inscription: Appendix 1.
22. *Monumenta Germaniae Historica, Scriptores* 2, 166; Ugolini 1957, 8; Partner 1966, 70; Partner 1972, 48.
23. Cf. Llewellyn 1971, 251-252; Partner 1972, 46; Wickham 1978a, 175. Wickham [pers. comm.].
24. Hadrian's pontificate is well dealt with in Llewellyn 1971, 231-245; Partner 1972, 29-37; Sefton 1980.
25. *Liber Pontificalis*, ii, 99-101; Llewellyn 1971, 262-263.
26. Llewellyn 1971, 283, 294-295, 301-302. Arab invasions of Italy: Daniel 1975, 49-79.
27. See in general Partner 1972, 50f; Ullmann 1972, 110-115; Marazzi 1985, 17.
28. Documents: Appendix 1; cf. Wickham 1978a, 137-139. Dedication to Saint Cornelius and Saint Peter: document number 40 in Fedele 1899, 70-71, to Saint Cornelius and Saint Ciprianus: *Pergamene del monasterio di SS. Cosma e Damiano in Mica Aurea*, number 132, unpublished. This last dedication reflects the close connection between the two saints, who shared the same feast day (16 September): cf. Thurston and Attwater 1956, III, 560-561. On the claimed presence of relics of Lucius and Felix at Santa Prassede: *Liber Pontificalis*, ii, 63-64, note 12; Nilgen 1974.

The possession of the body of Saint Cornelius was in fact claimed by the monastery at Compiègne in 876: this *translatio* is recorded in Migne, 1844-1888, volume 129, columns 1375-1382. Important relics of the saint were also claimed at Fulda in 838 and by the Korneliuskloster at Aachen. On the general trafficking of relics in the ninth century in particular, see Geary 1978, 51f. Geary (1978, 68f) notes how monasteries were eager to claim ownership of abundant relics in order to increase prestige and indeed to raise capital from patrons for building projects. In this case one may even see the revival of the early dedication at Santa Cornelia as an attempt to claim the continued possession of the relics of four notable martyr-saints.

29. See Llewellyn, this volume; Wickham 1978a, 137-139.

30. Llewellyn, this volume. From this time until its last reference, therefore, Saint Cornelius is recorded in the diocese of Porto.

31. Document 40 in Fedele 1899, 70-71: see Appendix 1.

32. Wickham 1978a, 177. Foundation charter: document 45 in Fedele 1899, 79-81.

33. Document 17 in Schiaparelli 1901, 473-477 of AD 1053; document 1 in Trifone 1908, 278-285 of 1081; document 47 in Schiaparelli 1902, 296-300 of 1158, and document 70 in Schiaparelli 1902, 331-336 of 1186. See Appendix 1 for full texts. The reference of 1238 by Abbot Ubertinus of Santa Maria di Farneta of the '*monasterium sancti Cornelii de Insula in Maceran[o]*'is misleading, and should probably read '*iuxta Macerano*'. On Macerano, see Wickham 1978a, 178-179.

34. Cf. Partner 1972, 90-92, 101-116. For the Crescenzi see Bossi 1915; on the Tusculani see Hermann 1973. The father of Stephanus, '*Leoni nomenculatori*', is named as the deceased brother of Petrus, '*nobili viro qui vulgo Caput longa vocor*' in 1011: document 23 in Fedele 1899, 32-34. Again there is no sign of a family tie to the Crescenzi. Partner 1966, 76-77 shows how the lands of many former *domuscultae* fell into the hands of the nobility, as for instance San Leuco, where the Crescenzi took a substantial share.

35. See Ferrari 1957, 402-407; Hamilton 1962.

36. Lawrence 1984, 80-87 discusses the spread of the Cluniac Order between *c.* 1000-1050, noting how monasteries which took up this Rule were either dependents of Cluny or, in special circumstances, remained autonomous (as with Farfa). Lawrence 1984, 109-111 outlines the boom in monastic foundations in the eleventh-twelfth centuries, and the steady stream of people seeking admittance. The monastery at Farneta: Felici 1972, 31-32.

37. Document 54 in Fedele 1899, 94-95. In 1081 *castrum Formelii* was confirmed in the possession of the monastery of San Paolo, Rome: document 1 in Trifone 1908, 278-285. Below, Appendix 1.

38. Cf. Lawrence 1984, 111-114. Wickham 1978a, 160-165; 1979, 77, 91-92 discusses the early medieval settlement pattern around Formello. Formello is first named in 1027 and its *castellum* in 1037.

39. For these donations, see Appendix 1.

40. Document 47 in Schiaparelli 1902, 296-300 (AD 1158) referring to earlier confirmations by Sergius II, Leo IV, Leo IX and Innocent II – possession of Saint Cornelius may be linked to any one of these four lost bulls. 1186 bull: document 70 in Schiaparelli 1902, 331-336.

41. 1188 bull: Kehr 1901-1902, 543-545, recording the '*monasterium sancti Cornelii cum ecclesiis suis*'. The monastery nonetheless remained within the diocese of Porto. On Santa Maria di Farneta and her possessions, see Felici 1972, 41-47.

42. Auvray 1890, 1103-1106, numbers 4478-4481; *Pergamene del monasterio di SS. Cosma e Damiano in Mica Aurea*, number 267, unpublished, a bull of Innocent IV which confirmed a bull of Gregory IX of 1238. At the time of transfer there is a reference to Clerimbaldus, abbot of Saint Cornelius (*Pergamene del monasterio di SS. Cosma e Damiano in Mica Aurea*, number 247, unpublished), though this records a former debt to Clerimbaldus, who may no longer have been abbot in 1238.

43. *Pergamene del monasterio di SS. Cosma e Damiano in Mica Aurea*, numbers 246, 247 and 265, unpublished.

44. *Pergamene del monasterio di SS. Cosma e Damiano in Mica Aurea*, number 298, unpublished, which refers to the *necessitatis subsidium deputant. multipliat molestentur nos volentes dicta abbatisse ac conventus providere quieti ac molestatoionis huimodi malitiis obviare difectioni . . .* , suggesting the churches listed had become somewhat run-down and that the convent of San Cosimato was having difficulty maintaining these.

45. Lawrence 1984, 192.

46. *Pergamene dei Agostiani di Santa Maria Novella, Bracciano*, numbers 9, 11, 12, unpublished – see Appendix 1.

47. See Appendix 1 for documentation relating to Santa Maria Novella. My thanks to Prof. Bombelli of Formello for first referring me to this documentation. Nibby 1837, 525 records the continued presence of a '*tenuta*' of Santa Cornelia '*al confine del territorio di Formello e di Sacrofano*' divided into quarters, and still held by the Augustinian monks of Bracciano. Nibby in fact offers an identification of this *tenuta* with that once held by the monastery of Saint Cornelius.

48. Nardini 1647, 233-234.

CHAPTER TWO. THE EXCAVATIONS

(i) THE CHURCHES

INTRODUCTION

The excavation of the church buildings was carried out over a number of seasons between 1960 and 1963. In 1960, a narrow north – south trench (trench I, extended southwards by trench Ia) was laid out across the centre of the second church, partly uncovering the apse of the first church; to the east, trench III uncovered the area of the campanile. In 1961 the northern half of the church zone was excavated (trenches A, B, A/D, B/E, D, E, F, G, H, K, L, M, N, P and Q). The southern half of the church complex was examined in 1962 (sectors R and S). The porch, whose western half was identified and excavated in 1961 (sector P) and 1962 (sector S), was fully uncovered in 1963 (sector Y) (cf. Fig. 2). The whole area, covering *c.* 38 × 25 m, was cleared to bedrock.

A sequence of six principal phases was identified.

PHASE 1a

In the southern half of the church zone a tufa-cut feature (001) was identified, 0.85-0.9 m wide, cut to a variable depth (up to 0.25 m) and running in a somewhat angled west – east direction for an almost continuous length of 29 m as far as the church entrance (Figs 3 and 4; Pl. 5). Traces of a possible additional west – east line (002) were recognised 13.5-14 m to the north, although the eastward course of this was obscured by later constructions. A rough, tufa-cut feature (003) *c.* 0.9 m wide was also noted nearby, this time of north-west – south-east orientation; the later crypt to the south had destroyed any trace of its southward extension. Nearby the bedrock was cut by a circular pit (004) of 1.1 m diameter. The bedrock also preserved a number of postholes, many of *c.* 0.3 m diameter.

Interpretation

Feature 001, and perhaps the vague features 002 and 003, can be interpreted as agricultural trenches, cut down into the tufa to provide greater soil depth. Examination of the series of similar trenches found elsewhere at Santa Cornelia suggests that these belong to a system of trenches placed consistently 6-6.3 m apart and crossing the whole site. These represent the agricultural activity of a nearby Roman farm, predating the existence of the *domusculta*. Some of the postholes may also relate to this farming. Pit 004 may belong to phase 3.

PHASE 1b

Trench 001 contained an earth fill, in places packed with tufa pieces. The remaining trenches featured tufa-coloured soil fills.

The packed fill of trench 001 was artificial, designed either to support the crop being grown or to ensure a firm fill to the feature once this became redundant.

PHASE 2a

The absence of additional tufa-cut agricultural trenches and other phase 1 features, as well as the lack of natural soil cover overlying the tufa bedrock elsewhere in the zone, indicates that the ground surface had been artificially levelled in preparation for the construction of the first church. As support for this, we can note a cutting-back of the tufa bedrock both east and south of the church. The survival of trench 001 implies that this feature had been cut to a somewhat greater depth than its neighbouring trenches and had thus escaped eradication: its packed fill may represent, therefore, careful packing to prevent later subsidence and damage to subsequent buildings.

(a) The church (Figs 4 and 5)

Immediately after clearance a building of dimensions 16 × 14.5 m was erected over the eastern half of the excavated area. This formed the first church at Santa Cornelia. Although construction work relating to a major remodelling of this church (below, phase 3a) had destroyed or obscured much of the early building, its basic layout nonetheless remained clear (Fig. 4, and see below Fig. 32). Traces of walling attributable to the first church survived on both its north and west sides, while fragments of its east and south sides may be identifiable in the foundations of the later church.

(i) West wall of the first church (006, 007, 008, 008a, 009)

A series of seven quadrangular tufa blocks (006, 007), forming the lowest foundation course of the west wall, was identified in sector N, running north – south for a length of 4.5 m (Pl. 5). Blocks 006, *c.* 0.6 × 0.6 m, ran from the north-west corner of the building up to larger blocks (007), *c.* 0.8 × 0.45 m, which projected eastwards into the church interior. These blocks were bonded with a strong whitish mortar and set into a shallow tufa-cut foundation trench. This foundation trench (008a) marked the southward continuation of the removed west wall, of which only a single block (008) survived. Graves 48 and 148 later cut up to the back of the wall foundations and help verify its course. The south-west corner of the church probably just underlay later feature 059 (Fig. 4).

The principal feature of the west wall was the shallow semi-circular apse (009), of 4.5 m diameter and internal depth 1.3 m (Pl. 6). Only the northern two-thirds of its foundations survived, set in a relatively deep tufa-cut foundation trench. These comprised six rough tufa blocks of irregular dimensions, 0.5-0.7 m wide. The junctions of the apse with the west wall had not survived.

(ii) North wall

The line of the foundations of the north wall (010) was preserved for a length of *c.* 9.8 m. The tufa-block foundations were generally part overlain by the later church north wall, and only the initial two blocks at the

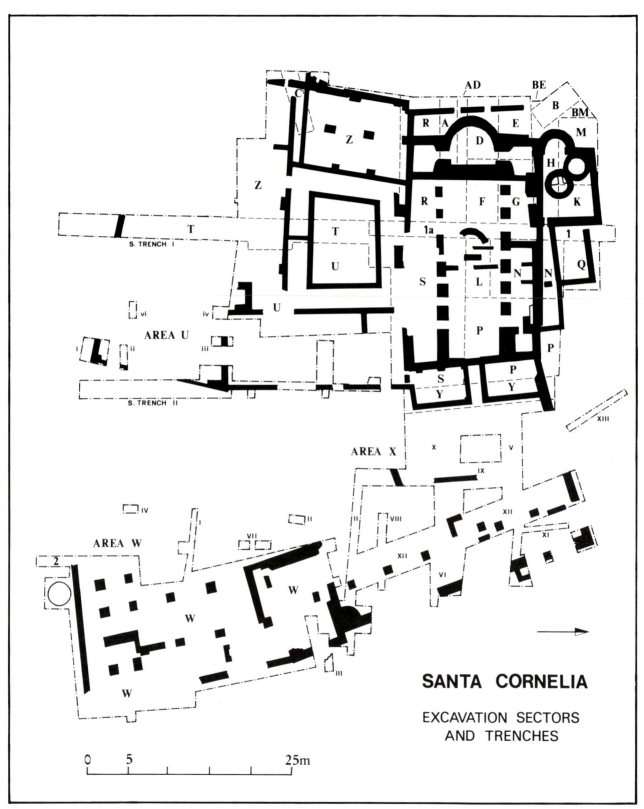

Fig. 2. Santa Cornelia: excavation sectors and trenches (NC)

north-west corner demonstrated the original thickness of the wall. This diminished eastwards from *c.* 0.7 m to just 0.3 m at the point of junction with the campanile (Pl. 16). The foundations comprised blocks of *c.* 0.7 × 0.45 m, though some squarer blocks were visible; there was no apparent internal foundation trench except at the north-west corner. The later construction of the campanile (phase 2e) at least partly destroyed the north wall course. While the crude external offset on the north face of the bell-tower could represent a direct reuse of the lowest foundation course of the original north wall, it is more plausible to argue that the deeper foundations required to support a campanile removed all trace of the earlier wall (010).

(iii) East wall: facade (Fig. 6)

We cannot be certain as regards the extent of reuse of the first church foundations in the east wall (052), although it seems likely that the basic length of the wall (*c.* 16 m) remained unchanged. Many phase 2a blocks could have been reused, though not necessarily *in situ*. The central entrance-way (011), 2 m in width, presumably corresponds to the original arrangement (Pl. 22 below).

(iv) South wall (005, 012, 013)

The poor state of survival of this badly robbed and ploughed-out area made it difficult to ascertain whether the later church had reused or wholly replaced the south wall of the early church. A crude foundation (012) of shaped tufa blocks 0.65-0.7 m wide survived for a length of 4.5 m in the south-east corner. Immediately south lay a lower-set tufa course acting as a buttress (013): this was probably a later addition (Pl. 7). West of the extant foundations, the line of the south wall was marked by a relatively deep foundation trench (005), designed to counter what was here quite soft bedrock. Graves 109 and 137 perhaps lay close to the wall's outer face. The total length of the south wall will have been *c.* 14.5 m.

(v) Internal arrangements

Internally the church comprised a central nave divided from flanking aisles by two rows of large tufa platforms (064-066, 056b, 070-072) for columns. Whereas the south arcade appeared to have been wholly replaced by later restructuring, traces of the north arcade survived in the foundations of the phase 3a bases, represented by large tufa blocks. Their dimensions were unclear, but were perhaps comparable to the phase 3a bases of *c.* 1.2 × 1.25-1.40 m. Blocks 007, incorporated into the church west wall, formed the westward termination of this early north arcade; likewise the isolated block 008 to the south marked the end of the south arcade. These arcades created aisles 2.8-3 m wide and a central nave of 6.5-7 m.

Three sections of crude walling (014, 015, 016), surviving as stumps in the north aisle and nave, originally formed a wall crossing the whole width of the church, *c.* 2.1-2.4 m from its west wall. Wallings 014 and 015 both retained fragments of marble facing on their eastern sides. In contrast, their west faces were rough, unshaped stone (Pl. 5). Set 0.8 m behind this dividing wall, and occupying a central position with respect to both nave and apse, was grave 160. This was a rectangular, north – south, tufa-cut

Plate 5. Santa Cornelia: general view of first church from west

Plate 6. Santa Cornelia: apse of first church, with line of second church *schola cantorum* and first church reliquary, grave 160

tomb of 2.10 × 0.60 m, 0.65 m deep, with an incurving north end. This end was tile-lined, the other sides featuring rougher stonework with neat facing. The grave had been badly disturbed.

Five additional graves lay within the area of the nave (Fig. 4): near the entrance, graves 110, 111 and 150 all certainly underlay the later church floor, and in the case of graves 110 and 150 the addition of an internal offset to the east wall in phase 3a had removed the feet of the burials (Pl. 17). Originally the graves extended up to the foundations of the facade. Grave 111 was in fact set into the phase 1a trench (001) and lay just inside the church doorway, displaced slightly to the south. Grave 150 lay against the line of the south arcade and comprised a deep, tile-lined tomb. For further discussion of the graves, see Chapter 3.

Exactly central to the church lay grave 39, a tufa-cut west–east tomb, of 2.6 × 0.9 m. A series of four post-holes (017, 018, 019, 020), two of circular form 0.35 m in diameter (018, 019), the other two quadrangular, lay north–south of the tomb and *c.* 1 m distant from it; their alignment also corresponded to the sides of the apse. Grave 40 lay to the north, near piers 065 and 066, and contained two skeletons.

The north aisle preserved a limited area of marble slab flooring (021), chiefly in the proximity of piers 065 and 066 (Pl. 8). Since fragments of this floor ran up to the inner face of the first church north wall, it is likely that this paving relates to phase 2. It was composed of broken slabs of white marble of variable dimensions (though at least two originally measured 1.2 × 0.95 × 0.1 m), bedded in a purplish mortar. For the most part the marble was *spolia*

(reused Roman materials), including inscriptions. A straight southern edge to these slabs existed opposite bases 065 and 066, widening from 0.23 m to 0.37 m from east to west; in the proximity of base 066 smaller marble pieces were used to fill the gap between this edge and base 066. No finds were securely associated with this paving.

The west edge of this marble floor was marked by a 1.35 m length of three small tufa blocks (022) of sizes 0.4-0.5 × 0.25 m, which lay directly opposite the fragment of wall 014: they were perhaps an original feature, reused in the later church.

No other area of phase 2 flooring was preserved *in situ*.

(b) The baptistery

A matching apsed structure of dimensions 9 × 8 m was erected immediately north-west of the church, lying just 1.7 m from its corner (Fig. 4, Pl. 9). This building followed roughly the same orientation as the church (west – east, tending slightly west-south-west – east-north-east), with its south wall (023) on virtually the same alignment as the church north wall. This building can be identified as the baptistery.

(i) Wall construction

The baptistery was constructed in large tufa blocks, 0.6-0.8 × 0.45-0.55 m, generally laid as headers, bonded with a strong white mortar cement. The foundations (the walls nowhere stood to more than a single foundation course) were set in tufa-cut trenches. The west wall (024), whose

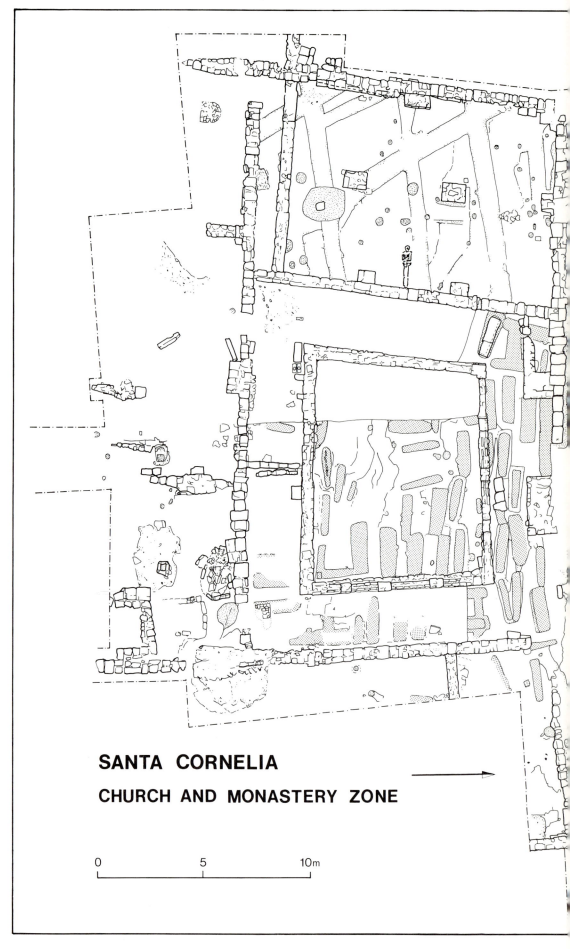

SANTA CORNELIA

CHURCH AND MONASTERY ZONE

0   5   10m

Fig. 3. Santa Cornelia: church and

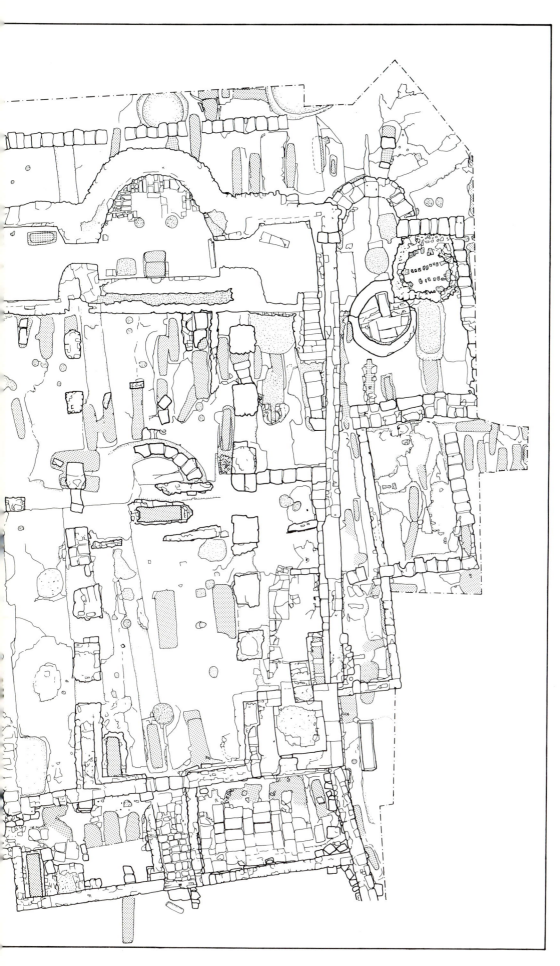

monastery zones, all phases (VW)

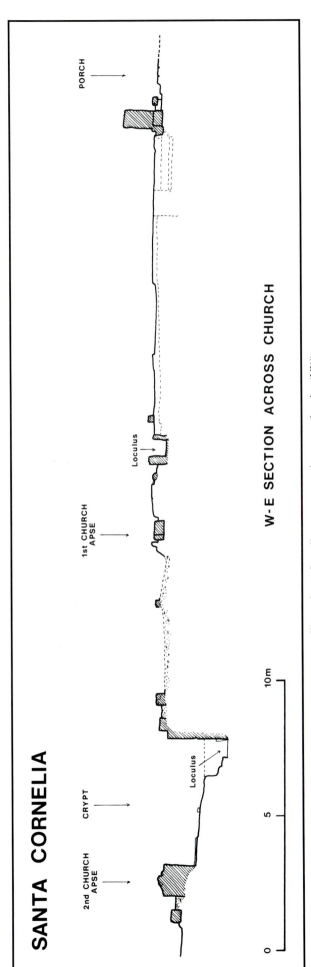

SANTA CORNELIA

2nd CHURCH APSE → CRYPT → 1st CHURCH APSE → Loculus PORCH →

Loculus

W-E SECTION ACROSS CHURCH

0 5 10m

Fig. 5. Santa Cornelia: west–east section across churches (VW)

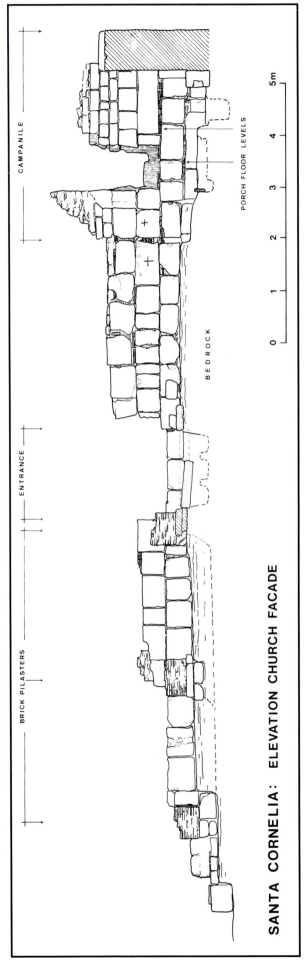

BRICK PILASTERS ← → ENTRANCE ← → CAMPANILE ← →

BEDROCK PORCH FLOOR LEVELS

0 1 2 3 4 5m

SANTA CORNELIA: ELEVATION CHURCH FACADE

Fig. 6. Santa Cornelia: elevation of church facade (east wall) (VW)

southern half had been removed by phase 3 constructions, was built of blocks 0.4 × 0.8 m in size. There was an indication that its foundation trench continued across the face of the apse, though this need not signify that the apse was a later addition to the original plan. The apse (025) was of semi-circular form, with an internal diameter of 2.5-2.75 m and a depth of *c*. 2 m. It comprised eight large tufa blocks of 0.6-0.75 × 0.55 m, buttressed externally on the south-west by a cordon of small blocks up to 0.35 m thick, giving an overall width of 0.9-0.95 m (Pl. 9). The central block featured two small holes on its upper face, suggesting reuse.

The north wall (026) was 9 m long and followed a slightly irregular course, accentuated near its east end. This eastern section and the north-east corner of the building were not fully excavated (Fig. 4). The facade (027) showed foundations 1.0-1.1 m wide, composed of irregular pairs of squared or rectangular blocks. In the centre of this wall, but slightly displaced to the north, two large blocks of *c*. 1.1 × 0.55 m provided the foundations for a threshold (027a).

The subsequent construction of the second church all but destroyed the south flank (023), with the later church north wall extending eastwards from over the south end of the baptistery apse and across its south-east corner. Five tufa blocks remained beside this corner to show a wall 0.75-0.8 m thick.

(ii) Internal features

Located almost in the centre of the building and set down into the bedrock was a baptismal font (028) of slightly irregular circular form, 3.2-3.3 m in diameter (internally 2.25-2.35 m) with walls 0.45-0.5 m thick (Fig. 7; Pl. 10). Its sides, surviving to a depth of 0.6-0.7 m were built of roughly coursed tile fragments and small tufa blocks (*tufelli*), bonded with white lime mortar. The font floor sloped gently westwards and was provided with a narrow drainage channel around its circumference. Both the sides and the floor retained the imprints in the plaster seating of thin marble slabs which had originally lined the interior. Sufficient fragments survived along the edges of the walls and the sides of the two pairs of steps to show the use of white Carrara marble as veneer. The steps were arranged in the west half, three to each side, descending eastwards to the mid-point of the font. They were divided into pairs by a cutting which narrowed from 0.58 m, at its west end, to 0.44 m.

To its west survived a small area of beaten yellow earth with traces of paving (029) in broken pieces of marble. Although this appears to have butted up to part of the font, it also ran up to the north wall of the later church and pit 004 (below, phases 3a and 3b) and we should be cautious in attributing this surface to the early baptistery. In the apse and east half of the baptistery, the bedrock was covered by a vague trodden soil level. No finds came from either context.

(iii) 'Ante-baptistery room'

Immediately east of the baptistery an additional structure was identified which appeared originally to have been attached to both the baptistery and the first church. The area was delimited to north and east by walls 030 and 031,

Plate 7. Santa Cornelia: south-east corner of church with depression 073c

SANTA CORNELIA

CHURCH AND MONASTERY ZONE

PHASES I & 2

0   5   10m

Fig. 4. Santa Cornelia: church and monast

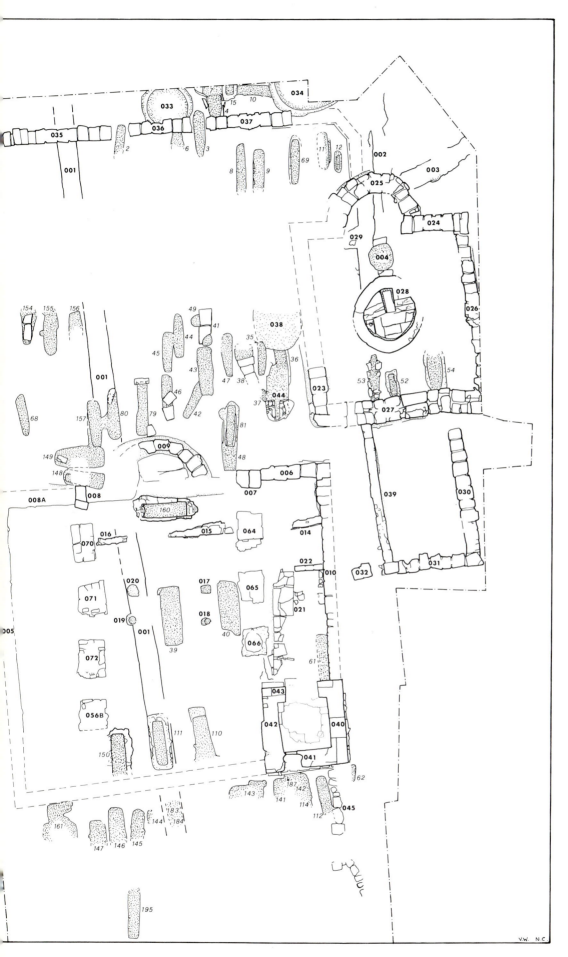

ry zones, phase 1 and 2 features (VW, NC)

Plate 8. Santa Cornelia: paving in north aisle of church near campanile

Plate 9. Santa Cornelia: view of baptistery from east

Plate 10. Santa Cornelia: baptismal *piscina*, cleared, from south-east

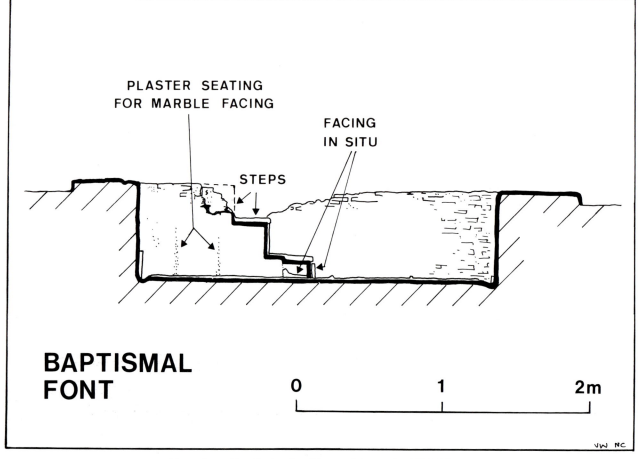

Fig. 7. Santa Cornelia: baptismal font or *piscina*, section (VW, NC)

both of which were constructed with large tufa blocks, surviving as a single foundation course set in a tufa-cut foundation trench (Fig. 4; Pl. 13). Wall 030 featured purplish blocks of 0.65-0.8 × 0.45-0.5 m, laid as headers and bonded with white mortar; it originally extended for 7 m, but the junction with the east wall of the baptistery had been lost, thus reducing its length to 6.3 m. The blocks of the east wall were less regular, and squarish in form (0.55-0.6 × 0.4-0.45 m). The wall ran on a slightly angled southward course for *c.* 4 m where it was interrupted by the junction with wall 039. Two tufa blocks (032) beyond this marked the probable continuation of the east wall up to the side of the church, at a point 5 m east of its north-west corner (Fig. 4). There was no evidence for a south wall or of any walling joining the north-west corner of the church to the baptistery south-east corner.

No trace of an associated surface existed, and the whole area had been badly broken up by late burials. There were no finds to date walls 030 and 031.

(c) The area west of the first church

At the west end of the site two large lime-pits were discovered, cut into the bedrock. The southernmost lime-pit (033), almost wholly excavated, was *c.* 2.3 m in diameter at ground level, diminishing downwards to *c.* 1.9 m, at a depth of 0.5 m. The second pit (034), 3.7 m to the north, was only partially excavated. Its overall diameter could not be accurately measured, but was in excess of 3 m. Both pits contained a thick lime layer throughout (Pl. 11).

Interpretation

Immediately after the initial clearance and preparation of the ground the first church was constructed. Although the construction of the second church later removed all but the lowest course of its walls, adequate details of its layout can be reconstructed (Figs 4 and 8, and see below Fig. 32). Arcades of five or six columns divided the nave from the aisles and provided support for the roof. The west end contained a raised presbytery formed over walls 014-016. Beneath this, and located directly in front of the apse, was grave 160 which most probably housed the principal relics of the church. The five other graves in the church nave need not all have been original features, and it is possible that tombs 39 and 40 belong to phase 3a. Graves 110 and 150 are certainly of phase 2, however, and these perhaps held the remains of two of the four pope-martyrs reburied at *Capracorum*. Postholes 017-020 around grave 39 are unlikely to relate to the position of a ciborium, but may rather indicate scaffolding points. The flooring preserved in the north aisle suggests the use of marble paving in the church aisles at least; much of the marble was *spolia*. There was no direct evidence for the setting of the choir screen or *schola cantorum*, for which abundant evidence was recovered in later levels in the form of fragments of chancel screens. While the main church entrance lay centrally on the east face, an additional doorway is postulated on the north, marked internally by walls 014 and 022.

The baptistery is of such similar orientation, plan and build to the church as to show contemporaneity of construction, although no finds were recovered to date directly the foundation of either structure. Access to the

Plate 11. Santa Cornelia: lime-pit 033 west of church and enclosure, with graves 6, 3 and 4

Plate 12. Santa Cornelia: graves 41-46, and 49 in nave of second church, between presbytery and *schola cantorum* north wall

baptistery may have been possible from the church north door. Walls 030 and 031 may therefore have formed a small enclosure in front of the baptistery. It can be noted in this respect that 031 apparently continued up to the church north wall and the east side of the presumed north entrance. However, the absence of blocks directly linking these walls to both church and baptistery leave it uncertain whether walls 030 and 031 were in fact part of the original scheme. The walls provided an area of 7 × 6.5 m in front of the baptistery, which may have been covered. The gap between the church and the south-east corner of the baptistery appears to have been left open, thus giving access from both church and baptistery to the area behind the church.

The two tufa-cut pits at the western limit of the excavated area clearly provided lime for the phase 2a building activity.

PHASE 2b

This may be defined as the early use of the church, but is not marked by finds or stratigraphy etc.

PHASE 2c BURIAL ENCLOSURE

The west end of the church zone revealed the foundation course of a solid wall (035, 036, 037) running south–north for a length of 13.5 m (Fig. 4). This was constructed in single, large tufa blocks of 0.7-0.8 × 0.5 m with the shorter sides forming the face, and bonded by a white lime cement. Its south portion rested partly on a thin layer of soil

overlying the bedrock and partly on the tufa itself. To the north it lay on the tufa and, as the tufa level rose, within a tufa-cut trench.

The wall ran across the east edges of both phase 2a lime-pits (033, 034). In order to support the weight of this wall the pits were filled with a dark, sandy, slightly clayey, soil, containing stones, and with larger stones directly underpinning the wall (Pl. 11). The fill of pit 033 contained both glass and pottery (including sherds from a single unglazed domestic ware vessel) of late eighth-early ninth century date (finds D/9-13), and that of pit 034 a sherd of similar date (E/7).

To the north the wall course was marked by the line of trench 037a. This continued northwards for *c.* 2 m before turning north-east and then east to run towards the baptistery apse (Fig. 4). An additional trench (037b) in fact continued beyond the apse as far as the baptismal font, though on a slightly different alignment to that of 037a. The construction of the later church south wall (058) and its extension (131) obscured the southward course of wall 035-037.

Underway by this phase was the series of burials made east, west and south of the church. Many graves (sixty-one in all) were found beneath the monastery cloister complex to the south: they belong primarily to phase 2 (see Chapter 3). Immediately east of the church fourteen graves were identified which predate construction of the porch (numbers 112, 114, 141-147, 161, 183, 184, 187 and 195). These were all tufa-cut tombs, mainly west–east oriented. More than one phase of burial was present since grave 142 was demonstrably later than graves 114, 141 and 187, and grave 112 (a charnel pit?) featured up to five skulls and additional bones.

Beyond the church west wall at least thirty-six graves can be regarded as of phase 2, although again burials had clearly been made over a long time span (see below, Fig. 17). The earliest of these included numbers 6, 8, 13, 36, 37, 46, 48, 49, 79, 80, 148 and 149. A significant grouping of burials in the proximity of the apse was apparent. It should also be noted that the phase 3a crypt had undoubtedly destroyed further phase 2 graves (Pl. 12).

At the east end of the excavated zone there was evidence for a tufa-built wall (045) running eastwards from the north-east corner of the church. A series of rough blocks, including one featuring a post-bedding socket, underlay the porch floor and partially underlay the foundations of the porch north wall (046) and its eastward continuation (Pl. 22). Its foundation trench was cut by grave 112.

Interpretation

Wall 035-037, erected over the redundant lime-pits, delimited an area west of the church, and should be interpreted as an enclosure wall. Although its southern extension could not be traced, it is possible that its line was followed by the later church south wall (058, 131). To the north we can assume that it attached to the back of the baptistery apse. The tufa-cut trench (037b), continuing east as far as the font, is difficult to explain, as is its absence further east. If cut to take the enclosure wall, we must argue either for its removal during construction of the baptistery or for an abandonment once construction work began in this area. Both hypotheses require that the enclosure wall predates, if only slightly, the baptistery. Alternatively, on the basis of the slightly different alignment, we may argue that trench 037b represents an additional phase 1a west–east agricultural trench, and has no relation to the enclosure wall. In each case the interpretation is hindered by the absence of the trench east of the font.

The area east of the enclosure wall and south and south-west of the first church contained a high number of graves ostensibly earlier than the phase 3 structures. These burials will have been made throughout the lifetime of the first church. The enclosure wall may have been built to define the west limit of this cemetery precinct. However, the location of graves close to the church facade demonstrates that burials took place outside this hypothetical precinct during phase 2.

The displaced fragments of tufa walling (045) are best interpreted as the early line of a perimeter or enclosure wall which extended east and then south to define additional zones related to the *domusculta*.

PHASE 2d

Burials continued to be made in this period. These may have included graves 41, 43 and 81 in the area west of the church. A large circular pit (038) up to 2.5 m in diameter was cut down into the tufa to a notable depth in the immediate vicinity of the baptistery south wall. In so doing it removed the west end of grave 36.

To the east, construction of wall 039 converted the former open area in front of the baptistery into a room of 7 × 4.5 m. This wall formed the south side of the building, parallel to wall 030. In construction it was quite different

from 030 and 031: of width 0.4-0.45 m, it rested on a foundation of smallish, squared, tufa blocks which gave an irregular internal offset of *c*. 80 mm, while preserving a slight tufa-cut foundation trench on its north side. To the east the wall survived two courses higher, these upper courses faced in small tufa blockwork (Pl. 13). Wall 039 butted neatly up to the east wall of the baptistery. At the south-east corner of the building a large tufa block indicated the nature of the second course of the east wall.

The room featured traces of a whitish mortar surface, badly disturbed by later graves. This ran up to the south wall, overlying its foundation trench. Towards the centre of the room a fragment of marble lay on purple mortar bedding; purplish mortar was also visible over the area of the baptistery entrance on wall 027. The presence of many plaster fragments in the disturbed soil over the floor and in particular against the inner face of the north wall suggest that this side at least had been plastered.

Interpretation

The construction of wall 039 created an enclosed room preceding the baptistery. This 'ante-baptistery room' presumably offered further space for the baptism rite.

Uncertain is the role of pit 038, whose fill yielded no significant finds. Its location within the cemetery zone may argue against a storage function.

Plate 13. Santa Cornelia: ante-baptistery room from east

PHASE 2e

(a) The area west of the church

Graves continued to be cut south and west of the church, some extending beyond the enclosure wall. In the case of graves 2 and 3, blocks had been removed from the wall's foundation in order to allow for the grave cuttings (Pl. 11). Similarly, the west end of grave 6 had hollowed out a foundation block. Graves 4 and 10 lay outside the wall.

The fill of pit 038 was chiefly of soil, but contained finds G/14 and 16, the material from the former of late ninth-tenth century date. This fill was probably contaminated during phase 3a.

East of pit 038 and south of the south-east corner of the baptistery, feature 044 was cut into the bedrock, in so doing cutting through grave 37. Of roughly circular form, 1 m in diameter, its walls were constructed chiefly in tile, except on its straight west face where the lower portions were of tufa (Pl. 14). The feature contained a central channel 0.65 m long and 0.25 m wide communicating with a larger channel *c.* 1.5 × 1 m cut to its west. This cutting had removed the east end of grave 36. Internally were found traces of a baked or blackened clay floor covering an area of diameter 0.55-0.6 m which partly extended over the central channel. The edges of this floor were slightly raised. At the back of the furnace a shallow rectangular cutting was noted in the tufa (cf. Pl. 14). Fragments of bronze were found within it and in its vicinity.

(b) The baptistery

It is probable that the demolition of the baptistery belongs to phase 2e. Its walls were reduced to their foundation courses, and at the same time the interior will have been stripped of much of its flooring and the marble lining of the font also detached. The font was partially filled with rubble from the building's demolition, which included some fragments of marble.

(c) The campanile

To this phase can be assigned the construction of the bell-tower, inserted into the north-east corner of the church and thus forming part of its facade (Pl. 22). It was of virtual square plan, *c.* 3.9 × 3.85 m, with walls 0.75-0.8 m thick, except on the south where the thickness was increased to 0.9 m, giving an internal space of 2.3 × 2.3 m. Its walls were built in both large and small tufa blockwork and a certain amount of brick, particularly in the interior. The solidity of the campanile was reflected by its survival to a height of up to 2.5 m, which allows a detailed structural analysis.

(i) North wall (040)

This rested on foundations of large tufa blocks *c.* 0.4 m high, set in a narrow foundation trench. Externally these provided an offset 0.15 m wide, marked to the east by the use of a row of tufa blocks 0.2 m high. Over this, at both east and west ends, were set two huge blocks of 1.0 × 0.7 m; between lay two masonry courses, the second 0.24 m high, the first of two larger blocks with tile packing between. Part of two upper courses survived, both composed of blocks 0.4 m high and 0.3-0.5 m long. The

Plate 14. Santa Cornelia: bronze furnace (bell-pit 044) with flue, cutting grave 36; pit 038 in foreground

Plate 15. Santa Cornelia: campanile, interior east and south sides, with east door and floor traces

wall here reached 2.1 m high.

Internally the facing was of brick to a height of 0.9 m except in the centre where tufa blockwork 0.2–0.24 m high occurred. Above 0.9 m ran a tufa course 0.35 m high, which continued on to the east wall. Over this was a band of two/three brick courses and part of a further 0.3 m tufa course. The brickwork featured a three module height of 0.15–0.16 m.

(ii) East wall (041)

Externally this too was predominantly tufa built with rare tile-packing, most notably above the lowest two courses, where construction was in large blockwork. The lowest course gave an offset of 0.1 m; the second consisted of blocks 0.45–0.5 m high and formed the level of the east door-sill. This (041a) was 0.75 m wide; concave cuts in the walls marked the setting of the door, while a raised tufa edge 0.35 m high on the internal face formed the threshold (Fig. 6; Pl. 15). South of the door one tufa block featured an incised cross, another example of which had been cut into the church wall close by. Above the second course lay two courses 0.35–0.45 m high, over which were set four further tufa courses each of 0.15–0.2 m. Wall 041 stood to 2.5 m.

The internal face was chiefly tufa-built but with some patching. The lowest course was of tufa c. 0.5 m high, over which ran a half-brick, half-tufa course (with an eight-course brick band to the north). Above lay four tufa courses of varied size, the first corresponding to that noted on the north face.

(iii) South wall (042)

The outer face of wall 042 was obscured by the later wall 055. At its west end 055 leant outward, and here the south wall exhibited tufa blockwork with a red plaster rendering. Internally, the lowest course formed a continuation of the largish tufa course of the east wall. Over an additional tufa course of 0.3 m came up to six tufa block courses, all quite heavily plastered. Almost central, at a height of 1.4 m was a small rectangular hole 0.4 m deep, topped by a long stone slab, perhaps a niche for a lamp.

(iv) West wall (043)

Externally, wall 043 was in large blockwork, though much of its face was obscured by the later church north wall 050, and wallings related to grave 61. This grave (see below, phase 3c) also obscured the junction of the first church north wall with the campanile. It seems likely, however, that the erection of the bell-tower necessitated rebuilding of at least the adjoining section of the north wall. Wall 043 featured the main entrance into the campanile, originally 1.55 m wide.

(v) Campanile floor

The early campanile floor comprised a broken tile surface set over a thin purple mortar bed, traces of which extended outside the west door. In the centre, the floor rested on a packed rubble and earth fill, while to the sides it was set over large tufa blocks which presumably formed part of the campanile foundations. This would suggest foundations up to 1.2 m wide.

(d) The porch area

Wall 045 running east from the north-east corner of the church was replaced in phase 2e by 046. This was built in smallish tufa blockwork with a rubble mortar core, of width 0.7 m. The wall butted up to the campanile at a slight angle, where it survived to six courses, 1.7 m high. Externally there was a rough tufa foundation which occasionally offered an offset, over which came facing in squarish tufa 0.25-0.3 m high, with occasional tile chocking. In the two lowest courses the wall featured two large blocks 0.6 m high (Pl. 22). The internal face was less regular, though the upper four courses corresponded to the external blockwork. Its rough foundations overlay stones of the demolished wall 045. The wall disturbed graves 59 and 62.

Interpretation

The construction of a substantial bell-tower in the north-east corner of the church necessitated the demolition of at least part of the church north wall and facade as well as a section of the enclosure wall to the east. The campanile may have reused the lowest courses of these walls in its foundations, which were reinforced internally by additional large tufa blocks. While the exact relationship between the north wall and the campanile is lost, on the east the homogeneity between the campanile and the church facade may be indicative of a substantial refacing or rebuilding of the facade with the construction of the bell-tower; alternatively, this facing may belong to phase 3a. The campanile exhibited primarily tufa construction, and it may be argued that the use of brick, particularly in the interior, was the result of later refacing; but brickwork may have been prominent in the superstructure of the tower. There was no evidence for an internal stairway.

The presence of limited scraps of bronze slag near feature 044 identifies this as a bronze furnace, supplied with a flue and central stoke-hole and a possible rear chimney. Its somewhat unusual form, however, combined with the evidence for only short-term use, indicates that this was a bell-pit, designed to provide a bell for the newly-built campanile. It was perhaps difficult to locate the furnace away from a cemetery zone given the apparently rapid spread of burials around the church.

The removal of blocks from the enclosure wall, and the spread of burials across and beyond it, denotes its redundancy as a cemetery boundary. By the time blocks were removed to make way for graves 2 and 3 it perhaps survived merely as a low foundation.

The changing fashion in the rites of baptism in the period 800-900 may be significant in the baptistery's demolition. The transfer of this ceremony to within the church itself will have negated the need for a separate baptistery.

PHASE 2f

Subsequent to the construction of the bell-tower, grave 61 was inserted against the internal face of the church north wall, with its east end against the west face of the campanile. Its earliest phase comprised a west – east tomb of c. 2.1 × 0.5 m cut down into the tufa to a depth of almost 0.9 m. This contained one articulated skeleton and most of another, and a disturbed fill with pottery and glass sherds in addition to a few iron objects (see below, phase 3a). Its top was formed by three pieces of marble (one from a strigillated sarcophagus), firmly mortared across the width of the tomb at ground level, though these did not cover the length of the grave (Pl. 16).

Other burials occurred: west of the church, grave 35 overlay the fill of pit 038, while graves 7 and 15 cut earlier graves west of the former enclosure wall. Burials were also made in the demolished baptistery: graves 52-54 were set up to the baptistery east wall; graves 52 and 54 showed a cutting for cover slabs (none preserved), while grave 53 retained a number of covering tiles along its edges, suggesting a form 'a cappuccina'.

Interpretation

Grave 61 probably denotes the burial-place of an important personage. However, since it was not among the original tombs within the church it is unlikely to have held the remains of one of the four pope-martyrs. Graves 52-54 testify to the swift use of the demolished baptistery as part of the cemetery.

Plate 16. Santa Cornelia: campanile, exterior, west face with grave 61 flanking church north wall and campanile stairs

PHASE 3a

(a) The second church

This phase saw the construction of a second, larger church which in its east half overlay the phase 2 edifice (Fig. 9, and see below Fig. 35). The new church was of dimensions 26 × 16.5 m, with entry retained at the east end, and a large semi-circular apse at the west. The building of a church twice the size of the former structure necessitated the demolition of the greater part of the phase 2 church. There was no indication that the first church had been abandoned or destroyed previous to this demolition. Much of the building material from the first church, and certain of its architectural elements, were reused in phase 3.

The walls of the second church were nowhere preserved to any significant height, except at the north-east corner, in proximity to the campanile. Indeed, its south side had suffered badly from ploughing and at best survived as a foundation.

(i) West wall (049)

The west wall and apse of the church survived at plough level externally as roughly-built foundations in irregular smallish stones, amply mortared and resting on bedrock (Pl. 20). Neat facing in tufa blockwork, *opus listatum* (tufa and tile), or brickwork, was present on the internal face, forming part of the crypt wall facing (see below). The foundations were 1.2-1.3 m thick, diminishing to 0.8-0.85 m towards the south-west and north-west corners. This rough stonework was presumably obscured by the contemporary ground level. Only near the north-west corner was there any trace of coursing, here resting on the naturally higher tufa bedrock (which sloped gently southwards): this consisted of two courses of roughly-squared small tufa, over which lay part of a brick band course.

The foundations of the west wall and apse lay just east of the early enclosure wall (035-037) and cut the east ends of a number of graves (2, 3, 6, 8 and 9) (Fig. 3). Sherds A/10, D/7, 8, 15, and E/12 and 15 came from the packing or from the mortar of the foundations, but these were all too small to confirm the chronology.

(ii) North wall (050)

The foundations of the north wall consisted of large tufa blocks 0.7-0.75 m thick. In the east, wall 050 overlay the north half of the first church foundations. To the west the wall ran over the soil-covered south-east corner of the baptistery and up to the south end of its apse, thus ignoring the line of the baptistery south wall. The foundations cut down to, but rarely through, the bedrock. An external offset was visible only towards the campanile, formed by rough packing in small stones: this should mark the contemporary ground level.

Over the foundations lay a faced tufa course with rubble-mortar core standing to 0.45 m and 0.65-0.7 m thick. This was broken at a distance of 5 m from the campanile by an entrance-way (051), 2.3 m wide. This corresponded to phase 2a internal wallings 014 and 022 (Pl. 13). The sill and jambs must have rested on a reduced second course.

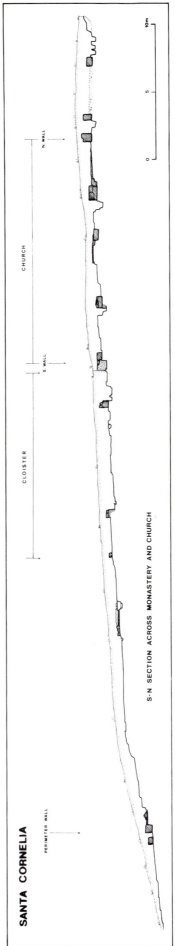

Fig. 8. Santa Cornelia: south–north section across monastery and churches (VW)

Only near the campanile was the wall preserved to any additional height, where it featured four courses of *opus listatum*, composed of single or dual brick band courses alternating with tufa courses 0.24 m high and up to 0.35 m long. On the internal face, however, longish tufa blocks were set over the remnants of wall 010 for a height of two courses, topped by five courses of *opus listatum* (cf. Pl. 8). To the west the internal face was less regular, but again showed the use of longish blocks with a hint of elevation in *opus listatum*.

(iii) East wall – facade (052)

As noted above, the homogeneity between the face of the campanile and that of the church east wall may signify that part of the phase 2e walling was retained unaltered here (Fig. 6). In its northern part the foundation blocks were of 0.5-0.65 × 0.35-0.4 m, and to the south were up to 0.55 m high, probably in order to counter the slope of the bedrock. Wall thickness was 0.6-0.65 m.

Probably repeating the first church arrangement, the main entrance (011) of the second church lay virtually central to the wall. The sill of this door was found in rubble close by (fragments 325a-e, 511-513). North of the entrance, the east wall stood to an additional two tufa courses, up to its junction with the campanile. These were 0.4-0.5 m high with tufa facing either side of a mortar core; some tile packing was evident.

An additional course (053, 054) was built up against the internal face of the foundations, providing an offset 0.25-0.3 m wide south of the doorway, and somewhat less to the north. This reinforcement was limited to either side of the doorway as far as the projecting walls 055 and 056 (see below), and presumably served to take the extra weight created by a larger entrance and facade arrangement. In two points these offsets required their own foundations, namely where they cut across the ends of graves 110 and 150. In the case of 150 rough mortared rubble foundations cut the skeleton below the shin and bones from the disturbed tomb were thrown into the mortar (Pl. 17). Finds S/30 and 31 from the tomb fill (sealed by phase 3d flooring) support an eleventh century date.

Part of a second tufa course survived south of the doorway for a length of 3 m. Beyond this the foundation course alone survived, and even this was lacking at the south-east corner.

(iv) South wall (012, 013, 057, 058)

As described above (phase 2a), preparation for the construction of the first church involved the levelling of areas of bedrock. This did not wholly eliminate the natural north–south slope of the tufa nor remove the softer tufa on the south side of the church site, so that we find that the south wall required buttressing and artificial terracing.

From the south-east corner, the wall (012) could be traced westwards for 4.5 m as a crude foundation of shaped tufa blocks, except at the west end where only a packed tile and mortar make-up remained. The top of this foundation was heavily mortared with a purplish cement containing some tile fragments, and seating preserving the outline of an overlying tufa course c. 0.65 m thick (Pl. 7). The wall was buttressed by wall 013, cut into the bedrock and

Plate 17. Santa Cornelia: grave 150 cut by addition 054 to internal face of church east wall

surviving for a length of 5 m. Its upper face, scored by the plough share, lacked mortar traces. The foundation trench (005) of the first church south wall probably also indicates the course of the phase 3a wall.

Beyond feature 059, the south wall reappeared as a single large tufa foundation course (057) with its foundation trench stepped into the bedrock. Initially laid as stretchers of 0.65-0.75 × 0.5 m for 2.5 m, the wall reverted to headers of 0.7 × 0.35-0.45 m. At the junction with the crypt, the wall (058) changed to double-faced work 0.75 m thick.

Internal arrangement of the church

The phase 3a building was divided into nave and aisles by the line of two arcades. These survived as two series of six tufa-built bases or stylobates (061-072, 056b) spaced c. 1.5 m apart, with additional bases probably located over wall 060, against the west wall and against the projecting walls 055 and 056a. These arcades delimited a central nave 7 m wide and side aisles of 3.0-3.3 m (Pl. 5).

(v) North arcade

At the west end of the church, the thickened foundations of the west wall, near the springing of the apse, and of wall 060, which formed the support for a raised presbytery, marked the positions of the initial bases of the arcades. Beyond these, in the north arcade, a series of six stylobates (061-066) ran towards the south side of the bell-tower. These were mainly rectangular tufa bases of 1.2 × 1.25-1.4 m set in shallow tufa-cut foundation trenches. The westernmost bases were less well-built, containing broken tufa, basalt and some marble in their foundations, mortared with a hard purplish cement. The dimensions of the central pier (063) were largest, owing to the apparent incorporation of blocks 007. This extra length maintained a spacing of c. 1.4 m between bases. Graves 35, 37, 38 and

48 were disturbed by the construction of these bases.

The north arcade terminated against wall 055. This wall flanked the south side of the campanile for a length of 2.9 m, and was 0.6 m wide, enlarging to 0.75 m where it matched the slight dog-leg of the campanile wall. The wall sat on a wide tufa foundation which extended westwards, flush with the west face of the campanile, offering an offset of 0.3-0.4 m; its foundation trench cut the bedrock. Built in *opus listatum* with a rough mortared core, it survived up to its fifth brick band at 1.5 m. The facing was in small tufa courses 0.25 m high, alternating with bands of one to three brick courses, though large tufa blocks 0.5 m high were used on the west face. Most probably as a result of the later collapse of the campanile, the wall exhibited a clear lean away from the campanile (Pl. 8).

(vi) South arcade

As with the north arcade, so the initial bases of the south arcade rested on the strengthened foundations of walls 049 and 060. To the east bases 067, 068 and 069 were poorly preserved, owing either to robbing or to plough action, and featured dimensions of just 0.8-0.9 × 1-1.3 m, creating irregular spacing between. Bases 067 and 068 were crudely built in small rough tufa; base 069, like the corresponding north base 063, may have reused blocks (008) of the first church west wall. This stylobate overlay graves 148 and 149, while 067 disturbed grave 156.

Bases 070-072 and 056b were set in a foundation trench up to 0.4 m deep. This was designed to counter the relative softness and friability of the bedrock in this sector. Accordingly the bases were solidly built, with large tufa block foundations, though with smaller, less regular tufa above, with occasional pieces of reused marble. The presence of clamp-holes in some of the larger tufa blocks showed their derivation from earlier structures. The irregularity in size and spacing of these bases, combined with the crude construction above their foundations, should indicate that much of their surviving structure was obscured by the phase 3a church floor.

Stylobate 056b formed the west end to wall 056a, which extended westwards from the church east wall for a length of 3.7 m. This wall rested on a rough stone foundation 1.25-1.3 m wide, set into a tufa-cut trench; its north side lay against the walling of grave 150 (Pl. 17). The wall was 0.6 m thick and probably of *opus listatum*, though it survived only to part of its second tufa course. Wall 056a matched wall 055, set south of the campanile.

(vii) West wall (060)

At a point 5-5.5 m from the west end of the church, wall 060, of variable thickness, ran across both aisles and nave. In the aisles it was 0.65-0.7 m thick, enlarging to 1.6 m opposite the apse through the addition of wall 074; the space (075) between the walls was filled with rubble and mortar. Both ends of this 'double-wall' were considerably thickened to create platforms of *c*. 2 × 1.7 m to support the second pier base of each arcade (Pl. 12). Construction was in rough stone and rubble with few shaped blocks. The wall disturbed graves 41, 154 and 155. In the north aisle the wall required additional foundations where it encountered pit 038. This section preserved part of a single course of smallish tufa blocks. To the north lay stairs giving access to the crypt (Fig. 9).

The west wall marked the front of the presbytery, the raised area containing the main altar and overlying the crypt; there was presumably stepped access from both nave and aisles.

(viii) Schola cantorum (077)

Running east from the north end of the 'double-wall' (060, 074) in the nave were the crude foundations of a narrow wall (077) *c*. 0.3-0.5 m thick, resting on a narrow spine of natural tufa created by the cutting of graves 41, 43 and 47. This extended for a length of 3.7 m at a distance of 0.55-0.6 m from the north arcade (see Pl. 13). Standing to between 0.13 and 0.44 m high, these foundations were crudely constructed, almost exclusively in small stones and reused marble fragments (fragments 367 and 368), and were amply mortared.

There was no trace of a corresponding south wall, unless the small fragment of mortared stonework found in grave 80 is related. To the east, however, between the apse of the first church and grave 160, there is an additional crude foundation wall (078), comprising a rough small stone base 0.4-0.5 m wide with purple mortar bonding, surviving for a length of 2.75 m; it lay in a shallow foundation trench, whose course could be traced south for a short distance (Pl. 6). These fragments should represent the foundations of the *schola cantorum* or chancel, which will have covered an area of *c*. 8 × 5.5 m and extended up to the mid-point of the nave (if we include the area of the presbytery). No trace of floor relating to the *schola cantorum* remained *in situ*. Its level here would probably have been raised with respect to the rest of the church and this would have accordingly minimized its survival.

(ix) Church flooring

Material found in the rubble of the crypts suggested a flooring of the elevated presbytery in marble slabs (generally *spolia*); there were also elements of a Cosmatesque floor (see below, phase 3d).

In the remainder of the west half of the church, no floor traces were found *in situ*, and very little survived of the mortar make-up, except in the north aisle. Again one should assume that many marble fragments, from the overlying rubble layers, comprised the original floor (as fragments 139, 144, 159-161, 172, 173, 175, 178-180, 191, 266, 278, 280, 365, 369-371, 373, 374, 400, 594, 595, 597, 599-605).

In the east half of the church, evidence for flooring was somewhat better. We should exclude, however, the phase 2 marble paving (021) near the campanile, which, given the height of both the phase 3a north wall and arcade bases, is unlikely to have been retained. Rather we should visualize a raised floor at the height of the remaining first church north wall foundations. This may be verified by the level of the steps of the campanile staircase (see below, phase 3d).

Within the nave a lime make-up was identified running as far as the east wall, covering the phase 2 graves 160, 39 and 40. One fragment of make-up (079) rested over the 0.3 m deep soil and tufa fill of the agricultural trench 001.

Find P/2 from the make-up supported a date of the first half of the eleventh century.

Some elements of the fragmented marble floor (080) within the entrance, to both west and south, should relate to the phase 3a building: there were in fact pieces underlying the blockwork of the east wall. However, the presence of cut shapes belonging to a Cosmatesque floor indicates notable later reflooring here (phase 3d).

Fragmentary traces of floor make-up also occurred in the south aisle near the foundations of wall 056a. In the church south-east corner the bedrock featured a rectangular cutting (073c) of 2.5 × 1.3 m. To its west lay two roughly circular features: the first (073b) was slightly raised above the surrounding bedrock, while the second (073a), c. 1.25 m in diameter, was slightly sunken (Pl. 7).

(b) The crypt

Beneath the presbytery at the west end of the church lay a large triple crypt, extending across the whole church width and covering an area of c. 15 × 3.5 m (Fig. 9). The crypt comprised a principal central chamber of horseshoe form, lying directly beneath the apse, which communicated with smaller adjoining chambers to north and south. The depth of the crypt meant that it had escaped substantial plough damage, and, in the case of the central and north chambers, its walls still stood to 2.5 m high. This allows a detailed analysis of the wall construction.

(i) Crypt stairs (082)

Access to the crypt was by means of stairs leading down from the north aisle (Pl. 18). These consisted of ten (surviving) steps, formed by single marble slabs 0.9-1 m wide and 0.25 m deep, though the second and third steps comprised two slabs each (perhaps replacements). It was likely that a further step existed at the top of the stairs, given that the cutting for these had removed the bulk of the south wall of the baptistery. The seventh step, preceding a recessed doorway, was 0.6 m deep, and gave space for opening the door.

The stairs were framed between the internal face of the church north wall and wall 076, which extended east into the north aisle for 2 m. It continued west to project into the north crypt for 0.5 m, with facing in brick and occasional small tufa blocks; this wall stood to 2.1 m. Later refacing of the north crypt (see below, phase 3d) saw the addition of an angled face to the north wall, reducing the width of the stairway.

(ii) North crypt chamber

Internally, the north crypt was originally of dimensions 3.8 × 2.8-3 m. As noted above, subsequent refacing obscured the face of the phase 3a north wall as well as that of the west side (Pl. 19). The original aspect of these walls survives in the east wall which avoided restructuring. Here the wall was built in *opus listatum*, alternating courses of small tufa blocks and brick bands, with tufa blockwork in the lowest course (Pl. 18). Its regularity was broken only at the top of the wall where two courses of tufa were set. In general the tufa was squarish, of height 0.2-0.25 m; the bricks were set in bands of two to four courses and demonstrated a three

module height of 0.18-0.2 m. At the south end, beginning at a height of c. 1.8 m, was the outline of a squinch for a cross or groin vault. The absence of a corresponding squinch to the north suggests a slightly awkward vaulting arrangement across the entrance.

The *opus listatum* of the first 1.6 m of the east wall continued west on to the wall leading to the corridor. It ceased, however, near the rounded corner, and became plain brick facing (as indeed occurred above the *opus listatum*). The brickwork formed a neat face to a rough rubble core which stood to 2.1-2.2 m; bricks were short and thin (c. 35-40 mm thick), set on mortar beds of c. 25 mm, giving a five module height of 0.29-0.3 m.

The west side of the corridor, featuring a shorter, curved connection with the west wall of the chamber, was also brick-faced rubble core, standing to 2.05 m. The brickwork again exhibited a five module height of 0.29-0.31 m. The corridor itself narrowed from north to south, from 1.3 to 1.2 m wide, and was 1.5 m long.

The floor was marked by traces of a purple mortar and sand level, presumably make-up for paving. Only one small fragment of marble was found embedded in this make-up.

(iii) Central or apse crypt

At the entrance into the central chamber lay a sill of 1.28 × 0.17 m, with an L-shaped west end. Its presence suggests that the various chambers of the crypt were sealed off by doors.

The central crypt, directly underlying the apse of the church, was of horseshoe shape, with an east facing wall 5.7 m long, and a depth of 4.7 m. To the north the crypt walls stood to c. 2.3 m, while to the south the plough had reduced this to 1.5-1.6 m (Pl. 20).

With the exception of the north entrance, the apse crypt was wholly faced in tufa. The walls all rested on a raised natural tufa ledge standing 0.23-0.3 m above the levelled bedrock of the floor. The curved west wall was faced with well-cut tufa, with squarish blocks 0.3 m high forming the bottom course, over which lay three courses of rectangular blocks 0.25 m high; the topmost surviving course again comprised squarish blocks of 0.3 m. In general this west wall survived to c. 1.55 m, although fragments of an additional course existed near the north corridor. The tufa face covered a rough mortared rubble core, as was clear in an exposed section near the north entrance. This showed how the foundations overlay steps cut into the natural tufa, descending to the crypt floor.

The east wall featured a bottom course of large, squarish blocks 0.6 m high, over which ran the remains of five small block courses of 0.2-0.25 m. This, like the west wall, appears to have been plastered and painted.

Virtually central in the east wall face, at 1.3 m above the floor level, was a brick-lined semi-circular niche (083) of diameter 0.54 m and depth 0.24 m. This lay directly above a rectangular feature (084) which had been cut into the tufa and stepped downward towards the wall to a depth of c. 1 m. Originally this feature was lined with thin marble slabs set on a 25 mm thick mortar bed, as shown by surviving base and back slabs. At floor level the feature was 1.1 × 1.3 m, diminishing through the presence of two steps to base dimensions of 1 x 0.7 m. A displaced tufa slab, originally of 1.15 × 0.65 m, located north-west of the feature and projecting slightly over its corner, may have

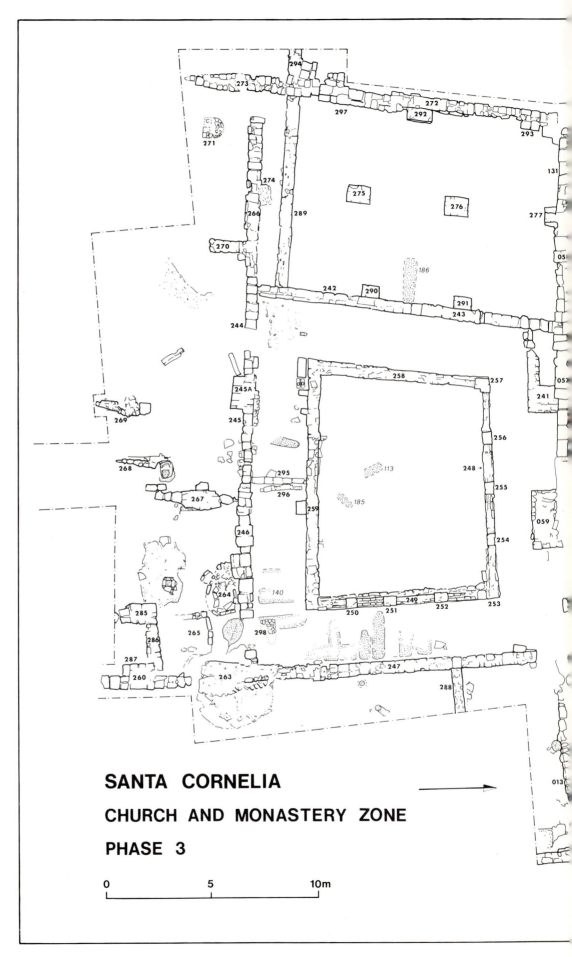

SANTA CORNELIA

CHURCH AND MONASTERY ZONE

PHASE 3

0   5   10m

Fig. 9. Santa Cornelia: church and mon

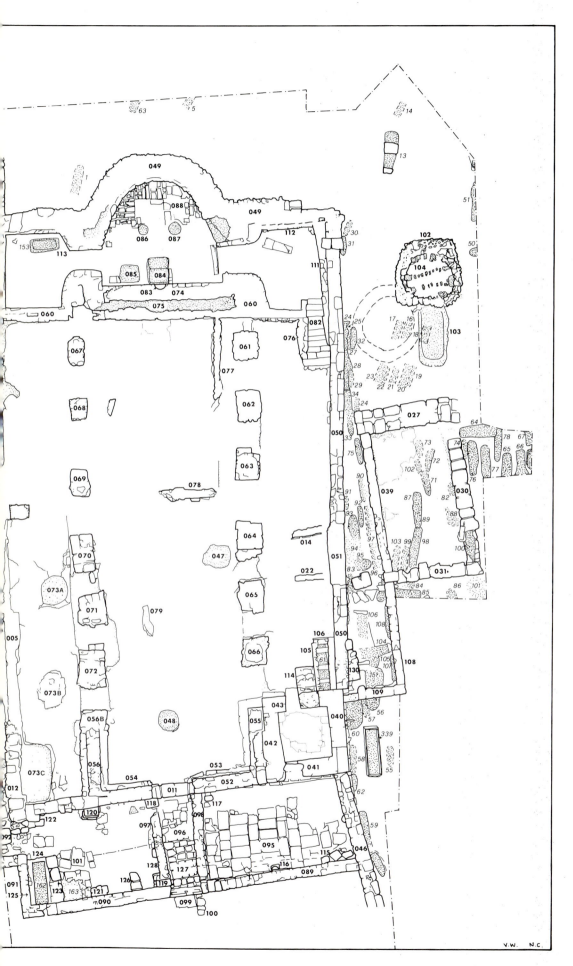

astery zones, phase 3 features (VW, NC)

Plate 18. Santa Cornelia: crypt, east and south walls of north chamber with stairs communicating with church north aisle

Plate 19. Santa Cornelia: crypt, north chamber, west wall with vault traces

Plate 21. Santa Cornelia: crypt, south chamber with grave 153, viewed from south

formed part of its cover. A shallow tufa-cut depression (085), 0.9 × 0.8 m and 0.3 m deep, lay 0.35 m south of feature 084. This was matched to the north, *c*. 0.8 m from the feature, by a similar, but shallower depression (unless this merely marked the position of a robbed floor slab).

Two further depressions (086, 087) lay 2.2 m from the east wall and 1.8 m from the west end. Their positions and circular form (diameters 0.45 m and 0.55 m) indicate column placings providing additional support for the vaulting.

The central chamber preserved traces of its floor (088). In the west thin marble slabs *c*. 15 mm thick and of variable size (many 0.15-0.2 m wide) rested on a 20 mm thick plaster bed overlying the tufa. This paving was best preserved around the edges of the apsed area of the crypt. The slabs respected features 086 and 087. In the east half of the chamber both paving and bedding were fragmentary; while in the immediate proximity of feature 084 three fragments of marble slab indicated its north rim. Additional fragments lay to the south, while traces of bedding were especially clear at the base of the east wall.

(iv) South crypt

Near the entrance to the corridor leading to the south chamber lay part of a door-sill. The corridor was 1.5 m long and narrowed from 1 m to 0.9 m. Initially the corridor walls maintained the tufa block construction of the central crypt, being likewise set on a raised bedrock ledge. At the entry to the south room, however, the face became predominantly brick, and this obscured any tufa ledge (cf. Pl. 21). This may denote later refacing.

Both west and south walls of the south chamber comprised brick facing over a lowest course of somewhat irregular tufa blockwork, which partly compensated for the uneven tufa floor level. The walls, surviving to *c*. 1.2 m, featured brickwork of five module height 0.3 m.

In contrast, the east wall was constructed in *opus listatum*, with the lowest tufa course resting on a slight tufa ledge (Pl. 21). The blockwork was somewhat irregular in courses *c*. 0.25 m high; the brickwork consisted of three to four courses, featuring a three module height of 0.15-0.16 m. The wall as a whole stood to the third brick band. Traces of a niche lay almost central, at a height of 1.3 m, but of this little more than its tile base survived (0.45 m wide); it had probably been 0.25 m deep and squarish in form. Only the lower half of the curved north wall running to the corridor was in *opus listatum*, to a height of 0.75 m. Above this came brick facing (five module = 0.3 m). The face was lost where the wall straightened, thus obscuring the joint with the neat blockwork to the north. The opposite joint was crude.

As noted, the natural tufa had been unevenly levelled, and traces of flooring were absent. A number of shallow, circular cuts were visible in the bedrock, particularly in the south-west corner, but offered no discernable pattern. The main bedrock feature was the tufa-cut grave 153, measuring 1.35 × 0.55-0.6 m.

(c) The porch – narthex

Contemporary with the phase 3a church was the construction of an east porch or narthex, providing an entrance hall preceding entry into the church. This covered the whole width of the church, extending up to wall 046 in the north: its overall dimensions were *c*. 16.5 × 4.5 m. It was divided into two roughly equal halves by a central causeway or approach (Pls 22 and 23).

(i) Construction of the porch walls

North wall (046)

Wall 046 running east from the church has been described above (phase 2e). This was probably reused unaltered as the porch north wall, though some of the tile patching on its internal face, particularly at its angled junction with the bell-tower, may denote repairs.

East wall (north half) (089)

Wall 089 was of tufa construction, *c*. 0.5 m thick, surviving to a height of two or three courses. In general it was built with single large blocks. In the foundations these were laid two abreast, providing an internal offset; above this single blockwork was present near the causeway, but to the north smaller, less regular, blocks formed the face to a mortared rubble core.

The internal face was uneven, and the blocks nearest the causeway were worn, indicating reuse. There was some brick chocking, chiefly between the second and third courses. The presence of a vertical join 1.8 m from the north-east corner, and the thickening of the wall to 0.55 m, suggest that the final segment of the east wall was a rebuild, perhaps a blocking of an entrance, though it was not possible to ascribe this to a definite phase.

East wall (south half) (090)

The wall here maintained a thickness of 0.5-0.55 m, preserved in general to just two courses. Externally it possessed an irregular foundation course of large tufa blocks. The second course was tufa-faced rubble core, with brick plugging. Internally the lower face was of small, irregular, tufa, over which came large, uneven blockwork. The south-east corner of the porch was occupied by grave 162, whose construction (phase 3d) perhaps blocked an entrance-way whose north end was marked by a vertical join; a hole 0.9 m to the south may mark the position of a door pivot.

Fallen facade wall (094)

A fortunate survival was that of part of the collapsed east wall, preserved directly beneath the plough level in front of the porch (Pl. 24; Fig. 11). This represented the wholesale collapse outward of the porch facade at a date subsequent to the site's abandonment (phase 4b, see below). Its survival offers the opportunity to examine part of the otherwise lost elevation of the phase 3a church.

Plough action had removed part of the rear face of the wall and reduced its thickness to between 0.11 and 0.48 m (greatest towards the porch). Since, however, the standing remains of the east wall were only 0.5-0.55 m thick, it is assumed that the original thickness of the fallen wall was 0.5 m. An area of walling 8 × 2.5 m was uncovered, lying

Plate 22. Santa Cornelia: second church porch and campanile from north-east, view of north compartment, with phase 3a floor

Plate 23. Santa Cornelia: porch causeway and south compartment

1.2-1.6 m from the north half of the east wall foundations. Additional material relating to this wall was accidentally removed before the feature was properly identified, for some brick was cleared away as 'rubble' in 1962, before the fallen wall was located.

The wall was predominantly of coursed brick/tile with occasional tufa blocks. On the piers of the arcades, the mortar between courses showed the use of 'falsa cortina' pointing. The original aspect of the porch facade will have consisted of a central doorway 1.5 m wide, flanked by coursed brick piers 0.9 m wide. The outline of the doorway lay almost directly in front of the sill of the east wall, with the top of the entrance marked by a travertine architrave 1.5 m long, lying c. 2.5 m from the sill. This featured two pivot-holes at each end, behind the raised fore-edge, and an additional hole in the centre of its upper face, presumably a bolt-hole. There were no separate jambs flanking the door. Immediately over the lintel was a flat brick arch 0.45 m high, over which ran horizontal courses.

Either side of the door piers, but only partially preserved to the south, lay a triple arcade supported by two slender columns with impost capitals (Pl. 24). Each arcade was 0.6 m wide and 1.4 m high; the two columns preserved *in situ* in the north arcade were 1.02 and 1.04 m long, thinning to the ends, with heads marked by two thicker bands 20 mm and 40 mm high, and bases (55-60 mm high) swollen and marked by raised vertical lines. Only one capital remained in place, of dimensions 0.45 × 0.13 × 0.16 m, with a base diameter of 0.12 m. These columns had been preserved through their inclusion in a later blocking of the arcades (phase 3f, see below). An additional triple arcade should have lain further north, beyond a 1 m wide pier, but only half of one of the arcades was revealed in the excavation. A similar series of arcades will have existed south of the entrance (cf. below, Fig. 38).

At a point 1.9-1.95 m above the first two arches of the preserved arcade, two lengths of travertine (of 1 m and 0.5 m) were incorporated into the facade wall. It is uncertain whether these formed part of a cornice or other decorative element.

Plate 24. Santa Cornelia: fallen porch facade wall, viewed from south

South wall (091)

This aligned with the south wall of the church, but did not join. Instead, a gap of 1.45 m was left for a doorway communicating south (Fig. 9). Wall 091 featured a large tufa block foundation with crude tufa and brick coursing, 0.45 m thick. The insertion of grave 162 may have necessitated rebuilding here. The wall turned at a right angle to run south for 2.8 m: it consisted of a single tufa foundation course (093).

A threshold (092) to the south doorway lay parallel with buttress wall 013, composed of three tufa blocks, and offering a 1.2 m wide entrance.

(ii) Porch interior

The porch interior can be divided into three distinct units, comprising north compartment, central causeway and south compartment.

North compartment

The area defined north of the causeway was of dimensions 7 × 4 m. Associated with the earliest phase of the porch was paving (095) in large square or rectangular stone slabs of 0.8 × 0.5 × 0.08 m or 0.5 × 0.5 × 0.08 m. In many points these were cracked and reddened, as a result of burning. Some had also broken and sunken downwards into the fill of phase 2 burials (numbers 112, 114, 141-143 and 187) (Pl. 22). The disturbed fills of these graves related to the construction of the porch, although it was apparent that later disturbances (the laying of the second porch floor and later robbing of the area) had contaminated these. In this regard we can note the absence of floor slabs covering the graves against the church facade. Finds from the graves thus covered a period between the eleventh and thirteenth centuries.

Central causeway

A central paved causeway (096) gave access from the porch entrance to the main door of the church. It comprised a raised stone slab pavement, 1.4 m wide to the east, widening to 1.6 m at the church entrance, flanked by low side walls (097, 098), up to which ran the paving of the north compartment (Pl. 23). The original height of these walls was unclear. The causeway was paved in large tufa slabs of similar size to those of floor 095 to the north. Here also, slabs had sunken inwards, partly over earlier graves (183 and 184), and partly over the phase 1a agricultural trench.

The porch door-sill was preserved *in situ* as a travertine block of 1.5 × 0.35 m with raised front edge, behind which was set a central socket-hole and at either end of which there were pivot-holes with related grooves (fragment SC325). Immediately outside lay a crude, large slab (099) of c. 0.95 × 0.5 m, which may have acted as a step. To its north lay four tufa blocks (100) which possibly flanked this step; two blocks, one displaced, may have flanked it to the south.

South compartment

This comprised an area of 6 × 4 m, preserving little of its

first period floor. Unlike the north compartment, where slabs were laid almost directly over the bedrock, here the tufa level was lower, and accordingly a soil fill was necessary to make the levels in the narthex even. Thus a trodden earth surface was identified in the east half of the compartment, which formed the bedding for a slabbed floor; to this paving (101) may have belonged three stone slabs just north-west of grave 162 and a further fragment near the later base 120. The removal of the remainder of this floor may have occurred prior to the laying of the second period floor (see below, phase 3d). The construction of the porch disturbed a number of phase 2 graves here (numbers 144-147, 161, 195), but the variable dates of the finds from these (S/18, 20, 23) reflect the confused stratigraphy of the west half of the room. Against the east wall lay the ruined grave 163, set into the tufa and given a rough tufa block surround. This was badly disturbed by the construction of grave 162 in phase 3d.

(d) The baptistery area

North of the church a significant spread of lime was found in the east half of the former baptistery. This apparently emanated from the rubble-filled baptismal font (028), suggesting the use of this feature as a lime-mixing pit. The lime spread extended over graves 52-54 at the east end of the demolished baptistery. Finds from this level and from the font were, unfortunately, contaminated, ranging from the ninth century to the twelfth century. It was unclear whether the lime layer spread west of the font.

Interpretation

Phase 3a marked the construction of a second church twice the length of the original building, and reusing in its east half elements of the first church plan. Much of the masonry and a number of internal fittings will have been reutilized in the structure.

The most imposing feature of the new church was the triple crypt, where the relics of the saints were undoubtedly rehoused. The principle reliquary was located in the apse crypt (features 083 and 084) while niches in the north crypt and the niche and grave 153 in the south chamber presumably contained additional relics. Cross or groin vaults were used to roof the chambers, although in the central crypt two columns provided additional support for this arrangement.

A porch completed the plan, forming a well-paved entrance hall. This featured an elegant arcaded facade, constructed in brick, and resting on tufa foundations.

Lime-mixing, designed to supply mortar for construction, was carried out in the area of the former baptistery.

PHASE 3a-b THE KILN

Further activity occurred in the baptistery zone with the construction of a large kiln (102). This was inserted into the north-west corner of the baptistery, with part of the make-up for the kiln's outer wall extending over the building's foundation blocks. In addition, the kiln cut the north-west side of the baptismal font. The kiln was roughly circular, of overall diameter c. 3 m (internally 2.1 m) and

had been cut down into bedrock to a depth of c. 0.8 m (Fig. 10; Pl. 25). Externally there was evidence for a broken tile facing at the north-west corner and along its west side. Otherwise its walls exhibited rough, small stone construction, standing to two steps, in what was presumably a stepped-domed roof. Internally there was a neater use of small blocks, and the faces were probably clay-lined, as suggested by the presence of a few hardened patches. The triangular mouth of the kiln was formed by two large stone slabs of unequal size, flanked by tufa blockwork. From this extended eastwards a flue channel (103), set at the same level as the mouth: U-shaped in form, the flue was 2.3 m long and 1.3 m wide at ground level, diminishing to c. 1 m wide on its floor. Its insertion removed the west end of grave 54 and clearly cut through the phase 3a lime layer.

A fortunate survival was that of the raised floor (104) of the kiln (Fig. 10). This was supported by a series of square piers of mortared tile, disposed around the circumference of the kiln interior, which rose from the kiln bottom and followed the curve of its walls to a height of 0.8-0.9 m. The floor was pierced by a series of ten large vents arranged symmetrically around its circumference, four of which lay at the back of the kiln. In the centre were set fourteen smaller vents arranged in two rows, with the rearward group consisting of eight vents spaced 0.1-0.2 m apart.

Interpretation

The kiln (102-104) probably served for the production of tiles for the roof of the church, and perhaps also of the monastery to the south. Although we do not know the total time taken to complete all building activity on the site, it should be assumed that this was not short. The presence of a tile-kiln demonstrates that an insufficient quantity of reusable tile was available and that on-site manufacture was necessary to complement this. The rock-cut base of the kiln allowed the generation of much heat, and the greater intensity of heat towards the back was reflected in the distribution of air vents.

PHASE 3c

Burials had begun to be made near the church north wall, although it is impossible to assign these securely to specific sub-phases, since burials were made throughout phase 3. We can discern, however, a number of graves which cut the tufa and which predate a series of higher-lying burials. In the area of the former baptistery graves 26, 30, 31, 33, 34, all of small dimensions, lay alongside the north wall, while the small tomb 32 cut the south edge of the font (see below, Chapter 3). Further small graves lay to the east, between the church and the ante-baptistery room (numbers 75, 92, 93 and 95). Near the campanile the larger tombs 104, 107, 108, 151, and perhaps also 56 and 62, can be noted. The majority of these tombs had been badly disturbed and most of the finds were thus late (late twelfth and thirteenth century in date).

Within the church, against the north-west face of the campanile, an upper tomb was added to grave 61 (see above, phase 2f). This involved construction of walling on its south side and over the foundations of the first church north wall, and the insertion of a sarcophagus fragment to the west (Pl. 16). The south side (105) was formed by

Fig. 10. Santa Cornelia: tile kiln in baptistery, section (VW, NC)

tile-faced walling, 2.1 m long and 0.2-0.25 m wide, which butted up to and ran slightly around the campanile west door, at which point it still stood *c.* 0.8 m high. On the opposite side crude tufa and tile coursing (106) rested over the foundations of the early north wall and against the internal face of the phase 3a wall; this coursing survived only near the campanile face. In contrast, the tomb's west face (107) was composed of what was originally half of the front of a strigillated sarcophagus featuring the lower half of a 'good shepherd' relief (fragment 507). This was set into a crude tufa and mortar bedding, with the northernmost fragment slotted in between blocks of the early north wall. The cover of the tomb comprised a large slab of Egyptian granite 0.5 m wide, the west half of which survived *in situ*. The base of the tomb was apparently provided by the marble slabs which had covered the lower tomb. The upper tomb contained a more or less complete skeleton. The construction of this tomb would have further disturbed the lower grave (given that the upper slabs did not form a solid base), already disturbed by phase 3a activity. Fills contained material indicating thirteenth-fourteenth century contamination.

Interpretation

Subsequent to the construction of the church and with the consequent redundancy of the tile-kiln, burials were resumed in the north, particularly near the church north wall. The frequency of small graves in this area, representing child burials, is difficult to explain. The insertion of an upper tomb to grave 61 is an interesting continuity and must mark a privileged tomb.

Plate 25. Santa Cornelia: tile kiln (104) in north-west corner of baptistery

PHASE 3d

(a) The area north of the church

Certainly now, if not in phase 3c, the superstructure of the kiln was demolished. Fills accumulated within and over the kiln containing much broken tile, bones (including the body of a dog), and a few sherds (M/5-6, 10 from fill, M/2, 4, 8 from over floor; K/8 from flue fill). A later twelfth century date for most of these finds again indicates late disturbance, no doubt caused by burial activity.

A layer of soil accumulated within the 'ante-baptistery room'. However, plaster appears to have been applied to the external face of the south wall (039), associated with which was a trodden earth surface, lying 0.3 m above the bedrock and running up to the external offset of the church north wall. This trodden level continued east, where it was bordered by walls 108 and 109. Wall 108 formed a 5 m extension to wall 039, though running on a slightly different alignment (Pl. 13). Butting up to the south-east corner of the 'ante-baptistery room', it comprised a tufa foundation, over which lay a wall 0.45-0.5 m thick, containing much tile. Off-centre in this lay traces of a doorway (110) 0.8-1 m wide. The foundations overlay graves 85, 107 and 108. The area terminated in an east wall (109) 3 m long and up to 0.52 m wide at foundation level, with fragments of tile coursing 0.4 m wide above. The wall butted up to the campanile, just east of the junction of the church north wall and bell-tower; a rough blocking was inserted between the church wall and wall 109. The latter overlay the centre of grave 151 and part-obscured grave 60. No finds were securely associated with the construction of these features.

(b) The church interior

Various important structural alterations were carried out within the crypt. The most extensive occurred in the north chamber, with much refacing in brick. The thickness of the north wall was increased from 0.65 to 0.95-1.15 m by the addition of a somewhat angled face (111) beginning from roughly the level of the third step of the crypt stairs (cf. Pl. 18). This had the effect of reducing the width of the lowest steps to 0.7-0.8 m. The new north wall was faced primarily in brick to a height of c. 0.95 m; over this ran a 0.25 m tufa course topped by three brick courses. In the subsequent tufa course were located three small squarish recesses spaced 1.1 m and 1.2 m apart. Over an additional tufa level in the north-west corner of the chamber and near the crypt entrance were the traces of the springing of the vault arches, beginning c. 1.8 m above floor level. These delimited a semi-circular area c. 2.2 m in diameter, composed chiefly of tufa blockwork. The vault squinches were preserved to a height of c. 0.8 m. Beyond the east squinch, the wall face was built in *opus listatum* of a reasonable quality of workmanship.

Traces of vaulting were likewise conserved on the refaced west wall. Here the 0.2 m thick refacing (112) was almost wholly brick built, featuring a five module height of 0.3 m. Tufa work was limited to the north half of the lowest course and to the area above and flanking a rectangular niche located slightly off-centre in the wall, c. 1.35 m above the floor. This was 0.33 m high, 0.28 m wide at its head and 0.32 m at its base, which was marked by a slightly projecting tile. The niche contained a few bones and skull fragments.

Two possible phases of vaulting were represented in this face: the first began at c. 1.4 m, replaced in this phase by new squinches for a cross vault at c. 1.75 m, corresponding to those of the north wall. The core of these squinches was preserved to the top of the west wall for a height of 0.8 m. A niche had been built up to the earlier of these squinches at the curve of the corridor wall.

There was no evident sign of restructuring in the central crypt. However, the crude transition from tufa to brick (113) at the entrance to the south chamber can probably also be related to phase 3d. Here the corridor wall angled sharply south-west to join the west wall: wholly brick-built, of five module height 0.29-0.31 m, this obscured any tufa ledge to the wall. Refacing may have continued to the south, since both west and south walls were brick-built over a tufa block course (Pl. 21). The walls of the south chamber, preserved to just 1.2 m high, showed no traces of the vaulting arrangement.

Rubble from the crypts relating to the paving of the overlying presbytery included a number of Cosmatesque elements (i.e. cut marble shapes, notably in porphyry). Further elements came from rubble over the church, and included part of an inlaid altar screen. Only near the church entrance was any of this floor (080) preserved *in situ*, here being overlain by collapsed masonry.

Perhaps at this same period the brick-built staircase (114) was added to the west side of the campanile, thereby reducing the width of the west door to 0.6 m. The staircase, resting on a low tufa rubble platform of 1.9 × 0.9 m set over the floor of the campanile, was constructed against the south side of grave 61, with its east face flush with the internal face of the campanile. Three slabs of white marble survived to mark the position of the lowest steps of this stairway, which stood to 1.5 m (Pl. 16).

(c) The narthex

In the narthex the phase 3a slabbed floor was covered in both north and south compartments by a packed earth layer, in general 0.2 m deep, but in some areas very fragmentary. Using data derived from finds in the fill of the graves here (e.g. P/17, 21, 24; S/23; Y/8) we can argue for a later twelfth-thirteenth century disturbance.

Contemporary with this raised level was the insertion of a series of pier bases (115-122), preserved best in the south compartment, and consisting of brick-built bases of 0.6-0.7 × 0.4 m set on tufa foundations (cf. Fig. 6). Piers were set in each corner of the compartments and at the mid-point of their west and east walls. To the north the tufa supports of only three bases remained (115, 116, 117): pier 117 in the south-west corner, flanking the church entrance and causeway, comprised a tufa block of 0.45 × 0.25 × 0.25 m, resting on a tufa support and mortared against the church foundations (Pl. 23). There was no trace of a corresponding base against the rear of the porch entrance.

In the south compartment, five bases (118-122) survived. Pier 118 lay south of 117 to flank the other side of the doorway. Resting on a rough rubble base which part extended over the causeway south wall (097), it survived to a height of nine courses, and featured a five module height of 0.275-0.28 m. The corresponding pier 119 against the inside face of the porch door was 0.7 × 0.3-0.35 m. Due south of pier 118, against the church facade, lay bases 120 and 122, spaced 2 m apart, and both consisting of brick-coursed piers set on tufa and tile foundations: pier 120 retained twelve brick courses (five module = 0.26 m) over a rough mortared base of 0.9 × 0.5 m; 122 lay at a lower level, resting on a rough tufa base 0.35 m high, with nine brick courses (five module = 0.275 m). Only a crude tufa base of 0.7 × 0.4 m remained for 121.

A south-east corner pier was apparently rendered unnecessary through construction of grave 162 (cf. Pl. 23), of dimensions 2.1 × 1 m, bordered by tufa- and tile-built walls 123-125, and containing two skeletons, lacking skulls, and a heap of loose bones. An additional phase 3d element was the double tufa block feature 126, located between piers 119 and 121.

The level of paving in the causeway was raised with new paving (127) of tufa slabs. These were 0.2-0.4 × 0.25-0.4 m, laid in north - south rows over a rough soil, tufa and *spolia* fill, covering the phase 3a slabs. This fill included part of a Roman inscription, and two fragments of ninth century interlace (fragment numbers 552a-b).

Interpretation

The soil level identified within the 'ante-baptistery room' signifies the room's redundancy and the demolition/robbing of its walls. Its south wall was retained, however, and extended to the east. The associated trodden surface formed a floor or the bedding for a floor. The area is unlikely to have acted as an independent room; rather, its proximity to the church north door suggests some form of passage-way or covered area. A door near the east end gave access to this 'passage'.

The extensive refacing that took place within the crypt probably countered structural deficiencies of the original plan. In the case of the north chamber, the added north and west faces and the reworking of the vault squinches may even signify that the ceiling here had collapsed or at least required major remodelling. The niches probably held lamps, although some may have held relics originally. The refacing visible in the south crypt may likewise point to a rebuilt vault.

Elements of Cosmatesque paving found within the church testify to a significant refurbishment of the interior in the second half of the twelfth-early thirteenth century, which may have gone hand-in-hand with the crypt refacing.

The brick staircase (114) built against grave 61 provided access to the upper levels of the campanile, perhaps replacing an earlier internal stair. Its construction may have coincided with a brick refacing of parts of the bell-tower (cf. above, phase 2e).

The raising of the floor level within the porch may have been necessitated by the sinkage of the phase 3a floor into underlying graves. A packed earth fill provided the bedding to this new floor, which was probably paved, though paving survived only in the causeway. The pier bases were inserted symmetrically, flanking both church and porch entrances, and set in the corners of the porch and centrally against the walls of both compartments. It seems unlikely that these bases acted as buttresses or provided support for internal vaulting. It is more logical to

regard them as bases for pilasters or small decorative columns: in support of this we can note how in the east their positions corresponded perfectly with the piers of the arcaded facade. These pilasters thus served to embellish the interior of the porch and to highlight the entrance-way.

Grave 162 may have been the tomb of an abbot of the monastery.

PHASE 3e

Graves were dug in the interior of the former 'ante-baptistery room', cutting through the mortar floor and partially cutting the bedrock (numbers 71-73, 82, 88, 89, 98-100, 102, 103) and in some cases (99, 100) cutting into the remaining foundations (Pl. 13).

Interpretation

These graves attest a spread of the cemetery area over the demolished 'ante-baptistery room'. The passage-way area to the south remained in use.

PHASE 3f

Within the porch the level of the side-walls flanking the paved causeway were raised with rough stonework, although this was only preserved to any significant height in the east half of the south wall (128). Its north face was of unshaped tufa with occasional brick, bonded with purplish mortar and standing to *c.* 0.5 m. Its south face consisted of very crude, uncoursed tufa. To the east this butted up to pier base 119. The foundations for the south wall extended down on to bedrock, further disturbing grave 144.

Simultaneously the arcades of the facade wall were blocked, with the blocking (129) comprising rough courses of brick with some small stonework. In the preserved section of collapsed wall two columns of the arcades were walled in, although the impost capital of one of these was removed (Pl. 24).

Within the 'passage-way', a crude tufa and rubble walling (130), 1.5 m long, was constructed against the external face of the church near the north-west corner of the campanile.

Interpretation

The crude raising of the causeway side-walls, combined with the blocking of the porch facade arcades, saw the transformation of the north and south compartments into two distinct rooms. The first was accessible only from the campanile, the second seemingly only from the monastery area. The function of these rooms is unclear. The removal of the phase 3d columns and some of their bases may have been contemporary: certainly the remnants of the causeway north side-wall appeared to run over into the space presumed to have been occupied by a pier. The absence of additional columns in the debris of the collapsed facade should indicate that not all the arcade columns were walled in *in situ*.

The function of the passage-way walling 130 was unclear, being in no way substantial enough to have acted as a buttress.

PHASE 4a

Within the campanile a fragmentary trodden earth surface up to 0.1 m deep was found overlying the original broken tile and mortar floor. Patches of burning were noted over this tread, in particular against the south wall where lay the remains of a crude hearth, covered by two tiles. The church interior featured no comparable earth surface, although a sandy soil 0.1-0.2 m deep, containing a few rubble fragments (fragments 164 and 165, including part of an interlace panel and a chancel post), was identified in the west half of the church.

A large oval pit (047), *c.* 1.25 × 1 m was cut down in to the bedrock to a notable depth towards the centre of the church nave. Its fill contained fourteenth and fifteenth century pottery (N/3, 4) and a wide assortment of fragments relating to the church's fittings. These included architectural fragments 262-265, 296-311, 386-393, 409-414, and comprised fragments of column bases, columns, capitals, floor elements, corbels, stamped tiles, choir screen panels with interlace, part of a ninth century inscription referring to *Pasqualis* – probably Pope Paschal I (fragment 265; see below, inscription number 1) – and part of a Cosmatesque screen (Pls 51 and 53).

Similar was pit 048, 0.9 m in diameter, set in the proximity of the church entrance and partly cutting grave 111. This contained fragments 686-700, 716-722, consisting of fragments of stamped tile, floor elements, interlace and a Cosmatesque altar panel.

The disturbance within the church of many graves, whose fills contain late material, should be contemporary.

Interpretation

The sandy soil can be regarded as fill consequent to the removal of flooring. The absence of *in situ* floor in much of the church interior indicates a general robbing of this in phase 4a, which can only relate to the abandonment of the church. The nature of the robbing appears somewhat selective, however, since overlying rubble and plough layers contained floor and other architectural elements, while pits 047 and 048 featured a surprising array of discarded marble items. Graves within the church likewise saw disturbance. Few finds were present to date this robbing, although pits 047 and 048 contained later fourteenth-fifteenth century material. However, robbing may well have begun well before this.

The hearth within the campanile suggests that this structure was now being utilized as a temporary shelter.

The situation inside the porch was unclear, although a similar stripping of the floor and of other reusable elements should be assumed.

PHASE 4b

Particularly in the east half of the church a dark layer with traces of burning overlay the make-up of the robbed church floor. Contemporary with this appears to be the collapse of walling over the paving (080) near the entrance (Pl. 26). Further burnt traces were noted over the marble paving (021) in the north aisle. In parts this dark layer was disturbed by ploughing: however, we can tentatively link

Plate 26. Santa Cornelia: fallen walling over phase 3d floor (080) inside church main entrance

finds G/2, 11, 13, 15, L/5, P/5, 6, and S/10 to this. These offer a broad thirteenth-fourteenth century date.

Burnt traces and occasional collapse debris were also identified within the porch, notably in the north compartment (north compartment: P/31, Y/29; south compartment: Y/6, 32 and S/22; burnt material also noted in the fill of grave 162).

Interpretation

If we interpret the dark layer within the church as a destruction level, it can be argued that the church was, subsequent to a period of abandonment and robbing (phase 4a), partly destroyed by fire. A direct consequence of this was the collapse initially of its roofing (large quantities of tile were found in the rubble debris), tower, and, soon after, of additional elements of its structure, such as its side walls and its raised presbytery. To this same moment should belong the outward collapse of the porch facade, probably as a result of an eastward fall of the church facade. Material from the accumulation over the courtyard surface underlying this wall (finds X/49) points to a fourteenth century date.

PHASE 5

The ruinous church complex will subsequently have formed a ready quarry of building stone for local farmsteads and quite probably also for nearby Formello. The sub-plough levels contained much disturbed rubble material, often indistinguishable from the plough level. This rubble layer extended across the whole area of the church. For the architectural fragments from this and the plough, see phase 6 below.

PHASE 6

Continued robbing of the site hastened the disappearance of its remains, allowing renewed agricultural activity over the area. Deep ploughing greatly disturbed the underlying levels and brought a large amount of the phase 4 and 5 debris to the surface. The pottery from this level is accordingly very mixed. A large quantity of architectural fragments was recovered, including column and capital fragments, floor material (cut marble and inscriptions), chancel screen fragments, corbels, and tile.

(i) From the west half of the church (including the crypt area): fragment numbers 126-130, 135-145, 154, 158-162, 164-191, 194-206, 214-220, 222-226, 230, 231, 235-237, 246, 252, 253, 255, 266, 278, 280, 344-374, 397, 400, 401, 403, 540-547, 554, 588-606, 653, 666-674.

(ii) From the east half of the church: fragment numbers 41, 45-47, 238-245, 257-265, 267-276, 282-325, 338, 343, 386-396, 398, 399, 402, 404, 405, 409-431, 433-444, 447-469, 479-482, 484-489, 491-496, 498, 507-511, 537-539, 561, 562, 573, 574, 577, 578, 582-585, 587, 633-638, 640, 651, 652, 686-692, 696-700, 716-722.

(iii) From the campanile area: fragment numbers 6, 38, 39, 45, 117, 149-153, 328-337, 339, 383, 384.

(iv) From the porch area: fragment numbers 326, 327, 341, 342, 375-382, 497, 500-506, 511-516, 552, 623, 624, 677-679, 685, 693-695, 701-711, 712(?), 723-725(?), 739, 742, 743, 748, 749, 797, 802, 804, 805.

(v) From the baptistery area: fragment numbers 176,

192, 207-213, 229, 232-234, 247-251, 277, 279, 340, 535, 536, 586.

(vi) From the area west of the church: fragment numbers 31, 84, 85, 88, 89, 109, 111, 146-148, 155, 157.

SEQUENCE WITH FINDS:

1. Area west of church

Phase 1: Bedrock features with fills.

Phase 2a: Construction of first church. Cutting of lime-pits.
Phase 2a-f: Laying of graves.
Phase 2b: Early use of church.
Phase 2c: Construction of enclosure wall.
    Fill of lime-pits: D/9-13, E/7.

Phase 3a: Construction of second church: A/10; D/7, 8, 15; E/12, 15.
    Disturbance of phase 2 graves: includes some of A/11; B/2, 3; D/6, 14, 17; E/9, 10, 13, 14, possibly 8.
Phase 3a-f: Laying of graves.

Phase 5: Sub-plough: A/3, 5-7, 9; B/4; BE/1; BM/2, 3; R/5, 6.

Phase 6: Plough: A/1, 7; B/1, 5; BE/1; BM/1; D/2-5, 24; E/1; M/1.

Unstratified material: A/12; D/1, 18.

2. The Churches

Phase 1: Bedrock features and fills: includes some of F/12(?), S/5, 9, 37, 39.

Phase 2a: Levelling of bedrock beneath and around church.
    Construction of the first church; insertion of saints' graves; laying of church floor.
Phase 2b: Early use of church.
Phase 2b-f: Laying of graves around church.
Phase 2e: Construction of campanile. Bell-pit: includes G/8, 10.

Phase 3a: Construction of second church: A/10; D/7, 8, 15; E/12, 15; P/2, 9 (unless phase 4); S/6, 7, 29, 38(?), 42.
    Fill of phase 2 graves: includes some of F/7-11, 13; G/6a; L/1, 5, 6; N/7, 8, 16; some of P/13; R/10; S/30, 31.
    Fill of bell-pit: G/9, 12, 14, 16.
Phase 3a-f: Duration of second church: may include some of N/2; P/2, 9; S/29.
    Laying of graves around second church.
Phase 3d: Internal refurbishment (Cosmatesque floor, etc.).

Phase 4: Abandonment, collapse, robbing of church: G/2, 11, 13, 15(?); L/5(?); N/3, 4, 9, 14; P/13, 15, 35; S/10, 28, 40(?).
    Crypt rubble: (upper rubble) A/2, 4, 8; D/23; E/4, 11,

16; F/4, 5; G/4, 7; R/2, 8; (lower rubble) D/19, 20; F/2; G/6b, 17.

Fill of grave 153 in crypt: R/3, 7, 9.

Fill of reliquary: D/22.

Phase 5: Sub-plough: F/1, 3, 6, 14; G/2, 3, 5; L/2(?), 4; N/1, 6, 7, 9(?); P/3, 4, 10, 11, 34; S/1, 2, 8.

Phase 6: Plough: D/1, 21; E/1; F/1; G/1; L/3, 4; N/12, 13; P/10, 12; S/1, 2.

Unstratified material: N/15; S/32, 40(?).

3. The Porch

Phase 2a: Levelling of ground around church area. Construction of first church.

Phase 2b: First use of church.

Phase 2c-d: Construction of perimeter wall.

Phase 2d-f: Graves in area preceding church.

Phase 2e: Construction of belltower.

Phase 3a: Construction of porch. First porch floor.
  Fill of phase 2 graves: includes some of P/18, 22-25; S/18, 20; Y/20, 23, 24, 33 (much relates to phase 3d and 4).

Phase 3d: Laying of second porch floor. Fill over earlier floor: P/32. Disturbance of graves (see 3a above): P/17, 21, 24; S/23; Y/8.

Phase 4: Abandonment and robbing of area: P/26; Y/8, 15, 18, 30, 32.
  Collapse and debris: P/31; S/17(?), 22(?), 24(?); Y/6, 26(?), 27(?), 29.

Phase 5: Sub-plough: P/7, 31; S/19; Y/5, 6, 9, 26(?), 29.

Phase 6: Plough: Y/13.

Unstratified material: P/33; S/17, 21, 24, 41; Y/28.

4. Baptistery area

Phase 1: Bedrock features and fills.

Phase 2a: Clearance of zone. Construction of first church and baptistery: perhaps K/7(?).

Phase 2b: First use of church.

Phase 2d: Conversion of area to east into ante-baptistery room.

Phase 2e: Demolition of baptistery. Fill of font.

Phase 2f: Insertion of burials into baptistery area.

Phase 3a: Construction of second church. Use of font for lime-mixing: M/7, 9.
  Fill of graves: K/10, 14. Earth layer under lime spread: includes some of K/11-13.

Phase 3b: Construction of kiln: M/4 (?).

Phase 3d: Demolition of ante-baptistery room. Construction of 'passage-way' to its south. Burials in ante-baptistery room.

Phase 3d-e: Fill of kiln: M/5, 6, 10. Flue fill: K/8.

Phase 3e-4: Fill of graves: K/3, 4, 9(?), possibly some of N/19-23.

Phase 4: Abandonment and robbing of church area. Fill of other graves: K/5, 6; N/19-22; Q/3, 5.

Phase 5: Sub-plough: H/3, 5, 6; M/2, 4, 8; N/10-12; Q/2.

Phase 6: Plough: H/1; K/1, 2; M/1; N/10-12; Q/1.

(ii) THE COURTYARD COMPLEX

INTRODUCTION

Area X covered the zone extending east of the church and porch complex, in the north-east corner of the site as a whole. The area was partly trenched in 1963 and extended in 1964; it was covered by east trenches II, V, VI, VIII, IX, X, XI, XII and XIII (see Fig. 2). Time was not available, however, to complete the excavations and to clear the whole area to bedrock. This fact, combined with the evident plough damage, meant that the sequence was at times confused and features isolated. Finds from this area were recorded under the heading X except in the case of material from the westernmost part of the area which was excavated as part of sector Y.

The area was presumed to have formed the courtyard preceding the church and its narthex, bounded to north and east by the perimeter wall. A sequence of six phases can be identified here.

PHASE 1a-b

The east half of area X preserved traces of a series of long tufa-cut features predating any structures on the site (Fig. 11). Of these, seven were oriented west-east (132-138) and the remaining two north-west-south-east (139 and 140). These were cut into the bedrock to a variable depth and were generally 0.8-0.9 m wide. Three periods were identified: the earliest consisted of those running north-west-south-east, where 139 was only partly visible, while 140 was traced for a length of c. 21 m. A second phase was marked by three west-east examples (133, 135, 137) c. 0.75 m wide. The trenches of the latest series (132, 134, 136, 138) were also west-east oriented and spaced consistently 6.0-6.3 m apart with an average width of 0.9 m.

These trenches contained a fill of tufa-coloured soil, lacking finds. There was no trace of a packed fill similar to that identified in trench 001 beneath the church. A similar light soil covered the natural tufa.

Tufa-cut post-holes were also present, scattered over much of the east part of area X. A concentration was found at the south end of east trench XII, some of 0.2 m diameter, others of up to 0.55-0.6 m diameter, but these yielded no discernable pattern.

Interpretation

The tufa-cut features can be interpreted as agricultural trenches, as indicated by their general regularity of size and spacing: three phases of trenching are visible. The orientation of the west–east trenches relates to the lie of the land, in that they follow the natural gentle slope of the low rise on which the site lies; the north-west–south-east trenches, however, will have run up this.

These agricultural trenches can be put in line with those recognized throughout the excavations, in particular in the south-east corner complex and in the west part of the monasterial zone. It is likely that they represent notable agricultural activity by a local Roman villa of later republican date.

PHASE 1d

To this phase may be ascribed the narrow, 0.15 m wide, feature 150 identified in the south-east part of area X over tufa soil. This was traced for a discontinuous length of *c.* 9 m, running north-west–south-east (Fig. 11).

Interpretation

Feature 150 resembles a series of trenches identified in area W to the south, which are identified as vine trenches. However, 150 was isolated and its narrow trench lacked postholes to mark the setting of vines or their supports.

PHASE 2a

The west traces of the phase 1a agricultural trenches appear to have been destroyed by the cutting back of the natural tufa bedrock to a distance of 8.4-8.5 m from the foundations of the porch facade (cf. below, Fig. 31). The tufa was bare except south of the narthex entrance, where it retained the cutting of grave 195 (see below). In this sector the natural tufa level was covered by an earth fill containing tile fragments. This contrasted with the phase 1b soil fill of the agricultural trench.

Interpretation

The cutting back of the bedrock represented a systematic levelling of the site for constructional purposes, relating to the preparation of the ground for the first church. A similar cutting-back operation can be claimed both for the area of the first church and for that of the monastery cloister complex. Over the reduced natural tufa level lay an earth layer containing some tile, presumably an artificial soil cover in front of the church.

PHASE 2a-b

The west half of area X contained a series of tufa blocks (142, 143, 144), many 0.45-0.5 m long. In east trench X these blocks formed a rough, incomplete line running west-north-west– east-south-east (144), to which can probably be linked the outline of a rough rectangular feature (141) of *c.* 2.0 × 1.7 m, incomplete on its north side, bounded by small tufa blocks and with a broken tile set off-centre in its interior. Further tufa blocks featuring traces of mortar lay to the east (145, 146); near 146, part of a fluted column (fragment number SC776) was found. Close by lay the traces of three badly ruined foundation

Plate 27. Santa Cornelia: courtyard, tufa tumble (144) in lower tread surface

walls (147, 148, 149), two of which followed a west–east (tending west-north-west–east-south-east) alignment and were between 0.7 and 0.9 m thick, while 148 was north–south and of uncertain thickness. The relationship between these foundation walls and the scattered tufa blockwork was uncertain, although orientation was similar (Fig. 11; Pl. 27).

At a point 1.5 m south of the porch entrance lay grave 195, overlain at its west end by the foundations for the later porch facade. No other graves were located in area X.

Interpretation

The series of tufa blocks identified in the west half of area X cannot be firmly interpreted. The blockwork overlay the earth fill covering the cut-back bedrock, and followed a predominantly west–east orientation, extending up to 8.5 m from the front of the porch. The fallen fluted column fragment also lay at this distance. The lie of these features is suggestive of fallen or demolished wallings. It is uncertain if the ruined foundation walls 147 and 149 were related to these tufa-block features or were later additions. The function of these features cannot be firmly established, but one possibility would be to hypothesize the existence of an atrium, forming a forecourt to the first church and predating construction of the porch. The fragility of these features prevents an accurate assessment of this. Grave 195 should be included among those burials made during

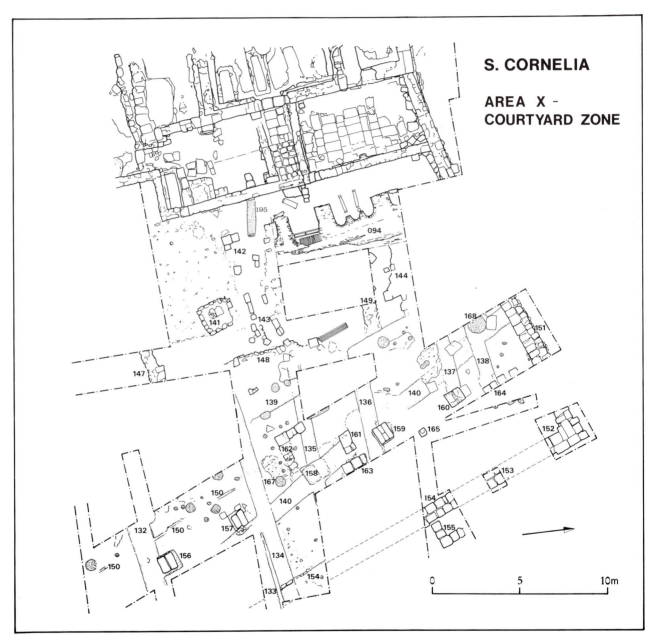

Fig. 11. Santa Cornelia: courtyard, all phases (VW)

phase 2 in front of the first church. It was the easternmost grave excavated at Santa Cornelia.

PHASE 2c-d

In the west half of area X, a trodden earth level was laid up to and around the tufa blocks and ruined foundation walls noted for phase 2a/b; in some cases it covered these features. It lay up to 0.5 m deep in the west, extending up to the porch foundations and covering grave 195, but became fragmentary to the east, dying out *c.* 7 m from the porch (Pl. 27). No finds were securely associated with this surface. The stratigraphical relationship between this trodden level and the sequence to the east could not be determined due to the heavy disturbance of the levels at this point. However, it seems probable that contemporary with it was the construction of the line of the perimeter wall to both north and east (151-154), and the insertion of a series of tufa-built pier bases (156-160) parallel to the east perimeter wall.

The section of wall running north-east from the church and incorporated as the north wall (046) of the porch has been described above. Its course was relocated *c.* 7.5 m from the north-east corner of the porch as a single foundation course (151) *c.* 1 m thick. This was built of large tufa blocks 0.55-0.6 m deep, laid as headers on the internal face and smaller blockwork externally, where a rough offset was present. The wall lay directly on bedrock. The north-east corner of the enclosure wall (152) was identified 3 m east, slightly displaced with respect to the line of wall 151. The corner itself was irregularly shaped with large tufa blocks *c.* 0.5 m thick. Subsequently the wall ran south-south-east with a thickness of *c.* 1.1 m. Its course was trenched at two further points, showing it to be *c.* 1.0 m thick with foundations faced on both sides in large tufa blocks (153, 154 and 154a). Immediately east of 154 lay an L-shaped feature (155) composed of five tufa blocks of 0.45-0.5 × 0.5 m, but lacking a corresponding feature to the north (Fig. 11).

To the south, the perimeter wall had been robbed out, although its course was clear and relatively straight. It butted up to the north wall (195) of room 5 in the south-east sector.

Five tufa-built pier bases (156-160), set in foundation trenches which occasionally cut down into the natural tufa, were constructed *c.* 4 m west of the internal face of the east perimeter wall (Pl. 28). These were spaced fairly regularly along the length of this, at a distance of between 3.5 and 4.25 m. Pier 160, however, was slightly displaced to the east of the general line of the bases. These bases were squarish, built of large tufa blocks bonded with white mortar, and in general comprised two tufa blocks at their base. Overall dimensions varied between 0.75-0.9 × 0.8-1.0 m. The robbed-out pier 158 survived only as a foundation trench. To the south-west of pier 159 rested a large, broken travertine slab (161) of 0.65 × 1.05 m, perhaps an additional pier base.

Contemporary with the piers should be the L-shaped walling (162), located west of the foundation trench of pier 158, and the tufa-block wall traces (163-165) running north-north-west–south-south-east, immediately east of bases 158-160. The L-shaped wall comprised a single course of tufa blocks, 0.45 m thick, part-fragmentary, with a length of 1.85 m on its west side and 2.1 m to the south. The absence of the blocks of both pier 158 and of the rest of

the south side of this wall made it unclear whether the wall was built up to pier 158 or vice versa. Of walling 163-165, a set of three 0.55 m thick blocks lay east of slab 161, and a further four blocks north-east of pier 160. The single tufa block set between piers 159 and 160 may also relate to this line.

West and south of wall 162 lay a series of post-holes of 0.2 m diameter, aligned with the wall and set at a distance of 0.3 m from this. These post-holes underlay the mortar floor of the room.

Interpretation

It is uncertain for how long the hypothetical 'atrium' may have existed. Its walls had been demolished, however, with the laying of a trodden earth surface in this area. Certainly the tread overlay or at least part-covered the remaining traces of its walls. The trodden level therefore comprised the early courtyard surface preceding the church. It spread south as far as the ruined foundation wall 147, while to the north and east its limits were formed by newly-constructed features.

To the north the enclosure wall (046, 151-154) ran north-east from the porch for a distance of 18 m before turning south-east and running for 33 m up to the south-east sector. The L-shaped wall (155), located *c.* 10 m south of the north-east corner of the enclosure, may mark the position of a formal gateway.

The line of five pier bases parallel to the east perimeter

Plate 28. Santa Cornelia: area of room 6, cleared to bedrock, viewed from north

wall should belong to the same phase as the enclosure wall, and document the construction of a piered building against the rear of this. No similar piers were identified on the north side. Although the west flank of this structure (designated 'room 6') was not identified, its dimensions must have been *c.* 33 × 11 m, extending as far as room 5 of the south-east corner complex. A structure of this size would undoubtedly have been partitioned into smaller units: connected with this may be the tufa blockwork (162-165) identified near the pier bases, although its relationship with the piers is unclear. No other possible partitions were identified.

The series of carefully spaced post-holes south and west of the L-shaped wall 162 may denote the position of scaffolding.

PHASE 2d

Following construction of the piers, a make-up of dark brown earth – visible occasionally as a burnt, black layer – was set over the phase 1b tufa soil and the phase 1d vine trench (150). Over this was laid white mortar. In some points, as for example near pier 158, the plough had removed this mortar level, and disturbed the make-up. Beside pier 157 were found traces of a broken tile beaten surface containing a few pieces of porphyry. Further south, the south-east corner of the structure featured a quarter circle or quadrant of radius 1.8 m, formed by marble or travertine slabs, with packing around (166). No floor traces were identified east of pier bases 159 and 160.

Interpretation

Room 6 was provided with a white mortar floor set over a dark earth make-up. It is possible that the mortar formed a bedding for a paved surface, given the presence of tile and porphyry fragments around pier 157 and quadrant 166. Material found in the disturbed layer over the floor level included a few pieces of marble, and an inscription fragment which may have come from marble flooring. In many places plough action and robbing previous to ploughing had removed the traces of the mortar surface.

The presence of tile fragments in the plough material over area X may indicate that room 6 was tile-roofed, though it is also possible that this material represents debris from the church and porch.

We lack finds to date the construction of room 6 precisely. The strata of packing of the quadrant vary from ninth to eleventh century date (finds X/4 and 5): the ninth century evidence may possibly help date the floor, the later levels the robbing of the zone.

PHASE 2e

In the west half of area X a soil layer, featuring some tile, overlay the trodden courtyard level. This extended to a depth of 0.2 m in the proximity of the porch, but diminished to the east to disappear at a point *c.* 5 m away. Towards the south end of trench IX a black layer overlay what was presumed to be the level of the lower trodden surface: X/38 from this offered a good tenth century group of material. A similar date was offered by X/73 to the north. Finds (X/12, 21, 43, 44) elsewhere in this level,

however, were mixed, dating from the tenth to fourteenth centuries and indicate a high degree of contamination from upper levels.

Interpretation

The soil represents accumulation over the phase 2c-d trodden courtyard surface. This need not relate to an abandonment: there was no associated rubble, and the depth of build-up was limited. Rather this should be regarded as accumulation during the use of this courtyard. The plough had in parts cut down into this layer, resulting in somewhat disturbed finds.

PHASE 3

The lower trodden courtyard with accumulation was subsequently sealed beneath a fairly consistent packed stone surface, containing some tile (Pl. 29). Towards the porch this was present as a compact surface, but diminished in thickness to the east, becoming very patchy. Traces of the packed surface were identified also under the section of fallen porch facade (094). Only fragments of the level were identified at the presumed east limit of the courtyard area. Finds from the packed stone level were quite mixed, suggesting contamination from the disturbed upper levels: however, finds X/30, 35, 36, 68, and 69 indicate an eleventh century date, as would be supported by the *denarius* of Otto I (967-973) found on the actual packed stone surface.

Its north limit was formed by the line of the perimeter wall. The east edge was uncertain, while its south extent coincided with the ruined west-north-west–east-south-east foundation wall 147. Immediately north of this the packed stone surface overlay a black layer which, as noted, probably related to phase 2e accumulation; to the south lay a plain soil fill.

Post-holes and small pits were cut down through the floor of room 6, in particular west of piers 157 and 160, and near feature 162. Eight of these were of diameter 0.45-0.6 m, but their spacing offered no coherent pattern. East of wall 162 lay a shallow depression (167). North-west of pier 160 and 1.2 m south of the perimeter wall, the floor was cut by a deep, bulbous pit (168) with mouth diameter of 1 m: its black earth fill contained some pottery, much tile and a few architectural fragments (finds X/72). In some points sparse traces of a dark brown accumulation overlay the mortar floor. The disturbed stratigraphy along the main axis of room 6, however, left it unclear whether the posts and pits noted above also cut through this accumulation.

Contemporary may have been the robbing of the zone for building material: within room 6 the blocks of pier 158 and part of wall 162 had certainly been removed. Robbing of the east perimeter wall disturbed part of the mortar floor.

Interpretation

The packed stone level represents a resurfacing of the courtyard. There was nothing to suggest that the pack was formed by demolition or tip material. It is tempting to regard this new courtyard as contemporary with the

Plate 29. Santa Cornelia: courtyard area, packed stone surface and tufa feature 141

restructuring of the church and its narthex; though few, the finds may support an eleventh century date. The coin of Otto I was somewhat worn and would fit an eleventh century context. There was no sign that room 6 underwent structural alteration or reflooring. Nor is restructuring evident for the perimeter wall, at least not at foundation level. Room 6 may briefly have remained in use, but more likely was already ruinous by phase 3a. Robbing of the perimeter wall for building material may have been underway by the eleventh century.

PHASE 4

Towards the porch a level of earth covered the packed courtyard level. Finds from this (Y/22, 25, X/24-27, 32, 49) comprised material mainly of late thirteenth-fourteenth century date. Likewise a layer of soil 0.15-0.3 m deep was identified beneath the fallen porch wall, the depth being greater closer to the porch foundations. This dark earth also covered the presumed entrance step (099) into the narthex.

Interpretation

This soil can be interpreted as accumulation: it lacked rubble material. While it is possible that it related to the period of abandonment of the church, it is equally likely that accumulation built up while the site remained occupied. The church may have been out of use for some time previous to its collapse.

PHASE 5

In the north-west, the remains of the collapsed portion of porch facade (094) were uncovered directly under the plough level: this feature overlay phase 4 accumulation. Some of the rubble located in the sub-plough east of the church complex may also have related to the collapse of masonry. This rubble included a fragment with an inscription (fragment 740, from X/52) found over the floor level of room 6, perhaps once part of the floor surface, and a stamped tile (fragment 840, from X/59), also from over the floor.

PHASE 6

The plough level overlying the whole courtyard zone was of very disturbed earth containing some sculptural and architectural material, including tiles, fragments of inscriptions, corbels from near the porch, and column fragments. The material comprised fragment numbers: 555-559, 565-569, 658, 680, 713-715, 733-736, 740, 774-776, 789, 790, 792, 793, 798-801, 806-808, 840, 961, 962.

SEQUENCE WITH FINDS:

Phase 1a: Bedrock features (trenches, post-holes) in east half of area X.
Phase 1b: Fill of phase 1a features.
Phase 1d: 'Palisade' trench in south-east.

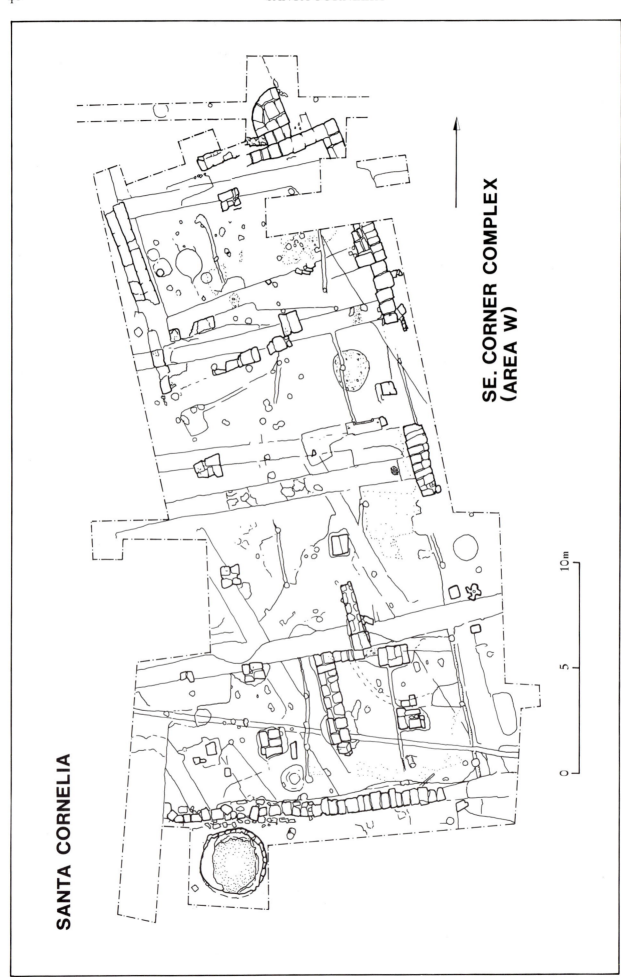

SANTA CORNELIA

SE. CORNER COMPLEX (AREA W)

0   5   10m

Fig. 12. Santa Cornelia: south-east corner, all phases (VW)

Phase 2a: Cutting back of tufa in front of porch and fill over.

Phase 2a-b: Construction of tufa-built features in west half of area.

Cutting of grave 195.

Phase 2c-d: Lower courtyard level covering or part-covering demolished phase 2b features: may include some of X/41, 42.

Construction of perimeter wall and insertion of piers parallel to east wall: X/61 (from cleaning foundation trench of pier B).

Phase 2d: Laying of mortar floor in room 6: some of X/4 and 5 (from packing of stones of quadrant).

Phase 2e: Accumulation of soil over lower courtyard: X/12, 21, 33, 38, 40-44, 69, 70, 73.

Phase 3: Laying of packed stone level over accumulation in court area: X/11, 25, 27, 30, 35, 36, 68.

Accumulation over floor of room 6: may include X/55, 56, 58, 60, 62, 63. Demolition of room and robbing of perimeter wall: X/3, 52, 53. Features cutting floor of room 6: fill of pit 168, X/72.

Phase 4: Accumulation over packed stone level: Y/22, 25; X/12, 24-27, 32, 49, 71.

Phase 5: Collapse of porch facade over courtyard accumulation.

Sub-plough: Y/7, 10, 12, 17, 57; X/8, 28, 34, 37, 45, 47, 48.

Phase 6: Plough: Y/11, 14, 51; X/1, 7, 9, 10, 14, 17, 39, 46, 50.

Unstratified material: X/15, 66.

Material from south end of area X, outside presumed 'courtyard':

Sub-plough: X/6, 13, 22, 23, 29, 30, 31.
Plough: X/2, 14, 39.

(iii) THE SOUTH-EAST CORNER

INTRODUCTION

The south-east sector was first investigated in 1960, with a single north–south trench (trench II). The area was more extensively trenched in 1962 with the long east trenches I, II, III, IV and VII, and then opened up and stripped to bedrock in 1963 (Fig. 12). The total area uncovered was c. 35 × 15-20 m. The area was regarded as the 'farm building quarter' of the domusculta Capracorum and in fact preserved significant data regarding activity on the site between Roman and early medieval times. An important stratigraphy survived for the early medieval phase.

The excavated zone was designated area W: all 'W' finds relate to this zone; in addition, a few 'X' finds belong to the northernmost part of area W, relating to east trench II.

PHASE 1a

The natural bedrock of the south-east sector showed the lines of eleven trench features (Fig. 13). A series of north-west–south-east trenches (169, 171-173) between 0.85 m and 1 m wide, spaced c. 5.5-5.8 m apart and relatively shallow cut, was identified. Part of a similar sized trench (170) was noted between 169 and 171. In the north half of area W were located two similarly shallow, west–east oriented, examples of c. 0.7-0.85 m width (176 and 178). The remaining four west–east trenches were 0.9-1.1 m wide, and spaced 6.2-6.5 m apart (174, 175, 177, 179). These were cut slightly more deeply into the bedrock. It is possible that the south line of the later perimeter wall (204) overlay the line of a further trench in this series (set c. 6.5-6.7 m distant from 174) (Pl. 30). Feature 174 narrowed c. 4 m from its west end, near the intersection with trench 171: here its north side swerved inward, narrowing the width from 1.05 m to just 0.4 m before curving outward again. The cause was uncertain, although it is possible that the natural tufa was too hard to cut through at this point.

Most probably to be associated with these trenches is the line of the deep tufa-cut trench 180, c. 0.2-0.3 m wide, running west-north-west–east-south-east across the south end of the excavated zone, between trench 174 and the later perimeter wall (Pls 31 and 32).

The bedrock also featured a number of post-holes, but these formed no coherent patterns; some had been cut down from later levels.

Interpretation

The area was dissected in the pre-domusculta period by a series of tufa-cut trenches, to be associated with olive or vine cultivation by a nearby Roman farmstead. Three phases of trenching were discernable: the earliest should be the five north-west–south-east trenches regularly spaced 5.5-5.8 m apart: the two shallow trenches 176 and 178 are probably also early in this sequence. The clearest, and probably also the latest, was the set of four trenches (174, 175, 177, 179) running west–east and spaced regularly at c. 6.5 m.

The narrow, deep-cut, feature 180 can be associated with at least one phase of trenching here. Its depth suggests that it acted as a drainage channel, carrying off surplus rainfall from the slope.

PHASE 1b

The bedrock was in general covered by a light tufa-coloured earth, although many of the agricultural trenches were filled with rammed earth (as 174) or with rammed earth and tufa pieces (as 175). Most material from these fills was Roman in date (e.g. W/96, 105, 106, 108, 124, 126 and 132).

Interpretation

The fill of the trenches, whether rammed earth or rammed earth with tufa, represents either packing or fill subsequent to the digging out of the trenches, perhaps prior to the cutting of new trenches across the area. On the basis of the pottery evidence, it seems likely that this agricultural activity relates to the period c. 200 BC–AD 100.

Plate 30. Santa Cornelia: south-east corner, rooms 2 and 4, and area 8 to bedrock

Plate 31. Santa Cornelia: south-east corner, rooms 1 and 2 to bedrock, viewed from east, with line and trench of perimeter wall, and phase 1a drainage trench 180

PHASE 1c

At least in the south half of area W the bedrock features and their overlying tufa earth fill came to be covered by a trodden or clay level, whose exact extension was not defined. There was an indication that the surface extended beyond the line of the later perimeter wall to the east, since patches of a baked brown clay surface were identified east of the later rooms 1 and 2. Find W/104 recorded from this surface has been lost.

Quite possibly associated with this surface were various post-holes, though some of these may well have cut this level. In the area of the later room 3 double post-holes were located in the spaces between the later piers 206 and 210, clearly indicating at least one period of post replacement. Two other features in this zone are noteworthy: a shallow pit (192) of 1.1 m diameter, and, to the north-west, over the drainage trench (180), feature 193, of roughly-circular form, 0.75 m in diameter (Fig. 13).

Interpretation

There is no clear explanation for the appearance of this trodden surface. No structures were associated with it, and it is thus difficult to regard it as a construction or floor surface. The post-holes revealed no distinct patterning in their locations, nor did their fills offer any indication of function. Features 192 and 193 are likewise anomalous.

PHASE 1d

A number of features cut down through the phase 1c surface on to bedrock. The clearest of these is a series of narrow north–south running 'palisade' trenches, 0.15-0.2 m wide (Pl. 34). The lines of three such trenches were identified (features 181-191), traceable for almost the whole length of the south-east corner excavations, set parallel to one another: the easternmost trenches (185-188 and 189-191) lay 3.0-3.5 m apart, while the central and western lines were 4-4.5 m apart. Various numbers of post-holes were present within the trenches, but occasionally these were not preserved and their spacing is thus uncertain: at the south end of the west trench (181-184) the post-holes were 1-1.5 m apart.

These trenches predated any construction in the area: the course of trench 189-191 in fact ran underneath the line of the later perimeter wall to east and south. Likewise, trench 185-188 ran beneath the south perimeter wall, pier base 212 and the door-sill of room 2.

In the area of room 5 at least one small pit (194) of 0.5 m diameter cut this trodden level.

Interpretation

It is difficult to perceive anything other than an agricultural function for the series of phase 1d 'palisade' trenches. Their narrowness and the irregular spacing of post-holes within them argues against a structural function, and we should regard them as vine trenches, with the posts marking the supports for the vines. A similar trench was traced in area X.

PHASE 2a

There was evidence for extensive burning over the phase 1c clay surface. This was particularly apparent in the area of the later rooms 2 and 3 where a thick, burnt, black level, containing much clinker, was recognized. The surface itself was in many places scorched or burnt, whilst the baked patch located outside the line of the east perimeter wall should also indicate burning.

Many of the post-holes cutting into the clay surface, including those of the phase 1d vine trenches and pits described above, were filled with burnt soil and some clinker. Finds from the palisade trenches (W/77, 92, 134, 136, and possibly 109) and from the various post-holes (W/80, 93, 102, 113, 119, 122 (?), 128, 133, 138), point to a later eighth-ninth century date for this phase of burning.

In the remaining area there was a build-up of soil over the clay level, of variable depth. The material from this level was quite limited, but contained W/22, 28, 29, 39, 76, 81-83, 116, and again attests to late eighth-ninth century activity.

Interpretation

Although the extent of burning was not traced throughout the excavation zone, the fact that much of the trodden surface showed traces of scorching should be an indication of consistent burning here. The thick burnt layer in the area of rooms 2 and 3 suggests the possibility of destroyed wooden constructions. On the basis of finds we can associate this burning with a deliberate clearance of the area, most probably contemporary with the foundation of the *domusculta*. It is difficult to explain the limited amount of clinker recovered as evidence of industrial activity.

PHASE 2a-b

Subsequent to this clearance operation was the erection of a building in the north part of area W. This building, of dimensions 12 x 7 m and oriented north-east–south-west, was formed by walls 195-198, which partly survived as single foundation courses (Fig. 14).

North wall 195 was preserved in its east half, built in single tufa blocks laid as headers of width 0.55-0.7 m; its robbed west course was marked by a foundation trench which slightly cut the bedrock. West wall 196 also lay in a shallow foundation trench and consisted of tufa walling one block thick (0.45-0.5 m). A tufa-cut foundation trench demonstrated the position of the south side wall (197), suggesting a width of *c.* 1.1 m and the use of double tufa block foundations. The foundations of the south-east corner of the room survived, indicating a width of *c.* 1.25 m. East wall 198, only partly uncovered due to the presence of a fig-tree, was *c.* 0.9 m wide with an external face of large tufa blocks laid as headers and an internal face of smaller stretchers.

A floor level was identified in only a few points. Finds from this were few (W/38, 112, 117, 120, 121), but indicated a late eighth/early ninth century date. A contemporary feature may have been pit 199, excavated into the tufa east of the later room 2 with a diameter of *c.* 1.15-1.2 m. Its west edge lay so close to the foundation trench of the robbed-out perimeter wall as to suggest that it predates the construction of this feature. Finds from this were of later eighth-ninth century date (W/18, 141).

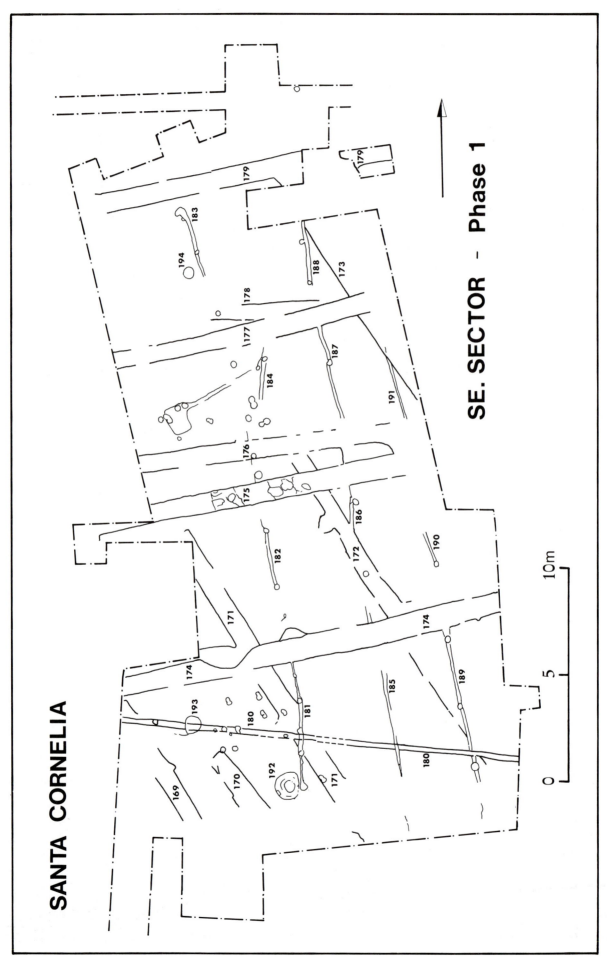

Fig. 13. Santa Cornelia: south-east corner, phase 1 features (VW)

Plate 32. Santa Cornelia: south-east corner, perimeter wall and area W to bedrock; room 1 viewed from south

Plate 33. Santa Cornelia: crop marks showing continuation of agricultural trenches to the south-east of the site

Plate 34. Santa Cornelia: south-east corner, clay level (phase 1c), with 'palisade' or vine trenches

Interpretation

This building ('room 5') appears to have stood in isolation: there are no other structures in the south-east corner complex which relate to this same phase. Room 5 perhaps formed an agricultural outbuilding, associated with the earliest phase of the *domusculta Capracorum*. No clues were offered as regards its function through the groundplan, and internal fittings were totally absent. However, we can note that over the fragmentary floor of this structure, and presumably predating the phase 2c-d surface, were fragments of a capital, column and sarcophagus; the small size of these pieces may indicate that they originally formed part of a pavement.

PHASE 2c-d

The line of the perimeter wall (154, 154a) traced in area X ran up to the side of the north wall of room 5 (195). The perimeter wall resumed a north-west–south-east course from the south-east corner of room 5 (up to which it butted), running south for a length of *c*. 26 m before turning at a right-angle to run west; from here it was traced for a length of 17 m (Fig. 14; Pls 31 and 34).

The wall cut through the phase 1c clay level and down on to bedrock. On the east it was preserved in just two points (200, 201) near room 5, being otherwise robbed out (202). Its south-east corner (203) was likewise lost, the wall (204) reappearing only 3 m from the corner. Construction was principally in single large tufa blocks laid as headers,

giving an average thickness of 0.75-0.9 m. Near the west end of its south side the wall was crudely built in smaller stonework, perhaps as a result of rebuilding. Scars along the top of the surviving blocks demonstrate plough damage. No finds were directly associated with the wall: W/107 from the fill of the foundation trench (near 200) was intrusive through robbing (phase 3a).

Contemporary with the construction of the wall was the insertion of a series of tufa-built pier bases (205-219) whose foundation trenches likewise cut through the phase 1c level to bedrock. In the south half of area W bases 205-208 lay roughly parallel to the south perimeter wall at a distance of 2.3-2.6 m and were spaced *c*. 2.3 m apart; a second series of bases (209-212) lay 2.2-2.3 m to the north with similar spacing between (Fig. 14; Pl. 34). Parallel to the east perimeter wall and 4 m from this were set piers 213, 215, 217, 218; piers 213, 215, 217 were spaced *c*. 3.75 m apart, while base 218 was displaced to the north, being 4.5 m from base 217. The remaining two pier bases (214, 216) formed part of a second pier line 4.5 m west of 215 and 217; there was no corresponding pier west of 218. A final pier, 219, may have been inserted at this time within room 5, close to its north wall: however, we should not exclude the possibility that this was a phase 2a-b feature. Each pier base was squarish (0.8-1.0 × 1.0-1.2 m), built of two or more large tufa blocks, bonded with white mortar; the presence of a socket-hole on one block of pier 208 should signify that at least some blocks were reused. Little remained of bases 205, 209 and 217. No associated finds were recorded.

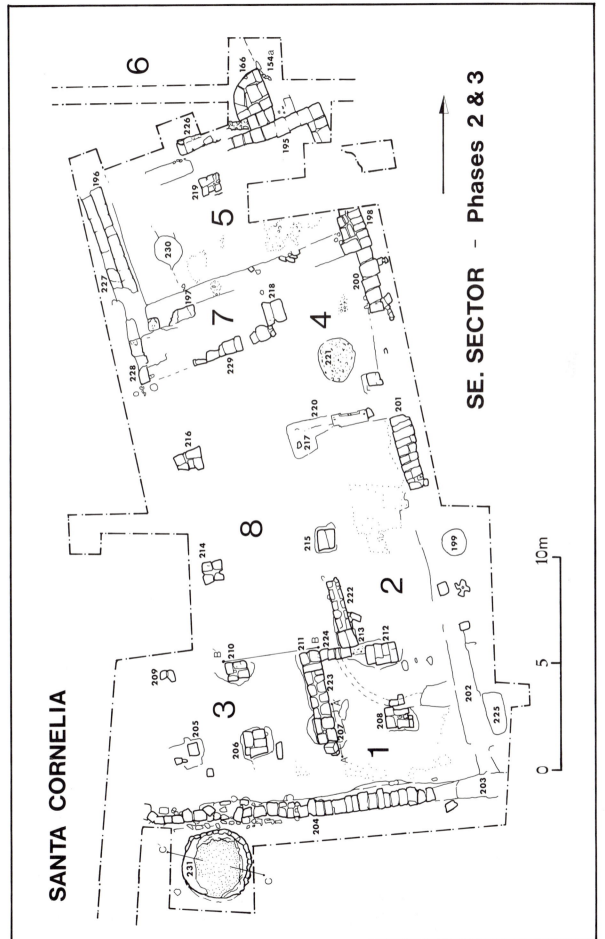

Fig. 14. Santa Cornelia: south-east corner, phase 2 and 3 features (VW)

SANTA CORNELIA

SE. SECTOR – Phases 2 & 3

The provision of these piers allowed the division of the area into a number of rooms, which were then provided with mortar floors. The floors were reasonably well preserved throughout the area, although the plough had scarred them in many places (cf. Pl. 35). In all, six rooms or areas were identified (Fig. 14), as discussed below.

Room/area 4

This area lay south of room 5, with its north side formed by the south wall of room 5 (197); its east side was formed by the line of the perimeter wall, which was here preserved only in the north-east corner as a single block wall 0.7 m wide and 3 m long (200). The south side of area 4 can be drawn to the point where a door-sill giving access to room 2, was preserved *in situ*; traces of the foundation trench (220) of this south wall were still visible and a single block of tufa lay beside the sill east side; pier 217, marking the probable north-west corner of room 2, was also robbed out. The west side of area 4 thus lay between piers 217 and 218, though there was nothing to indicate a wall between these. These confines give the room dimensions of *c.* 6.5-7 × 5.5 m.

Internally area 4 featured an earth make-up overlying accumulation over the phase 2a burning. At certain points patches of the mortar and plaster surface survived, and finds from here were mainly ninth century in date. Near the centre of the room, 1.5 m north of the door-sill, lay a circular feature (221) of 1.7-1.9 m diameter with its edges clearly defined, suggesting that raised stones had originally surrounded it. To the south-east a square tufa slab 0.6 m wide was set into the floor which had probably lain flush with the inside face of the perimeter wall.

Room 2

This room, of *c.* 11 × 5.5 m, lay south of area/room 4 and, as noted, was entered via the well-preserved threshold. The east side was formed by the perimeter wall 201, preserved only in the north-east corner of room 2 for a length of 3.5 m. The south extent of the room was probably delimited by pier 212 to the west, while to its east, two post-holes of irregular shape (0.3 m wide) denote a doorway 1.5 m wide leading south; a square central hole *c.* 0.1 m wide may mark the locking-hole of one leaf of the door.

The west flank of room 2 was formed by the line of piers 213, 215 and 217 with tufa blockwork 222 running for 2.5 m from pier 213, up to which it butted. This walling was 0.6 m thick, faced on both sides with blocks 0.35-0.5 m long, resting on a soil fill. It was robbed to the north, in the tract up to pier 215 and between piers 215 and 217 (Pl. 35).

The floor comprised thick white plaster, well preserved in the centre of the room where its surface showed plough scars at regular 0.55-0.6 m intervals; these scars continued to the east. The mortar floor ran right up to the perimeter wall and curved upward slightly to indicate that the wall thickness here was reduced over the foundations. The mortar floor rested on an earth make-up of variable consistency. Finds from the floor and its make-up (W/21, 62, 78, 87 and 89) offered a ninth century date.

Room 1

The area south of room 2, bounded to east and south by the perimeter wall, was denominated room 1 (Fig. 15; Pl. 32). Its west side appears to have been delimited by piers 207

Plate 35. Santa Cornelia: south-east corner, plough-scarred floors within rooms 2 and 1, looking west

and 211, between which was built a walling (223) 0.8-0.9 m thick, with tufa blockwork on each face, and with a foundation trench cutting the phase 1c surface but not the bedrock. The fill of this trench on its west side contained a ninth century sherd (W/95). Between pier 207 and the perimeter wall no walling survived, although there was the impression of a possible sill, up to which the floor appears to have run; the door width was uncertain. The north flank lay between piers 211 and 212 and the perimeter wall: as noted above, a doorway existed between pier 212 and the wall; west of this a single block walling (224), 0.45-0.5 m wide, linked the piers, though a gap of c. 0.65 m existed between the walling and pier 212. Although wall 224 butts pier 211, this need not represent a later revision to the original scheme. The enclosed area of room 1 was thus c. 7 × 6.5 m.

Its floor comprised a hardened lime surface overlying a slight earth make-up: the mortar formed bedding for a paved floor, since in a few areas a stone, porphyry and marble fragment flooring was preserved (fragments 642-650). Fragments in the overlying disturbed level must also relate to this (fragments 625-629, 661, 662). One piece of floor slab (number 656) was apparently found under the floor surface of room 1, but sherds here (W/57) were eighth and eleventh century in date, indicating contamination. The floor make-up included W/129, a ninth century sherd.

An oval pit (225) of c. 2.0 × 0.9 m was cut into the tufa east of room 1 and up against the presumed external face of the perimeter wall: the earliest of its fills contained ninth century material (W/3).

Room 3

This structure was of indeterminate size, but its length was in excess of 9 m: all traces to the west had been ploughed out. Its width was c. 7.5 m, running up to the second line of piers parallel to the south perimeter wall: however, no wall trace existed between piers 209-211 to mark the north side. The east side was formed by piers 207 and 211 and wall 223. The perimeter wall formed the south flank. Centrally the room featured pier bases 205 and 206.

Over the thick phase 2a burnt layer was laid a mortar floor with a slight earth make-up, present throughout much of the area of room 3, except the south, where it had been removed by the plough. The make-up contained finds of ninth century date.

Area 8

North of room 3 lay area 8, containing piers 214 and 216. The west side of this area was not identified with certainty due to plough damage, but it probably did not extend far beyond the piers. This suggests an overall area of c. 14-15 × 6 m.

Westwards only ploughed and disturbed earth was located. Within the area defined by the piers, however, a plough-scarred surface was identified, consisting of packed earth with slight mortar traces, but not such as to suggest a mortar floor. Finds from this again gave a ninth century date.

Rooms 5 and 7

Phase 2d saw the restructuring of room 5, involving doubling its north and west walls (195, 196) through the addition of a further tufa block walling against the external face of each side (226, 227). This additional face was preserved only on the west side of room 5; to the north its line was marked by a foundation trench 0.45 m wide.

Simultaneously the west half of the south wall (197) appears to have been removed (the trench fill contained the ninth century W/101) and a new structure, room 7, attached to the south. This room covered an area of 7 × 2.5 m, with its west side formed by a continuation (228) of the added face of the west wall of room 5. The poorly-preserved south wall (229) of room 7 was 0.5-0.6 m wide, built of poorly-shaped tufa blocks. Pier base 218 presumably formed part of its east side. A doorway may have lain on the south side near the south-west corner since on either side of a gap of 2 m lay possible pivot-holes.

The area of the combined rooms 5 and 7 was provided with a floor surviving as an earth make-up to a patchy mortar floor or merely as a trodden earth surface. This extended over the line of the removed south wall of room 5. Its make-up contained ninth century material.

Interpretation

The construction of both perimeter wall and piers saw the conversion of area W into a series of functional buildings in addition to the pre-existing room 5. The new rooms were nearly all equipped with mortar floors, and finds associated with these point consistently to a date in the first half of the ninth century. The insertion of wallings 223, 224 and 222 between pier bases need not denote later restructuring, as the phase 2d floors ran up to them. The ninth century unit W/95 in the foundation trench for wall 223, dividing rooms 3 and 1, supports this hypothesis.

Rooms 5, 2 and 1 were enclosed on four sides by walls. Area 4 lacked evidence for a west side but was presumably covered. While ploughing had destroyed much of the west end of room 3, there was no clear trace of a north wall, and room 3 may therefore have opened directly on to area 8. The latter lacked traces of a proper mortar floor, yet the presence of piers 214 and 216 would suggest that this area was roofed. Tile debris in the disturbed sub-plough and plough levels would indicate tile-roofing.

There was little evidence for internal fittings to help determine the specific functions of the rooms. Patches of marble flooring, perhaps of *opus sectile*, in room 1 set this room apart from the rest; similar floors may been robbed from the other rooms, but fragments of such paving are lacking (though four fragments (575a-d) of an inscription came from plough soil over rooms 2/4).

Taken as a whole, the rooms in the south-east complex form a compact, coherent, structural unit. It is difficult, however, to interpret this as a purely agricultural unit, designed for storage of materials or produce, given the location of the finely-floored room 1 at the back of the complex, and the presence of at least one reused Roman threshold at the entrance into another room (room 2). A few pits were identified in the area, such as pit 225 (east of room 1), but its location outside the perimeter wall may suggest a function as a rubbish pit rather than for storage. The framed circular feature 221 directly outside the entrance to room 2 is anomalous: although it was first identified as an oven, in fact this is unlikely given its proximity to the doorway.

Trenches made west of area W indicated heavy plough

damage and an absence of constructional activity. The area may have been open.

PHASE 2e-f

There was some evidence for burning within room 1: around the area of the paving much black, sooty soil was located, and the floor itself was burnt and hardened; on the west side of the room fallen chunks of plaster overlay the floor. Finds from this burnt level (e.g. W/5, 6), offered a date range of ninth-eleventh century, with evidence for some degree of plough disturbance. No other rooms in the south-east complex featured a comparable burnt layer, but a number did contain slight remains of a level of accumulation: no secure finds came from this. In room 5 pit 230, 1.3 m in diameter, was cut down through the mortared floor surface in the centre of the west half of the room: the fill of this contained sherds of ninth-tenth century Forum Ware (X/20) as well as two pieces of marble moulding (fragments 663 and 664).

Interpretation

There was no clear evidence for restructuring in any of the rooms. Heavy plough damage, however, had left many portions of the phase 2d floors badly scarred, making it difficult to assess the fate of the rooms.

The presence of burning in room 1 may signify destruction by fire. The absence of comparable levels elsewhere may suggest only partial destruction of the south-east corner complex, although the lack of evidence for continued occupation or use of the other rooms and areas would imply that the whole zone was abandoned. The cutting of pit 230 in room 5 indicates either continued activity in the area or early disuse of this building.

PHASE 3a

Subsequent to the destruction or abandonment of the rooms there was apparent robbing of the area for building material. The east perimeter wall suffered most, being robbed out for much of its length south of room 5; likewise the north wall and the east part of the south wall of room 5 were dug out. Robbing also may have occurred along the west side of room 2, although no robber trench was identified. In the entrance-way between rooms 1 and 3 the threshold at least appears robbed.

South of room 3, and just 0.5 m south of the perimeter wall, was identified a tufa-cut kiln (231) with a diameter of 3.3-3.4 m at its mouth, and a base diameter of 2.1 m (Fig. 16). Its mouth comprised a masonry surround of small tufa blocks 0.2 m high: half of this surround survived, with the faces of the exposed blocks burnt or badly scorched. Below the surround, the tufa was cut vertically to a depth of 0.25-0.3 m; the surface of this was also burnt. Below, the tufa was cut to a smaller diameter. The mouth of the kiln had a burnt lime or bituminous surface, polished

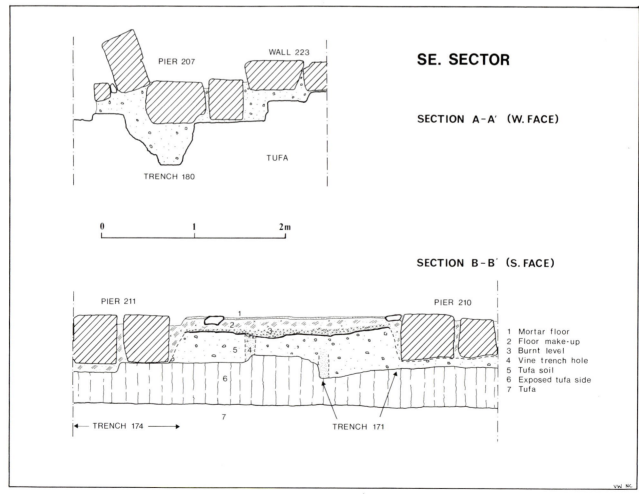

Fig. 15. Santa Cornelia: sections A-A' and B-B' (VW, NC)

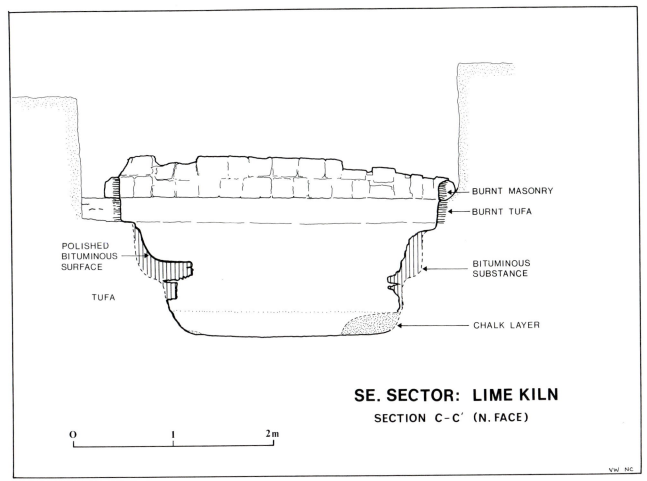

Fig. 16. Santa Cornelia: section C-C', lime kiln (VW, NC)

to the west and broken and rough to the east. Traces of this bituminous surface covered the sides of the kiln and descended to a depth of 1 m. At the bottom were remains of a 0.2 m thick lime layer. The total depth of the kiln from the base of the masonry surround was *c*. 1.3 m.

Interpretation

The robbing of the walls and the installation of the kiln relate to the construction of the second church and the monasterial complex to the north-west and to the use of the south-east complex as a quarry for building material. This assumes, therefore, that both buildings and perimeter wall no longer served a function.

PHASE 3b

Kiln 231 contained an eleventh century fill (W/97, 103, 140).

Interpretation

The kiln saw relatively short use. It clearly provided lime for the phase 3 buildings, and drew much of its material from this area.

PHASE 5

The sub-plough material was mixed and very disturbed

due to plough action. Material from this level is therefore an amalgam of finds of phases 2 and 3.

PHASE 6

This upper level contained finds of all periods, including tile and floor fragments; the tile may indicate tile roofing for the demolished buildings, unless this represents scatter from the church and monastery zones. Fragment numbers 560, 570, 571, 575, 576, 625-629, 641 (small Ionic capital), 654, 655, 659, 660, 662, 681, 964 are of this phase.

SEQUENCE WITH FINDS:

Phase 1a: Bedrock features (agricultural trenches, post-holes).
Phase 1b: Fill over bedrock, tufa soil: W/96, 98, 109.
   Agricultural trench fills: W/105, possibly some of 106, 126, 132 , and probably 124. Drainage trench fill: W/108.
Phase 1c: Lower clay surface: W/104.
Phase 1d: Palisade trenches cutting trodden surface.

Phase 2a: Clearance of zone for *domusculta*. Palisade trenches fills: W/77, 92, probably 109, 134, 136, 139.
   Post-hole fills: W/19, 80, 93, 102, 113, 119, 122, 128, 133, 138.
   Accumulation/burnt layer over trodden surface: W/22,

28, 29, 39, 48, 76, 81-83, 86, 88, 114, possibly 20, 90, 116-118, 131(?).

Phase 2a-b: Construction of room 5: W/98 (?).
 Use of Room 5: possibly W/38, 112, 117, 120, 121.
Phase 2c-d: Construction of perimeter wall: possibly W/107.
 Insertion of piers.
 Pit 199 fill: W/18, 141.
 Floors of the various rooms: W/14, 21, 22, 31(?), 32, 33, 40, 45, 54, 57, 58(?), 61, 62, 68(?), 74, 78, 79, 84, 87, 89, 99(?), 101, 121, 125, 129.
 Construction of walls: W/95. Pit 225 fill: W/4.
Phase 2e-f: Burning over floors: W/5, 6, and possibly 51, 66.
 Accumulation over floors: possibly W/137.
 Pit 230 in room 5, fill: X/20. Pit 225 upper fill: W/2, 3.

Phase 3a: Robbing of walls and piers: W/7, 23, 27, 30, 41, 50, 51, 56, 58, 63, 65, 72, 111, 130. Construction of kiln.
Phase 3b: Fill of kiln: W/97, 103, 140, and some of 94.

Phase 5: Sub-plough/disturbed accumulation: W/14, 25, 37, 42, 43, 51(?), 54(?), 55, 59, 66(?), 70, 71, 73, 100, 110, 137; X/19.

Phase 6: Plough: W/1, 8, 9, 11-13, 15-17, 20, 24, 26, 34-36, 44, 46, 47, 49, 52, 53, 55, 60, 64, 67, 69, 70, 75, 85, 94; X/2, 16, 18.

Unstratified material: W/10, 106, 115, 127, 131 (clinker), 135.

(iv) THE MONASTERY COMPLEX

INTRODUCTION

The monastery complex was identified to the south of the churches and was excavated in 1962 and 1964. An area of c. 21 × 28 m was cleared, covering roughly half of the monastery. Smaller trenches made in the remaining area, in particular near the south limit of the site, had demonstrated that plough damage was deep, often scarring the bedrock. The excavations therefore concentrated on the north half of the monastic zone where some stratigraphy survived.

The area was covered by excavation sectors S, T, U and Z (Fig. 2). Trench T (= long south trench I) was cut in 1962 and formed a south extension of 1960 trench I-IA across the church. Covering c. 36 × 3 m, it ran almost centrally through the cloister, extending south beyond the line of the south perimeter wall (cf. Fig. 8). Deep plough damage began c. 19 m from the church south wall.

Area U extended east of the line of trench T for c. 10 × 19.5 m, covering the east half of the cloister complex, room B and part of room A. The east wall of room A was revealed in the long south trench II (1962 trench) and parts of its south wall uncovered in the south 'holes' iii and iv (also 1962). South 'holes' i, ii and vi were laid out in 1962 south of room A. Finds from the south 'holes' and trenches were all grouped under U.

Excavation sector Z concerned an area of c. 20-21 × 15 m west of the north half of trench T and immediately south of the south-west corner of the second church. This revealed the west part of the cloister and the areas of rooms C and D. Part of the south side of the latter was first examined in the 1961 trench C (8 × 2 m): finds from this trench remained listed under the heading C. Not all of sector Z was cleared to bedrock.

It can also be noted that a few finds from sector S (1962), covering the south-east quarter of the church, came from the area south of the church south wall and thus related to the monastery zone.

PHASE 1a

Only in sector Z was there evidence for the series of tufa-cut trenches found elsewhere at Santa Cornelia. Here eight or nine trenches were identified (numbers 232-240), oriented north-west–south-east and west–east. The earliest appear to have been two north-west–south-east trenches (232, 235), c. 0.9 m wide, and spaced 3.6 m apart, to which may perhaps be linked the vague trace of trench 238, 4.5 m to the north-east. A further north-west–south-east trench (234), just 0.6 m wide, lay immediately east of the westernmost of these trenches. Five west–east trenches were present (233, 236, 237, 239, 240), of 0.7-0.9 m width (Figs 4 and 31). Two periods of west–east trenches can be recognized, the clearest represented by trenches 233 and 237 c. 6.6 m apart (Pl. 36).

A number of post-holes of diameter 0.15-0.2 and 0.4-0.5 m, also cut the bedrock, in particular in the east half of room D. However, they formed no discernable patterns.

Interpretation

The trenches relate to Roman agricultural activity as identified elsewhere on the site, most notably in the south-east corner. The latest phase of these comprised those west–east trenches spaced 6.6 m apart, to which can be linked trench 001 running beneath the church complex; this lay c. 6 m north of the northernmost of the room D west–east trenches.

PHASE 1b

At least in area Z the bedrock was covered by a thin layer of lightish tufa soil, in many points absent or indistinguishable from the overlying make-up for the fragmentary floor of room D. In the south part of room D the agricultural trench 233 was cut by an oval pit (240a) of c. 1.5 × 1.8-1.95 m.

Interpretation

There was little soil cover in this area before the constructional phases began. The fill of the agricultural trenches was of tufa-coloured soil, but this lacked finds. The Roman coin of Domitian from room D does not appear to have come from this tufa soil level. Although units Z/13, 18 and 23 were thought to be associated with this lowest level, these finds were chiefly of mid-late twelfth century date, with a few eighth or ninth century sherds: this demonstrates the difficulty of differentiating between the poorly-preserved floor of room D and the soil overlying the tufa.

Plate 36. Santa Cornelia: monastery, room D, to bedrock, looking north

Pit 240a also lacked finds, but was perhaps used for storage.

PHASE 2a

The absence of evidence for phase 1 from the remaining monastery zone to the east can be attributed to a cutting-back of the bedrock, similar to that noted immediately east of the church porch. The full extent of this operation cannot be determined. Its north limit was provided by the south side of the churches where the natural tufa had been cut back to a depth of *c.* 0.4-0.5 m. This appeared to run south for *c.* 11 m across the whole length of the cloister zone. The east limit was not clearly defined due to only partial excavation of room A. To the west, the survival of the agricultural trenches in the bedrock beneath room D shows that cutting-back did not extend this far; most probably the west limit lay between the east wall of room D (242) and the west wall of the cloister court (258), an area not cleared to bedrock.

Interpretation

The operation of cutting back was designed to accommodate the construction of the first church. The natural tufa on the south side of the church was less compact and more friable than to the north. The cutting-back here was quite extensive and covered an area of at least 15 × 14 m.

PHASE 2b-f

Sixty-one graves were cut down into the cut-back tufa (graves 109, 115-140, 166-182, 188-194: for a description of these see below, Chapter 3) (Figs 4 and 17). Most of these lay within the area enclosed by the later cloister. The south limit to this burial zone appears to have been the south wall (244-246) of the cloister. To the west, no graves were laid in the area of room D. Graves 139, 192-194 lay in the area of room A, where further graves perhaps remained to be uncovered. The tombs were generally west–east oriented adult inhumations, featuring cuttings for cover slabs (Pl. 37).

The greatest concentration of tombs lay closest to the church south wall, and here an uncertain sequence of burials occurred, with a number of graves cut or disturbed by others, or featuring secondary burials (e.g. graves 180-182, 188-191). A significant number of graves underlay and were cut by the foundations and walls of the later cloister (e.g. 115, 118, 123, 126, 127, 167, 169, 171, 172) and by other features of the monastery phase (numbers 132, 135, 136, 178, 188, 189).

Interpretation

The burials underlying the cloister complex denote an organized cemetery zone predating the construction of the monastery. Not all the burials need to predate the construction of the second church: there are indications of lengthy cemeterial activity, while the alignment of graves with the outer face of the second church south wall may signify that some burials belong to phase 3. If so, this may suggest that some time elapsed between the construction of the second church and the monastery. Alternatively, however, we may instead argue for the extensive use of the cemetery area solely during the lifetime of the first church.

The apparent concentration of graves within the area of the later cloister is noticeable: this raises the possibility that the confines of the cloister in fact followed the pre-existing outline of an early cemetery precinct. However, the fact that graves clearly extended into the area of room A calls for caution in this respect.

PHASE 2c-d

At the south limit of the excavation zone were identified the traces of a large tufa-built wall (278-280) oriented west-north-west–east-south-east, but almost wholly destroyed by plough action. In south trench II, the wall was marked solely by a stepped cutting in the bedrock designed to take its foundations. To the west, however, a 2.5 m length of wall was uncovered, c. 0.9-1.1 m thick, constructed in irregular-sized blocks, with larger stones, 0.75-0.8 m long, set on the external face. The wall at this point exhibited a slight dog-leg, as a result of the attachment here of a north–south wall belonging to phase 3c: this attachment may have necessitated the rebuilding of part of wall 279. Its course was relocated c. 11 m east, where the tufa had been stepped back to take the foundations. Part of only one face was in position, with squarish blocks c. 0.45 m long.

Interpretation

These wall traces can be equated with the remains of the perimeter wall. The south-west angle of this enclosure was projected at a point c. 20 m west of foundations 280, but this area was not excavated given the depth of plough damage. Its west flank can most probably be regarded as that later followed by the monastic structures, though in sector Z it was clear that this had probably been extensively rebuilt at the time of the foundation of the monastery (see below, phase 3b).

Only plough and sub-plough levels were found either side of the perimeter wall, with no indication of floors. No other structures relating to the period of the first church were identified in the monastic zone.

PHASE 3a-b

Subsequently the various graves were badly disturbed and the tombs filled with a light, tufa-coloured, soil layer containing some tile and purple mortar fragments. This soil also overlay the tombs and contained scattered human bone, relating either to the disturbed tufa-cut burials or to additional destroyed graves. In the area of the cloister court the disturbed grave fills contained finds T/15-17, 19-23, 43-57, and, in the tufa-coloured soil over these, T/4-6, 9, U/35. In the cloister surrounds the grave fills held S/12-16, U/59, 60, 61, 73, 98, 99, 107-111, and the overlying soil contained S/4, U/21, 61, 102, 106.

Disturbed tufa-like soil was also identified over a restricted area east of the cloister, containing finds U/42 and 75. To the south only limited traces of a tufa soil were encountered.

Plate 37. Santa Cornelia: monastery, cloister and garth viewed from south-east, with phase 2 graves cut into bedrock

Interpretation

This tufa-coloured soil probably only partly relates to the initial fill of the graves. On the basis of the material from the graves an initial disturbance of the whole area appears to have occurred in the eleventh century, presumably at the time of the construction of the monastery. The disturbance probably marks the preparation of the zone for building work through the levelling of the ground. However, the extremely variable dates of the material from the grave fills, ranging from the tenth to the thirteenth century, must indicate that subsequent work over the area, involving the relaying of the thin floors of the cloister surround and the digging out of the cloister court, meant a notable contamination of these earlier fills. Hence many of the secure levels claimed at the time of excavation have proved in fact to be unjustified. Disturbance was extremely extensive.

PHASE 3b

To this phase can be assigned the construction and foundation of the monastery south of the second church. The monastic buildings identified in the excavations comprised rooms A, B, C, D, E and F, and the cloister.

The cloister

The cloister lay due south of the central axis of the second church and was of trapezoidal form, *c.* 15 m wide, with its north side 15.5 m long, and its south side 18 m long. It was provided with a surrounding corridor or walkway 3 m wide, which faced on to a courtyard of similar trapezoidal form, of *c.* 8.5-9 × 10-11.5 m (internally 7.5-8 × 9-10 m) (Fig. 9; Pl. 37).

(i) The cloister walls

The north side of the cloister surround was formed by the outer face of the second church south wall. At *c.* 5 m west of the cloister north-east corner was set a low base (059) of 2.6-2.7 × 1.2-1.4 m built of rubble core with small tufa block facing; this feature lay slightly off centre with respect to the cloister north side. Its foundations appear to have overlain tomb 136. In the north-west corner of the cloister walk, built up to the external face of the church wall and originally against the cloister west wall (242) was set a large masonry construction (241) of 3.75 × 1.4 m (internal space of 2.5 × 0.75 m), whose rough foundations cut down into graves 132, 135, 188 and 189. Its walls were of rubble core with neat tufa facing. Inside lay the disturbed grave 178. Finds from here included two *denari* of Henry II, count of Champagne (1180-1197) and eleventh and twelfth century sherds (U/73, 109-111). The thickened east end of the feature preserved the traces of a single tufa-faced step (Pl. 38).

The cloister west wall (242) consisted in its north half of tufa walling of single block thickness, while to the south it was of double-block thickness using smaller-sized blocks; the wall thickness was a fairly constant 0.5 m. Like the other walls of the cloister, the foundations rested on, but did not cut, the bedrock. Originally an opening (243) existed between 3.3 and 5.25 m from the north-west corner, communicating west. To the south, wall 244-246

Plate 38. Santa Cornelia: monastery, cloister steps (059) connecting cloister north walk with church south aisle; view from south across centre of second church

was built in tufa blocks of somewhat irregular dimensions, giving a thickness of between 0.45-0.9 m, although in the west half the wall was more regularly 0.45-0.6 m thick. At a point *c.* 3.75 m from the south-west corner of the cloister the presence of four blocks (245a) against the external face of the wall gave a likely threshold of 1.45 × 0.55 m. To its west lay part of a 1 m long column (fragment number 987) which may originally have flanked the entrance. The absence of blocks near the south-east corner may mark the position of another doorway leading south. The wall in this area was badly ruined by plough action.

The east wall (247) featured foundations of large, somewhat irregular, tufa blocks, many reused, as indicated by the presence of clamp-holes; it also incorporated part of a dolium (fragment 843) and tombstone (fragment 856). Over the 0.5-0.55 m thick single block foundation course, the wall comprised a mortar core with double block facing; throughout there was much use of tile and small stones for packing. There was no clear indication of a doorway.

(ii) The cloister court walls

The walls (248, 249, 258, 259) containing the cloister courtyard all presented crude tufa blockwork foundations 0.5-0.6 m thick, over which lay a single surviving ashlar/tufa block course of faced mortar construction *c.* 0.35-0.4 m thick (cf. Pl. 37). The foundations cut down into a number of phase 2 graves, further disturbing their fills (graves 115, 118, 123, 126, 127, 167, 169, 171, 172, 175[?]). Finds were again very mixed, indicating later contamination. To the north the courtyard wall (248) still stood to a height of 0.7 m, reduced by plough damage to *c.* 0.35 m in the south. The top course of both the north and east court walls (248-249) preserved the position of a series of mortar pads or bases (250-257) 0.55 m long, and spaced 1.75-1.8 m apart, except near the south-east corner where the corner and adjoining bases were just 1.3 m apart.

Against the outer face of the courtyard wall near the south-west corner, lay a block of 0.8 × 0.4 m. East of this lay two medieval impost capitals (fragments 470 and 473) and two stones set up to the wall.

(iii) The cloister walks

In the walkways surrounding the courtyard the tufa bedrock and the thin phase 3a tufa-coloured soil layer were covered by a slight tread; in some places the phase 3a soil was absent and the trodden layer directly overlay the tufa, often sinking down into phase 2 graves. In the east corridor the trodden level was absent and in its place the worn surface of the bedrock alone was noted (as between graves 180 and 181). In the south corridor a later dividing wall (295, see phase 3d below) overlay a single piece of marble slab set into this trodden surface.

(iv) Cloister courtyard

Within the area enclosed by walls 248-249 and 258-259 the cloister courtyard contained a slightly trodden, lightish earth layer, 0.1-0.15 m deep, containing patches of mortar and some sherds (T/3, 8, 9, U/32, and Z/8). In the south half of the court this trodden layer rested over a scatter of broken tile. To the north the distinction between the phase 3b level and the underlying phase 3a soil was vague.

Interpretation

The cloister was directly accessible from the church by means of feature 059 built up to the church south wall and located central with respect to this. Given the cutting back of the tufa in this area this feature should equate with a stepped entrance-way. The construction of the cloister greatly disturbed the phase 2 burials, as indicated not only by the mixed finds but also by the general scatter of bone in the trodden soil layer of the courtyard, which can be equated with the first courtyard fill. The tile scatter noted in part of the courtyard may relate to destroyed tile covers of certain tombs, or to a deliberate scatter underlying the court soil to aid drainage. Bases 250-257 on top of the surviving second course of the north and east sides of the cloister court mark the pads for columns forming the low colonnades facing on to the courtyard. These were regularly spaced 1.75-1.8 m apart on the north wall, and likewise on the east side, except at the south-east angle where the corner and the adjoining bases were only 1.3 m apart; this was presumably repeated on the west side, while on the longer south wall the positioning of columns 1.3 m from each corner and then two spaced 1.8 m apart would have balanced out the remaining line. Thus five columns (including the corner columns) would have lain on each side except on the south, where the longer wall length required six. The colonnades featured small, slender columns *c.* 1 m high with impost capitals, such as were

found in the proximity of the south-west corner. Most capitals exhibited a cross carved in relief at one end, and were often reworked from classical marble elements. Fragments of both impost capitals and columns were found in the rubble and plough material over this whole area (corbels: fragments 470, 473, 517, 811-813, 815, 823, 825-828, 834, 836, 837; columns: 572, 817, 824, 829, 987) (Fig. 20).

There was no clear trace of an entrance into the courtyard nor of features such as a fountain or well within it.

The cloister surround was presumably covered with roofing pitched down on to the colonnades; a significant amount of tile was found in the cloister rubble, particularly in the south corridor. A thin trodden surface covered both bedrock and phase 3a soil, although the bedrock itself formed the floor surface in the east corridor. Doorways in the outer walls of the cloister gave access to a series of adjoining rooms.

(i) Room A

Room A covered an area of *c.* 21.5 × 9 m. It was delimited to the north by the church south wall and to the west by the cloister east wall (247) and an extension (260). Its east wall comprised a rough tufa walling (261) 0.5 m thick, extending north to join the south side of the porch. The south side (262) of the room was trenched in three points revealing foundations in large tufa blocks up to 0.7 m thick.

On its west side, an entrance-way (263) leading into room B was marked by a levelled area of white mortar up to 1.5 m wide and at least 2 m long. The plough had cut a central groove in this. Just to the south a saddle quern had been reused in the wall foundations. No connecting doorway with the cloister was evident.

Of the interior of room A only a narrow strip on its west side was excavated. Overlying the tufa soil was a scatter of tile with some pieces of purple makeup: further north the tufa soil was covered by a burnt, blackish soil.

(ii) Room B

The area of room B was bounded to the north by the south wall (244-246) of the cloister, to the east by the west wall (260) of room A, and to the west by the vague east wall of room C (see below). Traces of structures beyond 5 m to the south had been destroyed by the plough. This gave the room dimensions of *c.* 8 × 5 m.

Internally the bedrock was covered by a reddish soil (containing U/92, 101, 114) which may have formed the first floor level. Most probably originating in this phase was a hearth (264), built up against the north wall: this was of roughly semi-circular form *c.* 2.25 m in diameter with a rough tufa block surround 0.15 m thick. To its south-east lay the vague outline of an additional feature (265) framed by small tufa blocks. Fragments of three saddle querns came from room B, two incorporated into the internal face of its north wall (cf. Pl. 39).

(iii) Room C

Immediately west of room B lay the area of room C, whose

Plate 39. Santa Cornelia: monastery, area of room B with hearth 264

north wall was formed by the south wall of the cloister and its west continuation (266) towards the edge of the monastic complex. Access to this room from the cloister was by door 245a. Its east side was taken to be the line of masonry (267) c. 4 m east of this threshold, of crude workmanship and featuring a reused half millstone at its north end. Six blocks of an additional, irregular, walling (268) lay to the south-west, immediately west of which was a deep plough scar. A plough scar also underlay the trace of wall 269 to the west. The west limit of the room may have been formed by wall 270, of rough construction c. 0.55 m thick, running south for a length of c. 1.75 m. Ploughing had destroyed any features to the south. These confines suggest overall dimensions of c. 11 × 6 m. If correct, an additional area (= room F) of c. 8 × 6 m lay west of wall 270. No finds were recorded in this area, although a broken tile feature (271) almost 1 m long lay near its centre.

Within room C, a red, perhaps burnt, soil level containing some stone and tile was visible. Finds T/35 and 39 from this offered an eleventh century date. The east wall appears to have been constructed over the phase 3a level. However, ploughing had clearly disturbed the levels throughout the zone.

(iv) Room D

More clearly defined was the structure of room D, enclosed in an area west of the cloister and using the west wall of the cloister as its east side: it formed a slightly irregular rectangle of c. 13-14 × 10 m (shorter on its west side). Its north wall reused the south-west corner of the second

church as well as a 3.5 m extension (131) from this, built in large tufa blocks, and cutting or joining the line of the early perimeter wall (035-037). The west wall (272) ran parallel with the cloister and was built in both single tufa blockwork and double, smaller, blockwork, with a wall thickness of 0.55 m. It seems likely that the south wall of the room was originally formed by the west extension (266) of the cloister south wall: this, though ploughed and robbed, was 0.5-0.65 m thick and built in single tufa blocks, badly worn to the west, and bonded with a reddish mortar. The extant walling was lost c. 1.1 m from its junction with the west wall.

Contemporary with the original room plan was the line of central pier bases (274-277) spaced 3.5 m apart (Fig. 9; Pl. 36). Base 274 was set midway along the south wall, although this was very badly robbed out. To the north, and slightly west of the room's central axis, lay piers 275 and 276, of c. 1.10 × 0.75-0.8 m; pier 277 of 0.8 × 0.5 m lay against the north wall at a point corresponding to the south-west corner of the church.

A thin sandy level apparently provided the floor surface, but this was distinguishable only with difficulty from subsequent renewals of this surface. Hence associated finds Z/18, 19, 21 and 23 cover the eleventh-thirteenth centuries, indicating contamination from later levels. Doorway 243, 1.8 m wide, communicated with the cloister.

Interpretation

According to the customary arrangement of monastic rooms around a cloister, it seems likely that room A can be interpreted as the refectory. This need not have been more than a single storey structure. Entry to the refectory should probably be assumed in the south-east corner of the cloister; a further entrance lay at the junction with the church narthex to the north. The tile scatter and blackish soil identified over the phase 3a tufa soil was inconsistent, and it is difficult to see this as a true floor level. Most probably ploughing had destroyed the floor in the south part of room A; to the north a surface was preserved, but only beyond a later partition wall (see phase 3c below).

The principal feature of room B was the fireplace. This, combined with the room's location immediately adjacent to the refectory, should point to the function of room B as the kitchens. This may be further supported by the finding of three saddle querns in the room.

The role of room C is less certain since it preserved no obvious internal features. It can perhaps be interpreted as a storage area (the cellars?). Its east wall is problematic: walling 267 may in fact represent fallen masonry, toppled eastwards from its original north–south line c. 3.5 m from the threshold. It is possible that the fragments of walling to the west were ploughed topple from this same wall.

The presence of central piers running longitudinally across room D suggests a two-storeyed building: this can most probably be identified as the combined chapter-house and dormitory, with the dormitory located on the second floor of the structure. This interpretation helps explain feature 241 as the night-stair, giving external access to the dormitory. The floor level here as elsewhere was poorly preserved, consisting of a trodden level. The fragility of this surface seems to be reflected in the various patches of repair and renewal of the surface, often indistinguishable from the original trodden floor. This sequence of replacement and repair had clearly mixed the finds relating to the various phases. Finds in general, however, support a date in the first half of the eleventh century for the monastery's construction.

The lack of data for the small room F identified west of room C precludes any definite interpretation of its function, but its setting near room D may recommend an identification as a latrine.

Plough damage had removed any traces of structures south of rooms B, C and F, except for wall 278-280 which can be identified with the perimeter wall (see above, phase 2c-d). It is likely that construction of room D necessitated rebuilding of the west perimeter wall.

PHASE 3c

Wall 281-283, 0.4-0.45 m thick, built of smallish tufa blocks, was constructed from the south-east corner of room A running west-south-west to join with the perimeter wall c. 15 m distant. The course of this wall was traced 12 m distant (282) and again (283) at its junction with the perimeter wall (below, Fig. 35).

At the junction with room A the wall doubled to a two block course c. 0.85 m thick, to provide a doorway (284) 0.8 m wide. On the mortar bedding for the sill was preserved the imprint of a fragment of strigillated sarcophagus, used upside down as a threshold. Just inside the doorway lay part of a column base. Within the area west of the wall and south of room A, a tread of broken stone and tile was found which directly overlay the bedrock: this surface was preserved solely in this corner where it had escaped destruction by the plough. This level contained finds U/3 and 5, of eleventh-twelfth century date.

Against the west wall of room A and in the south-east corner of room B was inserted a small structure built in largish tufa blocks, with walls 0.5 m thick on the north and east sides (286, 287), but up to 0.9 m on the west (285). Its south side was not preserved, and the surviving foundation walls were plough-scarred. This room, at least 3.25 × 2 m in size, was designated room E. No internal features were recognized.

Perhaps to this phase belongs the partitioning of room A towards its north end by means of a 0.45 m thick wall (288), of rough, tufa with tile, chocking and some reused elements, including one piece of a capital (fragment 867). This wall does not seem, however, to have joined the east side of room A. The partition created a northern compartment of 4.5 × 9 m.

To the west, door 243 of room D was blocked with smallish tufa blocks covered in a red mortar. It is unclear where the new entry was set, but access into the cloister should have been maintained.

Interpretation

The area south of room A, bounded to the east by wall 281-283, contained a packed layer for a courtyard. It is possible that the enclosed area was a garden or orchard, but the evidence for this is lacking. The extent of the courtyard is likewise unknown. The construction of wall 281-283 is an indication that the monastery had maintained at least part of the phase 2c-d perimeter wall.

The function of room E cannot be ascertained, unless it can be regarded as an ancillary structure to the kitchens (room B).

The partitioning of room A should be connected with a change in the internal arrangement of the refectory, perhaps creating a separate dining space for visitors to the monastery.

PHASE 3d-e

There was a major remodelling of room D in this period, whereby the dimensions of the room were reduced through the construction of a new south wall (289) 0.8-1 m north of the existing wall (266) and on a slightly angled west–east course. This new wall was 0.55 m wide and faced in smaller, neater tufa blockwork either side of a rough core; its crude foundations featured some red and yellow tile as well as one piece of reused marble. The walling was cemented in a bluish mortar.

At the same time three or perhaps four tufa built piers were added to the inside face of the east and west walls (Pl. 36). On the east side pier 291 was set against the phase 3c blocking of door 243. Pier 290 lay 3.5 m south, 3.5 m from the new south-east corner of the room. Both bases were 0.8 × 0.55 m. On the opposite wall, pier 292, of 1.15 × 0.65 m, lay roughly central (5 m from the south-west corner, c. 6 m from the north-west), while base 293 in the north-west corner may be no more than a reinforcement of the west wall. All piers featured a bluish mortar.

No flooring was directly associated with this remodelling: additional 'tread' levels were noted in various places but these were fragmentary and inconsistent. In the proximity of pier 275 and against wall 289 lay traces of a hard tread with red mortar, while against pier 290 on the east wall lay a small spread of black soil: finds, however, suggested these were late surfaces.

In room C patches of a tufa-coloured, fragmentary, mortar level, up to 0.15 m deep, were identified over the phase 3b red surface; a single piece of marble embedded in this level was noted near the north end of the room. Much of this level, however, was scarred by the plough. Finds from this mortar level included twelfth century material. In room B, the phase 3b surface was part-covered by a layer of plaster (with U/82 – late eleventh-twelfth century) of limited spread. Around and over this lay the remains of a brown decayed mortar level, existing in places as an earth layer alone. This contained finds U/77-81 and 85, belonging to the first half of the twelfth century. Against the north wall the hearth was given a broken marble base (sealing finds U/90). Most probably also at this time a large tufa-packed post-hole of c. 0.25 × 0.25 m was inserted in the centre of the room.

In room A the north compartment featured a lightish tufa soil floor with brown mortar patches: U/40 from this dated to the second half of the twelfth century.

Within the cloister, the corridors showed little clear evidence of reflooring. As noted above, the floor comprised a thin trodden level which seems to have been restored rather than replaced by a new surface. In the south corridor a tufa wall (295), c. 0.3 m thick, was built on top of the trodden floor surface and thus divided the corridor into two roughly equal halves. Smaller blocks (296), 0.2 m thick, flanked this wall to the east, but were not attached to it. In the cloister court the light, presumed phase 3b, soil was overlain by a dark earth layer in places 0.3 m deep which became lighter as it descended; this layer was level with the offset of the court wall foundations. Its top surface was in some places traversed by the plough blade. Finds from this were again very mixed.

Interpretation

The remodelling of room D may have sought to counter a structural deficiency of the original plan through shortening the length of the building and adding extra piers along the walls. The central piers were not removed and probably remained in use.

Most rooms received new floors or their original floors were restored: rooms B and C showed traces of brown mortar floors, which were perhaps once paved or flagged. Flagging may have been present in the cloister walkways, since wall 295, dividing the south corridor into two, overlay one fragment. The reason for the division of the corridor is obscure, and it seems unlikely that this blocked access from one side of the corridor to the other. Blocks 296 may represent tumble.

The insertion of the large packed post-hole in room B may denote the renovation of the roofing or the need for additional support for this. It is also possible that this feature formed part of the original plan of the room, maintained into this phase.

The new surface within the courtyard shows some sign of mixing with the earlier levels, perhaps caused by the digging up of the courtyard soil for cultivation purposes.

Phase 3d as a whole should belong to the second half of the twelfth century and coincide with refurbishment within the church.

PHASE 3e

Additional restructuring of room D occurred with the reinforcement (297) of the internal face of the west wall in small tufa blockwork *c.* 0.25 m thick. This extra facing overlay the trodden floor surface and sealed sherd Z/21 (of eleventh, possibly late eleventh, century date).

In room C a large posthole of 0.25 × 0.3 m, set in a larger cutting of 0.7 × 0.5 m, cut through the floor near the east wall, perhaps to aid in supporting the roof.

PHASE 3f–PHASE 4

In the south-east corner of the cloister corridor a small hearth (298) of dimensions 0.75 × 0.75 m was constructed. On this had lain a large cooking vessel of the thirteenth century, containing burnt material (U/20). The hearth rested on a slight soil level overlying the corridor floor: this soil cover was clearest in the east half of the south corridor (finds U/65, 66, T/26; the corresponding level to the west held T/27, 28, U/67). This level was otherwise visible only in the east corridor. Finds from this related to the late twelfth–early thirteenth century.

Further east a similar build-up of soil was identified south of the partition wall in room A (U/9?, 39). The hearth in room B was covered by soil, suggesting that the fire had been moved to another position. Finds U/86-88 came from the fill, and relate to the later twelfth-thirteenth century.

The phase 3e post in room C may already have been

removed: its fill (finds T/37, 46) dated to the later twelfth century.

In room D there was a thickish deposit of light soil which contained finds Z/16 and 17 (thirteenth century) as well as a large column fragment (fragment 833).

Interpretation

The build-up of untrodden soil over many of the rooms and within the area of the cloister can be equated with accumulation subsequent to the abandonment of the monastery zone. Indicative of this was the presence of a fragment of fallen column in room D. Finds from these levels point to a broad thirteenth century context.

The hypothesis of abandonment is supported by the setting of a hearth in one corner of the cloister walk. This fireplace and its refuse may signify the presence of squatters or a temporary shelter.

PHASE 4b

In the south-east of the cloister surround the accumulation was overlain by a layer of tile, whose density was greatest closer to the dividing wall 295. The north-east spread of this tile layer formed a rough diagonal line from near the north end of this cross-wall to the south-east corner of the cloister. No similar tile level was identified elsewhere directly over this accumulation, although tile was a frequent feature of the sub-plough.

In excavating trench T, which uncovered only a small area east of this dividing wall, a level of burning was recorded: this may have been associated either with the tile or with the preceding phase 3f. It contained find T/25 (thirteenth century).

Two high-lying burials were made in the south half of the cloister court (numbers 113 and 185), cutting down into the phase 3b level. The dark fill of these graves contained T/15 (grave 113) and U/34 (grave 185) (thirteenth century). To the north, grave 186 cut through the accumulation layer in room D, its feet close to the room's east wall.

Interpretation

The thick tile level represents the collapse of the roofing of the cloister surround. The greater density of this layer towards the centre of the south corridor may reflect the inward collapse of the roof. Burning noted in trench T may predate the tile collapse and indicate that a fire led to the collapse of the roof. The accumulation below the tile implies that the monastery had lain abandoned for at least a short time before this collapse.

The absence of similar collapse debris over the rest of the area of the monastery may be the result of plough action. In the cloister surround the floor level was low with respect to the surrounding rooms and this protected the phase 4 levels from dispersal. The lack of tile collapse in the other cloister corridors is less explicable.

The high-lying graves in the cloister court and room D post-date the monastery, although the position of grave 186 shows that the outlines at least of buildings such as room D remained evident.

PHASE 5

Much rubble was present in both plough and sub-plough levels. As noted, the distinction between these levels and the underlying accumulation was vague, given the depth of plough disturbance, and the division of material is therefore difficult. The finds from this phase are listed below.

PHASE 6

The plough level contained much rubble and debris from the whole zone. In particular, a large amount of fragmentary marblework was recovered. Much of this may relate to flooring. Many of the pilasters and corbels found in the vicinity of the cloister undoubtedly belonged to the courtyard colonnades; a number of these corbels were reworked classical fragments. Most finds were from the general plough level and were not listed as coming from or over a specific area. Those that were, however, are listed below:

Cloister: fragment numbers 470, 473, 517, 769-773 (unless room A), 777-788, 811-817, 824-829, 836, 837, 857, 987; possibly also 518-524.

Room A: some of the material from 769-788; 849, 850, 856, 867-868, 870 (where 868 and 870 are fragments of medieval capitals).

Room B: 818-822, 862, 876 (with 819-821 saddle querns).

Room C: 835, 841, 851, 862, 875.

Room D: 833, 852-855, 861, 863, 865, 866, 871; and much of 750-767 (Z/1).

SEQUENCE WITH FINDS:

Phase 1: Bedrock features (trenches, post-holes); fills, soil over.

Phase 2a: Cutting back of tufa bedrock.
Phase 2b-e: Cutting of graves into tufa.

Phase 2c-d: Construction of perimeter wall.

Phase 3: Disturbance of phase 2 graves.
Grave fills: S/12-16, T/15-17, 19-23, 43-57, U/59-61, 73, 98, 99, 107-111. Disturbed soil: S/4, T/4-6, 9, U/21, 61, 102, 106 and probably Z/9 and 24 (much may belong to phases 3d and 4).
Tufa soil beyond cloister: T/40, U/42, 75, Z/6.
Phase 3b: Foundation of monastery. Construction of walls: Z/24.
Cloister court level: U/32, Z/8.
Laying of floors: U/40-42 (room A); U/90, 92, 95(?), 101, 114 (room B); T/35, 39 (room C); Z/18, 21, 23 and possibly 19 (room D).
Phase 3c: Surface south of room A: U/3, 5.
Construction of Room E: perhaps U/82.
Phase 3d-e: Remodelling of room D: possibly some of Z/13, 18-21, 23.
Refloorings: T/38, Z/7 (room C); U/77-81, 83?, 84, 85, 90, 95 (room B); U/40 (room A).
Construction of wall 295: T/29.
Phase 3e: Addition in room D: post-dates Z/21.

Phase 3f-Phase 4: Accumulation: T/3, 9, 26-28, U/20, 32, 37, 39, 40, 63, 65-67, 112 (cloister); U/9(?), 39 (room A); C/12, 13, Z/16, 17 (room D); T/35, 37, 46, Z/11 (room C); U/86-88 (fill of hearth, room B).
Phase 4b: Tile level: U/35 and possibly T/25.
High-lying burials, fills: T/15, U/34, Z/22.

Phase 5: Sub-plough: S/3, T/2, 7, 8, 10, U/2, 4, 9, 10, 13, 15, 36, 39, 67, 70, 72; C/2-7, 10, Z/16.

Phase 6: Plough: T/1, 10, 30, 31, 33, 41, 45, 47, U/1, 12, 14, 17-19, 22-24, 29-31, 36, 38, 76, 96, Z/1-5, 11, 12, 15, C/1.

Unstratified material: T/8, 44, 48, 97, 101, U/25-27, 62, 68, 69, 71, 74, 93, 94, 100, 113, Z/14, 20, 22, 25, 26.

Other finds. Material from unstratified levels west of room D: C/9, 14. From south of perimeter wall: T/13, 14, U/11, 12.

CHAPTER THREE. THE BURIALS

This section contains details relating to all the burials located in the excavations. Since no associated grave-goods, and thus no direct dating evidence, were present, the sequence of burials is drawn through location and relationship to other features and graves. The graves are considered according to zone and thus do not appear in numerical order, except within each sector considered. Interpretative notes follow each of these listings. It seems that most of the skeletal material was not retained: a separate section offers an osteological analysis of those bones which were kept.

(i) CATALOGUE OF BURIALS (Fig. 17)

All graves are tufa-cut, except where noted.

(a) GRAVES WEST OF THE SECOND CHURCH AND BAPTISTERY

Grave 1. High-lying, probably north–south oriented (head at north end) with tile near head. Disturbed. No finds recorded in fill.

Grave 2. West–east, feet underlying apse foundations. Dimensions c. 1.50 × 0.4 m, with provision for cover slabs (none remaining).

Grave 3. West–east, c. 2.20 × 0.5 m, east end under apse foundations. Likely cover slab surround. Fill included D/16.

Grave 4. West–east, probably originally tile-lined and covered, c. 0.6 m wide and at least 1 m long. Cut at west end by grave 7; east end extended up to enclosure wall. Fill of grave 4 or 7 contained D/17, and tile D/6 probably came from the side of grave 4.

Grave 5. Relatively high-lying, not tufa-cut, probably north–south. Overlay lime-pit (033). Dimensions uncertain.

Grave 6. West–east, dimensions uncertain. Skeleton cut from chest downwards by apse foundations; west end of grave perhaps hollowed out one block of the enclosure wall. Originally tile-covered? Fill with D/14.

Grave 7. North–south, dimensions unclear. Cuts grave 4, and was deeper and wider than this; feet of skeleton missing. Fill of grave 4 or 7 contained D/17.

Grave 8. West–east, c. 2.20 × 0.45 m, east end of grave under church wall foundations.

Grave 9. West–east, c. > 1.80 × 0.50/55 m, east end under wall foundations. Fill included E/14.

Grave 10. Shallow, north–south, c. > 1.60 × 0.45 m, arms by side or across pelvis; feet cut by grave 15; head looking west. Fill contained E/10 and 13.

Grave 11. Deep, west–east, c. 1.7 m long.

Grave 12. West–east, child's grave, 0.85 × 0.25 m, with probable cutting for cover slabs around.

Grave 13. West–east, c. 1.95 × 0.55 m, with two tufa cover slabs in situ, over chest and feet.

Grave 14. Very shallow tufa-cut tomb, west–east or north-west–south-east.

Grave 15. West–east, c. 0.35 m wide, cutting graves 10 and 7(?).

Grave 50. North–south, 0.4 m wide, only partially excavated. East of grave 51 and north of north-west corner of baptistery.

Grave 51. West–east, c. 1.8 m long, half-excavated. At north edge of trench M.

Grave 63. High-lying, north-west–south-east, plough-damaged.

Grave 69. West–east, c. 2.0 × 0.4 m, cutting for cover slabs.

Discussion

No graves predate the lime-pits (033 and 034), which contained ninth century fill. Graves 2, 3, 4 and 6 certainly post-date the enclosure wall. Outside this, grave 7 cut 4, and 15 cut 10. To the east, graves 8, 9, 11, 12 and 69 lay within the enclosure, and of these 8 and 9 predate the second church (both cut by the apse foundations). The enclosure wall was clearly out of use by the time the second church was built. Thus if the enclosure wall originally bounded the first church cemetery, burials had extended beyond this by the time of the second church. Graves 13, 50 and 51 respect the baptistery and may likewise predate the second church. High-lying graves 1, 5, 14 and 63 relate to phase 3.

(b) GRAVES WITHIN THE BAPTISTERY

Grave 16. Plough-damaged, high-lying over font, north-west–south-east or west–east, arms crossed over abdomen. Dimensions uncertain. Fill contained K/5.

Grave 17. High-lying over font, west–east, south of 16. Length c. 1.4 m. Head facing north, arms by side.

Grave 18. High-lying, west–east over flue of kiln, north of 16; length c. 1.6 m. Arms crossed over groin.

Grave 19. High-lying, west–east, size uncertain. Arms by side, head looking south.

Grave 20. High-lying, west–east; lower half of body removed by plough.

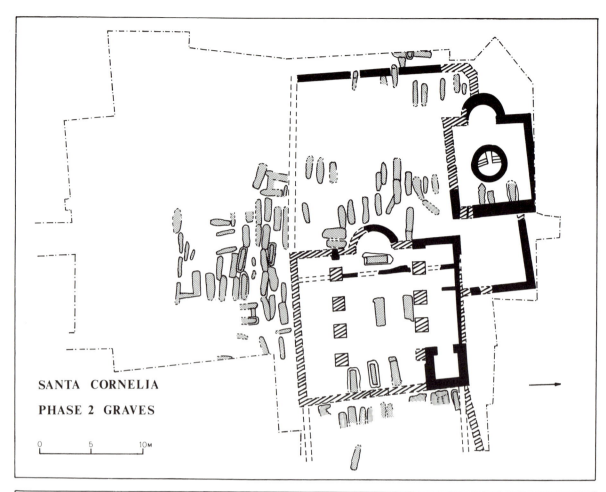

SANTA CORNELIA

PHASE 2 GRAVES

0   5   10м

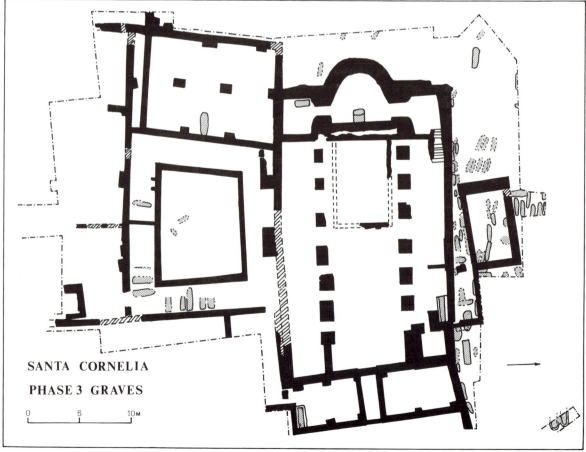

SANTA CORNELIA

PHASE 3 GRAVES

0   5   10м

Fig. 17. Santa Cornelia: graves, phases 2 and 3 (NC)

Grave 21. High-lying and disturbed, east–west (?); possibly crouched.

Grave 22. High-lying, west–east, c. 1.65 m long. Arms crossed over abdomen. Overlay 23.

Grave 23. Lower half lost through insertion of 22. Probably south-west–north-east.

Grave 24. High-lying, west–east, alongside church north wall. Lower half lost.

Grave 25. West–east, against church north wall, dimensions uncertain. Arms crossed over groin.

Grave 26. West–east, against church north wall, disturbed by 25.

Grave 27. Fragmentary west–east burial, disturbed by 25.

Grave 28. High-lying and plough-damaged, west–east, against church north wall.

Grave 29. As 28; set between 24 and 25.

Grave 30. North-west–south-east, child's grave against baptistery apse, with tile set at head of grave; unclear if tufa-cut. Fill with H/7.

Grave 31. West–east, c. 0.8 m long; against shoulder of baptistery apse and church north wall.

Grave 32. West–east, c. 0.95 m long, cutting font.

Grave 33. Small west–east burial, disturbed, with fragments of ploughed-out adult burial close-by; cut into baptistery east wall. Fill with K/6.

Grave 34. West–east, c. 1 m long, immediately west of 33, against church north wall; a stone marked west end of grave. Fill with additional skull and H/9.

Grave 52. West–east, c. 1.2 × 0.35 m, with surround for cover slabs; arms crossed over groin. Bronze armlet found in tomb, but unclear whether found on the skeleton itself or in grave fill; fill contained K/10. Tomb underlay phase 3a lime-spread in baptistery.

Grave 53. West–east, c. 2.1 × 0.5 m, against baptistery east wall. Remains of cover slabs over, and cutting at west end for head. Also beneath phase 3a lime-spread. K/13 from over grave but under lime.

Grave 54. West–east, > 1.5 × 0.7 m; cutting for cover slabs; against baptistery east wall, but cut to west by flue channel of tile kiln. Underlay lime spread. Fill with K/14.

In addition, the fill of the tile kiln contained broken tile, a skeleton of a dog, two human bones and part of a human skull. The fill post-dated the use of the kiln and predated the high-lying graves over the baptistery.

Discussion

None of the graves here predates the baptistery: the earliest post-date the font but predate the font's use as a lime-mixing pit (graves 52-54). Subsequent to these was a series of smallish tufa-cut graves (children?), which post-dated the lime-mixing and which followed the line of the outer face of the second period church north wall (graves 26, 30-34). Over these came disturbed high-lying graves (16-25, 27, 29), all of which post-date the kiln. The scatter of bone in plough and sub-plough levels signifies additional, destroyed high-lying graves.

(c) GRAVES INSIDE THE ANTE-BAPTISTERY ROOM AND 'PASSAGE-WAY'

Grave 71. High-lying, west–east, c. 1.5 × 0.35 m, in centre of room, cutting mortar floor, and partly into bedrock; plough-damaged.

Grave 72. High-lying, north-west–south-east, skeleton 1.67 m long. Arms crossed over chest. Probably lying just over mortar pavement. Sherd (1960, number 22) from fill.

Grave 73. High-lying, west–east, west of 71 and probably cutting floor; badly ploughed-out.

Grave 75. West–east, c. 1.13 × 0.3 m, in passage-way between ante-baptistery and church north wall. Sherd (1960, number 62) in fill.

Grave 82. High-lying, west–east, small grave over floor, near north wall.

Grave 83. Small, west–east, probably not tufa-cut; inserted between blocks on line of ante-baptistery east wall.

Grave 87. High-lying, west–east, overlying 89 near north wall.

Grave 88. West–east, cutting floor and part into bedrock. Fill with disturbed secondary burial and Q/3.

Grave 89. West–east, c. 1.6 × 0.4 m, cutting floor; cutting for cover slabs. Possible disturbed tiles from cover at east end.

Grave 90. Shallow, west–east, c. 1.5 m long; in passage-way parallel with church north wall.

Grave 91. Shallow, west–east, small; in passage-way against church north wall.

Grave 92. West–east, c. 1 m long; in passage-way.

Grave 93. West–east, disturbed; near church north door.

Grave 94. In disturbed area in front of church north door; grave contained at least two skulls. Fill with N/19.

Grave 95. Part tufa-cut, north–south; probably extended up to church north wall.

Grave 96. Shallow, west–east, dimensions uncertain. North of 95, against outer face of ante-baptistery south wall.

Grave 97. As grave 96, but to west.

Grave 98. North-west–south-east, *c.* 1.8 × 0.4 m, south-east of 88 against east wall. Tiles from possible cover. Perhaps cut west end of 89.

Grave 99. Shallow, west–east, over 1.25 m long; set in south-east corner, with feet cutting into two blocks of east wall.

Grave 100. West–east, *c.* 1.3 m long, cut into blocks of north wall.

Grave 102. High-lying, west–east, cutting ante-baptistery room floor.

Grave 103. Shallow tufa-cut, west–east, in south-east corner of room.

Grave 104. North–south, *c.* 1.7 m × 0.45 m; south end under buttress wall 130 against church north wall. Fill with N/23.

Grave 105. West–east. On tufa shelf south of 107.

Grave 106. Shallow, west–east, in east half of passage-way.

Grave 107. West–east, *c.* 1.3 m long; beneath foundations of eastward extension of ante-baptistery south wall (108).

Grave 108. West–east, at least 1.7 m long; under wall running eastwards from south wall of ante-baptistery.

Grave 151. West–east, *c.* 1.9 m long; centrally overlain by wall 108. Fill with P/29.

Discussion

Most graves in this area belong to the period subsequent to the demolition of the ante-baptistery room, since many cut through its floor and even into its foundations (numbers 71-73, 82, 87-89, 98-100, 102, 103). In addition, bones from the upper levels of the 1960 trench I should relate to further, destroyed, high burials. Graves 75, 96 and 97 may date to the lifetime of the building since these lay alongside the external face of its south wall, while 95 may have lain against the first church north wall. In the passage-way, graves 83, 90-95 and 106 were aligned with the second church north wall. To the east, in what is assumed to be a later extension to the passage, 107 and 108 were part overlain by the eastward extension of the ante-baptistery south wall. The buttress (covering 104) against the church north wall was probably contemporary with this extension.

(d) GRAVES OUTSIDE THE ANTE-BAPTISTERY ROOM

Grave 64. North–south, *c.* 1.7 × 0.5 m, east of baptistery east wall.

Grave 65. West–east, > 1.0 × 0.45 m.

Grave 66. West–east, > 1.15 m long; immediately north of 65.

Grave 67. West–east.

Grave 74. High-lying, west–east, disturbed; tile (from cover?) in fill.

Grave 76. West–east, *c.* 1.6 × 0.45 m, head facing north, arms crossed over chest; grave probably aligned with ante-baptistery north wall.

Grave 77. West–east, *c.* 1.5 × 0.4 m, north of 76.

Grave 78. West–east, *c.* 1.6 × 0.35 m, possibly cut by 64.

Grave 84. North–south, in corner between ante-baptistery east wall and passage-way wall, at level of the foundations of east wall.

Grave 85. North–south, > 1.25 m long.

Grave 86. West–east, small; north of 85.

Grave 101. Shallow cutting north of 86, containing three skulls.

In addition, a further, unnumbered tomb was located just north of 66.

Discussion

Graves north of the ante-baptistery room may belong to the lifetime of the baptistery and ante-baptistery, given that they respect the line of their foundations. However, loose bones recorded in plough and sub-plough levels in 1960 trench I signify destroyed higher, later, graves. Most graves east of the ante-baptistery should belong to phase 3.

(e) GRAVES NORTH OF THE CAMPANILE

Grave 55. West–east, small; north of sarcophagus 339.

Grave 56. South–north, against wall 109; child's burial with tile (cover?).

Grave 57. West–east, disturbed; lying across 56 and part over 60.

Grave 58. West–east, alongside campanile foundations.

Grave 59. East–west, flanking porch north wall; skull only preserved.

Grave 60. West–east, ploughed; over 56, part under 57. Fill with P/30.

Grave 62. No details given. May be small tomb partly underlying porch north wall.

Grave 151. West–east, *c.* 1.95 × 0.75 m; cut and overlain by east wall of passage-way (109). Fill with P/29.

Sarcophagus 339. Re-used, plain, classical sarcophagus of 2.15 × 0.65 m, with monolithic cover slab broken by plough. Single west–east inhumation.

Two further graves were identified in close proximity to the porch north wall, but left unnumbered. The first was a shallow tomb, west–east, c. 1.75 × 0.3 m, probably flanking the porch north wall. The second was also shallow, north-east–south-west, c. 1.15 × 0.35 m, perhaps part-underlying the porch north wall.

Discussion

The sequence here is confused: graves aligned with the campanile could belong to late phase 2. Some clearly underlay the porch north wall, and one (151) underlay the passage-way east wall; 56, 57 and 60, however, may be of phase 3. Since few graves were cut into bedrock (unless shallow), soil level here was possibly greater than elsewhere.

(f) GRAVES WITHIN THE AREA OF THE SECOND CHURCH

(i) Graves within the crypts

Grave 153. North–south, c. 1.4 × 0.6 m, with possible cutting for cover slabs. Lay close to west wall of south crypt. Fill with R/3, 7 and 9.

The rubble fill of the central crypt, at a level close to its floor, yielded remains of a skeleton. This suggests a burial sited in the overlying presbytery, or perhaps an unfortunate robber.

(ii) Graves in the western half of the second church

1. North aisle

Grave 35. West–east, c. 1.5 × 0.35 m. Lay across fill of pit 038 at west end of aisle. The foundations of stylobate 061 cut its south-west corner.

Grave 36. West–east, c. 2.1 × 0.55 m, with cutting for cover slabs. Arms crossed. West end and head cut by pit 038; east end cut by flue of bell-pit.

Grave 37. South-west–north-east, >1.65 m long. South-west end beneath stylobate 062.

Grave 38. West–east, at least c. 1.5 × 0.55 m, with tufa cover slabs. One slab preserved beneath stylobate 062, while grave west end (lacking cover slabs) part underlay base 061.

2. Nave of the second church: *schola cantorum* (Pl. 12)

Grave 41. West–east, >1.65 m long, with two tufa cover slabs of 0.85 × 0.45 m, broken to north-east. West end part cut by foundations of wall 060. Fill with F/8.

Grave 42. North-west–south-east, >1.75m × 0.4 m; north-west end cut by 43.

Grave 43. West–east, c. 2.15 × 0.7 m; parallel to bedrock foundation of *schola cantorum* north wall. Cut 42 to south-east. Fill with F/11.

Grave 44. West–east, c. 1.95 × 0.45 m; probable cutting for cover slabs; alongside wall 060. Fill with F/9.

Grave 45. West–east, c. 1.8 × 0.40/45 m; probable cover slab cutting. Cut to north-west by 44.

Grave 46. West–east, c. 2.05 × 0.5 m: east end covered by two large tufa blocks, originally a single cover slab of 0.95 × 0.45 × 0.19 m mortared over grave with purple cement.

Grave 47. West–east, 1.95 × 0.45 m; parallel to *schola cantorum* north wall.

Grave 48. Charnel-pit north of early apse, built up to back of wall 006; cut to west by 81. Originally may have been a west–east tomb subsequently disturbed by 81 and later by insertion of pier 063. Tile in fill may indicate cover. Fill with N/7 and 8.

Grave 49. North–south, child's grave, size uncertain; almost totally destroyed by insertion of 41: south end preserved, and trace of north end visible in bedrock foundation of *schola cantorum* north wall.

Grave 79. West–east, c. 2.3 × 0.45 m; west end terminates in rectangular tile-built feature of 0.7 × 0.25 m, perhaps to support cover slabs. West of first church apse.

Grave 80. West–east, c. 2.25 × 0.5 m; probable cutting for cover slabs on north side. Lay in line of phase 1a trench (001).

Grave 81. West–east, c. 1.85 × 0.4 m; probable tile cover. Part overlay 48.

Grave 148. North–south, c. 1.9 × 0.7 m, beneath stylobate 069. Originally against west wall of first church.

Grave 149. North–south, c. 2.65 × 0.95 m, east end under base 069.

Grave 157. West–east, c. 2.05 × 0.55 m; probable cover slab cutting around. Cut south side of agricultural trench 001, and was cut at east end by 149 and partly overlain by stylobate 068.

3. South aisle

Grave 68. West–east, c. 1.8 × 0.45 m.

Grave 154. West–east, >1.5 m long; two cover slabs *in situ* at east end. West end perhaps cut by crypt east wall.

Grave 155. Shallow, west–east, c. 2.0 × 0.6 m; possibly cut by crypt east wall. Fill with R/10.

Grave 156. Shallow, west–east, c. 0.6 m wide; east half under base 067.

(iii) Area of the first church

1. North aisle

Grave 61. West–east, *c.* 2.1 × 0.5 m. This was set against the foundations of the church north wall, with the east end against the west face of the campanile. The south side was formed by rough tufa and tile walling, which was flanked by the brick-built campanile stairway (114). The west face was composed of half of the front of a strigillated sarcophagus, crudely walled into the foundations of the church north wall, with a rough walling set over this and up to the campanile face, to provide support for the cover. The latter comprised a large slab of Egyptian granite *c.* 0.5 m wide, the western half of which survived *in situ*. The tomb was 0.65 m deep, its base marked by three pieces of marble (one from a strigillated sarcophagus) mortared across the tomb width: these did not create a complete base, however, but rather left wide gaps between. These slabs divided the tomb from an earlier, underlying burial. The upper tomb contained a more or less undisturbed inhumation, with a fill containing pottery (note that the grave was disturbed by robbers in winter 1961-1962). The lower tomb extended to *c.* 0.9 m deep and held one complete skeleton and most of another; its fill contained pottery, iron, and glass. Whereas the upper tomb clearly post-dated the construction of the second church, the lower should be of phase 2, but postdating construction of the campanile. Fills included P/13 (lower grave) and 15 (upper) (Pl. 16).

2. Church nave

Grave 39. West–east, *c.* 2.6 × 0.9 m; due south of 40. Contained just part of one skull, and a tufa block, perhaps part of cover. Fill with L/6 and N/5.

Grave 40. West–east, *c.* 2.25 × 0.95 m; containing two skeletons, one articulated, the other, earlier, fragmented and piled up by the former's legs. Fill with N/16.

Grave 110. West–east, *c.* 2.0 × 0.7 m; not emptied. East end cut by internal offset (054) to church east wall datable to phase 3.

Grave 111. West–east, *c.* 2.0 × 0.50/55 m; cutting for cover slabs. Lay in line of phase 1 agricultural trench 001, off-centre of church entrance, up to which it had been set. Covered by floor of second church.

Grave 150. Tile-lined, west–east, >1.6 × 0.6 m; cut at east end by foundations for internal offset (054), removing legs of skeleton below knees; these bones appear to have been thrown into the rubble foundations. Part of the skull of another burial also present. Covered by floor of second church. Finds from fill: S/30 (upper fill, under floor) and 31 (lower) (Pl. 17).

Grave 160. North–south, *c.* 2.1 × 0.6 m, with incurving south end. Lay immediately in front of first church apse. Tile-lined in north, with rougher, faced stonework for rest of tomb. Should equate with the reliquary of the first church. Filled with rubble, and contained L/1.

Discussion

Most, if not all, the graves within the area of the churches predate the second church, given that they are cut by or underlie phase 3 features. A few graves remain problematic. The following groups can be made:
Graves prior to the second church: 35-37, 41, 48, 49, 61 (lower tomb), 110, 111, 148-150, 154-156, 160.
Uncertain: 39, 40, 42-47, 68, 79-81, 157.
(Given the similarity in orientation, these probably belong to phase 2.)
Second church graves: 61 (upper tomb), 153 and likely burial in apse, signified by bones in crypt rubble.

It may be suggested that phase 2 burials were concentrated in the area west of the first church, particularly near the apse and in the area of the second church *schola cantorum*. Within the first church, the well-built graves 150 and 160 must have been important. Numbers 39, 40, 61, 110 and 111 were also burials set within the early church. We know that Hadrian I translated the bodies of four previous popes to *Capracorum*: their mortal remains were undoubtedly laid in certain of these tombs, and it is tempting to argue that pride of place was given to that of Cornelius, whose relics were perhaps redeposited in tomb 160. Subsequently these will have been re-located in the crypt reliquary.

(g) GRAVES FROM WITHIN THE PORCH

(i) North compartment of the porch

Grave 112. West–east, >1.8 × 0.5 m. Comprised two levels: uppermost featured up to five skulls and a few other bones; below lay three covering tiles from the disturbed lower grave. Grave may have cut the foundation trench of the earlier porch north wall (045). Upper fill contained P/17, 24 and Y/20.

Grave 114. West–east, >1.5 × 0.75 m. Fill with P/21, 25, and Y/23.

Grave 141. West–east, >0.8 × 0.55 m; west end cut by 142. Fill with P/20, 23.

Grave 142. North–south, *c.* 1.2 × 0.6 m. Overlay 187, and cut west ends of 114 and 141.

Grave 143. North–south, dimensions uncertain.

Grave 187. North–south, child's grave, tile at south end; set against church foundations. Underlay 142.

(ii) Causeway

Grave 183. West–east, dimensions uncertain. Under floor of first period causeway, probably in fill of phase 1 trench 001. Y/33.

Grave 184. West–east, dimensions uncertain. Against or partly under causeway north side wall, under first period paving; probably in trench 001 fill. Contained Y/33 (= general fill from causeway here).

(iii) South compartment

Grave 144. West–east, dimensions uncertain; overlain by causeway south wall.

Grave 145. Shallow tufa-cut, west–east, > 1.3 × 0.55 m. Underlay first porch floor. S/23 in upper fill.

Grave 146. West–east, > 1.5 × 0.75 m. Fill with S/18.

Grave 147. West–east, > 1.1 × 0.75 m. S/18 from top of fill.

Grave 161. North–south, c. 2.0 × 0.7 m; two tufa cover slabs at south end. North-east end overlain by porch floor slabs.

Grave 162. West–east, c. 2.05 × 1.0 m externally (including tile-built walls and cutting for cover); internally 1.95 × 0.6 m. Built into porch south-east corner, with sides added to north and west; north side perhaps disturbed area of grave 163. East end of 162 contained heaped-up bones and some metal; remainder held two articulated skeletons lacking skulls; there were burnt traces over fill. Fill with Y/30, 32.

Grave 163. Probably north–south, with tufa-block surround. Perhaps predated 162. Badly disturbed.

Discussion

All the graves, excluding 162, predate the first porch floor (phase 3a). However, the poor state of the floor meant a high degree of contamination of finds from graves, relating chiefly to later phase 3 activity. It was unclear whether any graves predated construction of the campanile.

(iv) Graves outside the porch

Grave 195. West–east/west-north-west–east-south-east, c. 2.0 × 0.5 m. Lay immediately west of porch south compartment, its west end perhaps just underneath porch foundations. Vertically set tile in east end. 195 should be linked with the pre-porch graves. No details recorded regarding skeleton.

In addition north of porch, c. 8 m from porch north-east corner, the east ends of two graves (164 and 165) were located in east trench XIII: both tufa-cut, c. 0.45 m wide, and west–east. No other details. Location indicates northward extension of cemetery (cf. tufa-cut burials north of ante-baptistery).

(h) GRAVES FROM THE MONASTERIAL ZONE

(i) Cloister court graves (Pl. 37)

1. Trench T graves

Grave 113. High-lying, north-west–south-east, dimensions unclear. Fill with T/15.

Grave 115. West–east, dimensions uncertain; part under court north wall.

Grave 116. West–east, c. 2.05 × 0.6 m. Fill with T/22 and U/56.

Grave 117. West–east, c. 0.65 × 0.2 m; child's grave. T/19 in fill.

Grave 118. West–east, c. 0.6 × 0.3 m; child's grave. Perhaps part-underlying cloister court north wall. Fill with T/20 and U/57.

Grave 119. West–east, half-excavated, width c. 0.35 m. T/16 in fill.

Grave 120. North–south, c. 2.0 × 0.6 m.

Grave 121. North–south, c. 1.7 × 0.35 m.

Grave 122. North–south, c. 1.95 × 0.35 m. Fill with T/17 and U/43.

Grave 123. West–east, size uncertain; part under court south wall.

Grave 124. West–east, c. 1.8 × 0.45 m, narrowing to east. Rough line of four tiles set down centre of base. Fill with T/21.

Grave 125. West–east, c. 1.75 × 0.35 m; possible cutting for cover slabs. Fill with U/54.

Grave 185. High-lying small grave, disturbed, north-east–south-west, overlying 125. Fill with T/7 and U/34.

2. Trench U graves (eastern half of cloister court)

Grave 166. West–east, c. 1.9 × 0.4 m; cutting for cover slabs. Fill with tile, horse bones, T/23 and U/44.

Grave 167. West–east, c. 2.0 × 0.45 m; cutting for cover slabs, (imprint of one surviving in purple mortar bedding; mortar also in fill). Part under court east wall. Fill with U/45.

Grave 168. West–east, c. 2.1 × 0.65 m; square-ended. Unclear whether north-east corner cut or was cut by 169. Fill contained purple mortar fragments, tile, stone, a nail, part of a child burial and U/46.

Grave 169. West–east, > 1.8 × 0.55 m, rectangular cutting. East end under court east wall. Fill with U/47.

Grave 170. West–east, c. 2.1 × 0.4 m; two shallow semi-circular cuts on each side; a fragment of purple mortar over east end may mark cover slab. Fill with tile fragments and U/48.

Grave 171. West–east, > 2.0 × 0.7 m. Skeleton badly disturbed, with skull smashed. Grave part under court east wall; south-west angle perhaps cut by 170.

Grave 172. West–east, *c.* 2.25 × 0.75 m, with squarish west end; it part underlay the court east wall. The disturbed fill contained U/50 and 51 (51 from beneath the court wall).

Grave 173. West–east, *c.* 2.3 × 0.75 m. Disturbed fill, with U/52.

Grave 174. North–south, at least 1.5 × 0.4 m, narrowing to north. Exact relationship with graves 173 and 175 uncertain. U/53 in fill.

Grave 175. West–east, *c.* 1.7 × 0.35 m, with a building block near east end, and cutting for cover slabs. May have part underlain court east wall.

Grave 176. West–east, *c.* 1.8 × 0.35 m; cutting for cover. Fill with U/55.

Grave 177. West-north-west–east-south-east, *c.* 0.9 × 0.25 m. Child's burial.

(ii) Graves from area of cloister surround

1. North-west corner

Grave 178. West–east, > 1.0 × 0.25 m; under area of night-stair (241). Area contained much disturbed bone, and some pottery, some perhaps from grave fill: U/73, 109-111. U/109 and 111 also contained two badly ruined bronze coins (coin numbers 3 and 6, below).

Grave 188. North–south, *c.* 2.25 × 0.5 m; north end under night-stair.

Grave 189. North–south, *c.* 2.1 × 0.55 m; also cut by night-stair.

Grave 190. West–east (tending north-west–south-east), *c.* 2.2 × 0.7 m; covered by two slabs (overlapping slightly and of different sizes). Some human bones found over slabs. U/107 from over cover, U/108 below.

Grave 191. West–east, > 1.0 × 0.65 m. Probably cut 188 and 189.

2. Cloister north walk

Grave 126. West–east, *c.* 2.25 × 0.45 m; south side part overlain by cloister court wall. Fill with S/16, and S/4 from over grave but under court wall.

Grave 127. West–east, *c.* 1.6 × >0.3 m; section of marble column reused as a cover slab (displaced somewhat over grave). South side overlain by court wall. Skull found over cover, presumably from nearby, destroyed burial; underlying skeleton intact, but with surrounding fill of bones, mortar and sherds: U/98 from over slab, S/15 and U/99 below.

Grave 128. West–east, *c.* 2.1 × 0.6 m; straight ends.

Grave 129. West–east, *c.* 1.95 × 0.45 m (narrowing to east); cutting for cover.

Grave 130. West–east, *c.* 2.1 × 0.5 m; three cover slabs over west two-thirds, westernmost slab partly over east end of 129.

Grave 131. West–east, *c.* 2.2 × 0.45 m; cutting for cover slabs. West end cut by 130. U/60 in fill.

Grave 132. West–east, *c.* 2.1 × 0.7 m; straight-edged. Part of west end under night-stair. Top fill with S/14.

Grave 133. West–east, *c.* 2.1 × 0.65 m (including rectangular cut for cover slabs); internally 1.7 × 0.3 m (narrowing to east).

Grave 134. West–east, *c.* 2.3 × 0.75 m; close to entrance to church (059).

Grave 135. West–east, > 1.75 m long; runs into 136 to east. Also cut by night-stair foundations 241, and perhaps disturbed by second church south wall.

Grave 136. Disturbed by or very closely set against church south wall; unclear if east end cut by entrance-way into church.

Grave 137. West–east, *c.* 1.8 × 0.4 m; perhaps cut by 109.

3. Cloister north-east corner

Grave 109. West–east, *c.* 2.05 × 0.7 m, sarcophagus. Fill with S/12.

Grave 138. West–east, *c.* 2.2 × 0.4 m; cutting for cover slabs. Perhaps cut 179 to south.

Grave 179. West–east (tending south-west–north-east), *c.* 1.8 × 0.35 m; cutting for cover slabs. U/59 in fill.

Grave 180. North–south, > 1.0 × 0.45 m, deeply cut into tufa. Disturbed by 182. Fill with U/61.

Grave 181. North–south, > 1.0 × 0.45 m, deeply cut into tufa; cutting for cover slab (one preserved). Primary burial intact, but disturbed bones from secondary burial appeared in fill and outside. Fill with U/61.

Grave 182. West–east, > 0.75 × *c.* 0.4 m; cut across tops of both 180 and 181. U/61 from fill.

4. East corridor of cloister

A number of depressions in the (unexcavated) floor level of the east side of the cloister indicate the positions of up to seven additional graves, five of probable west–east orientation. While apparently respecting the east cloister wall, their east ends may have been obscured by the foundation trench of this wall.

5. South corridor of cloister

Traces of three possible north–south graves were identified here, only one of which was numbered.

Grave 140. North–south, *c*. 1.75 × 0.6 m. Two skull fragments over sunken cover slabs (sinkage indicates slabs too small for cover); grave not emptied. U/21 from over slabs.

6. Graves from area of room A

Grave 139. West–east, *c*. 1.9 × 0.4 m, with squared west end.

Grave 192. West–east (tending to south-west–north-east), *c*. 1.75 m long, only partly visible.

Grave 193. Shallow, probably north–south, dimensions uncertain.

Grave 194. Shallow, north-south, > 1.0 m long.

7. Room D (west of cloister)

Grave 186. High-lying, west–east, no grave outline. Cut down into floor of room D, its feet close to east wall. Articulated skeleton, *c*. 1.6 m long, arms folded over chest. Fill perhaps with Z/22.

Discussion

In the cloister court, a tufa earth level underlay the fill forming the probable make-up for the courtyard surface. The same tufa earth fill was present in all the tufa-cut graves underlying the court. This suggests that the graves here predate the monastic cloister. Certainly the quantity of loose bone in this level argues for the disturbance of the graves at the time of the cloister's construction. The likelihood of burial within a cloister is small: the positioning of many graves may suggest that they respect the cloister walls, but this should be seen solely as a coincidence of orientation. More significant is the fact that many graves were clearly overlain by the cloister walls (115, 118, 123, 126, 127, 167, 169, 171, 172, 175[?]).

In the cloister corridors a similar situation prevails, for here the disturbed graves underlay a trodden floor level, which either directly covered the tufa bedrock or overlay a slight tufa earth cover. In the north walk, graves were cut by the dormitory night-stair and by the entrance into the church (132, 135, probably 136, 178, 188, and 189). Some graves respected the line of the south wall of the second church (109, 135, 136?, 137, 139, 178), though in its eastern half this of course followed the line of the first church south wall. The unexcavated graves in the east corridor do, however, show some sign of careful positioning.

The bedrock south of the church was cut back for some distance to accommodate the terracing for the south side of the churches (hence the absence here of traces of phase 1a agricultural trenching, although preserved, however,

below room D). Clearly all the excavated graves post-date this operation, and all the tufa-cut graves predate the monasterial buildings. We can thus argue that the graves are predominantly phase 2 in date and relate to the life of the first church, and therefore mark a significant cemeterial zone. The longevity of use is indicated by graves cutting others, secondary burials, and variable orientations. Given that some graves appear to respect the second church south wall, it is even possible that a few burials belong to phase 3a. It is impossible to conclude from these data, however, whether any substantial time elapsed between the construction of the second church and that of the monastery complex.

The few high-lying graves (113 and 185 from the cloister court; 186 in room D) relate to a post-monastery phase: 113 and 185 cut the upper soil level of the court, while 186 cut through accumulation over the floor of room D. This implies either that the monastery was abandoned before the church site was deserted, or that burials were still made near the church even after this too had been abandoned. These graves can perhaps be set in line with other high-lying burials both west and north of the second church.

(ii) THE HUMAN SKELETAL REMAINS

Valerie Higgins

INTRODUCTION

Although at least 194 burials were identified in the excavations at Santa Cornelia, very few skeletons were retained and were therefore available for examination. This report is accordingly concise and describes each preserved skeleton individually. It would not be justifiable to attempt to draw overall conclusions from such a small sample, and as there is no indication in the records of the criteria employed for keeping these particular skeletons it is impossible to assess their relationship to the burial population as a whole. In addition, it will be noted that almost every skeleton discussed below has some particular condition or abnormality.

METHODOLOGY

An inventory of the anatomical parts present was made, and data relating to age, gender, pathology and metrical analysis were recorded. Adult age was determined by assessment of tooth wear (Brothwell 1981, 72), pubic symphysis wear patterns (McKern and Stewart 1957; Gilbert and McKern 1973), the revised Todd method (Meindl *et al.* 1985), and auricular surface wear patterns (Lovejoy *et al.* 1985). Immature skeletons were aged on the basis of the total length of the long bones minus the epiphyses, and translated into chronological age (cf. Ubelaker 1978). Ages derived from long bone length alone should be regarded as approximate estimations. Tooth eruption is a more accurate method, but too little dentition was recovered here for it to be useful.

Sex was determined by morphological differences in the pelvis, skull and long bones. In the pelvis the following traits were recorded: shape of sciatic notch, presence/absence of well-defined pre-auricular sulcus, and the sub-pubic angle. In the skull the size of supraorbital ridges, mastoid process, posterior zygomatic process and nuchal crest was noted. The longitudinal length of the head of the femur was regarded as indicating male if it exceeded 44.5 mm and female if less than 43.5 mm. The bicondylar breadth of the femur indicated male if greater than 76 mm and female if less than 74 mm. The longitudinal head of the humerus indicated male if greater than 48.8 mm and female if less than 42.7 mm. The transverse width of the head of the humerus indicated male if greater than 44.7 mm and female if less than 36.9 mm. There is no reliable method of sexing immature skeletons.

The following cranial measurements were taken (based on Brothwell (1981, 81-83)):
Nasal height, from nasion to nasospinale (**NH'**)
Bimaxillary breadth, from one zygomaxillare to the other (**GB**)
Foraminal length, from basion to opisthion (**FL**)
Orbital breadth, from dacryon to the anterior surface of its lateral margin (**O'1**)
Orbital height maximum superior-inferior (**O'2**)
Maximum breadth of nasal aperture between the anterior surfaces of its lateral margins (**NB**)
Palatal breadth from one endomolare to the other (**G2**)
Basi-alveolare length, from the nasion to the alveolare (**GL**)
Foraminal breadth, maximum internal measurement of the foramen magnum (**FB**)
Upper facial height, from nasion to alveolare (**G'H**)
Frontal chord, minimum distance from nasion to bregma (**S'1**)
Parietal chord, minimum distance from bregma to lambda (**S'2**)
Occipital chord, minimum distance from lambda to opisthion (**S'3**)
Bi-dacryonic chord, minimum distance from one dacryon to the other (**DC**)
Simotic chord, minimum breadth of nasal bones taken along maxillo-nasal sutures (**SC**)
Mandibular bicondylar width between most external points of condyles (**W1**)
Minimum ramus breadth smallest distance between anterior and posterior borders of ascending ramus (**RB'**)

The following post-cranial measurements were taken:
Femur subtrochanteric anterior-posterior diameter (**FeD1**)
Femur subtrochanteric medial-lateral diameter (**FeD2**)
Femur midshaft anterior-posterior diameter (**FeD3**)
Femur midshaft medial-lateral diameter (**FeD4**)
Tibia anterior-posterior diameter at nutrient foramen (**TiD1**)
Tibia medial-lateral diameter at nutrient foramen (**TiD2**)

The presence or absence of each tooth was recorded. If the tooth was absent and there were signs of healing in the socket it was adjudged to have been lost ante-mortem; if there were no signs of healing, post-mortem loss was assumed. If the alveolar bone was missing it was recorded simply as lost, since it was not possible to distinguish ante- and post-mortem loss. The dentition is divided into four quadrants (left and right, maxilla and mandible) and assigned numbers beginning mesially – thus 1 signifies the central incisor and 8 the third molar.

ARTICULATED SKELETONS

1. Labelled 'Second burial'. Site location: Trench A.
Date: Phase 2.
Burial: Articulated single inhumation in sealed context. Found extended on back, oriented west–east.
Bones present: Fragments of frontal bone, both parietal bones, maxillae and mandibles. Vertebra C2. Right clavicle. Fragments of right humerus and ulna. Right radius. Sacrum. Fragments of left and right innominate. Left femur minus medial condyle at distal end. Proximal half of right femur. Shaft fragments of left tibia and fibula.
Age: Adult. Teeth lost ante-mortem. Pubic symphysis lost post-mortem. Long bones fully fused.
Sex: Female. Sciatic notch, preauricular sulcus and mastoid processes female.
Metrical data:

Right FeD1 25.3 mm	Left FeD1 24.95 mm
Right FeD2 33.6 mm	Left FeD2 33.3 mm
Right FeD3 30.55 mm	Left FeD3 30.6 mm
Right FeD4 26.2 mm	Left FeD4 26.3 mm

Dentition:

Right maxilla	8 –	Present. Slight mesial interproximal at cemento-enamel junction.
	7 –	Present. Gross interproximal mesial.
	6 –	Present.
	5,4,3 –	Lost post-mortem.
	2,1 –	Lost.
Left maxilla	8,7 –	Lost.
	6 –	Lost post-mortem.
	5,4,3,2 –	Present.
	1 –	Lost.
Right mandible	8 –	Lost.
	7-1 –	Lost post-mortem.
Left mandible	8-1 –	Lost post-mortem.

Pathology: The sacrum, open on the posterior surface, is consistent with the condition of spina bifida, while its abnormal curvature suggests that this individual had an abnormally curving spinal column. Unfortunately all vertebrae were lost, save for one cervical vertebra. The sacrum has just four segments, which may have been caused by lumbarization of the first sacral vertebra. Pathological changes in the innominate bones and the femora imply probable loss of mobility in the individual. Both femora show signs of remodelling, affecting the shape of the head and neck and giving an elongated appearance. There was no sign of a fracture, however, and we may assume remodelling over an extended period. The left femur has an inflammatory reaction around the facet of the head; the proximal and distal articulations showed moderate osteophytosis. The right femur has a moderate inflammatory reaction around the facet of the head and gross osteophytosis around the proximal articulation. In the innominates the left auricular surface is very irregular, and the lateral surfaces of both ilia show pleating causing striations along the stress lines and foramen in between. The right acetabulum bulges posteriorly due to the femoral head articulation; there is remodelling of the acetabular rim.

2. Labelled tomb 5. Probably trench D.
Date: Phase 2.
Burial: Disturbed single inhumation.
Bones present: Skull intact except for fragments of sphenoid, ethmoid and left zygomatic bone. Post-cranial bones may relate to skeleton 3.
Age: Young adult. M3 was erupted in all quadrants. Tooth wear was compatable with age range 17-25 years.
Sex: Male? Supraorbital ridges and mastoid processes male. Posterior zygomatic process and nuchal crest indeterminate.
Metrical data:

NH' 47.35 mm	GB 94.35 mm
FL 35.1 mm	Right O'1 38.75 mm
Right O'2 33.85 mm	Left O'2 34.6 mm
NB 22.7 mm	G2 40.1 mm
GL 86.3 mm	FB 47.55 mm
G'H 67.3 mm	S'l 103.2 mm
S'2 119.5 mm	S'3 89.95 mm
DC 21.9 mm	SC 11.6 mm
W1 115.1 mm	Left RB' 27.9 mm
Right RB' 30.6 mm	

Dentition:

Right maxilla	8,7 –	Present. Calculus supra gingival moderate inter-proximal.
	6,5,4 –	Present. Calculus supra gingival moderate inter-proximal and buccal
	3 –	Present.
	2,1 –	Lost post-mortem.
Left maxilla	8,7,6,5 –	Present.
	4,3,2,1 –	Lost post-mortem.
Right mandible	8-4 –	Present. Calculus supragingival moderate inter-proximal.
	3,2,1 –	Lost post-mortem.
Left mandible	8,7,6 –	Present.
	5 –	Present. Calculus supra gingival slight inter-proximal and buccal.
	4 –	Present, Calculus supra gingival slight inter-proximal, buccal and lingual.
	3 –	Present, Calculus supra gingival slight inter-proximal. Calculus supra gingival heavy buccal. Calculus supra gingival slight lingual.
	2 –	Present, Calculus supra gingival slight inter-proximal. Calculus supra gingival heavy buccal.
	1 –	Lost post-mortem.

Pathology: The nasal bone deviates slightly laterally to the left side and the nasal aperture is asymmetrical. This is consistent with a healed traumatic injury to the nose. The right maxilla has a patch of periosteal reaction that extends from the alveolar process to the infraorbital foramen. Both orbits have cribra orbitalia classification C (Brothwell 1981, 165).

3. Unlabelled. Possibly part of grave 5?
Burial: No data.
Bones present: Both humeri. Both radii. Both ulnae. Both innominates. Both femora. Right tibia. Left tibia, missing distal end.
Age: Middle 30s. Long bones completely fused. Pubic symphysis: McKern and Stewart 4/3/3, age range 19-39 years; corrected Todd phase VV, age range 36-40 years. Auricular surface age range 30-34 years.
Sex: Male. Sciatic notch and preauricular sulcus male. Femur longitudinal head length and bicondylar breadth male. Humerus longitudinal head length and transverse head length male.
Metrical data:

Right FeD1 28.0 mm	Left FeD1 26.5 mm
Right FeD2 32.6 mm	Left FeD2 33.6 mm
Right FeD3 28.7 mm	Left FeD3 28.9 mm
Right FeD4 27.3 mm	Left FeD4 29.1 mm
Right TiD1 36.7 mm	Left TiD1 39.33 mm
Right TiD2 25.45 mm	Left TiD2 25.0 mm

Pathology: Both tibiae show signs of inflammation. The left tibia has periostitis on the medial aspect, just inferior to the proximal articulation. The right tibia shows periostitis on the soleal line, with the surface slightly raised, suggesting that the infection may have penetrated the bone, causing osteitis. The right femur demonstrates exostosis adjacent to the fibular articulation at the distal end, and slight osteophytosis at the distal end. The left ulna had moderate osteophytosis at the proximal articulation and severe osteophytosis at the distal articulation. Moderate osteophytosis was observed at the ulnar notch distal surface of the left radius.

DISARTICULATED REMAINS

4. Site location and date unknown. Burial data lacking.
Bones present: One individual. One arch of thoracic vertebra. One right rib fragment. Right clavicle. Left scapula (glenoid and acromion only). Right ulna. Left third metacarpal. Left proximal phalanx hand. Right ischium fragment. Right talus. Right and left fifth metatarsal.

5. Site location D/22, from *loculus* in second church crypt.
Date: Phase 3.
Burial: Disturbed multiple inhumation, possibly accidental.
Bones present: Three adults and one child.
Adult bones: Skulls too fragmented to be fully recorded. C1 vertebra. Three fragments of cervical vertebrae. Four body and nine arches of thoracic vertebrae. One lumbar vertebra. One right and one left rib. Twelve midshaft rib fragments. One left clavicle. One right and one left scapula. One right and two left humeri. One right and two left radii. Two right and two left ulnae. One right second metacarpal. One right fourth metacarpal. One hand proximal phalanx. One hand middle phalanx. Two sacra. One right and one left innominate. Two right and three left femora. One right and one left patella. One right and one left tibia. Two right and one left fibulae. One right and

one left talus. One right and one left calcaneum. One right first metatarsal. One left fourth metatarsal. One left fifth metatarsal.

Age: Adult – no age indicators.

Sex: No data.

Pathology: The left and right fibulae show slight periostitis at the distal and medial aspect. The right orbit has cribra orbitalia. Slight osteophytosis occurs around the glenoid of the right scapula. One cervical vertebra has gross osteophytosis on the superior and inferior margins. One lumbar vertebra displays moderate osteophytosis on the superior and inferior margins.

Child bones: Occipital bone. Two arches of thoracic vertebrae unfused. Right scapula. Right radius missing proximal end. Left radius, missing distal end. Segment of sacrum. Left and right ilium. Left ischium. Left femur and left femoral epiphysis. Left tibia and left tibial epiphysis. Left and right fibulae.

Age: Child 4.5-5.5 years based on long bone length.

Metrical data:

Left tibial maximum length 180 mm

Left ilium maximum width 84 mm

Pathology: None.

6. Site location: P/34, rubble over church floor.

Date: Post-thirteenth century.

Burial: Disturbed inhumation in rubble.

Bones present: One individual. Left femur, distal end missing. Left tibia.

Pathology: The left femur has a healed fracture midshaft. The healing was almost complete, for the callus is well formed. A fracture has displaced bone in an anterior-posterior plane. The slight periostitis on the posterior surface had healed.

7. Site location: E/5, niche in west wall of north crypt.

Date: Phase 3.

Bones present: One individual, eight fragments of cranium.

Pathology: None.

8. Site location: G/11, near bronze furnace.

Date: Phase 2.

Burial: Possibly originally from grave 37.

Bones present: One fragment charred cranium. One fragment ilium. One charred midshaft ulna.

Pathology: None.

9. Site location: U/73.

Date: Phase 2.

Burial: Possibly originally from grave 178.

Bones present: Four loose teeth.

Pathology: None.

10. Site location: M/5.

Date: Phase 3.

Burial: In fill of tile kiln (with dog burial).

Bones present: One right parietal bone.

Pathology: None.

CHAPTER FOUR. THE FINDS

(i) COINS

Lucia Travaini

Six coins were recovered from the excavations at Santa Cornelia. Three of them are of special interest as regards medieval coin circulation in Latium: one *denaro pavese* of Otto I *imperator* and Otto II *rex* (967-973), and two *denari provisini* of Henry II Count of Champagne, mint of Provins (1181-1197). These coins represent, respectively, the beginning and the end of a long period of use of foreign currency in the region. The role of both Pavian and Champagne coinage in Latium has been well described by Toubert [1].

Between 975 and 984 the mint of Rome had ceased activity and had stopped striking papal *antiquiores*. By this time, Otto I had reformed coin production in the *Regnum Italiae*: whereas many mints, usually of minor size, existed in the rest of the empire, coin production in Italy remained strictly under royal control and was centralized in very few mints: namely Pavia, Milan, Lucca and Treviso (later substituted by Verona). This centralization permitted closer control and simultaneously a higher quality coinage [2]. As capital of the *Regnum Italiae*, the mint of Pavia was by far the most important and was supervised by nine *magistri monetari*, compared with just four at Milan. The Pavian *denari* became the 'national' currency, not only within the *Regnum Italiae*, but also, at various stages, in the area of Rome and in the south [3].

In Latium these *denari* formed the dominant currency between *c.* 1000-1150, after which, having become much debased, they fell from use. They were replaced at first by coins from Lucca, but already by 1160 the *denari provisini* of Champagne had become prominent, being of good silver content and deriving their success primarily from the importance of the Champagne fairs. These *provisini* were widely used in Latium until the early thirteenth century, when they were totally replaced by the *denari provisini Senatus*, imitations struck in the mint of Rome by the Roman Senate by arrangement with the Pope, from *c.* 1176-1177 [4].

The reverse type of the *provisino* bears a wool-comb, sometimes considered as a play upon words for Champagne (champ-peigne = comb in the field); the comb actually takes its origin from a deformed monogram [5]. Finds of *denari* of Pavia and Champagne *provisini* are quite widespread, both in hoards and as single finds [6].

CATALOGUE

1. Titus (for Domitian). Mint of Rome (AD 80-81)
   As, AE.
   Obverse: CAES DIVI VESP F DOMITIANI COS VII. Bust looking to left
   Reverse: AEQVITAS AVGVST SC. *Aequitas* standing
   [Bibliography: Mattingley and Sydenham 1923- (II, 1926), 136, number 163].
   Weight 9.76 g. Die position 190° 25-26 mm (worn).
   Findspot: From a layer underlying room D in monastery.

2. Otto I, Imperator, and Otto II, Rex. Mint of Pavia (AD 967-973)
   Denaro, AR.
   Obverse: + IMPERATOR. In the field, in cross OTTO
   Reverse: OTTO PIVS RE. In the field, PA/PIA
   [Bibliography: *CNI*, IV, 1913, 478 number 1].
   Weight 1.13 g. Die position 0° 18 mm (good preservation but black in colour).
   Findspot: From surface of phase 3a courtyard.

3. Henry II, Count of Champagne. Mint of Provins (AD 1181-1197).
   Denaro provisino, AR
   Obverse: + HENRICOMES. In the field, a cross around whose centre lie star, annulet and pellets
   Reverse: CASTRI PRVVINS. In the field, comb
   [Bibliography: Poey d'Avant 1862, 248, Pl. CXXXVIII number 22].
   Weight 0.98 g. Die position 180° 20 mm (good preservation)
   Findspot: U/111 (area of dormitory night-stair).

4. As coin 3, but of weight 0.99 g and die position 270°
   Findspot: U/109 (as U/111 above).

5. *Denaro* (?), Billon. Unidentified.
   Obverse: Cross
   Reverse: Uncertain motif
   Weight 0.45 g
   Findspot: S/41 (unstratified, from church south side).

6. *Denaro* (?), Billon. Illegible.
   Weight 1.2 g
   Findspot: U/111 (dormitory night-stair).

NOTES

1. Toubert 1973a, I, 577-601.
2. See Cipolla 1975, 13-24; Travaini 1988.
3. Cf. Grierson 1957. For the use of northern silver *denari* in the South, see Travaini 1981; Martin 1986.
4. Toubert 1973a, 583-584; Toubert 1973b, 180-189. *Provisini* of Champagne were also common in southern Italy: von Falkenhausen 1986. On exchange rates of *provisini* of Champagne and of Rome, see Spufford 1986, 67, 164-165.
5. Toubert 1973a, 584 note 1; Grierson 1976, 120, 130.
6. Cf. Toubert 1973a, 559, 578, 582-583; Capobianchi 1895, 122; Capobianchi 1896. For hoards, see Travaini 1980 (a hoard of *denari pavesi*); Balbi de Caro 1983, 16.

(ii) PAINTED WALL PLASTER

Ten main samples of painted wall plaster were collected, presumably representative of the material present in the excavations. The majority derive from the church and monastery zone, although some fragments were recovered in the south-east corner (W/50-55). Besides small, indecipherable, fragments, the larger elements comprised mainly plaster featuring more than one colour. Principal colours were red, yellow, orange, blue and black, with occasional green, and with white generally providing the background. Overall, the elements were too fragmentary to offer clues as to the various decorative schemes, although simple banded and floral designs were represented, along with tantalizing traces of figured and even lettered scenes. In particular, three tufa blocks (*Museo dell'Alto Medioevo* inventory number 2146a-c), probably from a side wall of the church, featured a single phase of plaster on a thin bed, depicting haloed heads. In 2146c it was clear that the red background had been painted first and then the white plaster featuring the figures was applied; the faces within the haloes were rendered with simple red brush strokes. Elements of black lettering were perhaps related to such figured scenes.

We cannot establish to which periods the fragments belong, but most will relate to the second church (eleventh-fourteenth century); demolition of the first church will obviously have broken up and destroyed any earlier works. In the second church more than one phase of painted mural decoration can be assumed.

Plaster groups included material from contexts G/3, 6; H/4, 7; K/2, 3, 9; P/12. Small fragments were found in many other contexts, too numerous to list.

(iii) METALWORK

Unfortunately, almost thirty years of storage without proper conservation has meant that much of the metalwork retrieved in the excavations has suffered irreparably, preventing any detailed analysis. Here we can merely point out that many of the iron finds were nails, principally round-headed and square-sectioned; length ran from *c*. 40 mm (for horseshoes, e.g. T/2) to 60 mm (T/2), and from 0.15 m (T/3) to 0.20 m (U/23). Most are assumed to have derived from timber construction or from graves. A few personal items such as belt buckles (e.g. K/3) were noted. Practical items included keys (e.g. Y/16), a small scythe blade (G/2), axe head (U/38), poker (0.35 m long – J/1) and strips which may derive from buckets or caskets (e.g. M/3). At least six horseshoes were recovered (e.g. Z/16) and a possible spur (Z/20). Bronze was poorly represented: we can note only a few small pins and a hollow-ended tube, perhaps for a stylus or hairpin (T/19). Elements of the material from the bronze furnace (bell-pit) were also kept (G/8).

Lumps of lead were recorded from contexts N/6, W/123 and Z/16, while Z/1 featured three pieces of lead sheet, perhaps from roofing.

(iv) GLASS

Dorothy Charlesworth

The following comprises a brief catalogue of some of the principal pieces of glass, compiled by the late Dorothy Charlesworth, and featuring a few emendations. A full, revised catalogue with discussion will be published shortly by Dr Charleston.

Most of the fragments are greenish-colourless glass deriving from beakers or lamps, whose plain, conical forms belong to the later fourth–sixth century (Crowfoot and Harden 1931, 197, Pl. XXVIII, 1-3). For this period the rim is generally rounded and thickened. Two examples of folded rims in the fragments listed below suggest second-fourth century material, while the heavy rim in blue-green glass and the base of an unguent flask are certainly of later first or second century date. The material includes post-Roman and medieval pieces and elements of window glass. It can be argued that much of the Roman glass relates to material scattered during agricultural operations by nearby farms; how much of the later material relates to the church and monastery is hard to ascertain.

DECORATED FRAGMENTS

Context: D/19 Fragment of a vessel apparently reused as part of a window; convex with ribbing forming a T-junction, plaster coating on outer surface.

M/3 Fragments of a multi-handled lamp in streaky blue glass, with an opaque white shoulder; of the surviving handles two are blue and one white suggesting a possible alternation of colour around the vessel. Base fragments reveal a pushed-in ring and concave centre with pontil mark, showing that although intended for suspension by the small eyelet handles, the vessel could also be set on its base (Crowfoot and Harden 1931, 205, Pl. XXX, 46).

M/3 Rim rounded at tip, colourless glass with clear blue marvered trail, flaking white weathering.

R/1 Applied oval with broken trail, colourless glass. Probably lower attachment and other fragments of a handle from a multi-handled hanging vessel.

T/8 Similar, with purple marvered trail, metal heavily striated, some weathering.

T/49 Tapering trail with horizontal tooled ridges; probably lower attachment of a handle.

Unstratified Small fragment of blue with unmarvered white trail.

Unstratified Thick amber glass shoulder of vessel with two horizontal cut lines and the top of a tooled rib.

Unstratified Greenish glass, perhaps part of a handle, but bearing a resemblance to a trailed 'cage' decoration.

UNDECORATED FRAGMENTS

D/13 Rounded rim and part of wall of a conical beaker or lamp; greenish metal with pinhead bubbles and striations. Fifth-seventh century.

G/16 Fragments, including base and head of small, narrow round flask or perfume bottle.

M/3 Base of conical vessel with a deep kick and pontil mark; greenish metal with pinhead bubbles.

M/3 Folded hollow tubular rim, colourless glass. Second-fourth century.

M/6 Small fragment of rounded rim in blue-greenish glass.

M/6 Base in greenish metal, with applied pad base ring.

T/15 As above.

R/1 Pushed-in base ring, perhaps third-fourth century.

U/53(?) Base of small drop-shaped unguent flask, irridescent green glass. First century.

WINDOW GLASS

T/10 Edge fragment of blown window glass; too small to determine whether cylinder or crown.

U/17(?) Small fragment of deep blue with a grozed edge, giving a triangular shape.

U/53(?) Folded fragment greenish glass: fold probably occurred immediately after blowing when the glass was annealed, and not resultant from fire.

See also D/19 above (Decorated fragments), reused in window.

OTHER

T/2 Single blue glass tessera.

Unstratified (plough, east side) Two opaque blue glass tesserae.

(v) THE ROMAN AND MEDIEVAL ARCHITECTURAL MATERIAL AND ROMAN SCULPTURAL FRAGMENTS

Janet DeLaine

ARCHITECTURAL MATERIAL

Section 1: Bases

1.1 Roman-Ionic bases

The Roman-Ionic base, comprising torus, double scotiae divided by an astragal moulding, torus and plinth, is a relatively common type from the early first–early third century AD, although the use of a single astragal only between the scotiae in fragment 1 suggests a date early in this period for these examples (cf. Strong and Ward-Perkins 1962, 5-8).

SC fragment number
1. (Fig. 18) Surface find. Height 0.29 m, plinth 0.79 m square. Material: greyish-white fine-grained crystalline marble, Carrara type.
Scotiae divided by single astragal. Two cuttings 90 × 90 mm on upper surface for dowels. Three corners of plinth cut back tangential to lower torus at some period of reuse.
Other examples: 60 (trench 1A, plough), 222 (apse crypt rubble).

2. (Fig. 18) Surface find. Height 0.27 m, plinth 0.79 m square, ?Carrara.
Scotiae divided by double astragal. Central square dowel hole. Brick and mortar adhering to underside. Part of plinth missing.
Other examples: 116 (reused as impost capital, see section 3, restored height 0.28 m), 223 (rubble in apse crypt).

1.2 Roman-Attic bases

This is the normal type of column base in use in imperial Rome from the late first century BC until at least the early fourth century AD. It consists of torus, single scotia, torus and plinth.

3. (Fig. 18) Surface find. Height 0.24 m, plinth 0.78 m square. Grey large-grained crystalline marble, Proconnesian type.
Lowered for reuse by recutting upper torus; original height c. 0.28 m. Central square dowel hole. Three corners of plinth missing.
Other examples: 41 (surface find, campanile), 528 (room D).

1.3 Medieval bases

Both comprise torus, single scotia, torus and plinth, a form clearly derived from the standard Roman-Attic base. The difference lies in the tall proportions, relatively high plinth, and coarse carving.

12. (Fig. 18) Surface find. Height 0.18 m, plinth c. 0.36 m square. Greyish-white fine-grained crystalline marble.
Plinth 50 mm high. Rough worked with tooling marks still visible.

16. Surface find. Height 0.22 m, plinth 0.45 m square.

1.4 Unidentifiable fragments

Large bases (?Roman): 263 (pit 047); 272 (rubble in N), 361 (apse crypt).
Small bases (?medieval): 270 (rubble in N), 375 (P, porch), 679 (porch).

Section 2: Columns

2.1. Standard Roman columns

Columns are arranged in descending order of magnitude, according to the probable original height of the shaft, calculated as either eight times the lower diameter or five-sixths of ten times the lower diameter (see Wilson-Jones 1989), and converted into Roman feet using a standard of one Roman foot = 0.295 m. All columns are assumed to have originally had Corinthian or Composite capitals, unless specifically indicated. No distinction is made between fluted and unfluted columns.

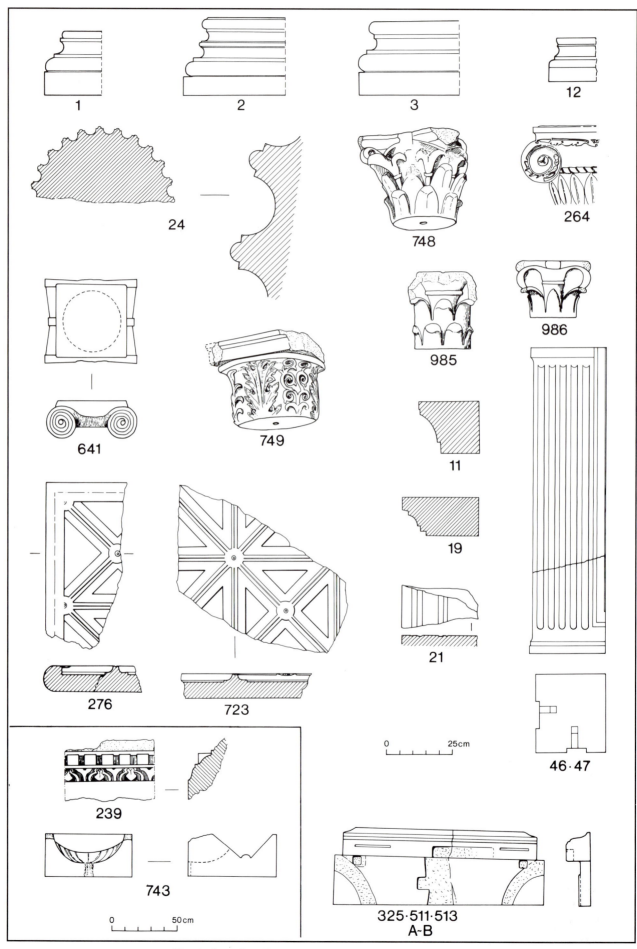

Fig. 18. Santa Cornelia: architectural fragments, various (SC, VW)

25 foot shaft:

459. South side of church. Two joining fragments: a) 0.27 × 0.29 × 0.075 m, b) 0.37 × 0.30 × 0.075 m. Flesh pink breccia with darker red-pink streaks, probably portasanta.
Distance between centres of flutes 0.12 m, giving diameter *c.* 0.92 m. From lower third of a fluted column, with convex channel. Reused (traces of mortar on face).
Joining fragments: 816a,b, reused as building material (plough, U).

15 foot shaft:

24. (Fig. 18) Surface find. Diameter 0.54 m. Giallo antico.
Fluted, flanges of flutes decorated with astragal. Section of shaft. The elaborate treatment of the fluting is relatively common in columns of giallo antico and pavonazzetto, especially in the second century AD (as at Hadrian's Villa, Tivoli).

72. Sub-plough, trench I. Height 65 mm, length 0.1 m, diameter *c.* 0.52 m. Fine grey crystalline marble.
Unfluted. Fragment of upper end. Height of upper moulding 47 mm.

471. South side. Height 90 mm, length 0.15 m, width 0.19 m. Pavonazzetto.
Fluted. Distance between centres of flutes 68 mm, giving diameter *c.* 0.52 m. Flanges of flutes decorated with astragal, as for fragment 24. Fragment of shaft.
Associated fragments: 287 (N, rubble), 460-462 (south side), 471, 474 (south side), 522 (Hole E), 533 (Hole E), 551 (surface find), 613 (T/1), 618-619 (T/1), 622, 754-755 (Z/1), 759-760 (Z/1), 767 (Z/1), and four unnumbered fragments (N/13, G/13, U/23, P/3).
A large section of the lower end of an identical column exists in the municipal garden at Formello, and probably derives from Santa Cornelia. The large fragments 287 and 471 have beading from some of the flutes trimmed off, and many of the remaining fragments appear to be the result of such trimming.

13.3 foot shaft:

385. Sector P. Height 1.87 m, diameter 0.48 m. Granite.
Unfluted. Upper end of shaft.

12.5 foot shaft:

5. Surface find. Height 0.70 m, diameter 0.41 m. Granite.
Unfluted. Upper end of shaft with square dowel hole.
Other examples: 167 (G, beside capital 166).

33. Plough, trench C. Length 0.55 m, width 0.38 m. Cipollino.
Fluted, distance between centres of flutes 53 mm giving diameter of 0.405 m. Lower end of column

reused as threshold block by slicing lengthwise.
Associated fragments: 245 (L), 520 (cloister).

802. Porch foundations. Height 0.21 m, diameter 0.43 m. Marble unidentified.
Fluted.

10 foot shaft:

323. Rubble, sector P. Two fragments: a) height 80 mm, b) height 0.12 m, diameter 0.35 m. Africano.
Unfluted.
Other fragments: 324 (P, south side rubble).

806. Porch. Height 1.87 m, diameter 0.355 m.
Fluted Doric with sharp arrises between flutes, ?lower end.

832. Room D, near south pier. Height 0.40 m, diameter 0.34 m.
Unfluted, upper end.

833. Room D. Height 1.57 m, diameter 0.35 m. Portasanta.
Unfluted, upper end with upper moulding blocked out, suggesting column came from stockpile of unused Roman architectural marbles (cf. Leotardi 1979, 35, numbers 96, 97).

835. Room C, on floor. Height 0.22 m, lower diameter 0.38 m.
Fluted, lower end of shaft.

8 foot shaft:

142. F, rubble over church floor. Height 85 mm, length 0.17 m, width 0.53 m, upper diameter *c.* 0.275 m. Weathered grey-white granular marble.
Unfluted, upper end.

987. Door of cloister. Height 0.97 m, lower diameter 0.28 m.
Unfluted, lower end.

?5 or 6 foot shaft:

17. Surface find. Height 0.50 m, diameter 0.19 m.
Unfluted, upper end.

248. K, rubble. Height 0.175 m, diameter 0.2 m; distance between flutes 30 mm. White fine-grained marble.
Spirally fluted, angle of spiral *c.* 30 degrees.
Associated fragments: 202 (north crypt); 776 (trench X).
As well as being fairly common in Roman contexts, spirally fluted columns were also used extensively in late antique and early medieval churches (Yegul 1986, 134-135). Despite Trinci Cecchelli's arguments (1976, 61-62) there is no clear evidence that these were not all of Roman manufacture.

Dimensions uncertain: unfluted granite columns – 203 (north crypt); fluted columns – 130 (E, church rubble), 242-243 (L, topsoil), 384 (P, north of campanile), 514 (porch, south side), 874, 972 (N/13).

2.2 Piers and pilasters

20.　Surface find. Pilaster veneer, edge of slab, upper or lower end. Height 0.2 m, length 0.32 m, width of flutes 0.125 m, thickness of slab 95 mm. Grey medium- to large-grained crystalline marble.
Back smooth, with later shallow moulding. Mortar on both faces suggests two periods of reuse of slab.
Associated fragments: 42 (trench I), 54 (trench I, reused as triangular floor slab 0.34 × 0.29 m), 132 (trench I), 213 (H, baptistery), 322 (P, rubble), 349 (apse crypt), 540-543 (R/1).

441.　P/8. Fluted pier, fragment. Length 0.15 m, width 90 mm, thickness 28 mm. Pavonazzetto.
Remains of five flutes, 27 mm wide, originally with sharp arrises, now worn. Reused as ?floor slab, mortar or plaster on one face.

668.　South-west corner of church. Fluted pier, corner fragment.
Height 0.14 m, length 0.1 m, width 0.1 m. Medium-grained white crystalline marble.
Two flutes 40 mm wide remain on both faces.

797.　Porch area. Fluted pier, upper end. Height 0.11 m, cross-section 0.215 m square. Coarse-grained white crystalline marble banded grey.
Four flutes on each face, each flute 50 mm wide.

Section 3: Capitals

3.1 Roman

3.1.1 Ionic capitals

458.　South side of church. Engaged capital, fragment of front face.
Length 0.19 m, height 70 mm; width of capital 0.165 m, diameter of volutes 50 mm. White fine-grained micaceous marble.
Shape roughly blocked out only; underside flat but roughly tooled.

875.　Built into north wall of room C. Diagonal capital, upper corner.
Length 0.24 m, height 0.175 m, width 0.16 m; height of abacus 80 mm, maximum radius of volute 65 mm, height of ovolo 80 mm. White fine-grained crystalline marble.
Upper surface roughly levelled with small dowel hole c. 25 mm square. Pointed egg with quarter palmette in corner extending over full width of egg at upper edge.

3.1.2 Decorated Corinthian capitals

51.　Unstratified. Acanthus fragment.
Height 70 mm, width 85 mm. Greyish-white, fine-grained crystalline marble badly decaying.
Leaf chiselled rather than drilled, large rounded cavity between lobes of leaf. Tooling on back signifies trimming for reuse.
Other fragments: 849 (room A rubble).
The rounded cavity and angular chiselled leaf in low relief relate more to Byzantine styles of carving than Roman, and suggest the late fifth-sixth century AD. (Cf. Kautzsch 1936, Pl. 51b; Krautheimer 1937-1977, III, 254-255.)

71.　Room A. Fragment of acanthus suppporting corner volute.
Length 90 mm. White fine-grained marble with grey streaks.
Hadrianic type with deeply drilled grooves between lobes and narrow vertical cavities between leaf points. Mid second century AD.
Other fragments: 74 (trench IA), 110 (trench I).

112.　Rubble west of campanile.
Intact, height c. 0.58 m.
Acanthus leaves have broad mid-ribs with slightly scalloped edges and central vein only lightly marked, narrow side ribs defined by deep vertical drill strokes continuing on upper register only to top of lower leaves, narrow wedge-shaped cavities between lobes, and broad points with oval tips. The leaf zone is about half the total height of the capital. Broad, shallow fluted cauliculi inclined slightly outward, with deep two-part caps of pendent rounded leaves above a row of scallops formed by the turned down tops of the stem flutes. Plain rosette stem rises from plain two-leafed calyx. Large volutes, inner ones not completely freed from block, possibly unfinished. The vertical leaves, general proportions and details of cauliculi suggest a Flavian date (last decade of the first century AD?) (cf. Pensabene 1972, numbers 225, 232).

137.　F, rubble. Corner of abacus with upper part of volute.
Height 95 mm, length 0.21 m; height of abacus 85 mm. Fine-grained grey and white crystalline marble. This and the following fragments belong to a single large capital which was cut down for reuse. Most are small fragments of acanthus but include angle volutes and one cauliculus. All show tool marks on the back. Some retain the shape of the acanthus leaves in the primary stage of working, suggesting that in its original position the capital had been set against a wall or in a corner. Mid-second century AD.
Other fragments: 32 (surface find), 49, 121 (surface find, possibly reused), 150 (campanile), 157 (E, outside church, traces of mortar on lower surface), 220 (rubble, north crypt), 416 (N, rubble), 420 (N, rubble), 444 (S, plough), 586 (Q/1), 588-589 (R/1), 609 (T/1), 611 (T/1), 675 (T/47), 729 (Y/13), 858 (U/28).
Fragments 71 and 477 may belong to the same capital.

166.　Rubble in G, beside column 167. Intact, volutes and corners of abacus missing.
Height 0.53 m, lower diameter 0.33 m.
Both ranges of acanthus have notched mid-ribs with deep drill groove marking central vein, on upper register extending full height of leaf; side ribs on lower leaves strongly curved, on upper leaves slightly curved, all defined by deep grooves; cavities between points broad, wedge-shaped and slightly

inclined. Narrow, vertical cauliculi divided into three sections by vertical drill strokes, single piece cap with zig-zag leaf decoration. Thick rosette stem rises from small two-leaf calyx, rosette with serpentine centre. The combination of deep drilling, curving lower leaves and vertical cauliculi is characteristically Hadrianic, although some Flavian details are retained (cf. Heilmeyer 1970, Taf. 58.3, 59.1,2; Pensabene 1972, numbers 247, 249).

477. Ante-baptistery room. Fragment of lower row of acanthus leaves.
Length 0.22 m, width 90 mm, height 80 mm. Greyish-white fine-grained crystalline marble.
From a large capital. Lower part of mid-rib groove visible between two leaves. Probably second century AD. Reused as corbel.

683. Room 5 (floor make-up?). Upper part including inner volutes.
Height 0.11 m, length 0.125 m; height of volutes 40 mm. Grey fine-grained crystalline marble.
From small capital, distance between centres of helices 70 mm. Upper surface flat, part of profile of abacus and boss of abacus flower; corkscrew volutes with tips of leaves below.
Other fragments: (?)781, fragment of angle corkscrew volute (U/30); 983, 984, joining fragments of inner helices of same size (Z/18).

867. Partition wall, room A. Fragment of lower part of bell.
Length 0.145 m, height 94 mm; lower diameter c. 0.34 m. Creamy white fine- to medium-grained crystalline marble.
Battered, but outline of lower part of two acanthus leaves with end of vertical mid-rib groove of upper acanthus leaf between them still visible. ?Second century AD.

Minor Corinthian fragments: 59 (trench IA), 404 (L, fill of grave 160; from reworked capital), 419 (N, rubble), 423 (N, rubble), 530 (room D, north-east corner; from reworked capital), 564 (T/13; from reworked capital), 585 (S/1), 652, 682 (room 5, floor make-up?).

3.1.3 Schematic Roman Corinthian

748. (Fig. 18) Rubble in porch. Almost intact, three corner volutes and abacus flowers missing.
Height 0.37 m, lower diameter 0.25 m.
Shallow v-shaped leaf profile, narrow near-vertical cauliculi, no boss for stem of abacus flower. Late second to mid-third century AD (cf. Pensabene 1972, 230ff, numbers 417-419).

3.1.4 Decorated Roman Composite

13. Surface find.
Height 0.47 m, lower diameter 0.35 m.
Single layer of acanthus only around bell; simple treatment of leaf with scalloped edges created by deep drill holes, ribs made by shallow grooves on surface of leaves. Leafy stem of rosette calyx worked but rosette a simple boss. Leafy stem on volute

channel continues almost to eye of volute. Ovolo of echinus has flat egg-and-tongue delimited by deep drill strokes, with outer eggs almost entirely covered by palmettes barely defined by shallow drilling; astragal has long beads with pointed ends and broad biconical reels. Low, poorly formed abacus. The nature of the acanthus, the use of the drill and almost total absence of any plastic qualities combine to suggest a late third–early fourth century AD date. Other examples: 414, fragment of volute (pit 047).

264. (Fig. 18) Pit 047.
Height 0.285 m, width abacus 0.48 m, lower diameter 0.32 m.
Squat type with volute zone taking up over half the total height of the capital. Channel of volute has leafy fill occupying half of spiral only. Volute zone divided from bell zone by horizontal astragal decorated with a twisted cord design. Single row of vertical 'water leaves' around lower part of bell.

3.1.5 Schematic Roman Composite

64. Monastery zone. Abacus and volute.
Height 0.125 m, length 75 mm; height of abacus 18 mm, diameter of volute 65 mm. Off-white fine- to medium-grained crystalline marble, weathered.
Five-petalled rosette fills volute. Unworked volute channel fill extends over rosette, cf. 506. Upper surface rough worked. Fourth century AD (cf. Pensabene 1972, numbers 520-521).

75. Trench IA, plough. Angle volute with abacus and part of acanthus.
Height 0.145 m, width 70 mm, diameter of volute 80 mm.
Greyish-white fine-grained crystalline marble. Fourth century AD.

386. Pit 047. Upper half, volutes and abacus flowers damaged.
Width across top 0.29 m, height 0.14 m. Greyish white fine-grained crystalline marble.
Volute zone has areas blocked out for corner palmettes, large projecting bosses for abacus flowers, bosses left for bell stems and flowers, and leaves with v-shaped profile and rib.
Cut off horizontally just below bell flowers, for reuse.
Top shows two superimposed sets of dowel cuttings. Late second–third century AD (cf. Pensabene 1972, numbers 468-469).

506. From fill of Grave 162. Schematic Composite capital.
Height 0.16 m, width across top 0.16 m, lower diameter 0.1 m. White crystalline marble with grey streaks.
Single band of four acanthus leaves supporting corner volutes, leaves joined at base in centre of sides. This simplified type is common from the second half of the fourth to the early fifth century AD (e.g. Ostia). (Cf. Pensabene 1972, 247, number 486; Herrmann 1974, 225-228, Type III numbers 196-200.) This capital could belong to an aedicular

construction decorating the arcosolium of the substantial grave 162 in the south-east corner of the porch (cf. Herklotz 1985, 143, Tav. 45).

640. Rubble near campanile. Schematic Composite capital, upper part, volutes missing.
Height 0.142 m, upper width 0.29 m. Fine-grained white crystalline marble.
Profile of leaves flat, volutes cut across profile of channel. Lower half cut off for reuse, cf. 386. Horizontal drill hole in upper part of centre leaf between volutes. Fifth century AD (cf. Herrmann 1974, 234-235 Type IV numbers 219-225).

868. Refectory, rubble. Schematic Composite capital, abacus and volute fragment.
Height 80 mm, length 0.16 m. White(?) medium- to large-grained crystalline marble, badly decomposed in places.
Width of abacus c. 0.31 m. Boss of volute channel fill extends across face of volute. Mid-fourth century AD (cf. Pensabene 1972, numbers 474, 476, 480, etc.; Herrmann 1974, 203-204, Type II/III, numbers 111-117).
Other examples: 876, volute zone and upper part of acanthus (built into north wall of room B/cloister).

870. Refectory, rubble. Schematic Composite capital, fragment of upper part with one angle volute.
Length 0.15 m, height 0.1 m, width 70 mm. Granular fine-grained white marble, partly decomposed; fracture face shows massive crystalline formation, mostly opaque creamy white with some clusters of clear crystals. Fourth century AD (cf. Herrmann 1974, Type II).

985. (Fig. 18) Unstratified. Schematic Composite capital, missing top of abacus and ends of volutes.
Height 0.28 m, width of abacus c. 0.29 m, lower diameter 0.215 m. White fine-grained crystalline marble.
Double order of acanthus, profile flat and leaves of both ranges joined together at base. Echinus moulding shallow. Lower curve of volute not differentiated from upper part of supporting acanthus leaf. Roughly square dowel holes on upper and lower surfaces, upper approximately 40 mm square, with filling channel. Chisel marks left on surface of volutes. Mid-late fourth century AD (cf. Pensabene 1972, number 496, etc. for volute; Herrmann 1974, Type II (plain style), numbers 74-90).

986. (Fig. 18) Unstratified. Schematic Composite capital, missing one volute.
Height 0.20 m, width of top 0.285 m, lower diameter 0.185 m. Creamy white fine-grained crystalline marble.
Single row of acanthus with flat profile, leaves joined above base. Echinus continues across top of volutes only. Late fourth–early fifth century AD (cf. Pensabene 1972, numbers 489, 501; Herrmann 1974, Type III, numbers 140-162).

3.2. Medieval

641. (Fig. 18) Over well in E/6. Schematic Ionic capital. Length 0.35 m, height 0.11 m, width 0.31 m, diameter of column seating c. 0.24 m. Grey fine-grained crystalline marble, badly weathered and encrusted.
Concentric scroll volutes, formed from four turns of narrow convex-profiled ridge starting with central flat boss and continuing across face of capital with a marked sag to separate echinus zone from abacus. Sides treated as simple boluster constricted at centre by raised band. Plain square abacus. Seating for column roughly dressed, upper surface smooth. The simplified design and lack of decoration on the echinus indicate either an unfinished state, or more likely an early medieval date. A similar capital in the 'Museo delle Terme' (MNR I/3, I.38) is dated tentatively to the late fourth century AD, but many features such as the low relief and tendency for abstraction are more often found on eighth-ninth century capitals (cf. MNR I/8, VIII.77).

749. (Fig. 18) Porch, rubble. Capital, part of abacus missing.
Height 0.32 m, width at abacus 0.455 m, lower diameter 0.32 m.
Bell-shaped body decorated with vertical acanthus leaves in low relief with pointed leaf tips set in centre of each face, alternating with vertical stylized acanthus-and-scroll motif consisting of two sets of three scrolls rising from pair of simple leaves; square, plain abacus. The stylization of the acanthus and the scroll design, the low relief and the poor quality of the carving connect this capital to the ninth century workshops producing interlace work. While the form of capital may derive from the standard Roman Corinthian, it also owes much to a series of decorated Tuscan capitals which feature a band of vertical acanthus leaves on a cavetto moulding below or in place of the echinus (cf. Pensabene 1972, numbers 72-76, 80-84, all Hadrianic; MNR I/3, VIII.5 for an example with a palmette design springing from acanthus calyxes on the cavetto).

Discussion

A number of near complete or large fragments of bases (1-3, 12, 16, 41, 236), columns (5, 24, 72, 142, 167, 323, 385, 471), and capitals (13, 112, 166, 264, 386, 640) were found in the body of the church, and all may have formed part of the main order of the nave arcades, despite the considerable differences in size and date of some of the pieces. A few possible groupings can be made. Bases 1-3 and 41, although of different types, were originally of the same size and probably belonged to columns whose total height was eighteen Roman feet; column shafts 24, 72 and 471, and the Corinthian capital 112, also belonged to columns of the same height. Fragment 385 may be from the column at the north-east corner of the church. Column 167 and capital 166, found together in the north-west corner of the church, belong to a column whose original full height was fifteen Roman feet. 5, also of granite, comes from a column of the same height, while a capital similar to 166 exists at Casale di Santa Cornelia: these may have formed a matching set to 166/167. The capitals 386 and 640 also seem to form a pair, as both have been cut down from Schematic Composite capitals of different date to a uniform height. Likewise we find the late Composite 13 and a closely similar example also at Casale di Santa Cornelia. The two columns with complex mouldings, 24 and 471, of different marble but of the same height, possibly also formed a pair. The presence of two medieval bases, probably contemporary with the second church, shows that *spolia* was supplemented when necessary. The smallest column shaft in this group is 142, the maximum height of which would have been eight Roman feet, or 2.36 m; if this were put with the smallest of the bases and capitals (12 and 386/640), the maximum height for the columns of the arcade would be about 2.7 m.

Several other column, capital and base fragments not belonging to the nave arcades can be assigned functions within the second church and monastery. The small unfluted column 17, and two spirally fluted pieces of the same diameter (202, and 776) from the church, and 248 from the baptistery, which can be assumed to have had an original height of five–six Roman feet, perhaps supported a ciborium. Two intact capitals of similar size from the porch rubble, 748 and 749, may be associated with the fluted column 514 and the small bases 515 and 375, suggesting a columnar decoration for the east door of the church, or, less probably, the porch. The miniature capital 506 probably belonged to an aedicular construction decorating grave 162. Two column fragments from room D in the monastery zone (832–823) relate to two masonry bases in the centre of the room and must have helped support the upper floor.

Section 4: Medieval impost columns

4.1 Column shafts

Columns are arranged according to context. All are of standard type with slightly swelling shafts thickened at both ends to create a rough base and a broad collar to support the capital.

Crypt zone:
354. Length 0.27 m, lower diameter of shaft 0.13 m, diameter of base 0.15 m.
Other examples: 35, 141, 199, 345, 346, 351, 355.

Campanile/porch zone:
39. Length 0.37 m, upper diameter 0.13 m, lower diameter 0.12 m.
Other examples: 151, 296, 301, 380, 381, and two complete (unnumbered) (height 1.02 and 1.04 m) from fallen porch facade.

Monastery zone:
482. Height 0.87 m, lower diameter 0.13 m, base diameter 0.15 m.
Greyish-white fine-grained crystalline marble.
Other examples: 469, 817, 824.

4.2 Impost capitals

26. (Fig. 19) Surface find. Length 0.38 m, width 0.185 m, height 0.12 m; seating for column 0.125 m square.

Rough worked, marks of ?claw chisel visible. ?From campanile.

38. East door of campanile. Length 0.53 m, height 0.17 m, width 0.225 m; seating for column 0.13 m.

116. (Fig. 19) Surface find. Height 0.19 m, maximum diameter 0.605 m, diameter of impost 0.14 m. White fine-grained crystalline marble.
Reused Roman-Ionic base, plinth removed, lower torus and part of scotia retained to give moulding at upper edge of capital.

470. Cloister. Length 0.44 m, height 0.13 m, width 0.165 m, diameter of seating 0.13 m. Underside of one half carved as simple cross.
Other examples from monastery zone (all have cross in relief on underside): 473 (reused; original face has half-column, width 0.15 m, cut back into block from face), 517, 815, 823, 836. These must have formed capitals for the cloister court.

Fallen porch wall. Length 0.45 m, height 0.16 m, width 0.13 m, diameter of seating 0.12 m.

Section 5: Corbels

5.1. Modillions

92. Trench II, plough. Length 0.28 m, width 0.168 m, height 0.145 m. Fine-grained marble, white with grey streaks, surface decomposed.
Schematic scroll modillion. Scroll and plain leaf with plain cyma reversa crowning moulding, length of projecting part 0.18 m. Triangular profile with small front scroll and leaf following curve of underside. Upper and lower surfaces worked with claw chisel, back and sides roughly dressed.

5.2. Medieval Corbels (Fig. 19)

The corbels are grouped according to context and then to height. All are of similar form, a long rectangular block with the front face carved as a quarter round with projecting fillet above. Many were cut from *spolia* and retain traces of the original mouldings or decoration.

Surface finds (over centre of church):
Height   0.13–0.12 m: 9 (0.40 × 0.15 m)
           0.11–0.10 m: 7 (0.56 × 0.15 m), 10 (0.48 × 0.13 m)
           90–80 mm: 8 (0.47 × 0.11 m)

North-west end of church (sectors D–H):
Height   0.13–0.12 m: 36 (0.43 × 0.135 m)
           0.11–0.10 m: 43 (0.36 × 0.12 m),
                118 (0.52 × 0.13 m),
                119 (0.32 × 0.125 m),
                120 (0.35 × 0.135 m),
                127 (0.37 × 0.12 m),
                145 (0.52 × 0.12 m),
                200 (0.45 × 0.12 m),
                208 (0.44 × 0.14 m),
                214 (0.46 × 0.13 m)

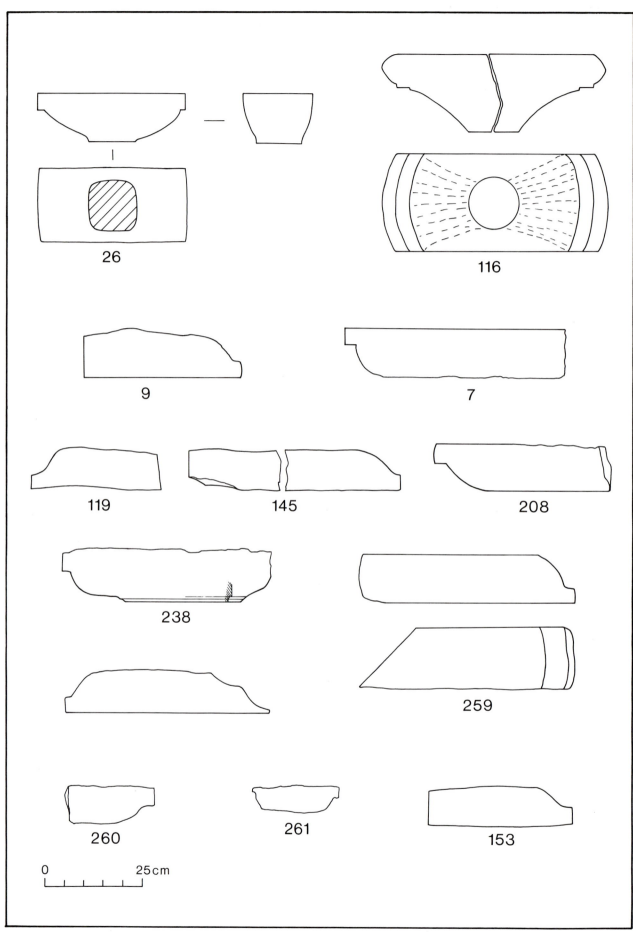

Fig. 19. Santa Cornelia: architectural fragments, medieval impost capitals and corbels (SC, VW)

90–80 mm: 44 (0.45 × 0.13 m),
128 (0.35 × 0.12 m),
181 (0.37 × 0.11 m),
207 (0.35 × 0.125 m)
Dimensions unknown: 357.

North-east end of church (sectors L, N, P):
Height 0.13–0.12 m: 238 (0.54 × 0.125 m),
259 (0.54 × 0.15 m)
0.11–0.10 m: 257 (0.50 × 0.145 m),
258 (0.52 × 0.145 m),
536 (0.48 × 0.11 m)
90–80 mm: 260 (0.20 × 0.14 m),
477 (0.22 × 0.09 m)
70–60 mm: 261 (0.20 × 0.07 m)
Dimensions unknown: 303, 387.

South-west end of church (sector R):
Height 90–80 mm: 672, 673 (0.425 × 0.10 m)

South-east end of church (sector S):
Height 0.11–0.10 m: 537 (0.40 × 0.16 m)
90–80 mm: 453 (0.24 × ? m),
492 (? × 90 mm)
Dimensions unknown: 493.

Campanile and porch (sectors P, Y):
Height 0.11–0.10 m: 152 (0.355 × 0.13 m), 153
(0.35 × 0.13 m)
Dimensions unknown: 117, 335, 337, 376, 377, 378,
381, 677, 804.

East of porch:
Height 90–80 mm: 556 (0.26 × 0.10 m),
800 (fallen porch wall, 0.50
× 0.10 m), 801 (fallen porch
wall, 0.29 × 0.10 m).

Monastery zone:
Height 70–60 mm: 834 (0.15 × 0.08 m)
Dimensions unknown: 534 (0.26 × 0.085 m),
811 (width 80 mm),
812 (width 0.11 m),
813 (width 0.10 m),
825, 826 (0.26 × 0.10 m),
827 (0.27 × 0.08 m),
828 (0.34 × 0.12 m)

Most of the thirty-four corbels from the area of the church lay on the north side, with only five from the south. These corbels formed part of the twelfth century campanile, which must have collapsed roughly westwards, in towards the church. A number of impost columns and capitals found with these corbels must also have come from the campanile. Corbels found around this and the porch presumably formed a decorative cornice on the facade of the building. This may well relate to the period in which the campanile underwent restructuring (late twelfth century). Those corbels which probably formed the cornice of the garden face of the cloister appear contemporary with the construction of the monastery (mid-eleventh century).

Section 6: Mouldings

This section covers a variety of fragments, the original function of which is not always clear, but distinguished by some kind of moulding in relief. Only those with decorated mouldings can be closely dated. For the rest, it is not always possible to differentiate between Roman and medieval, as some specific mouldings, especially the cyma recta, cyma reversa and cavetto, continued to be used and are often to be found in twelfth century Cosmatesque work. Fragments of large entablatures with signs of reuse are assumed to be Roman; the dating of others, usually the smaller elements, is left open.

6.1 Architectural elements

239. (Fig. 18) Sector L, topsoil. Decorated cornice.
Length 0.265 m, height 0.16 m. Light grey-white fine-grained marble. Dentils 50 mm high × 45 mm wide with spaces 20 mm wide × 40 mm deep; fillet 10 mm high × 10 mm deep; cyma reversa 50 mm high × 65 mm deep, pattern repeat 0.115 m. No bar between dentil blocks; profile of interstices is quarter round set back from face of dentils. Cyma reversa has continuous Y-shaped 'tulips' between splayed arches with small upper ring and broad tongue.
Other fragments: 97, 275 (rubble in N), 285 (rubble in N), 290 (rubble in N), 417 (N/17), 424 (rubble in N), 422 – corona fragment, anthemion decoration on face, plain underside (rubble in N).
In the municipal garden of Formello is a large cornice 0.55 m high × 1.66 m long with an identical arrangement of dentils and lower cyma reversa as the Santa Cornelia cornice fragments, and with the same distinctive broad tongue on the cyma reversa decoration. Here the upper part also survives; it comprises an ovolo with egg-and-tongue, corona with anthemion decoration of half palmettes in oval frames divided by tongues and plain underside identical with that of fragment number 422, astragal with bead-and-reel, and plain sima. It seems certain, therefore, that the Formello cornice originates from Santa Cornelia. The cornice was probably reused as part of the frame of the church north door (section 7 below). Marchei and Marvasi (1976) published this without provenance, dating it to the late second century AD. The individual mouldings, however, have their closest parallels in monuments of the Augustan or early Julio-Claudian periods. The distinctive cyma reversa belongs to the same family as those on the door of the Basilica Aemilia and on the Arch of Augustus (Leon 1971, Taf. 105.1-4, 106.1, 3-4); the square dentils with small half-filled spaces are usually mid-Augustan (Leon 1971, 186; Strong and Ward-Perkins 1962, 24, note 74); a similar ovolo is used on the Arch of Augustus and the capitals of the Temple of Castor (Strong and Ward-Perkins 1962, 17, 22); and the anthemion motif is found decorating the corona of a cornice in the Museo delle Terme (MNR 1/7(2) number IX.2) and on another cornice near San Nicola in Carcere (Leon 1971, Taf. 77.4), both of Augustan date. The cornice can thus be securely dated to the first decade of the first century AD.

325.   Rubble in sector P. A-B: cornice.
Length 1.58 m, height 0.18 m, width 0.53 m.
Marble.
Sima of fillet, cyma recta, astragal. Reused as
threshold (see section 7) of church east door.
Roman, imperial.
Rubble in P. C-E: architrave.
Length 0.97 m, height 0.19 m, width 0.55 m.
Marble.
Upper part of architrave, architrave cornice of
undecorated fillet, cyma reversa and astragal, start
of frieze. Reused as lintel of church east door.
Probably from the same entablature as 325a-b.

407.   Unstratified. ?Architrave cornice and frieze, small
fragment.
Length 90 mm, height 65 mm.
Undecorated fillet and cavetto with part of frieze
above. Roman.

432.   Plough, T. Frieze, fragment.
Length 0.20 m, height 0.15 m.
Lower part includes plain fillet of architrave
cornice; frieze decoration much worn, possibly
garland, with evidence of drillwork. Reused, mortar
on face of frieze. Roman, ?late first– third century
AD.

478.   Ante-baptistery room. Cornice.
Length 0.48 m, width 0.275 m. Grey medium-to-
large-grained crystalline marble.
Cyma reversa above astragal. Reused as threshold
(see section 7). Roman.

553.   Topsoil, south trench II. ? Sima.
Length 0.34 m, height 0.22 m. Greyish-white fine-
grained crystalline marble.
?Cyma recta with lotus and palmette decoration in
low relief.
This type of simple, classicizing lotus and palmette
decoration was used fairly frequently in the
Augustan period on tall, shallow or flat mouldings
such as the sima of the Lower Order of the Basilica
Aemilia (Leon 1971, Taf. 137.1), the coffering of the
Forum of Augustus (Leon 1971, Taf. 140.1), and on
the frieze below the Apotheosis of Augustus relief
(*Museo Nazionale*, Ravenna).

670.   South-west corner of church. ?Frieze and architrave
cornice, perhaps originally architectural veneer.
Length 0.123 m, width 0.116 m, thickness 42 mm.
Medium-grained greyish-white crystalline marble.
Reused slab, cut vertically; cavetto and fillet from
original moulding, with surface above fillet roughly
dressed, leaving fillet as raised lip. Back smooth with
traces of mortar. Roman.

6.2 Minor elements (plinths and cornices)

11.   (Fig. 18) Surface find. Cornice.
Length 0.70 m, height 0.19 m, maximum width
0.225 m. Marble.

Fillet, fillet, cavetto, fillet. Face of cavetto roughly
tooled. Roman, part of moulding reworked.
Associated fragment: 183 (rubble in G).
This probably formed the crown moulding for
either the *schola cantorum* screen or the east face of the
presbytery.

19.   (Fig. 18) Surface find. Cornice.
Length 0.145 m, height 0.14 m, width 0.29 m.
Fillet, cavetto, fillet, fillet. Top, bottom and back
surfaces smooth. Mortar on moulded face. ?Roman,
reused.

21.   (Fig. 18) Surface find. Cornice.
Length 0.17 m, height 0.14 m, width 0.29 m.
Medium- to large-grained pale grey crystalline
marble with darker grey streaks.
Fillet, fillet, cyma recta, fillet, astragal. Top and
back dressed smooth. Roman. Reused; back carved
in rough shallow moulding of two parallel concave
channels flanked by a v-shaped groove. Broad
tooling marks on sides suggest cornice deliberately
broken up (cf. Corinthian capital fragments 137,
section 3).
Associated fragment: 37, joins 21 (unstratified).

134.   Unstratified. Plinth.
Length 0.175 m, height 50 mm, width 85 mm.
White fine-grained marble.
Fillet 30 mm, cyma recta 20 mm, projection 25 mm.
Upper surface smooth, back and lower surface
roughly tooled.

138.   Sector F. Plinth.
Length 0.28 m, height 0.135 m, width 0.175 m.
Plain fillet 23 mm high, cyma recta 75 mm high ×
68 mm deep, astragal 26 mm high × 22 mm deep,
fillet 10 mm high.
Upper, lower and back surfaces roughly tooled,
with a smooth band 35 mm wide at rear of upper
surface. Two small drill holes, one on lower surface,
other on upper edge of astragal. Other example: 182
(length 0.5 m. Rubble in G. Vertical half-cylindrical
tongue on one end.).
Related small fragments: 140 (F); 224 (rubble apse
crypt). This probably formed a base for either the
schola cantorum or the east face of the raised
presbytery (cf. fragment 11).

408.   Unstratified. Cornice.
Length 0.12 m, height 55 mm, width 0.12 m.
Fillet 20 mm high, cyma reversa 35 mm high ×
30 mm deep.
Upper surface recut as square for reuse as floor slab.
?Roman.

442.   N/17. Cornice.
Length 0.15 m, height 61 mm, width 40 mm. Grey,
medium- to large-grained crystalline marble.
Torus, fillet, cyma recta. Upper surface smooth.
Other example: 624 (pilaster of church door).

455-456.   South side of church. Cornice or plinth, two
joining fragments.
Length 0.30 m, width 0.20 m. Greyish-white

medium-grained crystalline marble.
Cyma reversa above fillet.

485. South side of church. Cornice.
Height o.10 m, length 65 mm, width o.15 m. White crystalline marble with grey streaks.
Cyma recta, originally with fillet above, total height 80 mm, depth 40 mm; fillet 15 mm high; cyma reversa o.1 m high × 15 mm deep. Possibly reused as part of a wall, as upper flat surface shows traces of red and blue paint.

669. South-west corner. Plinth or cornice.
Length o.21 m, height 90 mm, width 35 mm. Pale grey fine-grained marble.
Astragal with three rough ?fillets above, poorly carved. ?Early medieval.

807. Unstratified. ?Plinth.
Length 0.32 m, width 0.35 m, thickness 40 mm. Grey-white fine-grained marble.
Very shallow cyma reversa moulding 50 mm wide, with type C decoration (see Strong 1953, 121 for classification of cyma reversa decorations), pattern repeat 70 mm. Probably second century AD.
Associated fragment: 612 (small fragment reused in floor T/1).

850. Rubble, room A. Cornice.
Length o.11 m, height o.1 m. Grey-white fine-grained marble.
Lower part of cyma reversa type C, pointed leaf with vertical groove and pointed tongue, pattern repeat 63 mm; astragal with semi-circular pendent leaf pattern on face alternating with same on underside, 18 mm high × 22 mm deep with pattern repeat 30 mm.

6.3 Veneer

6.3.1 Panels with decorated mouldings

50. Trench I, surface find.
Length o.145 m, height o.16 m, maximum thickness 32 mm.
Fine-grained white granular marble with grey streaks.
Very shallow profile, fillet 18 mm, cyma reversa 49 mm, pattern repeat 62 mm. Type C decoration coarsely carved with chisel marks remaining. Back of slab smooth. ?Late Roman.
Other examples: 63 (south slopes of site), 156 (unstratified), 864 (Z – pattern repeat 50 mm).

425. Top rubble, north strip.
Height o.255 m, length o.14 m, thickness 30 mm. White fine-grained marble with some grey streaks.
Very shallow cyma reversa decorated with type C pendent leaf and tongue, height 58 mm, pattern repeat 80 mm; above plain fascia with inverted vertical fluting, the bottom of each flute being filled in for one-fifth of surviving height of flute, pattern repeat 72 mm, width of each flute 55 mm. The profile of the leaf decoration on the cyma reversa, the absence of a tongue between the flutes, and the

high quality of the carving as a whole suggest an early Augustan date, the closest parallels being motifs from the entablature of the Temple of Apollo Sosianus (Strong and Ward-Perkins 1962, 20, 22).

6.3.2 Cornices

227. Surface find.
Length o.11 m, height 67 mm. Rosso antico.
?Astragal, fillet, cyma recta, fillet. Roman.

418. Top rubble, N.
Height 90 mm, length o.115 m.
Fillet, astragal, cyma reversa. Mortar on face suggests reuse.

707. Porch.
Length o.12 m, height 28 mm, thickness 53 mm. White fine-grained marble with grey streaks.
Cyma reversa with unfinished type C pendent leaf and tongue decoration engraved on surface, height 24 mm × projection 34 mm, pattern repeat 44 mm. Early medieval reinterpretation of Roman motif (cf. Raspi Serra 1974, number 168).

6.4 Screens

46, 47. (Fig. 18) Rubble west of campanile. Rectangular posts.
Length 1.125 m, cross-section 0.275 × 0.275 m. Both have five vertical flutes, the lower half filled in, on front face, vertical border on right-hand side, and vertical groove for screen panels on inner side. ? From *schola cantorum*.

276. (Fig. 18) Rubble in N. Panel.
Length o.59 m, height o.33 m, maximum thickness 95 mm. White large-grained crystalline marble with parallel blue-grey bands running through it; probably Proconnesian.
Common type in marble carved to imitate wood or metal fence, with horizontal, vertical and diagonal bars intersecting at circular bosses. Bars 90 mm wide have central grooved ridge. Related fragments: 100 (unstratified), 114 (surface find), 233 (plough, baptistery), 271, 274, 421, 472 (unstratified), 503 (porch south side), 504 (porch south side), 549 (S, topsoil), 723 (?porch).
This very common type of screen appears to have been in use since the early part of the first century AD (*MNR* I/7(2), number XV.35, 473-474) and continued through the imperial period, perhaps as late as the sixth century AD. It appears often in Roman *tituli* and other Christian centres in the fourth century AD (see Melucco Vaccaro 1974, 89, number 28). The careful profiling of the bars in this example precludes a date after the fourth century AD.

Section 7: Door frames

All fragments with evidence for reuse as part of door frames are collected here, although many also feature under the sections relating to the material in its original form.

33. Unstratified trench C. Threshold, reused column.
Length 0.55 m, width 0.38 m. Cipollino.
For details see section 2.

34. Surface find. Threshold, corner missing.
Length approximately 0.55 m.
Narrow raised lip and broad rebate with deep circular pivot hole 70 mm diameter at one end. Possibly reused sarcophagus fragment.

52. Unstratified. ?Threshold, fragment.
Length 75 mm, width 82 mm. White fine-grained crystalline marble.
Part of circular cutting approximately 80 mm in diameter, 7 mm deep, for pivot and rectangular slot 15 mm wide, 75 mm long and 11 mm deep. Cf. arrangement of 795. Remains of mortar on back. Possibly cut to a rough square for reuse.

239. Surface find. Lintel, reused Roman cornice.
Length 1.66 m, height 0.39 m, width 0.55 m. Grey-white fine-grained marble.
Cutting for door 0.19 m deep and 80 mm high in underside of block. From church north door. See also section 6.

325 = 511 = 513. (Fig. 18) Rubble in P. Threshold and lintel, five fragments.
A-B: Two joining pieces, reused Roman cornice.
Length 1.58 m, width 0.53 m, height 0.18 m.
Rebate 0.33 m wide, 90 mm deep has roughly square shallow pivot holes 60-65 mm set against doorstop and shallow curved cuttings either end, deeper large rectangular cutting with small offset in centre; doorstop has narrow slot 0.27 m long either end, centre worn down. See also section 6.
C-E: Two joining pieces and one fragment, reused Roman entablature.
Length 0.97 m, width 0.55 m, height 0.19 m.
Rebate 0.17 m wide, 85 mm deep has remains of rough pivot hole 80 mm wide, set 30 mm from edge. See also section 6.
These probably formed the threshold (A-B) and part of the lintel block (C-E) of the church east door.

478. Ante-baptistery room. Threshold, fragment, reused Roman cornice.
Length 0.48 m, width 0.275 m. Grey medium-to large-grained crystalline marble.
Remains of circular pivot hole 70 mm in diameter on rebate. Rectangular cutting 90 × 40 mm on tread 0.15 m wide.
For details of cornice see section 6.

743. Porch rubble. Door jamb, reused Roman ?sarcophagus.
Height 1.35 m, width 0.25 m, maximum diameter 0.25 m.
Outer face finished with claw chisel, inner face rough finished with raised lip 90 mm wide. Jamb tapers, with remains of head of crouching lion at wider end (see section 8 for details).

795. Unstratified. Threshold, complete block.
Length 0.7 m, width 0.245 m.

No rebate. Single pivot hole roughly 70 mm diameter at one end with narrow slot 0.11 m × 30 mm parallel to long side in front of it.
Other fragments: 484 (south side); 516 (south side porch).

The frames from the east (fragments 325a-e, 743) and north (239) doorways of the second church, probably retained from the first church, reuse large sections of Roman entablatures and a piece of sarcophagus. Both doorways were double-leaved, closing in the centre. The richly decorated cornice 239 is particularly fine, and it is interesting to find it used not as the frame to the main east door of the church but for the north door which, in the first church, gave access to the baptistery. Threshold 478 may come from a door of the ante-baptistery, but it could also be a fragment of the threshold of the north door; it, too, was made from a section of Roman entablature. There is no useful context for the other threshold blocks.

SCULPTURAL FRAGMENTS

Section 1: Undecorated sarcophagi

339. North of campanile. Three joining fragments, largely intact.
Length 2.25 m, width 0.72 m, height 0.65 m, walls 90 mm thick. Grey large-grained crystalline marble. Plain rectangular exterior with slight projecting edge at bottom of one long side. Floor curves up at one end
Other example: 799 (east of fallen narthex wall).

Section 2: Strigillated sarcophagi

2.1 Simple panels of double-curvature strigillated flutes

525. South trench II (monastery). Three joining fragments of lower left-hand corner.
Length 0.55 m, height 0.48 m. Creamy white medium-grained crystalline marble.
Strigillated flutes framed by fillet 23 mm high, cyma reversa 31 mm high. Distance between flutes 44 mm, v-shaped channel 12 mm. Side decorated with incised design of two crossed oval shields over shaft of ?spear; lower shield decorated with spirals. Reused as threshold (see section 7). For discussion of this type of shield decoration, see fragment 341. Cf. Matz 1975, number 286; Tusa 1957, number 42, for oval shields
Later third to fourth century AD.
Related example: 22 (surface find). Right-hand side of front panel.
Length 0.34 m, height 0.558 m, thickness at rim 70 mm. Creamy white fine-grained micaceous marble.
Side of sarcophagus roughly smoothed leaving clear tooling marks. Interior of sarcophagus smooth behind the flutes. Slab picked on side and base, with rough channel parallel to and 0.17 m from bottom edge, for reuse.
The well-formed cross-sections of both flutes and

mouldings suggest a date no later than the early fourth century AD.

2.2 Panels of strigillated flutes flanking imagines clipeatae

741. (Pl. 40) Cloister. Recomposed from several fragments.
Length 1.7 m, height 0.615 m, width ?.
Two panels of opposed strigillations frame central medallion with three-quarter female portrait bust, resting on altar with funerary inscription of Arria (inscription number 10, above). Full-face portrait wearing tunic and *pallium* looped from right to left shoulder. Fluted panels bordered above and below by fillet and cyma reversa moulding and framed by fluted pilasters with schematic Corinthian capitals and Attic bases. Sides have two diagonally crossed oval shields, overlying pair of crossed spears with heads in two front corners of each side; upper shield decorated with simple diamond pattern in centre.
Strigillated sarcophagi articulated with pilasters, central portrait medallions, and shield decoration on the sides are common from the late second to late third centuries AD. This example can be dated from the portrait, derived from the earlier portraiture of the Empress Julia Domna, wife of Septimius Severus (AD 193-211) (Meischner 1964, 11-17, 30-68); a very similar portrait, also of an Arria, appears on the lid of the Metropolitan Museum's Endymion sarcophagus (McCann 1978, 43, number 4). As Turcan points out (1966, 97-98), the hairstyles of women in portraits usually remain those they had in their twenties; since Arria died at the age of 65, the sarcophagus could date as late as AD 250. For the shield decoration see fragment 341.
Other example: 53. Surface find.
Length 0.24 m, height 0.26 m, maximum thickness 60 mm. White medium- to large-grained crystalline marble.
Lower part of *imago clipeata* of man in tunic and toga, clutching fold of toga in right hand and scroll in left. Frame of roundel rests on upper part of altar.
Third century AD.

783. U/30. Strigillated sarcophagus, part of central panel with *imago clipeata* and pastoral scene.
Length 0.23 m, height 0.18 m, thickness 60 mm. Medium-grained white crystalline marble with blue-grey streaks.
Joining fragments: 405 (L, fill of grave 160), 854 (room D, back of south pier).

Upper edge is fillet 15 mm high. Distance between flute centres 40 mm, deep rounded channel 12 mm wide. Roundel frame in high relief, 22 mm wide. Very small area of drapery only preserved within roundel. In angle between sarcophagus rim and outer edge of roundel is upper part of tree. Below and to right of roundel is upper two-thirds of standing male figure wearing short tunic (*exomis*), with milk-bag (*mulctra*) slung diagonally from right shoulder to left hip, and leaning with right elbow on staff (*pedum*) with right forearm raised. Left arm crosses body to rest on top of staff, head turns to right. From posture of upper body and fall of drapery, figure stands on left leg with right leg crossed in front of it. Little surface detail remains, but hair is heavily drilled, and folds of drapery are defined by linear drill strokes engraved on surface of the relief. Field containing figure is framed by narrow vertical fillet. Fragments of three strigillated flutes survive to right of this. Back roughly picked. Several examples survive of this combination of an *imago clipeata* above a pastoral scene, the best known of these being the sarcophagus of Baebia Hertofile in the Museo delle Terme (*MNR* I/8(1), III.11), dated to later third century AD. The figure of the shepherd in summer dress and leaning on his staff is common on bucolic sarcophagi from the late second century (Wilpert 1936, i, 64, and Tav. L.6, LXVIII.1, etc.). The part of the tree appearing at the top of the roundel is unusual. The deep profile of the roundel frame and the general style of carving suggest a date in the third century AD.

856. (Pl. 41) In room A/cloister wall foundation. Part of *imago clipeata*.

Plate 41. Santa Cornelia: sarcophagus fragment SC856 (*Museo dell'Alto Medioevo*, Rome)

Plate 40. Santa Cornelia: restored sarcophagus SC741 at Casale di Santa Cornelia

Height 0.37 m, width 0.14 m, maximum thickness
0.15 m, thickness at upper edge 70 mm. Large-
grained greyish-white crystalline marble.
Upper left-hand section of frame, 70 mm wide,
projection 45 mm.
Female portrait head, 0.17 m high, right-hand side
well-preserved. Head looks slightly to right; hair
parted in centre and slightly waved, with topknot
decorated in reticulate pattern to represent plaiting;
eye has drilled tear-duct and incised pupil. The
detail of the hair connects this portrait with the
earlier ones of Faustina the Elder, where the topknot
is created by a loop of plaited hair, usually
represented by a basket-weave design (cf. Wegner
1939, 26-32, Taf. 10-13; Fittschen and Zanker 1983,
numbers 13-15, etc.). This portrait type belongs to
the 130s AD; allowing for possible time lapse
depending on the age at death (cf. 741), the
sarcophagus can be dated broadly to the second
third of the second century AD. While it is likely
that the fragment formed part of a strigillated
sarcophagus, it is possible that the rest of the front
had a figured relief.

2.3 Panels of strigillated flutes with figured scenes at ends and centre

341. (Pl. 42) Porch rubble. Upper left-hand corner with
relief decoration on front and side.
Height 0.14 m, length on face 0.1 m, length
along side 0.24 m, thickness on side 65 mm.
Medium-grained white crystalline marble banded
with grey.
Joining fragments: 521 (hole E, monastery), 587
(S/2).
Front: full-face male head wearing traditional
winged hat of Mercury, almost certainly belonging
to herm. Round face rendered in high relief with
some plastic qualities although features – eyes,
nostrils, mouth, hair – show heavy use of the drill.
Side: upper corner of diamond-shaped shield, upper
edge concave, decorated with incised scroll design;
shield laid diagonally overlapping diagonal spear
and right side of double-headed axe probably set
vertically in centre of it. Along upper edge is plain
border 20 mm wide in low relief. Back roughly
tooled, apart from smooth band 30 mm wide at
upper edge.
Few examples of herms used as features on
sarcophagi survive, the best-known being that in the
cathedral of Cagliari (Pesce 1957, number 31), a
strigillated sarcophagus with herms of Mercury and
Hercules at either end and a portrait bust on a
plinth in the centre, datable to AD 260-280. A herm
relief in the Villa Doria Pamphilj (Calza *et al.* 1977,
number 217) with a Dionysiac head is believed to
come from a strigillated sarcophagus. A third
fragmentary example, also with a Mercury herm, is
in the Museo di Ostia (DAI neg. 57.1277). The
crossed shields on the sides form a common
decoration for strigillated sarcophagi, particularly
in the third and fourth centuries, although it
appears earlier on sarcophagi of a specifically
military nature (*MNR* I/7.2, 334-5). In later
examples the shield decoration is engraved on the
surface rather than rendered in relief. The treatment

Plate 42. Santa Cornelia: sarcophagus fragment SC341 (*Museo dell'Alto Medioevo*, Rome)

of the face suggests a relatively early date for the
sarcophagus, probably early third century AD.
Related example: 505. Porch, south side.
Length 0.265 m, height 0.41 m, thickness 65 mm.
Large-grained grey-white crystalline marble.
Joining fragment: 55 (surface find).
Two panels of opposed strigillated flutes separated
by Hercules herm in relief. Herm has bearded face
with hair, beard and eyes drilled, and tapering post
with residual arm stubs and genitals in low relief.
Back rough picked with smooth band 25 mm wide
inside upper edge. Late second-early third century
AD.

437. Rubble in P. Lower part of central figured panel.
Length 0.18 m, height 0.22 m, thickness 70 mm.
Medium-grained grey-white crystalline marble.
Lower part of draped female figure with left leg
relaxed; drapery falls vertically over right leg,
diagonally from right hip to left knee. Beside left leg
is vertical fold of drapery from cloak or curtain,
extending to just below knee. Main folds of drapery
of figure defined by heavy linear drill strokes, with
some plastic moulding of left thigh and calf. Folds of
vertical cloak or curtain represented by abstract
pattern of diagonal drill strokes. Back roughly
picked.
Joining fragments (strigillated): 526 (room A), 702
(porch).
Total surviving length 0.72 m.
The standing female figure as the central panel of a
strigillated sarcophagus belongs to one of two types:
the simple portrait figure, often holding a *volumen*,
which can be pagan or Christian (e.g. DAI neg.
65.2325, from San Liberato; Wilpert 1936, Tav.
CXVIII.4 from Anzio, Tav. LXIX.1 from Castel-
lammare di Stabia), or the Christian orant, with
both arms raised in prayer (e.g. Wilpert 1936, Tav.
LIX.1, LXXI.3, CXVII.1, CLXXVIII.2, all from
Rome). Both wear tunic and *pallium*, and are usually
framed by a *parapetasma* as a symbol of apotheosis
(Turcan 1966, 614f). Both of these types are
common in the third and early fourth century AD.
The general nature of the carving of the drapery
suggests a date in the second half of the third
century, the treatment of the hanging folds of the

curtain being closely paralleled on a sarcophagus in the Palazzo Farnese, dated to the late third century (Bovini *et al.* 1967, number 961).

507. West of campanile. Upper right-hand corner of front with start of figured panel.
Length 0.45 m, height 0.27 m, thickness 70 mm. Medium- to large-grained crystalline white marble streaked with grey.
Rim of fillet 32 mm high above shallow cyma reversa 24 mm high. Distance between flute centres 42 mm, deep rounded channels 12 mm wide. On right is section of 'Good Shepherd' relief, showing front of sheep with head turned back to right and forelegs held in right hand of figure. Only right arm and fragment of drapery of figure survive. Back roughly picked.
The figure of the 'Good Shepherd', usually young and beardless, dressed in a short tunic and carrying a sheep slung over his shoulders, appears frequently in early Christian iconography from the mid-third century AD. It is often found on strigillated sarcophagi, alone or in combination with other figures such as the orant (Wilpert 1936, i, 68–99). Although little remains of the relief here, the high relief and style of carving suggest a date early in the series, perhaps in the third quarter of the third century (cf. Wilpert 1936, Tav. LVI.3).

Other example: 705. Reused as front of grave 61. Lower left-hand corner of front with relief decoration.
Length 0.17 m, height 0.13 m, thickness 0.15 m. Medium-grained white crystalline marble with grey bands, badly weathered.
Lower part of legs and feet of standing figure with weight on right leg; rump and back legs of reclining sheep appear between feet of figure. Plain band at base of sarcophagus 30 mm wide. Back of relief and underside roughly dressed. From a 'Good Shepherd' sarcophagus, possibly the left-hand side of 507.
The position of the sheep, resting with its feet between the legs of the shepherd, is rare (the sheep are usually standing), but cf. Wilpert 1936, Tav. LVI.3.

559. Plough. East trench V. Fragment of engaged column.
Height 0.24 m, width 0.11 m, column diameter 65 mm, thickness 55 mm. Medium- to large-grained grey crystalline marble.
Column spirally fluted at 30 degrees. Back roughly dressed.
Probably part of a strigillated sarcophagus with side and/or central figured panels framed in columnar niches.

639. Unstratified. South hole V. Upper left-hand side of front with relief decoration.
Height 0.20 m, length 0.275 m, thickness 72 mm. Medium- to large-grained crystalline white marble with grey streaks.
At left end are head and shoulders of a female figure; head looks to the right, hair in short rough curls, possibly with wreath. Slightly upward gaze, pupil defined by drill. To right of body are start of four strigillations, width between flutes 0.4 m, v-shaped channels 12 mm wide; upper edge of sarcophagus defined by plain fillet 20 mm high. Appears cut for reuse.
From the torsion implicit in the pose, and the treatment of the hair, it is possible that the figure represented a maenad. The style of carving suggests a third century date.

798. East of fallen porch wall. Lower left-hand part with relief decoration.
Length 1.3 m, width 0.62 m, height 0.35 m.
At left-hand end is lower part of young male figure, an *eros*, standing on right leg with left leg crossed in front, leaning on a downward pointing torch, upper end under left arm, holding wreath in left hand. To right is panel with remains of ten strigillated flutes, maximum distance between flutes 45 mm. Lower edge is cyma reversa over deep fillet. Inside roughly picked. Strigillated sarcophagi with figures of *erotes* leaning on torches at either end are relatively common, usually of third and early fourth century date. The subject of the central panel varies, and can be either pagan or Christian. The *erotes* are thought to represent the spirits of the dead, the wreaths symbolizing immortality (Stuveras 1969, 33f; Sichtermann 1966, 30f). The elongated legs, compact pose, and style of carving suggest a date in the first half of the third century. Cf. Baratte and Metzger 1985, number 129, with central *clipeus* over crossed cornucopia; Wilpert 1936, Tav. LXXI.4, with central clipeus over pastoral scene; DAI neg. 65.2325 from San Liberato, with full female figure framed by curtain as central panel.

Fragments of fluting: 25 (surface find); 186 (apse crypt; cut to rectangle for reuse); 210 (baptistery, H); 445 (reused as front of grave 61); 480 (south side of church; possibly cut to rectangle for reuse); 510 (south side of church); 701 (porch; reused as floor slab); 861 (room D; reused as floor slab); 865, 866 (room D; reused for interlace).

Section 3: Sarcophagi with overall relief decoration

30. (Pl. 43) Unstratified, trench C. Fragment of upper edge of front.
Length 0.255 m, height 0.3 m, thickness 80 mm. Medium-grained white marble banded grey.
Fragment of "*in alberis*" sarcophagus. In centre is tree with straight columnar trunk, symmetrically spreading branches.
To left is upper part of bearded male figure in tunic, facing left; in front of him is hand of second figure holding a scroll, below which is fragment of third smaller figure or animal. To right of tree is beardless male figure in tunic, looking to right. Leaves of tree, beard of left-hand man, and eye of right-hand man defined by drill holes; tunics of both men carved flat with folds of drapery shown by vertical drill strokes. Back roughly picked. The "*in alberis*" sarcophagus forms a well-attested variant of the more common "*in columnis*" type, where biblical episodes, usually scenes from the life of Christ, or other Christian subjects, are framed in columnar niches. Our

Plate 43. Santa Cornelia: sarcophagus fragment SC30 (*Museo dell'Alto Medioevo*, Rome)

example has its closest parallels in those showing the miracles of Christ. From the iconography and the style of carving the piece can be dated to the mid-fourth century AD.

For a general discussion of the type see Wilpert 1936, III, 32-36, and Farioli 1966. For specific iconographic parallels see Wilpert 1936, Tav. CXXXXII, 3; CCXXVII, 2; CCXXVIII, 7; for stylistic parallels see Bovini *et al.* 1967, numbers 61, 215, and Farioli 1966, number 3, and 359-360 for dating to AD 330-340.

56.   Sub-plough, ante-baptistery. Fragment from lower edge.
        Length 0.17 m, height 0.215 mm, thickness 0.15 m. White medium- to large-grained crystalline marble. Draped left leg of female figure in high relief, bent at knee and moving to right. Fragment probably formed part of a large mythological scene; the leg is shown thrusting forward with the drapery clinging to it, suggesting rapid movement.

96.   (Pl. 44) Rubble, campanile. Section of front.
        Length 0.52 m, height 0.438 m, thickness 70 mm. White fine-grained micaceous marble weathered to honey colour.
        Joining fragment: 326 (P, east of church).
        Plain fillet 30 mm high at upper edge, irregular border maximum height 32 mm at lower edge. Back carefully worked. Unidentified mythological scene in sacro-idyllic landscape. Scene divided into two 'episodes' by large tree taking up full height of panel. Branches of tree spread out to left, with cloth forming canopy strung horizontally between, basket hanging from lower branch. Below canopy is

Plate 44. Santa Cornelia: sarcophagus fragments SC96, 326, and 711 (*Museo dell'Alto Medioevo*, Rome)

?female figure reclining on left side against rocks at foot of tree. Figure wears *peplos* pinned at shoulders, with *himation* draped around head, behind right arm, across lower abdomen covering legs, and under left arm. Right arm folded across chest, left hangs vertically over rocks. Head thrown back, appears to be wearing wreath or diadem. In front of figure is small rectangular object, possibly casket. Behind and to left of figure is ?horse, rearing to left with head (part missing) turned back to figure, cloth draped over back and rear. To right of tree is bearded ?elderly shepherd in short tunic (*exomis*) fastened over left shoulder leaving right bare, about to sacrifice ram; man stands behind ram, facing right with left knee pressing down on its back, large triangular knife in right hand, pulling head of ram back with left hand. Behind man is small tetrastyle Corinthian temple in three-quarter view with ashlar walls, wreath decorating pediment, and tiled roof.

There are no close parallels for this piece. Certain of the individual elements – the man sacrificing a ram, the basket hanging from a tree, the small temple, the reclining figure in *peplos* and *himation* (bearded male in this case) – appear together on a large *lenos* sarcophagus of late second to third century date in the *Museo Chiaramonti* in the Vatican (Matz 1968a, number 37, 135-138, tav 34-36). The style of carving and the arrangement of the figures are, however, quite different. The rest of the relief is devoted to the *vendemmia* and associated Dionysiac motifs, while Turcan (1958; 1966, 524-525) identifies the reclining figure as the ambiguous Dionysius Sabazius. It is not impossible that our sarcophagus also has a Dionysiac theme; the basket and canopy are common elements in scenes depicting the childhood of Dionysius, and these are often shown in a rural setting. The presence of the horse is harder to explain, and the pose of the shepherd is also unusual. This attitude, with knife raised in the very act of sacrificing, rather than already plunged into the animal's side as on the Chiaramonti sarcophagus, is derived ultimately from the Nike slaying a bull on the balustrade of the Temple of Nike Apteros in Athens. The Nike motif appears frequently on neo-Attic reliefs of all types (Campana reliefs, candelabra, architectural sculpture, etc.) from the late republic at least to the time of Trajan, occasionally with the Nike replaced by an *eros*; it is also the source of the standard representation of Mithras slaying the bull (Borbein 1968, 43-115). It is, however, found rarely in any other context.

From the style of carving and the episodic narrative treatment of the relief, a date in the early Antonine period seems most likely (cf. Turcan 1966, 48-53). The relief is stylistically close to that of the lid fragment 95 (section 4 below), which is similarly dated. Both lid and sarcophagus are in the same marble, and may belong together. This would give the sarcophagus a height to length proportion of 1:3.45, which is standard for the late Hadrianic-early Antonine period (Turcan, 1966).

Related example: 711. Porch. Lower edge of front.
Length 0.28 m, height 0.11 m, thickness 0.13 m.

Off-white fine-grained marble, surface badly decomposed. Poor state of marble makes details of relief difficult to decipher. Appears to be reclining animal, possibly sheep or goat, facing left, at foot of relief. Plain band 35 mm high at bottom of sarcophagus. Base smooth.

The type of marble, style of carving, subject matter and size suggest that this belongs to the same sarcophagus as fragment 96.

235-236. Apse crypt rubble. Section of drapery, two joining fragments.
Length 0.22 m, height 80 mm, thickness 0.14 m.
White, fine-grained marble.
Lower part of drapery of a large figure. Vertical asymmetrical folds carved in full plastic relief, with a deep re-entrant where two fragments join. Probably from female figure in a long robe belonging to a sarcophagus relief, the figure taking up the full height of the field. The base of the fragments is roughly tooled, and the area of tooling on the side at right angles to this suggests reworking.

433. Rubble in P. Fragment of front.
Height 0.263 m, width 0.135 m.
Part of head of wild boar in profile facing left, showing eye, ear and bristles on spine above ear, with ear pointing forward over eye, against plain background. Strong chiaroscuro treatment – details of bristles worked in combination of short, deep drill strokes, widely spaced, with shallow chisel strokes on areas between; eye shaped by chisel with deep drill hole for pupil.

The fragment could belong either to a simple hunting scene or one of several mythological types which include boar hunts (e.g. Meleager and the Calydonian boar hunt, Hippolytus or Adonis). The various types had long lives, the hunting sarcophagi continuing at least into the last quarter of the fourth century.

The details of the carving in this example have their closest parallels in, for example, the fragment in the Palazzo dei Conservatori, Rome (Andreae 1980, number 113), of AD 280-290, or the Meleager sarcophagus in Oxford (Koch 1975, number 156) of the second half of the third century.

Other example: 851. Fill, room C. Fragment of upper edge.
Length 0.20 m, height 0.15 m, thickness 45 mm.
Medium-large grained crystalline grey and white marble.
Rim of fillet 28 mm high. Only small section of relief remains, showing central part of bare arm from above wrist to below shoulder, held horizontally above ?back or head of boar. Boar bristles indicated by deep parallel vertical drill strokes over shallow irregular chiselled grooves.

684. Below floor(?), room 5. Fragment of upper edge of front.
Length 0.14 m, height 80 mm, thickness 17 mm.
Fine- to medium-grained white crystalline marble, badly weathered.
Head and left arm of ?female figure, facing left with arm raised to back of head; hair shows traces of

heavy drill work. Plain band 24 mm wide at upper

706. Porch. Fragment.
Length 0.20 m, height 0.19 m, thickness 35 mm.
Fine-grained white crystalline marble.
Part of major joint (shoulder or hip) of man or horse, in low relief. Probably from relief with large-scale figures.

710. Porch. Fragment.
Length 90 mm, height 50 mm, thickness 65 mm.
Greyish white, fine-grained marble.
Subject may be part of hair and right arm of figure with right arm raised above head.

712. Porch. Right-hand end of front, fragment.
Length 0.21 m, height 0.21 m, thickness 0.1 m, width 0.12 m. White large-grained crystalline marble, banded grey.
Surface of relief heavily weathered making details difficult to decipher. Appears to be bird perched on leafy branch facing right with head lowered towards ?nest among branches. Back of relief smooth. Cut to neat square for reuse.

728. Y/13. Fragment of ?garland, in deep relief.
Length 0.1 m, width 70 mm, maximum depth of relief 60 mm. Heavily weathered white marble. Poor condition.
Elements are long shapes, with either rounded or pointed ends.
From funerary altar or garland sarcophagus.

730. Unstratified.
Length 0.14 m, height 0.17 m, thickness 75 mm.
White medium-grained marble.
In lower left-hand corner is bent knee of ?male figure with area of drapery above and to right; below right is area of short drill strokes. Back roughly picked. Upper straight edge possibly recut.

731. (Pl. 45) Surface find.
Length 0.175 m, height 0.15 m, thickness 78 mm.
Medium-grained white crystalline marble with blue-grey streaks.
Fragment of a seated draped ?female figure, right hand resting on back of chair and holding piece of cloth, full swathe of drapery across lap. In front of chair is head of probable peacock. Section of drapery behind chair suggests a second figure. Back of relief smooth.
The fragment probably formed part of a mythological scene. Female figures seated on thrones occur in relatively few of the standard representations, and have a fixed iconography: Aphrodite with Eros on Adonis sarcophagi, for example, or Phaedra with Eros or a dove, and turning back to the nurse, on Hippolytus sarcophagi (Sichtermann and Koch 1975, numbers 6-7 and 26-30). In this example, the peacock's presence identifies the figure as Hera. The

Plate 45. Santa Cornelia: sarcophagus fragment SC731 (*Museo dell'Alto Medioevo*, Rome)

edge with inscription . . . S E Q . . . Part of straight edge by head suggests fragment recut for reuse.

subject matter is perhaps the Judgement of Paris, since in the versions of this on two similar sarcophagus lids in the Louvre, Hera is shown in a similar pose, holding a section of drapery in one hand, with a peacock under the chair, while Athena stands behind (Baratte and Metzger 1985, numbers 24, 41).

847. Over floor of room 6. Part of front with relief and *tabula ansata*.
Length 0.21 m, height 0.19 m, thickness 0.4 m.
Greyish-white fine- to medium-grained crystalline marble, weathered.
To left is lower part of figure of shepherd wearing short tunic and boots with milk-bag hanging on left side; figure stands on left leg with right leg crossed in front and leans to his right, probably on a staff. To right of figure is lower left-hand side of a *tabula ansata*. Back of relief smooth (cf. 783).

855. Accumulation, room D. Lower right-hand side.
Length 0.29 m, height 0.215 m, width 0.20 m. Pale grey fine-grained crystalline marble.
Surface of relief very weathered. Subject appears to be drapery in low relief over the lower part of the legs of perhaps two female figures. Plain fillet 50 mm high at base. Base smooth.

869. Plough in Z. Fragment.
      Length 0.1 m, height 0.25 m, thickness 53 mm.
      Greyish white fine-grained crystalline marble.
      Lower part of billowing drapery of ?female figure,
      possibly maenad or nymph. Back roughly dressed.

871. Support of pier C in room D. Relief fragment.
      Length 0.16 m, height 0.20 m, width 80 mm. White
      small- to medium-grained marble.
      Lower part of shaft, base, and pedestal of small
      column in high relief. Broad tooling marks on sides;
      reused as building material. Probably from the
      architectural frame of an "*in columnis*" sarcophagus.

Section 4: Sarcophagus lids

95,190,674 (Pl. 46) Campanile rubble; rubble north
      crypt; church south-west corner. Three fragments of
      front, missing short section from centre only.
      Total restored length 1.51 m, height 0.13 m, width
      0.14 m.
      Badly weathered, white fine-grained micaceous
      marble.
      95 has corner treated as a grinning Pan mask. To
      right of this is bearded male figure, in *himation*,
      facing right and lying on stomach with rear leg
      extended and front leg raised, extending right arm
      to female figure who faces him and supports herself
      on right arm. To right is start of third figure holding
      cup or jug. The next section, probably 0.38 m long,
      is missing.
      190 and 674 join. At left is right half of garland with
      trailing fillet, supported by putto with right arm
      raised to top of garland, legs extended to right with
      left leg crossed behind right leg at knee. To right of
      putto is ?naked figure facing right, seated on stool
      with far leg crossed over front leg, playing double
      flute. Next to this is bearded male figure wearing
      himation, reclining on left side, with head turned
      back to left and resting on left hand; to his right is

naked figure, female or beardless youth, facing right
and reclining on left elbow with right arm thrown
up and behind head, left hand holding two-handled
cup; to right is further male figure facing right and
reclining on left elbow, holding cup in right hand;
facing him is female figure, head and upper body
damaged, lower half draped, reclining on left elbow
and presenting back view. Slight remains of draped
curtain (*parapetasma*) forming background between
figures. The figures appear to recline on matresses
rather than *klinai*. Corner of lid treated as Pan
mask. The piece belongs to a group of sarcophagus lids
decorated with Dionysiac symposia scenes, whose
participants are men and women and/or satyrs; the
ends are treated as Satyr masks, or left plain (see
Matz 1969, 181, 184, 189, 194, 199). The lids are
mainly associated with Dionysiac sarcophagi, with
the exception of an example in the Louvre which
belongs to a Muses sarcophagus. These are all dated
to the early Antonine period, and appear to be from
the same workshop, which is identified by a limited
range of reclining figures or pairs of figures,
although no two lids have exactly the same
combination of elements. Typical are the male
figure lying full length on his front with one leg
raised, often combined with a female figure facing
him and supported on her right arm; a male figure
with right arm thrown back over head; a female
figure, half draped, reclining at full length and
presenting back view. The figures recline on
mattresses and the background is draped with
parapetasmai. All these are present in our example,
and the seated flute player can also be paralleled in a
related sarcophagus from the Villa Doria Pamphilj
(Matz 1968b, 129). There is no parallel, however,
for the putti holding a wreath which probably forms
the central motif in our example. Nevertheless this is
a common funerary motif, to be found on other
sarcophagi lids, such as one in the Museo Maffeiano
in Verona (Matz, 1968b, number 83), and on
funerary altars (e.g. *MNR* I/7.2, number IV, 13, of
the late first-early second century AD; see also
Turcan 1966, 88). The use of Pan faces instead of
satyr masks is found on the lid of a child's

Plate 46. Santa Cornelia: restored sarcophagus lid SC95, 190, and 674 (*Museo dell'Alto Medioevo*, Rome)

sarcophagus from Ince Blundell Hall (Matz 1969, number 186), of Severan date, and is not unexpected in a Dionysiac context. The unusual elements in our example suggest a date early in the series, perhaps in the late Hadrianic period.

363.   Near bell-pit. Fragment of front.
        Length 0.19 m, height 80 mm, width 0.105 m.
        Creamy-white fine-grained marble.
        To left are lower legs and feet of figure standing on right leg with foot turning to left, left leg relaxed. To right of figure are two vertical bands and corner of frame of central panel of lid. Below figure is horizontal band with inscription ..EBUERAT.. L-shaped cross-section, each arm 40 mm thick. Base roughly dressed.
        Lids with a central, almost square panel for an inscription, divided by vertical bars from figured scenes usually representing Biblical episodes, are relatively common in a fourth century Christian context (cf. Bovini *et al.* 1967 numbers 138, 143-147). The central panels are often framed by Victories or *erotes*, although in both cases a pose representing movement, with legs widely spaced and bent at the knee, is usual; a standing pose closer to that of our example does occur, however (e.g. Bovini *et al.* 1967, number 397). The figure could also belong to a narrative scene.

709.   Porch. Fragment of lower front edge.
        Length 80 mm, height 57 mm, thickness 43 mm.
        White fine-grained crystalline marble.
        Lower right leg and foot of standing figure with weight on left leg. Recut as rectangle and back smoothed for reuse as ?floor slab.

Discussion

Although only two complete sarcophagi (fragments 339 and 741) were found, sufficient survives of several others to suggest that these too were reused for burials. Fragments 437/526/702 were found in the porch or the area immediately south, and all show signs of burning; they probably come from a sarcophagus set up in the porch and damaged by fire at the end of the life of the second church. Fragments 798 and 799 from east of the fallen porch facade, where little building material would be expected, are both substantial pieces, including part of a sarcophagus base and back, and must also have been used for burials; these might also originally have been set up in the porch. Reused in a different way are fragments 705 and 445, which were built into one face of grave 61 as decoration; 507, found in the same area as grave 61, belongs to the same or similar sarcophagus as 705, and probably decorated the same grave. More problematic are 95 and 96. The presence of several fragments making up almost the complete front of the lid, and a large section of the relief decoration of what appears to be the corresponding sarcophagus, all in church and porch destruction layers

and none showing signs of reuse, suggests that the sarcophagus and lid may have been intact during the later life of the second church and broken up only after its abandonment. The fine figured scene, although pagan in character, would have been suitable for an important burial, perhaps located at the porch north end, near the campanile, where several fragments were found.

It is likely that there were originally more than the six examples of reused sarcophagi identified above. Sarcophagi would have been attractive targets for robbers after the abandonment of the church, particularly whilst the building still stood. With the increasing interest of the Renaissance in classical antiquity, mythological relief panels would have been particularly prized, which may explain why our only evidence apart from fragment 96 for this type of sarcophagus, other than those clearly reused for other purposes, comes from a few small fragments (e.g. 56, 235/236, 433, 706, 855). Other sarcophagi may have been broken up to provide raw material; this would account for fragments 783/405/854, three pieces from the central part of a strigillated sarcophagus with *imago clipeata* and bucolic scene, found widely scattered in plough over room A, in the fill of room D, and in grave 160. The fragments do not appear to be building rubble, and could easily come from another complete sarcophagus.

Fragments clearly reused for burial or to decorate graves include undecorated, strigillated and, probably, overall relief schemes. Only one group is of undeniably Christian content (fragments 507 and 705), and it is interesting that these are the only sarcophagus fragments reused in this way which definitely come from inside the church. It is probable, however, that the missing sections of fragments 437 and 798 also would have included Christian figures. The only other obviously Christian piece is the fragment of a mid-fourth century "*in alberis*" sarcophagus (fragment 30), which has no specific context. 783 and 847 both include the figure of a shepherd which also often has Christian connotations, but only the first is at all likely to come from a complete sarcophagus where the choice of motif may have been deliberate.

Other sarcophagi fragments were employed in a secondary context for their materials alone. The nature of the reuse varies; most easily identified are the thresholds (fragments 22 and 525), paving slabs (186, 584, 701, 861), and interlace panels (865 and 866). Several regularly shaped pieces with no firm context (e.g. 341, 480, 712) may have been paving slabs but could also have been facing blocks from walls. Other more irregular fragments were used as building rubble (856 and 871). Unfortunately, no evidence survives for the nature of the reuse of the remaining fragments.

As far as can be determined, the surviving fragments are predominantly from strigillated sarcophagi of various kinds, with both fewer and smaller fragments from those with overall relief decoration. There are also two undecorated examples. This may merely reflect the greater supply of the simpler types in the Roman period, and thus their greater availability for reuse, but other factors can be taken into consideration. Strigillated panels must have been far more suitable for reuse as floor slabs or for interlace screens than many of the overall designs in deep relief, since they already had a uniform face which did not require further dressing.

Section 5: Other sculptural fragments

58. Unstratified, south of campanile. Claw of lion.
     Length 90 mm, height 85 mm. Greyish-white fine-grained marble, possibly burnt.
     Possibly formed the foot of a table-leg.

184. Crypt rubble. Relief, edge fragment.
     Length 0.2 m, height 0.16 m, thickness 55 mm. Greyish-white medium- to large-grained crystalline marble.
     Border of narrow cyma reversa followed by opposed spirals of running hook design in flat low relief; probably from centre of panel. Rest of design undecipherable. Back smooth.

662. Room 1, south-east sector. Fragment of *oscillum*.
     Height 0.13 m, length 0.14 m. Marble.
     Low relief showing lower torso and upper legs of dancing satyr, in profile facing left, right leg advanced with left raised behind, and with lionskin hanging from arm outstretched. Relief on reverse is badly worn, but appears to be a male figure, probably also satyr, in profile, moving to left with right leg advanced and torso turned back on left side, left arm holding ?*pedum* resting on left thigh. Dancing satyrs feature in the standard repertory of many neo-Attic reliefs, including candelabra and *oscilla* (cf. Cain 1985; Corswandt 1982). Both of the figures on our example are unusual in that the far rather than near leg is advanced; the dancing satyr corresponds roughly to Cain's Satyr 6a, which, he notes, is less common than his Satyr 5, a similar type but with the opposite leg advanced (1985, 125). *Oscilla* with satyrs on both faces are also fairly rare – Corswandt's catalogue contains only four examples (1982, catalogue numbers 38, 43, 57, 131). Nevertheless, the fragment can probably be associated with Dwyer's Group 2, which he dates mainly to the second half of the first century AD (1981, 257, catalogue numbers 33, 74).

681. Unstratified, area 8. Relief slab, fragment of bull's head with garland.
     Length 0.18 m, height 0.165 m, thickness 28 mm. Creamy white fine-grained micaceous marble, surface decomposed.
     Low relief preserving main part of head, with pairs of small drill holes on centreline at forehead, nose and mid-point, on ears, at eyes and on garland, perhaps for the addition of metal ornaments.
     The low relief and delicacy of carving suggest a date in the first half of the first century AD.

743. (Fig. 18) Cloister. Sundial, upper corner missing.
     Length 0.35 m, height 0.295 m. Marble.
     Spherical type; eleven hour lines radiating from central rounded cutting for *gnomen*, no day curves. Sloping base with undecorated quarter round moulding in angle. Roman. Cf. Gibbs 1976, catalogue number 1005G.

The few pieces of sculpture which do not come from sarcophagi form an interesting and varied collection. The sundial (fragment 743) was probably reused in the monastery. The *oscillum* (662) and the *bucrania* relief (681) both come from the south-east corner complex and were found in contexts of the first church phase; both should be of early first century AD date. The other two fragments appear to have been used as building material in the second church, and it is difficult to assign a date to either. It is possible that all these pieces, including the sundial, come from the peristyle of a nearby villa of first century AD date rather than from a stockpile.

GENERAL DISCUSSION

Many of the architectural and sculptural fragments from Santa Cornelia, although Roman in date, must relate to three main events of later date: the building of the first church and possibly the south-east corner complex; the building of the second church and monastery; and the twelfth century alterations. The two churches required columns, capitals and bases for the main structure, large blocks for door frames and thresholds, slabs for paving, wall veneer, and other minor decorative elements, such as plinths and cornices for the face of the raised presbytery, and for the *schola cantorum* and other fittings. The monastery required more columns, paving slabs and thresholds; marble was also needed for small columns, impost capitals and corbels for the second church facade, for the cloister, and for the campanile. Some material must also have been brought in for the twelfth century Cosmatesque floor. In addition, complete sarcophagi for reuse as places of burial could have been brought in separately, as the need arose, any time within the lifetime of the second church. As much as possible of the precious material of the first church was no doubt reused in the second, either in the same capacity or recut for flooring or general building material.

Unfortunately, it is rarely possible to assign any individual fragment with certainty to a function in the first church. The Doric column (fragment 806) belonging to the atrium, and the two fragments of strigillated sarcophagus reused for interlace screens (865, 866), are the only firm examples among the reused Roman material. The two early medieval capitals (641 and 749) must also belong to the first church, as, of course, do the interlace screens, and the small fragment of early medieval veneer cornice (707). Columns, capitals and bases from the nave of the first church would have been retained in the second, but these can no longer be distinguished with certainty from the four extra sets required for the larger second church. It is also likely that the frames of the north and east doors of the first church were retained in the second (fragments 239, 325 and 743). Two sarcophagi fragments (fragments 684 and 847), the *oscillum* (fragment 662) and the *bucrania* relief (fragment 681) come from the south-east corner complex, and were possibly part of the *opus sectile* floors of rooms 1 and 5.

The reused material from the second church and monastery can be divided into three main groups: one where the pieces are used more or less intact and in a way which relates to their original function; a second where the fragments are clearly reworked for a different function to that for which they were originally intended; and a third which uses leftover pieces as general building rubble. In the first category come most of the columns, capitals and bases, the Roman screens, some of the wall veneer, and a number of sarcophagi; this includes a few early medieval pieces, e.g. capital 749. To this we should add several fragments selected for their decoration but not used in quite their original manner; the Roman cornice 239 reused as a door lintel is one example, while the reuse of the sarcophagus 705 as part of the front of the built grave 61 is another. There may be other instances among the many large fragments of decorated sarcophagi which can no longer be identified. The second category covers columns used as thresholds (fragment 33) or paving material (459); sarcophagi used as thresholds (525), paving material (186, 480, 584, 701, 861, etc.), or interlace screens (865, 866); bases used as impost capitals (116); and capitals (477) and inscriptions (672, 673) used as corbels. The backs of sections of pilaster veneer (20) and cornices (21) were reworked with a shallow decorative moulding.

The third category is harder to define, as it must include a number of small fragments found in the general rubble, but there are some examples from a specific context such as column fragments 806 and 843 used in the foundations of the porch and cloister respectively, and capital fragments 867, 875 and 876 and sarcophagus fragment 871 built into the monastery walls. Other fragments can be tentatively identified by the presence of mortar on the moulded face, or the working of the block to a roughly regular shape too thick to be a floor slab (e.g. sarcophagus 712). In contrast to the first two categories, it is unlikely that these fragments represent material brought in specifically for building rubble, as local supplies of tufa were readily available. Some fragments no doubt came from the first church (e.g. fluted pilaster 20 with back reworked but mortar on both faces), while others represent waste from material brought in for the second church, the clearest example of which is perhaps the building block fragments 816a,b from the monastery zone, cut from the same portasanta column as floor slabs 459a,b of the church. This last example also suggests that some at least of the material was reworked on the site. This seems confirmed by the evidence for tooling marks on the back of numerous acanthus fragments (e.g. 51, 59, 137 and related examples), although this trimming could conceivably date to after the abandonment of the second church. The same doubt exists for the trimming of the fluting of column fragment 471. Much of the unwanted material from the first church, and waste from working material for the second, would have been burnt as lime.

The most notable feature of the Roman material chosen for reuse is its variety. The columns, capitals and bases of the nave arcades are mixed in both date and type, yet show some signs of careful selection. The plain elements – unfluted grey granite and marble columns and schematic Composite capitals – contrast with the more colourful columns of pavonazzetto, giallo antico and africano and the more elaborate Corinthian and Composite capitals. It is tempting to assign the second group to the first church, which Hadrian I is said to have richly decorated. In keeping with this would be the ornamental lintel from the north door, a choice piece clearly intended to emphasise the importance of the doorway (cf. the lintel of the entrance to the San Zeno chapel in Santa Prassede); this makes most sense in conjunction with the first church, where it led to the baptistery. The difference in date, size

and type of even the most closely similar groups of material, e.g. the Schematic Composite capitals, precludes any possibility that they came from a single building or group of buildings; on the other hand, the presence of some elements matched for size and general type but of different date makes it unlikely that the material was collected at random. All this suggests that for the first church at least the material came from a stockpile, no doubt in Rome itself. The use of an unfinished column (fragment 833) in part of the monastery also suggests a stockpile, this time in conjunction with the second church phase, unless residual from the first church.

The reused sculptural fragments show a rather different face of the same basic picture. With the exception of only four pieces (section 5: 58, 184, 662, 681), which may derive from a nearby villa, and the sundial, all the identifiable fragments are part of sarcophagi. Of these, all the fragments which show signs of having been used for paving, or were recarved as interlace screens, are either panels from strigillated sarcophagi, or pieces from figured scenes in low relief, including part of a *tabula ansata*. This again suggests a careful selection of material, although it must also be borne in mind that the trimming required to turn a figured scene in high relief into a slab suitable for paving would probably render it anonymous. Fragments of inscriptions, however, account for a far higher proportion of the identifiable paving material than do fragments of sarcophagi, perhaps because of their even greater suitability for the task. The side and front of strigillated sarcophagi were also used to make two thresholds. In contrast, the few fragments which can be identified with some certainty as building material, are all in deep relief. At least two pieces (341 and 856) come from the figured panels forming the end and centre respectively of strigillated sarcophagi. No fragments from the base of sarcophagi have been identified amongst this reused material; the greater thickness of this part of a sarcophagus no doubt made it suitable for turning into corbels and impost capitals.

A quite distinct group of sarcophagi fragments are those that were reused for burials. These probably included undecorated, strigillated, and relief types (the latter is less certain), and both pagan and Christian subjects. The greatest concentration appears to have been in the porch, although this may be a late feature created by robber activity in the church itself. In addition, one complete sarcophagus was found in the cemeterial area north of the porch and another in the cloister. All of these burials are likely to date to the late eleventh and twelfth centuries, the period of greatest vogue for the reuse of antique sarcophagi by higher level ecclesiastics. Although such sarcophagi had been used for the bones of martyrs as early as the ninth century, the trend for contemporary burials was set by Pope Damasus II in 1048 (Agosti *et al.* 1984). Forty years later the abbot of Farfa, Bernardo I, was buried in a strigillated sarcophagus with central *tabula ansata* (Lucchi 1984, 178); this perhaps allows us to accept the strigillated sarcophagi 437, 741 and 798 as suitable for the final resting places of some of the abbots of Santa Cornelia. The prestige attached to burial in an antique sarcophagus no doubt led to the 'second best' solution of grave 61, where fragments from a 'Good Shepherd' sarcophagus were used to decorate a built tomb.

We are unfortunately poorly informed on the workings of the second-hand marble trade in medieval Rome (but now cf. Pensabene 1989). It seems unlikely, however, that whole sarcophagi were transported intact as far afield as Santa Cornelia except when required for burials, as they are both bulky and heavy. A sarcophagus could easily be divided into five panels of varying quality, the base the thickest but least worked and the front the thinnest and most regular, excluding those with high relief decoration. The front face could also, of course, have its own decorative value. Thus the material could be selected for its intended use – as a threshold, for example, or for paving. An 'unwanted' relief panel could be trimmed back for various purposes, the trimmings ending in the lime kiln or as building rubble. The reuse of sarcophagi in the late eleventh and twelfth centuries would have increased their value, especially for the highly decorated ones, making them less likely to be used merely as a source of material; this may explain the relatively small number of sarcophagi fragments used as paving slabs at Santa Cornelia compared with inscription fragments. On the other hand, the growing interest in antique sarcophagi may have led to their greater exploitation as a source of material also. While it must always be remembered that most available material would have been reused in the second church, it may be significant that the finds from Santa Cornelia include only four fragments of sarcophagi which can be associated with the first church, including only two out of many fragments of interlace, reflecting a disinterest in this source of marble in the early medieval period.

All this is highly speculative. More studies need to be made on the nature of Roman *spolia* in medieval buildings before a clear picture of this important and no doubt lucrative aspect of medieval society emerges.

(vi) EARLY MEDIEVAL AND MEDIEVAL SCULPTURAL FRAGMENTS

The following offers a brief catalogue of the various fragments of early medieval and medieval sculpture recovered from the Santa Cornelia excavations and provides a short discussion regarding their dating. A full catalogue is archived at the British School at Rome. The format for describing the various finds is that employed by the *Corpus della Scultura Altomedievale*. The pieces are listed here with the number provided in the excavation, and where joins exist between fragments these are specified. The material is now all – with the exception of a few fragments at the Casale di Santa Cornelia, Formello – stored in the *Museo dell'Alto Medioevo* (*MAM*), Rome.

(a) THE EARLY MEDIEVAL SCULPTURE

Fragment 717 – CHANCEL SCREEN POST FRAGMENT (Pl. 47)

Marble: Greyish-white fine-grained crystalline. Site findspot: pit 048 near church entrance. Dimensions: 0.24 (high) × 0.13 (broad) × 0.08 m (deep). *MAM* inventory number 2101.

Lower portion of a screen post, featuring the simple decorative scheme of interlinked circles formed by a wide, single grooved band. The piece has a wide, flat cornice on the base and on one side, the other side being narrower. The rear is plain, as is the angled right side; the left side has a continuous 30 mm wide central groove.

Plate 47. Santa Cornelia: fragments of chancel posts (*Museo dell'Alto Medioevo*, Rome)

There is no exact parallel to this simple design, though the scheme of interwoven or knotted circles is frequent: examples on pilasters exist at San Saba in Rome (Trinci Cecchelli 1976, 143-144, number 1156) and to the north at Otricoli (Trinci Cecchelli 1976, numbers 158 and 167) and Poppi (Trinci Cecchelli 1976, number 175). The latter design had a general ninth century currency.

Associated fragment: 725 (creamy white fine crystalline marble). Findspot: porch. 0.125 × 0.135 × 0.13 m. Fragment of a similar post, featuring 0.25 m wide grooved band on each side.

Fragment 500 – CHANCEL SCREEN POST FRAGMENT (Pl. 47)

Greyish-white fine-grained crystalline marble. Findspot: porch rubble 0.35 × 0.115 × 0.09 m. *MAM* inventory number 2100.

Upper portion of a post, with decoration on just one side: the rear is smooth, the sides feature a 35 mm central groove for the insertion of screen. The main face shows a close plait motif formed by a double-grooved wicker band; the decoration is framed within a plain cornice. The top of the piece preserves a roughly-carved spherical knob 60 mm high, set slightly off-centre.

This decoration type occurs regularly on both cornices and plutei from Rome and its environs. Similar examples come from the so-called Temple of Fortuna Virile (Melucco Vaccaro 1974, 238, numbers 249-251) and Santa Maria in Cosmedin (Melucco Vaccaro 1974, 161, numbers 123-124); similar plutei fragments occur at San Giorgio in Velabro (Melucco Vaccaro 1974, 67-69, number 5) and Santi Quattro Coronati (Melucco Vaccaro 1974, number 147). Outside Rome, examples occur at Civita Castellana and Castel Sant'Elia (Raspi Serra 1974, Tav. XXVIII-XXIX, Figs 50-52; Tav. CXVIII-CXX, Figs 193, 195, 197).

Ninth century.

Fragment 306 – CHANCEL SCREEN POST FRAGMENT

Greyish-white fine-grained crystalline marble. Findspot: pit 047 near first church apse. 0.9 × 0.21 × 0.1 m. *MAM* inventory number 2118.

Large fragment of post, apparently recut for reuse. One side has a 35 mm central groove. Decoration comprises a floral scroll made up of a double-grooved wicker band creating a series of interlinked hooks. A single grooved band marks the point where the band divides to define the hooks. The gaps between the divisions and the border contain small two-leaf and single-bud motifs. In the circular gaps within the hooks are four-armed helixes. See fragment 750a-c below.

Ninth century.

Associated fragment: 292(?)

Fragment 388 – FRAGMENT OF CHOIR SCREEN

Greyish-white fine-grained crystalline marble. Findspot: pit 047. 0.33 × 0.23 × 0.05 m. *MAM* inventory number 2070.

Edge fragment from a chancel screen, with plain, broad border. The decorative scheme is a series of interwoven circles formed by a double-grooved wicker band, combined with a sequence of diagonals which intersect at the centre of each circle.

This is a common design in eighth and ninth century sculpture and finds numerous comparisons in Rome and in Latium. Fine examples occur at Santa Sabina (Trinci Cecchelli 1976, 219, number 249) and San Saba (Trinci Cecchelli 1976, 133-134, numbers 102-104), and fragments are known at the so-called Temple of Fortuna Virile (Melucco Vaccaro 1974, numbers 233, 237, 238) and Santa Maria in Aracoeli (Pani Ermini 1974, number 33). Outside Rome, we can note pieces at Sutri (Raspi Serra 1974, number 302) and Tuscania (Raspi Serra 1974, number 386).

First half of the ninth century.

Associated fragments: 302, 434, 583, 617, 724, 739, 882, *Casale* 3 and 4; 312 (findspot: rubble in sector P; irregularly shaped edge fragment, with similar, but thinner circle and diagonal design and a space between the edge of the design and the border; joins 552a-b); 552a-b (findspot: in make-up of second period porch causeway. 0.49 × 0.44 × 0.11 m (0.7 × 0.44 × 0.11 m with 312); corner and edge fragments).

Fragment 344 – CHOIR SCREEN FRAGMENT

Greyish-white fine- to medium-grained crystalline marble. Findspot: rubble of apse crypt. 0.49 × 0.41 × 0.05 m. *MAM* inventory number 2096.

Corner fragment of a chancel screen. Features decoration similar to 388 above, but with a poorly balanced and irregular design, containing unequal sized circles and somewhat wavy diagonals. The plain cornice is somewhat crude. Spaces appear to have been filled with a two-leafed single-bud floral motif (cf. Santi Quattro Coronati (Melucco Vaccaro 1974, numbers 161, 162)), an insertion which further unbalances the design. The irregularities are paralleled in a pluteus at San Giovanni a Porta Latina (Melucco Vaccaro 1974, 96-97, number 35a), which, like

Plate 48. Santa Cornelia: restored fragments of ninth century choir screen with interlace design (*Museo dell'Alto Medioevo*, Rome)

fragment 344, stands in marked contrast with more elaborate panels from the same location.

Ninth century.

Associated fragments: 527, 787.

Fragment 304a-d – CHOIR SCREEN FRAGMENT (Pl. 48)

White-greyish fine-grained crystalline marble. Findspot: pit 047. 0.47 × 0.30 × 0.045 m. *MAM* inventory number 2074.

Corner fragments of a screen featuring decoration formed by a series of interwoven circles composed of a double-grooved wicker band; the circles are in turn interwoven with a double-grooved border which flanks a broad, plain edge. Within the circles are set four or six petalled flowers or eleven armed helixes; between the circles are various tendrils, volutes or flower motifs. The side features a 30 mm tongue. Numerous smaller fragments belong to this screen (see below). The reverse of the fragments has the outline of a gameboard.

The design is regarded as an alternative to screens featuring interwoven square panels. Examples of each occur at San Giovanni a Porta Latina (Melucco Vaccaro 1974, 95-96, number 34) and at San Leone, Leprignano (Raspi Serra 1974, 158-159, numbers 215, 216). Circular designs come from Santa Maria in Cosmedin (Melucco Vaccaro 1974, number 110) and from Tuscania (Raspi Serra 1974, Fig. 437). Few of these examples match the execution of the Santa Cornelia screen.

First half of the ninth century.

Associated fragments: 93, 253, 309, 310, 317, 319, 390, 413, 438, 439a-b, 501, 518a-b, 591, 592, 608, 610, 617, 657, 667, 716, 718, 719, 721, 757, 761, 777, 885, 886, 887.

Fragment 498 – FRAGMENT OF AN AMBO (Pl. 49)

White fine-grained crystalline marble. Findspot: east end of church, south side. 0.38 × 0.38 × 0.06 m. *MAM* inventory number 2094.

Triangular corner fragment, perhaps belonging to an ambo. Joins fragment 435. The lower design, set within a plain cornice, consists of a close plait of double-grooved

Plate 49. Santa Cornelia: restored panel from ambo stairs (*Museo dell'Alto Medioevo*, Rome)

wicker bands (above, fragment 500). The principal design comprises the start of an interwoven circle pattern intersected by diagonals (above, fragment 388). Tongue on bottom edge for insertion into another element.

First half of the ninth century.

Associated fragments: 435, 623.

Fragment 750a-c – FRAGMENT OF AN AMBO

Greyish-white fine- to medium-grained crystalline marble. Findspot: Z/1. a= 0.32 × 0.29 × 0.035 m, b= 0.16 × 0.17 × 0.035 m, c= 0.12 × 0.13 × 0.035 m. *MAM* inventory number 2103.

Triangular corner fragment, probably relating to an ambo. There is a plain cornice, between which is set a plant design with tendrils extending from a central branch and defining a series of circles terminating in a volute (cf. fragment 306 above). The points where the branches divide are marked by two bands. The circles contain five-armed helixes with a central disc.

The design is representative of the 'tree of life' motif frequently found on early medieval sculpture. Useful comparisons can be made with plutei from San Giovanni a Porta Latina (Melucco Vaccaro 1974, 91-93, number 31b; see also the well-head here, number 36), Santa Sabina (Trinci Cecchelli 1976, 213-214, number 244) and San Saba (Trinci Cecchelli 1976, 123-125, numbers 85, 86, 88, 89). Outside Rome, the motif occurs at Civita Castellana, Castel Sant'Elia and Tuscania, with that at Castel Sant'Elia forming the closest comparison with this fragment (Raspi Serra 1974, Figs 107, 170, 172 and 420).

First half of the ninth century.

Fragment 164 – FRAGMENT OF AN AMBO

Whitish fine-grained crystalline marble. Findspot: sector G, rubble. 0.64 × 0.36 × 0.055-0.06 m. *MAM* inventory number 2093.

Probable ambo corner fragment. Features a plain external border, narrower on one side, where a tongue is present. The border is flanked by one formed by a double-grooved wicker band to which are connected by means of small loops in the band a series of small interlinked circles; additional loops decorate the circles and border; the circles lack internal decoration. Joins fragments 318a-c, 704 and 884 to give a panel of overall dimensions 1.16 (upright) × 0.74 (base) × 1.14 (angled edge) × 0.19 (side) m.

Although we can cite examples featuring interlinked borders and circles (Santa Sabina, San Saba (Trinci Cecchelli 1976, numbers 114d and 239)), those pieces which show the additional 'looped' circles and borders

Plate 50. Santa Cornelia: fragments from ciborium arch (*Museo dell'Alto Medioevo*, Rome)

tend to possess floral motifs within the circles (Sant'Agnese (Broccoli 1981, 183-185, numbers 132-134), Sutri (Raspi Serra 1974, 220, Fig. 336)).

Late eighth-first quarter of the ninth century.

Associated fragments: 318a-c, 704, 884.

Fragment 497 – FRAGMENT OF CIBORIUM ARCH (Pl. 50)

White-streaked grey coarse-grained crystalline marble. Findspot: porch. 0.32 × 0.53 × 0.06 m. *MAM* inventory number 2098.

Lower portion of arch belonging to a ciborium. The principal element of the design is the quite chunky lower half of a bird, presumably a peacock, given the large tail. Its body is plain, but the tail is decorated with a fish-bone feather design, with the central spine featuring occasional buttons. The peacock stands on a cable moulding which follows the curve of the arch; beneath this is set an irregular double-grooved wicker band interlace design of poor composition. A plain cornice runs around the sides of the arch. Joins corner fragment 763.

The design of the bird's tail and body meets comparisons with examples in Latium, in particular Sutri, Castel Sant'Elia, Leprignano and Sant'Eutizio (Raspi Serra 1974, Figs 333, 163, 244 and 303). A more developed version of the peacock is seen at Santa Maria in Cosmedin (Melucco Vaccaro 1974, numbers 103 and 104). A similar, but tidier, border pattern with both cable and interlace occurs at Santa Maria Maggiore, Tuscania (Raspi Serra 1974, 253, Fig. 403).

First half of the ninth century.

Associated fragment: 763.

Fragment 883 – FRAGMENT OF CIBORIUM ARCH

White-streaked grey coarse-grained crystalline marble. Findspot: rubble in campanile. 0.04 × 0.24 × 0.055 m. *MAM* inventory number 2098.

Lower portion of a ciborium arch, presumably the opposite half of fragments 497, 763. This fragment joins

101 and 426. The outer cornice was plain; above this, following the line of the arch, run two irregular interwoven plaits formed by double-grooved wicker bands; a cable moulding borders this (see above, fragment 497). The principal field of decoration has a floral motif, resembling a spider. To the left is the end of a squarish tail, presumably belonging to a bird.

We lack parallels for the 'spider' motif, but similar squarish birds' tails are known (cf. Pani Ermini 1974, 60, number 43).

First half of the ninth century.

Associated fragments: 101, 329, 426 (reused: mortar on face).

Fragment 866 – CIBORIUM FRAGMENT (?)

Grey medium- to large-grained crystalline marble. Findspot: accumulation in room D (dormitory). 0.20 × 0.275 × 0.06 m. *MAM* inventory number 2628.

This corner fragment exhibits decoration to be associated either with a pluteus or more probably with the upper part of a ciborium. The top shows a wave design, flowing to the right with curled crests; these stand on a broad, flat border, which continues down the side of the piece. Within the border is part of a double-grooved wicker band design, perhaps two or three interlinked eyelets. The fragment may form the corner to the arch represented by 497 and 763. The reverse of the piece shows that it had been cut from a strigillated sarcophagus.

The wave motif is relatively common, particularly on ciboria: e.g. Santa Saba (Trinci Cecchelli 1976, number 79), Santi Bonifacio e Alessio (Trinci Cecchelli 1976, numbers 16 and 17), and Santa Maria Maggiore, Tuscania (Raspi Serra 1974, Figs 402 and 403). On plutei it usually occurs around semi-circular elements (for example, Santa Sabina (Trinci Cecchelli 1976, number 235), Tuscania (Raspi Serra 1974, Fig. 409)). For the interlace design we can cite the ciborium at Castel Sant'Elia, which also features the wave motif (Raspi Serra 1974, 139, 148-149, Figs 174, 202, 203).

Associated fragment: 356(?).

Fragment 865 – FRAGMENT OF CIBORIUM ARCH(?)

Greyish-white medium-grained crystalline marble. Findspot: accumulation in room D (dormitory). 0.27 × 0.19 × 0.55 m. *MAM* inventory number 2620.

Fragment of the base of a probable ciborium arch, recut from a strigillated sarcophagus. The poorly-executed decoration features part of a branch design similar to 750a-c above, whose individual tendrils terminate in 'trumpets'. The division of the branches is marked by two bands. No additional decoration occurs in the design. The sides have narrow plain borders, the base being slightly thicker.

First half of the ninth century(?).

(b) MEDIEVAL SCULPTURAL ELEMENTS

Fragment 105a-c – COSMATESQUE SCREEN (Pl. 51)

Grey medium- to coarse-grained crystalline marble. Findspot: Pits 047, 048 (church nave)? *MAM* inventory number 2144.

Plate 51. Santa Cornelia: fragments of Cosmatesque altar screen showing settings (*Museo dell'Alto Medioevo*, Rome)

Three joining fragments of the raised corner and side of a transenna or screen, featuring cuttings within the marble for Cosmatesque mosaic inlay. The design features a corner square of 95 × 95 mm, from which run two lines of triangular cuttings divided by diamonds. The triangles feature sides of 60 mm and the maximum width of the diamonds is 95 mm. Some red, white, green and blue tesserae were still in place, others were marked by mortar. There was no trace of the decoration of the main face of the panel which may have consisted of a large marble (porphyry?) slab. Joins 231, 305, 499, 722.

Early twelfth century (Glass 1980).

Associated fragments: 46, 47, 52, 231, 293, 305, 499, 722.

DISCUSSION

The fragments listed above can be divided into four main groups: posts, screens, and ambo and ciborium fragments. It seems likely that these form only a smallish proportion of the original fittings that existed in both the first and second churches at Santa Cornelia.

For the first church we have elements relating to at least three posts and six screens: the posts are all of early medieval workmanship, while the presence of fragments of large classical screens featuring 'union jack' type ornamentation (recreating in stone a metal screen) (Fig. 18) shows that contemporary chancel screens were supplemented by reused material. Indeed, fragments of one screen (*MAM* inventory number 2090) are clearly early medieval copies of these classical pieces. The medieval craftsmanship is variable: the quality of carving and the organisation of the designs is in some cases good (cf. fragment 388), yet crude and irregular elsewhere (cf. 344). Whether this reflects the non-contemporaneity of these elements remains unclear, for it is more likely that different sculptors of differing levels of skill were employed (in Rome or on site?) in their production.

The actual siting of the chancel screens is problematic. If we take the smallish number of elements at face value it may be possible to claim that the screen originally only ran across the church at the front of the raised presbytery, thereby forming an iconostasis [1]. However, given the limited depth of the presbytery, it is more reasonable to argue for a choir extending east from here into the nave, perhaps to the mid-point of the church (cf. Fig. 34). Since this will have rested directly on the church floor, or on plinths (such as, for instance, fragments 138 and 182), it is not surprising that we lack evidence on the ground for the choir.

Fragments 498, 750a-c and 164 with associated fragments belong to three tall, angled, screens flanking the steps of an ambo. Existing twelfth century chancel arrangements serve to show that the ambo generally lay along one side of the choir, often in the middle, and with its pulpit part-projecting beyond its side. Usually it stood opposite the stand for the lectern [2]. We have no obvious fragments relating to the pulpit. Finally, fragments of at least two arches of a ciborium were recovered. This most probably stood over the main altar which lay over or close by the reliquary (grave 160). The ciborium will have rested on four columns, set directly on the floor of the presbytery, thereby leaving no trace in the bedrock.

Taken as a whole, the group of early medieval sculpture from Santa Cornelia may be broadly attributed to the first half of the ninth century. This chronology must not be taken as fixed, since the problems of dating the various types are notable if we consider that many of the designs had a relatively long currency, covering the later eighth and much of the ninth century. Frequently, dates are assigned chiefly on the basis of the building history of the church to which they belong, and this leads to 'fixed' dates being preferred for certain designs. At Santa Cornelia the fragmentary inscription (fragment 265) referring to PASQUALIS, if indeed documenting the activity of Pope Paschal I (817-824), may suggest that the installation of the chancel and perhaps also the ciborium belonged to his pontificate. However, it is implausible that such elements were omitted from the original Hadrianic scheme and we should either visualize an arrangement in wood or metal, or regard the majority of the described pieces as belonging substantially to Hadrian's pontificate. The Paschal inscription may of course refer to something totally unrelated to the internal fittings (Pl. 53).

From the widely scattered findspots, it is difficult to ascertain whether these early fittings were readopted wholesale in the second church or whether they were disassembled and broken up for other uses. The discovery of a large number of fragments in the rubble in both sector P and the porch (e.g. 310, 312, 318, 434, 438, 439, 500) may for example be indicative that these had been incorporated in the church walling in these areas; certainly fragment 552a-b had been used in the make-up for the second phase of the porch causeway. Nonetheless, we lack sufficient examples of medieval fittings to suggest such total replacement. Although there is ample evidence for a twelfth century Cosmatesque floor in the second church, fragments from just one contemporary mosaic inlaid screen emerged from the excavations (105) and this may not belong to a schola cantorum. However, foundations for a choir covering half the area of the nave certainly existed in phase 3, and this undoubtedly supported screens. Even if we argue for a new series of screens in the twelfth century – almost all removed from the church some point after its abandonment – there remains the strong possibility that the original fittings were retained for part of the monasterial church's lifetime. The same may be true for elements such as the ambo and ciborium [3].

NOTES

1. Such an iconostasis, datable to the mid-ninth century, survives in situ at Leprignano near Capena: Raspi Serra

1974, 154f, Figs 210-235. Cf. San Liberato, this volume.

2. Cf. choirs at both San Clemente and Santa Maria in Cosmedin in Rome.

3. Perhaps significantly the craftsmen who worked at Santa Cornelia did not use the reverse of the early medieval screens, as occurs at Santa Maria in Cosmedin. Many eighth/ninth century elements are reused in the twelfth century churches of Santa Maria Maggiore and San Pietro at Tuscania, with Santa Maria featuring early ciboria fragments incorporated in the thirteenth century ambo: Raspi Serra 1974, 252-256, Figs 402-408.

(vii) ELEMENTS FROM A COSMATESQUE FLOOR AND OTHER VENEER (Figs. 20-23; Tables 1-6)

Amanda Claridge

Over 500 pieces of *opus sectile* paving and veneer were recorded during the excavations, variously scattered on the surface, in the ploughsoil and disturbed upper rubble levels in the area of the second church and further afield. A small group of fragments [1] came from the debris overlying room 1, at the far south-eastern corner of the site, where a patch of polychrome marble flooring was actually found *in situ* (see above p. 57); others were apparently concentrated in a pile to the north of room 6, not far from the fallen wall [2]. Unfortunately, many pieces were never given or have since lost their 'fragment number' and/or other marking, with the result that what were already tenuous archaeological contexts are now impossible to reconstruct except on the internal evidence of the nature of the fragments themselves.

The assemblage is dominated in equal measure by quantities of large square and rectangular slabs (Fig. 20) and narrow strips (Table 1) on the one hand, and by an impressive array of twenty-four roundels (Table 2) and sixty-eight pieces of Cosmatesque-type geometric mosaic floor (Fig. 21) [3] on the other. In their turn, some of the roundels may be associated with an assortment of *peltae* and other cusped shapes (Fig. 22), whilst an assortment of loose squares, triangles, hexagons and diamonds (Tables 3-6) for the most part matches those found in the mosaics.

Such a diversity of shapes and sizes is one of the hallmarks of 'Cosmati' church decoration in Rome and Latium during the twelfth and thirteenth centuries. So, too, is the distinctive choice of high quality "Imperial" stones: red porphyry (occasionally substituted in the mosaics by *rosso antico* or the odd piece of slate), green porphyry and the similarly dark green ophite *'granito della Sedia di San Lorenzo'*, giallo antico, pavonazzetto, grey granite, and white or greyish white marble (sometimes pale *portasanta*). A large and elaborate Cosmatesque floor laid in the second church probably accounts for a high proportion of the assemblage, though seemingly not all. The mosaic patterns certainly are readily paralleled among the pavements catalogued by Glass (1980, 141-149). All but one are motifs commonly used by all the Cosmati workshops (compare our Fig. 21 numbers 2, 2a, 3, 3a, and 5 with Glass numbers 1, 4, 7, 8, and 14). The exception is the herring-bone pattern (Fig. 21 number 2 = Glass number 23), a pattern associated particularly with the "Paulus" group, who were active in the first half of the twelfth century, predominantly in Rome, but sometimes

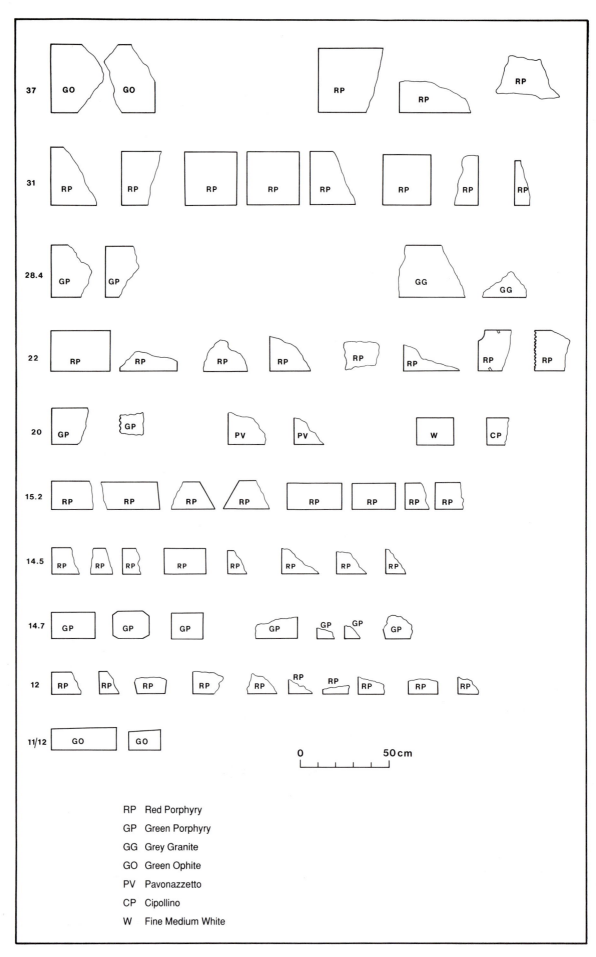

Fig. 20. Santa Cornelia: marble, rectangular fragments (SC)

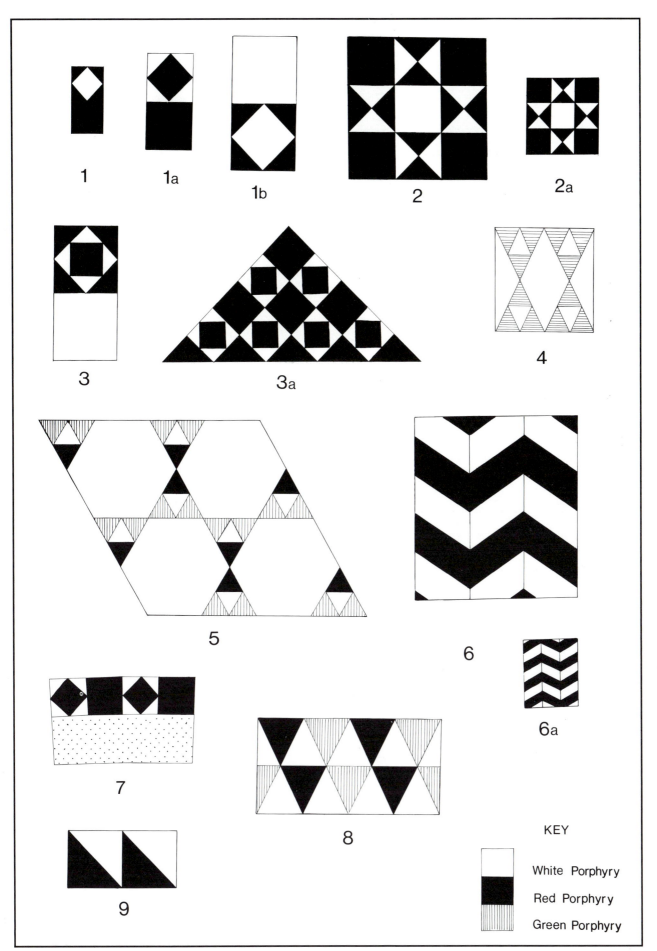

Fig. 21. Santa Cornelia: Cosmatesque decorative floor types (SM)

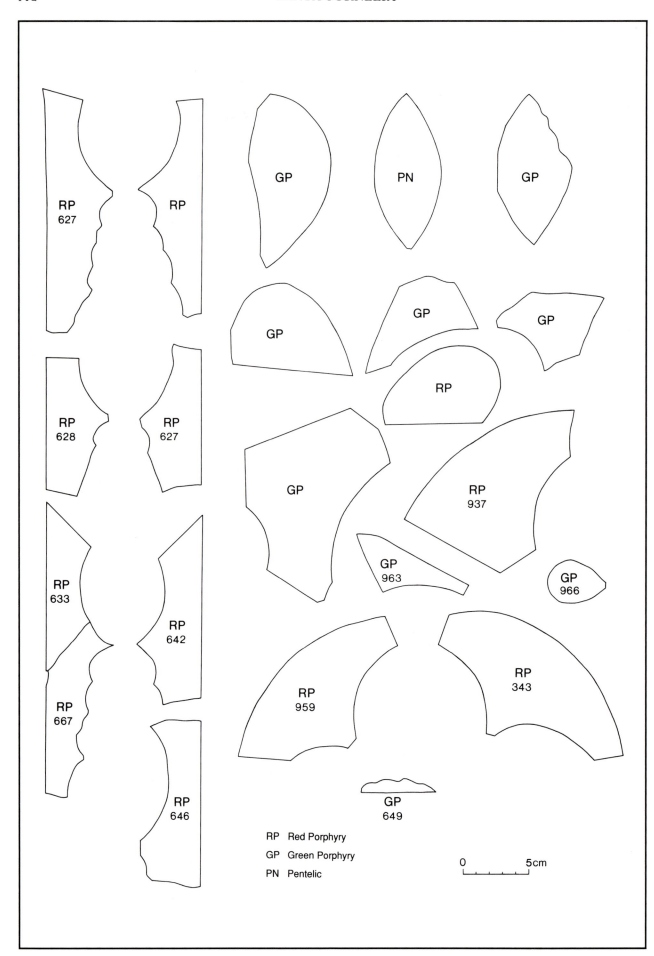

Fig. 22. Santa Cornelia: marble, cusp and wavy elements (SC)

elsewhere, as at Ferentino and Nazzano (Glass 1980, 18) (Pl. 52). If the pattern is truly diagnostic of their work we may extend the analogy to the roundels as well and imagine an overall design similar to those in Santi Quattro Coronati (see Fig. 23a, after Glass 1980, pl. 40-41, fold-out I) or Santa Maria in Cosmedin (Glass 1980, pl. 35), where a single quincunx (at Santa Cornelia this would be the largest red porphyry disc with green porphyry/ophite satellites?) is preceded and followed by a succession of discs interwoven with spirals of mosaic (cf. Fig. 21 number 7). Difficult to fit in with Paulus-type floors, however, are any

of the large square and rectangular slabs; those would be much more characteristic of the later 'Ranucius' group who had a penchant for alternating roundels and rectangles (see Fig. 23b, after Glass 1980, fold-out II), and worked at Castel Sant'Elia, Ponzano Romano and Tarquinia (Glass 1980, 19). It might also be noted that the triangular shaped fragment of a pattern from Santa Cornelia (Fig. 21 number 2a) rather than the corner of a panel, might derive from within a panel set with larger squares à la Ranucius (Glass 1980, 147, number 27).

But even for a Ranucius-type floor the numbers of

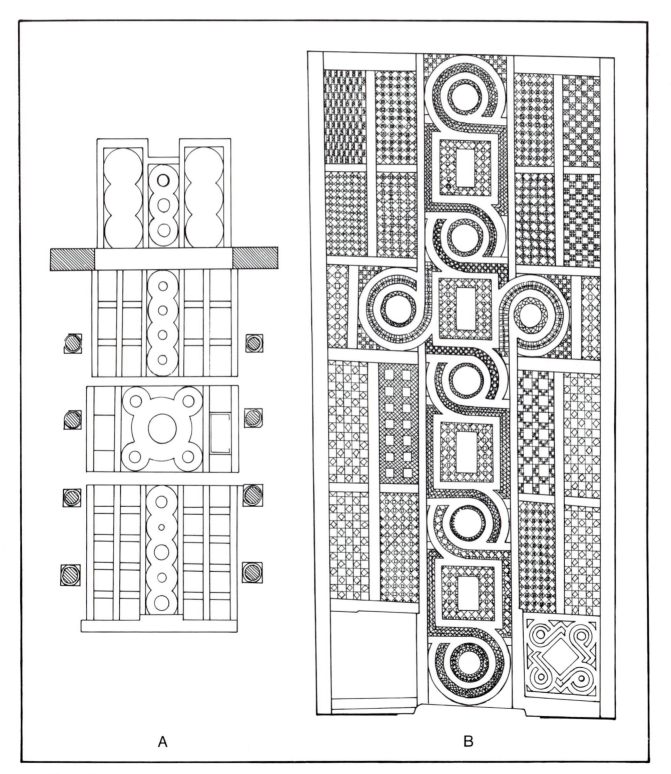

A   B

Fig. 23. Santa Cornelia: Cosmatesque floors a) Santi Quattro Coronati, Rome; b) San Andrea in Fiumine, Ponzano Romano (AH)

Plate 52. Santa Cornelia: elements of Cosmatesque flooring (*Museo dell'Alto Medioevo*, Rome)

green and red porphyry [5]. A few could derive from herring-bone pattern mosaic, or from other patterns, such as Glass number 25, but surely not all. They, too, are equally suited to forming decorative bands. It is suggestive in this respect that the broad rectangular slabs are mostly in red porphyry whereas the narrower strips are mostly in green porphyry. They could have alternated with one another in superimposed rows on whatever surfaces they adorned. To what one should attribute the *peltae*, leaf shapes and curiously cusped strips (Fig 22) – floors or walls – is a particularly vexed question. They are related to one another, and to the roundels, in materials and to some extent also in form, but they find no obvious parallels among any of the Cosmatesque floors. The cusped strips are all in red porphyry and form opposing pairs which could have framed a small roundel and some leaf-like shape within a broad band, suggesting a sort of frieze. But the findspots, in so far as they are known, are more in favour of an unusual floor in room 1 [6].

Notes

1. Numbers 627-629, 642-650, 656, 661.
2. Site notebook V, page 389 East trench XII, south, near south pier: "here much broken marble and porphyry etc".
3. Compiled from fragment numbers 226, 311, 651, 764, 765, 769-773, 791, 792, 814, 816, 835, 877-881, 889-935.
4. The large square and rectangular slabs are the least documented elements in the sample; only two are marked, one in grey granite came from the Baptistery area (H/2), the other, one of the red porphyry rectangles with a mitred corner, number 638, was found in the pile referred to above (note 2) and thus could derive from the facade rather than the interior of the church.
5. None of which is marked.
6. The likelihood is strengthened by the fact that the fragments retrieved from the patch of floor found *in situ*, with the exception of a *giallo antico* strip (656) found 'beneath' the floor (presumably set in the mortar as leveller), cannot be distinguished from the fragments found loose above it (however, see above pp. 57-59 for the sequence in the south-east sector).

rectangular porphyry slabs are excessive in proportion to the rest of the sample. Many reflect standard widths, suggesting borders or frames (two have mitred corners) rather than isolated elements. The broad borders and frames in Cosmatesque floors of all kinds, however, are never in porphyry, always in white or greyish white marble. That the Santa Cornelia sample is extraordinarily short on the latter is not necessarily to be taken as evidence to the contrary: the absence of white and grey marble is met with in the mosaics and their associated assortment of loose shapes. Both could be the result of preferential robbing, the robbers seeking marbles which could be burnt for lime. It is, therefore, very possible that we should exclude many if not all the big porphyry squares and rectangles from our hypothetical floor and place them elsewhere, on vertical surfaces instead: perhaps as panels on screen walls of the *schola cantorum*, or as decorative bands of colour along the architrave of the aisle colonnade, or outside on the facade of the church [4] as at San Lorenzo fuori le Mura.

The same may be said of the many narrow strips in

TABLE 1. STRIPS

Width		Material (total length present)
Inches	**centimetres**	
4	10.2	Green porphyry (19 cm)
3	8.5-9.5	Green porphyry (35 cm)
		Giallo antico (21 cm)
	7.0-8.0	Red porphyry (135 cm)
		Green porphyry (45 cm)
	6.3-7.3	Green porphyry (75 cm)
		Green ophite (13 cm)
	6.2-6.6	Giallo antico (14 cm)
		Pavonazzetto (11 cm)
2½	5.5-6.1	Red porphyry (82 cm)
		Grey granite (16 cm)

Width Inches	centimetres	Material (total length present)
2	5.0-5.6	Green porphyry (83 cm)
		Pavonazzetto (18 cm)
		Green ophite (14 cm)
	4.0-4.8	Green porphyry (45 cm)
		Green ophite (12 cm)
		Broccatello (12 cm)
		Pavonazzetto (10 cm)
	3.2-4.0	Red porphyry (264 cm)
		Cipollino (21 cm)
		Giallo antico (8 cm)
1½	3.3-3.8	Green porphyry (600 cm)
		Green ophite (10 cm)
1	2.2-3.0	Green porphyry (102 cm)
		Red porphyry (69 cm)
		Giallo antico (4 cm)
	1.4-1.9	Green porphyry (100 cm)
		Red porphyry (87 cm)
	0.8-1.4	Red porphyry (70 cm)

TABLE 2. ROUNDELS

Diameter Inches	centimetres	Material	Reference number
41	102	Red porphyry	SC635
27	66-68	Giallo antico (pink brecciated)	SC338
21½	53.4	Green porphyry	
21½	53.4	Green ophite	
16	40	Pavonazzetto	SC936
16	40	Grey granite	H/2
14	35	Giallo antico	SC144 inv. 2/21
14	35	Giallo antico	SC161 inv. 2/20
11	27.4	Breccia	SC 682
10	24.0	Breccia	SC 862A
9	23	Red porphyry	SC 428
9	22.6	Giallo antico	SC 969 (2667 + 2720)
8½	21.0	Grey granite	
7	18.0	Green porphyry	
7	17.8	Green porphyry	SC 778 U/30
7	17.0	Green porphyry	
6	15.5	Green porphyry	SC 967 (T/I)
5	12.6	Green porphyry	768
5	12.0	Green porphyry	Z/18
4½	11.0	White	430
4½	10.6	Red porphyry	971
4½	10.6	Red porphyry	648
3½	9.0	Green porphyry	N/3
3	8.0	White	

TABLE 3. SQUARES

Length of sides		Material, number of fragments
Inches	**centimetres**	**(reference number)**
4	10	Green porphyry (2)
		Red porphyry (1)
		Flecked grey/white (1)
	8.5	Green porphyry (1)
3	7.5	Cipollino (2) (K/1 N/10)
		Proconnesian (2) (K/1 H/3)
		Red porphyry (1)
		Carrara white (1) (K/1)
		Carrara grey (1) (P/8)
		Pentelic grey (1)
		Medium grain white (1) (P/3)
		Proconnesian grey (1) (K/1)
		Pavonazzetto (1) (K/1)
		Parian white (1) (SC752)
2½	6.0-6.5	Red porphyry (1)
		Green porphyry (1)
		White (1) (P/9)
2	5.0-5.5	Red porphyry (11) (includes K/11 P/10)
		Green porphyry (4)
		Green granite (1)
	4.5	Red porphyry (4) (includes K/11)
		Green porphyry (2)
		Giallo antico (1) (P/8)
		White (1) (K/11)
1½	3.5-4.0	Red porphyry (17) (includes P/8 N/8 L/4)
		Green porphyry (5)
		Green granite (1)
	3.0	Red porphyry (2) (includes N/4)
1	2.6	Red porphyry (2)

TABLE 4. TRIANGLES

Base length		Side length		Material	Reference
Inches	**centimetres**	**Inches**	**centimetres**		**number**
10	24.8	**7/8½**	17.7/20.6	Carrara variegated (1)	Inv. 2122
7	17-18	**5**	12	Green porphyry (2)	L/1
7	17.5	**5**	12.5	Cipollino (1)	M/2
5	13.0	**3**	9.0	Red porphyry (1)	P/5
5	12.5	**4**	10.0	Green porphyry (1)	
4	10.5	**3**	7.0	Red porphyry (1)	
3½	8.5	**3½**	8.0	Green porphyry (1)	
3½	8.5	**3**	7.0	Red porphyry (3)	
3½	8.0	**3½**	8.0	Green ophite (1)	
3½	8.0	**2½**	6.5	Green porphyry (1)	
3½	7.5	**3½**	9.0	Red porphyry (1)	N/12
3	7.0	**3½**	8.0	Green ophite (1)	
3	7.5	**2½**	6.0	Green porphyry (1)	
3	7.5	**2½**	6.0	Red porphyry (1)	

Base length		Side length		Material
Inches	**centimetres**	**Inches**	**centimetres**	
3	7.5	2½	5.5	Red porphyry (4)
3	7.0	2½	6.0	Green porphyry (1)
3	6.5-7.5	2	5.0	Red porphyry (4)
2	5.5	1½	4.0	Green porphyry (2)
2	4.5	1½	3.0	

TABLE 5. HEXAGONS

Length of sides		Material	Reference
Inches	**centimetres**		**number**
3	8.5	Proconnesian	SC835
	8.0	Proconnesian	SC907 (L/1)
	7.0	Proconnesian	SC226
2½	6.0	Fine grain white, Proconnesian grey	SC941 (N/3)
1½	3.75	Portasanta	SC440

TABLE 6. DIAMONDS

Length of sides		Material	Reference
Inches	**centimetres**		**number**
4	10.5-11	Green porphyry	
3	6-7	Red porphyry	N/3
		Proconnesian grey	N/17
		Pentelic	SC974 (N/10)
2½	5-6	Luna white	
1	3	Red porphyry	

(viii) ETRUSCAN AND ROMAN CERAMICS

Phil Perkins

Eighty-five sherds from the Etruscan and Roman periods were identified, the majority being body sherds. All sherds were small, and consequently a precise classification and identification was rarely possible. It was not considered worthwhile to produce detailed descriptions of fabrics nor to create a repertoire of forms. Furthermore, the area has been well served by excavation, and stratified collections of pottery from most periods have been adequately published (for example, for the Etruscan period see Murray-Threipland (1963) on Veii; Murray-Threipland and Torelli (1970) on Casale Pian Roseto: for Roman assemblages see Duncan (1964; 1965) and Perkins (forthcoming)).

The assemblage of pottery suggests uninterrupted frequentation of the area from the end of the seventh century BC through to at least the fifth century AD, and in some ways can be considered as a typical cross-section of the ceramics common in south Etruria.

For the Etruscan period the material can be divided into two qualitative groups, namely typical tomb goods and settlement refuse. In the first group, we can place the bucchero, particularly the *oinochoe*, and some of the coarse jars; in the second, the coarse wares, the *pithoi*, the internal slip ware and, possibly, a cooking stand. As a whole, the material suggests the presence of a nearby archaic necropolis and an archaic and classical period settlement.

There is no clear continuity between the Etruscan and Roman periods: the only pointer we have is ten unidentifiable fragments of black gloss ware. The Roman sherds, comprising mixed domestic refuse, fine ware, coarse ware and amphorae, are consistent with the local presence of a settlement site. The latest fine ware (?Hayes 32) dates to the third century AD, although fragments of African amphorae (e.g. Keay XXV s) and Palestinian bag-shaped amphorae attest some activity into at least the fifth century. Compositionally, the Roman material, fine wares, coarse wares and amphorae, is typical of central Italian collections.

CATALOGUE

Abbreviations

BO.S   Body sherd
B.S.   Base sherd
CPR   Casale Pian Roseto (Murray-Threipland and Torelli 1970)
Dr.   Dressel
Hayes   Hayes form (Hayes 1972)
HA.S   Handle sherd
K.   Keay form (Keay 1984)
M.   Morel form (Morel 1963)
Ras.   Rasmussen form (Rasmussen 1979)
R.S.   Rim sherd
V.D.W.   Van der Werff form (Van der Werff 1978)

IMPASTO

Y6		BO.S.	Local	Archaic	1

Dark red interior and exterior burnished slip

BUCCHERO

T3		BO.S.		?V BC	1

Greyish colour, junction of foot ring and body

T4		B.S.	Pesante	VI-V BC	1

Burnished exterior

W43		B.S.	Pesante	VI-V BC	1

Same vessel as above. Burnished exterior

P12	Oinochoe Ras.4	B.S.		625-575 BC	1

Very good quality fine bucchero well polished, double incised rays around base

P12	Oinochoe Ras.4	BO.S.		625-575 BC	1

Same vessel as above

BLACK GLOSS

T3		BO.S.		IV-I BC	1
T4		BO.S.		IV-I BC	1
U32		BO.S.		IV-I BC	2
W82		BO.S.		IV-I BC	1
W98		BO.S.		IV-I BC	1
Z17		BO.S.		IV-I BC	1
U106	Bowl	B.S.		III-I BC	1
SC?	Bowl	B.S.		III-I BC	1
P4	Bowl M.2480	R.S.		III-I BC	1

Reserved band 20 mm wide at rim on exterior

?BLACK GLOSS

P13	?Skyphos	B.S.		?V-IV BC	1

Very glossy metallic dark grey slip, three reserved bands on exterior

TERRA SIGILLATA ITALICA

P9	?Bowl	R.S.		I AD	1
W99	?Crater	BO.S.		I AD	1

Barbotine decoration

Y8	?Cup	B.S.		I AD	1
Y7	Platter	BO.S.		I AD	1

THIN WALL

W95	Cup	BO.S.		0-50 AD	1

Dark orange slightly metallic slip, rouletted exterior

AFRICAN RED SLIP

W96		B.S.	A1	75-250 AD	1
F5	Bowl ?H.32	B.S.	A/D	III AD	1
W27	Bowl H.3	R.S.	A1	75-150 AD	1

COLOUR COAT

U89		BO.S.		?I-II AD	1
Grey brown slightly glossy interior and exterior slip					
W100		BO.S.	Local	?I-II AD	1
Matt dark red exterior slip, grey brown slightly glossy interior slip					
W124		BO.S.	Local	I-II AD	1
Dark red slightly glossy slip					
X8		BO.S.	Micaceous	?IV-V AD	1
Dark red matt slip with finger striations on exterior					
W108	?Bowl	B.S.	Local	?I AD	1
Dark orange internal and external slip					

COARSE

T19		BO.S.	Local	VII-VI BC	1
Dark red exterior slip					
W118		BO.S.	Local	?I-II AD	1
Matt dark grey brown exterior slip in bands					
X3		BO.S.	Local	Roman	1
W84	?Bowl CPR Fig. 17A	R.S.	Local	V-IV BC	1
Cream slip					
W120	?Jar	B.S.	Local	V-IV BC	1
Thick internal oxidised slip					
W132	Jar	R.S.	Local	?IV BC	1
Wiped surfaces					
M6	Jar Stamnoid	HA.S.	Local	Archaic	1
Burnished dark red exterior slip					
W56	Lid	HA.S.	Local	?III-I BC	1
Same slip					

AMPHORAE

S3		HA.S.	?S. Spanish	I-II AD	1
W105	?Dr. 1	BO.S.	C. Italian	150-30 BC	6
Abundant small black augite inclusions					
W108	?Dr. 1	BO.S.	C. Italian	150-30 BC	1
As above					
W126	?Dr. 1	BO.S.	C. Italian	150-30 BC	3
Black augite rich fabric					
X8	?Dr. 1	B.S.	C. Italian	150-30 BC	1
X17	?Dr. 2-5	B.S.	Italian	I AD	1
W111	?K.LIII	BO.S.	?Syria	V-VI AD	3
Very micaceous fabric					
W25	?K.LIII	BO.S.	?Syria	V-VI AD	5
Rough exterior with poor horizontal bands					
W7	?K.LIII	BO.S.	?Syria	V-VI AD	2
As above					
W84	?K.LIII	BO.S.	?Syria	V-VI AD	1
As above					
X3	?K.LIII	BO.S.	?Syria	V-VI AD	1
Very micaceous					
W96	?K.LIII	BO.S.	?Syria	V-VI AD	2
Micaceous					
W72	African	B.S.	N. Tunisian	III-V AD	1
US	African	BO.S.	N. Tunisian	III-V AD	1
Salt water skin with vertical smoothing					
N18	African	BO.S.	N. Tunisian	III-V AD	1
Salt water skin					
N20	African	BO.S.	N. Tunisian	III-V AD	2
As above					
N22	African	BO.S.	N. Tunisian	III-V AD	1
As above					
P4	African	B.S.	N. Tunisian	III-V AD	1
X39	African	BO.S.	N. Tunisian	III-V AD	1
X24	African ?Grande	BO.S.	N. Tunisian	III-V AD	1
Dark yellow exterior with vertical smoothing					

Z4	African K.XXV S	R.S.	N. Tunisian	IV-V AD	1
Salt water skin					
R2	Dr. 1	HA.S.	C. Italian	150-30 BC	1
Black augite rich fabric					
X39	Dr. 1	B.S.	C. Italian	150-30 BC	1
As above					
X57	Dr. 1	HA.S.	C. Italian	150-30 BC	1
SC?	Dr. 2-5	HA.S.	C. Italian	I AD	1
W72	Dr. 2-5	B.S.	Tarragona	I AD	1
W63	Gallic Gauloise 4	B.S.	Typical	I-II AD	1
W88	Punic trad.	BO.S.	Typical	II BC-I AD	1
Salt water skin					
U30	Punic trad. VDW 2	R.S.	Typical	II BC-I AD	1
As above					

?STAND

P12		Flange	Local	VII-VI BC	1
?Flange of an archaic cooking stand with lug on flange, surface smoothed					

DOLIUM

P12		B.S.	Local	Roman	1
Flat base					
T45		BO.S.	Local		1

PITHOS

W4		R.S.	Local	Archaic	2
R.S. and BO.S. with lug handle on body					
Z19		BO.S.	Local	VII-VI BC	1
Burnished dark red interior and exterior slip					

TILE

W114			Local	Archaic	1
Y6	Pan tile		Local	Archaic	1
Smoothed surface					

(ix) THE EARLY MEDIEVAL AND MEDIEVAL POTTERY FROM SANTA CORNELIA

Helen Patterson

INTRODUCTION

The pottery from the excavations of Santa Cornelia has already been studied and published by David Whitehouse (1980a). The reassessment of the material presented here was undertaken for two main reasons. Firstly, when Whitehouse carried out his study the excavation report had not been prepared, and only a partial and preliminary phasing was available. Secondly, in recent years our understanding of pottery of the early medieval to medieval period from Rome and the surrounding area has increased dramatically. This is largely due to the excavations of the Crypta Balbi, Rome, directed by Daniele Manacorda, which have produced large quantities of stratified material of these periods (Manacorda 1984; Manacorda 1985; Manacorda *et al.* 1986). Detailed study of the pottery, particularly that by Paroli, has produced a datable typological sequence stretching from the late eighth century until the present day (Cipriano *et al.* forthcoming; Manacorda 1985; Manacorda *et al.* 1986; Saguì and Paroli 1990). The same pottery types appear to be characteristic of assemblages elsewhere in Rome and in the Roman

Campagna (for example, Berretta del Prete on the via Appia (Gai 1986), Pianabella, Ostia Antica (Coccia and Paroli forthcoming), Santa Rufina (this volume), Anguillara (Patterson forthcoming a), Castel Porciano (Mallett and Whitehouse 1967), Mazzano Romano (Potter 1972), Monte Gelato (material under study), Ponte Nepesino (Cameron *et al.* 1984) and Farfa). The importance of the pottery sequence established at the Crypta Balbi cannot be over-emphasized; for the first time material of these periods from excavation and survey can be dated with relative precision, thus opening up immense possibilities. In particular, a discussion of the economy and production and distribution of goods, fundamental to our understanding of developments in the early medieval and medieval periods, becomes possible.

In this context a re-assessment of the ceramic material from Santa Cornelia seemed justified. Despite the limitations imposed by the stratigraphic sequence (see below), the Santa Cornelia material offers an important contribution to our understanding of developments in the early medieval and medieval periods. It allows us to assess relations with an urban centre and the periphery and adds further new evidence to the emerging picture of ceramic production in the Roman Campagna.

(I wish to thank Dott.ssa Lidia Paroli for her invaluable help and advice in the study of the pottery.)

Chronology

A sequence of six phases was identified by the excavations: 1. Roman; 2. *Domusculta* (774-1000); 3. Second church and monastery (1000-1300); 4. Abandonment or decay of site (1300 onwards); 5. Sub-plough (1400 onwards); 6. Plough (1800-present). Material from the pre-*domusculta* phase (phase 1) consists mainly of a small amount of republican and early imperial pottery thought to relate to agricultural activity (see Perkins, this volume). The only material of possible early medieval date from this phase is fragments of amphorae (see section on domestic pottery). The pottery dates mainly from the late eighth century (phase 2), and the foundation of the *domusculta*, until the thirteenth century, with a relatively small amount of material of the fourteenth century. Material of a later date occurs sporadically, indicating some occasional use of the site after this date.

The phase 2 sequence can be relatively closely dated on the basis of the historical documentation for the site. From phase 3 onwards, however, the site has few historically dated features and absolute dating is limited to very broad chronological periods. Furthermore, the deposits are frequently very disturbed; residual and, in some cases, intrusive material is a frequent problem (see below). A relative sequence is possible, however, and absolute dates for this sequence have been proposed, based on parallels with pottery from other sites, in particular with the sequence from the Crypta Balbi, Rome. These dates should therefore be regarded as provisional, but the validity of this approach can be justified for two main reasons. Firstly, the relative sequence at Santa Cornelia largely corresponds with that of the Crypta Balbi and the chronology at Santa Cornelia is not based on parallels with just one particular type of pottery but on the entire range of types which characterize certain periods. Secondly, in the instances when the pottery can be dated from the structures (in particular in phase 2), these dates have usually conformed with those of the Crypta Balbi. From the end of phase 3 the appearance of certain glazed pottery types (in particular *ceramica laziale* or Rome ware and archaic maiolica), whose chronology is now firmly established, provides a further dating element.

The greatest uncertainty about the sequence at Santa Cornelia is caused by the presence of residual material. Material found *in situ* is, on the whole, limited to phase 2 (late eighth to tenth centuries); this phase includes some well stratified groups of pottery of the late eighth and ninth centuries. Given the rarity of deposits of this date (so far only recorded at Rome itself, Pianabella (Ostia Antica), Santa Rufina and Monte Gelato), these groups are of considerable importance. From phase 3 onwards, however, we are clearly dealing with redeposited material or contexts which have been disturbed by ploughing (see Christie, this volume) and the proportion of residual or intrusive material is often relatively high. The main effect of the presence of residual material is that it suggests excessively long life-spans for certain pottery types. Phase 4, for example, dated to the fourteenth century (see Christie, this volume) contains much material which would fit perfectly with a late twelfth to early thirteenth century date on the basis of parallels elsewhere.

The chronological divisions used for the pottery sequence are as follows:

Phase 2a-b: 774-815
Phase 2c-d: 815-850
Phase 2d-g: 850-1000
Phase 3 onwards is dated largely by comparison with the Crypta Balbi sequence
Phase 3a: early eleventh century
Phase 3b-c: eleventh to early twelfth century
Phase 3d-g: late twelfth to thirteenth century
Phase 4: fourteenth century, although the samples include a very high percentage of material of later twelfth and thirteenth century date
Phase 5: fifteenth century onwards, although, apart from some sporadic later material, the pottery is largely of the later twelfth and thirteenth to fourteenth centuries.

Methodology

In addition it should be noted that this reanalysis of the Santa Cornelia pottery has been somewhat selective. It has concentrated on the earliest and most securely dated groups of pottery of the late eighth and ninth to tenth centuries. Information about ceramic production of this period in Rome and the surrounding area is, as noted above, just emerging. Ongoing excavations at Monte Gelato (Potter and King 1988) have recently revealed large deposits of this date as well as the presence of a late eighth to early ninth century pottery kiln, producing a range of domestic pottery (*acroma depurata*) identical on typological grounds to that of Rome, Santa Cornelia, Santa Rufina and other sites in the Roman Campagna. In this context this material merits special attention. The later medieval glazed pottery from Santa Cornelia, such as *ceramica laziale* (Rome ware) and archaic maiolica, has been fully discussed by Whitehouse (1980a) in the original report on the pottery and is not repeated here. The characteristics of these classes are well known and their chronology is relatively well established. Furthermore, at Santa Cornelia they occur in disturbed deposits associated with a high percentage of residual material.

Quantification

The pottery from only two areas has been studied in detail and quantification carried out: the south-east corner and the monastery. These are the least disturbed areas and produced the best stratified sequences. The south-east corner is especially important as it is only in this area that deposits relating to the earliest (eighth century) phase of the *domusculta* were still intact. Quantification of the various classes of material by sherd count and weight was not possible since many plain body sherds had been discarded. For this reason, quantification of the assemblage is limited to a count of rim sherds (see Tables 7 and 8). On the other hand, all the early medieval and medieval glazed pottery (*ceramica a vetrina pesante* of the Forum Ware type) and sparse glazed pottery) was available for study. In the text percentages given for the different classes of material are based, unless stated, on rim sherds. For the remaining areas a sample of contexts was looked at, mainly for dating purposes, although if interesting groups or forms were found these were also recorded and in some cases drawn. Particular attention was paid to the deposits of phase 2d-g (mid-ninth to tenth century) from the courtyard area. These contexts revealed a series of closed pottery groups which conform with a tenth and early eleventh century date on the basis of parallels with the Crypta Balbi.

Fabrics

The term fabric refers to the composition of the fired clay body of a ceramic vessel. Fabrics can be divided into groups on the basis of their composition, that is size and number of inclusions. Each fabric group (1, 2, 3) will have its own distinctive composition. The fabrics of the pottery at Santa Cornelia have been divided into groups according to their visual characteristics following the criteria laid down by Peacock (1977, 6-7). Petrological analysis of the inclusions present in the fabric, however, has only been carried out for the Forum Ware and sparse glazed ware. It is hoped to undertake petrological analysis of the remainder of the sample shortly, but until then confirmation of the macroscopic groupings and a discussion of origins is impossible. The macroscopic description of the fabrics is given in Appendix 2. Unfortunately, for a series of practical reasons, it has not been possible to provide a catalogue of the illustrated forms.

THE POTTERY

The early medieval to medieval ceramic assemblage consists of the following classes of pottery: kitchen wares (55.8%), domestic wares not used for cooking (33.7%), painted pottery (0.9%), *ceramica a vetrina pesante* of the Forum Ware type and sparse glazed ware (9.6%). The later medieval glazed pottery includes *ceramica laziale*, archaic maiolica, miscellaneous glazed wares and maiolica: it is not discussed here (see Whitehouse 1980a).

(i) KITCHEN WARES (Figs 24 and 25)

Virtually all the vessels in this class of pottery show signs of scorching and have clearly been used for cooking. In phase 2 the kitchen wares comprise 31.8% of the ceramic assemblage. This percentage almost doubles in phase 3 when they represent 60.8% of the pottery recovered (see Table 8).

Forms

The kitchen ware forms are limited to jars and *testi* which first appear in the tenth century. *Testi* are earthenware covers which were placed directly over the food to be baked or cooked, usually bread although other foodstuffs were also cooked in the same way. The *testo* was generally placed on the hearth with the hot ashes of the fire heaped on and around it. The practice of baking or cooking under a *testo* has a long tradition and is well documented in the Roman period and earlier (Frayn 1978; Sparkes 1962; Whitehouse 1978; see in particular Mannoni 1965 and Cubberley *et al.* 1988 for further discussion of these vessels). The fabric of the *testi* is often coarser than that of the jar: this is a common phenomenon in both Roman and medieval assemblages (Cubberley *et al.* 1988, 106; Patterson 1989; Ricci 1986, 537), and presumably represents a deliberate attempt by the potters to increase the refractory properties of the clay. *Testi* occur from phase 2d-g, but their first appearance in the quantified contexts is in phase 3 when they comprise 35.4% of the coarse ware assemblage by rim count. In phase 5 this percentage drops to 26.2%.

The coarse ware forms are typical of those found in Rome and on sites in the Roman Campagna. The jars are globular or biconical vessels, which from at least the tenth century have two strap handles attached at the rim and extending to the widest point of the body. The bases are generally flat, although some earlier examples have slightly convex bases. At Rome convex bases appear in contexts of the ninth century only (Ricci 1986, 537). One example of a *paiolo* was also recovered (see below for a discussion of *paioli*). The *testi* have wide diameters and flaring or lightly curving walls, and a plain or down-turned rim. From the eleventh century onwards the vessel walls of both the jars and *testi* become thinner and the fabric more refined, this being accompanied by an increasing standardization of the forms. All the vessels were thrown on a fast wheel.

Fabrics

Three main fabrics have been identified: fabrics 1, 2 and 3. From the late eighth to twelfth/thirteenth centuries the majority of the coarse wares was manufactured in one fabric (fabric 1). Fabric 2 occurs in very small quantities (two rims only are of this fabric, Fig. 24.1,2) exclusively limited to the earliest eighth to ninth century contexts. During the twelfth (probably late twelfth) to thirteenth century a new, more refined fabric (fabric 3) appears alongside fabric 1. Schuring's study of the distribution of Roman and medieval coarse ware fabrics at Rome and from various sites in the surrounding area (Schuring 1987) included a sample of 82 coarse ware sherds from Santa Cornelia, mainly from phase 3 (eleventh to thirteenth century). Her fabric 5 corresponds to fabric 1 and comprised 51.2% of the sample studied; her fabric 1 corresponds to fabric 3 and represented 19.5% of the sample (Schuring 1987, Fig. 1). Fabric 1 (Schuring's fabric 5) is typical of coarse wares found at Rome and elsewhere in the Roman Campagna in the early medieval and medieval periods (see, for example, Schuring 1987, Fig. 1). In the tenth century this fabric is noticeably micaceous, but after this date the fabric becomes progressively more refined. All the vessels were thrown on a fast wheel.

Chronology

Relatively few coarse ware forms are present in the earliest levels of the late eighth to early ninth century. They comprise two examples of small jars with everted squared-off rims (Fig. 24.1,2) and these continue to be the most common forms in phase 2c-d (first half of the ninth century) (Fig. 24.3-5). At the Crypta Balbi these forms are typical of late eighth and ninth century levels (Paroli forthcoming a, Fig. 3.5; Ricci 1986, 536, Tav.XI,2,3). By the mid-ninth century production of these forms appears to have ceased, to be replaced by one, or two, handled jars with thickened, lightly everted or upright rims. The bases are generally flat and not wire-cut. One or two thick strap handles are attached at the rim (Fig. 24.8-11). These forms are characteristic of the coarse wares in deposits of the mid-ninth to tenth century and some (Fig. 24.10,11) may be of the early eleventh century. Two more complete vessels were recovered in contexts of the mid-ninth to tenth century, including one vessel with a convex base (Fig. 24.6,7).

The chronology of the forms from phase 3 onwards is

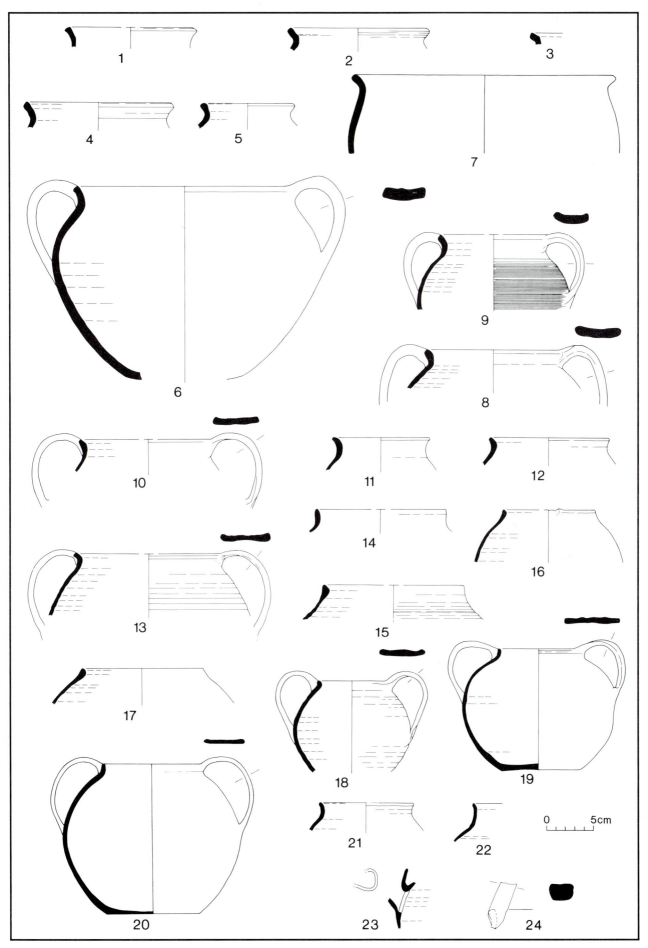

Fig. 24. Santa Cornelia: early medieval and medieval kitchen wares, closed forms (numbers 1-24) (SC)

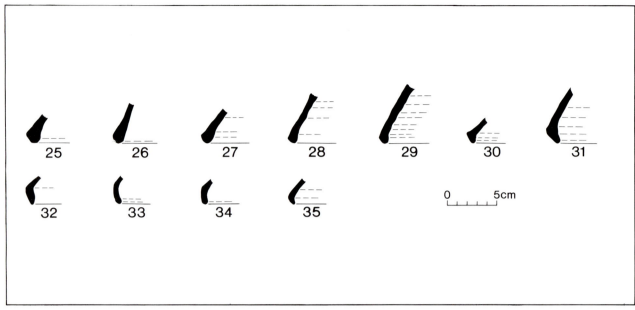

Fig. 25. Santa Cornelia: early medieval and medieval kitchen wares, the *testi* (numbers 25-35) (SC)

established partly on the basis of comparison with the sequence from the Crypta Balbi. With one exception (see below), the handled jar, with an ovoid to globular body and flat base, continues to be the sole closed vessel in use. The typology of the jar, however, undergoes a gradual evolution seen in particular in the rim and handle forms. The fabric becomes more refined and the vessel walls correspondingly thinner. From the eleventh century the jar rims become thinner, shorter and almost vertical (as Fig. 24.12 present both in a context of the early eleventh century and of the eleventh/twelfth centuries and Fig. 24.13,14 present in contexts of the eleventh/twelfth centuries). The strap handles are noticeably thinner than those of the tenth century vessels. During the twelfth/thirteenth centuries (phase 3d-f), not only does the standard coarse ware fabric (fabric 1) become much more refined, but it is joined by vessels of a new fabric (fabric 3). It is in this period that the vessel walls achieve a minimum thickness. The rims, although demonstrating a range of slight variations, are mainly short and vertical, in some instances no more than a simple upturned lip, the neck of the vessel having virtually disappeared. The strap handles become increasingly wider and thinner (Fig. 24.15-17 and 18-20). The same forms predominate in contexts of phases 4 and 5. At the end of phase 3 (late twelfth to thirteenth century) new rim forms appear (Fig. 24.21,22) which represent the latest development before the appearance of lead glazed kitchen ware. The presence of a short flaring spout in fabric 1 should be noted (Fig. 24.23 – phase 4): the form is identical to sparse glazed ware forms of the twelfth and thirteenth centuries.

One example of a *paiolo* was recovered from a context of the twelfth to thirteenth century (Fig. 24.24). *Paioli* are wide-mouthed vessels with an upright rim. Their distinguishing feature is an oval-section handle attached to the rim at two points and rising, like the handle of a basket, above the vessels, presumably to allow their suspension over the fire. This form is largely restricted to central Italy, examples occurring in Tuscany (Vannini 1974, 97, numbers 131f and 98; Maetzke 1974, 485-486, 490-492 and Pls VI-VII; De Marinis 1977, 172-183), Umbria (Blake 1981a, Fig.8), Romagna and the Po plain,

Lombardy (Brogiolo and Gelichi 1986; Gelichi 1986, 122-125, Tav. III.4, Tav. IV.1; Stoppioni 1984, Fig. 2, numbers 27-28) and the Marche (Mercando 1970, Fig. 17 and 19; Maetzke 1978, Fig. 5). In central Italy, at the above sites *paioli* were in use mainly in the thirteenth and fourteenth centuries; in the Marche, however, the earliest finds date from the eleventh and twelfth centuries and in Tuscany perhaps from the early medieval period (Gelichi 1986, 122). In Latium this form does not seem to have been common; only one example was recorded from the excavations at the Crypta Balbi (Paroli pers. comm.), and one example of medieval date was recovered from excavations in Rieti (Patterson forthcoming b).

Testi appear at Santa Cornelia in phase 2d-g (mid-ninth to tenth century). These are wide vessels, with flaring or curving walls, and probably had handles, as do the *testi* of the ninth century onwards at Rome (Ricci 1986, 537). Two main forms occur. The earliest, characteristic of phase 2d-g (mid-ninth to tenth century) (Fig. 25.25-27) and phase 3a (Fig. 25.26) and common in contexts of the eleventh/twelfth centuries (Fig. 25.28), has a plain thickened rim. The eleventh century examples of this form have thinner walls (note, for example, Fig. 25.28). Although these and similar *testi* are found in later contexts, they are unlikely to date beyond the twelfth century on the basis of comparison with the Crypta Balbi sequence where these forms are rare after the eleventh century. The second main form is the *testo* with a downturned lip. Examples first appear in deposits of the eleventh/twelfth centuries (Fig. 25.29,30) but by the twelfth/thirteenth centuries this form predominates, characterized by an increasingly emphasized down-turned lip and, like the jar forms, increasingly thinner walls (Fig. 25.31-35). At the Crypta Balbi forms such as Fig. 25.34,35 are dated to the thirteenth and fourteenth centuries.

(ii) DOMESTIC POTTERY NOT USED FOR COOKING (ACROMA DEPURATA AND SEMI DEPURATA) (Figs 26-28)

The pottery discussed in this section was not used for cooking. It forms a distinct and homogeneous group characterized by a pale coloured (ranging from very pale brown to pale pink), refined fabric. The term refined is used to refer to clays with few or no visible inclusions.

Forms

The forms are limited to closed vessels: jugs, jars and amphorae, sometimes with lids. Presumably these vessels were used to hold liquids although the amphorae may have been used to store other products. A few lamps were also recovered. The domestic vessels defined as amphorae were probably used for storage rather than transport. However a number of sherds, relating to large thick-walled vessels, recovered from the earliest eighth and ninth century levels of the sequence, may belong to transport amphorae. These are briefly discussed in the next section.

The vessels were without exception thrown on a wheel and the standardization of the forms and the refined fabrics reflect a high level of production throughout the early medieval and medieval periods. Like the kitchen wares, these vessels gradually become thinner walled. This class of pottery comprises a large proportion of the ceramic assemblage particularly in the earliest levels of the late eighth to mid-ninth century when it represents 68.6% of the pottery in use. In phase 3 the percentage drops to 23.8%, corresponding with, and probably directly related to, an increase in the quantity of glazed pottery. It seems probable that the sparse glazed jugs, which appear in large quantities in this period, substituted certain unglazed forms.

Fabrics

The domestic pottery was generally fired in a reducing atmosphere producing light coloured (very pale brown to pale pink) fabrics. The fabrics are usually fairly refined, often having very few visible inclusions, and for this reason the definition of these fabrics in particular must be regarded as strictly provisional; valid definitions may be impossible without petrological analysis. Four main fabrics were identified (fabrics 4, 5, 6, 7). The greatest range of fabrics occurs in levels of the eighth and ninth and, to a certain extent, the tenth century, comprising fabrics 4 and 5, used for the production of small- to medium-sized containers and some amphorae, and fabric 6, seemingly used exclusively for the production of amphorae. A common feature of vessels of fabric 4 is the very pale yellow exterior, and sometimes interior, surface. This surface treatment is clearly deliberate, achieved by the method of firing and not by the addition of a slip.

By the eleventh century the domestic pottery appears to have been made exclusively of fabric 5; although examples of vessels of fabric 4 and 6 still occur, they are probably residual. It is unlikely that fabric 4, in particular, continues beyond the ninth century. This corresponds with a reduction in the range of forms produced, becoming largely limited, certainly by the eleventh century, to one main form: the globular amphorae. Fabric 5 continues to be the standard domestic pottery fabric until sometime during the twelfth/thirteenth centuries when it is joined by vessels of fabric 7 (visually indistinguishable from the fabric of the contemporary sparse glazed pottery). Macroscopically fabric 7 closely resembles fabric 5. It is distinguished, however, by an oxidized pale reddish yellow fabric. Fabric 7 may reflect a change in firing techniques rather than a valid fabric grouping, and fabrics 5 and 7 may, in fact, represent colour variations within one fabric group. If this is the case, it raises interesting questions about changes in production techniques at this time, such as the possibility that the potters adopted larger kilns resulting in greater colour variation between the products (my thanks to Lidia Paroli for this suggestion).

Chronology

In the earliest phase 2 levels (late eighth and ninth centuries) the domestic pottery comprises a fairly wide range of standardized forms in a range of sizes, although small- to medium-sized containers predominate. The forms, which in some cases are reminiscent of late Roman and Byzantine potting traditions, include jugs, occasionally with tubular spouts, handled jars and amphorae. The bases of these vessels are usually wire-cut. Combed decoration, both in straight and/or wavy bands, is a common feature of these vessels, usually applied on the shoulder and/or the neck. As noted above, a further common feature of the jugs and jars in this period is a lighter surface colour which gives the appearance of a slip. The small number of lamp fragments recovered are all of this period.

The most common forms in contexts of phase 2a-d (late eighth and early ninth centuries) (twelve examples) probably belong to wide-mouthed jugs with a biconical body, one oval-section handle, and sometimes a tubular spout (Fig. 26.36-43, 41 is not illustrated). They recall Byzantine forms and are represented by one complete vessel and a series of rims. Four examples are present in phase 2a-b (774-815), and five examples, including the complete vessel (Fig. 26.38) occur in deposits of the first half of the ninth century. However, no examples were recorded from phase 2f (mid-ninth to mid-tenth century) and two later examples are probably residual. Other forms which occur in phase 2a-b (774-815) include a small two handled jar with a lightly flaring neck (Fig. 26.44) with bands of combed decoration around the neck and upper part of the body. The lower half of a vessel, which is probably of the same form (Fig. 26.45), is lightly burnished on the exterior in vertical streaks. Similar examples from the Crypta Balbi, Rome, are often finished in this way (Paroli pers. comm.; Romei 1986, Tav. VII,2-4). At Santa Cornelia other bases with this characteristic (Fig. 26.46,47) may be of the same form, although they occur in deposits of the mid-ninth to tenth century. One fragment, perhaps also of this form, may have originally had *pasta vitrea* inserted into the handle (not illustrated). Similar examples are recorded from the Crypta Balbi in ninth century contexts (Romei 1986, 526, Tav. XXI, 6-8). A common vessel of medium dimensions, whose complete profile is unknown (it may be a jug or a jar, possibly with two handles (Paroli pers. comm.)), has a tall neck and lightly collared rim (Fig. 26.48-55, 49 is not illustrated). It first appears in the late eighth/early ninth century (Fig. 26.48-50); two examples also occur in deposits of the first half of the ninth century; and one example is in a context of the mid-ninth to mid-tenth century. Six later examples are probably residual. It is interesting to note that the same form occurs at Santa Rufina in Forum Ware of late eighth or ninth century date (Fig. 92.P799), and at Pianabella

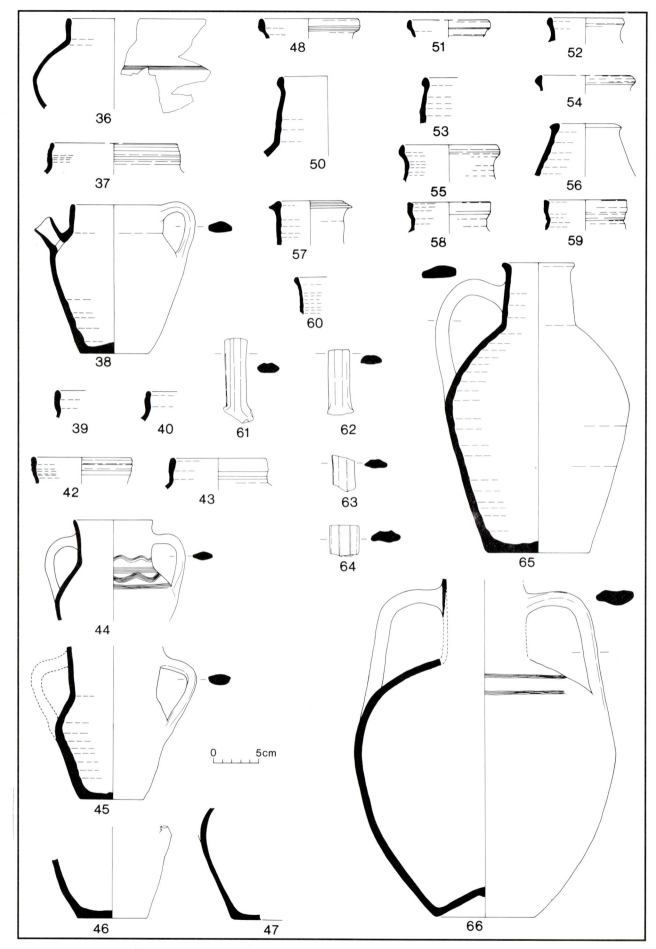

Fig. 26. Santa Cornelia: early medieval domestic pottery (*acroma depurata*) (numbers 36-66) (SC)

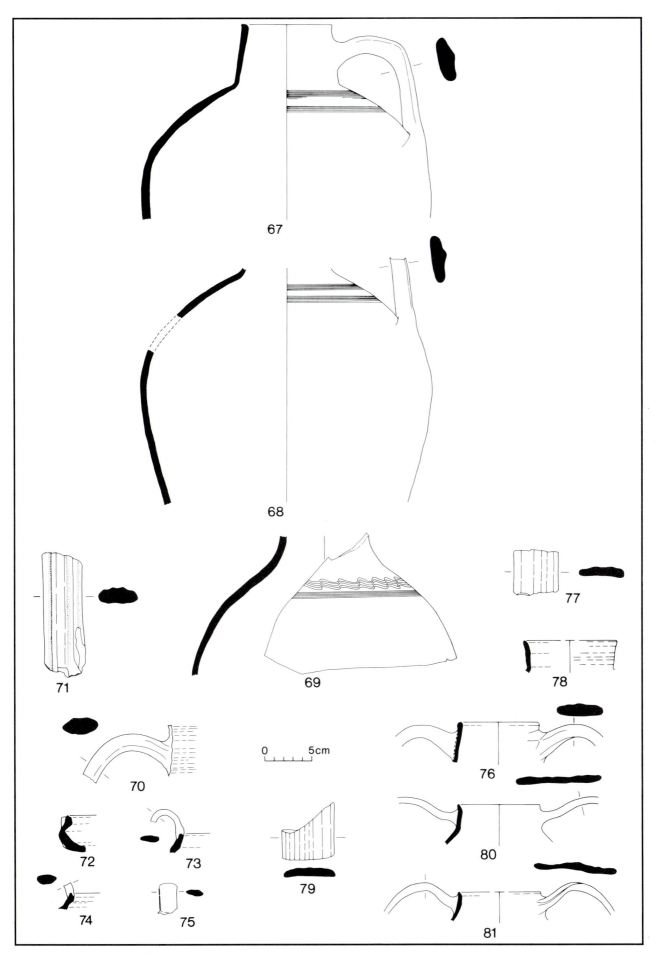

Fig. 27. Santa Cornelia: early medieval and medieval domestic pottery (*acroma depurata*) (numbers 67-81) (SC)

(Ostia Antica). These are the only examples known of this form in Forum Ware. Other rims, which may belong to similar vessels (Fig. 26.56-59) occur in contexts of the late eighth to early ninth century (one example) and of the first half of the ninth century (three examples). At the Crypta Balbi, eighth century examples of these forms have a cordon around the neck which disappears in the ninth century (Paroli forthcoming a, Fig. 3. 19-24; Romei 1986, Tav. VII.1). At Santa Cornelia, however, this cordon is lacking from examples in both the late eighth and ninth century deposits. One possible jug rim (Fig. 26.60) was recovered from a context of the early ninth century.

A series of distinctive handles probably belong to the above vessels. They are present in late eighth and early ninth century contexts (Fig. 26.61-64) and in levels of the first half of the ninth century. At the Crypta Balbi identical examples are dated to the eighth and ninth centuries (Paroli pers. comm.).

One larger vessel (Fig. 26.65), found in phase 3 (1025-1300), is similar in rim form to some of the above vessels and is probably residual; similar forms at the Crypta Balbi are dated to the ninth century (Romei 1986, 526, Tav. VII.1).

The only containers of large dimensions attested in this period are amphorae. It is not known if they were used for transport or storage. They have a globular body and an omphalos base, a tall, slightly inflaring neck and plain rim, two oval-section handles and bands of combed decoration on the shoulder (Fig. 26.66, Fig. 27.67-69). One example (Fig. 26.66) appears in a context of the first half of the ninth century and the remainder occur in contexts dated to the late ninth to tenth century. At the Crypta Balbi these forms are dated to the ninth century (Romei 1986, 526, Tav. VII.5). Some handles, which probably belong to the above vessels (Fig. 27.70,71), include one example (Fig. 27.70) similar to that of a painted amphora of eighth century date (Paroli forthcoming a, Fig. 5.5) and of ninth century vessels at the Crypta Balbi (Romei 1986, Tav. VII.1).

Finally, it is interesting to note the presence of seven fragments (Fig. 27.72-75) which belong to lamps of a type documented at both Rome (Paroli forthcoming a, Figs. 5, 7 and 8) and Naples, as well as at Reggio Calabria and in Sicily (Garcea and Williams 1987, 541-543, Fig. 2.9-11). At Rome and Naples these lamps are characteristic of deposits of the eighth to early ninth century. The Santa Cornelia examples belong to the latest variant of this form, dated to the early ninth century (Paroli pers. comm.). This date conforms with their appearance in the Santa Cornelia sequence; apart from one handle present of phase 2a-b, all the examples are of phase 2c-d (early to mid-ninth century).

Between the mid-ninth and tenth century (phase 2d-g) certain of the above forms persist in small quantities but they are unlikely to date beyond the ninth century in terms of their actual production. The evidence from the Crypta Balbi indicates that production of the jugs and jars of small- and medium- sized dimensions virtually ceases after this date (Romei 1986, 526). The domestic pottery of phase 2d-g is dominated by fragments of thick-walled vessels, probably amphorae of medium to large dimensions, the majority of which occur in pottery groups which would fit perfectly with a tenth century date, on the evidence from the Crypta Balbi. These vessels are exclusively of fabric 5. No complete examples were recovered, the evidence being limited to numerous body fragments often with bands of

combed decoration and thick strap handles (Fig. 27.76,77). Only one rim was recovered but in a phase 3a context (early eleventh century). The strap handles contrast with the oval-section, sometimes ridged, handles of the domestic pottery of the eighth and ninth centuries. They appear for the first time in this period and remain a characteristic feature of the ceramic assemblage throughout the medieval period.

These vessels characterize the domestic pottery of the tenth century at the Crypta Balbi (Paroli pers. comm.; for complete examples of these forms see Romei 1986, 526, Tav.VIII,3,4). They are probably the precursors of the globular amphorae which dominate the domestic pottery assemblage from the eleventh century (Romei 1986, 526).

A vast quantity of domestic pottery was recovered from levels of the eleventh to thirteenth/fourteenth centuries (phase 3 onwards). In phase 3 (1000/1025-1300) certain of the forms common in eighth and ninth century levels are still present, but are probably residual. Instead one witnesses a continuation of the trends first noted in the tenth century. The production of vessels of small to medium dimensions appears to cease, with production now limited to two main forms, namely globular amphorae and, to a small extent, lids which first appear in this period. These vessels, as in the tenth century, are manufactured solely in fabric 5. However, a feature of this period is the increasing thinness of the walls of the vessels. Combed decoration, which is a common feature of the domestic pottery from the late eighth to tenth century, no longer occurs.

The globular amphora is characteristic of the domestic pottery from the eleventh to thirteenth and possibly fourteenth centuries. It has an omphalos base and two strap handles attached at the rim or neck and at the widest point of the body (Fig. 27.78-81, Fig. 28.82-83). Eleven examples are of phase 3, twenty-four examples of phase 4 and forty-three examples of phase 5. All the examples found, however, are likely to date between the eleventh and thirteenth to fourteenth centuries on comparison with the Crypta Balbi sequence. The earliest examples at Santa Cornelia are of phase 3b-c, provisionally dated to the eleventh and twelfth centuries. The form evolves through time, from examples of phase 3b-c, with an upright rim and fairly thick strap handle, which are still similar to tenth century forms (Fig. 27.78,79, these forms at the Crypta Balbi dating to the eleventh century), to progressively thinner walled vessels of a very refined fabric (Fig. 27.80-81, Fig. 28.82-83). The strap handles become wider and thinner and, from at least the twelfth century onwards, expand towards the centre. The rims show considerable but slight variations, ranging from short upright rims, to tall rims sometimes with an everted lip, and to inflaring rims. The latter may belong to the amphorae with biconical bodies which at the Crypta Balbi appear alongside the globular amphorae from the thirteenth century and continue throughout the fourteenth century (Romei 1986, 529, Tav. IX.1). At Santa Cornelia this rim form occurs from the latest levels of phase 3 onwards.

The lids associated with these vessels occur in small quantities from phase 3e onwards (twelfth to thirteenth century). Fifteen examples were found, comprising two main forms: one has a vertical lip (Fig. 28.84,85), similar to contemporary sparse glazed lids and coarse ware *testi* forms, which at the Crypta Balbi is dated to the eleventh to

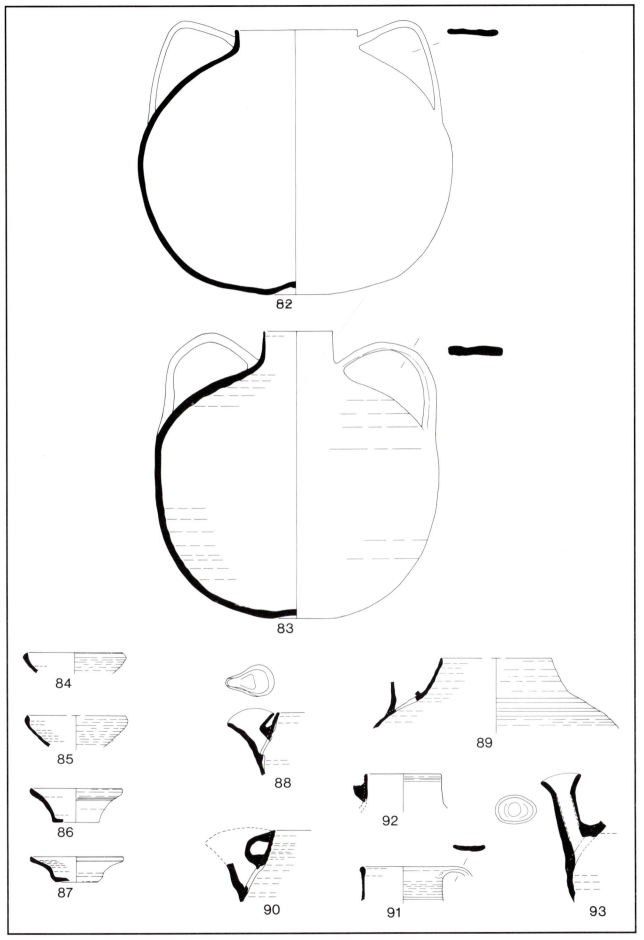

Fig. 28. Santa Cornelia: medieval domestic pottery (*acroma depurata*) (numbers 82-93) (SC)

twelfth century (Romei 1986, 529, Tav. VIII,5); the other is a form with flaring walls (Fig. 28.85,86), dated at the Crypta Balbi to the thirteenth and fourteenth centuries (Romei 1986, 529, Tav. IX,2).

Sometime during the later twelfth to thirteenth century new forms appear alongside the globular amphora: this includes a series of jugs in standardized forms with a flat base, usually inflaring neck and plain rim, sometimes rilled, a flaring spout and narrow strap handle (Fig. 28.88-92). The base is often knife-trimmed. The fabric of these vessels is usually oxidized and light red in colour (fabric 7). Two main forms have been identified: firstly, a jug with an inflaring neck, a plain usually rilled rim and a short flaring pinched spout (Fig. 28.88,89); secondly, a jug with an inflaring neck, plain rim and elongated flaring spout attached by a bridge to the rim (Fig. 28.90). A large number of rims recovered may also belong to these vessels or to the later globular amphorae (see above). The forms are the same as those of the contemporary latest sparse glazed ware and the fabric (fabric 7) appears identical. As a result it has not always been possible to distinguish between unglazed and sparse glazed vessels, especially since the glaze on the later sparse glazed ware forms is generally restricted to a thin application around the shoulder of the vessel. In cases where only the rims have been recorded it is, therefore, highly probable that at least some of these examples belong in fact to sparse glaze vessels. At the Crypta Balbi these forms first appear at the beginning of the thirteenth century (Romei 1986, 529, Tav.X.1,2,4) and unglazed examples continue to be produced after the disappearance of sparse glaze around the mid-thirteenth century (Paroli pers.comm.). At Santa Cornelia they appear in the later levels of phase 3 and in phases 4 and 5, that is from the late twelfth/thirteenth centuries onwards.

In phase 4 a few body sherds are present which are probably from amphorae of fourteenth century date, on the basis of parallels with the Crypta Balbi (Paroli pers. comm.; for a complete example of these vessels, see Romei 1986, Tav. IX,3). No forms were identified but the fragments are lightly rilled on the exterior. All the examples are of fabric 5. One other form worth noting is a tubular spout in a phase 3 context (Fig. 28.93).

(iii) AMPHORAE POSSIBLY USED FOR TRANSPORT

A number of fragments were recovered from thick-walled vessels, probably amphorae which may have been used for transport. The fragments, with the exception of one base, are all body sherds. Four main fabrics were identified (fabrics 8-11); although still fairly refined they are usually visibly coarser than those used for the domestic pottery. These vessels occur mainly in contexts of phase 1 and phase 2a-d and it is likely that they were in use no later than the mid-ninth century. They are the only possible examples of early medieval, as opposed to Roman, pottery found in secure phase 1 contexts, that is in the pre-*domusculta* phase. Nine fragments were recovered in phase 1 of fabrics 10 and 11.

(iv) PAINTED POTTERY

Apart from a brief period of production in the eighth and early ninth century as attested at Rome (Paroli forthcoming a) and at Monte Gelato (Patterson, material under study), pottery with painted decoration is not documented in Rome and the surrounding area until the thirteenth century. Finds are recorded from Rome itself (Paroli 1985, 204-205; Romei 1986, 529) and various sites in the Roman Campagna (Whitehouse 1978), including Tuscania (Andrews 1982, 110-111; Johns *et al.* 1973) and Civitavecchia (Mazzucato 1976, 16). At the Crypta Balbi, painted pottery appears in the late twelfth to thirteenth century but production seems to have ceased before the end of the thirteenth century (Paroli 1985, 205; Romei 1986, 529).

At Santa Cornelia one fragment with a broad band of painted decoration in red slip was recovered from a mid-ninth to tenth century context (phase 2d-g). The decoration recalls that of the eighth and early ninth century painted pottery from Rome and Monte Gelato. Other examples of painted pottery first appear in contexts of the late twelfth to thirteenth century and are identical to the painted pottery found in Rome and elsewhere in the Roman Campagna in this period (see above). The painted decoration on these examples is applied exclusively in narrow bands. This ware continues to be present in deposits dated to the fourteenth century. Although it is possible that painted pottery remained in use longer at Santa Cornelia, given the high proportion of residual material present, this date must be treated with caution. The painted decoration consists of narrow lines of usually red, occasionally black, slip painted on to the exterior surface of the vessel. The fabric appears identical to that of the contemporary domestic pottery (fabric 5). The few forms recovered are from closed vessels, probably jugs, with tall vertical or inflaring necks and plain rims, tubular spouts, thin strap handles and flat bases (for illustrated examples from Santa Cornelia, see Whitehouse 1980a, Fig. 12.120-127).

(v) CERAMICA A VETRINA PESANTE ALTOMEDIEVALE (FORUM WARE) AND SPARSE GLAZED WARE (Fig. 29)

The pottery discussed in this section belongs to the early medieval and medieval production of glazed pottery characteristic of Rome and the surrounding area and known as *ceramica a vetrina pesante* (Mazzucato 1972), or Forum Ware (Whitehouse 1965), and sparse glazed ware. These, it should be stressed, are not two separate classes of pottery but two successive phases of glazed pottery production. It is now clear that the original division of these glazed products into *ceramica a vetrina pesante* or Forum Ware and sparse glazed ware is somewhat over-simplistic and that the early medieval and medieval glazed pottery of Rome underwent a fairly gradual evolution, one of the main characteristics of which is a progressive diminution in the amount of glaze used and in the surface area of the vessel on which it was applied (see Paroli 1990 for a detailed description of the gradual changes in the application of the glaze). Nevertheless the distinction is useful for the purposes of description and in general terms has validity. Although recent work, in particular that of Paroli, has clarified many of the problems concerning the origins and the chronology of this early medieval and medieval glazed pottery (see Paroli 1986a; 1986b; 1990; forthcoming a, for detailed discussion of these wares), it has been and continues to be the subject of some debate.

Ceramica a vetrina pesante is the earliest medieval glazed pottery of Italian production; it is most common at Rome where vast quantities of the type known as Forum Ware have been recovered. The term Forum Ware is used here to refer specifically to this early medieval *ceramica a vetrina pesante* of Rome and the surrounding area, including the vessels from Santa Cornelia, which form a distinct and homogenous group. The vessels are predominantly closed forms, in particular jugs with spouts covered with a lead based glaze. The glaze is generally olive green in colour but frequently has a brownish or yellowish tone. The chronology of Forum Ware has been the subject of much controversy. It has been attributed, at various times, to the late Roman period (Cameron *et al.* 1984, 67; Reece 1982, 138-139; Whitehouse 1980b; 1981) to the early medieval period (Whitehouse 1965; 1980a, 153-155; Paroli 1986a; 1986b) and to the medieval period (Mazzucato 1972; 1976) (see Christie 1987 for a discussion of the arguments for dating). The sequence established by the excavations at the Crypta Balbi (Paroli 1986a; 1986b; 1990; forthcoming a), and now supported by finds from other excavations in Rome (such as at San Sisto Vecchio and San Clemente (information of Annis and Guidobaldi as quoted in Paroli forthcoming a and b)), finally seems to have established an initial date for the production of Forum Ware in the late eighth century, reaching a peak in the mid- to late ninth century. Production continues through to the thirteenth century, but with a gradual decrease in the amount of glaze used, (Paroli 1986a; 1986b; 1990). The same products are found, in smaller quantities, around Rome, and recently examples of the Rome production of *ceramica a vetrina pesante* of the Forum Ware type have been identified along the Tyrrhenian coast from Genoa, Savona, Marseilles, and along the Sardinian and Corsican coasts (Bonifay *et al.* 1986). *Ceramica a vetrina pesante* is found more sporadically in southern Italy, but here the forms and decoration follow a different development (Patterson 1989; Paroli forthcoming a).

Two main hypotheses have been proposed to explain the origins of early medieval glazed pottery. Firstly, it has been argued that these wares may represent continuity from late Roman glazed ware production as found widely in northern Italy and to a very small extent in Rome itself (Arthur and Williams 1981; Blake 1981b; *Ceramica Invetriata* 1985; Meneghini and Staffa 1985; Morgan 1942, 51-52). Although we cannot ignore the possibility of some continuity of production from the late Roman products attested in Rome in the fourth and fifth centuries (Meneghini and Staffa 1985; Whitehouse *et al.* 1985, 207), the evidence overall suggests that this is not the case and instead these late Roman products should be seen more in terms of the north Italian material as summarized by Blake (1981b). No direct link has yet been established between the late Roman glazed wares and *ceramica a vetrina pesante* of early medieval date which appears to be clearly distinct from the former both on morphological and decorative grounds. Despite this, the term *ceramica a vetrina pesante* is sometimes used to describe late Roman glazed products. To avoid confusion, Paroli has suggested that the term *ceramica a vetrina pesante altomedievale* should be used to distinguish the early medieval products from those of late Roman date (Paroli 1990, 314-315).

The second and more probable hypothesis is that the early medieval production of *ceramica a vetrina pesante* may have derived from earlier and similar Byzantine products (Hodges and Patterson 1986, 24-25; Paroli 1986b, 80-81; 1990; forthcoming a; Patterson and Whitehouse forthcoming a and b; Whitehouse 1965). Glazed pottery production is documented in the Byzantine world from the seventh century onwards (Bass and van Doornick 1982, vol. 1, 165-167; Hayes 1968, 203f; forthcoming). At the Crypta Balbi in late eighth century levels glazed chafing dishes occur alongside the first examples of *ceramica a vetrina pesante* of the Forum Ware type. Although of local production, these forms are typical of Byzantine pottery and some of the domestic pottery of this period also shows the influence of Byzantine forms (Paroli 1990; forthcoming a). Similarly, excavations at Otranto in Apulia found imported Byzantine glazed wares alongside *ceramica a vetrina pesante* of local production in contexts of the ninth to eleventh century (Patterson forthcoming c; Patterson and Whitehouse forthcoming a). The evidence suggests, therefore, that the revival of the production of glazed pottery may have been due, at least in part, to the contacts known to have existed between the Byzantine world and large areas of Italy in this period.

An additional, but less discussed, factor which cannot be ignored is the effect of Carolingian influence on the development of *ceramica a vetrina pesante*. It is noteworthy that the dramatic increase in the production of *ceramica a vetrina pesante* of the Forum Ware type occurs in the ninth century when Rome was under strong Carolingian influence and Byzantine power in Italy was at a low ebb. Despite the lack of evidence for a direct connection between the late Roman and early medieval glazed production, there are certain similarities between the products of the two periods. In particular the use of applied petal decoration is a characteristic feature of both late Roman and eighth and ninth century Forum Ware products, although the forms are different. This revival of ancient models is a characteristic feature of this period of Carolingian renaissance, the same phenomenon occurring in other aspects of material culture such as sculpture (Paroli 1990) and architecture. Furthermore, a common jug form of the ninth century Forum Ware (Whitehouse 1965, Fig. 16.2d, Fig. 17.3a-b; Paroli 1986a, Tav. III.7 and 9a-b) is very similar to a type widely diffused in northern Europe in the Carolingian period, and is a type which in its turn was derived from earlier Merovingian products (Paroli 1990). As Paroli states, '*accanto alla più scontata "connessione bizantina" si profila dunque nella storia della ceramica a vetrina pesante di Roma del IX secolo una "connessione carolingia", espressione dell'affermazione di un egemonia, puntualemente riflessa nella più umile tra le arti applicati, i cui effetti non mancheranno di farsi sentire nella progressiva emancipazione della produzione romana dall'influenza orientale*' (Paroli 1990, 318-319).

The typological and decorative evolution of the *ceramica a vetrina pesante* and sparse glazed ware from Santa Cornelia follows that documented at sites in Rome and other sites in the Roman Campagna. The *ceramica a vetrina pesante* has all the characteristics of the Rome products and is referred to as Forum Ware; the sparse glazed ware, as noted above, is simply a later development of this production. It is present from the earliest medieval levels (phase 2a-b: 774-815), relating to the foundation of the *domusculta*, until the final phase of occupation of the site, although it is probable that examples in phases 4 and 5 (1400 onwards) are residual. The production of Forum Ware persists throughout phase 2 (late eighth to tenth century) and it is only in the latest

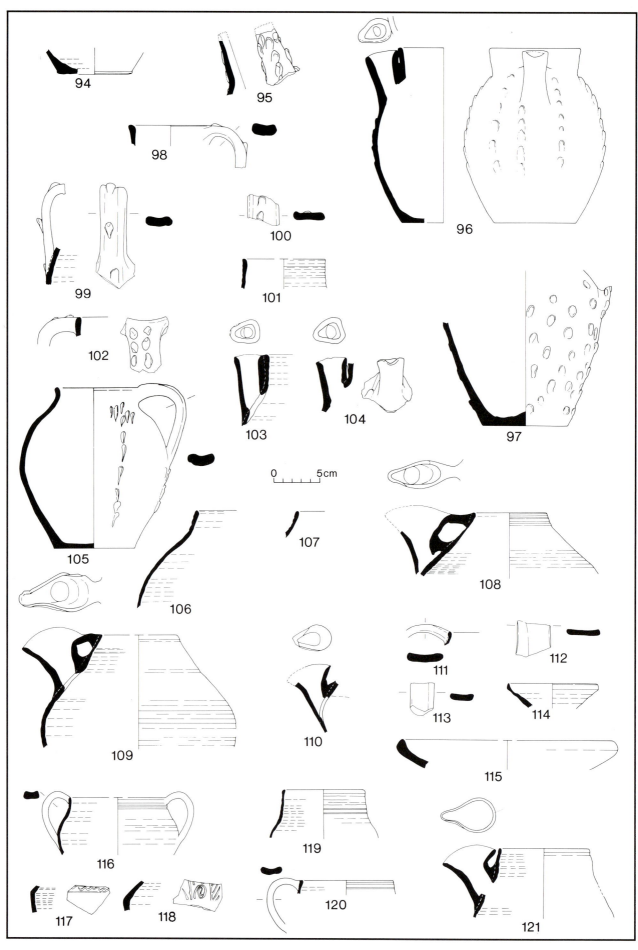

Fig. 29. Santa Cornelia: Forum ware and sparse glazed ware (numbers 94-121) (SC)

levels of this phase that the first examples of sparse glazed ware appear, the glaze no longer covering the whole of the exterior surface of the vessels. By phase 3 (eleventh to thirteenth century) finds of Forum Ware are clearly residual and the majority of the glazed pottery can be securely identified as sparse glazed ware. In phase 2 the glazed pottery comprises 6.8% of the assemblage, whilst in phase 3 this percentage has doubled (15.4%), indicating a notable increase in production in this period. There is a corresponding decrease both in the quantity and range of unglazed domestic pottery: in particular the jugs and jars of small to medium dimensions disappear. It seems likely that these factors are related and that sparse glaze forms now served many of the functions originally performed by the unglazed domestic pottery.

Forms

Virtually all the vessels recovered are jugs. Rare examples of lids and some possible open vessels were also found. In contexts of the ninth and tenth centuries the jugs have ovoid bodies, flat bases, a tubular spout, usually attached to the rim, and kidney section handles. Applied petal decoration is a common feature of these vessels. From the eleventh century onwards new jug forms appear with a biconical body, a flaring spout pinched at the lip, which is sometimes attached to the rim by a bridge, and a thin strap handle. Decoration on these vessels is rare and the use of applied petal decoration appears to have ceased completely.

Fabrics

The fabrics of the early medieval and medieval glazed pottery from Santa Cornelia were analysed petrologically as part of a large-scale thin sectioning project organized by Siena University, with the analysis being undertaken at Genoa University. This project comprised the analysis of a vast number of samples of both Roman and early medieval and medieval glazed pottery from all over Italy (Paroli forthcoming b). Samples of Forum Ware and sparse glazed ware from several sites excavated by the British School at Rome in the Roman Campagna were analysed. The results indicate a more complex picture for the production of this class of pottery than was thought previously (Patterson forthcoming b). These results are considered more fully in the discussion below. The analysis showed that at Santa Cornelia the Forum Ware is of two fabrics. The predominant fabric (fabric 11) is different to that of the majority of the Forum Ware of Rome. The origin of this clay is uncertain: it does not contain volcanic inclusions which is contrary to what one would expect given the geology of the area. The second fabric is, however, of a volcanic and sedimentary clay identical to that of the Rome products (fabric 12). The latest examples of Forum Ware (late tenth/eleventh centuries) and of the sparse glazed ware of the eleventh century onwards are again of a different clay (fabric 13). This clay is very refined, similar in fact to fabric 5 used for the production of unglazed domestic pottery; as a result the identification of a provenance is difficult. It is an alluvial clay, probably found near rivers, which could be local or sub-regional. It is not clear if it represents a different clay source or is simply a more refined version of fabric 11, but it is clearly different

to fabric 12 and to the fabric of the sparse glazed ware of Rome. The adoption of a very refined clay is, however, characteristic of the sparse glazed pottery in use throughout the Roman Campagna. From the later twelfth/thirteenth centuries some of the sparse glaze is of an oxidized light red fabric (fabric 7), indistinguishable macroscopically from that of some of the unglazed domestic pottery of the same period. The refined nature of this fabric makes valid macroscopic fabric groupings very difficult and it is possible that this clay is simply a refined version of fabric 13 fired in an oxidizing atmosphere (see fabric descriptions in Appendix 2).

Chronology

At Santa Cornelia, Forum Ware first appears in phase 2a-b (774-815); ten fragments were recovered from quantified deposits (Fig. 29.94), of which four have applied petal decoration in vertical lines. In contexts of the first half of the ninth century there are six fragments, including four with applied petal decoration. Similar fragments (Fig. 29.95) to one of the latter were present as residual material in a later context and may belong to the same vessel. These early examples of the late eighth to mid-ninth century have a noticeably coarse fabric, which is sometimes oxidized, and the glaze is thick and shiny, often brownish yellow as opposed to a green, and generally applied over both the exterior and interior surfaces.

In phase 2d-f (second half of the ninth to tenth century) the fabric of the Forum Ware becomes more refined and the glaze becomes thinner and less shiny. The glaze still generally covers the whole of the exterior surface but on the interior it is increasingly limited to splashes and drips of glaze. The glaze is usually green, often tinged with brown, examples with a yellow brown glaze no longer occurring. Applied petal decoration is still common. The material includes two almost complete vessels: both are jugs with ovoid bodies, flat bases and slightly flaring tubular spouts attached to the rim. Both vessels have applied petal decoration over the body (Fig. 29.96,97). Several rims and handles were recovered which probably belong to jugs. The rims are tall, often rilled, and in some cases have a kidney section handle attached to the top of the rim. The handles frequently have one or two vertical lines of applied petals (Fig. 29.98-102). Although the quantity of material recovered from phase 2 is relatively small it appears to conform with the sequence established for Forum Ware at the Crypta Balbi. Three other forms are likely to be of the ninth and tenth centuries respectively, on the basis of parallels with the Crypta Balbi material (Paroli pers. comm.), although they occur later in the stratigraphic sequence (Fig. 29.103-105).

Developments after phase 2 can be followed with less certainty. The first examples of sparse glazed ware appear in contexts dated to the late tenth to early eleventh century, and are characterized by a more refined fabric and a reduction in the amount of glaze used. It is likely that two forms (Fig. 29.106-107), although found in later or disturbed contexts, are of the late tenth/early eleventh century on the basis of parallels from the Crypta Balbi. One of these forms (Fig. 29.106) is clearly residual, the second form (Fig. 29.107), however, is present in contexts of the eleventh to the beginning of the twelfth century.

The material of the eleventh to thirteenth century (phase 3) is characterized by a further reduction in the amount of glaze, which becomes increasingly restricted to certain areas of the vessel, and the use of a very refined fabric (fabric 13). Only two decorated fragments (see below) were found and the use of applied petal decoration appears to have completely ceased by this period. It is probable that the examples of Forum Ware in these levels are residual. The glaze on the sparse glazed products of the eleventh century onwards is increasingly concentrated around the shoulder of the vessel with the rim, spout and base either being left unglazed or, more rarely, having a very thin covering of glaze. By the late twelfth to thirteenth centuries the glaze is often reduced to a smear around the shoulder of the vessel.

The vessel forms are now fairly standardized, characterized by jugs with thin strap handles, biconical bodies and thin inflaring rims, the neck of the vessel having disappeared, and a variety of flaring, elongated, pinched spouts being attached by a bridge to the rim (Fig. 29.108-110; Fig. 29.111-113). These are the standard forms of sparse glazed pottery in deposits of the eleventh and twelfth centuries and continue to be present in deposits of the late twelfth/thirteenth centuries. In the same period, from the eleventh or twelfth century onwards, rare examples of lids first appear (Fig. 29.114, 115) and there is one unusual form, possibly an open vessel (Fig. 29.111). Two fragments of an open carinate vessel are the only decorated examples recovered after phase 2 (Fig. 29.117,118). They are from phase 3 and have unusual incised decoration, with both the decoration and the glaze limited to the area above the carination.

Sparse glazed ware seems to have reached the final phase of its development in the latest levels of phase 3 (late twelfth to thirteenth century). These vessels are characterized by a very refined fabric and a further reduction in the amount of glaze, now limited to a smear around the shoulder of the vessel. The jug forms first attested in contexts of the eleventh/twelfth centuries continue (see for example Fig. 29.109) but they are accompanied by new jug forms (Fig. 29.119-121) with a lightly inflaring neck which is distinct from the shoulder, a thin strap handle and a squatter pinched spout detached from the rim. The flat bases of these vessels are often knife-trimmed. The forms are the same as that of contemporary unglazed vessels (see *acroma depurata*), as is the oxidized, light red fabric. The difficulty of distinguishing between the unglazed and glazed vessels has already been noted.

At Rome these late twelfth/thirteenth century forms represent the latest phase in the production of sparse glazed pottery which appears to end sometime in the early thirteenth century (Paroli 1986a; 1986b; 1990, numbers 337-341). It is impossible to determine how long sparse glazed pottery remained in use at Santa Cornelia: it is still present in phases 4 and 5 but the forms show no change and given the disturbed nature of these contexts it is highly likely that these finds are residual.

DISCUSSION

The ceramic sequence at Santa Cornelia closely follows developments at Rome, distinguished only, and not surprisingly, by the smaller variety of pottery types available at the *domusculta*. Material from excavations elsewhere in the Roman Campagna shows a similar picture.

The evidence suggests that a common potting tradition existed throughout northern Latium from the late eighth century onwards. Potters working on a fast wheel produced a range of standardized forms which reflect a fairly high degree of specialization. Even a more exotic ware such as Forum Ware, present in large quantities in Rome itself, seems to have been available, although to a much smaller extent, over a wide area of Latium.

The ceramic material from the earliest occupation phases of Santa Cornelia (phase 2a-d: late eighth to mid-ninth century) is characterized by a wide range of forms, many of which recall late Roman and Byzantine potting traditions. The unglazed domestic pottery (*acroma depurata*), in particular, is notable for the variety of its forms, the finishing techniques used (note the lighter surface colour and the knife-trimmed and wire-cut bases), and the ample use of decoration. The Forum Ware of this period, although present in small quantities, has similar characteristics; the products have a thick glaze applied on both surfaces and decoration is very common. All these elements indicate a high level of specialization and also a high labour investment in terms of time/energy and therefore cost.

During the tenth to eleventh century the ceramic assemblage underwent some significant changes and certain trends emerge which are to intensify in later periods. From the tenth century there are certain typological changes which mark a final break with late Roman and Byzantine potting traditions and the emergence of a purely medieval typology. A similar phenomenon has been noted in other regions of Italy in this period (Patterson 1989). In addition one notes an increasing standardization of the ceramic wares, probably reflecting an increasing trend towards specialized production on an 'industrial' scale: this is especially evident in the domestic and glazed pottery.

The most marked change occurs in the domestic pottery. In the tenth century the small- to medium-sized vessels which recall late Roman and Byzantine forms seem to disappear. The kitchen wares demonstrate a similar break with past traditions, and the general similarity to late Roman forms is no longer evident. The oval-section, sometimes ridged, handles of the domestic pottery are replaced by the strap handles which are to characterize the domestic and kitchen pottery throughout the medieval period. The kidney section handles of the glazed pottery may have persisted throughout the tenth century, but by the eleventh century they too have disappeared, to be replaced by strap handles. The tenth century pottery assemblage is therefore distinguished by the emergence of a purely medieval potting tradition. The same forms, although undergoing a gradual evolution, are to characterize the ceramic assemblage until the late twelfth to thirteenth century when the appearance of new kitchen and domestic pottery forms, soon followed by the presence on a large scale of both lead and tin glazed tablewares, marks a renewed vigour in the potting industries.

The medieval pottery assemblage of the tenth century onwards is marked by a reduction in the range of forms, which are increasingly limited to a restricted number of standardized vessels. The disappearance of the small- to medium-sized domestic ware containers is probably at least partly due to the increase in glazed pottery which occurs from around the eleventh century. However, the sparse glazed pottery of the eleventh century is limited to one main form, the jug with a flaring pinched spout. The kitchen wares are restricted to two standard forms, two handled jars and *testi*, whilst the domestic pottery is, by the eleventh century, overwhelmingly dominated by the globular amphora.

Contemporary with this reduction in the range of forms is the virtual disappearance of decoration on both glazed and domestic pottery, a marked decrease in the amount of glaze used, increasingly refined fabrics, and increasingly thin walled vessels. The use of combed decoration, characteristic of the late eighth to tenth century pottery, seems to have completely disappeared by the eleventh century, and the production of knife-trimmed wire-cut bases and vessels with a lighter surface colour ceases probably in the tenth century. The use of applied petal decoration on Forum Ware persists, although to a lesser degree, until the end of the tenth century, but by the eleventh century it is no longer attested and decoration of any sort is rare. Similarly the glaze from the mid-ninth century is increasingly thinner and more opaque, and by the late tenth to eleventh century the first secure examples of sparse glazed pottery appear. This trend towards increasing standardization intensifies from the eleventh century reaching a peak in the late twelfth to thirteenth century. It is characterized by the use of increasingly refined fabrics, thinner walled vessels, and a continued reduction in the amount of glaze used. All these elements suggest a trend towards specialist production on an 'industrial' scale in terms of reduced time and labour and lower costs.

These changes in the ceramic assemblage are important indicators of wider changes which were occurring in the production and distribution of ceramic goods. The analysis of the pottery from Santa Cornelia suggests the following phases of ceramic production. An initial phase in the late eighth and ninth centuries is characterized by heavy investment in ceramic production: a large range of forms was produced, demonstrating a variety of decorative and finishing techniques. This was followed, in the tenth or eleventh to twelfth century, by a phase of mass replication of standardized commodities, the refinement of vessel forms and an increasing streamlining of production. Finally, from the late twelfth to thirteenth century, a production phase characterized by an increased variety of forms as well as the appearance of new ceramic products may be identified. A similar sequence can be suggested for the pottery from other sites of this period in Rome and northern Latium.

Although it has some interesting implications for our understanding of social and economic developments in this period (note, for example, its close similarity to Rathje's cost-control model (Rathje 1975)), this abstract picture of pottery production is of limited use. The production sites, their location and nature, the systems by which products were distributed and changes in these through time, are fundamental aspects, of which we know virtually nothing. Furthermore, the evidence from Santa Cornelia must be seen in its regional context. It is only by understanding the mechanisms of production and distribution of pottery on a regional level that we can begin to approach an understanding of the wider socio-economic system to which they belonged. As noted in the introduction, it is only recently that the establishment of a datable pottery types series has meant that ceramic studies of this period

can now approach these wider problems. In northern Latium studies of this nature are only just beginning.

Production centres must have existed at Rome but none has yet been securely identified. Sherds of Forum Ware found in the Roman Forum included a possible waster (Whitehouse 1980a, 146), which may indicate a production centre in the vicinity. The only kiln site recovered so far is at Monte Gelato (Potter and King 1988; Patterson, material under study). The kiln produced a range of unglazed domestic pottery (and possibly painted pottery) types, identical to those at Rome and Santa Cornelia, of the late eighth and beginning of the ninth century.

Some petrological studies have been carried out which give some clue as to the distribution of ceramic goods and possible areas of provenance. Schuring's work on the coarse wares from Rome and various sites in the Roman Campagna is fundamental (Schuring 1986; 1987). The majority of the coarse wares of the medieval period, including those from Santa Cornelia, are of a volcanic clay which is found over large areas of Lazio. Analysis of Forum Ware and sparse glazed pottery from sites in Rome and several sites in the Roman Campagna produced some interesting results and indicated at least four, possibly five, production areas (Paroli forthcoming b; Patterson forthcoming b). A detailed examination of the clays of Rome and the surrounding area, however, has not been carried out yet; therefore the possible provenances of the clay sources of the fabrics have still to be identified on a systematic basis. Some preliminary observations, however, can be made relating to the distribution of the fabrics of these wares and to some of the possible provenances and therefore production areas of these fabrics, although these should be regarded as tentative.

Three broad fabric groups were identified. The fabrics of the Forum Ware and sparse glazed ware from the majority of the sites studied (Cencelle, Anguillara, Mazzano Romano, Pianabella (Ostia), Crypta Balbi and San Sisto Vecchio (Rome)), although showing some differences, are compatible with the geology of Rome and northern Latium. The fabric of the sparse glazed pottery is, however, noticeably more refined than that of the Forum Ware and it is possible that in this later production phase the clay was extracted nearer the surface (Annis forthcoming). The ninth and tenth century Forum Ware from Santa Cornelia and Santa Rufina, however, is more problematic. At Santa Cornelia only one part of the Forum Ware can be assigned to the above group; the remainder of the samples analysed, and virtually all of the samples from Santa Rufina, contained no volcanic inclusions and clay sources for these vessels must belong to a pre-volcanic geological phase. One example of this non-volcanic fabric has also been identified in the Forum Ware from Cencelle (Coccia and Nardi forthcoming). Pliocenic clays, belonging to the pre-volcanic phase, occur as outcrops in certain areas of Latium and a study of these clays is currently being carried out to ascertain if they represent possible clay sources for this fabric. The third fabric group is characteristic of the Forum Ware of the late tenth to eleventh centuries at Monte Gelato and Santa Cornelia, and of the sparse glazed ware from Santa Cornelia and Santa Rufina. It is a generic, alluvial clay which could be of local or sub-regional provenance and it is possible that it is a refined version of the non-volcanic fabric described above.

It is interesting to note that at Rome the Forum Ware

and kitchen ware are of the same fabric and were possibly produced at the same centres (Annis pers. comm.). This is compatible with the mode of pottery production defined by Peacock as urban nucleated industries (Peacock 1982, 39-40). These are specialist industries which manufacture a wide range of pottery types, including both coarse and fine wares, to meet 'the multifarious requirements of the urban market and its hinterland' (Peacock 1982, 40). At Santa Cornelia and Santa Rufina, however, it is likely that both the kitchen wares and domestic pottery were produced locally, but given that the Forum Ware in this period only occurs in small quantities it may have come from outside the immediate vicinity of these sites. From the late tenth to eleventh century the picture changes, and it is probable that the increase in the quantity of glazed pottery noted in this period, reflects an increase in the number of production centres manufacturing this ware.

The analyses so far raise more questions than they answer, but they allow us to make some observations and, in so doing, point the direction for future research. It is only by developing studies such as these that we can begin to make initial attempts at understanding the complexities of ceramic production and distribution in this area in the early medieval and medieval periods. Detailed quantified ceramic studies carried out on a regional level, incorporating systematic fabric sampling with petrological analysis, and a detailed study of the clays, as well as a careful study of the documentary sources, are fundamental for a valid discussion of these problems. In this way ceramic studies can make a valuable contribution to our understanding of the wider social and economic developments in this period.

Table 7. NUMBERS OF RIMS

	WARE			
PHASE	Kitchen	Domestic	Glazed*	Painted
2a-d	10	24	1	0
2e-f	4	3	2	0
3	79	31	20	0
4	84	39	10	3
5	61	47	8	1

* Glazed refers to Forum Ware and sparse glazed ware only.

Table 8. PERCENTAGES OF RIMS

	WARE			
PHASE	Kitchen	Domestic	Glazed*	Painted
2	31.8	61.4	6.8	0
3	60.8	23.8	15.4	0
4	61.8	28.7	7.3	2.2
5	52.1	40.2	6.8	0.9

* Glazed refers to Forum Ware and sparse glazed ware only.

(x) THE INSCRIPTIONS

Joyce Reynolds

The inscriptions from Santa Cornelia comprise a very small Christian group (numbers 1-3, two certain and one probable) and a large pre-Christian one, in which most stones seem to belong to the second or third centuries AD: almost all are in very fragmentary condition. It is reasonable to conjecture that number 1, of the ninth century, was designed for the site and is a record of some unknown action here by Pope Paschal I (817-824). Most of the other inscribed stones, and perhaps all, are likely to have been brought to the site as debris to be used in building, probably in building the church of Hadrian I; exceptions could be thé three inscriptions preserved in the *cortile* of the Casale di Santa Cornelia (numbers 5, 11, 17), which, since they are in much better condition than any found in the excavation, could have come from local tombs. Most of the remaining material may well derive from Rome; but since a Roman origin cannot be precisely demonstrated for any stone, as it can at Santa Rufina, the possibility that other sites, such as Veii, may have contributed cannot be excluded. Much of it certainly comes from funerary contexts, but numbers 4, 6 and 7 in particular need not. Very many items look as if they come from communal *columbaria* or the like, but some indubitably were from built family tombs (e.g. numbers 5, 9, 20). The social status of those recorded ranges from a senatorial family (number 4) to slaves (7, 27). There are even a few Greek-speakers (52, 53). I would suggest that the debris was of mixed origin from cemeteries on the north side of Rome.

The Christian texts are placed first as being in a special relation to the excavated buildings. With the pagan texts, references to senators come first, followed by those to *equites*, to a *collegium*, to soldiers, to civilians with stated functions, to other civilians (first those with surviving *nomina*, then those with surviving *cognomina* only – both in alphabetical order), and finally nameless groups of funerary formulae. Throughout this catalogue, numbers without a prefix are inventory numbers at the *Museo dell'Alto Medioevo*, Rome, and numbers preceded by SC are excavation fragment numbers. Stones are inscribed on one face unless otherwise stated.

CHRISTIAN TEXTS

1. 2109 = SC265. Fragment from top and right side of a marble panel (0.64 x 0.40 × 0.10 m). Letters, probably Carolingian [1]: 0.10-0.13; stops between syllables (Pl. 53).

```
        ...] PAS stop QUA stop LIS stop
          ...]ER stop SA stop LIS stop
   [...
```

Line 2, only part of serif of first letter survives, but it is enough to restrict the choice of words here to *anniversalis, universalis*.

The style of this inscription and its isolation within a long period of time which is anepigraphic at Santa Cornelia, justifies the suggestion that it may refer to the early ninth century Pope Paschal, although it is not clear what he might be recorded as doing; perhaps something connected with an annual festival of the saints buried in the church, cf. *an[niversari]o sanctorum mar(tyr)um* proposed in *ILCV* 2021. Whether or not that is the correct interpretation, this, which is the only inscription from the site contemporary with any of the buildings excavated, is evidence that *Capracorum* was touched, however slightly, by that aspect of the Carolingian revival which left a stronger mark in the wealth of inscriptions at San Vincenzo al Volturno (Hodges and Mitchell 1985). We may suspect that the breakdown of words into syllables on this stone is the mark of a craftsman who lacked confidence in his literacy.

[1]. I am grateful to John Ward-Perkins and more recently Dr R. McKitterick for advice here. [Ed. We must note, however, that recent reanalysis of this inscription by Dr G. Pani argues for a reading of the initial Ṗ as Ṛ, with ṚAS marking the end of a word not the start. He further points out that the form PASQUALIS does not occur in any known inscription – PASCHALIS is the form employed. Dr Pani nonetheless maintains an attribution of the inscription to the first half of the ninth century. (My thanks to Lidia Paroli for this information.)]

2. 1937 + 1964c = SC192 + 229. Two adjoining pieces from upper left corner of a white marble panel (0.25 × 0.15 × 0.35). Letters, perhaps fourth century: 0.025-0.03; uncial *u*.

```
   vac.  Chrism vac. [  ?vacat   ]
   stop D stop VLVENES[ ..?..    ?pare-?stop M stop]
     ntis stop dulci[ssimi...
```

Plate 53. Santa Cornelia: inscription number 1 (*Museo dell'Alto Medioevo*, Rome)

The lettering, although surely post-classical, shows none of the characteristics of number 1. The dating proposed for it is, of course, very tentative; the *chrism* places the stone in or after the reign of Constantine, but certainly continued in use for some time thereafter (Bruun 1963, 159). It is a reasonable conjecture (incorporated into the printed text) that the pagan formula *D(is) M(anibus)* was used here as in a number of Christian inscriptions, for which a tentative *terminus ante quem* in the second half of the fourth century has been proposed (Nordberg 1963, 211-222). If its presence is not accepted, the deceased used a *praenomen*, *D(ecimus)* which is very unusual indeed in Christian inscriptions (Kajanto 1963, 40-72). The name VLVENES[, although at first sight a barbarous single name, probably has connections with good Roman *nomina*, cf. especially Uluienus (*CIL* VI. 33857) and Uluius, and there could have been space for a short *cognomen* after it in the second part of line 1; the indications are that the man did not after all conform to the single-name system which began to prevail in the fourth century – which provides another argument for placing the stone earlier rather than later in the Christian period.

3. 2696 = SC565. Fragment of a white marble panel without cut edges, published from a photograph. Letters, perhaps fourth century.

```
                    ...]
         ...uixit] annis [...
    ... ?positus es]t kal.  stop S[ep]t(embribus) [...
```

The date preceded by a T suggests a funerary formula of the Christian period as proposed, but it is not certain; the letter forms could be rather earlier than suggested.

PRE-CHRISTIAN TEXTS

4. 8635 = SC124; 1929 (SC number not known); 1917 = SC693. Three pieces from a panel of coloured marble inscribed on both faces.

(a) With a top edge (0.21 × 0.25 × 0.03). Letters, second-third century, rustic capitals: (i) line 1, 0.045, line 2, 0.05; (ii) 0.08, less well cut than (i).

```
    (i) ..]nio stop  Ruf[...      (ii) ...]liae [...
        ...]riano c.u. Q[...           ...]i[...
        [...                           [...
```

(i) Line 1, final letter may be F, giving Ruf[o or Ruf[ino, or similar; line 2, final letter might be Q, C or G.

(b) Without cut edges (0.12 × 0.142 × 0.025). Letters, as in (a): (i) 0.05; (ii) truncated and not measurable.

```
 (i)        ...]              (ii)         ...]
      ...]IER[...                    ...]ÇEP[...
      ...]TRO[...                    [...
      [...
```

(i) Line 1, I might be any letter incorporating an upright; E might be L; R might possibly be A.
(ii) C might be S; P might be R or B.

(c) Without cut edges (0.195 × 0.165 × 0.03). Letters, as in (a): (i) line 1, 0.045, line 2, 0.05; (ii) 0.07.

```
 (i)             ...]          (ii)          ...]
      ...]riario [...                ...]ginia[...
      ...P]ostumo [...               ...]ME[...
      ...]IITET[...                  [...
      [...
```

(i) Line 1, first letter, though incomplete, is almost certainly R, suggesting the *nomina* Coriarius, Mariarius or Triarius, of which only the last is at all common.
(ii) Line 1, first letter, although incomplete, is almost certainly G, suggesting the *nomina* Fulginius, Garginius, Larginius, Longinius, Saginius, Taginius, Verginius, of which Fulginius and Verginius seem the most likely.

The title *clarissimus vir* in a (i), line 2 shows that the honorand was a senator; but I have not traced a senatorial family of the right date using any combination of the names or possible names that appear here. It is possible that the *nomen* of the man in a (i) line 1 was the same as that of the lady in c (ii) line 1, and, if so, it could be argued that the text on face (ii) was rejected as sub-standard and recut on (i). But it should be noted that while all the names on (i) are masculine, all those on (ii) are feminine so that the two texts may be unconnected. There is no clue to the purpose of the text, which may have come from a tomb or from an honorary monument.

5. In the *cortile* of Casale di Santa Cornelia. Two adjoining pieces of a moulded marble panel, probably Luna, the top missing, chipped along the break (0.885 × 0.45 × 0.08). Published in Reynolds (1962), whence *L'Année Epigraphique* 1969/70, number 193, Christol 1974, 119f, and so *L'Année Epigraphique* 1974, 319 bis. Letters, second-third century, rustic capitals: line 2, 0.055, lines 3 and 4, 0.04, lines 5 and 6, average 0.045. Lines 5 and 6 were added later, perhaps at different times; the hands are barely distinguishable, but the alignment is progressively weaker and the layout poorer – in line 5 the two penultimate letters are cut small and in line 6 the two final letters are cut one above the other, because, in both cases, insufficient space had been left.

```
     [ vacat    D(is)     vac. M(anibus)        vacat]
     Q. C[erelli Apo]llinaris c. m. u.
     vac. praef(ecti) [ui]g(ilum) proc(uratoris) rat(ionis) privat(ae)
     vac. proc(uratoris) Lud(i) M(agni) trib(uni) coh(ortis) V pr(aetoriae)
   5 et Cerelliae Veranillae c(larissimae) m(emoriae) f(eminae) fil(iae)
     et Aureliae Veranillae c(larissimae) m(emoriae) f(eminae) eius
```

For Apollinaris see *PIR²* C.665; this inscription adds important information to the previously known record that he was prefect of the *vigiles* on 11 April, AD 212. Christol stresses the unusual features of his career, demonstrates that he was under the patronage of the emperor Caracalla, who doubtless used him as an agent for control of key positions in Rome in his moves against his brother Geta, and suggests that the *clarissimate* here may as well have been the result of a grant of senatorial (?praetorian) *insignia* as of actual adlection into the Senate. The stone clearly came from a substantial built tomb befitting the status of this family and a location for it in one of the Roman cemeteries seems natural; but Caerellii (surely to be connected with these Cerellii) are buried at Veii (*CIL* XI. 3833) and Capena (*CIL* XI. 6856, 6691) and, although these are humbler bearers of the *nomen*, they may indicate the area of the family's origin and/or its estates, so that a local tomb is not to be excluded and might accord better with the modest quality of the letter cutting here.

6. 1940 + 1965 = SC625, 626. Two adjoining fragments of a white marble panel, without cut edges (0.32 × 0.26 × 0.03). Monumental capitals, very finely designed and cut, first or early second century: *c.* 0.17.

```
          ...]
     ...]EGI[...
       [...
```

Of the final letter only a bottom serif survives, but its position is sufficient to rule out Y here. This was clearly part of an important monument, even perhaps a public one; and in this context the most likely word to propose here is *legio* or an oblique case thereof.

7. SC397. Piece from a coloured marble panel, perhaps Phrygian (0.245 × 0.292 × *c.* 0.02), with cut edges of which top and right hand ones are certainly secondary, while left hand one is probably original and bottom one might be; inscribed on a worn face. Letters, probably second century, carefully designed and cut: average 0.025.

```
                    ...]
    conlẹgii [...
    vac. lustro[...
    Asclepiades stop PỌ[...
    v.    Aphrodisi ṣ[eruus ..?..]
        vacat        [ ? vacat ]
```

Clearly from a record of a formally constituted association, with officers in post for *lustra*, periods of 4 or 5 years. Its name will have stood in the second part of line 1, with the number of the *lustrum* in the sequence since the foundation of the association in line 2. The name in lines 3 and 4 is that of a slave, whose master's *nomen* is lost with the second half of line 3, although his *cognomen* survives in line 4, where the word *servus* may have been abbreviated or omitted. Asclepiades can only have been a *minister* of the association, not one of its senior officers, and the layout of the text suggests that all the *ministri* of the current *lustrum* were listed.

Numbered *lustra* appear in the headings of several inscriptions of the *collegia fabrum tignariorum (tignuariorum)* at Rome and Ostia, but not only is the title of these colleges rather long for the space likely to have been available (though *conlegii fabrum* alone would fit well), but in all such cases the genitive *lustri* is used. The ablative *lustro* seems rare; it appears in the cursus of an officer of the *collegium fabrorum tignariorum* at Tusculum (*CIL* XIV. 2630) and in a dedication made to a deity by a member of a religious association at Rome (*CIL* VI. 422), but so far not in the type of context we have here. *Ministri* also seem comparatively rare so far, but one dedication by the *ministri* of the *collegium fabrorum tignariorum* exists at Rome (Pearse 1975). The purpose of the text could have been related to a communal tomb maintained by the association or to a dedication to a deity (as in the case discussed by Pearse).

8. 1927a + b = SC568 + 680. Two adjoining fragments from upper part and right side of a piece of marble (0.265 × 0.16 × 0.04), either a panel or cut from a sarcophagus front inscribed within a moulded panel and on its upper moulding; an unexplained decorative feature, possibly part of a *tabella ansata* handle, extends into the panel from the right, shortening line 3 and itself cut into by the last letter of line 4. Letters, second-third century, quite well designed capitals, cut between visible guide-lines: lines 3 and 4, 0.015; line 2, 0.018; lines 5 and 6, 0.017; AV in line 4 in ligature.

```
        ...] v. RE[..c. 6 ..]
      ...]militi Ị[..c. 6 ..]
  ... ?frum]ẹntario leg(ionis) I
      ...]ONISỊỊ[..]IDEAAv.V
          ... ui]xit an(nos)
          ... ?die]s II
              ...] vac.
```

Line 1 presumably carried the name of the deceased soldier (line 2) whose career followed, its only recognisable stage being his probable service as *frumentarius* in line 3 (no other supplement seems likely). At this stage he belonged either to legion I Adiutrix, I Italica, or I Minervia, or to I Parthica if his career fell a little later than the letter forms suggest and so in or after the opening years of Septimius Severus' reign when that legion was first recruited. As *frumentarius* he was detached from his legion, however, and employed in a type of secret service activity, perhaps in Rome itself, and, if so, presumably with headquarters at the Castra Peregrina on Mons Caelius (cf. Mann 1988, 149-150). It is unclear what was stated in line 4, but he may have been promoted after leaving the corps of *frumentarii*, so that the opening letters could be from a noun in the dative, such as *optioni*, *centurioni* or from *legionis*.

Line 5 has a standard element of a funerary text, the subject's age at death.

9. 1926a,b,c = SC91 + 216 + 785 (Pl. 54). Three adjoining fragments of a moulded marble panel, perhaps Proconnesian, preserving a short section of the left edge and rather more of the bottom (0.39 × 0.195 × 0.05). Letters, probably third century, drawn under strong influence from cursive forms: lines 3-5, average 0.02; lines 6 and 7 average 0.018; A may have a straight (but sometimes slanted) bar, or a dropped one, and once in line 6 and again in line 7 has none at

Plate 54. Santa Cornelia: inscription number 9 (*Museo dell'Alto Medioevo*, Rome)

all; word divisions are rare, but the layout suggests that each word was drawn, and perhaps cut, separately; there has been a serious attempt to paragraph (one paragraph occupying lines 3-5, and a second lines 6 and 7), and to centre significant phrases.

```
        [ ? vacat    ]Ọ(is) vac. Ṃ(anibus) [ ? vacat
                ...]  vacat            [...
            ...]am  eorum  de  me  bene  ṃ[er- ...
        ...]nt libertis ][i]bertabusq[ue ...
   5    R.[.2-3.q]ue     v.   posterisque[...
        LVXV.[...1 or 2..]us aurariu[s ?.]RASINICV[...
            vacat          Pylades [te]mporis v. s[ui ...
```

Line 1, only the bottoms of the letters survive and their interpretation is not certain; *Di]s M[anibus* is one of the other possibilities.
Line 3, the first letter might be M; the second could, theoretically, be taken with what follows to give *meorum*, but the layout favours what is printed.
Line 5, the letters here are spaced more broadly than elsewhere, clearly in order to fill the line without introducing words from the next paragraph; after R at the start there is a trace of the base of the next letter, which almost certainly incorporated an upright.
Line 6, very little survives of the fifth letter except the bottom of its initial stroke which slants rightwards as it rises. At the end C might be G; if C is accepted, V could conceivably be A.
The text is certainly funerary and set up by the tomb-builder for his household, or perhaps only certain members of it who had deserved well of him. The formulae used include some for which I have not found a parallel in the Roman material, along with others which are banal. Any restoration must be conjectural; in lines 3-5 the sense should have been on the following lines:

```
[Memori]ạm  eorum  de  me  benem[eriti  qui]
[fueru]nt libertis ][i]bertabusq̣[ue libe]-
r[isq]ue  v.  posterisque [eorum]
```

The change from the genitive case in line 3 to the dative in lines 4 and 5 is inelegant, but understandable given the very common occurrence of the formula beginning with *libertis*; the conjectured position of the words *de me benemeriti* outside the relative clause would be designed to emphasise them.
Lines 6 and 7 must contain the name and some account of the tomb-builder. Two things seem

clear. First, since he had freedmen and freedwomen, he must have been of free status himself, so that the introduction of an owner's name in the genitive (e.g. [P.] Rasini Cu[pidi]) in line 6 is ruled out; he may well have been a freed slave, but did not use the standard way to indicate it, and in any case it was rare to do so, at the likely date, unless the patron was an emperor or member of the imperial family: in principle, however, something like *[P.] Rasini Cu[pidi l(ibertus)]* is possible. Second, he is to be connected with the world of entertainment in Rome; line 7 contains a formula of a type closely associated with successful performers, see *CIL* VI. 10060, 10106, 10107, *ILS* 5186, where it is used for *archimimae*, a charioteer and a pantomime (dancer), and it does not occur in *CIL* VI for anyone who is demonstrably outside this category. The name *Pylades* in line 7 recalls a famous pantomime of the reign of Augustus and another under Trajan (*PW* XXIII.2, columns 2082-2084), and is attested also, clearly as a stage name, for a number of other performers (not all pantomimes). It may have been the name (or stage name) of the tomb-builder, but, if so, the formula which followed must have been at least *temporis sui primus* (or some similar superlative adjective), perhaps combined with a description of his speciality; but that would have taken up the space at the end of the line which ought to have been left blank in order to balance the vacant space at its beginning and give emphasis to the words between. Either, then, the line length was longer than the proposed reconstruction of lines 3-5 (which is possible), or the name *Pylades* was being used descriptively – *Pylades temporis sui*, with the sense 'the (a) Pylades of his time'. Parallels exist, the closest in the *Scriptores Historiae Augustae*, e.g. *v. Alex. Sev.* 68, *Cato temporis sui*. The layout of line 7 seems to me to favour the view that it contained a new phrase, constituting a climax to, and/or a comment on what preceded, not a continuation of it, as a name would be.

Line 6 may have contained a series of names. If so, the first can hardly be restored as anything but the rare *Luxurius*, which is problematic because the remains of the fifth letter resemble more the first stroke of *M* than of *R* (but the shape of the first *R* in line 3 gives some support for the proposal); the second would be *Aurarius*, which is also rare; and next, unless there is the not so likely reference to a patron (see above), would be a *cognomen* [.]RASINICV[S ..c.4..], apparently the transliteration of a Greek personal name (e.g. Πασίνικος, which would give Pasinicus), but I have not found one which fits what stands here; a short second *cognomen* would presumably fill the remainder of the line, and *Pylades* in line 7 could be yet another, if the argument from the layout of line 7 is not accepted.

But, given two connections with public entertainment in the text, it is tempting to look for more. At the beginning of line 6, should we see an exclamatory description of a successful performer as *Lux*, perhaps *Lux unus* (but *N* is certainly no better fit for the fifth letter than the *R* of *Luxurius*), on the analogy of *Lux Victor* (sc. *pantomimorum*) in *CIL* VI. 10115 ? If so, the man's name is presumably simply *Aurarius*, with the *cognomina* as already proposed. Another, and still more interesting possibility is that after *Aurarius* we should restore *[P]rasini*, meaning *Prasini panni*, 'of the Green Faction', as in *CIL* VI. 33949, 33950. The 'Green Faction' was one of the four major organizations through which public entertainment is known to have been maintained in the imperial period in circuses, and in the Byzantine period also in theatres. If the tomb-builder was a pantomime, he performed in theatres; and his inscription strongly suggests that the factions operated in the theatres as well as in the circuses at a markedly earlier date than was previously attested.

There is a further possibility, if we take his name to be, after all, *Luxurius*, and interpret *aurarius* as an ordinary noun. *Aurarius* is well-attested with the sense 'goldsmith', 'gilder'; but it is also cited by Servius (*De Aeneid.* VI.204, 816) and some late Glossaries (perhaps simply following him) as meaning 'supporter' or 'fan' (see *TLL*, *sub voce*). In a recent discussion of Byzantine Factions, Alan Cameron has argued that it is this second meaning that should be attributed to the transliterated αὐράριος, which is found inscribed on seats in a number of theatres and *stadia* in the Eastern Empire, in late antiquity and the Byzantine period; and he takes it to refer to claqueurs responsible for organized applause (1976, 248-249). The view has been disputed, especially by linguists, and lacks the support of any text in which the alternative sense of 'goldsmith' is certainly impossible. At first sight this text might provide the missing support since it presents, on the interpretation under discussion, the only known collocation of an *aurarius* and a faction. Unfortunately, however, it is inconclusive; for associated with the performers in each faction were support staffs of considerable size, performing a variety of functions of which we are inadequately aware (for some of these see Skelton 1988, 73-138); that gilders or goldsmiths might be required to produce showy properties at entertainments (cf. the *argentatis choregiis* of Valerius Maximus 2.4.6.) is likely; and it is therefore possible that certain craftsmen were associated with particular factions, and perhaps on their payrolls. So the theory of applause organized through claqueurs called *aurarii* cannot be effectively advanced by this text. The tomb-builder may, then, have been a goldsmith/gilder, who later became a successful performer; but the loss of the end of line 6 deprives us of what should be essential information about his career. The first supplement suggested for it, suggested by surviving Roman inscriptions referring to factions, is *cu[rsor]* (cf. *CIL* VI. 33944), a word which may mean nothing more than a messenger; but it is certainly the case that some *cursores* connected with factions performed as runners in races (*CIL* VI. 33950). Less satisfactory palaeographically, but not quite impossible, is *ca[ntor]*; but in the present state of the text we can hardly progress further.

We have, I suggest, the following options:
(1) that line 6 consists of a long (and pretentious) name

```
either  Luxur[i]us Aurarius [.]RASINICV[S ..c.4.. ]
or      Luxur[i]us Aurarius,[.]Rasini Cu[ ..c.4.. ](ibertus)]
```

and that line 7 may have added a *cognomen*, Pylades, to it, but if it did, must have concluded on the following lines (which imply that the text extended further to the left than I have supposed throughout)

```
vacat Pylades, [te]mporis s[ui primus   vacat ]
```

(2) that line 6 comprised a short name, possibly preceded by a theatrical exclamation, and certainly followed by descriptions of activities to be related to the green faction.

```
Either  Luxur[i]us, aurarius [P]rasini, cu[rsor?],
        vacat   Pylades [te]mporis s[ui vacat ]
or      Lux unus, aurarius, [P]rasini cu[rsor? ],
        vacat   Pylades [te]mporis s[ui vacat ]
```

Punctuation is added to clarify the senses proposed for the modern reader.

(I am very grateful for discussion of the organization of Roman entertainment with Mrs Charlotte Roueché and Dr John Humphrey, of the word *aurarius* with Professors R. Coleman and Olivier Masson, and of various points of Latinity with Dr Janet Fairweather, but am solely responsible for the result.)

10. SC741. Striated sarcophagus almost completely reassembled from fragments, with a central feature on the front consisting of a female portrait head in a roundel, above an inscribed funerary altar, both in relief. Letters, third century, read from a photograph (cf. Pl. 40).

```
      vac. D(is) M(anibus) S(acrum)  vac.
      Arria Asellia Sita-
      ra uixit ann(os) LXV
      [       ..?..          ]-
 5    o fecit    vacat
```

Certainly funerary. The date is deducible from the hair style of the portrait. Lines 2 and 3, I can find no known *cognomen* which exactly fits the traces. Line 4 contained the name of the person who buried Arria, presumably a man whose *cognomen* ended in -o.

11. In the *cortile* of the Casale di Santa Cornelia. Marble stele with lower left corner broken away, inscribed on one face below an incised decoration comprising an ivy leaf between volutes. Letters, probably third century, designed under strong influence from cursive forms, but with reasonably well-cut trenches; superscript bars in line 7 above the abbreviation and figure.

```
      D(is) stop M(anibus)
      Arruntio  stop
      Ianuario  stop
      Ulpia stop  Successa
 5    coiunxs vac.                       sic
      quae uix(it) cu[m]
      eo stop an(nis) V[? stop m(enses)]
      X stop d(ies) I[?]
```

The husband's *cognomen* is common among slaves and freed slaves; the wife's *nomen* suggests a family enfranchised under Trajan. The spelling in line 5 reflects popular usage.

12. 1918a+b = SC76a+b. Two adjoining fragments from a panel of grey/ black marble without edges (0.14 × 0.11 × 0.025). Letters, perhaps second century, neat small capitals: 0.03.

```
                    ...]
    ...]eḭu[s ...
    ...]Decim[i - ...
    ...]VEṬV[...
    [...
```

Almost certainly funerary. Line 1 indicates the relationship of the deceased to the person who set up the monument, probably the wife.

Line 2, probably the *nomen* of the husband. Line 3, possibly the *cognomen* of the husband.

13. SC160. Fragment probably from upper left corner of a marble panel (0.155 × 0.12 × 0.045) inscribed on a worn surface within a simple moulding.

```
              ? ...]
    T stop Fla[ui- ...
      vacat A[...
      et M[...
      [...
```

Almost certainly funerary. The names here are probably those of the deceased, and may have been in the nominative, genitive or dative.

Line 2 presumably contained a *cognomen* for T(itus) Flavius, e.g. Aper.

14. 1948 = SC189. Fragment of white marble without edges (0.12 × 0.135 × 0.047). Letters, perhaps second century, fairly neat capitals: 0.035.

```
              ...]
       ...]ṣ vac. [...
    ... ?Fl]aui  stop  Aụ[...
          ...]VI[...
    [...
```

Almost certainly funerary. Line 2, it is not impossible that this was a T(itus) Flavius *Aug. lib.*, i.e. freedman of a Flavian emperor (AD 70-96).

15. 1923 = SC412 + 502. Two adjoining pieces from a white marble panel with a cut edge below (0.21 × 0.16 × 0.045). Letters, probably second century, neatly designed capitals: line 1, 0.03; line 2, 0.028; line 3 and 4, 0.025.

```
              ...]
        ...]ILEA[...
        ...]VRDIA[...
      ...]ri optimae[...
    ... Fl]auiae T.f. Nep[otillae ? ...
```

Almost certainly funerary. Line 2, presumably from a *nomen*, perhaps Murdia or Turdia, or from a *cognomen* derived therefrom. At this point the text may give the name of the person who set up the monument since at any rate one of those buried here appears in the dative in lines 3 and 4. Line 3, *mat]ri, soro]ri* or *uxo]ri*; presumably the lady whose name appears in line 4, Flavia T(iti) f(ilia) Nepotilla.

16. No SC number. Two adjoining pieces from the left side of a white marble panel, with cut edges at top and bottom, and, on left side, traces of the iron peg which upheld the panel, indicating the proximity of the left edge (0.10 × 0.145 × 0.035-4); inscribed between a roughly straight incised line above and a wavy line with dots in the loops below. Letters, perhaps second century: line 1, 0.03; line 2, 0.015; line 3, 0.018.

```
       L. Fu][...
    vac. Ap[...
       Fundi]l[la- ...
```

Almost certainly funerary. Line 1, a *nomen* like Fulvius or Furius, perhaps in the dative. Line 2, a *cognomen*, e.g. Aper, Appianus. Line 3, probably a feminine name for a wife or other relation.

17. In the *cortile* of the Casale di Santa Cornelia. Marble panel with upper right corner missing, chipped down the right side. Letters, perhaps third century, designed freehand and poorly cut (not measured).

```
    vac. D(is) [M(anibus) vac.]
    Iulius   V[a]-
    lens gene-
    r socer-
    o suo b-
    enemeren(ti)
    [?vac.f]ecit vac.
```

Presumably the deceased father-in-law's name appeared on another stone.

18. 1915 = SC570. Fragment from lower left corner of a white marble panel (0.11 × 0.14 × 0.03); the back shows traces of a bottom moulding indicating that the piece was reused. Letters, perhaps second century, designed under the influence of cursive forms: line 1, 0.04, line 2, 0.03; red paint survives in the trenches.

```
        ...]
    Nymp[hi-...
    v. Ar][...
```

Almost certainly funerary. Line 1 probably a name, Nymphidius, Nymphius, Nymphia or a derivative therefrom.

19. 1943 = SC771. Fragment, perhaps from the bottom of a panel of white marble (0.195 × 0.09 × 0.025). Letters, perhaps third century, cursives with uncial *u*: line 1, 0.037; line 2, 0.028.

```
         ...]
    ...] patri[...
    ...]ecilius ...
```

Almost certainly funerary. Line 2, a *nomen*, perhaps Caecilius, but Maecilius, though rarer, is another possibility.

20. SC256. Part of a white marble panel (not measured). Letters, second-third century, monumental capitals in line 1, but showing some influence from cursive forms in line 2; read from a photograph.

```
    ...]lius P(ubli) l(ibertus) Alb[...
    ...]millia C(aii) f(ilia) Lys[...
```

Line 1, B might be P. The block probably came from the facade of a built tomb for a household in which the husband was freed (line 1) and the wife freeborn (line 2), although her Greek *cognomen* (?Lysandra, Lysistrate) suggests that her family was of slave origin. For the husband's *cognomen* one might propose Albus or Alpinus, or a derivative of either. Husband and wife could have had the same *nomen*, but did not necessarily do so. There are too many ending -lius to justify speculation; for -millius one might think of Camillius.

21. 1922 = SC538. Fragment from a white marble panel without edges, but probably from near the top (0.08 × 0.12 × 0.02); the back carries a moulding showing that the piece was reused. Letters, probably second century, neat capitals cut between visible guide-lines: 0.025.

```
    ...] vacat [...
      ...]VE[...
    ...]elia[...
      ...]E[...
    [...
```

Almost certainly funerary. Line 2, probably from the end of a feminine *nomen* such as Aelia, Cornelia.

22. 1936 = SC399. Fragment of a marble panel without cut edges (0.16 × 0.13 × 0.045), inscribed on a worn face. Letters, perhaps second century: *c.* 0.03.

```
          ...]
    ...] lib(ert-) stop Eua[...
      ...]IB][]FIN[...
    ...]S[...
```

Almost certainly funerary. Line 1, a *cognomen*, feminine or masculine, e.g. Evander, Evagrius. Line 2, *s]ibi* is possible, but what follows does not seem to fit into any of the normal formulae which use *sibi*. *Vibi*, the genitive case of the *nomen* of one man, or the nominative plural for two persons, both living, is also possible.

23. 2640. Fragment from top of a marble panel. Letters, perhaps second century: 0.015.

```
    ...]us vac. EQ[...
    [...
```

Almost certainly funerary. This is most probably part of a name, the end of the *nomen* and the beginning of the *cognomen*.

24. SC175. Fragment from a piece of marble with four cut edges, of which only top and bottom could be original. Letters read from a photograph.

```
        ...] vac. [...
        ...]us v. M[...
        ...] vacat [...
```

Almost certainly funerary. This is most probably part of a name, the end of the *nomen* and the initial of the *cognomen*.

25. 2125 = SC273. Lower part of a white marble stele including the flange for insertion into the earth (0.245 × 0.25 × 0.05) inscribed within an area flanked on either side by an incised line. Letters, perhaps second century, neatly designed with use of ruler and compass: 0.017.

```
              ...]
        ...]ạ Tyche
    [?fecit m]ạter
```

Almost certainly funerary. Line 1, the mother's name might be Agatyche, but a *nomen* with the much commoner Tyche seems more likely.

26. 1649a = SC57. Fragment from a white marble panel without edges (0.085 × 0.08 × 0.035). Letters, perhaps second century: *c.* 0.035.

```
              ...]
        ...]IIA[...
      ...] stop Viç[tor? ...
      [...
```

Almost certainly funerary. Line 2, the stop is not certain but probable; the third letter could be G or O.

27. 1938 = SC861 or 869. Upper part of a marble stele with rounded top flanked by rudimentary acroteria (0.20 × 0.155 × 0.073-0.05) inscribed on a worn face which is partly encrusted with plaster. Letters, perhaps second century: lines 1 and 2, average 0.025; line 3, 0.03; there is some influence from cursive forms especially on A, M, R.

```
    D(is) M(anibus) S(acrum)
    Zosimo
    filio stop DRA-
    [...
```

The father's name may have been a single one, e.g. Dracon, in which case he and his son were probably slaves, or a citizen one, D. Ra[...

28. No SC number. Reused marble block, originally from an entablature with three fasciae, turned to show its underside, on which there is a square clamp-hole towards the right end; inscribed on this face. Letters, monumental capitals; the cutter has taken pains to avoid the clamp-hole. Read from a photograph.

```
    ...]llae fi v. [liae ...
```

The inscription, clearly meant for display on the facade of a monumental tomb, records the end of a feminine *cognomen* and the lady's relationship to the tomb-builder.

29. 1916 = SC436. Piece probably from the upper right corner of a white marble panel, perhaps Proconnesian (0.255 × 0.17 × 0.045). Letters, probably third century: *c.* 0.045.

```
        ...]nae    vac.
        ...]nae    vac.
    ... ?con]v. iuẋ vac.
    [...
```

Apparently a husband to his wife for whom the conclusions of two *cognomina* survive.

30. 1944 + 1945 = SC787 + 67. Two adjoining fragments from the bottom right corner of a white marble panel (0.31 × 0.25 × 0.045-55); on the back is part of a flat fascia showing that the piece was re-used. Letters, perhaps third century, poorly designed and cut: 0.045-55.

```
              ...]
        ...]unio
    ... ?infel]icissim(?)
          ...]vac. fec(it) v.
```

Line 1 either from the name of the deceased, in the dative, e.g. Fortunio, or from that of the person who buried him/her, in the nominative case.
Line 2 the relationship of the person who erected the monument, e.g. *pater* or *mater*, preceded the

adjective indicating his/her distress.

Line 3 probably the relationship was underlined here, e.g. by *filio*, but there may have been a reference to the tomb before *fec(it)*.

31. 1964t = SC789. Fragment from a white marble panel without edges (0.095 × 0.09 × *c.* 0.02). Letters, ?third century, badly cut: *c.* 0.055.

```
              ...]
        ...] G[...
     ... c]oiu[- ...
      [...
```

Almost certainly funerary. Line 2 from *coiux* or *coiugi*.

32. 1930c = SC508b+ one unnumbered piece. Two adjoining fragments without cut edges, from a white marble panel (not measured when assembled). Letters, small capitals, probably second century: *c.* 0.04.

```
               ...]
        ...]I[..]B[...
     ... c]ompar[...
        ...]PICT[...
      [...
```

Certainly funerary. Line 2, perhaps from *compar*, used for husband or wife, but the adjective *incomparabilis* to describe any deceased person is also possible, and the verb *comparauit* cannot be excluded.

Line 3, possibly part of the name of the person responsible for the monument, so perhaps Epictetus, which suggests a slave or freedman.

33. 1921 = SC65. Fragment of a white marble panel without cut edges (0.09 × 0.14 × 0.035) with traces of plaster on the inscribed face. Letters, probably second century, well designed and cut between visible guide-lines: 0.05.

```
              ...]
        ...]fi]l[i- ...
     ... ui]xit [annos ...
      [...
```

Certainly funerary. The deceased was probably the son or daughter of the person who erected the monument.

34. 1960 = SC736. Fragment from near the top of a white marble stele without edges (0.12 × 0.195 × 0.15); on the back is a moulding which shows that the piece was reused. Letters, perhaps second century: 0.03.

```
                    ...]
        ...fili]o pii[ssimo ...
     ... par]ent[es ...
      [...
```

Certainly funerary.

35. 1919 = SC779. Fragment of white marble without edges (0.12 × 0.075 × 0.018). Letters, perhaps third century, cut between visible guide-lines: *c.* 0.035.

```
                 ...]
     ... pa]renti[...
     ... ?di]es VIIII[...
      [...
```

Certainly funerary. Line 2 contained the age at death – *vixit annos? menses? dies VIIII*, but what survives may have been the number of months rather than days.

36. 1925 = SC614. Fragment from the left side of a white marble panel (0.114 × 0.11 × 0.045) inscribed within a frame consisting of two parallel incised lines. Letters perhaps second century, small neat capitals: 0.022.

```
         ...]
      ET[A[...
      uxo[r- ...
      fe[cit ?...
```

Certainly funerary. It is not clear whether the monument was for the wife or husband.

37. 1957 + 1954 = SC581 + ?690. Two adjoining fragments of a white marble panel with no cut edges (0.125 × 0.175 × *c*. 0.05). Letters, perhaps second century: 0.028.

```
                      ...]
              ...]R stop ḷ[...
              ...] vacat[...
          ...]ṚEID[...
              ...]VX[...
   5          ...]Ạ[...
          [...
```

Certainly funerary. Line 4, from *coniux* or *uxor*.

38. 1941 = SC715. Fragment from the bottom of a white marble panel (0.195 × 0.15 × 0.03). Letters, probably second century, well cut small capitals: 0.04.

```
              ...]
      ...]ṣ[...
      ...]eius [...
```

Certainly funerary. The last line clearly contained a statement of the relationship of the person who erected the monument to the deceased, e.g. *mater eius*.

39. 1951 = SC796. Fragment of a white marble panel without cut edges (0.07 × 0.10 × 0.02). Letters, probably third century: *c*. 0.045.

```
              ...]
      ...]sib[i ...
      [...
```

Clearly from some version of the funerary *fecit sibi et suis*.

40. 1924a + b = SC90 + 597. Two adjoining fragments from the lower left corner of a white marble panel (0.13 × 0.37 × 0.04) inscribed on one face within a frame defined by parallel incised lines. Letters, probably second century, neatly designed small capitals, quite well cut: average 0.023.

```
                              ...]
      pientiṣṣimae VṢ[ .. c. 11 .. et?]
      sibi et suis libert[is libertabus]
      que posterisqu[e eorum ? vacat]
```

Certainly funerary. Line 1 only the bottoms of the letters survive; the adjective is normally used of a relation, here presumably a wife, daughter, mother or sister; the name of the person who built the tomb, which was for the use of a whole household, followed.

41. 1956 = SC577. Fragment from the bottom of a white marble panel (0.15 × 0.13 × 0.035). Letters, probably second-third century: 0.035.

```
                  ...]
      ...p]osṭeṛ[isque eorum ...
```

From the funerary formula *libertis libertabusque posterisque eorum*.

42. 1950 + 1964 = SC757a,b,c,d. Four adjoining fragments, probably from the lower right corner of a white marble panel without cut edges (0.12 × 0.22 × 0.021). Letters, probably third century: *c*. 0.04.

```
                      ...]
      ... ?post]eṛi[sque eorum ...
            ...]VLA[...
      ... ui]xit[...
   [annos ? menses ? die]s VI
```

Certainly funerary. Line 1, cf. number 41 above.

43. 1932 = SC66. Fragment from a white marble panel without cut edges (0.072 × 0.12 × 0.035) inscribed on a face which has been plastered over. Letters, probably third century: *c*. 0.035.

```
                  ...]
          ...]ṭ[...
      ... ?lib]erṭ[is libertabusque]
   [posterisque eorum ...
```

Certainly funerary. Cf. number 41 above.

44. 1946 = SC159. Fragment of a marble panel without cut edges (0.16 × 0.10 × 0.035). Letters, probably second century, with some influence from cursive forms: 0.045.

```
                 ...]
... ui]xit stop a[nnos ...
    ...]ṣe stop ui[uo fecit ...
```

Certainly funerary. The name of the person who erected what was presumably a family tomb will have stood at the start of the last line.

45. SC244 or 158. Fragment of a marble panel without cut edges (0.13 × 0.10 × 0.035). Letters read from a photograph.

```
            ...]
...]ịNị[...
...] uix[it annos ...
[...
```

Certainly funerary.

46. 1934 = SC565. Fragment of a white marble panel without cut edges (0.175 × 0.17 × 0.022). Letters, perhaps third century, with rather distinctive serifs, roughly cut: 0.04.

```
              ...]
... uixit] annis [...
     ...]t kạr[i]s[sim- ...
```

Certainly funerary. Line 2 perhaps *fecit karissimo* or -*ae*.

47. 1920 = SC852. Fragment of a white marble panel without cut edges (not measured). Letters, perhaps third century: 0.04.

```
            ...]
... uixi]ṭ annọ[s ...
[...
```

Certainly funerary.

48. 1947 = SC630. Fragment of a white marble panel, probably from its right side but without cut edges (0.06 × 0.14 × 0.03). Letters, perhaps third century, poorly designed and cut: 0.022.

```
            ...]
        ...]o
        ...] stop
   ... uixit an]nis
[...
```

Certainly funerary.

49. 2662 = SC363. Fragment of a sarcophagus inscribed on the narrow *fascia* below the sculptured panel. Letters, perhaps third century: 0.018.

```
... m]eruerat [...
```

Perhaps from a sentence indicating that the deceased had deserved what those who set up the monument did, cf. *CIL* VI. 4373, 33466.

50. Three pieces from the same marble monument, each with remains of a corbel at the left side; it is unclear whether this shows that the pieces were reused. Letters, probably second century, well cut capitals.

(i) 1958a = SC673. 0.10 × 0.425 × 0.09. Letters, lines 1 and 2, 0.07; lines 3 and 4, 0.052.

```
          ...]
...]IS[...
...]QV[...
...]GI[...
...]VI[...
...]vac.[...
[...
```

(ii) 1958b = SC672. 0.075 × 0.355 × 0.10. Letters, line 2, 0.045, line 3, 0.04.

```
              ...]
      ...]ị[...
      ...]RV[...
       ...]VȦ[...
    [...
```

(iii) 1958c = SC342. 0.09 × 0.16 × 0.10. Letters, 0.043.

```
            ...]
     ...]ṚA[...
      ...]R[...
      ...]Rị[...
   [...
```

GREEK TEXTS

51. 1935 = SC61. Fragment from the lower right corner of a marble panel (0.145 × 0.12 × 0.02). Letters, perhaps third century: δ0.032 (Ψ, 0.042); lunate *epsilon*, cursive influence on *sigma*.

```
          ...]
    ...]ΣΙΑ  vac.
   ...]ΚΕψΕ  vac.
   ...]  vacat
```

Almost certainly funerary but hardly susceptible of restoration.

52. No SC number. Fragment probably from the top of a white marble panel (0.16 × 0.25 × average 0.035). Letters, perhaps second century: 0.042 (Φ, 0.071).

```
   ...]ΦΙΗΔȦ[...
  ...'ε]νκ[εν...
   ...]Φθι [...
   ...]ΜΟ[...
  [...
```

Probably funerary. Line 1, presumably from names, e.g. Ἀπφίη Δα[. . .
Line 2, cf. μνήμης ἕνεκεν in *IGUR* 1181. Line 3, perhaps from φθίνω, ἀπσφθίνω, words which are confined to use in verse in the series of *IGUR* texts.

OTHER FRAGMENTS

The following fragments give a small number of letters which cannot be interpreted at all.

1961a. Top of moulded panel of white marble; letters incomplete:

```
   ...]Ȧ[...
```

2123 = SC254. Top and left side of white marble panel; letters, 0.03:

```
   A[... / D[... / leaf [...
```

1930a = SC595. Fragment of white marble without edges; letters 0.038:

```
   ....]ḅ[... / ...]PAị[...
```

1952 = SC599. Fragment of white marble without edges; letters 0.033:

```
   ...]BIȮ[...
```

1964m = SC713. Fragment from top of white marble panel; letters *c.* 0.025:

```
   ...]ẸRị[...
```

1942. Fragment from bottom of white marble panel; letters incomplete:

```
   ...]ÇE[...
```

1964q = SC605. Fragment from bottom of white marble panel; letters, 0.028:

...]D[...

1964b = SC601. Fragment of marble without edges; letters incomplete:

...]E̦I̦[...

1964g = SC637. Fragment of white marble without edges; letters, 0.055:

...]E[...

SC594. Fragment of white marble without edges; letters, 0.035:

...]E̦EF[... / ...]ȘȚ[...

1961c = SC582. Fragment from bottom of white marble panel; letters, 0.023:

...]G[... / ...]M[...

1964o = SC790. Fragment from bottom of white marble panel; letters incomplete:

...]H̦[... / ...]V̦[...

1961b = SC509. Lower right corner of white marble panel; letters, 0.025:

...]I̦ / ...]I / ...]ae

1964i. Left side of white marble panel; letters, 0.023:

...]IO[...

1964d. Fragment of marble panel without edges; letters incomplete:

...]I̦[...

1959a + b. Two adjoining fragments of white marble without a complete letter:

...]I̦[...

SC276. Fragment from top of white marble panel; letters incomplete:

...]M̦[...

1390b = SC78a (508?). Fragment of white marble panel without edges; letters, 0.035:

...]N̦O[...

1964L = SC68. Fragment of marble panel without edges; letters, 0.045-0.05:

...] *vac.* I̦[... / ...]I̦I̦I̦R[... / ...] *vacat* [...

1962. Fragment of marble panel without edges; monumental letters, not less than 0.09:

...]RI[...

1964e = SC665. Fragment of white marble without edges; letters, *c.* 0.04

...]R̦[...

1965 = SC221. Fragment from right side of white marble panel; letters, 0.05, with traces of colouring in trench:

...] *vacat* / ...]s *vac.* / ...] *vac.*

1964h = SC70. Fragment of white marble panel without edges; letters incomplete:

...]SE[...

1964 = SC576. Fragment of white marble panel without edges; letters, 0.052:

...]SM̦[...

1949b. Fragment of white marble panel without edges; letters incomplete:

...]S[...

1963 = SC762. Fragment of white marble without edges; letters, 0.045:

...]I̦[... / ...]V[...

1964b = SC839. Fragment of marble without edges; letters, incomplete but not less than 0.04:

...]V̦[...

(xi) I LATERIZI

Lidia Paroli

I laterizi provenienti dallo scavo di Santa Cornelia attualmente conservati nel Museo dell'Alto Medioevo, Roma, ammontano complessivamente ad un centinaio di pezzi circa, dei quali settantaquattro sono muniti di bollo ed assegnabili, quasi senza eccezione, al periodo romano. È molto probabile quindi che questo materiale costituisca una selezione dei tipi principali rinvenuti nello scavo, considerato anche il suo carattere altamente rappresentativo. In assenza però di dati quantitativi complessivi non si è potuto tenere conto nello studio della distribuzione spaziale e nella sequenza stratigrafica che avrebbe condotto certamente a risultati maggiori, come nel caso emblematico di Ponte Nepesino nell'*Ager Faliscus*, reso più favorevole dalla scoperta di una grande catasta di laterizi perfettamente conservati sul posto (Stone 1984; in generale sui metodi per la campionatura e la pubblicazione dei laterizi romani, si veda ad esempio Young 1979). Un punto di riferimento essenziale è comunque offerto dalla fornace per laterizi scoperta sul sito, relativa alla fase 3b (*c.* 1025-1040) (cfr. *supra*) che funge da caposaldo cronologico per la produzione medievale di tegole non solo a Santa Cornelia ma per tutta l'area romana. A questa fornace si possono riferire infatti sia scarti di lavorazione che prodotti finiti.

Il nucleo più consistente è comunque formato dai laterizi di epoca classica (tegole, ma sopratutto mattoni), nessuno dei quali è stato ritrovato *in situ*. Essi costituiscono quindi l'esito del secolare riuso del materiale da costruzione 'cavato' dalle strutture insediative classiche presenti in gran numero nell'*Ager Veientanus* (Kahane *et al.* 1968, 145-160). In particolare il gruppo dei laterizi bollati è costituito da sessantaquattro esemplari con bollo epigrafico ed otto con bollo senza testo; altri due esemplari bollati, molto frammentari, sono menzionati nell'elenco redatto all'epoca dello scavo dalla Kahane, ma non sono risultati più reperibili. Uno di essi (frammento numero SC233) non era identificabile, ma poteva essere attribuito secondo la Kahane alla fine del secondo secolo d.C., l'altro (SC840) poteva forse essere identificato con *CIL* XV. 1474, databile in tal caso nell'ambito del primo secolo d.C. Questo gruppo, benchè decontestualizzato, riveste comunque il più grande interesse perchè, oltre a documentare più o meno estesamente i primi tre secoli dell'impero, ci offre una rara concentrazione di bolli tardo-antichi, assolutamente eccezionale per la Campagna romana (cfr. numeri 39-42).

Nella presentazione dei laterizi bollati si è prestata una certa attenzione anche al manufatto ceramico, non solo per quanto riguarda l'identificazione del tipo di laterizio su cui il bollo è stato impresso, ma anche dell'impasto e ciò con un duplice scopo: da una parte individuare le trasformazioni che potevano essere eventualmente intervenute nei processi produttivi nel lungo periodo; dall'altra verificare il valore diagnostico dell'impasto in relazione al problema della definizione delle officine di provenienza dei laterizi bollati, ovvero verificare la variabilità degli impasti all'interno di un centro produttore noto. Certamente questo genere di osservazione sarebbe senz'altro più feconda se applicata ad un campione molto vasto, ma anche nel caso di un campione molto limitato come quello di Santa Cornelia, essa ha dato delle indicazioni che, sebbene non possano essere considerate definitive, sembrano comunque piuttosto significative. È bene precisare che l'esame degli impasti è stata effettuato a livello di osservazione macroscopica, ad occhio nudo o con l'ausilio di una normale lente di ingrandimento così come la descrizione che ne viene data prescinde completamente (e volutamente) da termini specialistici, avendo il solo scopo di evidenziare le caratteristiche salienti dell'impasto per facilitarne il riconoscimento da parte di ciascuno in ogni occasione, senza l'intervento di mezzi particolari. Questa scelta è stata suggerita anche dalla consapevolezza che le componenti mineralogiche degli impasti di gran parte dell'opus doliare 'urbano' (per l'accezione da dare a questo termine, cfr. Steinby 1981a, 237-239) sono omogenee e quindi irrilevanti per la determinazione dell'area di fabbricazione, a meno di non adottare sistemi di analisi molto sofisticati. Ogni prodotto finito ha comunque una sua peculiarità in base alla quale si riesce talvolta a distinguerlo o accorparlo ad altri. Si tratta evidentemente solo di un primo livello di analisi i cui risultati possono però essere utili per orientare ricerche più approfondite, ma che possono fin d'ora, combinandosi con informazioni acquisite per altre vie, portare alla soluzione di qualche caso particolare.

Per quanto riguarda invece la presentazione del testo epigrafico, si è cercato di uniformare, nei limiti del possibile, l'organizzazione dei dati anagrafici a quella adottata in Steinby (1977-1978), a cui si rimanda per una descrizione dettagliata e per la spiegazione di tutte le convenzioni epigrafiche.

Nel commento ci si è preoccupati soprattutto di esplicitare le ragioni di alcune identificazioni o interpretazioni in modo da rendere possibili eventuali correzioni o modifiche. Non si è invece preteso di riportare la bibliografia completa dei singoli bolli, rimandando per questo alle opere principali attraverso le quali è comunque possibile risalire alle fonti. Si è ritenuto però opportuno fare un richiamo al capitolo delle concordanze degli *Indici complementari ai bolli doliari urbani (CIL XV. 1)*, nel quale è riassunta tutta l'eventuale vicenda seguita da un bollo, dalla pubblicazione nel *CIL* XV. 1 ad oggi. Si sono inseriti inoltre tutti quei riferimenti bibliografici che permettessero un primo inquadramento del bollo in relazione alla sua cronologia, fabbrica di provenienza, proprietà, ecc. In linea di massima tutto il materiale, bollato o meno, è stato ordinato in successione cronologica per ampie fasce, al cui interno non si possono tuttavia escludere fluttuazioni più o meno consistenti nel caso soprattutto di materiali molto frammentari.

(a) BOLLI EPIGRAFICI

1 – Frammento numero SC733 (MAM numero di inventario 1988). Bollo rettangolare. Sig. 9.3, 4; litt. 2; fr. 20+, 20+, 2.8.

    ] И AE [.   N inversa

Il bollo non è identificabile con sicurezza a causa della lacuna nella parte finale del testo dove rimane il tratto superiore di un segno, forse una A o una M (o un elemento decorativo ?). L'identifcazione con *CIL* XV. 1323c, l'unica eventualmente possibile, rimane comunque molto dubbia perchè nel nostro esemplare non appare il segno di interpunzione dopo la È e lo spazio residuo per le lettere finali del testo (AS) non sembra sufficiente. Può trattarsi pertanto anche di un bollo nuovo. Dal punto di vista della forma e dei caratteri epigrafici è particolarmente vicino a Bloch 1948, numero 343, di cui si veda una riproduzione in Steinby 1977-1978, numero 986, ed è databile, analogamente ad un gruppo consistente di bolli dei *Naevi*, in età augustea o negli anni immediatamente successivi (Steinby 1977, 67).

Il bollo è impresso su un laterizio non identificabile, con impasto di colore arancione spento (5 YR 6/3), grossolano con prevalenza di inclusi marrone-rossicci arrotondati, di dimensioni medie e grandi, disposti piuttosto regolarmente. È attribuibile, secondo l'ipotesi avanzata dalla Steinby per tutti i bolli dei *Naevi*, alle figline *Naevianae* (cfr. Steinby 1977-1978, numero 984).

2 – SC884 (numero di inventario 1967). Bollo semicircolare. Sig. 8 ca., 5; orb. 3 ca.; litt. 1.4-1.5; lin. 1, 2; fr. 17+, 12+, 3.1.

    C · VICC[I   ramus mali punicae vel papaveris]

Il bollo con lettere larghe, regolari ad estremità patenti è identificabile con *CIL* XV. 1510a o, meno probabilmente, con la variante d (cfr. Steinby 1977-1978, numero 1083; Steinby 1987, 398). Fa propendere per la prima soluzione l'ampio spazio residuo dopo l'ultima C che permette l'accoglimento del *signum*. È riferibile ad un gruppo di bolli databili nel periodo tra Claudio e Nerone prodotti in officine di identificazione molto discussa (Steinby 1977, 95-96). Nel caso specifico il bollo è impresso su un laterizio frammentario, forse un bessale, dall'impasto di colore arancione chiaro (5 YR 8/3), molto depurato e micaceo, con rari inclusi marrone-rossicci tondeggianti, di grandi dimensioni.

3 – SC737 (numero di inventario 1966). Bollo rettangolare. Sig. 7 +, 2.5; litt. 1.8-1.5 (O); fr. 7 +, 6.5 +, 2.5.

     ] ONI·L· [.

Bollo non identificato, probabilmente nuovo poichè l'ultima lettera, solo parzialmente conservata, può essere identificata solo con una E o una F. Ciò consente di escludere sia l'interpretazione come variante di *CIL* XV. 824 sia la coincidenza con il nuovo bollo Steinby 1987, 127, 387, numero 814/5, rispetto al quale il nostro esemplare presenta anche una diversa punteggiatura. La forma del timbro, con lettere in rilievo piuttosto grandi, i caratteri epigrafici, di cui si sottolinea la vicinanza con Steinby 1977-1978, numero 688, ed anche la formula, frequente su *dolia* (cfr. ad esempio Bloch 1948, numero 505 e 513; per le formule in uso nell'*opus doliare* del primo secolo d.C. si veda Steinby 1981a, 237-238), suggeriscono una datazione nell'ambito del primo secolo d.C.

Il laterizio, estremamente frammentario, ha un impasto di colore arancione spento (5 YR 7/4), grossolano, con inclusi numerosi ma prevalentemente medi e piccoli per lo più di tipo chiaro trasparente e angoloso; anche gli inclusi molto grandi, piuttosto rari, sono quasi tutti di questo stesso tipo; presenza di chamotte. Si sottolinea la notevole diversità di questo impasto rispetto a quelli, in genere più omogenei, di gran parte dei bolli rinvenuti a Santa Cornelia.

4 – SC569 (numero di inventario 1986). Bollo rettangolare. Sig. 7.5 +, 2.4; litt. 1.5; fr. 8 +, 7.5 +, 2.5.

     ] ŞCI CÂES

Bollo non identificato, probabilmente nuovo, con lettere molto accurate ad estremità fortemente patenti. Qualora appartenga alla produzione urbana, come si ritiene probabile, esso può essere datato sulla base del tipo del bollo nell'ambito del primo secolo d.C., probabilmente tra la metà e la seconda metà del secolo (cfr. Steinby 1977, 19ss.).

Il laterizio su cui si trova impresso, molto frammentario, ha un impasto piuttosto simile a quello del numero 9, ma di colore più rosso (10 R 5/6), ricchissimo di piccoli inclusi bianchi opachi e con qualche raro incluso scuro arrotondato, più grande.

5 – SC162 (numero di inventario 2148). Bollo circolare con orbicolo grande. Sig. 9.6; orb. 5.1; litt. 1-1.1, 1-1.3 (T̂I); lin. 1, 2, 1; fr. 42 +, 18.5 +, 4.3.

   M· CERCINI·FRVCTI̦ SEX
     ALLI·FORTVNAT̂I̦
        O̅

CIL XV. 923; Bloch 1947, 56; Steinby 1977-1978, numero 739 corregge la punteggiatura ed evidenzia il legame finale della seconda riga, poco visibile nel nostro esemplare; più difficile l'individuazione del punto dopo la M, presente nel bollo ostiense, a meno che non si debba interpretare in questo senso il piccolo apice in alto a destra di questa lettera. Il segno al centro rimane ancora di significato oscuro; si può interpretare anche come due lettere (CO) disposte perpendicolarmente alle altre due righe. Per una datazione tra la fine del primo e gli inizi del secondo secolo d.C. si veda Bloch (1947, 56) che ne sottolinea la presenza nei Mercati di Traiano inaugurati nell'anno 112 d.C. Il bollo è impresso su di un mattone di grandi dimensioni, con impasto di colore arancione (2.5 YR 6/6), non molto grossolano con inclusi angolosi assolutamente trasparenti e molto brillanti, di dimensioni medie e grandi e qualche incluso nero di dimensioni più piccole.

6 – SC446 (numero di inventario 1989a); SC842 (numero di inventario 1989b).

(i) Bollo circolare con orbicolo grande e centro in rilievo. Sig. 8 ca.; orb. 4 ca.; litt. 1; fr. 15 +, 7.5 +, 3.5.

DOL· ANTEROT· SEVER· CAE[S]

(ii) Bollo del tipo precedente ma di diversa matrice. Sig. ?; orb. ?; litt. 1.1-1.2; lin. 1, 2, ?; fr. 19 +, 15 +, 4.

DOL· AN[TEROT· SEVER·CAES]

CIL XV. 811 f o e; Bloch 1947, 15-18, Tav. A, Fig. 4; 111-112; Steinby 1977-1978, numero 684; Steinby 1981b, 316, numeri 61-62; Steinby 1987, 387.

Per il primo bollo l'identificazione con *CIL* XV. 811f si deve ritenere certa poichè è possibile scorgere ancora presso la linea di frattura la parte superiore del nesso AE (ben visibile anche nel calco); per il secondo esemplare, molto più frammentario, è possibile anche l'alternativa con la variante e. Si tratta comunque di bolli realizzati con matrici diverse, la prima coincidente perfettamente con quella di Steinby 1977-1978, numero 684 I.

A livello macroscopico gli impasti dei laterizi su cui si trovano impressi appaiono piuttosto dissimili sicchè sembra difficile pensare alla provenienza dalla stessa cava. Nel primo esemplare esso è di colore rosa chiaro (2.5 YR 7/4), non molto grossolano, con inclusi piccoli e medi non troppo numerosi, tra cui ben visibili quelli arrotondati di colore marrone, altri neri, spigolosi e brillanti oltre a qualche incluso trasparente, angoloso; nel secondo esemplare invece l'impasto, oltre ad essere molto più chiaro (5 YR 8/3), è più grossolano con inclusi dello stesso tipo del precedente ma molto più numerosi e in media più piccoli. È possibile dunque che alla varietà dei timbri, segnalata già dal Dressel e dalla Steinby (cfr. in particolare Steinby 1977-1978, numero 684), corrispondano officine con ubicazioni diverse nell'ambito delle proprietà imperiali in cui fu attivo *Anteros* (cfr. Bloch 1947, 15-18, 112, 337). Per una datazione nella prima età traianea (primo decennio del secondo secolo d.C.) si veda in particolare Steinby 1981b, 316, numeri 61-62).

7 – SC391 (numero di inventario 1983). Bollo circolare. Sig. 7.9; litt. 1-1.1; lin. ?; fr. 15 +, 10 +, 4.7.

CN DOMITI CRH[YSER]O   *sic*
    ramus palmae

CIL XV. 1105; Bloch 1947, 51, 55; Steinby 1977, 56; Steinby 1977-1978, numero 872; Steinby 1987, 392.

Il bollo è stato impresso con un timbro rotto in quattro parti su di un laterizio non identificabile delle figline dei *Domitii*, uno dei più grandi e duraturi stabilimenti per la produzione laterizia di Roma in età imperiale, di cui è stato possibile ricostruire la vicenda dalla età flavia all'età severiana e seguirne le tracce ancora in età tardoantica (cfr. Bloch 1947, 28-29, 297-298, 302, 311 e nota 30; Steinby 1977, 37-40, 47-58; Steinby 1986, 103-105). Per quanto concerne in particolare questo bollo esso è databile nel primo decennio del secondo secolo (cfr. Steinby 1977, 37-40, 47-58). In questo lungo arco di tempo, per lo meno dagli inizi del secondo secolo ai Severi, la produzione delle figline *Domitianae* conserva caratteri estremamente omogenei a giudicare almeno dagli impasti degli esemplari rinvenuti a Santa Cornelia (cfr. numeri 25, 34 e 35) mentre se ne distacca leggermente quello del bollo delle figline *Novae* (cfr. numero 33). L'impasto di colore sempre chiaro, variante dal giallo (2.5 Y 8/3) al giallo-rosa più o meno intenso (10 YR 8/3), è piuttosto grossolano, ricco di inclusi di tipi diversi, in genere medi o grandi ma talvolta anche molto grandi; tra questi ultimi figurano numerosi non solo quelli rossicci arrotondati ma anche quelli trasparenti angolosi.

8 – SC429 (numero di inventario 1981). Bollo circolare con orbicolo medio e centro in rilievo. Sig. 8 ca.; orb. 3.5 ca; litt. 1.1-1.2; fr. 25 +, 16 +, 3.2.

[B]ṚVT LVPI

CIL XV. 29e; Bloch 1947, 36, 68; Steinby 1977, 27; Steinby 1977-1978, numero 55 (ma di diversa matrice); Steinby 1987, 375.

Il bollo è impresso su un laterizio tipico delle figline *Brutianae*, le cosidette 'piccole tegole' descritte dal Gismondi (1953, 201) a proposito degli edifici ostiensi per le quali la Steinby (1974, 394) mette in dubbio molto fondatamente la destinazione come elementi di copertura. Questi laterizi presentano un margine sporgente, simile ad una cortissima aletta che si trova spesso segata come in tutti gli esemplari ritrovati a Santa Cornelia (cfr. numeri 9 e 23); lungo il margine corre una scanalatura più o meno profonda (cfr. Steinby 1974, 401, Fig. 8), un accorgimento dettato forse da considerazioni di natura estetica in quanto riduce l'altezza del letto di malta visibile in cortina. L'impasto è altrettanto tipico, anche se può presentarsi più o meno depurato e con una certa variabilità del colore dall'arancione spento (2.5 YR 6/4) al marrone rossastro (2.5 YR 5/4); la massa di fondo è in genere fine e compatta, punteggiata da radi inclusi marrone-rossicci, arrotondati che raggiungono talvolta anche dimensioni grandi, ricchissima in qualche caso di piccolissimi inclusi bianchi opachi (cfr. anche numero 9).

Le figline *Brutianae* furono di proprietà di M. Rutilio Lupo, *praefectus Aegypti* dal 113 al 117 d.C., dalla prima età traianea all'anno 123 d.C. (cfr. Bloch 1947, 316-320; Steinby 1977, 27-28). Questo bollo in particolare è databile nella prima fase della produzione, antecedentemente all'anno 110 o all'anno 114 d.C. (Steinby 1977, 27).

9 – SC561 (numero di inventario 1996). Bollo circolare con orbicolo grande. Sig. 9.5 ca.; orb. 4.4; litt. 1.3-1.5; lin.?; fr. 15 +, 12 +, 3.8.

[BRVT·M R·L·HAST· V]OP· COṢ
[Lupus ds. gradiens altero pede anteriore sublato]

CIL XV. 19 a o b; Steinby 1977-1978, numeri 32 e 33; Steinby 1987, 375.

Perduta larga parte del testo non è possibile stabilire a quale delle due varianti appartenga questo frammento. È impresso su di un laterizio tipico delle figline *Brutianae* di M. Rutilio Lupo (cfr. numero 8 e anche numero 23, a cui si rimanda per la descrizione dell'impasto e la bibliografia). Datazione consolare all'anno 114 d.C.

10 – SC395 (numero di inventario 1977). Bollo rettangolare a lettere incavate. Sig. 6 +, 2.2; litt. 2.2; fr. 19 +, 18.5 +, 3.5; piccolo bollo circolare anepigrafe in alto, in corrispondenza della R; presso il margine superiore punzonature circolari allineate o disposte a cerchio o semicerchio.

[SAL EX PR C]OR SEVE

Bloch 1947, 48; Bloch 1948, numero 125; Steinby 1977, 83; Steinby 1977-1978, numero 446 I; Steinby 1987, 381.

Alcune lettere sono lacunose: la prima E di SEVE manca della metà superiore del tratto verticale, nella seconda E il tratto superiore orizzontale è stato sostituito da due punzonature circolari esattamente come nell'esemplare sopra citato di Ostia; molti altri bolli a lettere incavate di questo stesso periodo presentano fenomeni analoghi. Nello stesso modo è caratteristica l'associazione con elementi decorativi punzonati (cfr. in particolare Steinby 1977-1978, numero 446 III dove il bollo è accompagnato da punti incavati disposti a forma di croce). Per altri esempi di lettere o elementi decorativi realizzati a punzone si veda da ultimo Steinby 1986, 440 nota 37 con elenco completo anche dei bolli di età traianea ed adrianea associati a bolli anepigrafi.

Il bollo è impresso su di un bessale ritagliato, conservato quasi per intero, appartenente all'*opus Salarese*, un complesso di figline specializzate nella produzione di bessali, dislocate sulla via Salaria, molto attive nei primi due decenni del secondo secolo d.C. Questo bollo in particolare è databile nella prima età traianea (Steinby 1977, 83; 83-86 per la cronologia delle figline *Salareses*; per l'identificazione di *Cn. Cornelius Severus*, proprietario di un'officina sulla via Salaria, si veda Bloch 1947, 179-180).

L'impasto, di colore arancione spento (5 YR 6/4) è poco grossolano, con inclusi non molto frequenti e quasi sempre di piccole o piccolissime dimensioni, marroni arrotondati. Un impasto abbastanza simile ricorre anche nel numero 16 e nel numero 26, delle stesse figline, mentre altri laterizi, pur recando lo stesso marchio di fabbrica, mostrano caratteristiche alquanto diverse (cfr. numero 15 e probabilmente anche il numero 17). La varietà degli impasti delle figline della Via Salaria costituisce comunque un fenomeno già noto (Steinby 1974, 396).

11 – SC84 (numero di inventario 1980). Bollo circolare con centro in rilievo. Sig. 7.8; litt. 1.4-1.5; lin. 1, 1; fr. 18 +, 14 +, 4.

    ṬVNN· ṢEX̣· VISM· HIMER·

Bloch 1948, numero 192; Steinby 1977, 99; Steinby 1977-1978, numero 545 con correzione della punteggiatura.

Nel nostro esemplare l'impronta è danneggiata quasi sempre in corrispondenza dell'interpunzione che non può pertanto essere confrontata con sicurezza. Il timbro sembra però corrispondere a quello dell'esemplare ostiense.

Il laterizio su cui è impresso ha un impasto di colore chiaro, giallo rosato (10 YR 8/3) non molto grossolano, con inclusi poco frequenti, di colore marrone-rossiccio arrotondati, grandi o molto grandi, che ricorre anche in altri esemplari delle figline *Tunneianae* da cui proviene anche questo bollo (cfr. numero 13, ma anche il numero 18). Per una datazione nel primo decennio del secondo secolo d.C. si veda Steinby (1977), a cui si rimanda anche per la cronologia di questa figline.

12 – SC219 (numero di inventario 1982). Bollo circolare con orbicolo grande. Sig. 7 +; orb. 4 ca.; litt. 1.5; lin. ?; fr. 10 +, 7 +, 4.5.

    palma SEX· Ṿ[IMATI HINIERI palma]   *sic sic*

CIL XV. 1517a; Steinby 1973-74, 113; Steinby 1977, 99; Steinby 1977-1978, numero 1089; Steinby 1987, 398.

È preferibile l'attribuzione alla variante a anzichè b perchè non sembra possa identificarsi una stella nel segno di interpunzione dopo SEX. Il bollo è distinto da lettere piuttosto alte come quello ostiense 1089, realizzato molto probabilmente con lo stesso timbro, per il quale si è ipotizzata una provenienza dalle figline *Tunneianae* (Steinby 1977, 99) dove si conoscono altri laterizi bollati da *Sex. Vismatus Himerus* (cfr. anche numero 11). Nel caso specifico il laterizio su cui è impresso il bollo ha un impasto che, almeno macroscopicamente, è completamente diverso da quello degli altri bolli delle *Tonneianae* presenti a Santa Cornelia (numeri 11, 13, ma si veda anche il numero 18): di colore arancione spento (2.5 YR 6/4), molto micaceo e poco grossolano, presenta inclusi quasi esclusivamente piccoli o piccolissimi tra cui numerosi quelli bianchi opachi. Per questo esemplare la provenienza dalla medesima cava degli altri prodotti delle *Tonneianae* sembra pertanto improbabile. Per una datazione al primo decennio del secondo secolo d.C. si veda Steinby 1977, 99.

13 – SC392 (numero di inventario 1979). Bollo circolare con orbicolo medio. Sig. 9 ca; orb. 5 ca; litt. 1.1-1.2, 1.1-1.3; lin. 1, 1, ?; fr. 11.5 +, 26 +, 3.5.

    [ramus palmae] ṬEG̣ [·TV]N·DOL·EVTYCHṾṢ ṢE̤
              IVḶIAE̤ PROCVḶAE̤
           ramuṣ palmae

CIL XV. 647; Bloch 1947, 178-179; Steinby 1977, 99.

Impronta poco profonda e piuttosto consunta, nondimeno ben identificabile, su laterizio delle figline *Tunneianae* di proprietà di *Iulia Procula*, databile nel secondo decennio del secondo secolo (per l'identificazione di questo personaggio si veda in particolare Bloch 1947, 179, nota 148; per la cronologia delle figline *Tunneianae* o *Tonneianae*, Steinby 1977, 94-100). L'impasto corrisponde a quello dell'altro bollo di queste figline rinvenuto a Santa Cornelia (numero 11) a cui si rimanda per la descrizione, e a quello di un altro esemplare ad esse attribuito (numero 18).

14 – SC394 (numero di inventario 1975). Bollo circolare con orbicolo medio. Sig. 9.5; orb. 4; litt. 1.1, 1.1; lin. ?, 2?, ?; fr. 16 +, 12 +, 3.

    M V̂ALERI[·PRISC · EX · PRED]I[palma]   *sic*
      PLOṬ[INAE· AVG]
      [nux pinea]

CIL XV. 702; Bloch 1947, 97, 166; Steinby 1977-1978, numero 598; Steinby 1987, 385.

Alcune divergenze nella punteggiatura e nelle linee ausiliarie rilevabili rispetto all'esemplare di Ostia sono dovute quasi certamente alla scarsa profondità dell'impronta, ma non si esclude la possibilità di una matrice diversa.

Il laterizio proviene da un'officina inclusa nei possedimenti di Plotina, moglie di Traiano, al quale subentrò nella proprietà delle figline *Quintianae* (Bloch 1947, 209-210; Bloch 1948, 30 per la loro ubicazione in Trastevere; Steinby 1977, 78-81; Steinby 1986, 442 nota 56; per altri bolli di Plotina si veda Alfonsi Mattei *et al.* 1974, 307, numero 18; Camilli e Taglietti 1979, 192, numero 11). L'impasto chiaro, di colore giallo rosato (10 YR 8/3) non è molto grossolano ma molto fessurato, con inclusi scuri prevalentemente di piccole dimensioni, ma in qualche caso grandi o molto grandi.

15 – SC188 (numero di inventario 1969); SC217 (numero di inventario 1992).

(i) Bollo rettangolare a lettere incavate. Sig. 8.2 + , 3.2; litt. 1.4-1.6, 1.4-1.5; fr. 21.5 + , 11.3 + , 3.2.

```
ḀPR ET PAE[T COS • PPB]
ṢALAR EX F̣[IG GTTT]
```

(ii) Bollo dello stesso tipo, ma forse di altra matrice. Sig. 7.5 + , 3.2; litt. 1.5, 1.5; fr. 17.5 + , 15 + , 3.8.

Altri esemplari dello stesso tipo: SC109 (numero di inventario 1993a); SC88 (numero di inventario 1993b).

```
[APR ET PAE̱T C]Q̱S• PPB
[SALAR EX FI]G̱ GTTT
```

CIL XV. 500a; Bloch 1947, 180 nota 150; Steinby 1977, 84.

I quattro esemplari sono relativi a bessali nei quali il bollo è stato dimezzato dal taglio dei *semilateres*. Nel primo si conserva la parte anteriore, negli altri tre la posteriore. Si può forse ipotizzare l'uso di due diversi timbri poichè il primo esemplare ha lettere più irregolari e di altezza variabile, ma non si può neanche escludere che ciò sia dovuto più semplicemente al suo peggiore stato di conservazione. L'impossibilità di confrontare la stessa parte di testo rende inoltre più difficoltosa la soluzione del problema.

Il bollo si riferisce a prodotti delle figline *Salareses* che nel periodo a cui esso risale (123 d.C.) erano suddivise tra diversi *domini* (per la proprietà di queste figline e la loro cronologia si vedano in particolare Bloch 1947, 164, 177-181, nota 150, 208, 337; Steinby 1977, 83-86). I proprietari della fabbrica da cui provengono i nostri bessali sono indicati dalle lettere G( ) T( ) T( ) T( ), tra cui si identifica *Trebicia Tertulla* (Steinby 1977, 84). Le iniziali P( ) P( ) B( ) dovrebbero corrispondere invece, secondo il Bloch, a quelle di un *officinator* che risulterebbe presente nello stesso periodo in altre figline (Bloch 1947, 164, 180-181 nota 150, 208). Tale interpretazione è comunque difficile da accogliere per l'anomalia creata dalla presenza di uno stesso *officinator* contemporaneamente in più fabbriche (Steinby 1977, 84).

Si è già sottolineato in precedenza (cfr. numero 10) la presenza di diversi impasti tra i laterizi della via Salaria, di cui si ha un immediato riscontro anche in questo gruppo di bessali con lo stesso bollo, tre dei quali (SC188, 109, 88) hanno un impasto di colore chiaro (10 YR 8/3-4), il quarto (SC217) di colore arancione rosato (10 R 6/6). Essi tuttavia non differiscono sostanzialmente per quanto riguarda il tipo di inclusi, per lo più rossicci tondeggianti, la loro grandezza (media e grande, qualche volta molto grande) e la loro distribuzione (poco frequente) né per la consistenza dell'impasto, friabile e molto polveroso. In questo caso dunque la differenza consiste soprattutto nel colore che può però dipendere da fenomeni di cottura, di trattamento dell'argilla e non necessariamente da una diversa fonte di approvvigionamento. Una variazione del tutto simile si osserva anche nel nostro gruppo di laterizi tardo-antichi con il bollo dell'officina di Benigno (cfr. numeri 41-42). Una cava separata deve invece essere ipotizzata per gli impasti dei numeri 10 e 26 che pur appartenendo all'*opus Salarese* hanno caratteristiche affatto distinte.

16 – SC981 (numero di inventario 1971). Bollo rettangolare a lettere incavate e margini visibili. Sig. 7 + , 3.5; litt. 1.2, 1.2-1.3; fr. 16 + , 11 + , 3.8.

```
PAET ET AP[R COS]
EX P IVḶ EV̱[T SAL]
```

CIL XV. 487 b o c; Bloch 1947, 146; Steinby 1977, 85; Steinby 1987, 381.

La L è solo parzialmente impressa: ne rimane la parte superiore del tratto verticale. Il laterizio, probabilmente un bessale, proviene dalla figline *Salareses* come i numeri 10, 15 e 26, a cui si rimanda per altre indicazioni. È caratterizzato da un impasto di colore arancione (5 **YR** 6/6), abbastanza simile a quello del numero 10, ma più grossolano. Per *Iulius Eutactus* si veda Bloch 1947, 172, 176, 185. Datazione consolare all'anno 123 d.C.

17 – SC230 (numero di inventario 1970). Bollo rettangolare a lettere incavate. Sig. 8+, 2.9; litt. 1.4, 1.4; fr. 22, 15+, 3.8.

```
APRO ET PAE Ç[OS]
M VIN HERCV[LAN]
```

CIL XV. 1529a; Bloch 1947, 129, 171, 176; Steinby 1973, 125 numero 66; Steinby 1977-1978, numero 1097.

L'identificazione con *CIL* XV. 1529a è la più probabile considerata anche l'identità con il bollo ostiense 1097. É impresso su di un bessale frammentario, ma non ritagliato, che ha un impasto affine a quello del SC217 (cfr. numero 15) delle figline *Salareses* da dove il Bloch riteneva potesse provenire anche il bollo *CIL* XV. 1529a (1947, 171). Datazione consolare all'anno 123 d.C.

18 – SC580 (numero di inventario 1997). Bollo circolare con orbicolo medio nel cui centro si trova una piccola cavità circolare. Sig. 9 ca; orb. 3; litt. 0.9, 0.8-1 (N̂I); lin. 1, 2, 2; fr. 16+, 8.5+, 2.5.

```
[L · A P· EX · F · FLAVIAES PROC]LAÊS OP · DO
    [PAETINO ET . APR] ON̂IAN
              SO⊃
    modius [ex quo pendent spicae]
```

(*v.3 linea recta* rigo capovolto.) *CIL* XV. 1157; Bloch 1947, 176; Steinby 1977, 76, 99-100.

Bollo attribuito già dal Dressel e poi dalla Steinby alle figline *Tonneianae*, ipotesi che trova un preciso riscontro nella assoluta identità dell'impasto di questo bollo con quello degli esemplari di Santa Cornelia recanti il marchio di queste figline (cfr. i numeri 11 e 13, con particolare riguardo a quest'ultimo pertinente a *Iulia Procula*, ai quali si rimanda per la descrizione). Datazione consolare all'anno 123 d.C.

19 – SC396 (numero di inventario 1968). Bollo rettangolare a lettere incavate. Sig. 8.5+, 3.2; litt. 1.5, 1.5; fr. 17+, 13+, 4.

```
[APRO]N ET PAE COS
[HEL]PISZONT          Z capovolta
```

CIL XV. 1175; Bloch 1947, 207-208; Steinby 1977, 79.

Il bollo proviene dalle figline di *M. Annius Verus* nei *praedia Quintanensia* per i quali si veda Bloch 1947, 204-210; Steinby 1977, 78-80. È impresso su di un bessale ritagliato, dall'impasto di colore arancione spento (5 **YR** 7/3), con una massa di fondo micacea e piuttosto depurata nella quale spiccano dei grandissimi inclusi marroni arrotondati, piuttosto frequenti. Datazione consolare all'anno 123 d.C.

20 – SC218 (numero di inventario 1972) (Pl. 55,a). Bollo rettangolare. Sig. 15.5+, 3.6; litt. 1, 1; fr. 18+, 12+, 3.9.

```
FLÂVI PHO EX FIG FLÂVI POŞ[IDONI]
VIA NOM PÂETINO ET ÂPRONIĹ·COS]
```

Bloch 1948, numero 205 di cui questo esemplare costituisce il completamento.

Nell'impronta, poco nitida, non si rileva con sicurezza il punto riportato dal Bloch dopo PAETINO. È impresso su un laterizio, probabilmente di grandi dimensioni, delle figline della Via Nomentana (cfr. Steinby 1977, 100-101).

Presenta un impasto abbastanza particolare con grandi chiazze rotonde arancioni o bianche, molto più depurate rispetto al resto dell'impasto, il quale è di colore arancione spento (5 **YR** 7/4), grossolano, con numerosi inclusi rossicci arrotondati, di medie dimensioni. Datazione consolare all'anno 123 d.C.

Plate 55,a. Santa Cornelia: tile stamp number 20 (*Museo dell'Alto Medioevo*, Rome)

21 – SC566 (numero di inventario 1985). Bollo circolare probabilmente con orbicolo medio. Sig. ?; orb. ?; litt. 1.2, ?; lin. 1, 2, ?; fr. 11+, 12+, 5.

```
[EX P IVLIAE ALB] OF MONṬ
   [APR ET PAE] ÇOȘ
```

CIL XV. 1216; Bloch 1947, 200, 203; Steinby 1977-1978, numero 930.

Bollo molto frammentario impresso su mattone di notevole spessore proveniente dall'officina *Montani* nei *praedia* di *Iulia Albana*, di cui non si hanno altre notizie.

L'impasto del laterizio è di colore chiaro, arancione rosato (5 YR 8/3), grossolano, nel quale si alternano sassolini ed altre grosse impurità ad una massa di inclusi rossicci tondeggianti, distribuiti irregolarmente. Esso appare singolarmente simile a quello del numero 27. Datazione consolare all'anno 123 d.C.

22 – SC563 (numero di inventario 1974). Bollo circolare con orbicolo medio. Sig. 8+; orb. ?; litt. 1, 1; lin. 1, 2, 2; fr. 8+, 13+, 4.

```
Ẹ[X · P·] C · Ñ · TI CḶ[AVDI · IRENAEI]
    ṖAEṬ · Ẹ[T · APRÓN]
       [SO]Ɔ
```

V.3 *linea recta* rigo capovolto. *CIL* XV. 704a; Steinby 1977-1978, numero 602.

Il bollo proviene dalle figline di proprietà dell'imperatore Adriano ed è impresso su di un laterizio non identificabile, dall'impasto chiaro, di colore arancione rosato (5 YR 8/3), con una massa di fondo poco grossolana nella quale si osserva però un numero consistente di enormi inclusi marroni arrotondati.

23 – SC653 (numero di inventario 1973). Bollo rettangolare. Sig. 2+, 4.2; litt. 1.4, 1.4; lin. 1, 2, ?; fr. 19+, 10+, 3.2.

```
EX [
ṖAẸ [
```

Bollo molto frammentario di difficile identificazione, impresso su un laterizio in tutto corrispondente a quelli tipici delle figline *Brutianae* descritti in precedenza (cfr. numeri 8 e 9 a cui si rimanda anche per la descrizione dell'impasto). Ciò consente di escludere l'identificazione con il bollo *CIL* XV. 71 = Steinby 1977-1978, numero 104 delle figline *Caepionianae*, molto simile al nostro anche nelle misure a differenza di altri bolli che hanno lo stesso inizio (si veda ad esempio Bloch 1948, numero 175 = Steinby 1977-1978, numero 504; Bloch 1948, numero 29; cfr. Bloch 1947, 191, Fig. 30).

Il bollo reca la data consolare all'anno 123 d.C., anno in cui si ritiene che anche le figline *Brutianae* siano già passate, come tutte le altre figline di M. Rutilio Lupo, ad un altro proprietario (cfr. Steinby 1977, 28 per le difficoltà di individuare un eventuale proprietario dell'anno 123 che preceda *T. Statilius Maximus Severus Hadrianus* che bolla i laterizi delle figline *Brutianae* a partire dall'anno 124 d.C.). Si deve sottolineare che nessun bollo di queste figline databile al 123 d.C. presenta una formula compatibile con l'inizio di questo frammento.

24 – SC655 (numero di inventario 1976). Bollo circolare con orbicolo medio. Sig. 9 ca; orb. 3.5; litt. 1.2, 1, 1-0.9 (O); lin. 1, 2, 2; fr. 10+, 12+, 3.7.

    EX · FIG PL · NEP · Q [D · VALERI · PR]ISCI

        SERVIAN[O $\overline{\text{III}}$] ET · VÂRO
           SO⊃

V. 3 *linea recta* rigo capovolto. *CIL* XV. 1366; Bloch 1947, 166, 181; Steinby 1973-74, 120; Steinby 1977-1978, numero 1009.

Si osservano lievi divergenze nella punteggiatura sia con il testo riprodotto nel *CIL*, che riporta un punto dopo FIG, che in Steinby 1977-1978, dove manca il punto dopo EX, ben visibile invece nel nostro esemplare. Il bollo appartiene alle figline di *A. Plaetorius Nepos*, eminente personaggio ed amico dell'imperatore Adriano, nelle quali ritroviamo l'*officinator M. Valerius Priscus* già visto nel bollo numero 14, relativo alle figline di proprietà di Plotina, moglie di Traiano.

Il laterizio su cui è impresso ha un impasto molto chiaro, appena rosato (7.5 YR 8/2), piuttosto depurato, con qualche raro incluso arrotondato. Datazione consolare all'anno 134 d.C.

25 – SC694 (numero di inventario 1990). Bollo circolare con orbicolo medio. Sig.9.2; orb.4; litt.1-1.1, 1-1.1; lin.1, 2, 2; fr. 21+, 18.5+, 4.

    QPV · DQ[L ⁚ EPAGA]THV · CLAVDI
        QV [INQVA] ŞER
          nux pinea

CIL XV. 1075a; Bloch 1947, 75, 345; Steinby 1977, 53; Steinby 1987, 391.

Bollo in parte corroso, ma comunque ben identificabile, proveniente dalle figline *Domitianae*. È attribuibile a *Domitia Cn. f. Lucilla* o a sua figlia *Domitia P. f. Lucilla* e databile nella prima età adrianea o poco prima (Bloch 1947, 75, 345; Steinby, 1977, 53). Per l'impasto cfr. numero 7 a cui si rimanda anche per altre notizie sulle figline *Domitianae*.

26 – SC403 (numero di inventario 1978). Bollo rettangolare a lettere incavate e margini appena visibili. Sig. 7+, 3.1; litt. 2.5; fr. 15+, 18.5+, 3.8.

    [S]AL F

Bloch 1947, 136; Bloch 1948, numero 149; Steinby 1977, 84.

Anche in questo esemplare dell'*opus Salarese* alcune lettere sono lacunose, in questo caso la A. I margini del bollo sono visibili sul lato destro, ma solo i tratti orizzontali. Si tratta di un bessale ritagliato di cui si conservano parte dei tre lati, con un impasto molto simile a quello del numero 10, prodotto nelle stesse officine. Per una datazione in età traianea o nei primi anni di Adriano, si veda la bibliografia.

27 – SC320 (numero di inventario 1995). Bollo rettangolare a lettere incavate. Sig. 7+, 2.2; litt. 2.2; fr. 19.3+, 12+, 3.2.

    [ƎVI Ⅎ]VꞨА Х₹Ş   *Testo retrogrado*

CIL XV. 823; Steinby 1977-1978, numero 693 I; Steinby 1987, 387.

In due lettere manca un tratto: nella E quello orizzontale superiore, nella X quello superiore destro; mancano inoltre i margini, visibili nell'esemplare di Ostia. Benchè lacunoso della parte iniziale si può escludere con sicurezza la sua identificazione con la variante SEAX (cfr. Steinby

1977-1978, numero 694) perchè si conserva presso la linea di frattura la parte superiore della S retrograda. Il bollo è impresso su di un bessale ritagliato con impasto di colore chiaro, grossolano, molto simile al numero 21 a cui si rimanda per la descrizione. Databile in età traianea o nei primi anni di Adriano.

28 – SC393 (numero di inventario 1994). Bollo rettangolare a lettere incavate. Sig. 7+, 2; litt. 1.8-1.9; fr. 19.5+, 18.5+, 3.2.

    [EX F CLA]V̦ IVLL̦

CIL XV. 931b.

Bollo con lettere piuttosto grandi, non del tutto regolari e mal impresse, proveniente dalle figline di *Claudius Iullus* alle quali si riferisce anche il nuovo bollo Steinby 1987, 56, 87, 389, numero 931/2?, da Torre Angela. È impresso su un bessale ritagliato conservato quasi per intero, con impasto colore arancione (5 YR 6/6), piuttosto micaceo e grossolano, con numerosi inclusi quasi tutti del tipo marrone-rossiccio arrotondati, sia piccoli che medio-grandi. È databile all'età traianea o adrianea in analogia con gli altri bolli di questo tipo.

29 – SC734 (numero di inventario 1987). Bollo rettangolare a lettere incavate. Sig. 7+, 2.2; litt. 2.2; fr. 17+, 12+, 3.2.

    ] · SC · [

Bollo molto frammentario con la parte iniziale del testo intenzionalmente cancellata sul laterizio ancora fresco. Sulla sinistra si identifica la parte inferiore di una lettera, una I o una T probabilmente, mentre sulla destra rimane la parte superiore di un segno verticale che potrebbe essere anche casuale (non di rado si osservano sui laterizi delle scalpellature regolari). In questo caso il bollo potrebbe essere identificato con *CIL* XV. 1393 = Steinby 1977-1978, numero 1030, databile in età traianea (Steinby 1977-1978, 334), altrimenti esso rimane non identificato. Il bessale su cui è impresso ha un impasto di colore arancione piuttosto vivo (2.5 YR 6/6), micaceo ma abbastanza depurato, con pochi inclusi trasparenti, angolosi.

30 – SC593 (numero di inventario 1999). Bollo circolare. Litt. 1.2; fr. 18+, 17+, 3.9.

    E]X · FIG · [
        ] · [

Bollo molto frammentario, non identificato, con almeno due linee di testo, databile nel secondo secolo d.C., probabilmente nel periodo traianeo-adrianeo. È impresso su un laterizio dall'impasto chiarissimo (7.5 YR 8/1), molto depurato, con rari inclusi scuri, tondeggianti.

31 – SC848 (numero di inventario 2001). Bollo circolare con orbicolo medio. Sig. ?; orb. 4; litt. 1.1, ?; lin. 1, 2; fr. 8+, 11+, 4.5.

    EX [
    ·[

Bollo molto frammentario, non identificato. La prima lettera della seconda riga potrebbe essere una I. É impresso su di un laterizio di notevole spessore con un impasto molto simile a quello del numero 19. Databile genericamente tra la fine del primo secolo ed il primo quarto del secondo secolo d.C. sulla base del tipo del bollo e dei caratteri epigrafici.

32 – SC89 (numero di inventario 2147). Bollo rettangolare. Sig. 12, 1.3+; litt. 1+; fr. 51.5, 23.5+, 3.

    ·] O [····

Bollo non identificato, con testo probabilmente di due righe, ma di cui si conserva solo la parte inferiore della seconda; il bollo è comunque mal impresso perchè mancano le ultime lettere sul lato destro del sigillo che si conserva invece fino al margine. É impresso su di una tegola dimezzata in senso longitudinale, dall'impasto rosato (5 YR 7/3) poco grossolano, con inclusi trasparenti molto brillanti e angolosi, ma piuttosto radi; scuri, arrotondati, in genere piuttosto piccoli e poco frequenti; chamotte. Sulla base del tipo del bollo si può ipotizzare una datazione nella prima metà del secondo secolo d.C.

33 – SC687 (numero di inventario 2003). Bollo circolare con orbicolo. Sig. ?; orb. ?; litt. 1.1-1.2, 0.9-?; lin. ?; fr. 20+, 12+, 3.3.

```
[OPVS DOLIAR]E · EX · PRAE[DIS]
[DOMINI · N · ET · F]IGL · NO[VIS]          sic
        [ piscis  ss.,]
        [ piscis  ds. ]
```

CIL XV. 204; Bloch 1947, 23, 302; Steinby 1977, 40; Steinby 1977-1978, numero 224; Steinby 1987, 378.

Si sottolinea la scomparsa nel nostro esemplare di due segni di interpunzione (dopo DOLIARE e dopo EX) e delle linee ausiliarie dovuta alla consunzione della superficie. Sulla base della identificazione proposta, il bollo è attribuibile alle figline *Novae* attivate secondo la Steinby già dall'età di Marco Aurelio e non dall'età severiana, come sostenuto dal Bloch (1947, 298, 312-314). Questo bollo in particolare è databile intorno alla fine del secondo secolo (Steinby 1977, 40). Il laterizio su cui si trova impresso presenta un impasto affine a quello delle figline *Domitianae* (cfr. numeri 7, 25, 34, 35), ma non identico. È possibile quindi che queste figline non fossero distanti dalle *Domitianae* con cui si trovano solitamente associate. Anche questo impasto è di colore giallo chiaro (2.5 Y 8/4), ma è meno grossolano, con inclusi analoghi, più radi e quasi sempre di grandi dimensioni.

34 – SC330 (numero di inventario 1984). Bollo circolare con orbicolo. Sig. 8+; orb. ?; litt. 1.2; lin. 1, 2; fr. 13+, 10.5+, 2.9.

```
[EX FIG DOM] MAIO DOM[INOR NN]
[tridens cui delphinus obvolvitur]
```

CIL XV. 165; Bloch 1947, 297, 303; Steinby 1977, 38; Steinby 1977-1978, numero 193; Steinby 1981b, 306, numero 9.

In questo esemplare l'impronta del *signum*, benchè presente, è illeggibile. Il laterizio proviene dalle figline *Domitianae Maiores* che all'epoca a cui si riferisce questo bollo (198-211 d.C.) erano già passate in mano ai Severi (Bloch 1947, 297; Steinby 1977, 38). Per gli altri bolli delle *Domitianae* presenti nel gruppo di Santa Cornelia cfr. numeri 7, 25, 35 ai quali si rimanda per la descrizione dell'impasto e altre informazioni.

35 – SC660 (numero di inventario 1998). Bollo circolare con orbicolo piccolo. Sig. 10; orb. 2; litt. 1.1-1.2, 0.9-1; lin. ?, 1, ?; fr. 19.5+, 11+, 2.8.

```
OP DOL EX PR AVGG NN FIG DOMIT
  IAN MAIOR LANI PISENTINI
  nux pinea [foliis circumdata]
```

CIL XV. 166; Bloch 1947, 297, 302; Camilli e Taglietti 1979, 201 numero 42; Steinby 1973, 123 numero 44; Steinby 1977, 38; Steinby 1987, 377.

Bollo quasi completo ma molto consumato da una parte, dove è molto difficile individuare con sicurezza la presenza di eventuali altre linee ausiliarie. Il bollo, databile tra il 198 e il 211 d.C. (cfr. Bloch 1947, 297, 302; Steinby 1977, 38), appartiene come il numero precedente alle figline *Domitianae Maiores*, ora di proprietà dei Severi. Per la descrizione dell'impasto cfr. in particolare il numero 7.

36 – SC658 (numero di inventario 2696). Bollo circolare con orbicolo piccolo. Sig. ?; orb. 2; litt. 1.2, ?; lin. 1?, 1?; fr. 7+, 7.5+, 3.1.

```
[OP · DOL · EX PR DOM AVG N] FI
      GL[INAS GENIANAS]
[Protome galeata ds., ad d. iaculum]
[ad s. tridens?; in orbiculo stella?]
```

CIL XV. 237b; Steinby 1977-1978, numero 247; Steinby 1987, 378.

Malgrado l'estrema lacunosità dell'esemplare, sembra del tutto probabile l'identificazione con *CIL* XV. 237b che potrebbe coincidere, secondo quanto ipotizzato dalla Steinby (cfr. Steinby 1977-1978, 107), con la variante a, il cui *signum* sarebbe stato mal interpretato dal Dressel. La leggera prominenza visibile nell'orbicolo corrisponde verosimilmente con la *stella* indicata nella descrizione del *signum*. Il bollo, in uso sotto Caracalla, proviene dalle figline *Genianae*, entrate anch'esse a far parte delle proprietà imperiali dei Severi (Bloch 1947, 295-296, 300, 302; Steinby 1977, 43-44; Steinby 1986, 103). É impresso su di un laterizio con impasto di colore arancione spento, grossolano, con inclusi di vario tipo, in genere piccoli, ma sporadicamente anche molto grandi.

37 – SC562 (numero di inventario 2000). Bollo circolare. Sig. 9 ca; litt. 1.2-1.3, 1; lin. 1, 2, 1; fr. 11 + , 7.5 + , 3.

```
[OP]VS · DOL · E[X · P · AVG N EX · FIG]
        [PV]BLILI[ANAS]
   [ Protome solis radiati et pileati ]
```

CIL XV. 424; Bloch 1947, 298, 302, 339; Steinby 1977, 39, 78.

Identificazione molto probabile, ma non del tutto certa per la grande lacunosità del testo. Rispetto al *CIL* questo bollo presenta inequivocabilmente un punto dopo le prime due parole della prima riga. Per l'identificazione del *signum*, anch'esso molto frammentario, si veda Steinby 1977, 39. Proviene dalle figline *Publilianae* lungamente attive nel corso dell'età imperiale (per la loro cronologia si veda Steinby 1977, 75-78), le quali divennero proprietà dei Severi solo con Caracalla (212-217 d.C.), periodo al quale risale anche questo bollo. Si osservi in particolare la formula ex seguito dall'accusativo, corrente in età severiana. Il laterizio su cui questo bollo è impresso ha un impasto chiaro, rosato (5 YR 8/3), non molto grossolano, con inclusi rossicci anche di dimensioni medie o grandi, ma poco frequenti.

38 – SC738 (numero di inventario 2002). Bollo circolare a lettere incavate. Sig. 8 ca.; litt. 1.3; lin. 1; fr. 3 + , 4 + , 2.5.

```
[Hed]era OF [
        [Hedera]
```

Bollo molto frammentario per il quale non è possibile indicare il numero di *CIL* corrispondente, ma che può essere riferito con certezza alla serie 4a dei bolli tardo-antichi con la formula OFF SRF seguito dal nome dell'officina ridotto a tre-quattro lettere, datata all'età di Diocleziano e Massenzio (Steinby 1986, 118-119; per i bolli diocleziani si veda anche il capitolo dedicato alle terme di Diocleziano in Bloch 1947, 303-316). Un esemplare del tutto corrispondente al nostro è illustrato in Cozzo 1936, Tav. XIX, Fig. 58, relativo alle figline *Oceanae* (*CIL* XV. 1622).

Il laterizio su cui è impresso ha un impasto chiaro, di colore rosato (5 YR 7/3), depurato, con rari inclusi marroni arrotondati, di piccole dimensioni.

39 – SC631 (numero di inventario 1991) (Pl. 55,b). Bollo rettangolare incorniciato da una linea continua in rilievo. Sig. 10 + , 3.2; litt. 1.6-1.8, 1.3 (O); fr. 10 + , 14 + , 3.

```
]IЯ8YⵏO           testo retrogrado
```

Bollo nuovo che presenta la stessa forma (con cornice) del bollo Bloch 1948, numero 254 proveniente dalle Mura Aureliane (Pfeiffer *et al.* 1905, 54, numero 224, Tav. II,8), anch'esso con testo retrogrado ma diverso per formula, caratteri epigrafici e misure. Il *dominus* menzionato nel nostro bollo è probabilmente lo stesso del bollo già ricordato Bloch 1948, numero 254 e del bollo *CIL* XV. 1705, che può essere identificato con un membro della famiglia degli *Anicii*, *Q. Clodius Hermogenianus Olybrius*, *praefectus Urbi* del 369-370 e console nel 379 ovvero con *Q. Anicius Hermogenianus Olybrius*, console nell'anno 395 d.C. (cfr. Steinby 1986, 133; Steinby 1987, 42-43, numero 82). É impresso su un laterizio di colore arancione spento (5 YR 7/3), poco grossolano, con inclusi di vario tipo, medi e piccoli non molto frequenti.

40 – SC654 (numero di inventario 2004). Bollo circolare con forte linea ausiliaria. Sig. 8.5; litt. 1.5-1.7; fr. 19 + , 14 + , 2.8.

```
[IЯ]OⵏℲ AⵈIƆIℲO crux         testo retrogrado
            crux
```

CIL XV. 1689; Cozzo 1936, Tav. XXII, Fig. 69; Steinby 1986, 129, serie 32.

Per la datazione (quinto secolo d.C.) ed altre considerazioni cfr. numero 42.

41 – SC692 (numero di inventario 2006) (Fig. 30). Bollo circolare con forte linea ausiliaria. Sig. 8.5; litt. 1.5, 1.9 (F, B, G); fr. 35.5, 16.5 + , 2.5-3.

Altri esemplari dello stesso tipo: SC86, 163, 574, 845 (numero di inventario 2007a).

```
crux OFICI · BENIGNI
         crux
```

Plate 55,b. Santa Cornelia: tile stamp number 39 (*Museo dell'Alto Medioevo*, Rome)

CIL XV. 1678a; Cozzo 1936, Tav. XXI, Fig. 64; Steinby 1986, 129, serie 32.
Per la datazione (quinto secolo d.C.) ed altre considerazioni cfr. numero 42.

42 – SC690 (numero di inventario 2005) (Pl. 55,c). Bollo circolare con forte linea ausiliaria. Sig.
8.5; litt. 1.5-1.7, 1.9 (F, B, G); fr. 26.5+, 27+, 2.4.
Altri esemplari dello stesso tipo: SC87, 410, 415, 579, 686, 727 (numero di inventario 2007b). Per
altri otto esemplari non si può stabilire se appartengano a *CIL* XV. 1678 a oppure b, a causa del
loro stato di conservazione: SC401, 411, 578, 596, 689, 691 (numero di inventario 2007c); 85
(numero di inventario 2008); 838 (numero di inventario 2009).

```
    crux OFICI · BENICVI        G e N capovolte
             crux                   e retrograde
```

CIL XV. 1678b; Steinby 1986, 129, serie 32.
I numeri 40-42 comprendono ventuno esemplari appartenenti alla serie 32 della
classificazione dei bolli tardo-antichi (Steinby 1986), dei quali solo uno è relativo a *CIL* XV.
1689 (numero 40), tutti gli altri appartengono a *CIL* XV. 1678, varianti a e b. Per quest'ultima si
possono forse distinguere due timbri che si differenziano unicamente per la diversa larghezza dei
tratti delle lettere mentre l'altezza e la distanza rimangono invariate. Non si esclude pertanto che
la differenza sia dovuta solo al diverso grado di essiccamento delle tegole al momento della
siglatura che può aver determinato un'impronta più o meno nitida e profonda.
Tutti gli esemplari, per quanto frammentari, possono essere attribuiti a tegole fabbricate in
un'unica officina. Esse presentano un impasto molto omogeneo quanto a grado di depurazione e
tipo di inclusi, più variabile per quanto riguarda il colore che oscilla dal giallo molto chiaro (2.5
Y 8/3) al giallo rosato (7.5 YR 8/3) al rosa più scuro (5 YR 7/4). Queste gradazioni coesistono
talvolta nello stesso esemplare e ciò può dipendere dalle condizioni di cottura dei pezzi.
L'impasto, sempre piuttosto depurato, presenta pochi inclusi appartenenti quasi esclusivamente
al tipo arrotondato, di colore marrone-rossiccio, di dimensioni piccole o medie.
Poichè nessun esemplare ci è giunto intero, non conosciamo le misure del telaio che ci

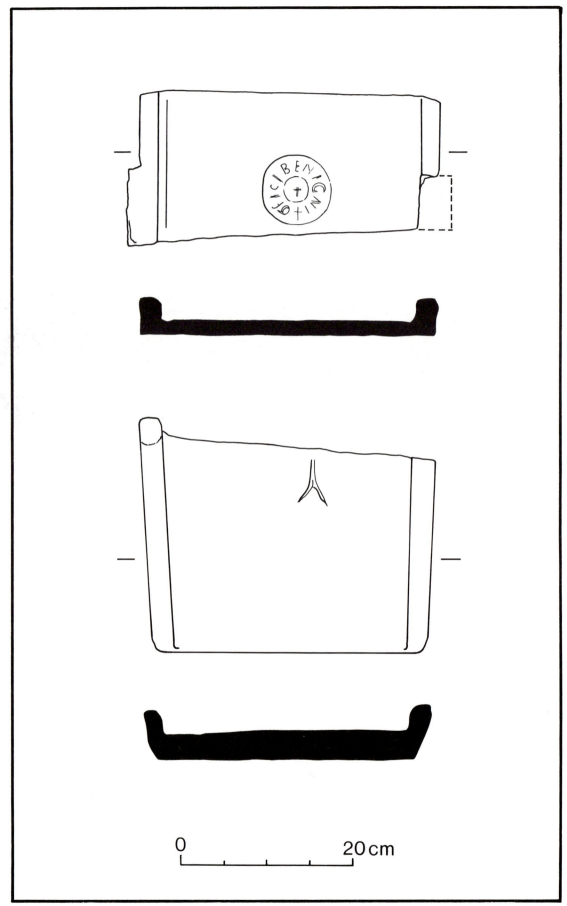

Fig. 30. Santa Cornelia: tiles, stamps and sections of numbers 41 and 53 (SC)

Plate 55,c. Santa Cornelia: tile stamp number 42 (*Museo dell'Alto Medioevo*, Rome)

permetterebbero di fare un confronto con la tipologia delle tegole di Santa Maria Maggiore (Steinby 1973-1974). Le poche misure rilevabili (larghezza minima di cm. 35.5, lunghezza della risega di cm. 9, spessore del piatto oscillante tra cm. 2.4 e 3.2, con valori prevalenti intorno a cm. 2.5) mostrano comunque maggiori analogie con il gruppo VII di età teodoriciana (Steinby 1973-1974, 124ss, Figg. 20-22), provvisto solitamente, come sottolinea la Steinby, di una scanalatura alla base e sulla sommità dell'aletta, che non si trova mai nelle tegole di Santa Cornelia. In queste ultime si osserva solo una lieve marcatura alla base di una delle due alette, dal profilo semplicemente arrotondato (Fig. 30). Nei nostri esemplari è più distintiva la rifinitura dello spigolo inferiore dell'aletta mediante spatola o coltello che si trova non solo in corrispondenza della risega ma lungo tutto il margine esterno, che risulta così smussato obliquamente e allisciato. Il bollo è di norma apposto a breve distanza dal margine più corto della tegola, al suo interno.

Bolli di questa serie erano noti fino ad oggi esclusivamente in ambito urbano, molto spesso in connessione con chiese. Solo di recente è stata segnalata la scoperta di un esemplare dell'officina di Benigno nei pressi del castello di Scorano sulla Via Tiberina (informazione Diletta Romei). La loro datazione sembra potersi circoscrivere nell'ambito del V secolo d.C., probabilmente intorno al secondo terzo del secolo (Steinby 1986, 129, 145-146 e tabelle A e B). Il ritrovamento di un nucleo così numeroso in un sito della Campagna romana costituisce quindi un fatto abbastanza eccezionale, considerata la generale rarità dei ritrovamenti di bolli tardo-antichi al di fuori di Roma. Le ragioni di una simile concentrazione non sono comunque semplici da ritrovare anche perchè il contesto archeologico di provenienza non offre elementi sufficienti per una interpretazione univoca. La maggior parte dei bolli è stata infatti ritrovata nell'area della chiesa ma in strati che non consentono di trarre conclusioni certe sull'utilizzazione di questo materiale. La connessione topografica suggerisce tuttavia un legame con l'edificio di culto nel cui ambito le tegole possono essere state riutilizzate. Si tratterebbe infatti di un reimpiego, dato il divario cronologico esistente tra le tegole, di età tardo-antica, e la chiesa, di età carolingia (per la cronologia della prima fase della chiesa cfr. *supra*, fase 2; per i laterizi di età altomedievale cfr. *infra*, numero 53).

Per quanto riguarda l'origine del materiale di spoglio non si può dire nulla di certo; sembra però abbastanza probabile che la fonte di approvvigionamento non fosse molto lontana. Questa ipotesi è rafforzata dalla ricorrenza nello scavo di Santa Cornelia di molto altro materiale di recupero sia di età classica che tardo-antica (elementi architettonici, epigrafi, sarcofagi, ecc.) che sembra indicare la vicinanza di un insediamento romano sottoposto, come accade solitamente, ad una sistematica spoliazione. In mancanza di dati sicuri tuttavia, non si può escludere anche l'ipotesi di un trasporto da più lontano, ad esempio dalla stessa Roma, anche se ciò appare molto più improbabile.

Ammessa l'ipotesi di una provenienza delle tegole dalle vicinanze del centro altomedievale si aprirebbe un'interessante prospettiva sul problema dell'ubicazione delle figline tardo-antiche in cui operarono Floro e Benigno.

Le notizie disponibili per la localizzazione delle figline classiche e tardo-antiche sono ancora molto scarse e ancor meno sappiamo dei sistemi di immagazzinamento e vendita dei prodotti laterizi (Steinby 1978, col. 1507ss; Steinby 1981a, 237-239; Steinby 1986, 153-154). Nondimeno l'omogeneità del ritrovamento sul sito di Santa Cornelia, dove le tegole bollate appartengono quasi tutte a questo gruppo, potrebbe indicare forse, dal momento che ci troviamo in area extraurbana, una vicinanza anche del centro di produzione. Diverso è il caso di Roma dove la concentrazione di bolli di uno stesso tipo in un edificio non ha relazione con l'ubicazione del centro di produzione, ma sembra dipendere piuttosto da altri meccanismi, purtroppo ancora ignoti, in relazione verosimilmente con i sistemi di stoccaggio e vendita dei laterizi. Del resto anche la zona di Santa Cornelia si prestava egregiamente alla produzione di laterizi come dimostra l'impianto in quel sito di una fornace databile in età pienamente medievale (cfr. *supra*, fase 3), destinata a produrre tegole utilizzate, si suppone, nella copertura della nuova chiesa e del monastero (cfr. *infra*, numero 53). Ma impianti produttivi sono noti nell'area anche per i secoli precedenti. Si segnala il recente ritrovamento a pochi chilometri a sud del centro altomedievale, in località Ospedaletto Annunziata sulla Via Veientana, di due grosse fornaci per laterizi incluse nelle strutture di una villa romana, datate purtroppo solo molto genericamente in età tardo-antica (Messineo *et al.* 1984, 192-196; Petracca e Vigna 1985).

In conclusione, la scoperta di questo importante gruppo di laterizi tardo-antichi solleva una serie di quesiti a cui non è possibile dare ancora risposte definitive. Le ipotesi che si sono qui avanzate in via preliminare dovranno quindi essere verificate alla luce di nuove e più ampie conoscenze sulla distribuzione dei bolli di età tardo-antica nel suburbio di Roma.

(b) BOLLI SENZA TESTO

43 – SC658 (numero di inventario 2158c) (Pl. 55,d). Bollo di forma quadrangolare comprendente una cornice in rilievo sui cui lati insistono quattro semicerchi ribassati. Sig. 3+, 3.5; fr. 7+, 7+, 2.4.

Questo bollo, anche se privo per ora di confronti puntuali, può essere inquadrato senza difficoltà nel gruppo dei bolli detti ornamentali o senza testo che contraddistinguono i bessali di età severiana e sono ancora presenti in gran numero nelle Mura Aureliane (per i bolli severiani cfr. in particolare Broise e Scheid 1987, 131ss; per quelli delle Mura Aureliane, Pfeiffer *et al.* 1905, 72-85, Tav. III-X; Steinby 1986, 110-111; altri piccoli nuclei editi sono quelli di Santa Maria Maggiore: Steinby 1973-74, 116, Figg. 6-7 (di età teodoriciana), 121, Fig. 9 (del terzo secolo d.C.); di Ostia: Steinby 1977-1978, numeri 1273-1305; dell'Area Sacra di Torre Argentina: Steinby 1981b, 332, numeri 152-158; alcuni esempi sono illustrati in Cozzo 1936, Tav. XVII, Figg. 47-48; sono di recente pubblicazione quelli provenienti dall'esedra della Crypta Balbi: Saguì e Paroli 1990, 562-564; per una discussione generale del problema dei bolli anepigrafi si veda infine Steinby 1986, 138-139).

Il bollo è impresso su un laterizio dall'impasto di colore giallo (2.5 Y 8/3), non molto grossolano, con una prevalenza di inclusi trasparenti, angolosi, di medie dimensioni e con qualche incluso marrone-rossiccio arrotondato, di grandi dimensioni.

44 – SC735 (numero di inventario 2158g) (Pl. 55,e). Bollo composto di due parti: la più piccola, circolare, reca al centro un incavo un po' decentrato; la maggiore è a forma di fungo, con decoro a volute contrapposte alla base. Sig. circolare 2; sig. a fungo 3.8; fr. 16.5+, 13+, 3.

La decorazione a volute è molto diffusa nei bolli di età severiana e ben documentata anche nei laterizi delle Mura Aureliane ma nessuno degli esemplari editi coincide perfettamente con il nostro (cfr. Pfeiffer *et al.* 1905, Tav. V, numeri 4-5, 9-10; Steinby 1973-1974, 121, Fig. 9; Steinby 1977-1978, numero 1282; Broise e Scheid 1987, 132-134, numeri 1-9, 11, per i quali si ipotizza una matrice formata con guarnizioni dell'equipaggiamento militare).

L'impasto è di colore arancione chiaro (7.5 YR 8/3), poco grossolano, con inclusi prevalentemente medio-piccoli, di colore marrone e arrotondati.

Plate 55,d. Santa Cornelia: tile stamp number 43 (*Museo dell'Alto Medioevo*, Rome)

Plate 55,e. Santa Cornelia: tile stamp number 44 (*Museo dell'Alto Medioevo*, Rome)

Plate 55,f. Santa Cornelia: tile stamps numbers 47 and 48 (*Museo dell'Alto Medioevo*, Rome)

Plate 55,g. Santa Cornelia: tile stamps number 49 (*Museo dell'Alto Medioevo*, Rome)

45 – SC79 (numero di inventario 2158f). Bollo circolare con centro incavato. Sig. 5.4, 1.9; fr. 12+, 9+, 3.

È lacunoso da una parte e pertanto non sappiamo se potesse esservi associato un secondo bollo dello stesso tipo o di altro tipo, come avviene di frequente (cfr. Pfeiffer *et al.* 1905, Tav. V, 11 in particolare; Broise e Scheid 1987, 138, numero 27). Il laterizio su cui è impresso è molto friabile, 'polveroso', di colore molto chiaro, rosato (10 YR 8/2), piuttosto depurato, con qualche raro incluso marrone-rossiccio, arrotondato, di dimensioni medie o grandi. Impasti molto simili ricorrono anche in altri due esemplari con bolli anepigrafi (cfr. numeri 46 e 47).

46 – SC III 64 (numero di inventario 2158e). Bollo circolare con anello concentrico delimitato da larghi solchi. Sig. 5 ca., 3 ca.; fr. 9+, 6+, 2.8.

Bollo di struttura elementare abbastanza simile anche nelle dimensioni ad un esemplare della Magliana, databile all'età di Caracalla (Broise e Scheid 1987, 138, numero 31; si veda anche un esempio più piccolo a p. 143, Figg. 180-181; Saguì e Paroli 1990, 564, Fig. 168, 21). Il tipo è rappresentato anche nelle Mura Aureliane (Pfeiffer *et al.* 1905, Tav. VI, 11 e 15, ma con alcune diversità che indicano matrici diverse). L'impasto del laterizio è di colore chiaro, friabile e molto depurato, in tutto simile a quello del numero 45 e del numero 47.

47 – SC80 (numero di inventario 2158d) (Pl. 55,f). Il bollo è composto di due cerchi accostati, ma non tangenti, di diverse dimensioni: il maggiore racchiude due anelli concentrici e reca al centro un incavo irregolare; il minore racchiude anch'esso dei cerchi concentrici, il primo formato da una sottile linea in rilievo, seguito da un anello più largo, con il margine interno dentellato e decentrato rispetto al cerchio esterno; al centro incavo rettangolare. Sig. maggiore 4.5, 3, 2.5; sig. minore 3.5, 2; fr. 9+, 8.5+, 3.4.

Il bollo è piuttosto consumato anche a causa dell'estrema friabilità dell'impasto del laterizio su cui è impresso; è di colore molto chiaro (2.5 Y 8/2), ben depurato con qualche raro incluso marrone-rossiccio arrotondato, ed appare in tutto simile a quello dei numeri 45 e 46. È confrontabile solo genericamente con i numerosi bolli a cerchi concentrici di età severiana e successiva che mostrano una straordinaria varietà di combinazioni sia degli elementi interni che tra di loro (cfr. ad esempio Broise e Scheid 1987, 135-139, numero 16ss, in particolare numero 22 e 23; Pfeiffer *et al.* 1905, Tavv. VI-VII; Steinby 1977-1978, numero 1283-1287).

48 – SC232 (numero di inventario 2158d) (Pl. 55,f). Bollo composto di due cerchi tangenti di diverse dimensioni, ad anelli concentrici di vario tipo: nel maggiore si vedono due sottili linee in rilievo seguite da un anello in rilievo ripartito in sei settori trapezoidali; il centro è incavato; il cerchio minore presenta una duplice coppia di sottili linee in rilievo, seguite da altre due linee che racchiudono il centro incavato. Sig. maggiore 4, 3, 1.5; sig. minore 3.1, 1.5; fr. 17+, 15+, 3.2.

Il cerchio minore trova notevole corrispondenza in esemplari editi (cfr. ad esempio il numero 29 della Magliana: Broise e Scheid 1987, 138, ma si vedano altri esemplari simili tra i laterizi delle Mura Aureliane: Pfeiffer *et al.* 1905, Tavv. VI-VII), mentre il maggiore costituisce un tipo nuovo, privo di confronti. Il bollo è impresso su di un bessale dall'impasto rosato (5 YR 7/3), depuratissimo, ma meno friabile rispetto a quello dei numeri 45-47.

49 – SC98 (numero di inventario 2158b) (Pl. 42,g). Bollo di forma circolare composto da impronte cuneiformi disposte a raggera. Sig. 4; fr. 11+, 10+, 1.6. Altri bolli dello stesso tipo: SC398 (numero di inventario 2158b)

I due bolli compaiono su laterizi assolutamente identici, forse parti di un'unica tegola, dallo spessore notevolmente ridotto. L'impasto, di colore giallo chiaro sfumante nel grigio (5 Y 8/2), è depuratissimo e poroso e sembra accostarsi molto di più a quello dei laterizi medievali ritrovati a Santa Cornelia che non a quello dei bessali con bolli ornamentali ed in genere ai laterizi di età classica, sebbene anche tra i primi figurino impasti molto depurati.

Anche se il tipo di bollo radiato non è sconosciuto in età classica (cfr. Pfeiffer *et al.* 1905, Tav. V, numero 6), esso sembra più frequente in periodo medievale, in particolare in area toscana, lungo la costa, fino a Luni e nell'interno, nella zona del Valdarno (Paoletti 1987, 469-470). Di dimensioni variabili, il bollo radiato si trova applicato, da solo o in combinazioni multiple, sulle anse delle anforette cosiddette 'pisane', su brocche e boccali, forse con funzione ornamentale o, in qualche caso, come sigillo o come misura di capacità. Il Paoletti ne rivede la datazione spostandola al pieno medioevo (dodicesimo-tredicesimo secolo) (Paoletti 1987, 472, Figg. 5-16, 474, Fig. 18). Analoga cronologia è attribuita anche alla tegola con bollo radiato rinvenuta a Roma, nell'Esedra della Crypta Balbi (Saguì e Paroli 1990, 568, Fig. 169, 3). Una datazione in età medievale per i due esemplari di Santa Cornelia sembra pertanto molto probabile.

(c) LATERIZI CON SEGNI PARTICOLARI

50 – SC774 (numero di inventario 2158a).

Tegola frammentaria con impronta di zampa di cane; altre due impronte simili si trovano su di un grosso mattone in due frammenti (SC720a-b – numero di inventario 2158a).

51 – SC409 (numero di inventario 2158h).

Frammento molto probabilmente di tegola recante al centro un cordone filiforme in rilievo a forma di U. Altro frammento in tutto corrispondente: SC846 (numero di inventario 2158h).

Per questi due esemplari si può forse ipotizzare una datazione in età medievale sulla base del tipo di impasto, rosato (7.5 YR 7/3), depuratissimo, e del genere di decorazione, a cordone applicato, che ricorda molto quello del numero 53 (databile certamente nel pieno medioevo (cfr. *infra*), come del resto le due tegole con decorazione a rilievo dalla Crypta Balbi (Saguì e Paroli 1990, 567, Fig. 169, 1-2).

52 – SC165 (senza numero di inventario).

Frammento quasi certamente di tegola recante al suo interno una decorazione incisa a reticolo di maglie rettangolari un po' irregolari. Un altro frammento certamente dello stesso esemplare: SC573 (anche esso privo di numero di inventario).

Oltre la decorazione, è molto caratteristico di questo laterizio il tipo di impasto, molto chiaro (10 YR 8/2), friabilissimo (polveroso), piuttosto ben depurato, ma molto poroso, che conserva al suo interno frammenti incombusti di paglia. Questo tipo di incluso non era mai stato rilevato finora nei laterizi di età classica, nè si troverà tra i laterizi di epoca medievale, pertinenti ad una fornace, che vedremo più oltre. Esso è comunque più simile agli impasti medievali che non a quelli classici e pertanto, considerata anche la notevole sottigliezza della tegola, si può ipotizzare anche in questo caso una datazione in periodo medievale, probabilmente anche in una fase piuttosto avanzata (tredicesimo-quattordicesimo secolo ?).

(d) LATERIZI MEDIEVALI

53 – SCIII (numero di inventario 2152-2153) (Fig. 30).

Tegola parzialmente ricomposta da cinque frammenti, recante al centro del piatto una decorazione in rilievo a forma di Y. Lunghezza 26 +; larghezza 32.5; spessore 1.5-2; lunghezza risega 6.5-7; h. aletta 1.5-2; larghezza aletta 2.2-2.5.

Appartengono allo stesso tipo di tegola tre frammenti provenienti rispettivamente da SC III.67, I.7, III.78 e tutte le tegole deformate e fuse in cottura, molte delle quali tuttavia dal profilo ancora rilevabile, prodotte in una fornace installatasi nell'area del primitivo battistero nella fase 3a-b (1000-1040 ca.) (cfr. supra). Si tratta in particolare di due esemplari abbastanza conservati (I.22), due frammenti di alette (III.73, A/1), cinque frammenti della parte centrale (I.5, I.6, I.9, III.73, III.85, quest'ultimo completamente deformato), un blocco di due tegole fuse insieme (K/1), un blocco di quattro tegole fuse insieme (III.85), ed infine un gruppo di frammenti completamente vetrificati (K/1, K/9). Nei pezzi più deformati non è sempre possibile distinguere con sicurezza, quando sono anche piuttosto frammentari, se si tratti di tegole o embrici.

Tutte queste tegole hanno le alette di dimensioni piuttosto modeste, basse e squadrate, con la parte superiore appiattita anche se con i margini arrotondati; all'interno, nel punto di congiunzione con il piatto, sono rifinite con una ditata che lascia un'impronta piuttosto nitida presso il margine esterno. Anche alle estremità sono rifinite in modo da risultare stondate e leggermente oblique. Ma ciò che è più caratteristico e la risega che interessa solo lo spigolo inferiore dell'aletta e non quello superiore. Essa è realizzata cioè mediante un taglio obliquo anzichè verticale il quale, invece di partire dalla sommità dell'aletta parte ad 1 cm circa al di sotto, tagliando di netto lo spigolo inferiore e riducendone quindi lo spessore solo in parte, senza risultare visibile da sopra. Visto dall'alto quindi, il profilo dell'aletta appare continuo (cfr. Pl. 42,9a), anche in corrispondenza della risega. Questo particolare tipo di risega che ha precedenti in periodo classico compare anche in età carolingia a Roma dove è documentato in una tegola della chiesa di Santa Maria Maggiore recante un bollo monogrammatico attribuito concordemente dagli studiosi a papa Adriano I (772-795) (Steinby 1973-1974, 117-118, Fig. 8).

Rispetto alle nostre, la tegola carolingia ha dimensioni leggermente più grandi, almeno per quanto riguarda la larghezza, poichè la lunghezza complessiva degli esemplari di Santa Cornelia ci è ignota, anche se può essere stimata intorno ai 40-45 cm.

Sembra così profilarsi anche nella produzione dei laterizi di Roma una specifica tradizione altomedievale, già operante in età carolingia, ma forse già presente in precedenza dal momento che ci è noto un bollo di papa Giovanni VII (701-705) (cfr. Steinby 1986, 115-116 con precedente bibliografia). Questa tradizione persiste immutata almeno fino all'undicesimo secolo, se questo è il periodo a cui si debbono assegnare gli scarti di fornace di Santa Cornelia, ma non sembra perdurare molto oltre questa data dal momento che la risega è già scomparsa nei laterizi di Ponte Nepesino, attribuiti ad una fase di poco posteriore (Stone 1984, 108-121, in particolare 111, Figg. 33 e 34) ed è estremamente sporadica nel consistente nucleo di tegole bassomedievali (tredicesimo-quattordicesimo secolo) dell'esedra della Crypta Balbi (Saguì e Paroli 1990, 565). Qualche indicazione più puntuale sul momento della scomparsa della risega nelle tegole medievali si potrebbe forse ricavare dall'esame delle tegole bollate da Innocenzo II (1130-1143), ritrovate in gran numero sulla Via Nomentana (Gatti 1909).

Se dunque le tegole altomedievali non si discostano completamente sotto il profilo morfologico dalla tradizione classica conservando, seppure modificata, la risega, la loro struttura appare però molto più leggera e maneggevole grazie alle proporzioni e agli spessori più ridotti e ad un impasto molto elaborato che, almeno negli esemplari di Santa Cornelia, appare sempre molto depurato. Anche sotto questo aspetto assistiamo alla conclusione di un lungo processo che vede il progressivo 'raffinamento' degli impasti di tutti i laterizi nel corso della tarda antichità, compresi i bessali, tradizionalmente più grezzi dei grandi laterizi, che mostrano invece nel terzo secolo, stando al campione di Santa Cornelia, una percentuale molto alta (50% circa) di impasti molto depurati. Molto depurato è anche l'impasto del laterizio con il bollo di età tetrarchica (cfr. numero 38) così come sono in genere piuttosto depurati gli impasti dei ventuno esemplari della serie 32 (cfr. numeri 40-42). Non conosciamo l'impasto delle tegole di Adriano I, ma si può supporre, dato l'alto livello tecnologico della ceramica coeva (Schuring 1986, in particolare 199; Annis, in corso di stampa), che esso fosse piuttosto elaborato analogamente a quello dei laterizi riferibili al tipo numero 53, riconosciuto come distintivo della produzione della fornace medievale di Santa Cornelia.

54 – SC III.71, A/2 (senza numero di inventario).

Embrici molto frammentari dal profilo ad arco ribassato, quasi appiattito ai lati. L'impasto è molto simile a quello delle tegole viste al numero 53, in particolare nel primo esemplare che mostra tra l'altro di aver subito una cottura eccessiva. Questo materiale è attribuibile con certezza alla produzione medievale, probabilmente anche locale, che si inserisce in una tradizione artigianale attiva in area urbana fin dai primi secoli del medioevo (cfr. *supra*, numero 52). Per alcuni confronti a Roma e nel Lazio si veda Stone 1984, 119, Fig. 33,8; Saguì e Paroli 1990, 569, Tav. LXXXV, 789-795).

CONCLUSIONI

Ricapitolando rapidamente quanto è stato esposto nel catalogo si può osservare a proposito dei laterizi bollati che essi si distribuiscono in un arco cronologico che dagli inizi del primo secolo d.C. giunge al pieno quinto secolo d.C. in queste proporzioni: 7.8% nel primo secolo; 48.4% in età traianea-adrianea; 7.8% in età severiana; 1.5% in età tetrachica; 34.3% tra il tardo quarto e il quinto secolo d.C. Le attestazioni del terzo secolo raddoppierebbero se ai bolli epigrafici si assommassero quelli senza testo, sei dei quali sono certamente databili in quell'ambito cronologico (cfr. numeri 43-48). Rispetto ai dati di altre situazioni (un accenno è in Steinby 1981a, 243), le percentuali di Santa Cornelia hanno un andamento anomalo a causa dell'alto numero di bolli tardo-antichi ivi attestato, che altrove si riscontra difficilmente in queste proporzioni. Nello stesso ambito territoriale un confronto può essere istituito con i bolli provenienti dalle ricognizioni nell'Ager Veientanus (Kahane *et al.* 1968, 197-198, 208, Fig. 34), con valori più vicini alla norma. Lo stesso varrebbe per il gruppo di Santa Cornelia se si escludesse per un momento l'anomalia costituita dal folto gruppo tardo-antico: la maggioranza assoluta spetterebbe allora ai bolli della prima metà del secondo secolo, seguiti a grande distanza dal bolli del primo e del terzo secolo. Le figline più attestate sono in assoluto le *Salareses*, seguite dalle *Domitianae*, dalle *Tonneianae* e dalle *Brutianae* con due o più esemplari; si deve però tener conto che i laterizi dell'*opus Salarese* provengono da più fabbriche riunite sotto la stessa denominazione e potrebbero quindi avere un significato relativo. Tuttavia il significato più generale di queste presenze, del loro maggiore o minor peso nell'ambito del gruppo, ci sfugge completamente sia per la carenza di informazioni sulle strutture a cui erano destinati in origine sia per la scarsità dei dati sulla distribuzione dei bollo di mattone nell'Agro Romano.

Come si è già accennato all'inizio, solo una piccola parte dei laterizi esaminati (meno del 25%) appartiene al periodo medievale, ed è costituita esclusivamente di tegole ed embrici. Come è noto, furono questi gli elementi che continuarono ad essere prodotti a Roma nel corso dell'alto medioevo allorchè furono occasionalmente bollati dai papi tra cui il pontefice Adriano I, fondatore della *domusculta Capracorum*. Questa tradizione non è comunque limitata all'area di Roma, ma si trova bensì diffusa ad esempio in territorio lombardo nell'altomedioevo (Fiorilla 1986). La fabbricazione di piccole quantità di laterizi è documentata anche nel resto della penisola, quasi sempre in relazione a qualche grande centro abbaziale (Farfa, Cassino, San Vincenzo al Volturno) (Arthur e Whitehouse 1983, 526-531; Mitchell 1985, 165, Fig. 6.39).

Nessun esemplare con il bollo di questo pontefice è però tornato alla luce a Santa Cornelia; non credo tuttavia che questo fatto debba meravigliare troppo se si considera la rarità dei ritrovamenti anche in ambito urbano, a cui fu certamente diretta in modo preferenziale la produzione laterizia che dovette essere comunque piuttosto limitata. Dalla descrizione della tegola di Adriano I presente sul tetto di Santa Maria Maggiore (Steinby 1973-1974, 117, numero 1) si evince che la produzione altomedievale conserva un tratto tipico delle tegole romane, la risega, che ritroviamo ancora nelle tegole della fornace di Santa Cornelia databile all'undicesimo secolo, testimoniando così una continuità della tradizione artigianale nel corso dell'alto medioevo che viene superata solo più tardi (dodicesimo-tredicesimo secolo?). La produzione successiva adotta un modello semplificato, privo di risega (Stone 1984, 111), che troviamo poi enormemente diffuso nei siti bassomedievali di Roma e del Lazio, ma di cui manca una testimonianza diretta tra i materiali di Santa Cornelia che ci sono pervenuti. In quest'epoca (quattordicesimo-quindicesimo secolo) l'industria laterizia conosce di nuovo a Roma e nel Lazio una fioritura imponente (Cortonesi 1986, 293-307), anche se non paragonabile a quella di epoca classica.

CHAPTER FIVE. INTERPRETATION AND CONCLUSIONS

From the excavation data recorded above we can draw some significant conclusions as regards the three main phases of activity on the site of Santa Cornelia. These can be broadly classified as (1) Roman, (2) *Domusculta* (774-1000), and (3) Monastery (1000-1300).

PHASE 1: ROMAN ACTIVITY

The excavations at Santa Cornelia failed to identify any secure indication of classical Roman construction underlying or preceding the foundation of the *domusculta Capracorum*. This conclusion was to some extent unexpected, given that early medieval church builders frequently utilized at least the foundations of pre-existing Roman buildings (cf. San Liberato, this volume). The 1950s field survey of this area indeed located a relatively high number of Roman farmsteads and possible villa structures in the immediate vicinity, datable to various points between the first century BC and the fourth-fifth century AD (Appendix 3) [1]. These were seen as belonging to 'representatives of the well-to-do middle class', many of course acting as weekend retreats [2]. However, with the exception of AV 232, which surface finds suggested was continuously occupied from republican into late Roman times, none of the identified sites was particularly opulent.

A thorough examination of some of the nearest of these farms (namely numbers AV 232, 234, 235, 237, 238, 241) – now unfortunately almost completely destroyed through deep ploughing and modern villa construction – might once have enabled us to discern the survival of one of these sites into the eighth century. Certainly the *Liber Pontificalis* makes plain the fact that the *domusculta* was created around an existing *fundus*, inherited by Pope Hadrian I. It is unlikely that this area had become badly depopulated by this time or that the land lay uncultivated; rather, as Wickham argues, we should visualize at least small scale continuity [3].

Roman agricultural activity was discernible beneath the site of Santa Cornelia. In each of the four principal excavation zones was located a series of trench features which had been cut down into the tufa bedrock (feature numbers 001-003, 132-140, 169-179, 232-240) (Fig. 31). At least three periods of trenching were identified, with two series of west–east oriented trenches and at least one of north-west–south-east orientation: the former followed the natural contours of the slight slope on which the *domusculta* was later positioned, while the north-west–south-east trenches ran up the slope, though on a slightly angled course. Cropmarks revealed the continuation of the west–east trenches beyond the site (Pl. 33). The clearest, and quite probably the latest in the sequence of trenches, was a west–east series spaced consistently 6.0-6.3 m apart, best identifiable in the south-east sector (numbers 174, 175, 177, 179) (Fig. 31). Trench 001 beneath the church complex should also belong to this group. The trenches were of variable depth, presumably reflecting the depth of the overlying soil cover in antiquity, and in general were cut to a width of 0.9-1.1 m.

Despite the relative softness of the tufa bedrock, the cutting of these trenches would have been a sizeable operation, requiring a significant number of man-hours. The task was clearly designed for the planting of crops, to increase soil depth, to aid drainage capacity, and to provide a secure bedding for the crop. This may be related to the Roman practice of *pastinatio*, a method of trenching a plantation, normally by means of a deep foot-rest spade (*altum bialium*). Columella, who describes the operation, relates that this practice was expensive in terms of labour, requiring up to eighty man-hours per *iugurum* or 120 man-hours per acre. White suggests that trenching of this type may have been done by contract and carried out where labour, not being scarce, could be readily offset by the returns [4]. *Pastinatio* was the preferred treatment of the ground for vineyards; olives, in contrast, were generally planted in pits and spaced 8-10 m apart, although in Roman Italy the practice was to grow crops between the rows of olives, thus increasing the space between rows to 13-20 m. According to the Roman agronomists, vines were spaced 1 m apart between plants and 2-3 m apart between rows [5]. Such figures are, of course, a generalization and in practice spacing could vary greatly, depending on soil type, climate, and vine or olive type.

Whilst the 6 m gap between trenches at Santa Cornelia might initially suggest an olive plantation, the use of trenches as opposed to pits makes this doubtful; simultaneously, the spacing appears too great for vine cultivation alone. A plausible explanation may be mixed cultivation, whereby vines were grown between trees (often olives) which provided support, shade and protection against frost; this method of wooded vine (*vitis arbustiva*) often gave high yields. Columella indicates that this was an essentially Italian system, not practised elsewhere [6], and indeed is a system still visible in many parts of Italy today. At Santa Cornelia it is the absence of pits between the trenches which makes its presence doubtful. Nonetheless, the spacing recommended by Pliny for cultivation of this type does offer a useful comparison [7].

Surprisingly few trenches comparable to the type

identified at Santa Cornelia have been properly excavated and recorded elsewhere. For instance, a number of rock-cut trenches *c.* 0.7 m wide were uncovered beneath a Roman *villa rustica* at site 11 in the locality of Tor Bella Monaca on the via Gabina east of Rome, but their function was not defined by the excavators [8]. More significant results emerged at Tor Pagnotta, near Rome, where the bedrock featured numerous trenches 0.5-1.0 m wide, of varied

orientation. A principal system was recognized, comprising north-east–south-west trenches 0.7-0.8 m wide and *c.* 3.7 m apart; near the hilltop the trenches attained a depth of 0.4 m. The excavators noted regular enlargements in the trenches, which suggested the setting of trees in a system of 'wooded vine' with the possibility of grain cultivation between trenches. In one case the trenches extended for at least 89 m. Two phases of vineyards were recognised, both

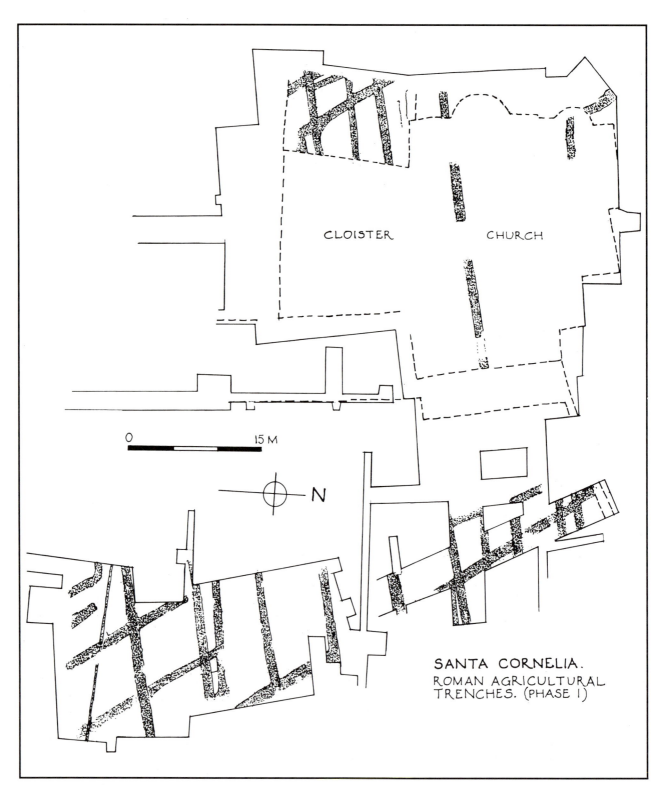

Fig. 31. Santa Cornelia: phase 1 plan (SG)

assignable to the third–second centuries BC [9]. Similar data come from the Apulian Tavoliere, where vine trenches were cut into the bedrock ('*crosta pugliese*') in rows 2.15 m apart, with rectangular tree-pits set at regular intervals. The space between rows may again have allowed cultivation of a cereal [10].

A few pieces of pottery were recovered from the fills (phase 1b) of the agricultural trenches at Santa Cornelia – though it remains unclear whether the packing (rammed earth or rammed earth and tufa) represented the infill of redundant trenches or the packing of the trenches whilst still in use to support the crop – and these covered a period extending from the second century BC to the first century AD. We can note in this context that surface finds made during the general Ager Veientanus survey highlighted republican and early imperial activity in the immediate zone; to this we can add the coin of Domitian (80-81 AD) found in a probable sub-floor level of room D in the monastic complex (coin 1, above, Chapter 4, i). These data may suggest a notable development in local farming in the late republic-early empire with heavy investment by a farmer in trench cutting.

A narrower, V-shaped, trench (180) was excavated in area W, of west-north-west–east-south-east orientation. Whilst an isolated feature, it can probably be associated with one of the periods of west–east agricultural trenches, designed to aid in drainage.

In the south-east corner (area W) somewhat later, but undated, Roman activity was attested by the presence of an extensive clay surface covering much of the excavated zone (phase 1c). There was no evidence to suggest that this surface was in any way associated with constructional activity. However, postholes were noted which cut the surface and which predated the phase 2b floors here, and given that some of these posts were replaced, we may argue for the presence of certain fixed features, most probably agricultural in scope. Postdating this clay level was a series of three roughly parallel, narrow, north-south running trenches (181-191), featuring post-holes (phase 1d). In the case of feature 181-184 the trench could be traced for a distance of 28 m. Their dimensions roughly correspond with those offered by Columella and Pliny for vine cultivation: the post-holes identified within the trenches may thus denote the positions of stakes to support the vines (*vitis iugata*), while the gap between rows may have been sufficient to allow the cultivation of a cereal crop. The trenches were quite different from the wide, flat-bottomed tufa-cut trenches of phase 1a, and do not appear to allow sufficient space for the growth of roots. One may perhaps argue from this that the vines – if these were being grown here – were no longer supported by trees as in phase 1a and therefore no longer required the wider trenches which gave sufficient space and depth for these. If this interpretation is correct, then vines alone were being

cultivated in rows running with the contours of the site. Any other function is difficult to envisage: they would have provided too flimsy a support for any structure, and their arrangement does not suggest stock-enclosures or fencing of any kind.

A single trench (150) of similar form, but lacking internal postholes, was noted in area X, on a slightly different north–south course. Stratigraphically, however, it belongs to the same period of land use as those identified in area W.

PHASE 2: THE DOMUSCULTA (AD 774-1000) (Fig. 32)

THE CHURCH OF POPE HADRIAN I

Immediately previous to the construction of the first church at Santa Cornelia there occurred a significant clearance of the surface around and directly beneath the church (phase 2a). At least to the south and east this clearance continued down into the bedrock removing any trace of phase 1a agricultural trenches; beneath the church itself trench 001 alone survived, showing that this had perhaps been cut to a greater depth than its neighbours and that the cutting-back of the tufa was not quite as extensive here. To the south the cutting-back partly terraced the south side of the church; the bedrock in this zone was somewhat softer than to the north and thus offered a less stable foundation to any wall. To the east the area of cleared bedrock extended up to 14 m from the church facade. In the south-east corner clearance operations appear to have comprised burning, destroying the presumed phase 1d vine cultivation; the intensity of the burning is reflected in the scorching of parts of the phase 1c clay surface. Finds associated with the burning and the fills of the vine trenches included amphorae, *acroma depurata* and two fragments of Forum Ware, which combine to offer a later eighth century date. The clearance as a whole was sizeable in terms of man-hours and will have required a large workforce.

The cutting-back removed any tangible traces – if any ever existed – of phase 1 Roman structures in the area. Given that the church appears not to have reused any existing walls as foundations, it is likely that the edifice was built on virgin ground. However, it incorporated a large quantity of tufa blockwork obviously culled from local ruinous or demolished structures, with many reused blocks featuring chiselling, dowel-marks, etc; local quarries could have provided the remaining stone. Some of the marble supplied may have been gathered locally, but the bulk, given its quality and variety, was clearly drawn from stockpiles in Rome; the same may be true of the tiles used to roof the early medieval edifices, given that the majority relate to the early second and late fifth centuries AD (see Paroli, above).

The date of cutting-back undoubtedly relates to *c.* 774-776 when the *domusculta Capracorum* was founded and the decision made to build a church. This was formally dedicated in *c.* 780, by which date the building should have been complete, or at least sufficiently complete for Pope Hadrian I to impress the Rome clergy and nobility.

Lime for mortar was mixed in a pair of large circular pits (033, 034) west of the church; the furnace to burn down marble for this lime, not located in the excavations, presumably lay close by. Additional lime-pits may have been required elsewhere on site, as for instance in the vicinity of the south-east corner structures.

The late eighth century church complex comprised three principal components: church, atrium, and baptistery (Figs 33 and 34). The church followed a west–east alignment (with western apse), an orientation fairly typical of early medieval churches in Rome and in Latium, and featured the somewhat squat dimensions of 16 × 14.5 m. Adequate comparisons exist in Rome to verify that this was not an unusual plan [11]. In contrast with fourth to sixth century churches in Rome where the nave measured exactly twice the width of the aisle, Santa Cornelia, like San Clemente, was given a wider nave to counter

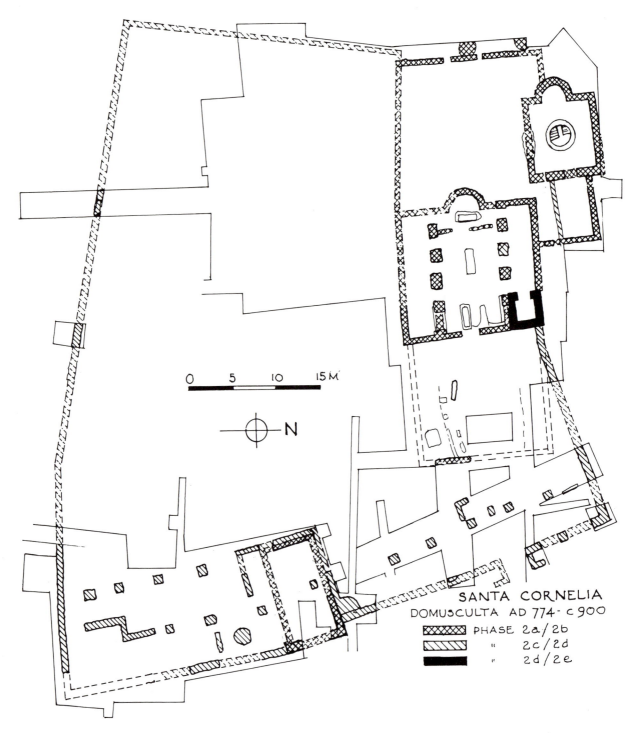

Fig. 32. Santa Cornelia: phase 2 plan (SG)

a reduced length. This will have necessitated the provision of a somewhat low roof (see Fig. 34). The reasons for this squarish plan are uncertain, being dictated neither by the availability of space (which was certainly available for a longer and narrower structure of more traditional design, as adopted in phase 3) nor by the reuse of Roman foundations.

The walls of the church (005-013) survived at best as single large tufa block foundation courses 0.6-0.7 m wide, bonded with strong white mortar. A foundation trench, cutting the bedrock, was in evidence on at least the south and east sides. The ready availability of tufa, freshly quarried or as *spolia*, dictated that the greater part of the construction was carried out in tufa blockwork, some of which was certainly reused in the second church. This supply was enhanced by a sizeable quantity of peperino and travertine, also probably of local derivation. Brick, a feature of the phase 3 church, need not have been present. Such plain tufa construction can be seen in many south Etrurian churches, including those of Tuscania and Viterbo, and San Liberato near Bracciano [12]. Blockwork in this area, however, shows very little variation between c. 850-1150 except in the general transition from larger to smaller blocks, and thus cannot be closely dated as in the case of brickwork. A useful comparison is nonetheless formed by the *enceinte* of Cencelle, a fortress founded by Leo IV in

854, where the earliest masonry consists of large tufa blocks 0.45-0.5 m high and 0.5-0.6 m long; elsewhere in the circuit occur blocks 0.3-0.4 or 0.4-0.5 m high [13]. At San Liberato the period I (ninth century) church employed in its lower courses large, often worn, blocks taken from the ruins of *Forum Clodii*; somewhat smaller blocks and roughly-coursed rubble formed the upper courses. We do not know the size of the upper course blockwork of the church at Santa Cornelia; the huge blocks of 0.6-0.7 × 0.5 × 0.5 m are unlikely to have been used throughout; more probably smaller blocks, 0.25-0.3 or 0.35-0.4 m high, similar to those noted in the phase 2e campanile, were present. By contrast, in Rome, where brick was the principal building material, tufa, where available, was used primarily in church foundations; the upper courses occasionally featured small tufa blocks or *tufelli* of 0.12-0.2 × 0.06-0.08 m, rarely used consistently with brick to form *opus listatum* [14]. There is no clear evidence for such small tufa blocks in phase 2a at Santa Cornelia.

Internally the church was divided by two lines of pier bases into a nave with flanking aisles. The foundations of these bases were substantially reused in phase 3, suggesting that the latter church simultaneously reutilized the existing series of columns. Calculations made from the column fragments found in the church rubble indicate that

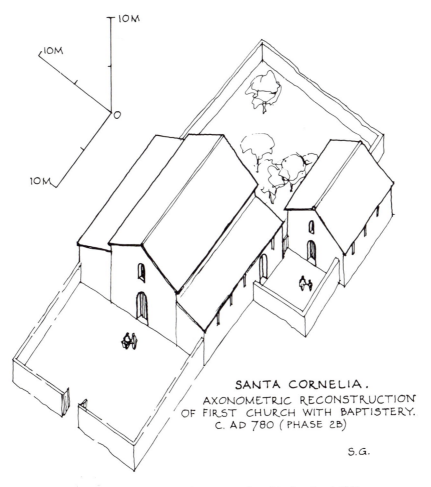

SANTA CORNELIA.
AXONOMETRIC RECONSTRUCTION
OF FIRST CHURCH WITH BAPTISTERY.
C. AD 780 (PHASE 2B)

S.G.

Fig. 33. Santa Cornelia: axonometric reconstruction of the first church (SG)

the average height of these was in the order of 15-16 Roman feet; with the additional height of the bases and capitals we can envisage an overall height of *c.* 18 Roman feet. Despite the fragmented nature of the finds, one can argue that a varied collection of roughly similar columns was employed; the probability exists that these columns relate to selected material from stockpiles in Rome. On the basis of the capitals, much of the marblework is second century in date, a fact which may support a derivation from a single source. The same is true for the roof tiles, whose stamps belong principally to the second and fifth centuries. There was minimal evidence for an entablature borne over the columns, and we should instead visualize arcades, which provided support for a clerestory – an arrangement characteristic of Roman church building between the fifth and thirteenth centuries [15]. The arcades ran up to both west and east walls where we can assume the use of engaged columns (see DeLaine, above).

Towards the shallow-apsed west end, walls 014-016, featuring marble facing on their east sides and crude construction behind, delimited an area *c.* 2.1-2.4 m deep, covering the whole width of the church: this can be interpreted as the front of a raised presbytery, set at least one step above the floor of the church nave. This gave access to both the altar and grave 160, located centrally before the apse and exhibiting tile and stonework facing to its tufa-cut sides. Grave 160 was undoubtedly the centre of veneration in the first church, being the location above which the church rites were carried out. As a *confessio*, it may have housed the relics of the apostles recorded by the *Liber Pontificalis*, relics of all four of the martyr-popes translated to *Capracorum*, or, more probably, the remains of one specific saint: since Saint Cornelius subsequently became the most venerated of these martyrs it can be argued that grave 160 marks his late eighth century resting-place. Additional phase 2 graves within the church can be interpreted as the tombs of the other popes buried here (Fig. 17). Although anular crypts were in vogue in the late eighth and ninth centuries, reviving as their model the covered *confessio* of Saint Peter's, it may be that the cutting of such a crypt at Santa Cornelia would have been too arduous, or was simply considered superfluous [16].

Grave 160 and the main altar probably lay beneath a ciborium, fragments of which (fragments 497, 865, 883, etc.) were found scattered in the church rubble. Given that its reconstructed size is of *c.* 1.3 × 1.3 m and that it will have rested on four columns set on the presbytery floor, it is likely that only part of grave 160 will have actually been visible or accessible, perhaps by means of a grille. Evidence for this may be the raised sides of the tomb which will have brought it level with the presbytery.

Graves 39, 40, 110, 111 and 150 are all phase 2 burials and thus candidates for the remaining papal tombs. Significantly they all lie within the nave, and numbers 110, 111 and 150 congregate near the entrance. Grave 39, however, occupies a singularly prominent position exactly central in the church, presumably beneath the area of the *schola cantorum*, where it may have been marked out by a distinctive tombslab. Post-holes 017-020 located in the bedrock north and south of grave 39 do not relate to the choir, but rather to scaffolding used during construction.

According to the *Liber Pontificalis*, Hadrian I 'lavishly decorated' his church. To a great extent this probably refers to the abundance of fine quality reused marblework, in the form of columns, capitals, and paving. Of the floor only a limited zone was preserved *in situ*, demonstrating that the aisles at least featured plain marble slab paving. Elsewhere within the church and in particular over the area of the raised presbytery one can visualize the use of *opus sectile*, as may be suggested by cut coloured marble fragments found in the general rubble which do not appear to relate to a phase 3 Cosmatesque floor. The use of *opus sectile* is further attested in room 1 of the south-east corner complex, and in a limited area of room 6 east of the church (see Claridge, above). The material is too fragmentary to reconstruct the designs employed, although contemporary pavements at Farfa and in churches like San Giorgio al Velabro and Santa Maria in Cosmedin exhibit designs characterized by central granite or porphyry discs with checkerboard surrounds [17]. There was no indication that an apse mosaic was ever present – a feature common to churches built or restored in the ninth century, particularly under Paschal I [18] – as only a few tiny pieces of Roman mosaic were found from the whole site (fragment number SC788). Rather, the Hadrianic church will have been richly adorned with mural frescoes, though the fragmentary nature of the finds prevents any reconstruction of decorative schemes [19]. The *Liber Pontificalis* abounds with references to donations by Hadrian and his successors to churches in Rome of textiles (particularly curtains to hang between columns), liturgical vessels, candlesticks, books and other mobile elements: no doubt these also formed part of the 'lavish' decorations [20].

To a secondary phase may belong the provision of the series of interlace-decorated chancel screens and posts, which, on the basis of their decorative designs and motifs can be broadly assigned to the first half of the ninth century, and perhaps tied down to the pontificate of Paschal I (817-824) if we take the inscription of *Pasqualis* to refer to activity on the part of this pope (inscription number 1, above, Chapter 4, xi). Certainly the embellishment of the church at this date would fit well with Paschal's extensive building programme in Rome [21]. Yet, as argued above, it is difficult to see Hadrian omitting the provision of these fittings, and unless we accept that metal or wooden screens were initially employed, it may be necessary to ante-date the sculptural material to his pontificate. The *schola cantorum* should have run east from the

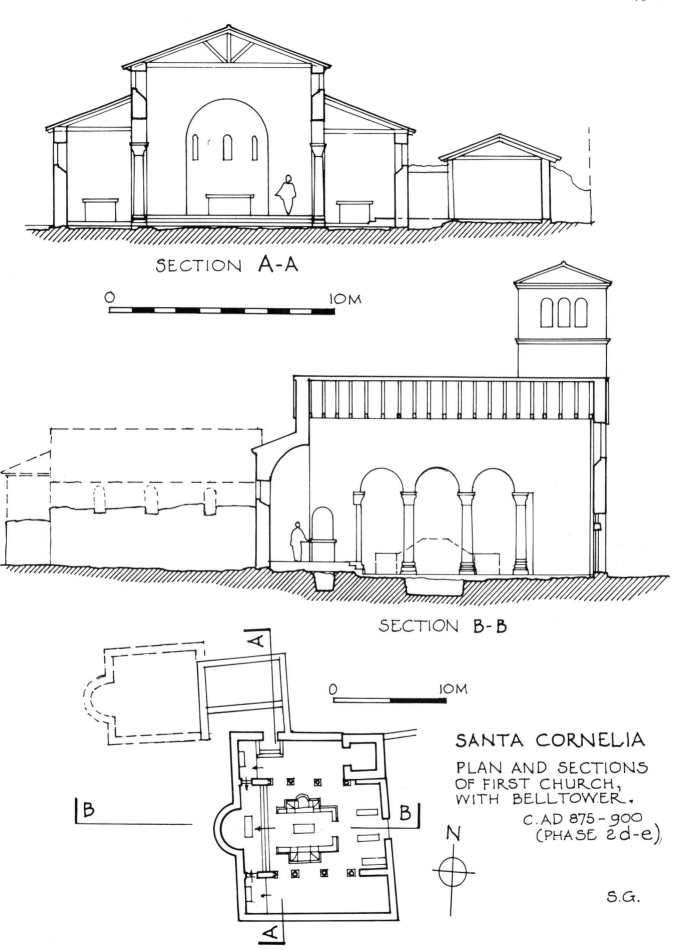

SECTION A-A

0 10M

SECTION B-B

0 10M

SANTA CORNELIA

PLAN AND SECTIONS
OF FIRST CHURCH,
WITH BELLTOWER.
C. AD 875-900
(PHASE 2d-e)

S.G.

Fig. 34. Santa Cornelia: plan and sections of the first church (SG)

presbytery to the mid-point of the nave, perhaps as far as the east end of grave 39, thus giving dimensions of at least 6.5 × 4 m. Its walls rested directly on the church floor and have thus left no trace in the bedrock. Pulpits, indicated by the presence of ambo screens, are hypothesized on either side of the choir, partly projecting over its sides: this arrangement would still allow space for the insertion of grave 40 immediately north of the choir (Fig. 34).

The building of this church and *domusculta* coincided with the beginnings of the general programme of building, rebuilding, restoration and embellishment of churches prompted by the so-called Carolingian renaissance of the later eighth and ninth centuries [22]. In this setting, Santa Cornelia lacks many of the features that characterize churches erected in the full of this renaissance, notably the presence of a continuous transept and of an architrave over the colonnades, both derived from fourth and fifth century models. Yet if Hadrian was eager to impress the Roman clergy and nobility, we should not be surprised if he incorporated at least some elements of the new trends in church architecture: such may be seen in his adoption of the atrium and in the insertion (admittedly lacking an associated anular crypt) of a *confessio*. As noted above, Hadrian's building and restoration programme was not restricted to Rome but extended to sites in its environs, particularly his *domuscultae*. Santa Cornelia thus represents one of the earliest stages in this architectural renaissance and with the *domusculta* as a whole thereby expresses the vigour of a revitalized papacy.

THE BAPTISTERY

A structure to be seen as contemporary with the Hadrianic church is the baptistery, a tufa-built building of 9 × 8 m located immediately north-west of the church. Central in this was a marble-lined circular font or *piscina* 3.2-3.3 m in diameter set into bedrock (Pl. 10). This was provided with a low parapet surround, giving a depth of 0.6-0.7 m; steps led down from the west to the floor of the font. While in theory it is possible that the catechumen (the person to be baptized) could have undertaken the rite of baptism through total submersion by lying down, placing his legs in the gap between the two flights of steps, it is more realistic to visualize baptism by semi-immersion (with the catechumen standing in shallow water) with the subsequent act of triple immersion or affusion of the head (with the priest pouring water over the catechumen) [23]. The two flights of steps signify either that the rite of baptism could be administered to two persons simultaneously or that the catechumen descended into the font by one flight and left by the other. The evidence from surviving Italian baptismal fonts suggests that the basin parapet featured a colonnade supporting a canopy, with curtains hung between the columns to ensure privacy of the rite. No traces of a colonnade setting were noted [24]. A useful, contemporary parallel is the font excavated recently at Monte Gelato and located within a separate baptistery building immediately north of the church: this was of external diameter *c.* 2 m (internally 1 m) and at least 0.5 m deep, but lacked surviving steps; this font was rebuilt once and later robbed [25].

According to the known sequence of baptism, subsequent to the immersion and the laying on of hands by the bishop or priest, the newly-baptized were anointed by oil and then clad in white robes before partaking of their first communion at the altar housed within the baptistery [26]. The space required for these stages is adequately catered for in the baptistery at Santa Cornelia, with the altar located in the semi-circular apse. Unfortunately no partitions or other features were noted in the interior. The baptized would then process into the church, presumably through the north door, to join the congregation. The area preceding the baptistery, bordered by walls 030 and 031, may have provided a covered entrance-way (Pl. 12). Although the gap between the baptistery and church north-west corner offered access to the baptistery without passage through the church, nonetheless the ritual would not have prohibited the catechumens from proceding through the church along the north aisle to the baptistery. This movement seems appropriate if we consider that the zone west of the church was initially enclosed.

The presence of a baptistery here is not an unexpected feature. In the face of changing fashions in the rest of western Europe, where, from the late eighth century, the rite of baptism was administered to infants (as opposed to adults) and a small standing font came to be preferred over the sunken baptismal font, Italy conservatively retained the primitive ritual and its associated baptistery and tank. Baptisteries indeed continued to be built into the eleventh and twelfth centuries, as demonstrated by extant buildings at Pisa and Parma [27]. It may even be argued that Hadrian I decisively went against the trend prevalent in the Carolingian Empire by actively promoting the construction and restoration of baptisteries – though the *Liber Pontificalis* only specifically records this pope as restoring those at Santa Rufina and at Sant'Andrea on the via Appia (perhaps San Tommaso near Cisterna). However, his work at many other churches in Rome and its environs quite probably included any attached baptisteries [28]. Hadrian's successor, Leo III (795-816) continued his policy, restoring baptisteries at Santa Susanna, and Sant'Andrea on the via Appia (perhaps near Ninfa) [29]. Hadrian's foundation of the *domusculta* of *Galeria Aurelia* at Santa Rufina (*Silva*

Candida) included the restoration of the basilica and its baptistery (this volume, Part II); and, as noted above, a baptistery occurs at Monte Gelato.

Baptisteries were the mark of a parish church or *pieve*, providing for the religious cares of local communities. In the case of Santa Cornelia this status is attested only from 1026 when it is named with seven subordinate *tituli*: most probably this status goes back to its foundation as the mother-church of the *domusculta Capracorum*.

However, the laying of three graves (numbers 52-54) at the eastern end of the baptistery previous to the phase 3a lime-mixing conclusively testifies to the demolition of the baptistery at a relatively early stage in the lifetime of the church (phase 2d-e). The structure appears to have been systematically stripped and reduced to its lowest foundation course. Although, as noted, Italy was somewhat backward in its retention of separate baptisteries, it seems likely that by the mid-ninth century Rome at least had begun to adopt the use of the small font, generally a marble tub set in the north aisle of the church. This changeover was in response to the growing prevalence of infant baptisms and the consequent superfluity of large sunken fonts. This may be confirmed by the recommendation of Pope Leo IV (847-855) that every church should have a standing font [30]. That this did not form a wholesale ban on baptisteries is shown in the restoration by Benedict III (855-858) of the baptistery of Santa Maria in Trastevere [31]. However, a date of *c.* 850 would certainly fit the sequence identified at Santa Cornelia. Unfortunately no fragments of a replacement tub-font have survived, relating to either phase 2d-e or phase 3. The font probably lay within the south aisle of the church, and both the slightly raised platform in the bedrock (073b) and the sunken circular feature (073a) are candidates for its position.

Subsequently the former baptistery was included within the phase 2 cemeterial zone, with burials continuing into phase 3. Curious, however, was the high number of phase 3 child burials (numbers 24-34) in this zone, perhaps relating to unbaptized, still-born infants; whether this is merely a coincidence of location or a memory of the role of the demolished baptistery cannot be ascertained. Significantly, a similar sequence of burials exists at Monte Gelato [32].

The east wall of the baptistery was retained and incorporated into a new building, the 'ante-baptistery room', created by the construction of wall 039 on the south side of the former open area facing the baptistery. This new wall was of quite different construction, using smallish tufa; there was a white mortar floor, and plaster covered at least one wall. The room may have co-existed with the baptistery for a short time, but we lack finds to date its erection. Its function is also uncertain.

THE CEMETERIAL ENCLOSURE (*Figs. 17 and 33*)

From the enclosed area preceding the baptistery access was available to a zone west of the church. At a date soon after the church's construction wall 035-037 was constructed in well-cut, large tufa blocks set parallel to the church, defining an area almost equal in extent to that of the church itself. Its construction necessitated the in-filling of lime-pits 033 and 034, an event datable to the early ninth century (finds D/9-13, E/7).

The south extent of the wall was not identified: it seems unlikely that the west wall of the later room D reuses the wall in the south; more plausible is the hypothesis that the wall turned towards the south-west corner of the first church and that elements of this were reused in the second church south side. To the north, tufa-cut trenches indicated the turn of the wall towards and up to the apse of the baptistery; there was even an indication that the trench continued beyond the apse as far as the font. However, given that wall 035-037 most clearly post-dates the phase 2a lime-pits and that the baptistery was an integral part of the original building scheme, we must argue that this 'foundation' trench in fact relates to phase 1 agricultural activity. We should therefore see the construction of this wall rearward of the first church, perhaps running from the church south-west corner and extending to the baptistery apse; walls 030 and 031 denote the completion of this enclosure and defined the space preceding the baptistery. Access was via the church north door.

At least thirty graves lay within this area, all of which should predate the second church; additional graves were undoubtedly destroyed when the crypt was built. A number of graves (numbers 42, 46, 48, 79, 80, 81, 148, 149, 157) group around the apse of the Hadrianic church. From this we may argue that the function of this enclosure was cemeterial. Although its area was not filled, burials spread both west and south before the end of phase 2: to the west, graves 2, 3 and 6 removed or cut blocks of the surviving enclosure wall foundations; to the south many burials occur in the later cloister, and these must be regarded as predominantly of phase 2. Whether this south grouping of graves necessitated the creation of an additional cemeterial enclosure is unknown, but it is interesting to note that only in the case of graves 139, 192-194 do burials extend beyond the confines of the later cloister surround.

Few parallels exist for this cemeterial precinct, even if the practice is presumed to have been relatively widespread [33]. A useful comparison may perhaps be drawn with the eighth-ninth century imperial abbey of Farfa: here, immediately west of the church apse and crypt, has been excavated an area of *c.* 14 × 20 m, delimited to the east by the end wall of the church and by a curved ambulatory, and to the south and west by the lines of partially destroyed walls; the north side was not excavated. This space, dubiously designated as the 'atrium' by the excavators, was subdivided by two west–east walls running west from the edges of the ambulatory. The south portion, delimited by the first of these walls, contained numerous burials, whilst graves were also noted in the larger central area. The enclosed space was interpreted as a cemetery for monks, buried near the relics stored in the crypt; to the south-west of the church, on the other hand, lay a probable 'lay cemetery', but it was unclear whether this too was enclosed [34]. It overstretches the evidence to claim a similar incidence of distinct burial zones at Santa Cornelia.

That graves soon extended beyond the west enclosure wall demonstrates the relatively rapid growth of the cemetery. From phase 2e graves may have begun to spread north, including over the demolished baptistery, while to the east graves were set near the church facade. The greatest concentration of burials, however, underlay the monastic cloister. The absence of grave goods and the general similarity in grave orientation prevent an accurate assessment of the time-span involved here and make it impossible to gauge whether there was a break in burial activity previous to the construction of the second church. Nor does the evidence allow clarification of whether the construction of the phase 3a church predated that of the monastic complex: although certain graves (numbers 132, 135, 136, 178) appear to respect the line of the south side of the second church, this may be coincidental or indeed may reflect the existence of an earlier south side to the cemeterial enclosure discussed above.

THE PHASE 2 BURIALS (Fig. 17)

As is to be expected with Christian burials of this period, the phase 2 graves are conspicuous for their plainness. The minimal soil cover required that these be cut into the tufa bedrock, though the operation of cutting and shaping them was a relatively easy matter.

They were cut to a roughly rectangular form with somewhat rounded corners, and frequently the grave narrows slightly towards the feet. The few graves featuring a tile lining were limited to the interior of the first church (numbers 61, 150, 160) and can presumably be regarded as prestige burials. It seems unlikely that phase 2 saw the reuse of classical sarcophagi for important burials – as argued below, such reuse fits better with phase 3. The orientation of the graves was predominantly west–east (head to the west), following the alignment of the church, though in a few instances (e.g. 120-122, 148, 149, 180, 181) a north–south orientation was followed – in the case of graves 148 and 149, however, this was conditioned by their insertion into a restricted space near the apse of the first church. The provision of tufa cover slabs was common: even where the grave lacks an inset surround, it seems probable that slabs were still employed, as in the case of graves 46 and 170 where mortar was used to position these. Few examples contained tile debris to suggest pitched tile covers 'a cappuccina' (e.g. numbers 48, 53, 81, 166, 168). No grave goods accompanied the burials in either phase 2 or 3, with the sole possible exception of a bronze armlet (lost) claimed from grave 52.

The disturbed nature of the majority of the burials obstructs any detailed assessment of grave ritual. While the head was normally placed in the west, it was not apparently turned to face any particular direction; likewise the arms of the skeletons were variously positioned, in general by the side of the body, but occasionally crossed over the groin or abdomen (cf. grave 52). Little was unfortunately recovered from the graves to show whether the bodies were placed in wooden coffins or simply wrapped in shrouds. Nails were noted, but very few pins recorded. An extremely limited range of bones was gathered from the excavations, a procedure which prevents detailed osteological analysis: most of the bones preserved in fact demonstrate slight abnormalities, suggesting that primarily 'unusual' bones were collected. This leaves a considerable gap in our understanding of factors such as the social conditions, health, and diet of the inhabitants of both the domusculta estate and the later monastery (see above, Chapter 3).

As regards the hypothesis of distinct lay and clergy cemeterial zones (see above), this general homogeneity in burial type offers no verification. The maintenance of this rite likewise makes it impossible to discern any such division in phase 3, and difficult to differentiate between phase 2 and 3 graves [35].

Blake has recently summarized the data regarding burials between c. 400 and 1000 and examined the principal changes and variations in rite. As he points out, Italy lacks any body of published medieval cemetery excavations, with the exception of those of Torcello (fifty-nine tombs) and Bellinzona (twenty-five tombs) [36]. In the regions immediately north of Rome, we can note graves recently uncovered at Farfa, Santa Rufina and Monte Gelato. At Farfa the numerous eighth-tenth century graves congregate in an area behind the crypt of Siccardus and consequently follow somewhat varied orientations, tending principally to be north–south or west–east. Three main grave types were present: simple earth-cut burials, occasionally featuring tile lids; stone or mortared rubble graves with stone covers; and tile-lined graves, often with tile floors. Further, some headstones were recovered [37]. At Santa Rufina two main periods of medieval cemetery activity were identified: the ninth-twelfth century (phase V) burials were shallow tufa-cut trenches without covers; in some cases tufa ledges were left to support the head. Period VI (twelfth century and later) burials included two ossuaries and plain tombs (this volume). At Monte Gelato, the early medieval burials comprised west–east and north–south tombs, many tufa-cut and with five at least so far known of '*a cappuccina*' form; surprisingly, a certain number of tombs contained grave-goods, of modest composition, though in one instance a glass pilgrim's flask was recovered [38].

THE COURTYARD ZONE AND THE PERIMETER WALL

The area in front of the church (area X) was also affected by the operation of cutting-back or levelling in preparation for building activity (phase 2a). This work extended for a distance *c.* 13 m east of the church facade.

In this area a series of displaced large tufa blocks (142-143), preserving a rough west–east orientation, were recognized extending as far as the edge of the cut-back bedrock, where was identified a ruinous foundation wall (148) running north–south (Fig. 11). To the north lay part of a column (fragment 806) and the line of another ruinous foundation (149). In its vicinity lay further 'tumble' (144). From these very fragmentary traces one may tentatively hypothesize a structure built contemporaneously with the phase 2a church. This structure will have predated the porch, and the laying of any of the graves located in front of the church. Its location immediately suggests the existence of an atrium or forecourt. We lack sufficient data to establish the form of this hypothetical atrium: its length will have been *c.* 13 m, marked to the east by the ruined foundations 148, whilst its width may have been *c.* 10 m if we argue that features 149 and 144 belonged to its north flank. More probable, however, is the view that the fragmentary walling (045) noted beneath the later porch north wall forms the north side of this atrium, thus offering an area almost identical in size to the church itself (Fig. 32).

The existence of porticoes around the whole atrium would seem unlikely: quite possibly the north and south sides were plain tufa-built walls, while colonnades perhaps extended across just the west and east ends. In this respect we can note the fragment of fluted column (fragment 806) in the immediate vicinity of wall 148 which certainly predates the phase 2c-d trodden level. The original Constantinian church of Saint Peter's may have presented a similarly arranged atrium, though lateral porticoes were added to this in the sixth century. In this instance the atrium was preceded by an arcaded gatehouse, which was elaborated in the eighth century [39]. Unfortunately the fragility of the surviving remains precludes discussion regarding the existence of a similar gatehouse at Santa Cornelia.

A final element associated with the hypothetical atrium is feature 141, comprising an outline of small tufa blocks and a broken tile lying off-centre. To what

this related must remain obscure, unless it formed the base to some ornamental structure.

We cannot be certain as to the longevity of the presumed forecourt. No finds were securely associated with this nor with the subsequent lower courtyard surface. In phase 2c-d, however, the atrium was systematically demolished and some of its material most likely reused in the construction of a perimeter wall which came to define an enlarged area east of the church. Contemporary with this event was the laying of a trodden earth surface over much of area X, which at least partly covered the few surviving remnants of the atrium. This surface can be equated with a courtyard level.

In area X, the perimeter wall (046, 151-154) was traced running east-north-east from the north-east corner of the church for a distance of *c.* 22.5 m before turning to run 33 m in a south-south-east direction towards the south-east sector where it joined the north side of room 5 (Fig. 32). It survived mainly as a foundation course 0.95-1.1 m thick built in large tufa blocks of *c.* 0.6-0.7 × 0.45-0.6 m laid as headers, resting on bedrock or occasionally set into this. Only against the campanile, where wall 046 was reused as the north side of the porch, did the perimeter wall survive to any significant height, demonstrating the use of tufa blockwork 0.25-0.3 m high above the foundations. However, the construction of the campanile (phase 2e) and of the porch (phase 3a) undoubtedly required the rebuilding of at least the superstructure of wall 046. It is uncertain why the north wall (045) of the presumed atrium was not reutilized for the perimeter wall; perhaps it did not provide solid enough foundations for the enclosure wall, or else other factors determined the outline of the perimeter.

Against the east face of the perimeter remained traces of an L-shaped foundation (155) built in similar large tufa blocks. A corresponding foundation perhaps lay in the unexcavated area to the south. It may be possible to regard this as the base of a formal entrance, perhaps even a gatehouse.

The perimeter wall resumed a south-south-east course beyond room 5 and continued for a length of 26 m before turning at a right angle to run west for 17 m to the limit of the area W excavation. Enough survived of the foundations to show a wall 0.75-1.0 m wide, generally built with single large tufa blocks laid as headers. The foundation trench slightly cut the bedrock. There was nothing here to indicate openings within the wall, though a number of sections had been totally robbed out, thus making such an identification difficult.

The westward course of the enclosure wall was located in trenches south of the monastic buildings both as a foundation trench stepped into the bedrock and as ruined foundations 1 m wide (278-280). Wall 279 exhibited irregularly-sized blocks, with larger stones up to 0.8 m long on the external face; to the west, in contrast, construction 280 was primarily in blocks *c.* 0.45 m long. The remainder of this south side and the south-west corner were not excavated due to evident plough damage. Although likely that the west side of the monastery adopted the line of the west perimeter wall, the excavation of room D made it plain that little, if any, of the original structure survived. Indeed, much of the perimeter wall in this quarter of the site may have been rebuilt. The circuit presumably joined the line of wall 035-037 behind the church, but this junction was not preserved.

The perimeter wall defined a roughly trapezoidal enclosure of irregular form, measuring 65 m long to the east, 75 m to the south, and *c.* 50 m to north and west (Fig. 32). Its construction can be assigned to phase 2c-d, the period of *c.* 815-850, as indicated by finds from the fill of lime-pits 033 and 034, and in particular by Forum Ware sherds associated with the initial phase of use of the structures in the south-east sector (see Patterson, above). No finds were directly associated with the perimeter in area X or south of the monastic complex.

The relative thickness of the perimeter wall (in general *c.* 1-1.1 m) may argue against a simple enclosure wall and points rather to a defensive function, designed to afford the somewhat exposed location of the *domusculta Capracorum* some degree of protection. No towers were identified along its length, however, nor was there any indication of an external ditch – though excavation immediately outside the line of the enclosure was minimal. As has been noted, the foundation of the various *domuscultae* under Hadrian I followed a period of papal decline in the face of military strongmen, and marked an attempt to re-establish papal domination in and around Rome. Subsequent events seriously threatened the existence of these estates: firstly, in 816, the Roman nobility rebelled against papal harassment and burnt down various *domuscultae*. Later, in 846, Rome was attacked by Arabs who succeeded in sacking Saint Peter's; they then ravaged the immediate countryside, destroying the estate of *Galeria* and the basilica of Santa Rufina. Further raids across Latium, the Sabina and southern Tuscany are recorded for the period 880-890. *Capracorum* cannot have been unaffected by these insecurities. Indeed, in 846, Leo IV utilized the *militia* of *Capracorum* as a workforce to help build the defences around the Vatican: it is not unlikely that Leo simultaneously recommended the construction of circuits around the surviving papal estates.

In the Sabina to the east, the abbey of Farfa is recorded by the *Chronicon Farfensis* as girded in the ninth century with a wall and towers, making it 'like a fortified town' [40]. Details are absent regarding contemporary monasteries like Montecassino, Subiaco and San Vincenzo al Volturno, although often the natural location of such sites and the composition of their plans negated the need for actual defensive precincts. Interestingly, at Santa Rufina

the northern corner of a tufa-built enclosure wall 1 m thick was exposed, surviving on its western flank for a length of 20 m (see this volume, Part II); the construction of this wall appears to have been contemporary with the use of Forum Ware (fill of gully F6) and we can therefore tentatively suggest a similar role to that at Santa Cornelia.

Built up against the inner face of the eastern line of the perimeter wall in area X was room 6, based on a series of piers (156-160). Despite dimensions of *c.* 33 × 11 m, running from the perimeter's north-east corner as far as room 5 in the south-east corner, there were no definite partitions along its length, although blockwork 162-165 was traced along its main axis towards its northern end. The structure featured a plain mortar floor, except beside pier 157 where a broken tile beaten surface containing a few pieces of porphyry was noted, and in the far south-east corner of the room where a quadrant (166) of travertine slabs lay. The basic design of room 6 is utilitarian, comprising a series of pier bases, which may have supported a roof sloping down from the perimeter wall – the west side of the building was nowhere identified with certainty, and this may have been partly timber-built. We must assume partitions, creating a series of smaller rooms. While the lack of finds precludes any interpretation as regards function, the simplicity of plan recommends a possible storage role, except perhaps in the southern half of the structure, where the tile and travertine floor traces may denote residential status. Again we should note the possible formal entrance-way east of piers 158 and 159. Room 6 is to be regarded as contemporary with and thus directly related to the presumed residential structures identified in the south-east corner (area W).

THE SOUTH-EAST CORNER COMPLEX

The earliest stone-built phase 2 structure in the south-east corner appears to have been room 5, a simple rectangular tufa building of 12 × 7 m, set on a slightly different orientation from that of the church. This lacked definable internal partitions, and its floor was very fragmentary. Finds (principally *acroma depurata*) ascribed to the occupation of this room belong to the later eighth and ninth centuries and may be sufficient to indicate that room 5 was contemporary with the foundation of the *domusculta* (phase 2a). Whether residential or agricultural in scope must remain undetermined.

In phase 2c-d the perimeter wall was built up to the north side of room 5 and continued southwards from its south-east corner. Contemporary was the construction of additional rooms built around a series of pier bases set parallel to the perimeter and lying south of room 5; at the same time, room 6 was constructed east of the church. Material associated with the floors and occupation of these rooms included *acroma depurata* and a small but consistent group of Forum Ware sherds which, when combined, indicate an early to mid-ninth century date (see discussion by Patterson, above, Chapter 4, ix), tallying well with the proposed historical context for the construction of the perimeter wall. The south-east sector provided one of the few coherent ceramic sequences for the site as a whole and was particularly crucial for clarifying, through comparison with material from the Crypta Balbi in Rome, the chronology of the early medieval occupation at Santa Cornelia.

At least three rooms (1, 2 and 5) of this south-east sector were enclosed by tufa wallings (Fig. 14). Room 3, badly damaged by the plough, apparently had an open north side facing area 8, which, given the presence of piers was probably at least partly covered; area 4 likewise seems to have been unenclosed. Most of the rooms had mortar floors, while in the case of room 1 patches of *opus sectile* floor were found. Although marble paving may have been totally stripped from other rooms, no imprints of slabs were visible. A reused Roman threshold led into room 2 and a further fixed entrance was identified leading south into room 1; no internal partitions were noted.

The presence of both thresholds and well-laid floors suggests a probable residential function for at least rooms 1 and 2, and perhaps also for room 5 which in this period (phase 2c-d) was extended through the addition of room 7 on its south side. Since access to these rooms was via areas 8 and 4, it seems unlikely that the latter were used for storage of animals or produce. Rather we can postulate possible workshop functions – as indeed for room 3 [41]. Altogether the south-east corner presents a compact complex of structures of relatively simple design and construction, nestled against the inner face of the newly-erected perimeter wall. Though the evidence is scanty, one can tentatively hypothesize that this zone formed the administrative centre of the *domusculta*, and that areas for workshops, storage and for the accommodation of the estate workers lay close by. If, as seems plausible, the erection of the perimeter wall denoted a fortification of the site between *c.* 815 and 850 (see above), the construction of adjoining structures may signify a related nucleation of the estate, bringing together storehouses and workers and directly replacing former scattered outbuildings. Without detailed survey and excavation – now almost pointless in the light of continuous plough activity – the location of such outbuildings cannot be determined, though they need not have been in the immediate proximity. As regards the phase 2c-d storehouses and workers' rooms, the area of room 6 must be a candidate, as well as the ploughed-out south and south-west side of the enclosure.

THE CAMPANILE

On the basis of the structural sequence of the phase 2 church, we can ascribe the construction of the campanile to the period *c.* 875-950 (phase 2e), certainly predating the erection of the phase 3a church and its associated porch.

The tower itself was of virtual square form and was inserted into the area of the first bay of the north aisle, standing flush with the church facade. It featured solid, large tufa block foundations at least 2 m high, above which the walls were perhaps built in alternate tufa and tile courses (*opus listatum*). In this and in parts of the foundations was noted a sizeable quantity of tufa blocks 0.24 m high. The appearance of similar blockwork employed in the phase 3a church north wall and crypts suggests either the availability of blocks ready-cut to this size in the period between phases 2e and 3a (*c.* 875-1041) or the reconstruction of a substantial part of the campanile in phase 3a. That it is a rebuild is in fact supported by the homogeneity in construction of the church and campanile east faces (Fig. 6; Pl. 22). In effect we have a tenth century belltower heavily restored or remodelled in the eleventh century.

Unfortunately, in the absence of a modern, detailed study of Italian campanili, we lack precise comparisons for these two periods. However, the essential elements of the structural typology of the belltowers are clear and allow some general conclusions [42].

Bells had become an important part of the church ritual by the sixth century as a means to indicate the times of the divine offices. Only in the mid-eighth century, however, do we find reference to a belltower, constructed by Pope Stephen II (752-757) at Saint Peter's. The appearance of this undoubtedly prompted the construction of a host of campanili throughout the city, though surprisingly we find no mention of these in our sources [43]. One of the earliest surviving Roman campanili forms an entrance tower preceding the atrium of Santi Quattro Coronati. This belongs in all probability to work undertaken by Leo IV (847-855) on the church as a whole, and represents a northern, Carolingian addition in terms of its placement [44]. The tower rises in plain brickwork in somewhat undulating courses and lacks divisions into different levels; towards its top each face is pierced by an arcaded triple window divided by squat columns. Of tenth century date is the campanile of Santa Sabina: this too is predominantly brick-built, but features some large tufa blockwork in its lowest courses; although not originally divided up into distinct zones, the tower featured a series of double-windows divided up into brick piers on each face [45]. Additional tenth century examples in Rome appear to be absent. To the north, early belltowers occur at Santa Maria della Cella, Viterbo, and Santa Maria della Pieve,

Basanello, both plain structures built in large tufa blockwork [46].

Eleventh century Roman campanili are more elaborate in design. The principal structural change was the segmentation of the tower into distinct floors marked by projecting brick courses including a serrated or toothed course of triangular bricks. The upper storeys feature double windows on each face, divided by a pier or impost column. This arrangement is well illustrated in the late eleventh century campanili of Santa Maria in Cappella, San Lorenzo *de Piscibus* and the tiny San Benedetto in Piscinula. Twelfth century elaboration comprised principally the use of mensoles in the mouldings, double or triple windows separated by slender columns, 'bacini' or imported glazed bowls inserted into the brick face above the windows, and a general heightening of towers into four or more storey structures. Fine mid- to late twelfth century examples occur at San Bartolomeo all'Isola, Santa Cecilia, Santi Giovanni e Paolo and Santa Maria in Cosmedin [47].

Roman belltowers are variously positioned. Free-standing examples are rare, and most frequently they stand in the first or last bay of either aisle of the church. The towers at Santa Cecilia and Santa Maria in Cosmedin resemble that at Santa Cornelia in their position left of the church entrance and behind an added porch [48].

Too little of the Santa Cornelia belltower survives to enable us to place it securely in this general sequence. Unlike the Rome campanili, construction was predominantly in tufa, reflecting its ready availability; similar in this respect are towers in the Viterbo region [49]. The brick used on the tower interior may have come from nearby ruins or from stockpiles in Rome; the similarity in three and five module heights with brickwork in the phase 3 crypt and porch supports the likelihood of remodelling. Finds from the rubble and plough debris within the campanile and its immediate vicinity showed a significant quantity of corbels (fragment numbers SC117, 152, 153, 335, 337, 383), capital fragments (numbers 38, 150, 328, 331, 334) and column fragments (numbers 39, 151, 384). This may be sufficient to show that in elevation the tower, most probably as a result of restructuring first in phase 3a and perhaps later in phase 3d, was divided into levels marked by mouldings containing corbels and featuring single or double arched windows supported by impost columns (Fig. 33). Given its solid foundations the campanile may have attained four storeys in height.

A representation of the church and campanile exists in a map of 1547 preserved in the Vatican Library, which shows the church still standing with a tall, spired tower. The design is obviously standardized and probably bears no relationship to the real church (the campanile is indeed shown in the wrong position), and the map as a whole is certainly a copy of a much older original, now lost [50].

An important feature associated with the construction of the campanile was the bronze furnace (044) located within the cemeterial zone west of the north aisle of the first church. This was chiefly tile-built, of 1 m diameter and featuring a central flue channel: over this lay an area of hardened clay with slightly raised edges, defining a circle 0.55-0.6 m in diameter. The plan of this feature bears notable similarities with a series of medieval (twelfth to fifteenth century) bell-pits recently examined by Blagg [51]. Although the pit at Santa Cornelia predates these examples by up to three hundred years, the mode of production need have undergone little change over this period, and feature 044 serves to show that the practice was already well-established by *c.* 900 (Pl. 14).

Figures derived from these pits and from extant thirteenth century bronze bells in Rome demonstrate that although size varied considerably, in general bells were produced to a diameter of 0.5-1 m in this period, becoming increasingly larger in successive centuries. Few early bells survive, but a useful comparison is the Canino bell, presumed to have belonged to an early ninth century abbey near Viterbo, and featuring a mouth diameter of 0.39 m [52]. The bell-pit at Santa Cornelia would have produced a bell *c.* 0.5 m in diameter.

Blagg further notes that bell-pits were frequently constructed in close proximity to the tower in which the bells were to be hung [53]. Useful examples in this context are the late Saxon bell-pits found within churches such as Winchester, and the thirteenth century bell-pit excavated in the Cloître Saint Martin, Tours in 1982, which was inserted into the monastic cloister, disturbing a number of early medieval and medieval burials; burials continued to be made in the zone after the pit had become redundant [54]. The location of the presumed bell-pit in the midst of an existing cemetery at Santa Cornelia is not therefore as surprising as it might seem.

How long the original bell lasted is not known, but additional bells were cast in the lifetime of the monastery. In 1647, however, Nardini records that the inhabitants of Formello had long since made off with the monastery's bells.

THE END OF THE DOMUSCULTA

Few clues exist with which to argue the fate of the *domusculta Capracorum*, whether abandonment, destruction or demolition. According to the scarse documentary sources, Santa Cornelia was a parish church overseeing no less than seven dependent churches in 1026, nine years before it is recorded as a monastery. This fact alone suggests that the church, if it had been abandoned or destroyed, had been long enough back on its feet to establish itself as a parish church. That it fulfilled this role from its outset in the late eighth century can be claimed from its possession of a baptistery [55]. The charter of 1041 in fact claims the continued residency of all four of the martyr-popes translated by Hadrian I. The relics of Saint Cornelius at least should have remained, given the subsequent dedications of the monastery church, but we should be hesitant in accepting the presence of the other martyrs, whose relics are recorded elsewhere in ninth century churches in Rome, such as at Santa Prassede; admittedly Saint Cornelius too appears to have been disseminated across much of Francia and parts of Rome, with relics (and even bodies) claimed at Fulda, Compiègne, and at Santa Maria in Trastevere in Rome. Certainly, if the church at *Capracorum* had lain empty for any length of time the saints' relics will have rapidly been whisked away and variously sold off to the highest-bidding church. The chances of such an event happening were quite high, given the notorious level of relic thefts in eighth to tenth century Italy and western Europe, but the frequency of falsification was equally high, and it is equally reasonable to see the church of *Capracorum* maintaining Cornelius' relics throughout this period. Of course, if these had indeed been stolen, the church was unlikely to admit to this and would no doubt have found suitable replacements to work miracles on its behalf [56].

The actual role of the *domusculta*, by contrast, will have necessarily fallen by the wayside during the course of the later ninth and tenth centuries, when the popes were losing their grip on Rome and its countryside to the Roman nobility; likewise the persistent Arab threat will have worn away various of its lands. Certainly by the time of the official foundation of the monastery of Saint Cornelius in 1041, the land around the church was in the possession of a wealthy Roman nobleman, Stephanus, son of Leo *de Nomiculatorem*, and neighbour of one of the Crescenzo family. How long this had been the situation is unclear. We have seen how in phase 2c-d the *domusculta* became nucleated within a tufa-built perimeter wall, a process dated to *c.* 815-850. This undoubtedly affected the running of the site and may well have drastically altered its original role, transforming it from a papal estate providing food for the poor of Rome into a virtual papal fortress.

While the estate name of *Capracorum* was preserved into the eleventh century (*Capracozio, Crapario*), this in no way signifies the survival of the estate itself; similarly, the appearance of the name *castrum Capracorum* at Monte Gelato in the area of Nepi in the eleventh century need not indicate a transfer of the estate centre or its role northwards at some stage in the ninth or tenth century, but rather the adoption of the name of the estate to which it once belonged [57].

The excavations provide no clear answer to these problems. The phase 3a church ostensibly overlay the late eighth century church in its eastern half and retained the positions of its arcades; much of the

building material and some of the internal fittings for the new church also came from the original edifice. There is no evidence that the latter was burnt down or had lain long abandoned previous to phase 3a. Most probably, therefore, the first church was systematically or partially demolished in order to build the phase 3a structure and that during this operation useful building material and marblework was set aside for reuse and reworking, and other marble burnt down for lime; there was no clear evidence for other fragments being discarded or buried – most of the material could be of some use. Rubble did, however, fill grave 160, the presumed *confessio* of the Hadrianic foundation.

The burials provide only a vague hint of the continuity postulated in the church sequence. It is argued that burials continued right up to phase 2g and the church's demolition (e.g. the insertion of graves 52-54 within the baptistery, and the apparent demolition of part of the enclosure wall west of the church to make way for graves 2, 3 and 6) but none demonstrably span phase 2g – 3a. The courtyard preceding the church presented a confused sequence, which is of little help in this discussion, except for the presence of a coin of Otto I (967-973) on the phase 3a courtyard surface, which may offer a sign of frequentation in the late tenth century, but more likely verifies the construction of the second church and the laying of a new courtyard surface in the early eleventh century (see Travaini, above).

More significant are the data drawn from the south-east corner complex, the 'administrative' quarter of the *domusculta*. Constructed only in phase 2c-d (*c.* 815-850), its rooms featured single phase mortar floors with no apparent relaying. They appear to have fallen into disuse, and, in the case of room 1 at least, to have been burnt down in phase 2e-f. Plough activity had, unfortunately, badly disturbed the upper levels, often scarring the mortar floors, and mixing finds; the few finds from the burnt layer (W/5, 6) offer a late ninth-tenth century date. That the zone was no longer in use by phase 3a is evident from extensive robbing of the rooms and perimeter wall, and construction close by of a lime kiln: finds from the robber trenches and the fill of the kiln pointed to an eleventh century date, demonstrating that the south-east corner was fully exploited as a quarry for building stone and marble for lime. The same is true for room 6, where the perimeter wall was in many parts wholly robbed out; although heavy plough disturbance had contaminated the levels, robbing appears to have begun in the eleventh century.

Thus, by the time the decision was taken to rebuild the church on a grander scale, the structures associated with the *domusculta Capracorum* were perhaps in an advanced state of decay or abandonment, and the church alone stood intact, within a delapidated enclosure. The ruinous structures offered a ready source of building material and were fully exploited. How much of these remained once the new church had been erected cannot be ascertained, but it is unlikely that the area was wholly scoured of tumbled buildings.

PHASE 3: THE SECOND CHURCH (Figs 35 and 36)

THE CONSTRUCTION OF THE PHASE 3a CHURCH

To phase 3a relates the rebuilding of the church on a larger, grander scale, involving the extension of the church westwards to create a plan of dimensions *c.* 26 × 16.5 m (Fig. 35). Despite some irregularities in plan, one can calculate that the unit of measurement employed was a foot of 295 mm, giving external dimensions of 88 × 56 feet and internal dimensions of 83 × 51 feet.

As building work began on site it appears that lime for the mortar was being prepared in at least two areas: in the former baptistery the font (028) was converted into a lime-mixing pit, and lime was found spread over much of the eastern half of the building. Sherds below the lime (including K/10 and 14 from graves 52 and 54 and M/7 and 9 from the font fill) suggested an eleventh century date, but here too there were intrusive sherds, highlighting again the absence of secure sealed deposits in the church area. A lime kiln (231) was excavated into the bedrock just south of the buildings in the south-east corner and derived marble for burning from these (Fig. 16). The demolished baptistery also saw the insertion into its north-west corner of a large well-constructed tile kiln (102-104) of 3 m diameter preserved to its pierced floor level 1.4 m above the bedrock base (Fig. 10; Pl. 25). The kiln was almost certainly domed, reaching up to 3 m in height: its reddened sides showed that it had been frequently fired, and fused, misfired, tiles (K/1, 9) related to this. Its use immediately followed the lime-mixing activity (it cut the former font to the south-east), and provided tile to supplement the large amount of reused Roman tile for roofing both church and monastery (see Paroli above, Chapter 4, x) [58]; it continued in use into phase 3b.

In its eastern half the phase 3a church overlay the phase 2a plan, but only in the case of the facade wall do the foundations and perhaps even walling of the earlier structure appear to have been reused; on the south and north sides, in contrast, the phase 3a walls only part followed the earlier foundations or otherwise flanked these. Building stone was certainly taken from the demolished phase 2 edifice, and in some cases recut. In general, construction was characterized by the use of large tufa foundations between 0.7-0.8 m thick, over which ran courses of smaller tufa blocks 0.25-0.3 m high, which, on the north wall at least, alternated with brick bands to form elevation in *opus listatum*. On the facade largish

blockwork alone was preserved, while elsewhere, as in the crypts, brickwork was much in evidence (Fig. 18). The occurrence of *opus listatum* both in the crypts and on the projecting walls 055 and 056 mark this out as the principal building technique.

The transition from large tufa blockwork in phase 2a to smaller blocks in phase 3a reflects a general trend in masonry types in northern Latium at least in the period 1000-1150, as demonstrated in the walls of Cencelle, where eleventh century work is marked by tufa blocks 0.2-0.27 m high [59]. We lack data on eleventh century monuments in Rome, though a greater frequency in the use of brick can be noted, a trend reinforced in the twelfth century [60]. Bricks here were pilfered from Roman ruins, and it is plausible that those used at Santa Cornelia were similarly obtained, if in somewhat smaller quantities. Interesting is the occurrence on the brick piers of the porch facade of '*falsa cortina*' pointing, whereby the mortar-beds were scored by a horizontal incised line. This was current in twelfth century Rome, but probably derives from Roman practice [61]. *Opus listatum* similarly represents a likely unbroken tradition; in twelfth century Rome the small tufa blocks are between 0.09-0.24 × 0.09-0.17 m in size and occur with greater frequency in the second half of the century, perhaps due to diminishing brick supplies.

In their adaptation of the phase 2 outline, the phase 3a builders maintained the original location of the arcades, to some extent reinforcing these by creating larger bases which incorporated *spolia* in their foundations. Despite the additional length of the new church, it seems probable that many phase 2a columns were reused; additional columns and capitals were most likely brought from Rome. The arcades divided a 7 m wide nave from aisles of 3-3.3 m: in the east these extended up to projecting walls (055, 056a) which acted as buttresses to the facade; engaged columns formed the termination of the arcades. The setting of stylobates 063 and 069 behind the foundations of the west end piers of the first church (007, 008) recommend provision of central double piers. To the west the arcades extended into the raised presbytery, an area of 15 × 4 m, dominated by a 3 m deep semi-circular apse, and probably reached by steps from the church nave (over walls 060, 074, 075). The roof was probably carried on a relatively high clerestory with windows set above the arcades (Fig. 36).

The principal feature of the new church was the triple crypt underlying the presbytery, entered by means of stairs (082) leading down from the north aisle. These comprised a set of three chambers, those to north and south squarish in plan, the central crypt repeating the overlying horseshoe design of the apse. The side chambers were roofed with simple cross vaults, whereas the main room showed vaulting supported centrally by two lowish columns *c.* 0.5 m in diameter (086, 087). The crypt was paved throughout in marble slabs, generally *spolia*, though paving

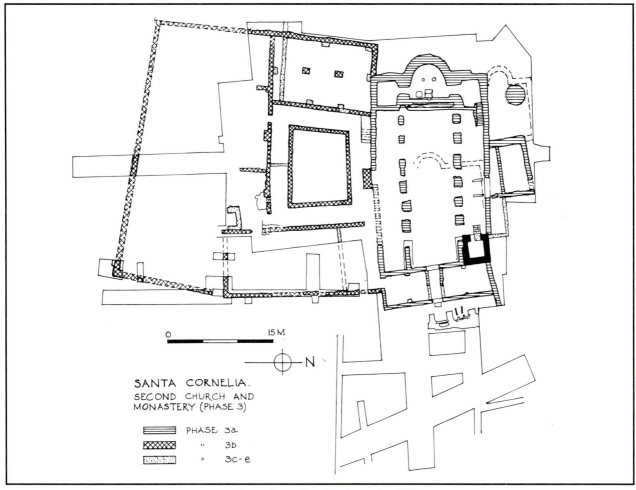

Fig. 35. Santa Cornelia: phase 3 plan (SG)

survived only in the central chamber. Niches were present in both the north and south rooms, but the principal feature of the crypt was the marble-lined reliquary (084) set in the floor of the central chamber against its eastern face and presumably holding the relics of Saint Cornelius; the wall itself held a wide semi-circular niche (083). What arrangement existed for exhibiting the relics is uncertain, but we should expect an associated altar placed over the reliquary, perhaps set on low columns; the sunken features (085a and 085b) north and south of the reliquary pit may denote the setting of additional altars. Traces of fallen plaster on the floor suggested that the walls of the central chamber featured painted designs, but these cannot be reconstructed.

In the main body of the church the crude foundation walls 077 and 078, featuring numerous marble fragments (numbers 367-368), mark the north and east bases of a *schola cantorum*, extending 8 m from the front of the presbytery into the exact centre of the church. Although its south side was not preserved we can visualize a choir of 8 × 6 m, lying just within the line of the arcades, repeating an arrangement found in many twelfth century churches in Rome. There is no indication that new chancel screens were carved for this, and it seems plausible to argue that at least initially the earlier fittings were

re-employed. Only in a few instances can we definitely state that elements had been broken up for other uses – in the case of 552a-b as part of the make-up for the phase 3d porch causeway. The ambo and ciborium should probably likewise have seen reuse, whether wholesale or fragmentary, being incorporated into new structures of similar function. Later on the church saw Cosmatesque embellishment which included flooring and at least one transenna; noticeably, however, the craftsmen did not use the reverse of any of the existing screen panels, an event which occurs in a number of Roman churches. The phase 3a floor cannot be accurately reconstructed given the later insertion of Cosmatesque work, and while we can probably argue against the continued use of the phase 2 floor, it is likely that many of its elements saw reuse. Fragments of marble floor were indeed preserved in the area of the church entrance (080) and traces of its make-up (079) were noted elsewhere in the eastern half of the church; fragments of marble slabs were also bountiful in rubble in the crypts.

Phase 2 graves within the church (numbers 39, 40, 110, 111, 150, 160) were disturbed to varying degrees, with grave 160 being filled with rubble, after its contents presumably had been transferred to the main altar or crypt reliquary. To the west, building

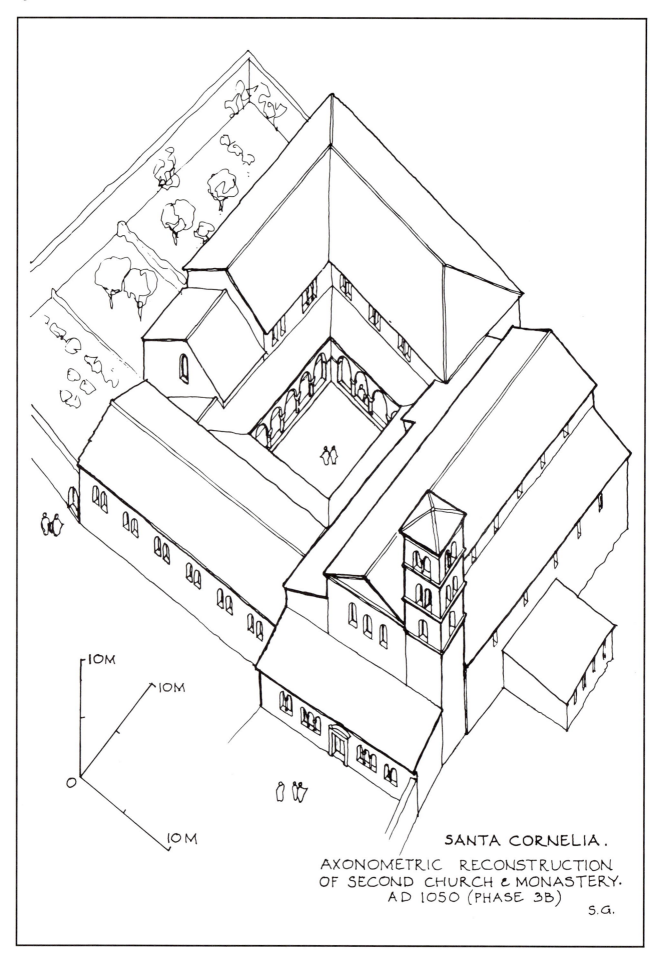

SANTA CORNELIA.
AXONOMETRIC RECONSTRUCTION
OF SECOND CHURCH & MONASTERY.
AD 1050 (PHASE 3B)
S.G.

Fig. 36. Santa Cornelia: axonometric reconstruction of the second church and monastery *c.* 1050 (SG)

work disturbed various graves, many of which were overlain by elements such as stylobates (e.g. numbers 35, 37, 38, 148, 149, 156). The apparent alignment of certain of these tombs (e.g. 41, 43, 81) with phase 3a church structures should be regarded as coincidental. The practice of burying high-ranking members of the clergy beneath the floor of a church became commonplace only later in the Middle Ages and perhaps outside the lifetime of the church at Santa Cornelia [62]. Nonetheless, at least two graves, numbers 153 (in the south crypt) and 61 (against the belltower) belong to phase 3. While grave 153 was a simple tufa-cut burial, grave 61 had some pretensions, exhibiting parts of a Roman strigillated sarcophagus on its western face. If these are not to be seen as burial places for abbots, they must be regarded as replacement resting-places for the bodies or relics of the saints brought here in 780. We can also speculate that sarcophagi fragments found in the church rubble relate not to flooring but to further 'showy' tombs in the church aisles. (One such location may be cutting 073c in the south-east corner, of dimensions c. 2.5 × 1.25 m.) The re-employment of classical sarcophagi was adopted by the popes after c. 1054 when Leo IX was buried in a marble sarcophagus set above ground in Saint Peter's – previously burials were below ground, sometimes in sarcophagi, with only epitaphs set over the grave or on the wall nearby as visual indicators [63]. After Leo IX there was a fashion for fine, often figured sarcophagi: in the case of the popes, imperial sarcophagi such as those of Hadrian and the empress Helena were utilized, and porphyry was especially prized [64]. Lesser clergy and the nobility readily followed the papal lead in this reuse of classical *spolia* (see DeLaine, above).

THE PORCH

A major element of the new church was the narthex or porch. This comprised an area of 16.5 × 4.5 m covering the whole church width and extending north to join the line of the former perimeter wall (046). Its lower wall courses were of tufa, though the surviving foundations featured quite worn blockwork, implying reuse. The preservation immediately east of the northern half of the porch and directly under the plough level of a large portion of the collapsed facade wall (094) of the porch enables a reconstruction of its elevation (Pl. 24; cf. Fig. 38). Built chiefly in coursed brick or tile with occasional small tufa blocks, the facade exhibited central piers framing the 1.5 m wide entrance, to either side of which ran small triple arcades set over two 1 m high impost columns and standing on a parapet formed by the porch foundations (089, 090). Further triple or double arcades lay either side of brick piers of 1 m width and ran to the corners of the porch. The north wall (046) lacked an opening, although a door (093) communicated southwards towards the monastery.

The sill of the porch entrance lay *in situ*, and the travertine lintel lay in position in the collapsed walling, indicating a height of 2.25 m. Over this ran a flat brick arch 0.45 m high. In the walling above the preserved triple arcade ran lengths of travertine which perhaps formed a cornice element (Pl. 24). Finds from the porch rubble indicated the likelihood of a sloped tile roof.

Internally the narthex contained a slightly raised central approach (096) flanked by low side walls (097, 098); paving here and to both north and south was in large tufa slabs of 0.5-0.8 × 0.5 × 0.08 m. Construction disturbed a number of phase 2 graves, and the finds from their fills are suggestive of an initial disturbance in the eleventh century. Subsequent restructuring in the porch later led to further disturbance.

In the church elevation (Fig. 38), at least a single window should have existed over the porch roof in the facade to allow adequate lighting of the church interior, and the triple window arrangement postulated for the first church may have been retained. The occurrence of brick patching and the use of tufa blocks 0.24 m high on the bell-tower point to notable rebuilding at the time of the erection of the second church. Further elaboration of the campanile is postulated during the twelfth century.

The narthex was preceded by a courtyard, bounded to the north by the former perimeter wall (046, 151, 152), but of uncertain extent to south and east. Its packed stone and tile surface survived best near the south side of the porch, becoming fragmentary eastwards; it seemed not to extend beyond walling 148 or over the area of room 6. Room 6 was not retained, although its west side, if still standing, may have formed an eastern edge to the courtyard. Evident robbing of the phase 2c-d perimeter wall in this period makes its retention likewise doubtful. Association of the courtyard with the phase 3a church is supported by the finding from its surface of a silver *denaro* of Otto I of 967-973 (coin 2, Chapter 4, i).

North of the church the 'ante-baptistery room' saw continued use into phase 3c-d. Its exact function in this period cannot be determined, although a role as guest house for visitors to the monastery seems plausible. In the meantime, burials were made around the building and against the north wall of the church, congregating near the north door (051).

CHURCH PLAN – DISCUSSION

As noted above, there are few surviving structures of contemporary foundation with which to compare Santa Cornelia in phase 3a. In most cases the eleventh century plans have been obscured by twelfth century or later modifications, rebuildings, etc. and may only become discernable with excavation or detailed structural analysis. We can cite the cases of

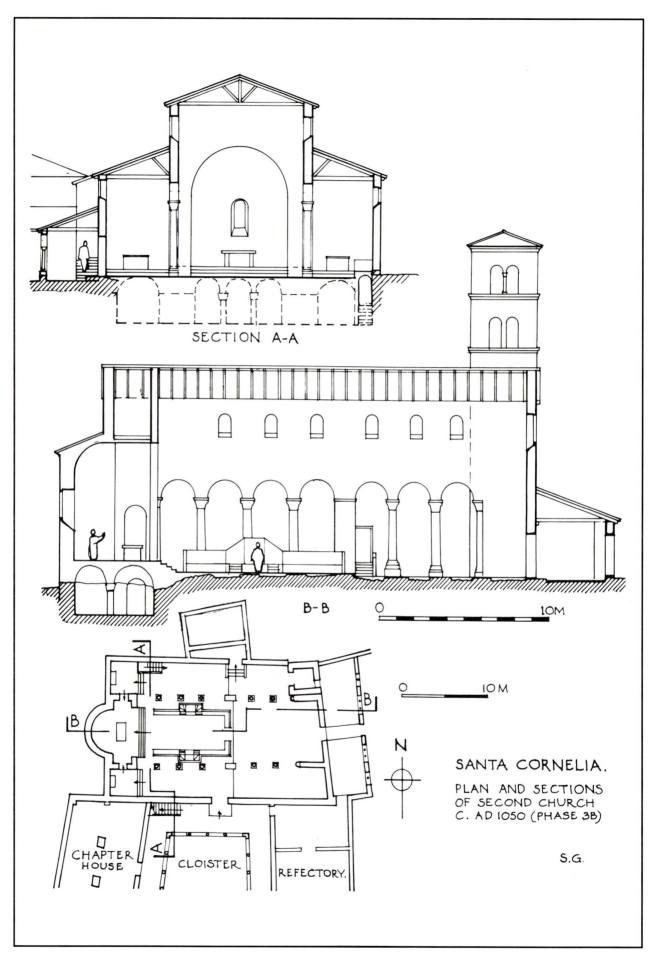

SECTION A-A

B-B

SANTA CORNELIA.

PLAN AND SECTIONS
OF SECOND CHURCH
C. AD 1050 (PHASE 3B)

S.G.

CHAPTER
HOUSE   CLOISTER   REFECTORY.

Fig. 37. Santa Cornelia: plan and sections of the second church (SG)

the basilica at Castel Sant'Elia near Nepi and the church of Santi Abbondio e Abbondanzio at Rignano Flaminio, both known to have been in existence *c.* 1000, but expanded or rebuilt in the twelfth century. At the same time, both preserve eighth-ninth century sculptural material, indicating that here, as at Santa Cornelia, the buildings are of older origin still [65].

The plan of the second church at Santa Cornelia is typical of many churches founded between the tenth and thirteenth centuries whose principal element is the inclusion of a crypt, often covering the whole width of the apsed end of the church. Crypts were the architectural expression of the cult of relics which reached its peak between the mid-ninth and eleventh centuries: their design allowed pilgrims to process past or near a reliquary without cluttering access to it [66]; frequently access to the crypt was by stairs beneath one aisle and exit by stairs on the opposite side. The Santa Cornelia crypt exhibits a single stairway (082) in the north aisle with a central landing, signifying that access could be closed off; in the central chamber two columns allowed an organized mode of circulation past the reliquary. This conforms to a type designated 'corridor crypt' with a corridor linking its three chambers, a type adopted throughout much of Italy, in particular northern and central Italy, from the early ninth century [67]. Its origin is closely linked to the revival of Benedictine monasticism, which took deep roots in Rome in the tenth century, and whose architecture was quickly disseminated across the peninsula. Our crypt, however, belongs to the transitional phase of the later tenth and eleventh century, when 'room crypts' became increasingly popular, being characterized by a large underground chamber vaulted across a number of low columns [68].

Cornelius was a popular saint in this period, with his relics being claimed at various locations in Europe. The clergy and monks here no doubt vociferously stressed the genuineness of their own relics to help make them an important focus of veneration. The flow of pilgrim trade will have magnified the site's prestige and helped pay for the monastery's upkeep [69].

Porches too were prominent additions to churches in the eleventh to thirteenth centuries. In Rome narthexes were relatively open affairs with high columns standing over a low parapet and supporting an architrave (e.g. San Giorgio in Velabro, Santi Giovanni e Paolo) or with tall arcades (e.g. San Giovanni a Porta Latina) [70]. The smallish pairs of triple arcades at Santa Cornelia should probably be seen as primary and are features which find comparison in the twelfth century porch at San Liberato where triple arcades, resting on columns of varied heights, flanked the entrance; the north flank featured a single opening, while the south fronted on to the bell-tower (see this volume, Part III, Fig. 108).

ALTERATIONS TO THE CHURCH
(c. 1125-1175)

Various alterations and embellishments at Santa Cornelia can be associated with the renaissance which affected Rome and much of Italy in the twelfth century, prompting the flowering of Romanesque art and architecture. Many of the roots of this renaissance lay within the revival of the monastic world under the influence of Cluny II and the Cistercian movement and covered most of western Europe. This rebirth affected not just the principal towns and monasteries but almost every rural diocese, and accordingly a large proportion of Italian churches today owe some major element to this [71]. Santa Cornelia was no exception to this wave of architectural energy, and its proximity to Rome ensured a ready assimilation of new styles. The extent of this assimilation is, however, relatively small scale.

In the course of the twelfth century the 'ante-baptistery room' was demolished and soil accumulated over its floor. Graves subsequently extended over the room, and a few (numbers 99, 100) cut into its surviving foundations. The south wall (039) remained standing, however, and plaster was applied to its south side; a 5 m long extension (108) was made eastwards, running on a slightly different alignment; wall 109 joined the campanile near its junction with the church wall. Both 108 and 109 overlay phase 3 graves (numbers 60, 85, 107, 108, 151), whose fills lacked finds. Within the long quadrilateral 'corridor' was a trodden earth surface level with the church wall offset and covering a number of graves. An enclosed passage can be hypothesized, linked to the church north door. Burials later occurred around this structure to both east and north.

Within the church itself, a major twelfth century development was the insertion of a Cosmatesque floor. Few elements of this marble carpet were preserved *in situ*, reinforcing the picture of extensive robbing of the church prior to its collapse. Near the church doorway, however, north of wall 056a and over grave 150, lay one small area of floor (080), comprising chiefly quadrangular white marble slabs, but also featuring occasional shapes such as triangles. Few coloured pieces survived, suggesting selective robbing. These traces reveal Cosmatesque flooring in at least the nave, extending as far as the entrance: mosaic should have filled the *schola cantorum* and the presbytery, and quite probably ran into the aisles; it was absent in the crypts. Its design cannot be fully reconstructed, but its basic components are clear. We can visualize a decorative scheme of roundels progressing from the doorway into the apse, flanked by a series of smallish rectangular panels featuring colourful and varied patterns (Fig. 23) – repeating a design found in many existing pavements in Rome and its environs. Glass has shown that the Ranucius family of marbleworkers, active from *c.* 1150 to the early thirteenth century, were responsible for a limited number of works in northern Latium, as at Tarquinia, Tuscania, Ponzano Romano and Castel Sant'Elia, while the earlier Paulus group (*c*. 1100-1150) worked mainly in Rome. We may tentatively attribute the Santa Cornelia floor to one of these groups [72]. Later robbing was aimed primarily at the (mainly porphyry) roundels, for components such as flanking strips and decorative panel patterning were too small to see reuse. The prizing out of these roundels would have badly broken up the floor, hence the paucity of traces of floor *in situ*. Marble patterning is also likely to have adorned the church facade (see Claridge, above).

In general, such embellishment of a church interior would extend to the *schola cantorum* and the decoration of the altar. As noted, however, at Santa Cornelia the possibility exists that the original phase 2 chancel fittings were reused in phase 3a, perhaps supplemented by additional, plain screens; this set-up may have continued given the lack of definite Cosmatesque chancel panels. The twelfth-thirteenth century churches at Tuscania offer examples of recomposed early medieval chancels and ambos [73]. Nonetheless, fragments of at least one mosaic-inlaid screen survive from Santa Cornelia, which may form the front of a new altar; above this, however, the late eighth-early ninth century ciborium was probably retained.

Painted murals existed throughout the church and were undoubtedly embellished, modified or replaced at various moments during the church's lifetime. Yet the frustratingly small fragments of painted plaster recovered in the excavations, whilst demonstrating a rich use of colour in evident floral and pictorial scenes, preclude any reconstruction of the designs.

Important structural modifications involving much brickwork were carried out in the crypts during phase 3d. Work centred on the north and south chambers: in the north, new faces (111, 112) in *opus listatum* were added to the west and north walls, contemporary with which was a revision of the vaulting arrangement, creating new corner squinches for a cross vault beginning at a height of *c*. 1.75 m (Pl. 19). This probably replaced a failed cross vault, though we cannot say if this had collapsed or had simply threatened collapse. The same problem may have been encountered and rectified in the south crypt, where extensive brick refacing (113) was apparent on both west and south walls; however, none of the vault squinches were preserved here.

Brickwork within the campanile may also record refacing. Contemporary may have been the insertion of brick-built stairs (114) which reduced the west entrance to 0.6 m; a slightly angled line was due to their positioning against the south side of grave 61. The stairs stood to *c*. 1.5 m and preserved three steps, the lowest of which indicates the relatively high level of the church floor. These stairs presumably replaced earlier timber stairs which perhaps ascended the tower from its interior. Updating of the campanile

exterior in the second half of the twelfth century can be claimed on the basis of the numerous corbels identified in the church rubble which relate to decorative mouldings marking the different storeys of the tower: such mouldings should have comprised mensoles set between saw-toothed courses formed by projecting triangular brickwork. A likely reconstruction of the tower elevation in phase 3d is provided in Fig. 36.

There may have been a contemporary reworking of the church and porch facade and roof line comprising the insertion of similar corbels and triangular brickwork, such as is visible on churches like San Giorgio al Velabro in Rome (Pl. 89). Within the porch itself, the phase 3a slabbed floors were covered by a 0.2 m deep packed earth layer which probably formed the bedding for further paving, none of which was preserved. Late twelfth-early thirteenth century sherds (e.g. P/17, 21, 24) from the fills of graves near the facade are an indication of the date of this restructuring. This event suggests that the original floor had become uneven through sinkage into underlying graves.

Simultaneously, brick piers (115-122), resting on rough tufa foundations, were arranged in each corner of the porch compartments and midway along their west and east sides. They were best preserved in the south compartment (piers 118-122), where pier 120 retained twelve brick courses over a base of 0.9 × 0.5 m. Piers in the middle of the walls corresponded to the brick piers of the facade wall and thus will have been invisible from outside. The absence of pilaster fragments from the porch rubble indicates that the piers were brick built in elevation and that they acted as supports for the roof trusses. More ornate, however, may have been piers 117-119 plus another (lost) which flanked the entrances of both church and narthex. Prominence was given to this approach by raising the level of the paved causeway (127) and its side walls (97, 98): the make-up for the causeway pavement included part of a Roman inscription and two joining fragments from a ninth century choir screen, indicating that not all the earlier interlace panels had been retained.

In the south-east corner of the porch the insertion of grave 162 negated the need for a pier opposite base 122. The tufa-cut tomb featured well-built brick sides (124, 125) except to its north where rough masonry walling 0.6 m thick with brick facing (123) survived to the height of the porch wall (090) (Pl. 23). The tomb is comparable with a series of twelfth century '*tombe ad arcosolio*' known in Rome, frequently sited within porches. A useful comparison is the tomb of the *camerarius* Alfano (d. 1123) located in the porch of Santa Maria in Cosmedin: set against the wall of the church it comprises a stone plinth bearing a sarcophagus divided by upright members into three plain square panels over which rises a tympanum borne on two slender columns and set into the wall behind [74]. Alternatively, wall 123 formed a high base over which was set a reused classical sarcophagus [75]. We may associate one small classical capital (fragment 506) with this tomb and offer the hypothesis that sarcophagi fragments from the rubble here relate to this or to other notable burials within the porch. Grave 162 contained a jumble of mainly disarticulated bones: originally the tomb probably held the body of an abbot, and was strategically sited near the entrance to the claustral zone.

To late in phase 3 (3f?) can be set the transformation of the porch compartments into distinct rooms through the raising of the causeway side walls (preserved only on the south, 128) with crude stonework presumably to roof height, and through the blocking (129) of the arcades of the facade with rough courses of brick and small stone. In the surviving section of fallen wall two columns but just one impost capital had been walled in *in situ*. How the enclosed rooms were put to use remains uncertain. Access to the south room was via door 092, and to the north room via the campanile.

PHASE 3b: THE MONASTERY (Figs 36 and 38)

Although the site is first recorded as *monasterium sancti Cornelii* in 1035, the foundation charter of the monastery belongs to 1041, suggesting that only by this date had construction work been completed. The probability exists that the monastery represents a foundation distinct from that of the phase 3a church, post-dating the latter by at least a decade, though the evidence for this is circumstantial, related primarily to the possibility of phase 3a graves underlying the monastic cloister and to the documentary reference to a pre-existing parish church in 1026. The pottery offers no real clarification. If the graves are all regarded as predating the monastery, we should expect a major disturbance of their fills in the early eleventh century. However, the thin floor levels throughout the monastery and the constant digging of the cloister court meant much additional disturbance of the graves. Eleventh century material was certainly present, but it was not possible to pinpoint the earliest date of activity here – some ninth and tenth century sherds are also present, relating to pre-monastic activity.

The monastery was founded in the wake of a great monastic revival which had taken shape in Rome in the tenth century. The majority of these monasteries were Benedictine, but strongly influenced by the Cluniac observance of the Rule following Saint Odo's reforms in *c*. 936.

The layout of the buildings at Santa Cornelia conforms to the basic plan of a Benedictine abbey [76]. The monastery lay immediately south of the second church, with its focus, the cloister, positioned centrally along the church flank. The cloister was of trapezoidal form, an accidental arrangement or perhaps produced by building walls

242 and 247 at right angles to the somewhat irregular church south wall. This gave a northern width of 15.5 m, enlarging to 18 m on the south side; a 3 m wide walkway ran around the trapezoidal cloister courtyard or garth (8.5-9 × 10-11.5 m). The courtyard walls stood to *c*. 0.7 m and offered a parapet for a low colonnade on all four sides: its columns rested on mortar pads (250-257) spaced *c*. 1.75 m apart except near the south-east corner where spacing was 1.3 m. Entry to the garth was from the south-west corner. There was no trace of internal features such as a fountain or *lavabo*, which may indicate cultivation within the garth. The walls, of variable quality of tufa construction, cut down in many points into underlying graves (e.g. numbers 115, 118, 123, 126, 127, 167), and it is presumed that preparation for building work here required clearance of the ground surface down to bedrock, thus exposing the majority of these graves. As noted, the corridor floors consisted of little more than a covering of soil, and in places the bedrock itself had been used.

The cloister gave access to structures on all sides: to the north a low base (059) of *c*. 2.6 × 1.3 m formed a stepped entrance into the church. In the north-east corner of the corridor there was a narrow entrance-way into room A; access may also have been available near the south-east corner of the cloister and certainly via room B (Fig. 9). The large building (21.5 × 9 m) designated room A and defined by walls 247, 260-262, may be identified as the refectory, where the monks took their meals while listening to holy readings. Its position is in contrast with some monastic plans, where the refectory often lay on the south side, parallel to the axis of the church, the east flank being taken by the chapter house or warming room [77]. Wall construction here was fairly typical of the monastery as a whole, comprising rough tufa walling 0.5 m thick, occasionally with large tufa blocks in the foundations; the worn nature of some blocks may indicate a provenance from demolished *domusculta*-period buildings. Further *spolia* included small fragments of marble, and, in the case of walls of rooms A, B and C, millstones or quern-stones; the west wall of A also featured part of a dolium. No internal features were traced in the refectory, though only a small portion of its interior was investigated. The reader's pulpit was usually sited along one side of the room, but this need not have been of stone; the monks will have been provided with wooden tables and chairs, since no wall benches were identified here. This was probably a two-storeyed structure (cf. Fig. 36) with piers set along the central axis (cf. room D, below). The upper storey may have formed the vestiary.

The identification of room A with the refectory is bolstered by examination of the adjoining room B. Its lost south side probably lay parallel to that of room A, giving dimensions of *c*. 8 × 6 m. Its principal feature was a hearth (264) set against the north wall

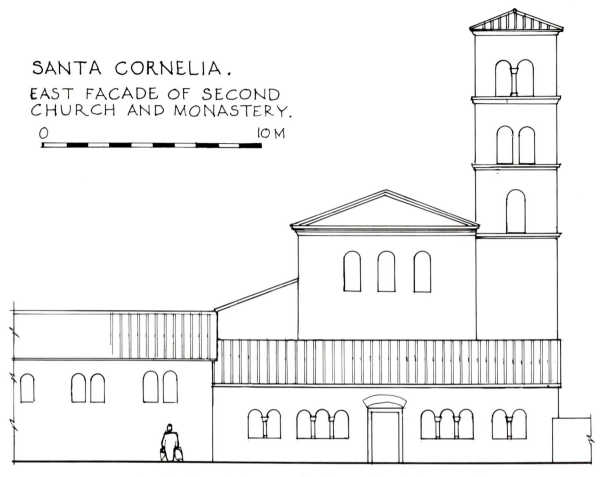

SANTA CORNELIA.
EAST FACADE OF SECOND
CHURCH AND MONASTERY.
0 _____ 10 M

Fig. 38. Santa Cornelia: east facade reconstruction of the second church and monastery (SG)

(244-246), of roughly semi-circular form defined by a rough tufa block surround. Feature 265 to its south-east is unlikely to have been another oven given its proximity to the entrance to both the cloister and room A. The room can be identified as the kitchen, lying in immediate communication with the refectory. There was no trace of fixed work surfaces or storage areas within the room [78].

Close by will have lain the cellar, a structure of two-storeyed height, the lower equipped with wine barrels, the upper perhaps forming a larder. Wine was an essential element in Italian monastic life and we know from the documents that vineyards were cultivated by our monastery [79]. A cellar need have no distinctive internal fittings but merely form a large open storage space. It is plausible, therefore, to consider the featureless room C, adjoining room B to the west, as the cellar: there was no obvious passage from B to C, although a threshold (245a) existed for access with the cloister. Plough damage was severe here, but the room's dimensions should have been c. 11 × 6 m.

As Horn and Born argue for Saint Gall, 'the monks' cellar and larder is the only one of the three principal claustral structures to communicate directly with the service yard to the south of the cloister. This connection is indispensible, since in addition to wine and beer, all the meats and staples stored in the larder

above the cellar had to be brought in from the outer areas' [80]. However, extensive plough destruction beyond room C determined only minimal trenching of the southern half of the monastery, the only structural trace being the ruinous perimeter wall (278-280). It is logical to assume that at least this section of the phase 2c-d enclosure wall was retained to form the southern line of the monastic precinct. On the west flank the perimeter was perhaps rebuilt when room D was constructed. In areas W and X, however, robbing indicates that these stretches of perimeter wall no longer functioned and its stones were instead reused in the new buildings (as evident in weathered blocks in the porch and claustral zone). The eastern limit of the monastery was formed by the east wall (261) of room A and by a slightly angled extension southwards (281-283) of c. 15 m length. This wall, 0.4 m thick, built of smallish tufa blocks, compares poorly with the enclosure wall (279) with which it joined. The walls were not defensive in scope, but merely served to shield the monastic world from the outside. More substantial was the refectory wall, and since this formed part of the claustral complex which was designed to be the most enclosed sector of the monastery it is reasonable to argue that its east windows were set high to ensure privacy. In total, the monastic precinct was c. 35 × 35 m and the area south of rooms A, B and C c. 35 × 15 m (Fig. 9).

At the junction of wall 281-283 with the south-east corner of room A lay an entrance-way (284) 0.8 m wide; within lay fragments of a column base, a small piece of a column, and part of an acanthus (fragments 528-530), perhaps part of an ornamental frame to the inner face of the door, unless fragments which had been incorporated into the wall here. The entrance gave access to an area of tread formed by broken tile and stone which almost directly overlay the bedrock; the extent of this surface was uncertain, but it may have belonged to a path leading to buildings in the south enclosure. We should doubt the presence here of a large contingent of novices and thus of a novitiate. An infirmary was a relatively fixed element of any monastery and its various components (dormitory, refectory, warming room and kitchen) could have been included in a compact unit, perhaps towards the west end of the enclosure. Workshops, stores, and other ancillary buildings, probably timber-built, may be postulated, along with the monks' vegetable and herb gardens, but the actual arrangement must remain obscure.

We reach firmer ground with room D. This irregular rectangular structure of c. 13-14 × 10 m, utilized the church south wall and its extension (131) as its north side, and the rebuilt perimeter wall as its west flank (272); its south side was originally formed by a westward extension (266) of the cloister south wall. An upper storey was supported by a series of tufa pier bases (274-277) along the central axis of the room spaced 3.5 m apart. Door 243 communicated with the cloister west walk. Inserted against the flank of the church and in the north-west corner of the cloister lay the well-built tufa foundation 241 with the face of one step preserved on its eastern side. This can be interpreted as a night-stair, giving access to the dormitory on the upper floor of room D, and simultaneously allowing monks to descend into the church for nocturnal services. On the basis of the dimensions of room D one may calculate a community of thirty to thirty-five monks.

In monasteries such as Saint Gall and Cluny II, a privy or latrine (the rere-dorter) was situated on the same upper level, reached by a connecting corridor [81]. Exactly where such a privy was sited at Santa Cornelia is uncertain, though a location immediately south seems logical. There was an indication of walling (294) west of the south-west corner of room D, but the excavations did not pursue this.

The ground floor of room D provided the chapter house, where much of the temporal business of the monastery was transacted. Alternatively it may be viewed as a warming room, although no traces of an underfloor heating system were found. In a calefactory the monks would have warmed themselves in wintertime, dried clothes and perhaps carried out basic indoor chores. In a mediterranean climate, however, a calefactory may have been a luxury for the monks.

The final phase 3b structure located was room F, set south of room D but of uncertain dimensions (c. 8 × 6 m?), being defined to the east by wall 270. The entrance was not apparent, but access may have been via rooms C and D. The sole internal feature was a vague arrangement of broken tile, perhaps a hearth. If the upper storey of this room formed the latrine, the ground floor may have housed the laundry and baths. Yet no trace of drains existed, and tubs, etc. will have been wooden [82].

The early floors of the various rooms only partially survived: in rooms B and C reddish soil levels were noted, in A the floor was nowhere clear, and in D lay traces of a thin sandy level. This general fragility necessitated relaying and patching of the floors, and finds (e.g. Z/18, 19, 21) are accordingly mixed, running from the eleventh to the fourteenth centuries. Plough disturbance was proportionately greater to the south.

Problematic is the question of accommodation for the abbot. In the ninth and tenth centuries the abbot was frequently housed separate from the general community to enable him to eat with guests and visiting pilgrims and by so doing maintain the isolation of the claustral complex [83]. But the eleventh century Cluniac reform revoked this privilege and the abbot again slept within the monks' dormitory and set an example to his fellows [84]. If this situation prevailed at Santa Cornelia we need not seek a separate residence, which otherwise would have lain north of the church. It remains possible, however, that in this area the 'ante-baptistery room' formed a guest room or an additional dining hall for visitors where they could be met by the abbot.

As regards water supply, the foundation charter refers to wells and water mills. Traces of a likely medieval mill lie downslope of the site on the Fosso di Pantanicci.

PHASE 3 BURIALS (Fig. 17)

Graves soon began to be laid north of the church, with a number of child burials occurring in the area of the former baptistery (e.g. numbers 24, 31, 32) and adult inhumations around the ante-baptistery (e.g. numbers 64-67, 76-78) and the campanile. Few burials appear to have been made west of the church. It is difficult to perceive any organization in these cemeterial zones. In the case of Cluny II (942-c. 981) a monks' cemetery was sited rearward of the church, while a lay cemetery flanked the church's north side; a similar layout is envisaged for ninth-tenth century Farfa [85]. At Santa Cornelia excavations west and north of the church complex were restricted, limiting our data in this argument. However, field-walking in 1986 and 1987 north of the church identified a wide scatter of bones, indicating ploughed-out burials; this scatter was less pronounced to the west. It can be noted that graves 164 and 165 were identified in a trench 10 m north of the porch and should belong to a much larger cemeterial zone.

Little can be said about grave ritual. Some were cut into bedrock, but often only lightly, indicating somewhat greater soil depth; many later graves (e.g. numbers 16-24) were simple earth burials overlying ruinous buildings. There was slightly more variation in terms of orientation, though west–east remained the norm. No grave goods were present. As noted above, a surprising number of child burials lay within or near the former baptistery, a practice which need not relate to the building's former function but may have conformed to some other religious requirement.

Caution is necessary when discussing the possibility of burials within the monastic cloister. There is apparent regularity in the setting of certain graves, in particular in the east and south corridors, across the width of the walkways, and this suggests burials made in the cloister's lifetime. The practice of burial within cloisters began only in the later twelfth century, although before this date some abbots in Germany and France were indeed laid to rest beneath cloister floors [86]. Abbots' graves also occurred within churches, and examples of these may be grave 162 in the porch and grave 61 near the bell-tower. The paving in the cloister walks, if any existed, had been thoroughly robbed out. Yet surprisingly, Santa Cornelia lacks fragments of tomb covers which would be expected for such burials [87]. Burials under the garth and north corridor walk, however, should predate the cloister (see Chapter 3, above).

SUBSEQUENT STRUCTURAL ALTERATIONS

A series of structural alterations was made at imprecise points in the monastery's lifetime (phases 3b-3e), none of which changed the basic claustral composition.

In room A, a northern compartment of 9 × 4.5 m was created by the crude partition wall 288, although its eastern end was not traced. Since this area communicated with the porch via door 092 and possibly also with the cloister north walk, a function as parlour may be offered, providing a space where monks could converse with each other or with friends and relatives and thus forming 'the only legitimate place of contact between the monks and the outside world' [88]. On the other hand, the area may have become the guests' dining room, adjoining (but distinct from) the monks' refectory (and kitchens), with a door in its south-east corner. Such a hypothesis may be strengthened if we argue for the demolition of the 'ante-baptistery room' (postulated above as a guests' hall) at a similar date – this structure being razed to its foundations and subsequently being given over to burials. We lack dates for both events.

Near the back of room B and against the refectory was built a small room (room E, walls 285-287) with internal space 1.75 × 1.5-2 m. The lack of finds or distinguishing features may signify that this was some kind of kitchen store, yet the thickness of its walls may cast doubt on this. In room B itself, traces of a plaster floor datable to the early twelfth century were found, but of limited spread. Centrally in the room was inserted a large timber upright for roof support.

Phase 3d saw a major remodelling of room D (chapter house), whereby its length was reduced to c. 12 m by the construction of a new south wall (289) c. 1 m north of the former wall (266). This was of reasonable build with small tufa blocks either side of a rubble core, its foundations containing some tile and one piece of marble. Contemporary were three tufa piers (290-292) built against the inside of the east and west walls: on the east wall 290 and 291 were spaced 3.5 m from the corners, with 290 blocking the former entrance. A new door probably lay between these bases. Roughly central on the opposite wall was a wider pier (292). The reduction in length and the insertion of new piers presumably afforded greater structural stability to room D (had there been a collapse?); the central piers appear to have remained in use (Pl. 36).

No floor surface was directly associated with this restructuring: the various 'tread' levels noted were fragmentary and inconsistent and suggest merely a patching of the old surface. Against the new south wall, for instance, a portion of trodden floor with a patch of hard red mortar contained finds primarily of the eleventh to late twelfth century, but with two later sherds (thirteenth and fifteenth century). A late twelfth century date is, however, supported by other finds. Contemporary may have been the provision of a 0.25 m wide additional face (297) to the southern half of the west wall, perhaps offering a wall bench.

In rooms C and B fragmentary, brownish mortar levels overlay the presumed phase 3b surfaces, both plough scarred (T/32, 38 from C, U/77-81, 85 from B) and again twelfth century in date. In the kitchen the oven was given a broken marble surface, sealing twelfth century sherds. The latest cloister corridor floor was a slight soil cover, clearest in the south walk; finds here (including T/26-28, U/65, 67) provided a late twelfth–early thirteenth century date (on principal pottery types for this period, see Patterson, above) (Pl. 39).

In the cloister garth an uncertain stratigraphy was revealed which suggested an initial, phase 3b lightish earth level containing mortar, bone, and, in its southern half, a scatter of broken tile (from graves?). Over this was identified a darker soil up to 0.3 m deep, which lay up to the internal offset of the court wall foundations. Finds from both layers cover a wide period, belonging chiefly to the later twelfth and thirteenth centuries but with residual tenth and eleventh century material, and signify that the garth saw continuous cultivation.

A narrow tufa wall (295-296) 0.3 m thick was built over the trodden floor of the south corridor of the cloister, effectively dividing the corridor into two halves. On its west side the wall overlay a single fragment of marble slab, perhaps part of the pavement (lacking, however, beneath the rest of the wall). Why the corridor was partitioned is unclear: it seems unlikely that it marks the division of the cloister into distinct halves reserved on the one hand for choir monks and on the other hand for lay-brothers: although lay-brothers (*conversi*) – employed to carry out such tasks as cooking, gardening, carpentry, etc., thereby leaving the choir monks to devote themselves wholly to religious activity – became an increasingly frequent element of monasteries from the late eleventh century, there is no written evidence for their employment at Santa Cornelia [89]. To insert *conversi* into the social organization here would have required large-scale conversion of the claustral structures into separate lay- and choir-monk zones, a situation not reflected by structural remains.

THE ABANDONMENT OF THE MONASTERY

Our documents indirectly describe a running-down of the monastery in the second half of the thirteenth century. Mismanagement on the part of the new owners, the Clarisse of San Cosimato, may have played a role, but more significant was the irreversible decline in new recruits to traditional monastic life. By 1273 the church alone is mentioned, a plausible sign of the redundancy of the monastic structures. The chronology is broadly confirmed by the archaeological data. In the kitchen, the oven was covered by soil and its fill contained coarseware of the thirteenth century. In the south-east corner of the cloister, a hearth (298) rested on soil covering the latest corridor floor; on this lay the remains of a large mid-thirteenth century cooking pot and burnt material (U/20): evidently the kitchens no longer functioned and this part of the cloister was briefly used for cooking purposes. A build-up of accumulation seems evident in room A, and in room D this part-covered a fallen fragment of column (fragment 833); associated finds pointed to a late thirteenth-fourteenth century date. There are few finds relating to the period post 1300 (see Patterson, above).

Lack of maintenance or disuse led to the collapse or demolition of the monastic buildings. In the eastern half of the cloister south corridor there was evidence for burning over which came a layer of tile, whose density was greater near wall 295-296 and which may denote a collapse of the roofing. Given the relatively limited quantity of tile and building stone over the zone in the sub-plough and plough levels, we may argue that while some robbing of buildings occurred, overall the area must have been ruinous and rubble-strewn.

The church itself remained in use for some time afterwards as the monastery ruins became overgrown with weeds etc. During the remaining lifetime of the church at least three high-lying burials were made here: grave 186 cut through accumulation in room D, its feet close to the east wall – suggesting this was still visible; over the southern half of the garth graves 113 and 185 were made, while similar high-lying graves had probably been destroyed by the plough. We cannot exclude that these graves post-dated the church.

THE END OF THE SECOND CHURCH

The decline of the monastery unquestionably fell hard upon the adjoining church of Saint Cornelius. By 1273 the church alone is recorded on the site and the implication is that its days were numbered. Although we find no further reference to the site until 1448 when the area is recorded simply as the church-less '*Casale sancto Cornelio*' (see Appendix 1), it seems improbable that the church itself persisted long into the fourteenth century. The heyday of the cult of relics had long since dissipated and the waning of the importance built up around the holy remains of Saint Cornelius and his fellow martyr-popes quickly made the church of Saint Cornelius a somewhat ponderous, isolated edifice. As we have seen, the church and monastery had attracted no immediate satellite settlement and nearby Formello had evolved into an established community with its own churches. This church of Saint Cornelius will no longer have served as a parish church but probably catered for a few local farms.

If the traditions later recorded by Nardini regarding the removal to Formello of the head of Saint Cornelius and the bells of the monastery are accurate, we may argue that at some point around *c.* 1300 the church was deconsecrated and its relics and elements of its internal furnishings transferred to the town. The quantity of such robbing may have been small if we consider that the churches of the Formello region had themselves been quite long established and thus did not require additional columns, capitals, chancel screens or other fittings. Nonetheless, Saint Cornelius contained a rich array of small marblework such as flooring, and sections of this, such as the porphyry roundels, would have attracted the eye, and perhaps found their way to Formello; smaller elements from a Cosmatesque floor could not have been easily reused and were thus simply rooted out in order to obtain more prized fragments. Unfortunately, however, Formello lacks evidence of such *spolia*, unless it remains to be discovered beneath its churches' floors. Local farms clearly reutilize building material and other spoil derived from the site, and in the case of the Casale di Santa Cornelia a good selection of marblework now adorns its *cortile*. Robbers could have rapidly denuded the church, leaving only the larger structural elements such as the columns in place.

It remained a shell only a short time. Traces of burning in both the church and its narthex indicate that a fire prompted the initial stages of collapse. Material from the porch destruction debris (e.g. Y/26, 27, 29) points to the collapse of at least the roof in the late thirteenth-early fourteenth century, whilst similar material comes from the dark destruction layer overlying the mortar make-up of the robbed-out church floor. The roof would have succumbed first to the fire and collapsed inward, bringing down masonry. The remaining structure will have been seriously weakened, prompting a sequence of gradual collapse of the walls, progessively reducing the building's height. Elements of masonry found over the broken-up floor near the church entrance and the distorted, battered nature of the floor itself relate to this decay (Pl. 26).

The porch facade wall collapsed outward to lie over courtyard accumulation. This event was probably prompted by the eastward fall of the church facade, to which much rubble within the porch belonged. The preservation of the porch facade immediately beneath the plough level was fortunate; however, more careful excavation here as elsewhere might have provided fuller data regarding the elevation of the church walls as well as their collapse.

Most dramatic was the collapse of the campanile, which for a short while, on the evidence of a hearth, was used as a temporary shelter. Buttressing to its south by wall 055, and the presence of somewhat deeper external foundations to north and east seem to have conditioned a westward fall of its superstructure. This is verified by plotting the various corbels found in the church rubble: the excavations discerned a concentration of these in the north half of the church, particularly in the north aisle and in the crypt rubble (fragments 43, 44, 118-120, 257-261; 127, 128, 200, 214). Similarly, fragments of impost columns found in the central crypt (fragments 35, 199, 345, 346, 351, 354, 356) may originally have featured in the uppermost storey of the campanile. We can envisage two or three storeys of the tower falling westwards and splaying out on impact, perhaps bringing down with it a section of the church north wall, and causing the collapse of the presbytery floor into the crypts.

Much of the collapsed masonry was perhaps reusable, and the site undoubtedly provided a useful quarry. Two pits (047, 048) in the nave of the first church – perhaps an area relatively free of rubble – appear to be the results of fifteenth century robbing: exactly what they were in search of is unclear, for the fill of their deep pits contained no small quantity of broken marble fragments belonging to both churches, including chancel screens, a Cosmatesque transenna and part of the 'Pasqualis' inscription. Most treasure hunters would merely have scoured the debris rather than dug pits down. Much later, a rent contract of 1835 expressly forbad the quarrying of materials from the 'tenuta di San Cornelio', in particular from the church ruins (see Appendix 1). By this date the land around and across part of the site was under cultivation, and continued robbing eventually al-lowed plough activity across areas of the former *domusculta* and monastery. When Nardini wrote in 1647, however, there was 'ancor in piedi gran parte delle mura, e del campanile' – vestiges of what had once been an imposing and important ecclesiatical complex.

NOTES

1. Kahane *et al.* 1968, 153; cf. Potter 1979a, 120f.
2. Kahane *et al.* 1968, 157-159.
3. Wickham 1978a, 176; 1979, 86-87.
4. Columella *De re rustica* III, 13.6f; White 1970, 236-237. Columella says that trenching was usually to a depth of 3 feet on sloping ground, and 2.5 on level land.
5. Columella *De re rustica* III, 15.1-2; Pliny *Naturalis historia*, xvii, 35, 167-172; cf. White 1970, 225-227, 229-237.
6. Columella *De re rustica* III, 3.2; Pliny *Naturalis historia*, xvii, 35, 199f; cf. White 1970, 236.
7. Pliny *Naturalis historia*, xvii, 35, 202-203 recommends spacing of '40 feet behind and in front and 20 at the sides' if the soil is to be ploughed 'but if it is not to be ploughed, 20 feet each way . . . It is essential to plant the vines in a trench 3 feet deep, with a space of a foot between them and the tree'.
8. Widrig 1980, 120; Oliver-Smith and Widrig 1981, 103-104.
9. Valenziani and Volpe 1980, 206-209.
10. Jones 1980, 90, 96, 99-100. We may add the traces of vine trenches at Ponte di Nona, *c.* 0.4 m wide and set 0.5-0.7 m apart, and belonging perhaps to the fifth century: my thanks to Dr T.W. Potter for this reference.
11. See, for example, the plans of Santa Balbina, Sant'Agata dei Goti, Sant'Angelo in Peschiera, San Clemente: Krautheimer 1937-1977, i. N.B. his comments regarding Sant'Agata and San Clemente, 11, 135.
12. Tuscanian and Viterbo area churches: Raspi Serra 1972. San Liberato: this volume.
13. Andrews 1978, 391-395, noting similar blockwork of at least 0.4 m high in late tenth-early eleventh century circuits at Castel Paterno and Corneto-Tarquinia.
14. Bertelli *et al.* 1976-1977, 163-164, listing eighth-ninth century examples, 125-160.
15. Cf. Krautheimer 1937-1977; 1980, 122f, 161f.
16. Annular crypts: Toynbee and Ward-Perkins 1956, 216f; Magni 1979, 41-43: see the discussion below regarding San Liberato.
17. McClendon 1980, 157-158, 162; Guidobaldi and Guidobaldi 1983, 460f, 477f ('opus sectile geometrico con motivo a scacchiera'). Contra McClendon, they claim that much of the marble for these works is early, as opposed to later, imperial *spolia*: p. 482. Note also the variant 'sectile-tessellato marmoreo/mosaico marmoreo a grandi tessere con elementi di opus sectile' p. 349f, N.B. 415-459.
18. See Krautheimer 1980, 123-134.
19. Eighth century wall-painting in Rome: Krautheimer 1980, 128.
20. E.g. *Liber Pontificalis* i, 499f, 504, 508, 510-511; Llewellyn 1970, 244; Krautheimer 1980, 112.
21. Cf. *Liber Pontificalis* ii, 52-68; Krautheimer 1980, 123f; Bertelli *et al.* 1976-1977, 163-164.
22. On the *renovatio* see Krautheimer 1942, especially 15f; 1980, 109f.

23. Bond 1908, 12-17; Cabrol and Leclercq 1907-1953, II.1, 251f on baptism; Thomas 1981, 204-206.
24. Cf. Bond 1908, 21, 23.
25. See Potter and King 1988; Marazzi, Potter and King 1989. My many thanks to Dr Potter for providing interims and discussions regarding this site.
26. Bond 1908, 23.
27. Bond 1908, 18-19; Cabrol and Leclercq 1907-1953, II.1, 382ff, especially 421-429, listing surviving Italian baptisteries.
28. Restoration of baptisteries: *Liber Pontificalis* i, 501-502, 508. The Lateran baptistery is also recorded (i, 504), where in 781 Hadrian baptized Carloman and Louis, the sons of Charlemagne.
29. *Liber Pontificalis* ii, 3, 9.
30. See Bond 1908, 28-31; Cabrol and Leclercq 1907-1953, II.1, 306-309; on fonts, Cabrol and Leclercq 1907-1953, II, 1873-1874, and Bond 1908.
31. *Liber Pontificalis* ii, 147.
32. See note 28 above. The graves here follow the sides of the building, showing that at least part of it remained visible.
33. Cf. Blake 1983, 188; Thomas 1971, 49-50.
34. McClendon and Whitehouse 1982, 327-329; Whitehouse 1985, 250: the atrium is far more likely to have lain at the church entrance to the east. On the desire to be buried near saints' graves or their relics: Herklotz 1985, 28-32.
35. On the simplicity of Christian graves after *c.* 500 see Herklotz 1985, 24f, reflecting papal practices: 85-91. See also Bullough 1983.
36. Blake 1983, 177-178. Torcello: Leciejewicz *et al.* 1977. Bellinzona: Meyer 1976. See also von Hessen 1978, and Grilletto and Lambert 1989.
37. My thanks to Martin Hicks for supplying information on the Farfa burials.
38. See note 28 above. For San Vincenzo al Volturno, Coutts and Mithen 1985 show how the early medieval graves so far discovered belonged to the higher ranks of the monastic community and were relatively well-built, often featuring painted sides; the ordinary monks' graves lay elsewhere and remain to be identified.
39. Krautheimer 1937-1977, IV, 261-271. Krautheimer 1942, 20-21 shows that the atrium was readopted in the early stages of the *renovatio* (*c.* 810-850), as at Santa Prassede and Santa Cecilia, but was short-lived and never replaced the plain arcaded narthex form.
40. *Chronicon Farfensis* I, 31; cf. Whitehouse 1985, 246.
41. Workshops have been identified at San Vincenzo: Moreland 1985. On a possible medieval attribution to the *opus sectile* floor in room 1, see Claridge, Chapter 4, vii, above.
42. Serafini 1927 is fraught with misconceptions and is therefore frequently misleading; he does, however, provide excellent photographs. More up-to-date, but too cursory in detail, is Spartà 1983. See also the discussion on the campanile at San Liberato: this volume, Part III.
43. *Liber Pontificalis* i, 454; Serafini 1927, 20-24; Spartà 1983, 23; cf. Krautheimer 1937-1977, IV, 270 note 3. The use of bells: Serafini 1927, 1-6; Spartà 1983, 11f.
44. Cf. Krautheimer 1980, 139. Wall construction: Bertelli *et al.* 1976-1977, 153-155. The tower is decribed in full by Serafini 1927, 223-224; Spartà 1983, 34-35.
45. Serafini 1927, 94-96; Spartà 1983, 36.
46. Serafini 1927, 87-89 with pl. VIII.

47. See the photographs in Serafini 1927.
48. Serafini 1927, 25f on positions of towers; Krautheimer 1980, 173.
49. Viterbo area towers: Serafini 1927, 85-91.
50. Map by Eufrosino della Volpaja, in the Bibliotecha Vaticana: see Ugolini 1957, between 36 and 37.
51. Blagg 1978, 425-427 with Fig. 27.1.
52. Canino bell: Serafini 1927, 75-76, Pl. Ia; De Rossi 1980, 1-9. On thirteenth century bells, see Serafini 1927, 77-81, Pl. Ib-IV; Spartà 1983, 18.
53. Blagg 1978, 423.
54. Tours: Galinie *et al.* 1982, 172-174. My thanks to Georgia Clarke for this reference. In Britain, late tenth century bell furnaces lay in the naves of the Minsters at Winchester and Hadstock in close proximity to their towers: Biddle 1965, 254-256 with Fig. 5; Rodwell 1976, 66-67 with Fig. 2.
55. Parish churches (*Pievi*) and baptisteries: see, for example, Violante 1977 and Vasina 1978.
56. On the mechanics of the relic trade see Geary 1978, especially 51-67.
57. Potter and King 1988; Marazzi, Potter and King 1989.
58. Cf. Arthur and Whitehouse 1983, 527-528, arguing against its use for brick production.
59. Andrews 1978, 396.
60. Avagnina *et al.* 1976-1977, 242-244; Barclay Lloyd 1985, 243-244.
61. Barclay Lloyd 1985, 227, 237-238.
62. Herklotz 1985, 90. For burials within English churches in the Middle Ages see Rodwell 1981, 146-147.
63. Herklotz 1985, 85-91.
64. Herklotz 1985, 95-107.
65. Castel Sant'Elia: Raspi Serra 1974; Rignano Flaminio: Rossi 1986, 79-88. Rossi also provides the similar example of Santa Maria dell'Arco, Civita Castellana, whose bell-tower perhaps closely resembles the form that at Santa Cornelia may have taken (pp. 35-41).
66. Relics: Geary 1978. Exhibition of relics: Magni 1979, 81-83.
67. Magni 1979, 44f, 82-83. We can note parallels in plan with the ninth century church of Santa Maria delle Cacce, Pavia, and, interestingly, the half-built church of San Martino near Farfa of *c.* 1097 (see Tosti-Croce 1985, 59).
68. Magni 1979, 56f, 84-85. Examples of multi-columnar crypts occur in the cathedrals at Sutri and Nepi.
69. Geary 1978, 126; Conant 1959, 346-347.
70. See individual churches in Krautheimer 1937-1977.
71. Twelfth century expansion and renaissance: see in general Krautheimer 1980, 161f. Monastic contribution: Conant 1959, 110f (Cluny II); Brooke and Swaan 1974, 99f; Lawrence 1984, 146-149. Romanesque architecture in central Italy: Conant 1959, 225f; Salmi 1961, 6f; Raspi Serra 1972, 13f; Tosti-Croce 1985; and the series *Italia Romanica*. Rural dioceses: see the example of Civita Castellana, in Rossi 1986, especially 161-163.
72. Glass 1980, 10-12, 18-19.
73. Raspi Serra 1974, 250f; Glass 1980.
74. Osborne 1983; Herklotz 1985, 143f, with Fig. 45.
75. Herklotz 1985, 161f with Figs 56-60, a type seemingly dating from the mid-thirteenth century: examples exist at San Lorenzo fuori le mura and Santa Maria Maggiore.
76. Cf. plans of Cluny II and Saint Gall: Conant 1959, 19-23, 107f; Eschapasse 1963, 18-19, 32, 70-71; Horn and

Born 1979, I, especially 271f. Monastic planning was not totally rigid and could and did vary in practice.

77. Cf. layout at Saint Gall: Horn and Born 1979, I, 281-284; Heitz 1980.

78. Horn and Born 1979, I, 284-289 on the monks' kitchen, noting that the kitchen at Cluny was *c.* 9.5 × 8 m.

79. Vineyards: see Appendix I – *Pergamene del monasterio di SS. Cosma e Damiano in Mica Aurea*, numbers 45, 63, 87, 133, and 218. Of course the *domusculta Capracorum* also provided wine to Rome's poor: *Liber Pontificalis* i, 501-502. See Horn and Born 1979, I, 292f on cellars, wine and the larder.

80. Horn and Born 1979, I, 305.

81. Horn and Born 1979, I, 259-262.

82. Horn and Born 1979, I, 262-267.

83. Horn and Born 1979, I, 22, 323-324.

84. Horn and Born 1979 II, 338.

85. Cluny II: Horn and Born 1979, II, 335; Farfa: see note 37 above.

86. Horn and Born 1979, I, 249.

87. Cf. graves from San Vincenzo: Coutts and Mithen 1985, 75.

88. Horn and Born 1979, I, 307, noting also the service of *mandatum* or feet-washing.

89. Lawrence 1984, 149f, referring in particular to Cistercian use of *conversi*: at Riveaulx, he points out for the mid-twelfth century, 'segregation was observed in the cloister, where the *conversi* were confined to the walk on the west side, which was commonly separated from the rest by a wall' (p.150).

APPENDIX 1. The Documents

AD 774-776. *Liber Pontificalis, v. Hadriani*, 501-502: Foundation of the *domusculta Capracorum*.

Hic beatissimus praesul fecit atque constituit noviter domocultas IIII, una quidem quae vocatur Capracorum, posita territorio Vigentano, miliario ab urbe Roma plus minus XV. Ex qua primitus fundum ipsum Capracorum cum aliis plurimis fundis ei coherentibus ex hereditaria parentum suorum successione tenere videbatur, eius proprii olim existentes; ubi et alios plures fundos seu casales et massas, data iusta reconpensatione ad vicem a diversis personis emere et eidem domui cultae addere visus est. Quam videlicet domoculta Capracorum cum massis, fundis, casalibus, vineis, olivetis, aquimolis et omnibus ei pertinentibus, statuit per apostolicum privilegium sub magnis anathematis obligationibus ut in usum fratrum nostrorum Christi pauperum perenniter permaneat; et triticum seu ordeum quod annue in locis eiusdem domocultae natum fuerit, diligenter in horreo sanctae nostrae ecclesiae deferatur et sequestratim reponatur. Vinum vero, seu diversa legumina quae in praediis ac locis ipsius antefatae domocultae annue nata fuerint, simili modo curiose in paracellario praenominatae sanctae nostrae ecclesiae deducantur et separatim reponantur. Sed et porcos qui annue in casalibus sepius dictae domocultae inglandati fuerint, capita centum exinde occidantur et in eodem paracellario reponantur. Decernens eius ter beatitudo atque promulgans sub validissimis obligationum interdictionibus ut omni die centum fratres nostri Christi pauperum, etiam et si plus fuerint, aggregentur in Lateranense patriarchio et constituantur in portico quae est iuxta scala que ascendit in patriarchio, ubi et ipsi pauperes depicti sunt; et L panes, pensantes per unumquemque panem lib. II, simulque et decimatas vini II, pensantes per unamquamque decimatam lib. LX, et caldaria plena de pulmento; et erogetur omni die per manus unius fidelissimi paracellarii eisdem pauperibus, accipiens unusquisque eorum portionem panis atque potionem vini, id est coppu I, capiente calices II, necnon et catzia de pulmento. Ita videlicet statuens eius almifica ter beatitudo promulgavit una cum sacerdotali collegio ut in nullis aliis utilitatibus ex frugum reditibus vel diversis peculiis antefatae domocultae erogetur aut expendatur, nisi tantummodo in propriis subsidiis et cotidianis alimentis predictorum fratrum nostrorum Christi pauperum cuncta proficiant atque perenniter erogentur.

AD 776-780. *Liber Pontificalis, v. Hadriani*, 506-507: Foundation of the church at Capracorum.

Hic idem sanctissimus praesul in domoculta quae appellatur Capracorum, quam ex iure proprio suo offeruit pro alimoniis pauperum beato Petro apostolorum principi nutritori suo, a solo fundavit atque edificavit ecclesiam, simulque speciose ornavit, et in nomen eidem Dei apostoli fautori suo dedicavit, recondens in ea reliquias Salvatoris domini nostri Iesu Christi et eiusdem Dei genetricis semperque virginis Mariae atque XII apostolorum et aliorum venerabilium martyrum; in qua sacratissima ecclesia cum cuncto clero suo senatuique Romano pergens, cum nimia gloria seu exultatione pariter ovantes et in pauperes ibidem magna consueta elemosina faciente, translatavit atque infraduxit in ea corpora sanctorum martyrum simulque pontificum, videlicet corpus sancti Cornelii martyris atque pontificis, successorisque eius sancti Lucii martyris et pontificis, et corpus sancti Felicis simili modo martyris seu pontificis, pariterque corpus sancti Innocentii confessoris atque pontificis; quos et patronos in Domino, almus sacerfruens ob amorem sancte sedis apostolicae, in qua et praesederunt, sicut decuit honoravit.

AD 846. *Liber Pontificalis* 518; Tomassetti 1913, 148: Leonine Wall inscription.

```
Hanc turrem - et pagine una
f - acta a militiae - Capracorum -
tem[pore] dom. Leonis - quar[ti]
pp ego Agatho e...
```

AD 1026. Marini 1805, 73f, number 46: Papal bull confirming to the bishop of Silva Candida a series of parish churches (*plebes*) and subordinate churches (*tituli*).

. . . Item Plebem S. Cornelii in (Capracozio) Crapario, et per hujus privilegii nostri et decreti paginam in perpetuum confirmamus in predco vro Epio Silve Candide cum terris, vineis, et olivetis, et titul. ss., titulum S. Pancratii cum terris ss., titulum S. Marie cum terris, et prato suo, titulum S. Valentini cum terris, et oliveto suo, atque prato, titulum S. Donati cum terris ss., titulum S. Marie cum terris ss., titulum Sci Laurentii cum terris suis, titulum S. Anastasii in Cannetolo cum terris et vineis ss., titulum S. (Vita non longe a Civitella) Viti cum terris ss . . .

. . . Confirmamus etiam vobis casalia, et colonias, atque castellum in integrum, quod appeliatur Dalmachia, Balneo, Stabla, Massa Juliana, vel si quis aliis vocabulis nuncupantur, una cum familiis masculis et feminis, seu colonis per singula loca pertinentibus, cum casis, vineis, terris, silvis, et pratis, aquis perhennibus, vel cum omnibus ad supradicta casalia, et colonias, atque castellum pertinentibus, posit. territorio Nepesino miliar. ab Urbe Roma plus minus XX. inter affin. ab uno latere via, que est inter Militiam de turre de Capracorio, et terram de Pastoritia S. Petri, ab alio lat. terra de Monte Arsitio, et Focazan, quod vocatur Columella, et terra de turre de Crapacorio, que appellatur Matera, et a quarto latere terra S. Laurentii, que appellatur Salicara, et rivus qui pergit per Bussetum, et Maclan . . .

AD 1035 (3 February). *Pergamene del monasterio di SS. Cosma e Damiano in Mica Aurea*, number 40, published in Fedele 1899, 70-71: Donation by Maia of a house in the *castello* of Pietra Pertusa to Leo, abbot of the monastery of Santi Cornelio e Pietro.

Quoniam certum est me Maia honesta femina filia quondam Maio, seu Stephania honesta femina quondam iugales, consentientem in oc mihi Petrus, v. h. filio meo, hac die sub usufructu dierum vite meae, do, dono, cedo, trado et irrevocabiliter largior, simulque concedo ex propria mea substantia propria spontane a mea voluntate, vobis domnus Leo presbitero et monacho atque coangelico abbate de venerabili monasterio sancti Cornelii et Petri apostoli, tuisque successoribus que ibidem sunt et in a[n]tea intraturi sunt in perpetuum largire et concedere placueritis, pro Dei omnipotentis amore, mercedeque anime meae, simulque pro vestra sacra sancta orationem qua pro salutem christianorum mearumque anime die noctuque exiberi nitimini, quaprobter remunero et dono tibi post decessum meum in perpetuum. Idest cubucella due in integrum de domo terria scandolici a una in integrum cum iferiora et superiora sua a solo terre et usque ad summo tecti cum introitu et exoitu suo et cum omnibus ad eas pertinentem. Posita intro castello quod vocatur Petra pertusa, . . .

AD 1037. Marini 1805, 79f, number 48: Papal bull confirming to the bishop of Silva Candida a series of parish churches and subordinate churches.

. . . Confirmamus etiam vobis Casalia & Colonias atque Castellum in int. qui appellatur Dalmachia cum fundis & casalibus videlicet Attici Dalmachia Balneo Stabbla Massa Juliana vel quibuscumq. aliis vocabulis nuncupantur una cum familiis masculis & feminis seu colonis per singula loca pertin cum casis vineis terris silvis pratis aquarumque decursibus vel cum omnibus ad predca Casalia & Colonias atque Castellum pertin pos. territorio Nepesino mil. ab Urbe Roma plus minus vicesimo inter affin ab uno lat. viam que ducit inter Militiam de Curte de Capracorio & terram de Pastoricio S. Petri ab alio latere terram de Monte Arsitia & Focazan que appellatur Columpnell. a tercio lat. terra de Curte Capracorio qui appellatur Matera & a quarto lat. terra S. Laurentii que appellatur Silicara & rivum qui ducit per Buxitum & Madulanum . . .

AD 1041 (2 April). *Pergamene del monasterio di SS. Cosma e Damiano in Mica Aurea*, number 45, published in Fedele 1899, 79-81: Donation by Stephanus to Abbot Leo of the monastery of Saint Cornelius of lands around.

. . . Et ideo quoniam constad me Stephanus nobili viro domnus Leo qui vocatur de Nomiculatorem olim filio presentem et consentientem in oc mihi Marozza nobilissima femina coniuge meam, hac die do, dono, cedo, trado et inrevocabiliter largior simulque concedo ex meo iure in tuo iam iure do[mi]nioque obtimam legem trasoffero atque trasscribo, nullo me cogentem neque contradicentem aut vim facientem, set propria spontanea mea voluntate, vobis domnus Leonem virum venerabili presbiterum et monachum atque coangelico abbate de venerabili monasterio sanctorum Christi martirum Cornelii, Felis, Luci atque Inocentii, qui situm est in territorio Silbe Candide, et per vos namque in cuncta congregatione monachorum fratrarum introeuntibus in servitio et laudem Dei commorantibus vestrisque successoribus in perpetuum, pro Dei omnipotentis amore omniumque sanctorum nostre anime salutis . . . Idest totam vel integra meam videlicet portionem de terra sementaricia de quantacumque infra subscripti affines conclauduntur, cum portionem de vineis et ortuis, sive de aquimolum unum qui per tempore moleant infra se abentibus et de terris rationalis, campis, passcuis, pratis, scoropetis, montibus et vallibus, plageis et planizeis, cultam vel incultam, vacuam et plenam, cum finibus terminis limitibusque suis, et cum omnibus a suprascriptam

mean videlicet portionem generaliter et in integrum pertinentibus. Constituto territorio Silbe Candide in circuitu iam dicto vestro monasterii, quod est inter affines, ab uno videlicet latere ribo decurrentes fine fontana que vocatur Becla usque in caba qui dicitur de Ponticelli, et sicuti dividit ibso rigo inter ibsa videlicet terra et alia terraque est de heredes de Crescentio Domini gratias olim prefectus, et aliis consortibus, et a secundo latere iam dicta caba de Ponticelli, sicuti vadit per ibsa caba usque in via carraria, et sicuti dividit ibsa caba inter ibsa terra et terra et silba de heredes de quondam Britto qui vocatur de Agella cum aliis consortibus, et a tertio latere iam dicta via carraria, et sicuti vadis usque i staffile qui est possitus in capo de valle Capogatti, et deinde vadit usque in cabartina qui dicitur de Cornalitu, et da ibsa cabartina sicuti vadit per via qui descendit de monte qui vocatur Acuzzo, usque in alio staffile qui est possitus iusta via, et a quarto latere sicuti vadit da ibso videlicet staffile per arboribus designati et petre ficte, usque in iam dicta fontana Becla, et recte in suprascripto rigo. Infra os vero fines de totam meam videlicet portionem de terris, pratis, vineis et ortuis, sive de aquimolum unum in integrum, nullam reserbationem exinde facio. Iuris cui existens . . .

AD 1050 (9 April). *Pergamene del monasterio di SS. Cosma e Damiano in Mica Aurea*, number 54, published in Fedele 1899, 94-95: Donation by Adam and Maria, inhabitants of the *castello* of Formello, to Leo, abbot of the monastery of Saint Cornelius of '*nobe uncie*' of their inheritance.

. . . Quoniam certum est nos Adamo v. h. seu Maria h. fem. sue coniu[ge] abitatore de castello quod vocatur Formello hac die [spontanea voluntate] nostre cessissemus et cessimus ac donassemus, [et] donavimus, largimus et tradimus propria spontaneaque nostre voluntatis vobis domno Leone religiosus abbas [de venerabili] monasterio sancti Cornelii et tuisque successoribus in perpetuum ad opus [suprascripto monasterio] pro amore Dei omni[pot]enti domini nostri Iesu Christi et pro amore . . . sancti Cornelii pro r[edem]ptione anime nostre. Idest donavimus et tradimus in suprascripto monasterio nobe uncie in integrum prencipalis de totius rebus supstantia ereditatis nostre movile vel immobile a seseque mobentibus de quantucumque modo abemus et antea parare et acquidere potuerimus diebus vite nostre de . . . vineis et terris et de movile vel immovile a seseque mobentibus de quan[tu]cumque modo abemus et acquidere potuerimus vite [nostre] diebus . . .

AD 1053. Document 17 in Schiaparelli 1901, 473-477: Leo IX confirms to the archpriest of Saint Peter's and to the canons of that church established in the monastery of San Stefano Maggiore the properties and privileges bestowed by Pasqual I, Leo IV, John X and John XIX.

The bull includes this confirmation:

. . . Pariterque concedimus et confirmamus fundos qui vocantur Tracquata, Cornelianum, Vivariolum, positos in Macorano iuxta Capracorum et iuxta rivum Gralli et prope curtem de Macorano . . .

AD 1062 (20 March). *Pergamene del monasterio di SS. Cosma e Damiano in Mica Aurea*, number 63, published in Fedele 1899, 384-386: Donation by Bonizzo de Rosa to Abbot Pietro of the monastery of Saint Cornelius of a vineyard in the locality 'Balle longa' in the territory of Nepi, in exchange for one set in 'Gripanula'.

. . . Quoniam certum est me Bonizzo [v. h.] qui vocor de Rosa, hac die cessisse et cessi anc commutasse et commutavi, largi[or] et trado, propria spontaneaque mea voluntatem, vobis donno Petrus gr[atia] Domini abbas de venerabili monasterio sancti Cornelii et tuisque successoribus in perpetuum ad opus suprascripto mo[nasterio], pro ideoquem tu suprascripto Petrus abbas dedisti a me suprascripto Bonizzo petiu de vinea illo[co] qui vocatur Gripanula, pro ideo idest dono tivi ad opus suprascripto monasterio vinea mea omni a cum introito et exoito suo et cum omnibus ad se pertinentibus, posita territorio Nepesi[no i]lloco qui vocatur Balle longa, quod est inter affines, a primo latere vinea de Silvestro v. h., a secundo latere tenientes Maria ohnesta femina que vocatur de Crista, et a tertio vel a quarto latere tenientes filii de Adinolfo vone memorie, omnia vero dono tivi suprascripto Petrus abbas in commutatione ad opus suprascripto monasterio quantacumque infra suprascripti affini conclauduntur. Unde et anc commutationis charta manibus meis tivi contradidit. Pro quam etiam ipsa suprascripta vinea cum poma et arboribus suis et cum introito et exoito suo et cum omnibus ad se pertinentibus, possita territorio Nepesino illoco qui vocatur Balle longa sicud scriptum est ud superius legitur, et ab odiernam die in vobis vestrisque successoribus in perpetuum ad opus suprascripto monasterio sit potestatem abendi, bendendi, donandi etiam com[mu]tandi in vobis vestrisque successoribus in perpetuum ad opus suprascripto monasterio sit potestatem . . .

AD 1079 (12 January). *Pergamene del monasterio di SS. Cosma e Damiano in Mica Aurea*, number 87, published in Fedele 1899, 424-425: Abbot Dominicus of the monastery of Saint Cornelius sells a vineyard to Stefanus, which will be restored to the monastery at his death.

. . . Quoniam certu est me donno Dominicus abbas de monasterio sancti Cornelii consentientes mi cuncta congregationem de eiusde monasterii ac dicessissemus et cessimus, vendedissemus et venumdavimus, largimus et per singulos anno pensione redendum in monasterio denario uno, propria spontaneaque nostre voluntatis, vobis Stefanus vir honestus et tuisque erhedibus largire et concedere placueritis. Idest venumdamus tivi una petia de vinea cum introito et esoito suo posita in loco qui vocatur Grieti, et a primo latere Iohannes presbiter de Verta, a .II. latere vinea donn[i]ca, et a .III. latere Benedicta de Mauro, et a .IIII. latere via pulvica, infra isti affini conclauduntur. Sup tale videlicet ratione post obitum tuum reverta in suprascripto monasterio et pro anima tua, unde et ac venditionis charta manibus nostri tivi contradimus. Pro quam suprascripta petia de vinea cum introito ed esoito suo et cum poma et arvoribus suis et cum omnibus asse pertinentibus sicut scritum est ud superius legitur, unde accepimus nos suprascripti venditori da te suprascripto conparatore in arienteis denariorum numerum solidi sex tivique placavile in omne vera decessione . . .

AD 1081 (14 March). Document number 1 in Trifone 1908, 278-285: Gregory VII takes under his protection the

monastery of San Paolo and confirms all its rights and properties.

The properties listed include:

. . . Castrum quoque Formelli, cum omnibus suis pertinentiis. Fundumque Maceranum positum iuxta ecclesiam Sancti Cornelii . . .

AD 1124 (May). *Pergamene del monasterio di SS. Cosma e Damiano in Mica Aurea*, number 115, unpublished: Stefano and Guittimanno sell to Abbot Guido of the monastery of Saint Cornelius all the land they hold in the Casale Gavisle in the territory of Nepi, for the price of 12 *denari pavesi*.

AD 1158 (10 February). Document 47 in Schiaparelli 1902, 296-299: Hadrian IV confirms to the church of Saint Peter the possessions and privileges bestowed to four monasteries – this repeats earlier confirmations by Popes Sergius II, Leo IV, Leo IX and Innocent II.

The properties listed in the bull include:

. . . castrum Capracorum cum terris, fundis et casalibus suis cum ecclesia Sancti Iohannis diruta cum aquimolis et molaria sua . . . monasterium Sancti Cornelii, quod est positum in territorio Vegentano cum omnibus suis pertinentiis, sex pedicas terrarum in fundo qui dicitur Vallis de Pertica, terram de Macerano positam ad Petram Pertusiam . . .

AD 1159 (12 May). *Pergamene del monasterio di SS. Cosma e Damiano in Mica Aurea*, number 132, unpublished: Nastilia, with her husband Bovacciano, renounces the quarrel with Abbot Domenicus of the monastery of Santi Cornelio e Cipriano; she receives thirty Provence *soldi*.

AD 1160 (11 January). *Pergamene del monasterio di SS. Cosma e Damiano in Mica Aurea*, number 133, unpublished: Andrea and his wife Gemma present to Abbot Domenicus of the monastery of Saint Cornelius half a house, with half the cellar, and part of a vineyard set in the Petoli farm in the territory of Cesano.

AD 1186 (13 June). Document number 70 in Schiaparelli 1902, 331-336: Urban III confirms to the church of Saint Peter the possessions and privileges bestowed on four monasteries – this repeats the confirmation given by Hadrian IV in 1158 (see above).

The properties listed include:

. . . castrum Capracorum cum terris, fundis et casalibus suis cum ecclesia Sancti Iohannis dirruta cum aquimolis et molaria sua . . . monasterium Sancti Cornelii quod est positum in territorio Vegentano cum omnibus suis pertinenciis, sex pedicas terrarum in fundo qui dicitur Vallis de Pertica, terram de Macerano positam ad Petram Pertusiam . . .

AD 1188. Document in Kehr 1901-1902, 543-545: Clemens III puts the monastery of Santa Maria di Farneta of the Arezzo diocese and all its properties under apostolic protection.

The properties of the monastery include:

. . . monasterium sancti Cornelii cum ecclesiis suis. .

AD 1190 (4 April). *Pergamene del monasterio di SS. Cosma e Damiano in Mica Aurea*, number 160, unpublished: Giovanni di Paolo Saccer admits receiving from Philippus, abbot of the monastery of Saint Cornelius, ten Provence pounds which he had lent to him and renounces any quarrel over this loan.

AD 1221 (27 March). *Pergamene del monasterio di SS. Cosma e Damiano in Mica Aurea*, number 219, unpublished: Romana, widow of Angelo, gives to Abbot Iohannes of the monastery of Saint Cornelius two parts of a vineyard set in the territory of Cesano.

AD 1238. Documents 4478-4481 in Auvray 1890, 1103-1106: Transfer of the rights of lands from the monastery of Santa Maria de Farneta in the Arezzo diocese to the monastery of Santi Cosma e Damiano in Rome.

4480: In Christi nomine. Amen. Ego donnus Ubertinus, abbas, et nos conventus monasterii Sancte Marie de Farneto, Aretine diocesis -, constituimus, facimus et ordinamus sindicum, actorem et procuratorem nostrum et dicti monasterii te, fratrem Ubertum, ipsius monasterii monachum, ad dandum et permutandum – monasterium nostrum Sancti Cornelii de Insula in Maceran[o], Portuensis diocesis -, monasterio Sancti Cosme in Transtyberim de Urbe -. Actum in claustro predicti monasterii nostri de Farneto -, anno Domini MCCXXXVIII, XIIII kalendas julii, indictione XI . . .

4481: Gregorius episcopus, servus servorum Dei, dilecto filio magistro J[ohanni] de Sancto Germano, capellano nostro, salutem et apostolicam benedictionem . . . discretioni tue per apostolica scripta mandamus quatenus ad abbate et conventu predicti monasterii de Farneto super concessione ab eis de ecclesia Sancti Cornelii, cum omnibus juribus et pertinentiis ejus, monasterio nostro Sancti Cosme trans Tiberim perpetuo facienda, prius recipias publicum instrumentum. Dat. Laterani, XVIII kalendas julii, pontificatus nostri anno XII . . .

AD 1238 (14 December). *Pergamene del monasterio di SS. Cosma e Damiano in Mica Aurea*, number 246, unpublished: Gregorio, archpriest of Formello, renounces to Bentevenga Economo of the monastery of San Cosimato, for himself and for the monastery of Saint Cornelius and of Fargeto, six Provence lire, lent to the abbot of Saint Cornelius.

AD 1238 (15 December). *Pergamene del monasterio di SS. Cosma e Damiano in Mica Aurea*, number 247, unpublished: Angelo and Romana acknowledge to Bentivenga Economo of San Cosimato receipt of eight Provence lire, formerly lent to Clerimbaldus, abbot and rector of Saint Cornelius.

AD 1247 (18 June). *Pergamene del monasterio di SS. Cosma e Damiano in Mica Aurea*, number 264, unpublished: Innocent IV orders Cardinal Stefano to maintain the monastery in the possession of the church of Saint Cornelius in the diocese of Porto.

AD 1248 (18 June). *Pergamene del monasterio di SS. Cosma e Damiano in Mica Aurea*, number 265, unpublished: Innocent IV gives papal acceptance to the new ownership of Saint Cornelius by the female order of the monastery of Santi Cosma e Damiano.

AD 1248 (14 July). *Pergamene del monasterio di SS. Cosma e Damiano in Mica Aurea*, number 265, unpublished: Bull of Innocent IV confirming the transfer of 1238 when Albertino, abbot of Santa Maria di Farneto, ceded to the monastery of San Cosimato the church of Saint Cornelius near Isola di Castel San Pietro, in the diocese of Porto, in exchange for the 'spiritually badly-run' (*lapsu temporalium iminente in spiritualibus*) monastery of San Crispolto di Bettona, in the Assisi diocese (Pl. 3).

AD 1273 (8 February). *Pergamene del monasterio di SS. Cosma e Damiano in Mica Aurea*, number 298, unpublished: Gregory X orders Alberto, canon of Saint Peter's, to defend the monastery which was vexed with its churches of San Lorenzo, Sant'Iacopo, Saint Cornelius, and Santa Maria of the dioceses of Porto and Sutri.

AD 1448 (29 October). *Pergamene dei Agostiani di Santa Maria Novella, Bracciano*, number 9, unpublished: Nicholas V entrusts to Roberto Cavalcanti, bishop of Volterra, to carry out the sale of the Casale di S. Cornelio (described as *ruintupato*) in the area of Formello, diocese of Nepi, property of the Clarisse of San Cosimato, and to deposit the money in a bank – a request made by the Clarisse (Pl. 4).

AD 1449 (19 April). *Pergamene dei Agostiani di Santa Maria Novella, Bracciano*, number 11, unpublished: The abbess of San Cosimato sells to Orsino of the Orsini, *cancelliere* of the Kingdom of Sicily – who buys in the name of the convent of Santa Maria Novella at Bracciano – the *casale* of Saint Cornelius in the territory of Formello: it is described as an area of 194 *rubbia* near the *castello* of Formello, bordering with the casale di Monte Tiberio of the church of San Lorenzo in Damaso, the *ponte mutilo* Santo Spirito, Spezza Maria, the territory of Scrofano and San Piero. Sale price of 650 florins.

AD 1449 (12 May). *Pergamene dei Agostiani di Santa Maria Novella, Bracciano*, number 12, unpublished: Roberto Cavalcanti, bishop of Volterra, reports completion of the task entrusted to him in 1448 (above, perg. 9) at the request of the abbess of San Cosimato: namely the sale of the *casale* of Saint Cornelius (*mitupano?*) in the territory of Formello (*Castri Formelli*) and attached area in order that the nuns might buy more convenient property within the city. The *casale* is recorded as bought by the *cancelliere* of the Kingdom of Sicily, Orsino of the Orsini, for 650 florins.

AD 1481 (3 January). *Pergamene dei Agostiani di Santa Maria Novella, Bracciano*, number 21, unpublished: Inventory of the possessions of the Augustinian brothers of the monastery of Santa Maria Novella, Bracciano. The list includes:

. . . Item in territorio Formelli una possessio que vocatur sancto Cornelio iuxta casale Sepezzamezzo et iuxta bona sancti Laurentii in damaso de Urbe . . .

AD 1637. *Pergamene dei Agostiani di Santa Maria Novella, Bracciano*, number 32, unpublished: Plan of the *tenuta* of Saint Cornelius, held by the monastery of Santa Maria Novella. The plan divides the holding of 194 rubbia into four main areas.

AD 1835. *Collezioni di disegni e piante*, cartella 94, number 826, unpublished: Plan of the *tenuta* of Saint Cornelius, drawn for the Augustinians of Santa Maria Novella, Bracciano. This forms a copy of a lost plan of 1830. The holding of 194 rubbia is divided up into twelve areas, of which area F comprises: '*Terra lavorativa con vestigie della Chiesa di S. Cornelio, e ripe de fossi sodive con fonte in vocabolo le Muraccie di m.*'.

Also present is a rent document related to the '*tenuta di S. Cornelia*'. Condition 14 of this expressly forbids quarrying or excavating in the holding, noting: '*anche per i trasporti di colonne, concimi di marmo, perperino o di qualunque altra sorta di pietra esistente in detta tenuta, ed in specie nella fabrica diruta di S. Cornelia scoperti o sotterrati che siano*'.

APPENDIX 2. Pottery Fabrics: Macroscopic Descriptions

Helen Patterson

FABRIC 1: this fabric is usually oxidized red brown, but it is often unevenly fired and heavily scorched. It is hard, with a rough feel and hackly fracture. During the ninth and, in particular, the tenth century this fabric has abundant inclusions, often large, characterized by large plates of biotite mica visible on the surface, frequent small yellowish white inclusions and some angular transparent inclusions. After this date it becomes progressively more refined, reaching a peak in the late twelfth to thirteenth century.
Kitchen ware: standard kitchen ware fabric in phases 2 to 5.

FABRIC 2: this fabric is dark reddish yellow to brown. It is compact, hard with a slightly rough feel and a slightly hackly fracture containing abundant small matt white inclusions, occasional large rounded red or black inclusions and much fine mica.
Kitchen ware: phase 2 only.

FABRIC 3: this fabric is dark reddish yellow, hard with a slightly hackly fracture and slightly rough feel. It is a fairly refined fabric but has frequent small inclusions including matt yellowish white inclusions, larger rounded matt black and red inclusions and some fine mica.
Kitchen ware: from end of phase 3, that is from the late twelfth to thirteenth centuries.

FABRIC 4: this fabric is usually pale red, sometimes very pale brown. Vessels of this fabric commonly have a very pale yellow exterior (and sometimes interior) surface. This surface treatment is clearly deliberate, it is not a slip and must be a result of firing. It is a hard fabric with a lightly rough feel. It has a clean fracture containing frequent to abundant small inclusions, characterized by small, rounded, matt white inclusions sometimes visible on the surface, some small, rounded, matt red inclusions and mica.
Domestic pottery: phase 2 only.

FABRIC 5: this fabric is pale brown to pale reddish yellow. It is hard with a smooth feel and has a clean fracture. This fabric is very refined with very few visible inclusions: fine mica, very occasional matt white inclusions and minute rounded matt red inclusions.

Domestic pottery and amphorae: from phase 2 onwards; from phase 3 it is the standard domestic fabric.

FABRIC 6: this is a very pale brown to pale reddish yellow fabric. It is hard with a slightly rough feel and clean breaks characterized by abundant angular shiny black inclusions sometimes visible on the surface of the vessel.
Amphorae: phase 2 only.

FABRIC 7: this is usually oxidized pale to dark reddish yellow. It is hard with a smooth feel and clean fracture. It is very refined with some small, occasionally larger, matt white inclusions, occasional rounded red or black inclusions and fine mica.
Late sparse glazed and domestic pottery, may be the same fabric (but oxidized) as the domestic pottery fabric 5: from the end of phase 3, that is from the late twelfth/thirteenth centuries.

FABRIC 8: this is a reddish brown fabric. It is hard with a rough feel and hackly fracture containing numerous inclusions characterized by abundant angular white inclusions which are also visible on surface.
Amphorae: phase 2 only.

FABRIC 9: this fabric is very pale brown. It is hard with a slightly rough feel. It is a very refined fabric containing few visible inclusions: mica and some small matt red and black inclusions.
Amphorae: phase 2 only.

FABRIC 10: this fabric is reddish yellow with a lighter coloured outer surface. It is hard with a slightly rough feel and clean breaks characterized by abundant fine mica and some matt white inclusions.
Amphorae: phase 2 only.

FABRIC 11: this is brown with a smooth exterior surface. It is hard with a smooth feel and clean breaks. It is very refined with occasional small pale brown inclusions.
Amphorae: phase 2 only.

FABRIC 12: this fabric is reddish yellow to grey. It is hard with clean breaks containing frequent small inclusions including mica, rounded matt red and black inclusions and some small white inclusions.
Thin section analysis revealed an absence of volcanic inclusions which are characteristic of the Forum Ware at Rome.
Forum Ware of ninth to tenth centuries, most common fabric.

FABRIC 13: this fabric is reddish yellow. It is hard with sandy breaks containing abundant small, matt white inclusions.
Forum Ware, thin section analysis showed this to be identical to the fabric of the majority of the Forum Ware at Rome.

FABRIC 14: this fabric is usually a very pale brown, sometimes pale reddish yellow. It is hard with a clean fracture, very refined with frequent to some small matt white inclusions and fine mica.
Thin section analysis showed this to be a generic alluvional clay, which could have a local or sub-regional provenance.

The latest examples of Forum Ware (late tenth/eleventh century) and sparse glazed pottery. This fabric becomes progressively more refined and the latest examples of the twelfth/thirteenth centuries are very similar macroscopically to fabric 7 used for the manufacture of the latest domestic pottery and latest sparse glazed ware. It seems likely that fabrics 14, 5, and 7 are of similar or identical clays and that the differences noted macroscopically are simply ones of differing degrees of fineness and different methods of firing.

APPENDIX 3. Settlement Traces in the Area of Santa Cornelia: Results of the Ager Veientanus Field Survey

The following provides a summary listing of the survey findings related to the Roman and medieval occupation of the area around Santa Cornelia. The results of the Ager Veientanus survey are listed in more detail in Kahane et al. 1968.

1. ROMAN ROADS

In Kahane et al. 1968, Santa Cornelia (AV 236) lies in area 4, bounded by Roman roads 3, 4, 8 and 9A, of which only 9A was definitely paved (Kahane et al. 1968, 74-75, Figs. 8 and 9); of these, 3 and 4 had Etruscan origins (Kahane et al. 1968, 19). The principal road appears to have been 9A, along which were located various large wealthy villas, perhaps linked to the proximity of the basalt-flint quarries at Monte Aguzzo (AV 163 zone: Kahane et al. 1968, 118-119).

2. ROMAN FARMS IN THE IMMEDIATE PROXIMITY OF SANTA CORNELIA

(a) SITES ATTESTED NORTH OF SANTA CORNELIA:

AV 163 (859593) – Large villa close to roads, c. 1 km distant from Santa Cornelia; architectural finds; pottery to RP II (Kahane et al. 1968, 119).

AV 188 (865591) – Building, south of paved road, c. 750 m distant. Only terra sigillata noted.

(b) SITES TO THE NORTH-EAST:

AV 237 (866586) – Substantial site north of via di Santa Cornelia, c. 300 m distant. RP I (Kahane et al. 1968, 119).

(c) SITES TO THE EAST, BESIDE FOSSA DI MONTE AGUZZO:

AV 238 (870585) – Sherd scatter east of via di Santa Cornelia, c. 600 m distant. RP I (Kahane et al. 1968, 121).

AV 239 (872582) – Substantial site on small knoll, with plaster, etc. Set c. 850-900 m distant. RP I (Kahane et al. 1968, 121).

(d) SITES TO THE SOUTH-EAST:

AV 241 (867578) – Large Roman building on hill above Casale Muracciole ('Farmhouse of the Ruin'); c. 600 m distant. RP I and II (Kahane et al. 1968, 97).

AV 341 (873572) – Extensive villa site on top of ridge east of via di Santa Cornelia, with brick walling, glass, porphyry, RP I-III. Lay c. 1.5 km distant (Kahane et al. 1968, 106).

(e) SITES TO THE SOUTH:

AV 232 (865575) – 'Important villa' on north-east slopes of La Selvotta ridge, c. 900 m distant. With plaster, glass, marble, RP I and III – perhaps linked with AV 233 (below, section 5) (Kahane et al. 1968, 97).

(f) SITES TO THE SOUTH-WEST:

AV 140 (857580) – Sherds from a poorly-built Roman structure on a promontory, 'probably reused in the Middle Ages' (cf. section 5, below). With tile, tufa blocks, TS, RP I and II. Located c. 750 m distant near the Casale Due Torri (Kahane et al. 1968, 90, 177-178).

AV 234 (860580) – Roman building, on north edge of Selvotta ridge, c. 500 m distant. With RP I and II (Kahane et al. 1968, 97).

3. SMALLER SCATTERS OF ROMAN FINDS IN THE VICINITY OF SANTA CORNELIA

(a) TO THE NORTH OF THE SITE:

AV 164 (862593) – Scatter of Etruscan and Roman (RP I) sherds, on south slopes of Monte Aguzzo (Kahane et al. 1968, 119).

AV 187 (862591-2) – Sherds by road cutting (Kahane et al. 1968, 119).

(b) FINDSPOTS TO THE SOUTH:

AV 236 (Santa Cornelia) – Residual Etruscan and Roman (TS, RP I and II) pot.

AV 240 (567580/568580) – Sherds and building material.

(c) FINDSPOTS TO THE WEST:

AV 235 (861583-4) – Scattered sherds of RP I and II and coarseware on spur east of Fossa di Pantanicci (below, section 5).

AV 143/144 (858585-6) – Scatter of Etruscan and Roman sherds.

4. MAIN ROMAN SITES IN THE AREA FEATURING RP III

(a) SITES NORTH OF SANTA CORNELIA:

AV 190 (extensive villa over the Fossa di Monte Aguzzo).

(b) SITES TO THE SOUTH:

AV 341 (extensive villa – see above, section 2d).

AV 232 (important villa – above, section 2e).

AV 326 (extensive villa, set 1.5 km distant – Kahane et al. 1968, 98).

AV 373 (prominent villa site, c. 2.5 km distant – Kahane et al. 1968, 99).

(c) SITES TO THE WEST:

AV 4 (large villa, c. 2 km distant, on Veio-Formello road, south of via di Santa Cornelia junction – Kahane et al. 1968, 76).

(d) SITES TO THE EAST:

AV 249 (villa – Kahane et al. 1968, 117).

AV 302 (building – Kahane et al. 1968, 110).

AV 344 (widespread site – Kahane et al. 1968, 110).

(e) ADDITIONAL SITES WITH RP III:

AV 177 (extensive building remains on south slopes of Monte Stallone, set further north towards Formello along via di Santa Cornelia – Kahane et al. 1968, 92).

AV 161 (catacomb on Monte Stallone, with RP I-III – Kahane et al. 1968, 92)

Further RP III sites are recorded in zone between Fossa di Malviata and Fossa della Fontanaccia (Kahane et al. 1968, 207, Fig.33).

5. SITES WITH MEDIEVAL ACTIVITY NEAR SANTA CORNELIA

AV 140 (857580) – See section 2f above: find of a medieval bracket in travertine similar to those from Santa Cornelia (Kahane et al. 1968, 177-178).

AV 233 (862578) – See section 2e above: small group of medieval coarse ware with some Roman wares (Kahane et al. 1968, 178).

AV 235 (861583) – See section 3c above: medieval strap handle in a scatter of Roman sherds.

SITES TO THE SOUTH WEST OF SANTA CORNELIA, OUTSIDE THE IMMEDIATE ZONE:

AV 376 (873557) – Grotte Vecchiarelli: small promontory site on ridge west from Spezzamazze plateau, overlooking Fossa di Pantanicci; rock-cut ditch over neck of promontory, and traces of a tower nearby; large cave and many pits; area of c. 1500 m² within defences. One sparse glazed sherd, and various coarse wares; no Roman pottery, though a Roman cistern lay to south (Kahane et al, 1968, 173-175 with Figs. 23-24).

AV 332 (871560) – Castel dei Ceveri: a small but strong promontory at south end of a steep plateau between Fossa di Pantanicci and Fossa dei Costaroni; ditch across neck, but no defensive structures; area of c. 2,200 m². Plain and glazed sherds (probably late medieval) (Kahane et al. 1968, 173).

AV 337 (876564-877564) – Large villa site on slopes of Spezzamazze ridge near via di Santa Cornelia, c. 500 m east of Castel dei Ceveri (Kahane et al. 1968, 106): one Forum Ware sherd found below site (876563 – Kahane et al. 1968, 179).

AV 375a (872557) – Promontory opposite Grotte Vecchiarelli (AV 376), across Fossa di Pantanicci: scatter of medieval sherds, coarseware and one sparse glazed sherd (Kahane et al. 1968, 179; Wickham 1978a, 173 suggests also a Forum Ware sherd).

6. MILLS

A mill was identified near Santa Cornelia (862580) in the Fossa di Pantanicci, c. 250 m south-west of the excavation (Kahane et al. 1968, 178).

7. MEDIEVAL ROAD SYSTEM NEAR SANTA CORNELIA

There was probably a general maintenance of most of the Roman roads of the area, and the regrowth of many old ridgeway communication routes. Kahane et al. 1968, Fig. 21 shows a road running north-west from the zone of findspots AV 392-393 towards Santa Cornelia via AV 337 (Forum Ware findspot) over the Spezzamazze ridge and over that of Muracciole before cutting westwards north of *Capracorum* over the Passo dello Scannato to link with the north–south road to Formello. The modern via di Santa Cornelia follows the line of this road. The route basically follows an unpaved Roman road (number 7) up to its junction with road 4 between the Muracciole and Spezzamazze ridges (between AV 241 and 341): the Muracciole ridge road seemingly follows no Roman or Etruscan line, but rather crosses earlier roads at the Passo dello Scannato. However, the presence of the substantial site AV 237 north-east of Santa Cornelia suggests at least an unpaved *diverticulum* from Roman road 9a, which perhaps extended south past AV 241 (large building) to join Roman road 7. A further road appears to have run north-west from Santa Cornelia via Monte Aguzzo and Monte Stallone to reach Formello.

PART II

Santa Rufina
A Roman and medieval site in
South Etruria

by
M. Aylwin Cotton, Margaret Wheeler and David Whitehouse

with contributions by
Neil Christie, Federico Guidobaldi, Peter Llewellyn, Demetrios Michaelides,
Joyce Reynolds, Frank Sear and Bryan Ward-Perkins

INTRODUCTION

Santa Rufina (798455), nine kilometres north-west of Rome on the ancient *Via Cornelia*, was rediscovered in 1963 (Fig. 39). As previously at Santa Cornelia, the site was identified immediately. 'The most exciting fresh discovery' John Ward-Perkins wrote in *Antiquity*, 'is that of the long-lost site of the church of Santa Rufina . . . the traditional site of the burial of, and centre of cult to, the martyred Santa Rufina in the late third century; about the year 500 it became the seat of the bishopric of *Silva Candida*, comprising the whole area between Rome and the sea; it was restored by Pope Hadrian I in the late eighth century, becoming for a time the centre of a considerable settlement' (1964).

The site was excavated by the Istituto Pontificio di Archeologia Cristiana and the British School at Rome in 1965-1967 and 1969. In the field, Mgr. Jacquand represented the Istituto and Lady Wheeler the British School at Rome. The first, short season revealed a catacomb and a building with a mosaic, thought at the time to be a chapel. The second, longer season provided the raw material for a provisional assessment of the entire site, which had been occupied or frequented, perhaps continuously, for more than a thousand years. Again we have the words of Ward-Perkins in *Antiquity*: '[we found] structures and associated remains of four successive periods: a small Etruscan or early republican country settlement . . .; outbuildings and the rock-cut water supply of a considerable Roman villa . . .; the heavily robbed remains of a circular, late Roman mausoleum and, around and overrunning it, part of the large chapel . . . and a section of defensive walls . . . a cobbled *piazza* and timber huts, all belonging to . . . [a] medieval settlement' (1966, 90). The third season saw the lifting of the mosaic, which after temporary conservation at the British School at Rome was placed in the Museo dell'Alto Medioevo, Rome, for full conservation. The other finds were also deposited in the same museum.

After the excavation, Lady Wheeler produced the first draft of the report, while Dr Cotton worked on the finds [1]. At this point, in circumstances beyond their control, the project was set aside. In 1981, with the blessing of Lady Wheeler, Dr Cotton and Dr Bryan Ward-Perkins (his father's literary executor), all the relevant documents – draft reports, notes, drawings and photographs – were reunited in Rome. The result is the report which follows. In preparing it, I have followed the original drafts as far as possible; the method of presentation is the same and the final version was approved by Lady Wheeler [2]. I record with great sadness that Molly Cotton, who had followed the revival of the project with characteristic enthusiasm, died before its completion. Late in the day, Mr Peter Llewellyn kindly agreed to provide an account of the written evidence for the martyrdom of Santa Rufina and the history of the site which bears her name. In Chapter 4, I discuss the site in the context of rural settlement in the environs of Rome in the first millennium AD.

David Whitehouse (Corning, 1986)

[1] The project was the work of many hands. We owe particular debts of gratitude to Father Felice Darsy OP of the Istituto Pontificio di Archeologia Cristiana and Dr John Ward-Perkins, then director of the British School at Rome, neither of whom, alas, lived to see the results of their efforts appear in print. The Italian authorities kindly granted permission for the excavations to take place, and the landowner, Sig. Parigi, gave every possible assistance. In the field, the volunteers included Julian Cheyne, Charles Freeman, Sheila Gibson, Peter and Estelle Hansen, Stephanie Judson, Herbert MacTaggart, Jo McIntire, Campbell McKnight and Eleanor Millard, ably assisted by Antonio Fantini, a veteran of Santa Cornelia and Quattro Fontanili. Doris Rogers and Kay Stratton were responsible for lifting and restoring the mosaic. In the *camerone*, John Hayes gave valuable advice on the pottery, much of which was sorted by Martin Beddoe and Jeremy Johns. Susan Collingridge worked on the glass. The plates are from photographs by John Ward-Perkins, Peter Hansen and Frank Sear. The figures were drawn by Alison Barrett, Sheila Gibson, Caroline Hananiya and Patricia Mallett – time, however, has had an adverse effect on many of the original drawings and we are extremely grateful to Sally Cann for preparing them for the present publication. Dr Graeme Barker (director of the British School at Rome 1984-1988) and the Chairman and members of the Publications Committee ensured that the site – at last – can receive in print the attention it deserves. To these, and all others in the project, Lady Wheeler joins me in offering our warmest thanks.*

[2] In the interest of accuracy, I must explain that it was not always clear to me whether the recorded numbers of pottery fragments and other objects represented the quantities excavated, or the quantities retained for study.

*[With deep regret I must record that Lady Wheeler died in December 1990, before the publication of this volume. (ed.)]

213

CHAPTER ONE. THE HISTORICAL RECORD
THE BISHOPRIC OF *SILVA CANDIDA* AT SANTA RUFINA

Peter Llewellyn

The shrine of the sisters Rufina and Secunda, martyrs under Valerian and Gallienus, was probably the site of a church built by Pope Julius I (337-352) and renewed by Pope Damasus I (366-384). Their cult is first firmly attested early in the fifth century in the entry for 10 July of the Latin *Hieronyman Martyrology*, drawing from a local Roman *Depositio Martyrum*:

> *Via Cornelia mil. VIIII Rufinae Secundae.*

A pilgrim guide of between 650 and 680, the *De locis sanctis martyrum quae sunt foris civitatis Romae*, includes the shrine in its itinerary; the saints' cult was known to Aldhelm of Malmesbury (d. 709), who used the legend in his *De Virginitate*, and to the Frankish martyrologists of the ninth century [1]. Their feast entered the Roman calendar early in the eleventh century, in the *martyrology* of Saint Peter's. Just before his accession to the papacy, Anastasius IV (1153-1154), as Cardinal Bishop of Sabina, transferred their relics to the Lateran. The author of the *Descriptio sanctuarii lateranensis ecclesiae*, who was present at the ceremony, describes the group of chapels behind the basilica which Anastasius created from the portico of the old baptistery, and names that containing the *altare sanctarum Rufinae et Secundae sororum in quo eorum condita sunt corpora* [2].

The bishopric was established at the shrine early in the sixth century. It suffered severely during the Investiture conflict and in 1120-1124 Pope Callistus II combined it with the cardinalitial see of Porto, although holders of the united see continued commonly to use the shrine's dedication as their title until the mid-twelfth century. This survey does not deal with its geographical extent or structure – well dealt with elsewhere [3] – but with its institutional and political relationship with Rome. Exceptionally a rural see, it developed into one of the cardinalitial bishoprics closely bound to the Roman episcopate, whose holders included some of the papacy's most influential assistants. Three moments are paramount in its history: its establishment at Santa Rufina, its status as a reflection of Lateran preoccupations in the eighth century, and its role in papal and Roman policies in the tenth and eleventh centuries.

(i) THE BEGINNINGS OF THE BISHOPRIC, *c.* 500-550

The first mention of a Bishopric of *Silva Candida* is at the Roman Synod of 501, when Adeodatus signs as *episcopus ecclesiae Silvae Candidae*; this represents the very recent transfer of an existing bishopric from the Antonine imperial villa of *Lorium* on the nearby *Via Aurelia*. At the synod of 499 an Adeodatus features in the attendance list as *lorensis* in the same relative position, indicating seniority by consecration. The probability is high that he was bishop of a community based on *Lorium* and successor to the Petrus *lorensis* named in 487. Virtually nothing is known of this community; some Christian inscriptions, which include the names Rufina and Candida have survived but no hagiographical traditions [4]. We have therefore a change of title and possibly of residence (although no *episcopium* or baptistery is mentioned until the late eighth century) from a historic settlement to a cult centre. The dates indicate the Laurentian schism in the Roman Church, from 498 to 507, as the context for this transfer, and the general, if not the precise, circumstances, may be suggested by the legends that developed around the shrines of Trastevere and the *Viae Aurelia* and *Cornelia*. The major impulse behind the relocation came from the rivalries for patronage of great senatorial families.

We can begin by way of comparison with a bishopric which follows closely Adeodatus' signature in the lists of 499 and 501. In 499 Dulcitius was *episcopus ecclesiae Sabinensium*, but in 501 *episcopus ecclesiae S. Anthimi*: a similar change from a geographical to a cult designation. The single acts of the martyrs venerated along the *Salaria*, which individually date perhaps to the late fourth century, had by the late fifth century been edited into a continuous account of the Salarian-Picene saints around the figure of Anthimus, patron of Cures. The expanded legend was linked to members of a specific Roman family; Lucina, Pinianus and perhaps Anicia Fultonia Proba. This reflects the patronage of a great Roman house of the late fifth century over the churches and cult centres of the *Salaria* in association with its estate ownership, such as the *fundus Pinianus*, on which the church of Saint Anthimius was built, mentioned in the *Registrum Farfense* in the eighth century [5].

The legends of Trastevere, the *Aurelia* and the *Cornelia*, a region severely contested during the Laurentian schism, were never edited into so continuous a whole; they leave us with a much more diffuse scatter of indirect indications and associations, reflecting the many interests at issue *c.* 500. Although the schism had its major ecumenical and political aspects with the Church and Court of Constantinople, more immediately important were domestic issues, senatorial and clerical. Members of a revived and self-conscious senate were anxious to compete for office and to offer traditional largesse and patronage over the Church as over society as a whole. Such competition was expensive and burdensome but continued into the 540s by when with government support the senate had in practice established its predominance. But with the subsequent demise of the senate's economic and political clout, individual churches came more directly under the Roman episcopate. This may be seen in the change in style of designations of *tituli*, from those of the synods of the early sixth century by founders' names, to those of the end of the century when the saints hold sway. There was also tension within the clerical body; the Roman Church was host to a considerable number of Catholic refugees from the Vandals in north Africa, concentrated in Trastevere. There were the strains of schism itself, the existence of two rival popes, Symmachus and Laurentius, and the needs to justify and validate the claims and status of each. Senatorial and papal competitors alike sought personal re-inforcement by largesse and extravagant building and by attaching to their own interests the heritage of the martyrs. All this induced a flourishing propaganda activity and the production of polemical texts, synodal acts, foundation legends and the reworking of historical records [6].

These elements may be seen at play in Trastevere and along the *Aurelia* and *Cornelia*. The *Passio S. Calisti*, for example, commemmorated the early third century pope against the reputation of his rival, Hippolytus; the surviving text is certainly a sixth century reworking [7]. Along the *Aurelia*, other disputed pontificates were brought to bear. The Laurentians developed the memory and shrine of the fourth century antipope Felix II with the *Passio Felicis* as an anti-Symmachan tract; they also controlled the shrine of Saints Processus and Martinianus, who as Saint Peter's gaolers were ripe for development. In response, the Symmachans revived the memory of Felix's rival, Liberius, with the *Gesta Liberii*. Symmachus himself, accused by his enemies of extravagance in building and largesse to win popular support, devoted much attention to Trastevere and the *Aurelia*, where he built or authorized the building of the churches of San Pancrazio and of the Sicilian saint Agatha of Catania. Nevertheless, it is possible that dissident groups survived along the road until the end of the sixth century [8].

Further out we find family rather than papal interests at work. The *Passio SS. Marcellini et Petri* gives an explanation of the name *Silva Candida*. Candida and Paulina were converted by the saints, and all condemned by the *vicarius*:

'*cumque vicarius omnia quae gesta fuerunt cognovisset, iussit eos duci in silvam nigram, quae hodie in honorem sanctorum silva candida appellatur*'

The two clerics were buried there in a *cubiculum* by their relation Lucilla who later, after a vision, removed and reburied them in what became their permanent shrine, three miles along the *Labicana* [9].

The *Passio SS. Rufinae et Secundae* itself, tells of the two daughters of Asterius and Aurelia, whose fiancés tried to win them from Christianity; they fled but were arrested and interrogated by the prefect Donatus, proving remarkably resistant to argument, torture and capital execution by boiling alive and drowning. The prefect, meeting his match, handed them over to his *comes* who

'*iussit eas duci in silvam in via Cornelia ab urbe Roma miliario decimo in fundum quod vocatur Buxo et illic unam caedi capite aliam percuti et sic earum inhumata corpora derelinqui luporum morsibus commedenda*'.

This proved definitive and the landowner, Plantilla, had a vision of the sisters in their heavenly glory: this brought about Plantilla's own conversion and the building of a shrine [10].

This *passio* has several points in common with others of the region. One is the name Asterius. In Trastevere the legend of Santa Caecilia, her husband Valerian and brother-in-law Tiburtius were brought before the prefect Turcius Almachius; the *Passio S. Calisti* mentions the spectacular series of conversions among the Roman judiciary set off by the priest Asterius (or Austerius) before being thrown into the Tiber. In the *Passio SS. Marii, Marthae et Audifacis*, venerated just beyond Santa Rufina, at the twelfth mile of the *Cornelia*, Asterius is the *princeps* of the prefect Calpurnius, is converted and releases all the Christians in his prison. Other shared elements include a fondness before magistrates for Trinitarian discussion, more appropriate to a Rome under Arian Ostrogothic rule, with refugees from the Arian Vandals and faced with the issues of the Acacian schism, than to those on trial for their lives before pagan officials [11].

The indications are of a transfer of a bishopric from *Lorium* on the *Aurelia*, open to the Laurentians, to a shrine on the *Cornelia* under the patronage of a family well-disposed to Symmachus and contending with its peers for prestige and influence. Certainly Symmachus was willing to accommodate actual or potential senatorial allies in the acquisition and development of such sites; he consecrated the basilica dedicated to Saint Peter which Albinus, *cos.* 493, and his wife Glaphyra built on their *fundus Pacinianus* near Fiano [12]. Turcius Rufius Apronianus Asterius, *cos.* 494, the editor of Vergil, had found his consulship a proud but expensive burden and the development of such potential influence may have been a welcome lure. We might speculate on Lucilla, the builder of the first shrine at *Silva Candida*. It is not a common name in Rome, but one does stand out, the celebrated broker of ecclesiastical and spiritual power mediated through the martyrs and their shrines, the *potens et factiosa femina* of early fourth century Carthage. Perhaps behind the use of this name in a milieu with strong African connections there lurks some lady of early sixth century Rome, such as Stephania, sister of

Faustus, Symmachus' staunchest senatorial ally, and herself married to an Asterius [13].

Primarily senatorial interest is also suggested by the bishopric's next substantial appearance. In 545, during the Gothic War, Pope Vigilius, in Catania on his way to Constantinople, sent back to Rome his *vicedominus* Ampliatus, and Bishop Valentinus:

> 'retransmisit Romae Ampliatum presbiterium et vice-dominum suum et Valentinum episcopum a sancta Rufina et Secunda ad custodiendum Lateranis et gubernandum clerum'.

Supplies of wheat for Rome were also sent but the fleet was intercepted off Ostia by Totila, who cut off the hands of Valentinus accompanying it [14]. Valentinus survived and made his way to Constantinople. In 553 Vigilius and his entourage signed the condemnation of Theodore of Caesarea; among the first signatories was Bishop Zacchaeus of Squillace and then

> 'Zacchaeus episcopus rogatus a fratre Valentino episcopo Silvae Candidae, ipso praesente et consentiente et mihi dictante, huic constituto pro ipso subscripsi' [15].

Valentinus was perhaps a former Roman priest, attending the synod of 531, and so one who had held office through the troubles of the 530s which ended with the consolidation of the senate's influence over the Roman Church and especially over papal (and other episcopal) elections as alone able to afford the expenditure required [16]. These are the circumstances of his elevation to the episcopate. Vigilius had left Rome in 545 amid accusations of responsibility for the death of the husband of his niece Vigilia, the 'consul' Asterius. Asterius' filiation is uncertain but he may have been a son of Stephania. In Catania in 545, according to the *Liber Pontificalis*, Vigilius was 'permitted' to hold ordinations:

> 'in civitate Catinense permissus est facere ordinationem per mensem Decembris presbyteros et diaconis, in quibus retransmisit Romae Ampliatum . . . et Valentinum'.

Valentinus may have been bishop for only a few months before his capture, and may therefore have been chosen for a specific function by specific interests in unusual circumstances. The compiler of that passage, presumably a Roman cleric well-versed in official usage, chose to draw attention to the shrine, while Bishop Zacchaeus, at Valentinus' dictation, used his proper style [17].

The signatures of 553 are also interesting. Zacchaeus, as bishop of a not very distinguished see, signs in his own right above several metropolitans, and it is possible that he was signing as episcopal representative of the Roman senators then in Constantinople, who included Cassiodorus and Cethegus. Why did Valentinus ask him to sign on his behalf? More natural, if he were a former Roman priest, would be one more closely his peer, such as Redemptus, bishop of another suburban see, *Nomentum*. The answer may lie with Cethegus, *cos.* 504, *princeps Senatus* in 545, who

probably succeeded Cassiodorus as *magister officiorum*. If Valentinus was made bishop in Catania in 545, then this was on Cethegus' home territory; he had major interests there, in 559 requesting Pope Pelagius I to consecrate a Bishop of Catania [18]. What part he played in the Laurentian schism is not clear, but his father Festus may be identifiable with the accuser of Pope Symmachus in 501, the leading supporter of the Laurentians, who retained control of Church property until a royal order in 507 forced him to disgorge it. In that case we may see in Symmachus' building of the church on the *Aurelia* dedicated to the Catanian Agatha a successful move to win over or neutralize an important man with influence in a delicate and contentious area, and the beginning of an extension of his patronage at the expense of the Asterii, until by the 540s it had gained the bishopric itself to the personal disadvantage of Valentinus, caught up in Totila's vendetta against the senate.

(ii) THE BISHOPRIC IN THE EIGHTH AND NINTH CENTURIES

From the mid-sixth century the record, like that of so many sees, is reduced to occasional synodal mentions of bare names, the formal style remaining as it had begun, *Silva Candida*. The *De locis* indicates a frequented shrine but there is no direct evidence of an episcopal seat until the late eighth century when Pope Hadrian I restored the *basilicam sanctae Rufinae et Secundae quae ponitur in epioscopio Silvae Candidae*. *Episcopium* is an episcopal residence, not necessarily the principal or cathedral one; in the eighth century the popes themselves built alternative *episcopia* away from the Lateran, and in the tenth and eleventh century the bishops of Porto and of Silva Candida had *episcopia* on Tiber Island, just as the suffragans of Ravenna had houses in Ravenna or north Italian bishops in Pavia. Hadrian's action will be considered below; but it is tempting to consider that Santa Rufina's survival from the late sixth to the late seventh century was due more to its status as a shrine than as the seat of a bishop. However, the bishopric, a product of vanished senatorial patronage, against episcopal tradition unassociated with a city, survived and grew to influence through its consititutional and administrative links with the papacy where historically better-rooted sees disappeared or at best left only fitful traces. These links, unlike those of bishoprics like Ostia and Albano whose position was secured by traditional roles in the consecration of new popes, were the results of domestic developments and preoccupations of late seventh and eighth century Rome.

From the 680s the pope's position changed; to his Petrine and patriarchal status was added that of a presidential figure over Roman society. There were consequent administrative and ceremonial adjustments; he governed the City and Duchy directly through regular Lateran officials, the later *iudices palatini*, and his new representative role could be delegated, where before his purely personal Petrine one could not. So by the 730s we have clear notice of the regular assignment of episcopal celebrations in the Lateran to the bishops of sees immediately adjacent or historically linked to Rome, who thus became 'cardinal' bishops. The same pattern was adopted in the other patriarchal basilicas by the priests of the *tituli*, the 'cardinal' priests. This was matched by developments within the Church as a whole, both East and West, which saw the reassertion of the ecclesiastical province and the city-based diocese as the proper form for episcopal jurisdiction [19].

A major concern of the eighth century Lateran was preservation of the integrity of the city-based diocese, the fundamental social and legal unit, from the sort of erosion it had experienced in Francia through the chances of partial conquest, settlement or family interest. A major feature of the papal correspondence of the eighth century is concern for the integrity of *territoria*, with their *loca et saltora*, the lesser settlements and borderlands vulnerable to detachment from urban authority. The issue was not simply retention or recovery of imperial cities; to palatine officers the risk of control passing from urban to rural forces was a present one. Pressures were growing to remove the episcopate from the growing monopoly of clerical officials, while the laity was becoming intrusive; in 744 the young married layman Sergius seized control of the see of Ravenna; in 766 Duke Stephen became Bishop of Naples. In 767 Duke Toto of Nepi entered Rome and installed his brother Constantine as pope, a defeat not so much for the Roman clergy as for the Lateran *iudices* and cubiculariate which had increasingly dominated papal successions. In summer 769 Toto and Constantine were expelled, with the support of Duke Theodicius of Spoleto, by the *primicerius* Christopher and his office-holding family, the supreme representatives of the Lateran oligarchy [20].

The synod which they and their pope, Stephen III, held later in 769 was an assertion of the Lateran's deeply held constitutional convictions. It was attended by metropolitans from Francia, where the provincial idea was beginning to gain roots, a renewal of close contact with Rome after a certain distancing in Pepin's latter years. City-based jurisdiction was reaffirmed; candidature for the papacy was restricted to cardinal-priests and Roman deacons, and country-people were forbidden to enter Rome during papal vacancies. In effect a large part of the Duchy of Rome was disenfranchised in the choice of their president-pope, to the advantage of the Lateran officers.

From the signatures at the synod we may see something of the peculiar status of *Silva Candida*. Successive designations of bishops had been:

679 Synod. *Novita, Silva Candida.*

710 Entourage of Pope Constantine I on the journey to Constantinople. *Nicetas episcopus de Silva Candida.*

721 Synod. *Tiberius, Silva Candida.*

732 Synod. *Epiphanius, episcopus sanctae ecclesiae Silvae Candidae.*

743 Synod. *Theophanius Silvae Candidae.*

745 Synod. *Theophanius Silvae Candidae.*

At the synod of 769 all bishops signed in the most formal way, i.e. *X, episcopus de civitate Y.* There are two exceptions, both cardinalitial sees: *Silva Candida* and Albano signed in the form *Gregorius (Eustachius) episcopus territorii Silve Candide (Albanensis).* For *Silva Candida*, neither a *civitas* nor a *municipium*, the point was clear: it was to be regarded as having the same administrative and legal status and integrity [21].

It is shortly after this synod, in an entry of the *Liber Pontificalis* datable to 782-783, that the *episcopium* first appears, in the record of Pope Hadrian I's repairs:

'*Immo et basilicam SS. Rufinae et Secundae quae ponitur in episcopio Silvae Candidae, quae ab olitana vetustate marcuerat, una cum baptisterio summo studi renovavit*'.

The entry must not be taken in isolation. In 774-776 Hadrian, continuing the resettlement of this area begun by Pope Zacharias with the establishment of the *domusculta* of *Lauretum* (possibly old *Lorium*), had founded two more *domuscultae* at *Galeria*, one '*posita via Aurelia, miliario ab urbe Roma plus minus decimo ad Sanctam Rufinam*', and a third not so far distant at *Capracorum*. The 780s were worrying times for the papal administration, with Charlemagne backtracking on his initial euphoric confirmation of Easter 774, bypassing Rome in his dealings with Benevento and prising Farfa and with it much of the Sabina away from its traditional association with Rome. The need for such foundations was clear. The region may have suffered severely in Aistulf's siege of Rome in 756, or Duke Toto's rising of 767, or his suppression in August 769. Following the foundation of the *domuscultae* in 774-776, the restorations of 782-783 were intended to make the site a major social and administrative centre [22].

These restorations were part of a programme of repairs lasting until about 786 and concerned mainly with suburban shrines. The initiative most probably came with Charlemagne's third visit to Rome for Easter 781, a visit important not only for the baptisms of his young sons Carloman-Pepin and Louis and their anointing as Kings of Italy and Aquitaine, major extensions of Carolingian dynastic and constitutional ties with the papacy, but for a final delimitation of the papal lands. In return, Charlemagne may have undertaken to subsidize various rebuilding works; over the next few years Hadrian was writing to remind him of the materials promised for this, including 2000 lbs of lead for roofing. The programme is important for an internal reason as well: the *Liber Pontificalis* entries for this period suggest a new hand in the compilation and perhaps also in the direction of the works, that of the *vestararius*

Sergius, in office from *c.* 781-785, who drops the attributions of spiritual motives for such undertakings and applies more 'civic' epithets, such as *vates*, to the pope [23].

The close association of the bishopric with the Lateran seems, as far as we can judge, to have continued into the mid-820s. Hadrian's successor, Leo III (795-816), had been Sergius' successor as *vestararius*, and as pope continued the shift in emphasis of Roman government from 'presidential' association with the nobility and the *iudices* to greater use of officers strictly of his own appointment, the *vestararius* and the *bibliothecarius*, never members of the municipal college of *iudices*, and the *cubicularii*. The vast sums coming to Rome after the capture of the Avar Ring in 795 allowed him to swamp the city nobility in the exercise of social and artistic patronage, the *domuscultae* allowed him to control the countryside, and agents of the vestiariate continued to pursue claims to lands in the Sabina. The resentment of Roman society was shown not only in the assault on Leo by Hadrian's nephews, both *iudices*, in 799, but also by the sack of the *domuscultae* by the Romans at the end of his life. Leo's successors, Stephen IV (816-817) and Paschal I (817-824), faced increasing discontent in Rome and appeals to Louis the Pious. Bishop John of *Silva Candida* was an active legate to the emperor to explain away the charges being brought. Lothaire's *Constitutum Romanum* of 824 increased Frankish supervision of Roman affairs and reduced the tension of Roman domestic affairs, but Bishop John appears again in 826 as *bibliothecarius* defending Roman interests against Frankish relic hunters and their supporter, Abbot Ingoald of Farfa (*c.* 815-830), the leading protagonist of Frankish interests in the neighbourhood of Rome [24].

Our record of the see's importance comes more from its holders' role in papal government than from its own pastoral functions. It is possible that popes in the ninth century did attempt to advance the latter, but the evidence is negative, drawn from the fortunes of its neighbour, Cere. A bishop of Cere was at the synod of 769 but is not mentioned again until the late ninth century with the extraordinary careers of the future Popes Marinus (882-884) and Sergius III (904-911), both of whom had been bishops of Cere but seemingly either as an honorific or a means of relegation for a dangerously ambitious cleric. The region was in any case badly afflicted by a general depopulation rather than Arab attack, a useful alibi for a failing government. In May 905 Sergius III strengthened *Silva Candida*; the *Massa Cesana* he gave to the bishopric, probably beyond the diocesan bounds as then established, was for the support of the *episcopium*, whose clergy were to provide much-needed prayers for Sergius' salvation, three masses weekly and a daily litany of 100 *Kyrie* and 100 *Christe eleisons* [25].

(iii) THE BISHOPRIC IN THE TENTH AND ELEVENTH CENTURIES

It is from the mid-tenth century that the bishopric peaks. Rome's government in the tenth century has been misunderstood and calumniated by both contemporaries and historians. In simple terms, the balance between the various components that had emerged from the late seventh century was readjusted; the lead was taken by an officer of the private papal administration, the *vestararius*, whose strength lay in his control of the privy purse and of lands in the Sabina, the essential point of contact in creating the coalition of Rome, Spoleto and the rural aristocracy needed in central Italy to oppose the Arabs of the Garigliano. The pope remained a spiritual leader, whose relative but often exaggerated lack of effectiveness was due less to domestic controls than to the fragmentation of western rulership in general and the identification of metropolitans with their regional dynasts. However, domestically he did lose some authority over the individual Roman churches, or rather, the Roman aristocracy regained what its predecessors of the early sixth and mid-eighth centuries had held. With the *vestararius* leading the *iudices palatini*, the pope was left with one sure official of his own appointment, the *bibliothecarius*, librarian, personal theological and canonical adviser, and head of his private administration. Tenth century popes chose fairly widely for this post, but the *bibliothecarius* was always a bishop. Sutri, Bomarzo, Nepi, Bieda, Porto, Narni, Labico, Albano, Ostia, Preneste are recorded. Three times before the 1020s a bishop of *Silva Candida* held the office: Benedict between 939 and 944; Guy (or Wido) between 966 and 975, and another Benedict, in 1013. It is the second of these who contributed most to the fortunes of the papacy and of his bishopric [26].

Guy was *bibliothecarius* in delicate years. He first appears as bishop at the synod of December 963, when Otto I deposed Pope John XII, the first imperial deposition of a pope for over three hundred years. Otto had misjudged; only five bishops from the kingdom attended, and even his Archchancellor for Italy, Bishop Guy of Modena, took three weeks to appear. His new pope, Leo VIII, was resented not as an intruded stranger (he was Roman and had succeeded his father as *protoscriniarius*) nor as a layman, but as one outside the oligarchy of Rome's rulers. He was expelled, first by John XII and then in favour of the deacon Benedict, much respected in both Rome and Germany. But Otto's prestige demanded Leo's reinstatement. Bishop Guy survived to become one of the architects of a restored *modus vivendi* between Saxon emperors, popes and Roman nobility. In succession to Leo, the bishop of Narni, formerly *bibliothecarius* to John XII, became pope as John XIII (965-972). He was a member of the Crescentian branch of the nobility, which now rose to pre-eminence; his niece was married to Benedict, rector of the Sabina, who was granted lands to the east of Civitavecchia, with Cere as a strong point. John XIII also reached accommodation with Otto notably by developing the identification of the Saxon emperor with the figure of Constantine the Great. Guy's period as *bibliothecarius* shows a growing exclusion of the secular *iudices palatini* from the papal administration and a greater control by the papacy of its own affairs. Papal co-operation with the Empire is shown by the approval given for the creation of new metropolitan provinces, such as Magdeburg, at the synod of Ravenna in 967, with Guy as papal legate to the consecration of Magdeburg in October that year, and of Benevento in 969.

Guy was also active in the recovery of *Silva Candida*'s lands, matching John's resumption of direct administration of papal properties. He survived the turmoil following the deaths of Pope John in September 972 and Otto in January 974. Late in 972, after an attempted coup by one Franco, Benedict VI was elected to succeed John but in May 974 the Crescentii seized power, installed Franco as Boniface VII and had Pope Benedict strangled. Boniface was in turn expelled by Sicco, Count Palatine to Pandolf *Capodiferro* of Capua and Spoleto, the strongest imperial supporter in Italy, and replaced by Benedict VII (974-983), a member of the high nobility and a continuer of the policies of John XIII. Guy's political skill is suggested by his retention in office by both Benedicts until his last mention in 976, and his survival of Franco's two coups. Indeed, it was from Franco, as Boniface VII, that he acquired a major resource for the resettlement of his bishopric, the newly-established *castrum* of Pietra Pertusa [27].

Imperial-Roman relations were always fragile, susceptible to chances of personality and considerations of prestige, depending largely on the techniques of indirect control. Otto III's establishment of his court in Rome renewed tension by swamping the legitimate aspirations of the local nobility and overshadowing the papal administration, but his cousin Henry II secured once again a fruitful co-operation, especially with the popes of the Tusculan House (1012-1045). It is noteworthy that a bishop of *Silva Candida*, Benedict, was serving as *bibliothecarius* in 1012-1013, at the moment of accession of Benedict VIII, the first Tusculan pope. However, only after the deaths of Benedict and Henry in May and July 1024 do we see in two documents of Pope John XIX of 14 and 17 December 1026 and that of Benedict IX of 1037 the full importance of the bishopric. The topographical aspects have been well studied elsewhere; here, some of the political implications will be considered.

By the mid-1020s south Etruria was part of a nexus of interests and alignments, in part dating back to the Crescentian establishment under John XIII and including the Sabina and Latium, from where many of its baronial families of the tenth and eleventh centuries had come. In 998 Count Benedict, John XIII's nephew, had opposed Gregory V in Cere; in 1012 his sons John and Crescentius led the opposition to the newly elected Tusculan Benedict VIII, from bases in Preneste and Farfa. Farfa too had important interests in south Etruria: since 883 it had held the church of Santa Maria on the Mignone river, the southern boundary of the county of Civitavecchia, where Abbot Campo (*c.* 936-963) established a community; this connection extended into Trastevere, when Santa Maria's prior became abbot of the monastery of Santi Cosma e Damiano *in Mica Aurea* founded *c.* 936-945 [28].

These factors impinged on the wider imperial and papal scene. The position of Conrad II, elected king in Germany in 1024, was not particularly strong, but his coronation was secured in March 1026. His southward move was resisted by Rainier of Tuscany who had been Count of the Sabina in 1003-1006 and Marquis of Tuscany since 1012, retaining considerable influence around Rome. He was removed, and by July 1028 at the latest had been replaced by Boniface of Canossa. Pope John XIX, successor to his brother Benedict VIII, also required stability if the traditional opponents of his house were to be restrained and if the pretensions of Aribert for Milan, to whom Conrad had promised precedence after Rome in the Italian Church, were to be checked.

Bishop Peter was Pope John's nephew; his mother, the pope's sister, was born in 979 so he was perhaps just twenty-five on becoming bishop in 1023. On 14 December 1026 the pope heard an appeal by the churches of Galeria against the bishopric. The hearing was well attended; all the cardinal bishops were present, Velletri, Preneste, Porto, Albano, Ostia and Labico, with the pope's brother Alberic, Count Palatine, and John Tocco, Count of Galeria. The pope was angered at Peter's failure to collect the full revenues due to him from the churches of Galeria, which were not paying him the customary one-third of their receipts; he was depriving his Church, the *episcopatus S. Rufinae*. This and the pope's investiture of Peter, presumably already consecrated, with the staff of public jurisdiction, indicates that comital rights were the main point at issue.

Three days later Pope John issued a major confirmation of the lands of the bishopric, with other rights attached. These included possession of some churches within Rome, such as the chapel of Santi Rufina e Secunda in the Lateran portico and the church of Santa Maria in Monte Augusto; authority over the four monasteries of the Leonine City that provided the offices in Saint Peter's, as well as rights over all the churches and consecrations within the Leonine City and all the alms given at Saint Peter's after the third hour of the day. He was given corresponding duties; to reform the Vatican's liturgy and to exercise jurisdiction over the clergy of the Leonine City. He was given an episcopal residence on Tiber Island and was to take the leading role among the episcopate at the coronation of an emperor.

These measures, the confirmation of possessions, rights over churches and comital powers, are good illustrations of the Tusculan family's methods of government. In origin one branch of the hydra-headed Roman oligarchy, it developed and retained power from 1012 by asserting the institutions of the papacy, by-passing its rivals through greater use of the cardinal-bishops in the administration of the Roman countryside. So the habit of direction by the cardinal-bishops in the service of the pope was established before the Reform movement came to give it a spiritual and canonical content. The services and the administration of the Vatican were reformed to make them a model for Rome, an aid in regaining control of the city churches and a fitting object to the growing numbers of distinguished visitors [29].

Pope John was aligning himself with the approaching Conrad, following his brother Benedict's policy of close association (amounting almost to conjoint sovereignty) with Henry II. He was elevating *Silva Candida* into a powerful lordship to counter the south Etrurian influence of the family of Conrad's opponent, the Marquis Rainier. In granting Peter an *episcopium* on Tiber Island and a sharing in the privileges there recently confirmed to Porto, we may perhaps also detect concern with the prestige of the Tusculan dynasty, a rebuke to Bishop Benedict of Porto, who had spread stories of the posthumous and infernal sufferings of Benedict VIII, but who was now made to pronounce the solemn malediction on any infringement of the grants of 1026 [30].

But the immediate benefit to the bishopric and the dynasty came with the actual coronation of Conrad on 26 March 1027. This was the most spectacular of all medieval coronations: over seventy archbishops and bishops and most of the secular magnates of Germany and Italy attended, as well as the impressive figures of King Rudolf of Burgundy and Canute of Denmark and England. To the holder of the Vatican concession the profits from the offerings must have been immense, even if the pope's design to make the ceremonial an exclusively Roman affair was defeated; Ravenna and Milan had a tug-of-war over Conrad's right hand in Saint Peter's, leading Conrad to induce John to confirm Milan's supremacy [31].

It was perhaps from this influx as much as from the confirmation of land-holdings and rights over churches that the bishopric's status as a major lordship stemmed, marked in 1037 when Peter's cousin, Pope Benedict IX, confirming his uncle's acts, referred to Peter's fortification of Santa Rufina:

'*fundum in integrum qui vocatur Buxus, in quo basilica SS. Rufinae et Secundae constructa esse videtur, quem etiam tuo studio muro et fossato vallastri et circumdedisti atque populo atque sacerdotibus bene sufficienter replevisti*'.

From the mid-1020s we see from the designation of the successive bishops that the bishopric's interest lay as firmly in the importance of the site and in the family connection as in its constitutional and administrative relationship to the papacy. In 1026 it was the *episcopatus S. Rufinae*, and thereafter the dedication was used as much as the territorial style. The diocesan and his staff were major figures in the distinguished circle of the Tusculan popes, which included Lawrence of Amalfi and Bartholomew of Grottaferrata, and which the young Peter Damian had expressed a willingness to join; in 1037 Bishop Peter was patron of the monastery of San Pietro in Perugia and the priest Bonizo, *vicedominus S. Rufinae*, was bishop-elect of Tuscania.

The great place given to Santa Rufina was dynastic and personal, and depended on the character and affiliation of the bishop; this led to a certain weakness through loss of continuity as popes switched control between Santa Rufina and Porto. Peter was dead by 1043; by a judgement in 1049 his successor Crescentius lost his share of jurisdiction over Tiber Island to Porto. We know very little of Crescentius, of his attitudes in 1044 to the expulsion of Pope Benedict IX or the defence of that pope by the Trasteverini and Count Gerard son of Rainier, but he must have ceased to be bishop by May 1050. We know more, however, of John of Porto. He was a former Roman cleric, who had become bishop of Tuscania before being transferred to Porto to become a major adjutant to Pope Leo, advising on the Church's relationship with the emperors [32].

Santa Rufina was soon given to a leading reformer. The great Cardinal Humbert of Moyenmoutier came to Rome in 1049 with Leo IX and was consecrated archbishop with intended metropolitan and legatine powers over Sicily; in May 1050 he signed a Lateran Synod as *Archepiscopus S. Rufinae*. German sources preferred this designation; in 1052 we find *Humperto Sancte Rufine ecclesie episcopo*; in 1057 *Humbertus scilicet episcopus Sanctae Rufinae*, and, in the *Vita* of Saint John Gualbert, we have *dominus Ubertus sanctae Romanae ecclesiae qui unus erat de septem cardinalibus . . . qui de titulo sanctae Rufinae episcopus extitit*. On the other hand he subscribed to Nicholas II's Lateran Synod of 1059 as *s.e. Silvae Candidae*. His successor Mainard, cardinal-bishop from 1061 to the early 1070s, is also designated in either form.

Papal control of the Roman Church and of the cardinalitial sees was not yet absolute; as the reforming programme and its ideology developed there was room for less than total commitment to innovatory trends. John of Porto had been handpicked by Leo IX both for the bishopric and for *Silva Candida*'s former jurisdiction, but is not heard of after 1050. His successor but one, John II, is known from 1057, and certainly attended a synod of 1059 which by the decree on papal election retrospectively legitimised the reformers' actions. But at the end of a long episcopate he was in 1082 one of the cardinal clergy who withdrew support from Gregory VII. It may have been considerations of Humbert that had led Victor II in May 1057 to regrant to *Silva Candida*, in modified form, the powers removed by Leo IX from Crecentius [33].

The circumstances are comprehensible. The family of the former Marquis Rainier and of his son, Farfa's *advocatus* in Tuscany, still commanded considerable influence. Count Gerard had in 1044 successfully supported Benedict IX and the Trasteverini against the Romans, his rivals among the nobility and the pope they proclaimed, Bishop John of Sabina (Sylvester III). In 1046 Henry III probably appointed him Count of Galeria, but there would have been continuing unease in reforming circles at so prominent an associate of the Tusculans so powerfully entrenched. Tusculan influence in sensitive areas was by no means over yet [34].

On the death of Pope Stephen IX in March 1058, the first real test for the reforming circle came. Peter Damian of Ostia, Humbert of *Silva Candida*, Boniface of Albano, Hildebrand and others of that small coterie gathered in Tuscany and by December had made the revolutionary selection, outside Rome and by a minority of the cardinal-bishops, of Gerard of Florence as Pope Nicholas II. The Roman clergy and laity, under the leadership of Benedict IX's brother Count Gregory II of Tusculum and of Count Gerard of Galeria, had already elected John of Velletri as Pope Benedict X. In customary form, it was a good election and John, probably a Tusculan, was a man of recognised honest life. But the impulse behind his nomination was dynastic rather than spiritual (Benedict IX had died in retirement that same year, depriving the Tusculans of their natural candidate); his only open supporter among the cardinal-bishops was Rainier of Palestrina, who, probably from 1041, had been abbot of Santi Cosma e Damiano in Trastevere, and who first appears as bishop in 1058, but retaining authority as *rector et dispensator* of the monastery [35].

The suppression of Benedict early in 1059 shows the importance of these links; Hildebrand preceded the reforming army from Tuscany into Rome and specifically to Trastevere where he made contact with Peter, the head of the Pierleoni, dominant between Santa Maria in Trastevere and the island, and with this help Duke Godfrey of Tuscany's troops entered Rome and seized the island. Benedict X fled the Lateran, first to the Crescentian Castel Passarano and then to Count Gerard at Galeria, where after a fierce assault by the reformer's Norman allies he was captured. By February 1059 Bishop Rainier was again simply 'priest and abbot', last being mentioned in 1061. In 1060 the Normans renewed their operations, ravaging Tusculan lands in the Sabina and Mentana, then crossing the Tiber to assault those of Count Gerard as far as Sutri.

This was by no means the end of Count Gerard. 1061 was a busy year. In May Cardinal Humbert and late in July Pope Nicholas II died, and Gerard immediately led a delegation of Roman notables to the young Henry IV in Germany, bearing the insignia of a patrician of the Romans and begging him to take up his duties as *rector* of the Roman Church. He was presumably at Basle at the end of October when the chancellor of Italy, Bishop Cadalaus of Parma, was elected pope as Honorius II against the reformers' Anselm of Lucca, Alexander II, and did homage to Cadalaus at Sutri in March 1062.

Alexander and the reformers did not fully control Rome until summer 1063 and even then the reformers continued to be divided on several major issues. The position of Gerard and his family continued to grow; a brother, Saxo, had become count of Civita Castellana, and Saxo's son Count Rainier in 1066 made substantial grants to Farfa in the county of Civitavecchia, followed in 1068 by his cousin. As known imperial supporters they were probably not hindered by Humbert's successor as bishop of *Silva Candida*. Mainard is first named as bishop in May 1061. From 1047 to 1056 he had been abbot of Pomposa near Ravenna, a house which had traditionally displayed great loyalty to emperors, even during times of schism and antipopes. Mainard's appointment provided a mutually acceptable intermediary between pope and king during the pontificate of Alexander II; he was Alexander's first legate to Germany, to make initial preparations for imperial coronation, and in 1063 Henry rewarded him by reappointing him to the abbacy of Pomposa. He was a moderate; like Peter Damian and Alexander II he was a resister of the growing intransigence being displayed by Archdeacon Hildebrand, having a spirit of accommodation which made it difficult to maintain his bishopric against a member of the territorial nobility which also enjoyed the favour of Henry IV [36].

Peter Damian, Mainard and Alexander II all died in 1073, leaving the field open to Hildebrand as Pope Gregory VII. When in the 1080s mutual exasperation between pope and king had reached the point of armed conflict and Henry IV attacked Rome to install his own Pope Clement III and himself be crowned emperor it was the House of Galeria that gained. In 1083, during one of his incompetent blockades of Rome

'*Heinricus rex Pascha celebravit apud Sanctam Rufinam*'. In his entourage was Rainier son of Count Gerard's brother Hugh who, after Henry's occupation of Rome, was appointed *dux et marchio* of Tuscany, which his grandfather had held. Gerard's family had, on the local front, defeated the reforming papacy.

The extent of the defeat is revealed by the record of the bishopric after Mainard's death. No pope of the line deemed by Church historians to be the canonical one appointed a replacement to Mainard; instead, Gregory VII attempted to build up San Paolo fuori le mura – with which he had close connections – as the major force in the area. Early in his pontificate he confirmed to San Paolo alleged donations of Galeria by Popes Paschal I (817-824) and Marinus II (942-946). This was repeated in March 1081, at a crucial moment for the Gregorian papacy, a fortnight after the second papal excommunication of Henry IV and as the king with his antipope Wicbert (Clement III) was approaching Rome. With Henry's final entry into Rome and the installation of Clement in mid-1084, south Etruria, and with it Santi Cosma e Damiano, passed largely under Clementine control. That year the king confirmed to Farfa the death-bed grant made by Count Rainier in 1072 of half of Civitavecchia. The Clementines continued to appoint bishops to *Silva Candida*, one of whom, Albert, named in 1089 and 1098, was elected pope against Paschal II in 1102. Albert's predecessor as antipope, Theoderic, elected on Clement III's death in 1100, was probably Clementine cardinal of Albano, but the *Annales Romani* reflect Santa Rufina's place as a major centre of anti-Gregorianism in calling him *episcopus S. Rufinae*. Gregorian jurisdiction within Trastevere seems to have been assigned to Porto, for Cardinal Maurice consecrated an altar there in 1098 [37].

The motives for the amalgamation with Porto are not precisely determinable; it was in general a period of reorganization of diocesan structures. Porto's contribution to the Reforming movement had not been as distinguished as that of *Silva Candida* or, with its special position as consecrator of a Pope-elect, of Ostia. Both Ostia and Porto remained in Gregorian hands from 1087 and through the pontificate of the antipope Clement III. The determining factor was probably the achievement of Bishop Peter of Porto in late January 1119. The election of Gelasius II a year before had been a critical moment. The conclave in Santa Maria in Pallara had been attacked by Cencius Frangipane and the new pope, John of Gaeta, physically assaulted. The Emperor Henry V, on the advice of Irnerius of Bologna, declared the election invalid and appointed the Portuguese Archbishop Maurice Burdinus of Braga as Pope Gregory VIII, installing him in Saint Peter's. Pope Gelasius was again assaulted by the Frangipane and made his escape to Cluny, dying soon after. The emperor had an antipope, the nobility of Rome was divided, so too, geographically, was the College of Cardinals. Many of its more active members, like Lambert of Ostia, were north of the Alps, either on legations or in attendance on Gelasius, and it was they who swiftly selected the redoubtable Archbishop Guy of Vienne, a kinsman and long-standing opponent of the emperor, as Pope Callistus II. It fell to the bishop of Porto, left as Gelasius' vicar in Rome, to gather the remaining cardinals behind the distant choice and to organize full endorsement in the most formal terms for their brethren's action, preventing renewed schism. Yet the transfer of title was not immediately effective. In 1130 the disputed elections of Cardinals Gregorio Papareschi (Innocent II) and Pietro Pierleone (Anacletus II) brought another, eight year, papal schism. The choice of Pierleone was directed by

Peter of Porto, who consecrated him as pope in Saint Peter's. It was probably out of respect for this dutiful *venerabilis senex* that his Innocentian replacement, Theodwin of Gorze, did not use the title of Porto; during his service as papal legate in Germany from 1135 until the mid-1140s, Theodwin consistently styled himself *sancte cardinalis episcopus* or *cardinalis episcopus de titulo sancte Rufine* [38]. Only following the translation of the relics was cardinalitial authority north of the Tiber assigned to Porto alone.

NOTES

1. *Martyrologium Hieronymianum* 89. Valentini and Zucchetti 1942, 106-118. Aldhelm of Malmesbury, *De Virginitate* 367.
2. Journel 1977, 254, 374. John the Deacon, *Descriptio sanctuarii lateranensis ecclesiae*, in Valentini and Zucchetti 1946, 319, 353.
3. Wickham 1978a; 1979. Useful summaries of the history of Santa Rufina and the bishopric of *Silva Candida* are to be found in Motta and Ungaro 1986 and Sacchi Ladispoto 1987.
4. In the attendance list of 499, *Adeodatus lorensis* is 26th in the signature list, as *Adeodatus episcopus ecclesiae Cerrensis* in 31st place. His relative order is the same in each:

Attendance	Signature
24. Vitalianus, Amati	28. Vitalianus
25. Serenus, Nomentum	29. Serenus
26. Adeodatus, Lorensi	30. Iustus
27. Stephanus, Nursini	31. Adeodatus, Cerrensis
28. Dulcitius, Sabinensis	32. Stephanus
	33. Dulcitius

(*Cassiodori Senatoris Variae* 400, 407). The normal adjectival form of Cere is Caeretanus, and Mommsen in his index gives Cerrensis as a misreading for Lorensis. Synod of 501: *Cassiodori Senatoris Variae* 438. *Lorium* inscriptions: *CIL*, XI.3738, 3742, 3756, 3758. See also De Rossi *et al.* 1968, 19-20.
5. Salarian legends: Mara 1964a and 1964b.
6. On senatorial rivalry during the Laurentian schism, see Barnish 1983. The strong African presence in Rome and especially in Trastevere is suggested by Llewellyn 1976; 1977, 245f.
7. *Passio S.Calisti*; Dufourcq 1900, I, 115. Kirsch 1924; Verrando 1981.
8. Verrando and Liberio 1981. Symmachus' buildings: *Liber Pontificalis* i, 262.
9. *Passio SS. Marcellini et Petri*; Dufourcq 1900, I, 88, 163.
10. *Passio SS. Rufinae et Secundae*.
11. *Passio SS. Marii, Marthae et Audifacis*. Asterius: Dufourcq 1900, I, 311-312. The *Passio S. Caeciliae* dates to the years 486-523 (Dufourcq, 1900, 293-296).
12. *Liber Pontificalis* i, 263.
13. Martindale 1980, II, Asterius, 173; Stephania, 1028. On Lucilla, Brown 1981, 34.
14. *Liber Pontificalis* i, 297-298; Procopius, *De Bello Gothico*, VII, xv, 13-15.
15. *Constitutum de tribus Capitulis* in Mansi 1759, IX, col.106A.
16. The regularity with which Roman clerics in the sixth century were appointed to the smaller neighbouring bishoprics cannot be accurately determined. Redemptus of

Nomentum, who also signed the *Constitutum* of 553, may be identifiable with a Roman priest of 531, in a sequence of other possible Roman promotions to this see; the priest Romanus of 489, bishop in 501-502; the deacon Felix of 519-520, bishop in 531; *defensor* Constantius of 591, bishop in 600.

17. *Liber Pontificalis* i, 297.

18. Cethegus: Martindale 1980 II, 281-282; his Sicilian connections, Pelagius I, *Epistolae* 33 (Migne 1844-1888 72, col.747); Gregory the Great, *Registrum Epistolarum* IX, 72.

19. Kuttner 1945; Llewellyn 1979.

20. Llewellyn 1986, especially 59.

21. Signature of 679, Mansi 1759, XI, col.179; of 710, *Liber Pontificalis* i, 389; of 721, Mansi 1759, XII, col.261; of 732, *Liber Pontificalis* i, 422, note 13; of 743, 745 and 769, *Leges 3, Concilia 2, Concilia Aevi Karolini*, i, 22-23, 41, 43, 75.

22. *Liber Pontificalis* i, 501-502.

23. Hadrian I to Charlemagne on lead: *Monumenta Germaniae Historica, Epistolae* III, 609-610; Geertman 1975, 34-35.

24. Odilo, *Translatio S. Sebastiani* i, 383-384; Santifaller 1940, 41, note 5. Most of Leo III's extra-Roman building work in 801-803, immediately after the imperial coronation, was concentrated on the cardinal-bishoprics.

25. Marinus (pope, 882-884) was subdeacon under Leo IV (847-855) and deacon by 862-866; as legate and bishop of Cere he presided at the Ecumenical Council of 869-870 in Constantinople. But in 879 he was in Naples, describing himself as *arcarius sanctae Sedis*, a unique tenure of a palatine office by a bishop (cf. Duhr 1934). Sergius III (904-911) was deacon under Stephen V (885-891) and a bitter opponent of the controversial Bishop Formosus of Porto who when pope (891-896) made him bishop of Cere, perhaps to exclude him from hope of the papacy. He reverted to a deacon in 896-897. Sergius' grant of 905: Migne 1844-1888, 131, col.973.

26. Benedict II of *Silva Candida, bibliothecarius c.* 939-944:

Zimmermann 1969, notes 152, 170, 177. Benedict III: Zimmermann 1969, notes 1113, 1118. Santifaller 1940, 80, 126.

27. Bishop Guy: Zimmermann 1969, note 397 (*bibliothecarius* in 966), 547 (last reference 975); Santifaller 1940, 95-104. Fabre and Duchesne 1910, I, 348. Toubert 1973a, ii, 1009-1010, 1027. Cecchelli 1935.

28. In general, Fedele 1898; 1899. Respighi 1956.

29. Toubert 1973a, ii, 1035-1036. See also Maccarrone 1974. The list of witnesses to the 1037 document is significant; so too is the emphasis of the two documents on the shrine, whereas Bishop Guy had styled himself only *episcopus et SSA, bibliothecarius* and Benedict III *Silvae Candidae*.

30. Jotsald, *Vita Odilonis* II, 14 (published in Migne 1844-1888, 142, 927-929).

31. Coronation: cf. letter of Canute in William of Malmesbury, *History of the Kings of England* II, 182.

32. Leo IX and John I of Porto: Marini 1805, note 49. Huls 1977, 117-118.

33. John II of Porto: Huls 1977, 118-120. Victor II to Humbert, May 1057: Migne 1844-1888, 143, 828-829.

34. Fedele 1899, note 33.

35. Fedele 1899 notes 46, 49, 51-58, 62; Huls 1977, 108-109; *Annales Romani, Liber Pontificalis* ii, 331, 334-335.

36. Gatto 1962.

37. Trifone 1908, 278-285, note 1. Testini 1975, attributes the abandonment of the see to the spread of malaria. Huls 1977, 136-137 for the Clementine cardinal and antipope Albert, and 264-265 on Clementine control of Trastevere.

38. Peter of Porto and the election of Callistus II: Huls 1977, 122-123. Peter's reputation and role in the election of Anacletus II: Palumbo 1942, 207, note 3, 226, note 1, 227. Peter was succeeded as Anacletan Bishop of Porto by John, from 1134-1136. On the fate of the structures at Santa Rufina after the twelfth century see Motta and Ungaro 1986, 334-346; Sacchi Lodispoto 1987, 54.

CHAPTER TWO. THE EXCAVATION

The site occupies the summit of a low promontory overlooking the Fosso Galeria, on the east side of the Via di Boccea (the ancient *Via Cornelia*) and only a short distance from the casale of Santa Rufina (Fig. 39). The excavated features, which originally were divided into four periods (Etruscan or early republican, late republican and early imperial, late imperial, and medieval), are believed now to represent six principal phases of occupation:

I. Republican, *c.* 400–100 BC
II. Late republican, *c.* 100–30 BC
III. Imperial, *c.* 30 BC–fifth century AD
IV. Late antique, fifth–seventh century AD
V. Early medieval, ninth century or earlier–twelfth century AD
VI. Late medieval, twelfth century AD and later.

(In discussion of the finds, the references relate to the figure in which the object is illustrated and the number within that figure.)

(i) PERIOD I: REPUBLICAN, *c.* 400–100 BC

1. Areas C, D and F: cuniculi
2. Areas B and D: pits
3. Finds
4. Date

1. AREAS C, D AND F: CUNICULI

Area C contained two connecting tunnels (C1 and C2), each entered by a single shaft, one rectangular in section and the other round (Figs 40, 41 and 52; Pl. 56; section D-D'). The rectangular shaft (C2) measured 1.0 × 0.8 m and had been dug carefully to a depth of 2.2 m with footholds or sockets for crossbars in the east and west walls. This gave access to a tunnel, which extended to the north and south-south-west along the contour of the hill. The tunnel was explored for 15 m to the north and 14 m to the south, beyond which it was blocked with mud. It had been excavated from the shaft, as the direction of the pick-marks in the sides indicated. It was approximately 1.7 m high and 0.7 m wide: just sufficient to allow a person to pass through without stooping unduly.

The circular shaft (C1) was 0.8 m across and 3.2 m deep. It, too, had footholds and led to the second cuniculus, 1 m deeper than the first. The lower channel makes a number of angular turns and its north section crosses the line of cuniculus C2. Exploration beyond approximately 14 m north and south of the shaft was abandoned because the tunnel was blocked, perhaps in the vicinity of other shafts.

When cuniculus C1 was dug, the rectangular shaft of C2 was deepened to provide additional access. The two cuniculi, therefore, were connected. Thus, if their purpose was to carry water, C2 was earlier than C1. The access shafts were blocked in the late first century AD.

In area D, one debris-filled cuniculus (D) was discovered, but not explored. The tunnel was 0.7 m wide and probing showed that it extended at least 4 m towards the north. The south end had been destroyed by quarrying in period IIIb (see below).

Excavation in area F revealed two parallel cuniculi (F1 and F2), aligned north–south, each 0.5 m wide and 1.4 m high (see below Figs 58 and 59; section A-A'). A shallow gully (F6), leading towards them from area E, may have been connected with a water catchment system.

2. AREAS B AND D: PITS

In area B, the excavators found a rectangular pit (B31) measuring 0.9 × 0.75 × 0.75 m, with three semicircular scoops (0.4 m deep) round the edge, which gave the feature a trefoil-like plan (see below Fig. 53, section C-C'; Pl. 57). The lower filling of the pit contained nothing later than period I (though see *Date* below).

In area D, three pits were found: Da, Db and Dc. Pit Da, which was roughly rectangular and measured 0.75 × 0.75 × 0.81 m, was packed with fragments of dolia, jars and other pottery. Pit Db was slightly larger, but not so deep; it was filled with sterile black soil. The north side, only, was excavated. Pit Dc measured 2.0 × 1.0 × 0.57 m; again, only the north part was excavated.

The presence of rubbish-filled pits suggests domestic occupation, while the cuniculi indicate drainage of the area, presumably in connection with cultivation. We conclude, therefore, that a farm, perhaps of modest dimensions, occupied the site in period I.

3. FINDS

Cuniculus F1:
Black slip, 12 (including 73.2, 73.11 and cf. 73.9)
Internal slip, 8 (including 71.12 and two similar pieces)
Red burnished, 2
Amphora (80.1)

Plate 56. Santa Rufina: period I – cuniculi C1 and C2

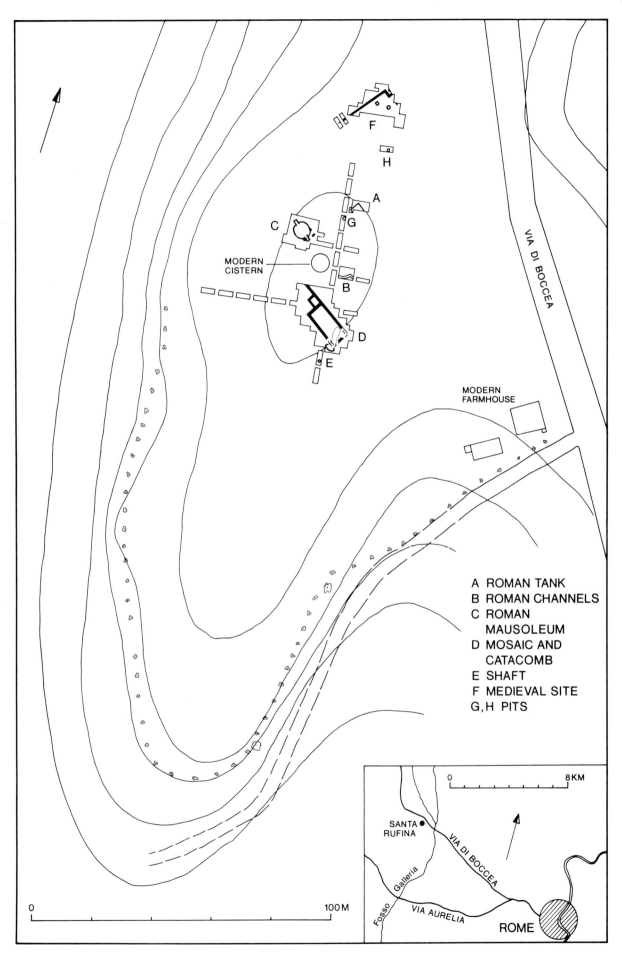

Fig. 39. Santa Rufina: general plan

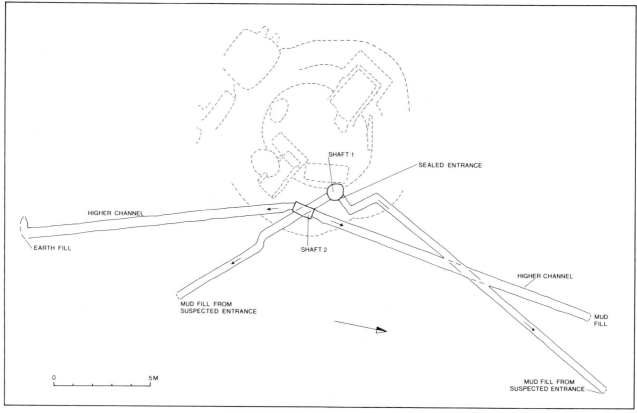

Fig. 40. Santa Rufina: area C, cuniculi beneath mausoleum

Cuniculus F2:
    Bucchero, 1 (bowl fragment)
    Black slip, 8 (including 73.6, 73.9 and cf. 73.9)
    Other pottery, 9 (including 72.1 and two similar, and 72.3)

Pit B31, unit 2:
    Etruscan painted (71.3)
    Black slip (73.9)

Pit Da:
    Black slip, 3
    Internal slip (89.6)
    Dolium, 1 red burnished
    Other, 3 (including 87.1 and 89.1)

Pit Dc:
    Etruscan applied painted (71.5b)
    Black slip (73.4)
    Internal slip (72.4)

4. DATE

The earliest datable pottery was Etruscan: applied painted ware (probably of the fourth century BC), bucchero, internal slip ware and coarse pottery, some of which

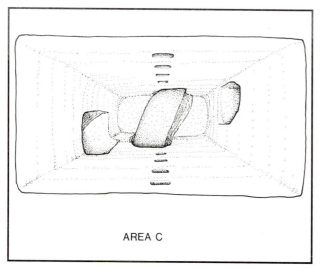

Fig. 41. Santa Rufina: area C, shaft of cuniculus 2, seen from above

Plate 57. Santa Rufina: period I – pit B31

resembles material from Casale Pian Roseto, deposited not later than *c.* 390 BC. However, almost every substantial unit contained sherds of late republican black slip ware, some of which may belong to the second or early first century BC. Thus, while the earliest recorded occupation of the site began in (or not long before) *c.* 400 BC, the earliest excavated features may have been backfilled or abandoned as late as *c.* 100 BC.

(ii) PERIOD II: LATE REPUBLICAN, *c.* 100–30 BC

1. Area A: cuniculus
2. Area D: *opus quadratum* building
3. Area F: unit sealing cuniculi F1 and F2
4. Finds
5. Date

1. AREA A: CUNICULUS

A short stretch of cuniculus (A4) was found at the east end of area A (see below Fig. 44, plan and section B-B'). Like the earlier cuniculi, it was aligned north–south. The channel, which measured 0.5 × 0.75 m, was only 0.5 m below the surface of the tufo. A tributary channel, which diverged to the west, was blocked by the wall of a vat, built in period III (see below).

2. AREA D: OPUS QUADRATUM *BUILDING (Fig. 42)*

Here, the excavation revealed traces of structures in *opus quadratum*. The main east–west wall (B) survived as a row of eight well-cut tufo blocks, each measuring 1.0 × 0.6 × 0.2 m. Only three blocks survived of the south wall (C). The walls, together with the missing east and west walls, enclosed a room *c.* 10 m long and at least 3 m wide. A slightly smaller structure stood almost immediately to the north of wall C. Only the north and east walls (U and M) remained; they were built of tufo blocks, which rested on bedrock (Pl. 58). All the walls were constructed without mortar. A thin accumulation of dark soil lay against the outer face of wall M. This, and a deposit 0.2 m thick, to the south of wall Z (see Pl. 58), were the only undisturbed units in area D attributable to period II.

3. AREA F: UNITS SEALING CUNICULI F1 AND F2

Where the roofs and sides of the cuniculi had collapsed, farther south than the line of section A-A' in Fig. 59, it was possible to excavate the debris that filled them. The associated finds are of period II.

4. FINDS

Area A: cuniculus
Earthenware lamp (62.1)

Area D: *opus quadratum* building
Black slip, 15 (including 73.15, 73.17, 74.4, 74.5 and 74.9)
Others, several (including 87.19, 87.20 and 1 similar, and cf. 85.1)

Plate 58. Santa Rufina: period II – area B, wall M running north-east into V

Area F: unit above cuniculi F1 and F2
Bronze object (66.12)
Red burnished, 1
Black slip, 3 (including 73.6)
Others, several (including 86.31 and cf. 83.15)

5. DATE

The evidence for the date of period II is largely negative.
The most common variety of fine pottery is late republican
black slip ware, and the absence of Arretine suggests that
the period ended before *c.* 30 BC.

(iii) PERIOD III: IMPERIAL, *c.* 30 BC–FIFTH CENTURY AD

Period III, the first occupation of which substantial
remains survive, may be subdivided into three:
  IIIa,   *c.* 30 BC–AD 75
  IIIb,   *c.* AD 75–200
  IIIc,   *c.* AD 200–fifth century

PERIOD IIIa: *c.* 30 BC–AD 75

  1.   Area B: tank, pits and other features
  2.   Area D: gully

  3.   Area C: blocking of shafts C1 and C2
  4.   Finds
  5.   Date

1. AREA B: TANK, PITS AND OTHER FEATURES

A tank and overflow channels occupied the highest part of
the promontory. It was not clear when these features were
constructed, but neither the tank nor a curved channel
leading from it contained any material later than period
IIIa. The tank (B23), which was 0.6 m deep, had been
covered by a vault of tufo blocks bonded with mortar,
which sprang from narrow ledges cut in the bedrock (Fig.
43; Pl. 59). The curved channel joined a wider gully (B22)
of undetermined date.

   The largest deposit of occupation debris of period IIIa
lay between walls M and U of the earlier building in *opus
quadratum* (above, period II). Contemporary deposits
rested on bedrock to the south of wall B and in gully W.
Two rectangular pits (B26 and B27) also may belong to
this period.

2. AREA D: GULLY

A gully (Dd), 0.15 m deep, ran across the area from east to
west. At the west end, it was blocked by a wall (Z) of tufo
bonded with mortar. The area had been disturbed by pits,

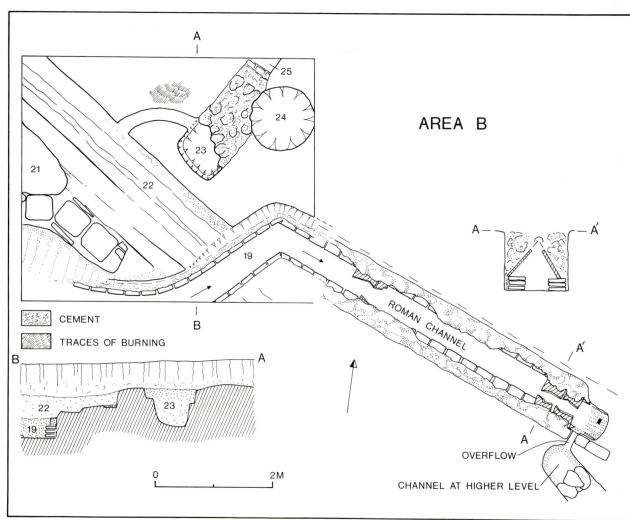

Fig. 43. Santa Rufina: area B, channel 19 and other features

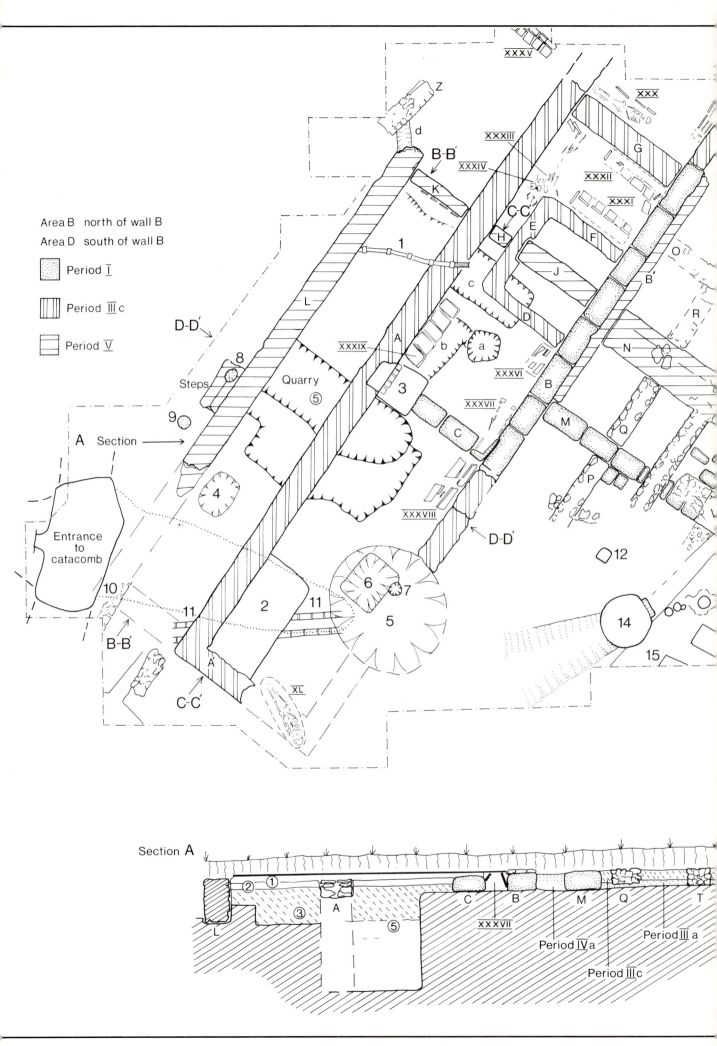

Area B north of wall B
Area D south of wall B

Period Ⅰ

Period Ⅲc

Period Ⅴ

Z

d

B-B'

K

1

XXXV

XXX

XXXIII

XXXIV

G

C-C

H

E

F

c

XXXII

XXXI

J

D-D'

L

Quarry
⑤

A

XXXIX

b

a

D

B'

8

Steps

3

XXXVI

B

N

9

XXXVII

C

M

Q

A Section

XXXVIII

P

D-D'

12

Entrance
to
catacomb

6
7

5

14

10

15

11

2

11

B-B'

A'

C-C'

XL

Section **A**

② ①

A

C
B
M
Q
T

L

③

⑤

XXXVII

Period Ⅳa

Period Ⅲc

Period Ⅲa

Fig. 42. Santa Rufina: areas B and D, structure in *opus quadratur*

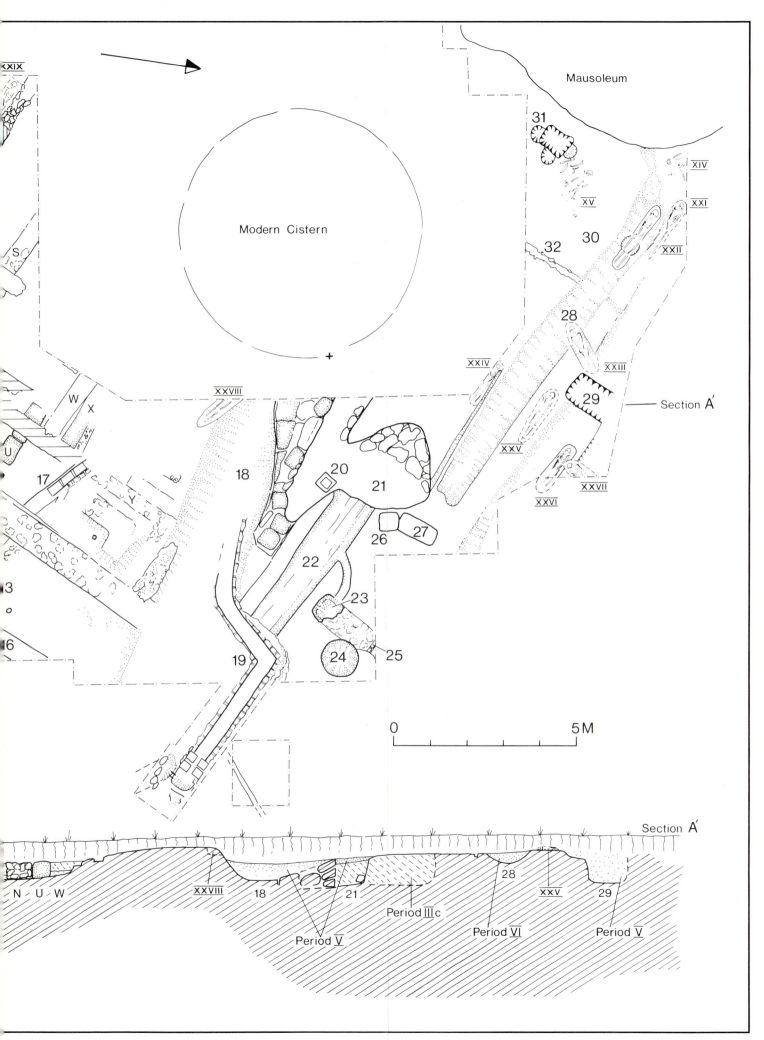

Mausoleum

Modern Cistern

Section A'

Section A'

N U W $\overline{XXVIII}$ 18   21   28 $\overline{XXV}$ 29

Period $\overline{III}$c

Period $\overline{V}$ Period $\overline{VI}$ Period $\overline{V}$

0   5M

(period II), cemetery walls (period IIIc) and room with mosaic (period Va)

Plate 59. Santa Rufina: period IIIa – tank B23 with channels

robber trenches and the foundation of wall L. Nevertheless, it was clear that the gully and its immediate vicinity contained sealed deposits of period IIIa.

3. AREA C: BLOCKING OF SHAFTS C1 AND C2

Shafts C1 and C2 were backfilled at the end of period IIIa; the two features contained fragments of the same vessels and it was clear that they were filled simultaneously.

4. FINDS

Area B: the tank and the curved channel
  Arretine, 1 (base of dish, early first century AD)
  Unguentarium, 1
  Thin walled, several (including 74.20 and 1 similar)
  Other, 1 (cf. 84.2)

Area B: (i) pit B24
  Late Italic terra sigillata, 1 (cf. 76.16)
  Reduced common ware, 1 (87.21)
  Amphora, several
  Other, several

(ii) various deposits
  Lamps, several (including 1 cf. 64.13)
  Iron object (67.7)
  Black slip, 13 (including 73.8-10, 73.13, 74.12 and 74.15)
  Internal slip, 1 (cf. 71.9)

Arretine, 4 (including 75.4, 75.6 and 76.14)
Thin walled, 15 (including fragments similar to 74.16-18, 74.28 and 74.33)
Unguentarium
Fine painted (79.24)
Pottery with light surface, many (including 81.8, 81.11, 82.6-7 and 91.8)
Reduced common ware, many (including 84.1 and 1 similar, 84.17, 85.12 and 1 similar, 86.25, 87.14, 87.17, and 87.20)
Amphora, 10 (including 80.16)
Other (91.3)

Area D: gully and adjacent deposits
  Black slip, 2 (73.13 and 73.19)
  Arretine, 8 (including 75.6)
  Fine painted, bowl (cf. 79.24)
  Oxidized common ware, 3 (81.5, 82.6 and cf. 81.8)
  Dolium, 1 red burnished

Area C: (i) filling of shaft C1
  Earthenware lamps, 5 (64.11 and 1 similar, 64.13 and 1 similar, and 64.14)
  Iron object (67.2 and 67.4)
  Black slip, 1
  Internal slip (71.9)
  Arretine (75.1, 75.7, 75.9, 76.12-13)
  Late Italic terra sigillata (75.8 and 76.16-18)
  Imitation terra sigillata, 2
  Colour-coated beaker, 29 (including 74.16, 74.18 and 74.24 and 1 similar)

Plain beaker (74.26-27)
Colour-coated bowl (74.17 and 74.28)
Plain bowl (74.31)
Fine painted (79.25, fragments of this also came from the filling of pit C2)
Amphora, 6 (including 80.2 and 80.5)
Reduced common ware, 16 (including 83.3 and 2 similar, 84.1-6, 87.2-3, 87.6)
Mortarium (88.2)
Dolium (89.5)
Other (91.2 and 91.4)

(ii) filling of shaft C2
Hellenistic red slip, 1
Fine painted (79.24, 79.25 (see above) and 81.1)
Reduced common ware (83.11, 87.5 and 87.7)
Dolium (89.4)

5. DATE

The diagnostic pottery consists of Arretine ware, Italic terra sigillata and thin walled table ware, including colour-coated beakers. This material is consistent with a date between c. 30 BC and c. AD 75.

PERIOD IIIB, c. AD 75–200

1.   Area A: pit C4
2.   Area D: quarry D5
3.   Area D: deposit in gully Dd
4.   Areas B and D: channels B17, B19, B25 and D11
5.   Area A: cistern
6.   Area B: pit B21 and feature B20
7.   Finds
8.   Date

1. AREA A: PIT C4

An oval pit, measuring 1.25 × 0.75 × 0.70 m, had been excavated in the tufo bedrock (Figs 42 and 44). The fill contained nothing later than the second century AD.

2. AREA D: QUARRY D5

A quarry, measuring 4.25 × 1.50 × 2.50 m, was sited immediately outside the east wall of the republican building, which by this time may well have gone out of use. The quarry had cut through a cuniculus of period I (see below Fig. 57, sections B-B', C-C' and D-D'; Pl. 60). The filling, which appeared to have accumulated gradually, belonged to period IIIb.

3. AREA D: DEPOSIT IN GULLY Dd

There appears to have been a gradual sequence of accumulation in this area. This deposit lay above period IIIa material and was sealed by a layer attributable to period IIIc.

4. AREAS B AND D: CHANNELS B17, B19, B25 AND D11

The several tanks and channels described below were constructed at various times between the first and third centuries AD; they became choked with mud and were abandoned during period IIIc.

(a) B19, the longest channel, carried water from the top of the slope to the west to lower, cultivable ground to the east. It had a mortar bed, sides lined with three courses of bricks and mortar and was capped with two rows of tiles, which together made a pitched 'roof'. The channel was 0.25 m wide and (from the bed to the apex of the cover)

Plate 60. Santa Rufina: period IIIb – quarry D5 cutting cuniculus

Plate 61. Santa Rufina: period IIIb – area A, Roman vat or cistern

0.75 m deep. A narrow overflow channel, blocked with lumps of tufo, fed another channel, which carried water towards the east (Fig. 43).

(b) B25, of which only a small section was exposed, north of tank B23, had the same construction as B19.

(c) D11 was designed to carry water from the top of the slope towards the south. The bed and sides were constructed in the same manner as B19 and B25, but in this case there was no evidence for a cover.

(d) B17 carried water down the slope towards the south-east. Although almost completely destroyed by erosion or ploughing, sufficient remained to show that the bed consisted of a row of tiles set in mortar; the sides were lined with mortared bricks.

5. AREA A: THE CISTERN

Although no firm evidence was found for the date of the cistern, it is attributed with confidence to the Roman period, before the establishment of the cemetery which put an end to cultivation in the immediate vicinity of the site. It occupied the highest point on the promontory. Its construction involved the incidental cutting of the republican cuniculus. The sides were lined with rubble, with a plaster surface. The cistern was a rectangular structure, 4.0 m wide and more than 4.0 m long, with rounded angles (Fig. 44; Pl. 61). It was more than 1.30 m deep; the top did not survive. The filling was attributed to period IVa.

6. AREA B: PIT B21 AND FEATURE B20

B21 was a large, irregular pit (not completely excavated). On the south side, where the bedrock had cracked, it was lined with well-cut tufo blocks. On the west side, it bellied out in a circular feature, 3.0 m across, which had been filled with tufo blocks. On the east side, near the wall, a rectangular recess (feature B20) was cut into the floor.

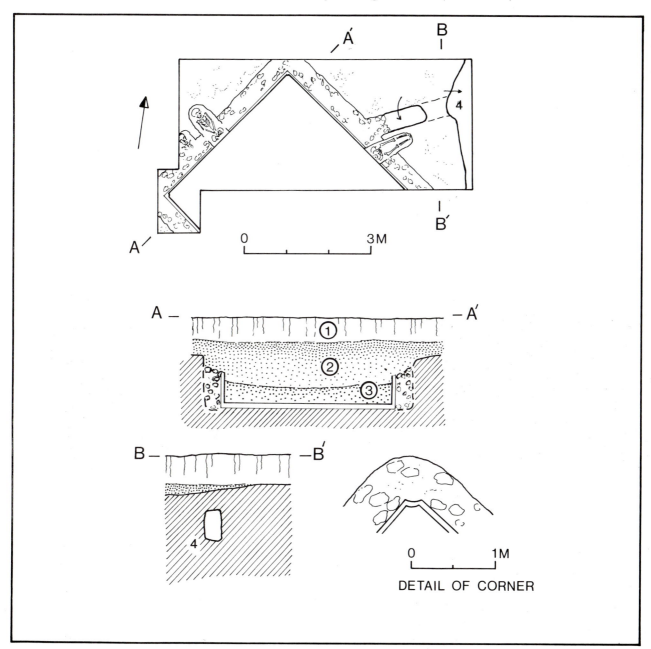

Fig. 44. Santa Rufina: area A, cistern

Neither the function of the pit, nor the circumstances of its partial filling with blocks, was apparent. The rest of the filling belonged to period IIIc (see below).

7. FINDS

Pit C4
Black slip, 1
Arretine, 1
African red slip, 1 (second century)

Quarry D5
Metallic slag
Lamps (64.9 and 64.12)
Black slip, 4 (including 73.3 and cf. 74.5)
Arretine, 3 (including 75.2 and 75.5)
Colour-coated (74.23 and 74.33, 5)
Painted (79.26, 2)
African red slip (78.1-2, 78.8 and 79.22)
Amphora (cf. 80.16)
Light surfaced (81.8 and 81.11)
Reduced (83.5, 84.1, 84.3, 85.3, 87.3, 87.8 and 87.23)
Pompeian red (91.1)

Deposit in gully Dd
Arretine (76.11)
African red slip, bowl (mid- to late second century)

8. DATE

The latest datable material consists of fragments of African red slip ware of Hayes' forms 8A (which remained in use until at least c. AD 160), 9A (also current until c. 160) and 23B (which was in use from the mid-second century until the early third century). Period IIIb, therefore, may have ended in c. AD 200, although a date in the second half of the second century or the first half of the third century would be equally defensible.

PERIOD IIIc: c. AD 200–FIFTH CENTURY

Santa Rufina continued to have an agricultural function for most of the third century and a substantial layer of soil accumulated round the ruined republican building, burying the quarry and covering the east, south and west slopes of the promontory. Eventually, cultivation was abandoned. A catacomb was excavated and, at the same time, or slightly later, the area became a cemetery; by the fourth century, it contained, in addition to graves, a circular mausoleum.

1.   Area D: latest agricultural activity
2.   Area D and E: catacomb
3.   Area D: cemetery
4.   Area D: abandonment of tanks and channels
5.   Finds
6.   Date

1. AREA D: LATEST AGRICULTURAL ACTIVITY

This was represented by the following deposits of cultivable soil:
(i) Area D, the quarry (see below Fig. 57, sections B-B' and C-C'). The quarry floor was covered with lumps of blackish tufo and sterile soil (unit 3). Above this lay a deposit of cultivable soil (4), which also extended on either side of the *opus quadratum* wall (B). The channels, it appeared, remained in use.
(ii) Area D, in and around gully Dd. Soil accumulated steadily until the construction of the building with a mosaic (see below).
(iii) Area D, near walls B and M-H-N. Here, too, the excavators found a layer of agricultural soil.

2. AREAS D AND E: CATACOMB

The catacomb was discovered when work on the south-west side of area D disclosed the collapsed roof at the junction of four galleries. The excavators explored the north gallery and probed the other three; all four were blocked with earth and rubble (see Figs 45-48).

The north gallery was 6.5 m long. The lengths of the other galleries were not determined, and the original entrance was not located. At the junction, the galleries were 2.8 m high, with a tufo 'roof' barely 0.8 m thick. The south gallery was 2.0 m wide, with loculi on either side. Due to the presence of earth and rubble, these were only partly investigated. They included six on the east side of the gallery (I-V and IX) and four on the west side (VI-VIII and X) (Fig. 47; Pl. 62). Loculi I-IV, VI and X were simple rectangular niches, each sealed with three upright tiles embedded in mortar. In some cases, tiles had fallen off, revealing an extended skeleton, lying on its back. Loculi IV and VII were more elaborate, with marble slabs, which measured 1.6 × 0.7 × 0.04 m, forming the floors. Loculus IV was sealed with tiles, but VII had seven courses of bricks and mortar, and a tile at the north end; in addition, the roof was lined with four and a half tiles held in position by mortar. Both the marble slab and the roof projected into the passage. The excavators found two lamps *in situ* on the upper projection and five on the lower (Figs 48 and 49).

The catacomb collapsed in antiquity. Some time after the roof had given way and the galleries had become partly filled with debris, the tufo beneath loculus IV crumbled,

Plate 62. Santa Rufina: period IIIc – west side of catacomb

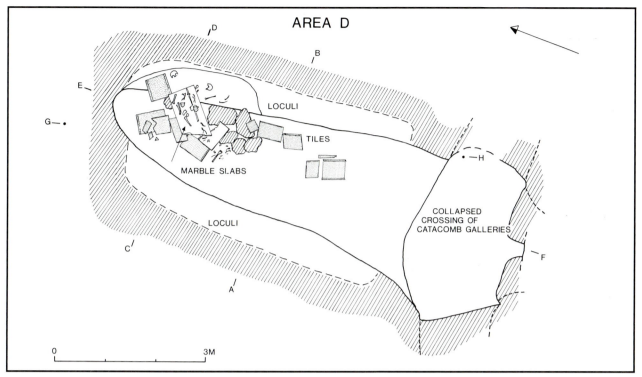

Fig. 45. Santa Rufina: area D, catacomb

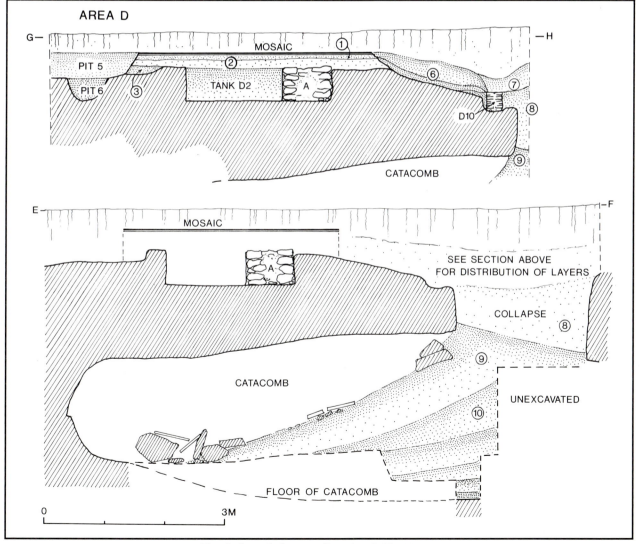

Fig. 46. Santa Rufina: area D, sections G-H and E-F

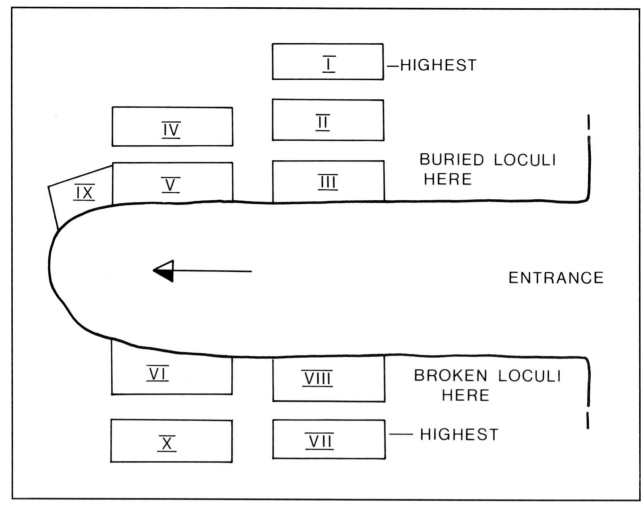

Fig. 47. Santa Rufina: area D, catacomb, with positions of loculi

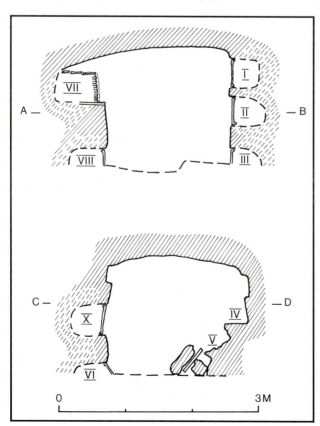

Fig. 48. Santa Rufina: area D, catacomb, sections A-B and C-D

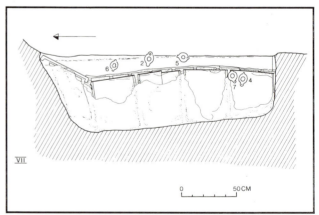

Fig. 49. Santa Rufina: area D, catacomb, plan of loculus VII, showing lamps *in situ*

and the marble slab, together with the remains of two skeletons, fell into the passage. Tiles from some of the other loculi fell to the floor. It is interesting to note, however, that none of the skeletons had been removed deliberately.

Excavation in area E revealed the top of a rectangular rock-cut shaft, 1.2 m long and 0.9 m wide (Fig. 50). It was excavated to a depth of 0.9 m. The top was reinforced on the north, east and west sides with three courses of bricks and mortar. The north and south sides had two pairs of footholds or sockets for rungs. Above these, on either side of the shaft, were post-holes, which may have supported a windlass. It is possible that the shaft was a *lucernarium* (light-well) in the south gallery.

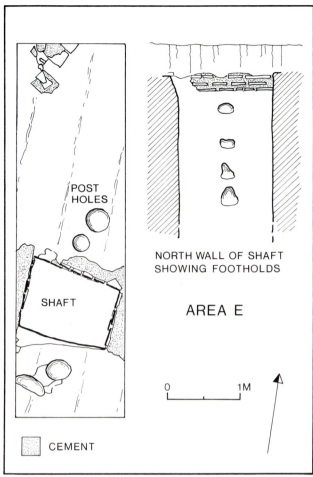

Fig. 50. Santa Rufina: area E, shaft, perhaps associated with catacomb

3. AREA D: THE CEMETERY

The cemetery was enclosed by walls A, A' and B. Wall B was built on the one surviving course of *opus quadratum* wall of period II, which was now extended in both directions, giving a length of *c.* 20 m. Parallel to this, and 3.0 m to the south, was A, a rubble and mortar wall 0.7 m wide. At the south-west end of A, wall A' returned towards the north. Walls A and A' enclosed a mortar-lined tank (D2), which measured 2.0 × 1.3 × 0.5 m and appeared to be contemporary with them. D3, which consisted of three courses of bricks and mortar above a stone platform, may be the threshold of an opening in wall A, through which one entered the cemetery. The same wall was pierced by a drain (D1) which continued for 3.0 m towards the south (Fig. 42).

The cemetery was divided by partitions of mortared tufo rubble into plots. The plot at the west end contained two graves, both constructed '*a cappuccina*', with a row of imbrices along the apex of the cover: XXIX, beside the north wall, with the skull to the west, and XXX, beside the partition (G), with the head to the north.

Graves XXXI and XXXII, also '*a cappuccina*', were aligned north–south; they were not investigated.

Details of the other graves were as follows:

(i) XXXIII and XXXIV (Pl. 63), beside wall A, had been disturbed in period V (see below);

(ii) XXXVI was the grave of a child, 0.8 m long and covered with fragments of earthenware pipes (Pl. 64);

(iii) XXXVII, 1.4 m long, was cut through the *opus quadratum* masonry of wall C;

(iv) XXXVIII was also 1.4 m long;

(v) XXXIX lay beside wall A. It was covered with a single row of tiles leaning against the wall;

(vi) XXXV was outside the cemetery zone, to the south of wall A. It had a vertical tile at the head and was covered with a row of three tiles sealed by three additional tiles, which covered the joints.

On the north side of wall B, the excavators found a number of partitions (walls O, P, Q, R, S, T and V), all built of tufo rubble bonded with mortar. Some (such as P and Q) abutted wall M, others (such as T) were cut through it. The area did not contain a single burial and it was assumed that it had been subdivided into plots which were never used.

Plate 63. Santa Rufina: period IIIc – graves '*a cappuccina*' in the late Roman cemetery. Graves XXXIII and XXXIV

Plate 64. Santa Rufina: period IIIc – child's grave XXXVI

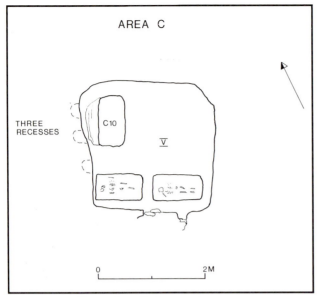

Fig. 51. Santa Rufina: area C, grave V

Plate 65. Santa Rufina: period IIIc – grave V with associated pit and niches

Farther north, the excavators discovered an important grave: V (Fig. 51; Pl. 65). This consisted of a pit, the bottom of which was 1.5 m below the surface of the tufo. It was roughly 2.5 m square and contained, in addition to a tile grave, an empty space; moreover, the west side of the pit contained three small niches and the floor beneath them had a small trench (C10), all of which may have been intended to accommodate lamps and other offerings. The grave itself was covered with both flat and curved tiles, the latter serving as ridge-tiles above the inclined pieces which formed the cover.

Beneath the tile grave were two small graves, each measuring 0.8 × 0.5 × 0.15 m and containing the remains of an infant. Neither yielded evidence for its date, the only finds being residual (see below).

East of grave V lay the robbed remains of three rectangular rock-cut graves: VI, VII and VIII.

Some time after the late third or early fourth century, a mausoleum was constructed on the north side of the cemetery. Unfortunately, the entire structure had been demolished, presumably to collect building materials, as a result of which nothing but the empty foundation trench remained. This showed that the mausoleum was circular, with an internal diameter of about 6.0 m and walls up to 1.0 m thick (Figs 52-54; Pl. 66). The foundation trench had been excavated to a depth of 1.0 m below the surface of the tufo, and had cut the debris-filled shafts of two Etruscan/republican cuniculi (C1 and C2).

Plate 66. Santa Rufina: period IIIc – mausoleum with later ossuaries

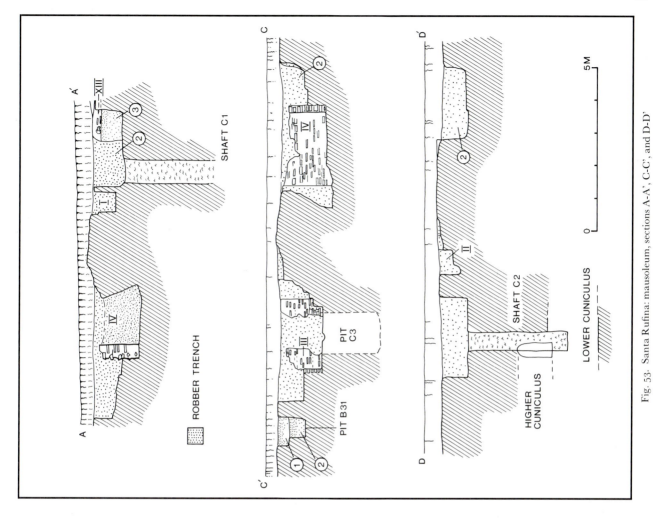

Fig. 53. Santa Rufina: mausoleum, sections A-A', C-C', and D-D'

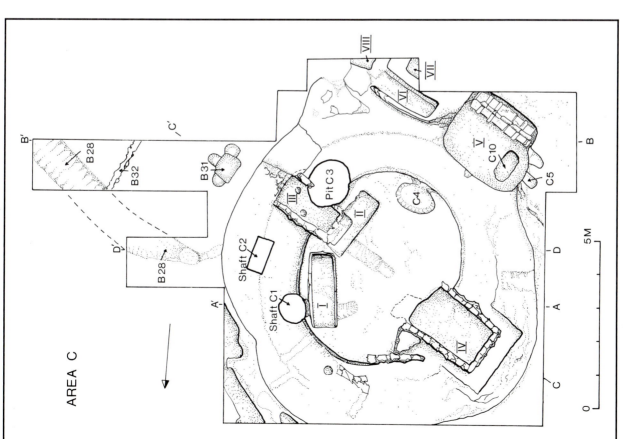

Fig. 52. Santa Rufina: area C, mausoleum

AREA C

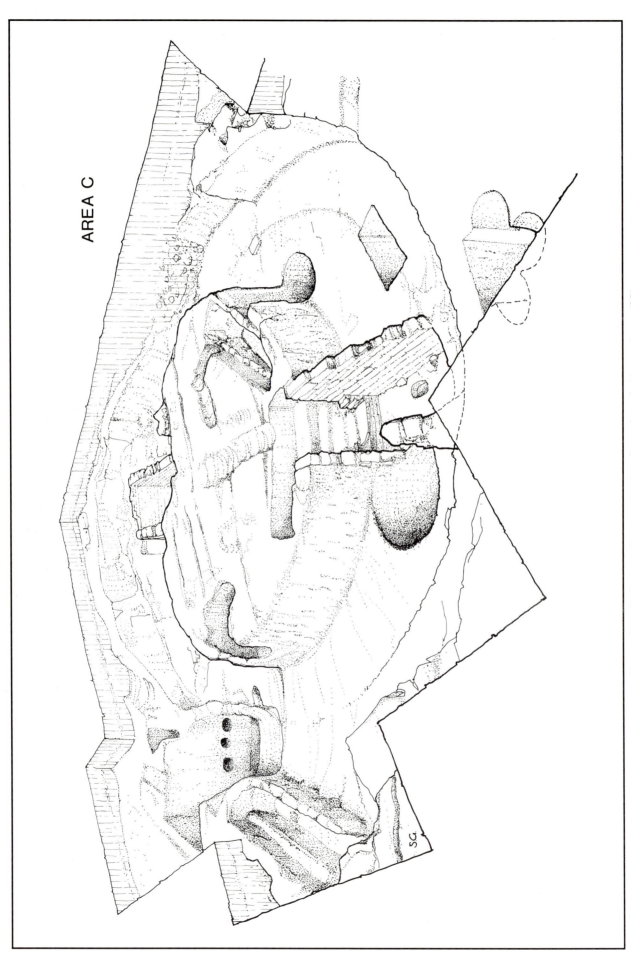

Fig. 54. Santa Rufina: area C, perspective view of mausoleum, looking north-west (SG)

The two primary graves (I and II) lay near the east wall, suggesting that the entrance was to the west. Grave I, which measured 2.25 × 0.9 × 0.75 m, had been lined with slabs of marble, fragments of which remained *in situ* on the walls and floor; a narrow rebate round the top of the grave marked the position of the cover, and this too may have been marble. Grave II also measured 2.25 × 0.9 × 0.75 m; no trace of lining or cover survived. The floor of the mausoleum also had been completely removed. Scattered throughout the area of the mausoleum were fragments of tubular tiles, presumably from a dome. These, and the many fragments of marble, glass tesserae (evidently from a wall or ceiling mosaic) and painted wall plaster suggest that the mausoleum was lavishly finished.

4. AREA D: THE ABANDONMENT OF THE TANKS AND CHANNELS

With the establishment of the cemetery, agricultural activity in this area was abandoned and the channels went out of use. Channels B19 and B25 became filled with earth, as probably did the tank (pottery from the fill consisting mainly of residual fragments, but there was one undiagnostic sherd of African red slip). Channel D11 was destroyed when the cemetery wall and tank D2 were built. The new tank did not last long, but had become filled with earth before the end of period IIIc; indeed, by this date, the whole system of irrigation had been abandoned.

5. FINDS

Area D: (i) unit 3
Bronze bell (66.1)
Black slip, 7 (including 73.12, 74.5 and 74.16)
Arretine (75.7)
Thin-walled beaker (74.33 and 1 similar)
African red slip, 10 (including 78.7, 78.10 and 79.22)
Amphora, 10 (including cf. 80.6, 80.12 and cf. 80.15 and 1 similar)
Late Roman colour-coated (cf. 90.1 and 1 similar)
Reduced (83.6, 83.9-10, 85.1 and 1 similar, 87.3 and 3 similar, cf. 84.19 and cf. 87.20) Dolium (89.3)

(ii) Unit 2
Glass (65.6-7)
Black slip (73.8, 73.12 and 1 similar, 73.14, 74.14 and 1 similar, cf. 73.9, cf. 73.19, cf. 74.5 and cf. 77.12 and 1 similar)
Arretine, 2
Thin-walled beaker, 2
Painted (cf. 79.24)
African red slip (79.22 and cf. 78.8 and 1 similar)
Light surface pottery (81.7, 81.10 and 1 similar, 81.17 and 1 similar, 82.1-2)
Reduced (83.13, 84.11, 85.1 and 3 similar, 85.4, 85.9, cf. 83.10, cf. 84.3, cf. 84.12 and 1 similar, cf. 87.3 and 3 similar, cf. 87.4 and cf. 87.11)
Amphora (80.4 and 80.9)

Area D: unit west of wall L and overlying gully Dd
African red slip, 1
Light surface pottery (cf. 81.8)
Reduced (83.14)

Areas B and D: unit north and south of wall B
Etruscan (71.9)
Black slip (73.7, 73.9 and 1 similar, 74.3 and 74.5 and 1 similar)
Thin-walled (74.17)
African red slip, 1
Light surface pottery (81.2, 81.21-22)
Reduced (83.2, 83.15, 84.2, 84.10, 84.12, 85.11-12, 87.16 and cf. 85.1)
Amphora (80.6 and 3 similar, 80.10, 80.14 and 2 similar, and cf. 80.8)

Areas D and E: catacomb
Loculus VII
Lamps (62.2, 63.4-7)

Lucernarium
Reduced (cf. 84.3 and cf. 87.18)

Area C: filling of grave V
Coin (number 4)
Black slip, 2 (including 74.7)
Arretine, 1
Internal slip, 2 (including cf. 71.10)
Light surface pottery, 1

Area B: channel B19
Lamps, 4 (including cf. 63.5 and 2 similar)
Arretine, 2
African red slip, 1

Channel B25
African red slip, 1
Reduced, 2 (including 83.2)

Area D: tank D2
Unguentarium (cf. 74.34)
African red slip, 1
Light surface pottery (81.4 and 81.13)
Reduced (cf. 87.20)
Amphora (80.18, cf. 80.8 and 1 similar, and cf. 80.17)

Area B: tank B21
Etruscan (71.4a)
Internal slip, 2
Black slip, 2
Fine ware (74.30)
African red slip, 1
Light surface pottery (82.10)
Reduced (84.15-16, 85.5, 85.13 and 86.23)
Mortarium (88.7)
Dolium (89.2)

6. DATE

The date at which period IIIc ended is difficult to establish. The latest African red slip ware is Hayes' form 52, which went out of use in the fourth century. The lamps, however, include Bailey's type R (current until the early fifth century) and type U (which probably belongs exclusively to the fifth century). There is in fact a hint that the closing date may be even later. The glass includes fragments of stemmed goblets (Isings form 111). Although Isings (1957, 139-140) believed that vessels of this type came into use in the fourth century, they were completely lacking from the Schola Praeconum when the earlier deposit was sealed, perhaps in the decade 430-440. They are common, however, in later contexts as, for example, at Carthage in the sixth century (see Tatton-Brown 1984, 200-202).

(iv) PERIOD IV: LATE ANTIQUE, FIFTH–SEVENTH CENTURY

1. Areas B and C: repairs to mausoleum
2. Area A: abandonment of vat
3. Area D: collapse and abandonment of catacomb
4. Latest occupation
5. Finds
6. Date

1. AREAS B AND C: REPAIRS TO MAUSOLEUM

A continuous, somewhat irregular trench was dug around the outside of the mausoleum (cf. Pl. 66). This served as the foundation trench for a series of buttresses, evidently to support the structure at points where it threatened to collapse; part of one such feature survived near ossuary III. Between the buttresses, the trench was backfilled with earth. The filling (unit 3 in Fig. 53, section A-A') remained intact when the mausoleum itself was demolished.

On the south-east side of the mausoleum, a channel (feature B28) was cut into the tufo. It was 1.0 m wide and 0.3 m deep, and extended down the slope for 11.0 m. Outside the mausoleum, a cavity had developed in the floor of the channel. The feature is identified, therefore, as a drain for rainwater from the roof. At an unknown date, feature B30, a hole 0.5 m across and 0.3 m deep, was cut in the channel.

South-west of the drain, feature B32 was a small structure, 0.1 m high, made of tufo bonded with mortar.

A small area between walls B and M had been excavated down to the tufo and backfilled with earth.

2. AREA A: ABANDONMENT OF VAT

The vat fell into disuse and became filled with earth (unit 3 in Fig. 44, section A-A').

3. AREA D: COLLAPSE AND ABANDONMENT OF CATACOMB

At a point where two galleries meet, the roof collapsed and earth and rubble cascaded into the catacomb (Fig. 46, section E-F'). This deposit consisted of three units: 8 and 9 (above) and 10 (below). The lower units yielded a fragment of African red slip ware of Hayes' type 91 (c. 350-550); the upper unit contained sherds of Hayes' 61b (late fourth to fifth century) and 64 (early to mid-fifth century). The character of the deposit and the evidence for its date are consistent with the following hypotheses: (1) the deposit accumulated gradually, or (2) the hole was filled deliberately, the earlier sherd being residual (as, indeed, were many other fragments: see below). However, since nothing was found to suggest that the catacomb had been robbed – lamps, for example, remained in situ – the second hypothesis is perhaps more likely.

Feature D10, the bottom of a trench-built wall of unknown date, was buried beneath unit 8.

The three holes in pit B31 became filled with earth. Other units attributed to this period sealed graves XXXI and XXXII.

4. LATEST OCCUPATION

The latest excavated feature was in area B, and consisted simply of a channel (B22), cut in the tufo. However, coins of Heraclius (610-642) and Constantine IV (668-685) and a scatter of African red slip ware, mostly from later contexts, imply that at least in the seventh century the site experienced rather more than occasional visits from cultivators, shepherds or scavengers. This conclusion is supported by the presence of two early medieval inscriptions (numbers 8 and 9e), although we cannot rule out the possibility that they arrived as spolia in, perhaps, period V.

5. FINDS

From the mausoleum: (a) unit 3
Black slip, 2
Arretine, 1
Late Roman slip (90.1)
Reduced (84.8, cf. 84.3 and cf. 87.23)

(b) Filling of features B28 and B30
Bone pin (68.2)
Sherd with graffito (68.12)
Tubular tile (cf. 69.4)
Black slip (74.8)
Amphora (including cf. 80.5)
Other coarse pottery

From the vat: unit 3
Arretine, 3
Early colour-coated (74.19 and 74.25)
African red slip (77.2)
Amphora, 2 (80.12 and 1 similar)
Other coarse pottery (including 74.12 and 72.4)

From the catacomb: (a) units 8 and 9
Building materials: 4 black tesserae, 1 yellow marble fragment and painted wall plaster
African red slip, Hayes 91 (79.16)
Amphora, 10
Other coarse pottery (including 81.8, 81.11, 81.14, 83.1, 87.10 and cf. 84.3)

(b) unit 10
Coin (number 5)
Iron (including spike 0.13 m long)
Glass fragments
Building material (including 1 black and 1 white tessera)
Lamps (including 62.3 and 1 similar)
Arretine, 1
Early colour-coated, 1
African red slip, including Hayes' 61b and 62 (78.4, 78.11 and 78.13)
Late colour-coated, 4 (including 90.2)
Amphora, 5

Mortarium (88.3)
Other coarse pottery (including 83.5, cf. 83.1, cf. 83.3
and cf. 87.22)

Sealing graves XXXI and XXXII
Shell (68.7)
Black slip, 2
Coarse pottery (including 81.3 and 1 similar, cf. 87.3
and cf. 87.11)

Unit between walls B and M
Tile (70.1)
Black slip, 4 (including 73.5)
Early colour-coated (cf. 74.33)
Unguentarium (74.35)
African red slip (78.15)
Late colour-coated (90.4)
Amphora (80.3)
Mortaria (88.1, 88.5-6)
Other coarse pottery (including 87.13, cf. 87.7 and cf.
87.3)

Pit B31
Bronze (66.14)
African red slip, 2
Coarse pottery (including cf. 83.5 and cf. 83.23)

Channel B22
African red slip (including Hayes 105, 79.20-21)
Coarse pottery (including cf. 84.2 and cf. 87.3)

6. DATE

The occurrence of African red slip ware of Hayes' form 105
shows that the site was occupied or frequented until at least
the late sixth century. Indeed, the discovery of coins of
Heraclius and Heraclius Constantine (*c.* 620) and
Constantine IV (668-685) suggests, but does not prove,
that activity continued in the seventh century. The
fragmentary inscription (number 9, below, Chapter 3,
xxviii) records a donation to the church, in or about the
sixth century.

(v) PERIOD V: EARLY MEDIEVAL, *c.* 800 OR
EARLIER– TWELFTH CENTURY

The site was transformed in period V, through the
demolition of the mausoleum, the construction and use of a
building with a mosaic floor in area D (the 'chapel' of the
preliminary notices in *Antiquity*: Ward-Perkins 1964; 1966;
1968) and of a walled complex in area F (the 'walled
settlement') and the establishment of a new cemetery. The
period can be divided into two phases. Units which
contained pottery with sparse glaze were attributed to
period Vb, while earlier units without it were attributed to
Va.

PERIOD Va

1.   a) Area D: room with mosaic
        b) The mosaic, by Demetrios Michaelides
2.   Area C: demolition of mausoleum
3.   Area F: walled complex

4.   Area F: cemetery
5.   Other features
6.   Finds
7.   Date

1. (a) AREA D: ROOM WITH MOSAIC

This was a rectangular structure, 14.0 m long and 7.0 m
wide, constructed in the south-east corner of the Roman
cemetery (Figs 42 and 55; Pls 67-68). The orientation was
determined by that of the republican building with *opus
quadratum* masonry (above, period II). Thus, wall B, which
had been incorporated in the north wall of the Roman
cemetery, was now rebuilt and extended to form the north
wall (B1) of the new structure. Boundary wall A of the
cemetery was demolished, but the north arm survived and
dictated the position of the east end of the structure, which
was completed by extending the wall in the corner of the
cemetery and building walls to the south and west (Pl. 67).
The new walls were of tufo rubble bonded with mortar.
They had foundations of varying quality. The south wall
(L) was built in a rock-cut foundation trench. The bottom
of the trench was generally 0.7-0.8 m below the level of the
mosaic, but where the wall crossed the loose earth in the
abandoned quarry, it was 1.60 m deep; at the west end,
too, where the accumulation of soil was deeper, the trench
was deepened, to allow the builders to set the foundations
on bedrock (Fig. 57). The west wall (J, H, K), in contrast,
was flimsily built, with foundations only 0.25 m deep.

The interior of the structure was levelled, in the course of
which several period IIIc graves were damaged. The
builders next laid a bed of very coarse mortar, 0.1-0.15 m
thick. Above this, they set a thin layer of fine, compact
mortar: the bedding for the mosaic. The mosaic was not
the only opulent feature. At the west end, the wall retained
the lower edges of marble revetments, and part of a white
marble column lay on the floor (cf. Pl. 68).

The room was entered through a doorway *c.* 1.4 m wide,
placed near the centre of the south wall. One approached
the doorway up two steps made of bricks and mortar, with
a rubble core. The function of the room, described at the
time of excavation as a chapel, is discussed below.

1. (b) THE MOSAIC (Pls 69-71)
Demetrios Michaelides

This was made up of large coloured tesserae and smaller
black and white tesserae. The former measured 25 × 25 ×
20 mm. They were made of green and red porphyry and
white marble, and were cut from *spolia*. Among the latter,
the visible surface usually measured 10 × 10 mm; the
black tesserae were about 20 mm long, while the white
ones were up to 50 mm long. They were made of basalt and
limestone, and could have been cut at any time.

The central design was framed by a border, which
survived only on the north and west sides of the room (Figs
55 and 56; Pl. 69). The north border was relatively wide,
the west border narrow. We have no means of knowing
whether there was a border on the east side, but, to judge
from the dimensions of the main design, the south border
was omitted; the result, it seems, of inadequate planning
before the tesserae were laid. Spaces between the borders
and the walls of the room were filled with a chevron
pattern of rectangular white tesserae.

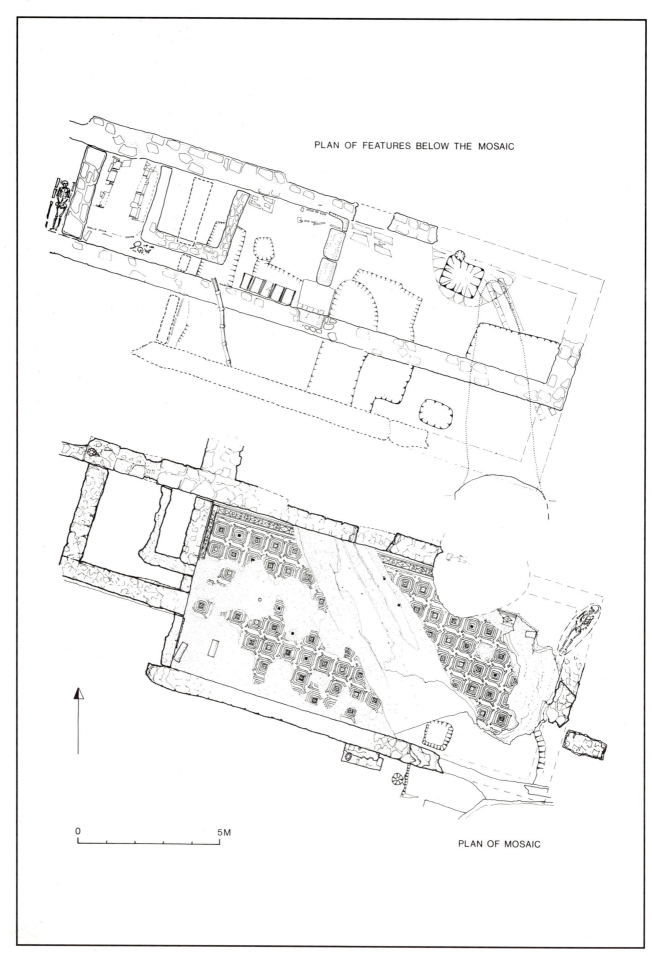

PLAN OF FEATURES BELOW THE MOSAIC

0   5M

PLAN OF MOSAIC

Fig. 55. Santa Rufina: area D, room with mosaic (below) and earlier features (above)

The *north border*: on the outside, a black band ran for the entire length of the design. Inside this came the border proper: a row of continuous interlocking swastikas enclosing lozenges (a variation of Blanchard *et al.* 1973, number 260 = Balmelle *et al.* 1985, R38e). This design is outlined in black on a white background. The centre of each lozenge is decorated with a diagonally placed 'fleurette' or crosslet (Blanchard *et al.* 1973, number 106), mainly in alternating red and green porphyry. The inner edge of the border is formed by the black outline of the swastika pattern, which makes up the main design.

The *west border*: although narrower, this is basically similar to the north border, the only difference being that on the inside it is not bordered by the black outline of the main swastika pattern, but by the white body of the swastikas themselves.

The *main design*: this consists of a repeated geometric pattern in black and white, with a coloured motif in the centre of each component part (Pl. 70). The design consists of an orthogonal pattern of adjacent octagons worked in swastika meander (Blanchard *et al.* 1973, number 345 = Balmelle *et al.* 1985, R166b), the meander white bordered by black. The octagons are white, containing a smaller, concentric black octagon, within which is a central coloured motif on a white ground. The complete design was eight units wide and at least eighteen units long.

There are three main types of central motif. They are arranged in diagonal rows, each containing a single motif. Starting in the north-west corner and moving towards the east, the rows develop in a regular sequence: ABACAB, and so on (Fig. 57). The three motifs are:

A.   Simple fleurettes with red centres and green right-angled leaves, or green centres and red leaves.

Plate 67. Santa Rufina: period Va – area D, room with mosaic ('chapel') viewed from west

B.   Chequerboards in green and white.
C.   Red squares with green corners, enclosing green
        squares with white centres.
[For further discussion of the date of the mosaic, see the assessment of Federico Guidobaldi in Appendix 1.]

2. AREA C: DEMOLITION OF THE MAUSOLEUM

The mausoleum was completely dismantled; even the foundations were removed, and the only indication of the position of the outer walls was the massive rubble-filled robber trench (cf. Pl. 66). An oval pit, measuring 1.50 × 1.25 × 1.80 m, dug in the floor of the robber trench, was apparently contemporary with the dismantling of the mausoleum. It contained pieces of worked marble, including a capital (below, Chapter 3, xxvi, number 34), and two sherds of Forum Ware. After the filling of the pit, ossuary III was constructed above it. When the filling subsided, the mortared brick sides of the ossuary collapsed.

3. AREA F: WALLED ENCLOSURE

Excavation revealed the north corner of a walled enclosure (Fig. 58; Pl. 72). The outer wall was built of tufo blocks which varied considerably in size, the largest measuring 2.0 × 0.5 × 0.6 m and the smallest 0.5 × 0.5 × 0.5 m. They were laid in a double row, which together made a wall 1.0 m thick. The west wall of the enclosure was traced for 20 m. One course only survived, except where the wall

Plate 68. Santa Rufina: period Va – room with mosaic from east

crossed the gully (F6) and the collapsed cuniculus (F1), where two extra courses had been required to fill the depressions in the surface. The large blocks were laid without mortar, which occurred only where small, irregular lumps were used. On the north side of the

0   40cm

Centres of the patterns of the mosaic floor

Alternating centres of border

▨ Green Porphyry
◻ Red Porphyry

0   20cm

Fig. 56. Santa Rufina: area D, detail of mosaic (SG)

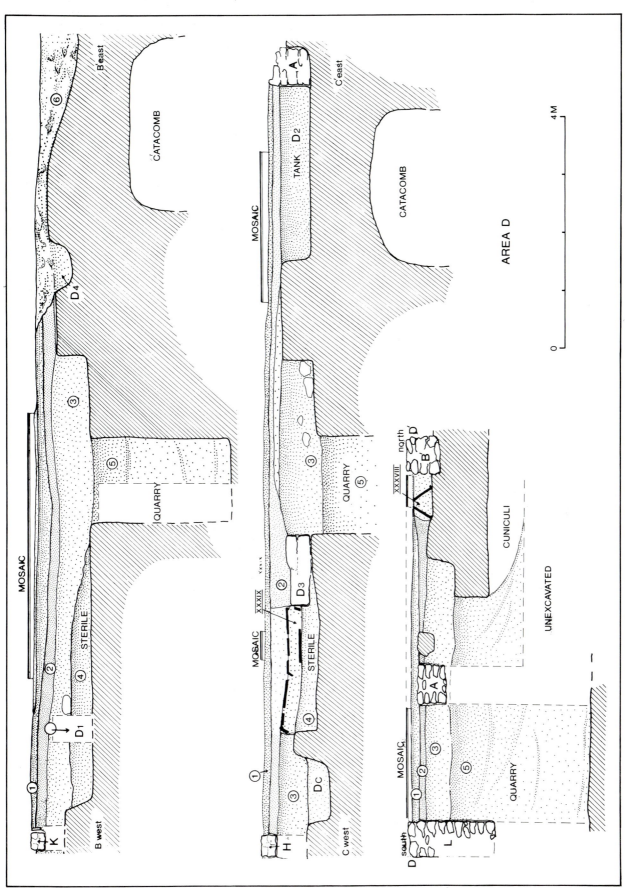

Fig. 57: Santa Rufina: area D, sections B-B', C-C' and D-D'

Plate 69. Santa Rufina: period Va – fragment of mosaic border

Plate 70. Santa Rufina: period Va – main design of mosaic

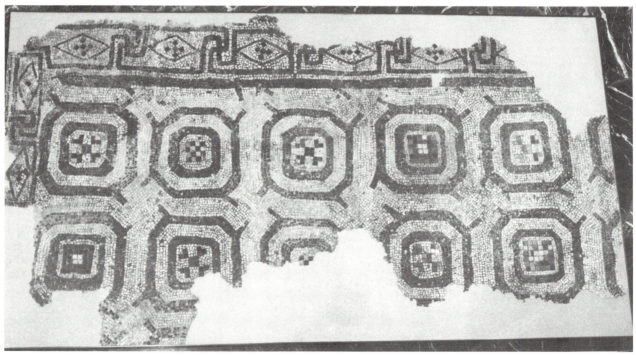

Plate 71. Santa Rufina: period Va – restored mosaic (*Museo dell'Alto Medioevo*, Rome)

enclosure the excavators uncovered 8 m of the wall, two courses of which survived. Three metres from the corner lay a gateway, 2 m wide. On each side of the gateway was a posthole. The hole to the west was rectangular and that to the east circular; both, however, had maximum dimensions of 0.6 × 0.44 × 0.75 m. The east posthole had been recut. Outside the gateway, there was a hint of a protecting wall, but further excavation would be needed to confirm or deny its existence.

Several other features require comment:

(i) Filling of gully F6. It was thought that the gully served as a feeder for cuniculus F1. Pottery from the filling included both republican black slip ware and sherds of

Forum Ware. This might be explained by supposing that the gully went out of use at the same time as the cuniculus and filled with earth. Much later the builders of the enclosure cleared part of the filling, in order to found the west wall on bedrock. The earth was then replaced, at which time recent material (i.e. Forum Ware) became mixed with sherds from the original fill (black slip ware).

(ii) Holes Fa and Fb in gully F6. These too were refilled when the enclosure wall was built. They contained sherds of Forum Ware. Hole Fc, on the other hand, did not contain a single artifact and its filling cannot be dated.

(iii) Units 8, 9 and 10. All three units accumulated against the outer walls of the enclosure (Fig. 59, section B-B').

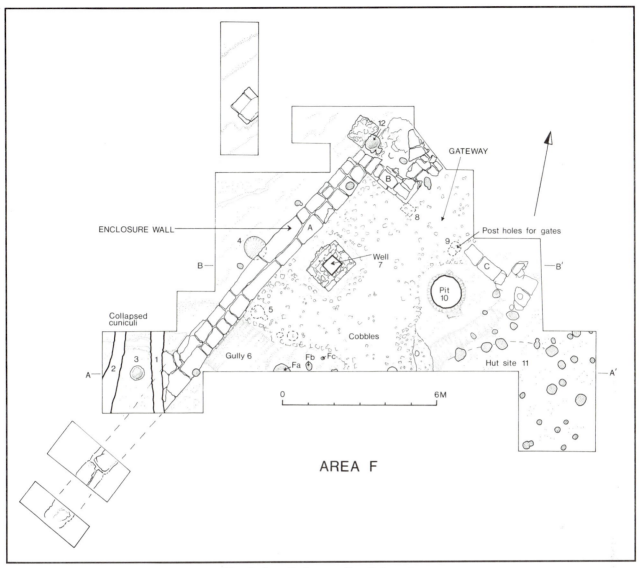

Fig. 58. Santa Rufina: area F, walled complex

Plate 72. Santa Rufina: period Va – north corner of enclosure wall looking towards the courtyard

(iv) Feature F11 and unit 12. Inside the enclosure, the area to the east of the entrance contained a large number of post-holes of uncertain function, identified collectively as F11. These were sealed by a layer of dark earth (unit 12 in Fig. 59, section A-A').

4. AREA F: CEMETERY

A new cemetery now developed on the site, with graves of a type entirely different from those of period III: shallow trenches without covers. The new graves extended south from the walled enclosure in no discernible order and without a common alignment. The users of the cemetery may have respected the site of the mausoleum, or adjacent graves; they showed no such regard for the room with the mosaic, although grave XL was cut through the north-east corner after the structure had been demolished. It was virtually impossible to assign graves to specific periods; most lay directly beneath the ploughsoil and some had been partly destroyed by cultivation.

The graves nearest to the walled enclosure were those cut into the Roman vat (Pl. 59), and six burials left

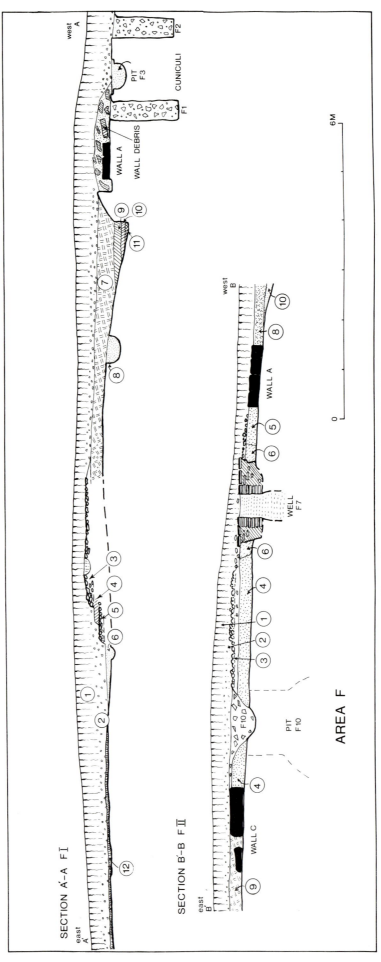

Fig. 59. Santa Rufina: area F, sections A-A' and B-B'

unexcavated in a trench to the west of area A. The former were badly damaged in period VI.

The area of the mausoleum (Fig. 60) contained, in addition to shallow graves, two ossuaries cut into the filling of the foundation trench, one of which also cut primary grave II (Pl. 73) and the filling of pit C3. Both had been excavated in the tufo and were lined with brickwork rendered with mortar. They had been robbed, with the result that neither their covers nor contents (apart from the disarticulated bones on the floor of ossuary IV) survived. Evidently, the ossuaries were built after the demolition of the mausoleum and the filling of pit C3, which contained sherds of Forum Ware.

Among the adjacent graves, IX-XIII and XX contained articulated skeletons, while XIV and XV had been disturbed, when the final robbing of the mausoleum took place. Indeed, only one of the graves cut into the earlier filling of the robbed foundation trench remained intact: XIII, the west half of which lay on the one small section of buttress infill not disturbed by the later stone robbers. Grave XIX contained an articulated skeleton, but without the skull. This was missing because, in graves excavated into the tufo, ledges were left at one end to support the head which, being at a higher level than the rest of the body, was more liable to damage by ploughing. Graves XXI-XXVII, east of the mausoleum, contained articulated skeletons. Grave XXII was cut through the filling of feature B30.

5. OTHER FEATURES

(i) Area G: pit G. This rock-cut pit had a circular mouth 1.6 m across, a maximum diameter of 1.6 m and a total depth of 1.25 m. The filling included coarse pottery and a sherd of Forum Ware.

(ii) Area B: pit B29. This was a rectangular pit, measuring 1.0 × 0.6 × 0.5 m. It was only partly excavated, but contained broken bricks, tiles and the strap handle of a medieval amphora.

(iii) Area D. A small pit was investigated west of wall L.

(iv) Area B: pit B14. At the east edge of area B, a circular pit was found, 1.3 m across and 1.75 m deep. On the north-west side, the lip shelved slightly, with a shallow gully which led away towards the south-east. On either side of the pit was a post-hole 0.48 m deep. It was not clear whether the holes (B12 and B13) were associated with the pit or not. The filling of the pit (B14) was excavated in three arbitrary spits, each of which was 0.5-0.6 m deep. The uppermost filling consisted of broken roof tiles (tegulae and imbrices); the lowest fill contained fragments of charred wood and, at the bottom, a layer of 'grain', 40 mm thick. Other finds (see below) included iron nails, a grinding stone and a wide range of pottery, including Forum Ware.

(v) Area B: pit B15. This rectangular pit was only partially investigated. There were no finds and its attribution to this period is uncertain.

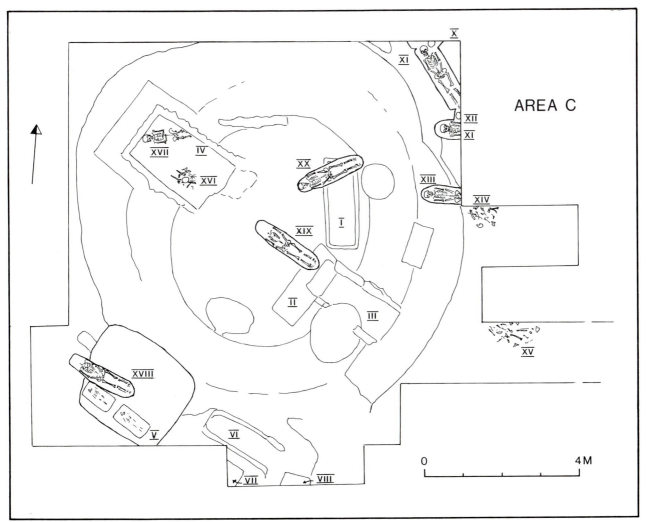

Fig. 60. Santa Rufina: area C, ossuaries and graves on site of mausoleum

Plate 73. Santa Rufina: period Va – ossuary II cut into the robbed-out mausoleum

6. FINDS

Area D: room with mosaic

(i) Unit 1, under mosaic
Glass (65.3 and 65.8)
Black slip (74.10)
Late Roman colour-coated (cf. 90.1)
Reduced (83.4, 84.3, 86.20 and 1 similar, 86.24 and 1 similar, 86.32, 94.8, cf. 84.1 and cf. 86.20 and 1 similar)
Amphora (80.13)

(ii) Foundation trench for wall B'
Black slip, 7 (including 74.9)
Arretine, 3
Light surface pottery (82.14)
Reduced (84.12)
Amphora, 20
Forum, 5

(iii) Foundation trench for west wall of room
Black slip, 4 (including 74.3)
African red slip, 1
Light surface pottery, 7
Forum, 1

(iv) Foundation trench for south wall and contemporary ground surface
Coins (numbers 1, 2, 10-12)
Marble (number 27)

Black slip, 2
African red slip, 1
Reduced (86.32, cf. 86.24 and cf. 87.3)
Forum, 1

Area C: pit C3
Bronze (66.8)
Glass, fragments (including 1 blue tessera)
Iron, 1 nail
Painted wall plaster
Marble (fragments of two columns, cornice, etc.)
Pottery (including 2 Forum)

Area F: walled enclosure

(i) Filling of gully F6
Black slip, 5 (including 73.1)
Painted (cf. 79.24)
Forum (cf. 92.6)

(ii) F1, unit 10
Black slip, 2 (including 74.6)
Internal slip, 2 (including 71.10)

(iii) F1, unit 11
Black slip, 1
Reduced (cf. 94.3)
Forum, 1

(iv) Filling of Fa
Forum, 1

(v) Filling of Fb
Reduced (86.24)

(vi) Unit 8
Glass, fragments
Pietra ollare (68.5)
Thin-walled beaker (74.22)
Reduced (cf. 86.24)
Amphora (95.15 and 1 similar)
Forum, 2

(vii) Unit 9
Light surface pottery, 5 (including 95.15 and 1 similar)
Reduced, 1
Forum, 4

(viii) Unit 10
Stone (68.5)
Arretine, 1
Early imperial glazed (79.27)

(ix) Unit 12
Marble (number 30)
Reduced, 3 (including cf. 94.3)
Forum (92.2 and 92.13)

Area B:

(i) filling of channel B18
Black slip (73.18)
Unguentarium (cf. 74.34)
Reduced (86.29, 86.33 and cf. 84.15)
Forum, 1

(ii) post-hole B13
Black slip, 1
Coarse pottery, various
Mortarium (88.4)

(iii) pit B14
Stone (68.13 and fragment of red porphyry and marble, and 1 white tessera)
Glass (68.11)
Iron, including 3 nails
Bucchero (71.1-2)
Black slip, 1
Internal slip (cf. 72.5 and 2 similar)
African red slip, 3
Dolium, 6
Storage jar (91.7)
Reduced (83.8, 85.6, 86.29 and 1 similar, cf. 84.2 and 1 similar, cf. 85.12, cf. 86.24, cf. 94.6 and 1 similar and cf. 87.1)

(iv) pit B29
Light surface pottery, 1
Amphora (cf. 95.15)

Area G: pit G
Light surface pottery (81.15, 94.5, 94.7, 95.10, 95.13 and 95.16)
Reduced (94.1 and 1 similar, 94.2, 94.3 and 1 similar, 94.4 and 4 similar, 94.6, 95.9, 95.11-12, 95.14 and cf. 86.29)
Forum (92.4)

7. DATE

The most important developments in period Va were the construction of the room which included the mosaic and the walled enclosure, and the demolition of the mausoleum. The evidence for the date of the room with the mosaic consists of material from beneath the floor and from the foundation trenches of the north, west and south walls. Beneath the floor, unit 1 (Fig. 57, section D-D') was deposited to make up the level before the laying of the coarse mortar bed. It contained much residual material, and the sagging base of a jar (see below Fig. 94.8), which finds parallels (associated with Forum Ware) in pit G. The north side of the room consisted of an earlier wall, strengthened by the addition of a trench-built jacket, some 3.5 m long. The filling of the trench contained five sherds of Forum Ware. The foundation trench for the west wall was dug in three sections (J, H and K). The trench for section H cut into the top of Roman grave XXXIII, which is attributed to period IIIc (see above). On the south side of the room, the unit that formed the ground surface at the time of construction yielded a coin of Heraclius and Heraclius Constantine, minted c. 620, and one sherd of Forum Ware.

The construction of the walled enclosure and the demolition of the mausoleum were also associated with Forum Ware. In the former, gully F6, which was partly cleared and then backfilled to accommodate part of the outer wall, contained Forum Ware, as did the filling of postholes Fa and Fb. In the latter, robber-pit C3 yielded two sherds of Forum Ware. None of these features contained a single fragment of pottery with sparse glaze decoration.

Period Va, therefore, is attributed to the period in which Forum Ware was current, and before the introduction of sparse glaze. Opinions on the date of Forum Ware have for long varied widely, from the sixth century to c. 1000: the problems associated with this type of pottery are discussed, in relation to Santa Cornelia, by Patterson (above, Part I, Chapter 4, ix). However, well-stratified deposits in the Crypta Balbi in the centre of Rome (Paroli 1986a) now securely attest Forum Ware in contexts dating at least from the later eighth century and extending into the tenth century.

PERIOD Vb

1. Area F: walled enclosure
2. Area D: room with mosaic
3. Finds
4. Date

1. AREA F: WALLED ENCLOSURE

The courtyard was resurfaced with broken tile, pottery and pebbles embedded in yellowish clay (F11). The new surface extended outside the entrance to the south and west. It may have extended towards the east too, but a later pit (F10) had removed the evidence. Deposits associated with these features (F11, units 1-6 in Fig. 59, section B-B' and F1, units 6-7 in Fig. 59, section A-A') were all roughly contemporary.

The courtyard contained several features, including a well and a storage pit (Figs 58 and 61). The well was dug through unit 6 in F11. It had a square well-head and a circular shaft (Pl. 74). The well-head, constructed from fragments of brick and tile bonded with mortar, was recessed to support a cover. The shaft was 0.5 m across. The uppermost 0.6 m was lined with brick fragments and mortar, below which it was rock-cut. It was excavated to a

Plate 74. Santa Rufina: period Vb – well-head within enclosure

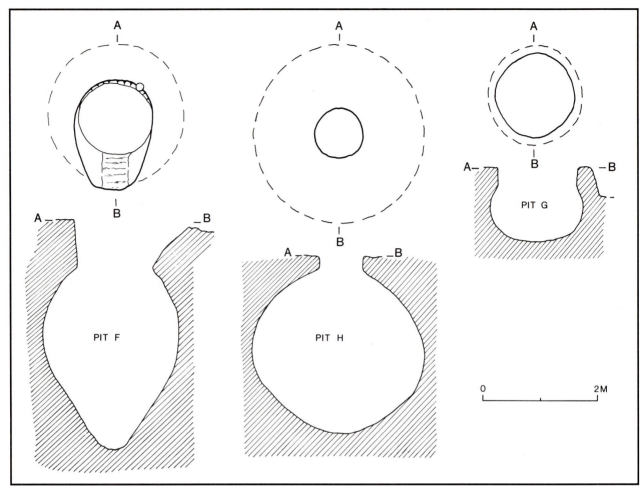

Fig. 61. Santa Rufina: area F, pits F, G and H

depth of 1.5 m only. The area to the east of the entrance was riddled with post-holes. Unfortunately, no coherent structures were discerned and it is not clear whether the post-holes formed part of a domestic building, a storehouse, or served some other purpose.

Storage pit F10 was pear-shaped with a roughly circular, shaft-like mouth, up to 1.25 m across and 0.75 m deep. Below this, the diameter of the pit increased to 2.4 m, before tapering to a pointed base. Although the filling contained pottery of the thirteenth century or later, the pit itself may be attributed to period Vb.

A second storage pit (H) in area H, had a circular mouth, of 0.75 m diameter, and a spheroid body, 3.0 m in diameter and nearly 3.0 m deep. Again, despite later pottery in its fill, it was thought to belong to Vb.

2. *AREA D: ROOM WITH MOSAIC*

The following features contained pottery with sparse glaze, but nothing later:

(i)   A deposit on the south side of the room, which ran up to the steps;

(ii)   A pit outside the south-west corner;

(iii)   Pit B16, near the complex of pits, post-holes and trenches (B12-15). The pit, which may have been contemporary with B12-15, measured 0.6 × 0.5 × 2.0 m.

3. *FINDS*

Area F:

(i) F11, units 1-2
Forum, 6
Sparse glaze, 2
Other, 12 (including cf. 95.15)

(ii) F11, unit 3
African red slip, 1
Forum, 17
Sparse glaze, 2
Other (82.9)

(iii) F11, unit 4
African red slip, 1
Forum, 4
Sparse glaze, 3

(iv) F11, unit 5
Forum, 5
Other, 2

(v) F11, unit 6
African red slip, 1
Forum, 6

(vi) F1, unit 6
Forum (92.15)
Sparse glaze (93.5)

(vii) F1, unit 7
Etruscan red burnished, 1
Forum, 2 (including 92.6)
Sparse glaze, 2 (including 93.7)
Other, 10 (including 84.14 and 95.14)

Area D: room with mosaic
(i) Deposit to south
Glass (65.2)
Black slip, several (including 74.13 and cf. 73.19)
African red slip (cf. 78.8)
Forum (92.1)
Sparse glaze, 1

(ii) Pit outside south-west angle
Sparse glaze, 1
Other (81.9)

(iii) Pit B16
Glass, 2 blue tesserae
Marble, scrap
Sparse glaze (93.1)
Other, several

4. DATE

The type-fossil for period Vb is pottery with sparse glaze, which seems to have enjoyed a long currency between the tenth and the twelfth centuries. The beginning of period Vb is marked by sparse glaze; we do not know when it ended.

(vi) PERIOD VI: LATE MEDIEVAL, TWELFTH CENTURY AND LATER

After period Vb, the site was virtually abandoned. The discovery, however, of a number of graves and a small quantity of late medieval and post-medieval pottery indicates some form of activity, undoubtedly modest and perhaps intermittent.

1. Area F: walled enclosure
2. Area A: tank
3. Area C: cemetery
4. Area D: room with mosaic
5. Features of uncertain date
6. Finds
7. Date

1. AREA F: WALLED ENCLOSURE

Storage pits F10 and H were backfilled. Among the debris in F10 was the skeleton of a cow.

2. AREA A: TANK

There may have been an attempt to reuse the tank. The upper filling was removed, in the course of which a number of graves came to light. Perhaps for this reason, the operation was abandoned before the tank had been emptied. Subsequently, unit 2 accumulated in the depression created by the digging.

3. AREA C: CEMETERY

Ossuary IV (described above) was broken open, as a result of which the skeleton was disturbed. Later, the tomb was filled with a deposit containing fragments of a screen and other marble objects, tesserae, scraps of painted wall plaster, and two coins (numbers 9 and 13), one Roman and the other perhaps of Conrad II (1027-1039). Cut into the deposit was a grave containing a skeleton in a contracted position. Another late grave (XVIII) was dug into the earth above grave V.

Ossuary III was also robbed. The tomb had been constructed in the rubble-filled robber-trench of the mausoleum and it was impossible to distinguish between the fillings of the earlier and later features. Indeed, the only uncontaminated deposits in this area were unit 3, the filling of ossuary IV and a pocket of soil containing post-medieval material near the bottom of the robber-trench on the north side.

4. AREA D: ROOM WITH MOSAIC

Nothing of the room survived above ground and, apart from footings and a fallen piece of wall A', all the masonry had been removed. The mosaic, however, was left substantially intact. The following features accumulated or were constructed after the abandonment of the room:

(i) Grave XL, on the site of the east wall;
(ii) A layer of earth overlying the mosaic (Fig. 46, section G-H);
(iii) Several other deposits, including units 6-7 in Fig. 46, section G-H and unit 6 in Fig. 57, section J-K;
(iv) Pit D4, which measured $1.0 \times 0.8 \times 0.4$ m and contained tesserae from the mosaic;
(v) A shallow pit (D5), 3.0 m across, cut through the remains of the north wall;
(vi) Post-holes D8 and D9, both $c.$ 0.3 m in diameter, one of which was cut through the steps.

5. FEATURES OF UNCERTAIN DATE

Three features, although demonstrably 'late' in the overall sequence, could not be assigned to a specific period:

(i) Area B: pit B24, 1.0 m in diameter, was cut through the north end of feature B23 (period IIIa). The bottom of the pit was 0.6 m below the surface of the tufo;
(ii) Area C: pit C5, 0.5 m across and 0.2 m deep, was cut into grave V (of period Va);
(iii) Area D: features D6 and D7. D6 was a rectangular pit, measuring $1.0 \times 1.25 \times 0.3$ m. D7, a post-hole, was cut through the north-west corner of the pit. The filling of D6 contained Forum Ware and is, therefore, no earlier than period Va.

6. FINDS

Area F: filling of pit F10
Glass, including 2 tesserae
Marble, 1 fragment
Iron, 1 nail

African red slip, 1
Forum, 3
Sparse glaze (93.3)
Late medieval glazed, 5 (including 96.4)
Other, 5 (including 84.14, cf. 93.3-4)

Area H: filling of pit H
Bronze, 2 pins (including 66.2)
Marble, 1 fragment
African red slip, 2 (including cf. 78.1)
Forum, 5
Sparse glaze (cf. 93.4)
Late medieval glazed, 11 (including 96.2)

Area A: tank, unit 2
Black slip, 1
African red slip, 1
Forum, 5
Sparse glaze, 3
Late medieval glazed (96.3)
Other, several (including 86.24, 86.30, 87.15, 87.18 and cf. 84.3)

Area C:
(i) ossuary IV
Coins (numbers 9 and 13)
Marble, carved and inscribed fragments (including numbers 1-6 and 29)
Glass tessera, 48 blue, 2 opaque white
Bronze, several (including 66.6-7, 66.9, 66.13, 66.16 and cf. 66.10)
Iron, several (including 66.3, 66.8 and 66.37)
Painted wall plaster, several fragments, mostly plain reddish brown, but with 3 polychrome
Black slip, 1
African red slip, 1
Forum, 7
Sparse glaze, 22 (including cf. 93.4)
Other, several (including 82.12, 86.26, 91.6 and 95.15)

(ii) Unit above grave V
Marble, fragments
Sparse glaze
Late medieval glazed (96.1)
Other, several (including 86.26 and 86.35)

(iii) Ossuary III
Tubular tile, 5
Forum, 1
Post-medieval glazed, 2

(iv) Robber trench of mausoleum, unit 2
Coins (numbers 6 and 8)
Bronze, several (including 66.4, 66.10-11, 66.17 and 66.1)

Iron, several (including nails, 67.11-12)
Tubular tile, 34 (including 69.4 and cf. 69.2)

(v) Pit C5
Glass, including tesserae
Iron, including nails
Painted wall plaster, 4 scraps
Etruscan applied painted (71.4a)
Other, 5

Area D:
(i) unit resting on mosaic
Horn (68.9)
Tile (70.3)
Pottery (cf. 86.24)

(ii) Features D6 and D7
The finds were amalgamated with those from D5: before this occurred, however, Forum Ware was noted in D6.

Area B:
(i) pit B13
Black slip, 1
Mortarium (88.4)
Other pottery

(ii) pit B24
Tessera, 1 green porphyry, 1 black stone, 1 glass
Tubular tile, 1
African red slip, 1
Roman glazed (91.11)

(iii) pit B28
Tubular tile (cf. 69.4)
Black slip (74.8)
Other pottery (including cf. 69.4 and cf. 80.5)

(iv) Unit 6 (Fig. 59, section B-B')
Marble, capital (number 31)
African red slip (including 78.14 and 78.19)
Roman glazed (91.10)
Other pottery (80.7, cf. 84.1 and cf. 87.23)

7. DATE

The thin scatter of pottery and other objects attests to limited activity on the site in the late medieval and early modern periods. This consisted of treasure-hunting and the salvage of building materials (ossuary IV was 'robbed' some time after 1027), and, presumably, a certain amount of cultivation.

CHAPTER THREE. THE FINDS

(i) *COINS*

Bryan Ward-Perkins

1. Small bronze in bad condition. Probably Greek colonial, second or first century BC. K2.4.
   - Obv.   Perhaps head facing right.
   - Rev.   Horse's head facing right.

2. *Quadrans* in bad condition. Republican, *c.* 150-70 BC. EEE1.9
   - Obv.   Head of young Hercules facing right, wearing lion skin. Three dots behind.
   - Rev.   ROMA below prow facing right, with three dots in front.
           Inscription or moneyer's mark lost.

3. *Quadrans* in bad condition. Almost certainly Claudius (AD 41-54). Mint of Rome. JJ1.3.
   - Obv.   Almost certainly a *modius* on three legs. Legend lost.
   - Rev.   SC large in centre. Legend lost.

4. *Dupondius* in bad condition. Almost certainly first century AD. YY1.3.
   - Obv.   A head.
   - Rev.   Illegible.

5. Probably a *dupondius*, but in bad condition. Early third century AD. OO1.3.
   - Obv.   Imperial bust, laureate and draped, facing right.
           Legend: IMP C[. . .
   - Rev.   Probably Providentia AVGG type SC.

6. *Sestertius* of Valerian I (*c.* 253). K2.4.
   - Obv.   Laureate head of Valerian, facing right. IMP [C P LIC] VALERIANVS A[VG]
   - Rev.   Winged victory standing, facing left, with wreath in right hand and palm in left. [VICTORI]A AV[GG]. S.C.
   - (Cf.   Mattingley and Sydenham 1923-, 52, number 177.)

7. Small bronze coin in very bad condition. Possibly third century AD. T2.3a.
   - Obv.   Perhaps radiate head.
   - Rev.   Illegible.

8. Bronze coin in very bad condition. Possibly early fourth century AD. 00 Ex.1.5.

9. Small bronze coin in bad condition. House of Theodosius (378-388). T2.3.
   - Obv.   Imperial head facing right. Legend lost.
   - Rev.   VOT V MVLT X within wreath.
   - (Cf.   Carson and Kent 1960, 88.)

10. Ae 4 of Valentinian III (425-455). Mint of Rome. K2.4.
   - Obv.   Bust of Valentinian, laureate and draped, facing right. D N VALENTINO P F AVG
   - Rev.   VOT XX within wreath; RPM in exergue.
   - (Cf.   Carson and Kent 1960, 63, number 856.)

11. 20 *nummia* of Heraclius and Heraclius Constantine (*c.* 620). Mint of Rome. K2.4.
   - Obv.   Bust of Heraclius on left, smaller bust of Heraclius Constantine on right, each draped and crowned. Above, cross. Border of dots. Legend lost.
   - Rev.   XX above cross. ROM in exergue. Border of dots.
   - (Cf.   Wroth 1908, 242-243.)

12. 20 *nummia* of Constantine IV (668-685). K2.4.
   - Obv.   Bust of Constantine, beardless, facing, wearing cuirass and helmet.
   - Rev.   XX above cross. ROM in exergue.
   - (Cf.   Wroth 1908, 328, number 93.)

13. Silver *denaro* of Lucca, possibly Conrad II (1027-1039). 00 Ex.1.5.
   - (Cf.   *CNI* vol.XI, 68f.)

PROVENANCES:

Period IIIc:	2
Period IV:	7
Period V:	1, 6, 10-12.
Period VII:	4, 5, 8, 13.
Not stratified:	3, 9.

(ii) GLASS (Fig. 65)

1. (20) Jar with rounded, outsplayed rim. Opaque dark purple rim, with thin transparent purple wall. Bubbly. Lemon yellow trails round rim and body.

2. (57) Neck of bottle. Thick, bubbly greenish glass; trailed decoration.

3. (58) Goblet with thickened rim. Pale green with opaque cream trails. (Cf. Whitehouse *et al.* 1985, 165, number 26.)

4. (18) Base of unguentarium. Bluish glass.

5. (19) Lamp. Very thin pale green wall with pale green vertical handles. Variant of Isings form 111.

6. (41) Stemmed goblet. Yellowish green glass with irridescent weathering.

7. (42) Bottle with bulbous body and tall, cylindrical neck. Thick yellowish glass with severe weathering.

8. (58a) Goblet with hollow stem. Bluish glass.

9. (26) Ring base. Greenish colourless glass, bubbly.

10. (26a) Ring base formed by winding trail four times round bottom of body. Body transparent pale green, base trail opaque dark green. (Cf. Whitehouse *et al.* 1985, 170, numbers 55-58.)

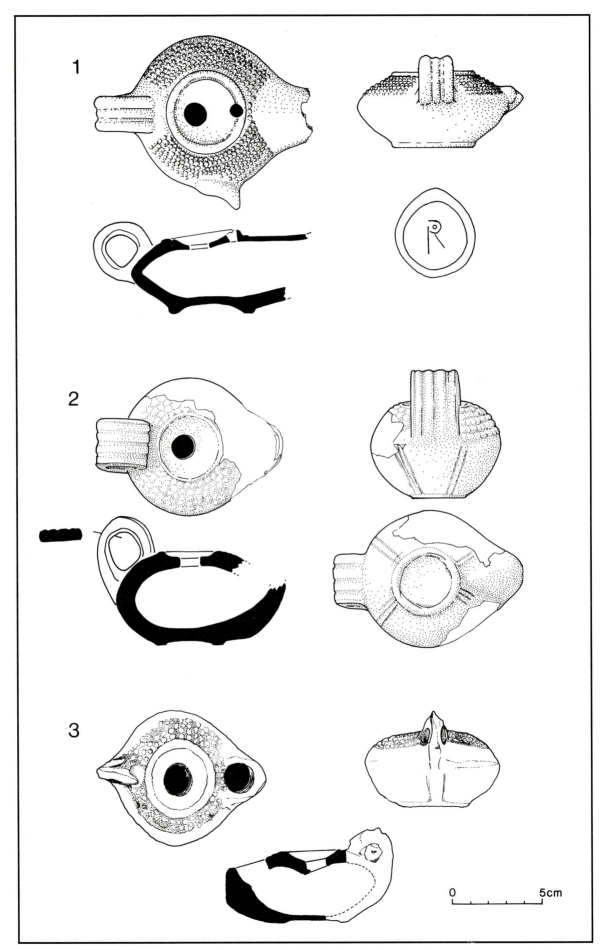

Fig. 62. Santa Rufina: lamps

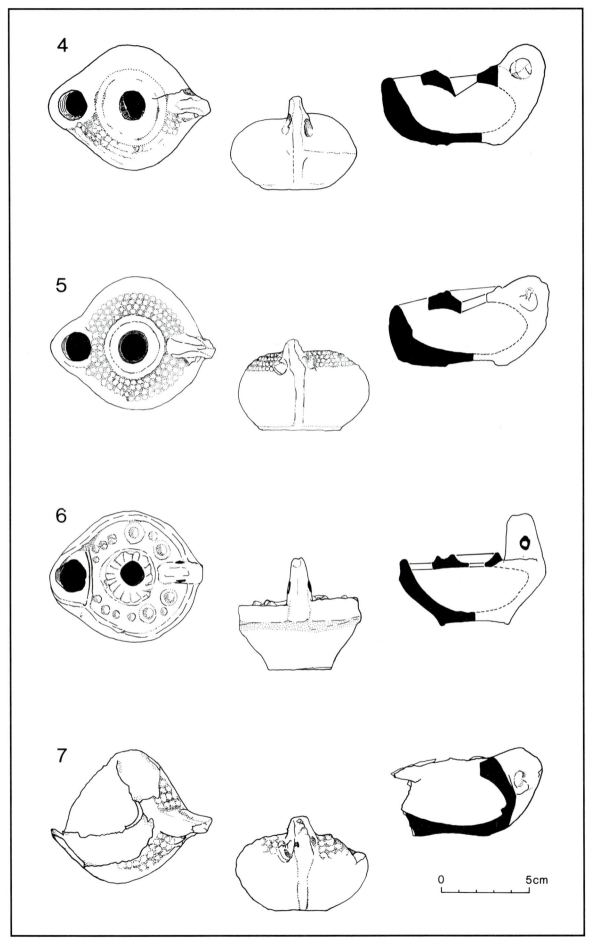

Fig. 63. Santa Rufina: lamps

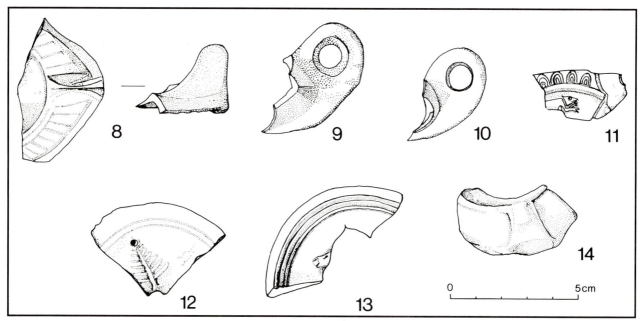

Fig. 64. Santa Rufina: lamps

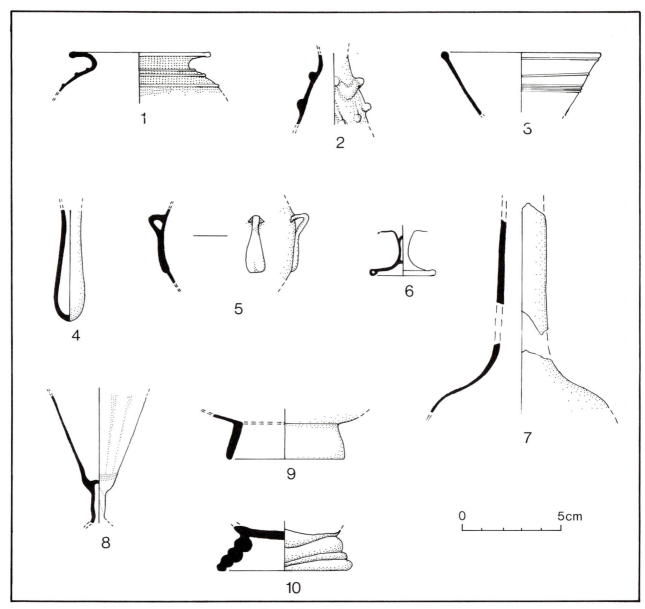

Fig. 65. Santa Rufina: glass

PROVENANCES:

Period IIIc:	6, 7.
Period V:	3, 8.
Period VI:	2, 9.
Period VII:	1, 5.
Not stratified:	4, 10.

(iii) BRONZE (Fig. 66)

1. (43) Bell with iron clapper, now very corroded. Attached to top, bronze loop. B.3.
2. (33) Two studs with short stems and domed heads. Pit H.
3. (85) Strip, slightly convex, with V-shaped section and hook or loop at one end. B.3.
4. (90) Ring with oval cross-section. DDD 1.4.
5. (87) Ring. HHH 1.2.
6. (27) Hook with one link of chain attached. oo Ex.1.5.
7. (38) One of two identical buckles with iron pins, found on either side of the pelvis of skeleton XVII, in ossuary IV.

8. (23) Pin with globular head. Pit C3.
9. (88) Wire, hooked at one end. oo Ex.1.4.
10. (28) One of two strips, possibly fittings from a wooden object. oo Ex.1.5, ossuary IV.
11. (40) Similar to 10. oo AA1.2.
12. (89) Handle.
13. (24) Chain, of which five links were recovered. oo Ex.1.5, ossuary IV.
14. (91) Disc with one flat and one concave surface. BB 1.2a.
15. (32) Perhaps part of bit. CCC 1.4.
16. (39) Buckle. oo 1.2, ossuary IV.
17. (92) Buckle. oo AA 1.2.
18. (86) Ring-headed pin. CCC 1.5.

PROVENANCES:

Period II:	12.
Period IIIc:	1, 3.
Period IV:	14.
Period V:	8.
Period VII:	2, 4, 6, 7 [2], 9, 10, 13, 15-18.
Not stratified:	5.

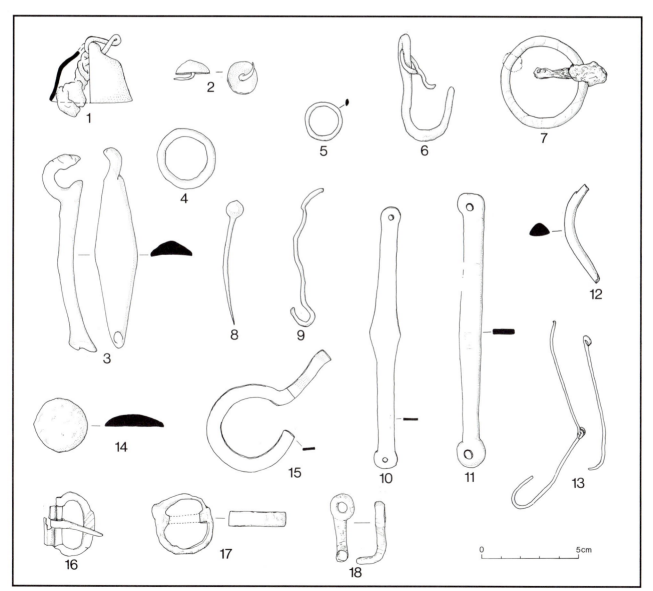

Fig. 66. Santa Rufina: bronze

(iv) IRON (Fig. 67)

1.   (30) Nail, one of seven, length 0.15 m. 111.6. In all, forty nails were recovered, all with square shafts. Here, three different sizes are illustrated.
2.   (78) Nail, one of two, length 0.10 m. DDD 1.9.
3.   (83) Nail, length 75 mm. oo Ex.1.5.
4.   (77) Disc with rectangular perforation at centre. DDD 1.9.
5.   (75) Perhaps split pin. 18.1.
6.   (74) Ingot. oo Ex.1.5.
7.   (76) Snaffle bit with two-link mouthpiece. 22.2.
8.   (28) Key with perforated, lozenge-shaped bow, solid shank and squarish bit. oo Ex.1.5.
9.   (37) Bar with lozenge-shaped terminal, which has looped staple attached. oo Ex.1.4.
10.   (81) Perhaps a ring. oo Ex.1.5.
11.   (31) Buckle with two tongues. CCC1.4.
12.   (82) Bar, looped at one end. CD1.4a.
13.   (79) Ring or collar. oo Ex.1.5.
14.   (80) Object. oo Ex.1.5.

PROVENANCES:

Period IIIa:	2, 4, 7.
Period IV:	cf. 2.
Period VII:	3, 6, 8-14.
Not stratified:	1, 5.

(v) MISCELLANEOUS SMALL FINDS (Fig. 68)

LEAD

Ten lead objects were found, mostly unidentifiable and from late deposits. A flattened lead fragment with signs of cutting was recovered beneath the floor of the room with the mosaic; the period V foundation trench for wall L yielded two cames, one of which is illustrated.

1.   (84) Came with H-shaped section, length 0.10 m.

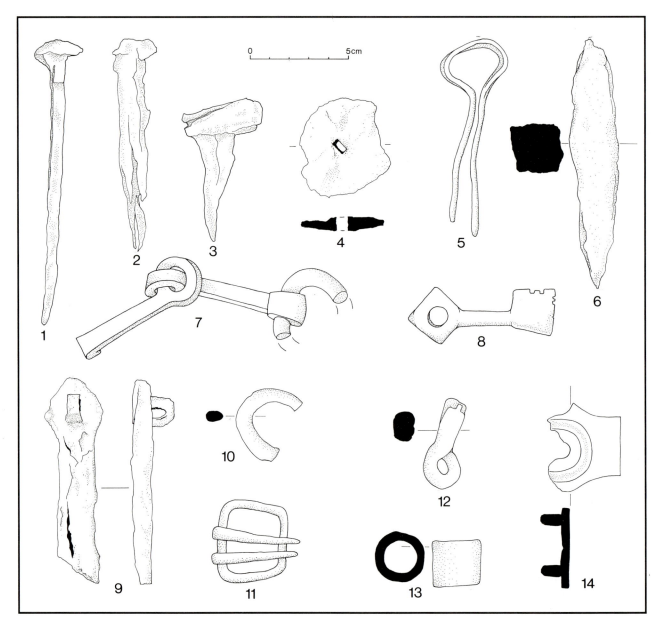

Fig. 67. Santa Rufina: iron

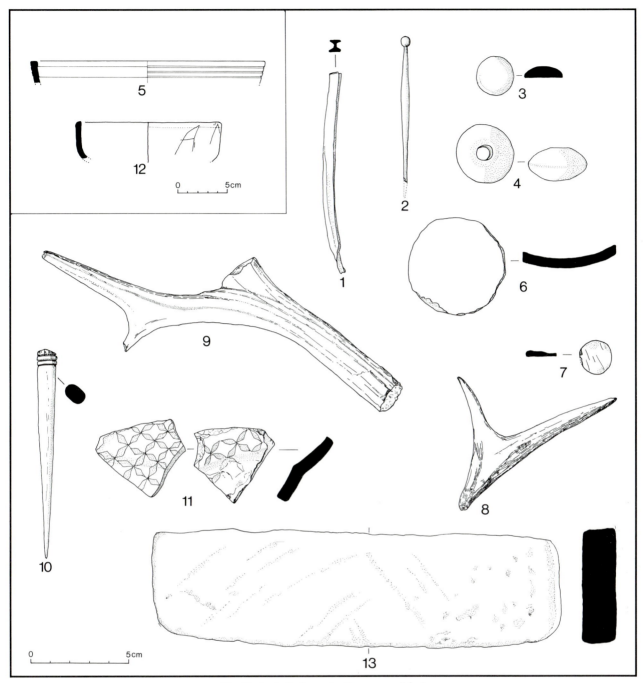

Fig. 68. Santa Rufina: miscellaneous small finds

BONE

2.   (29) Pin with globular head, carefully polished. (Cf. Davidson 1952, Pl. 119, number 2326.)

3.   (8) Gaming piece.

(94) Not illustrated: bone button with central perforation, incised and polished. Decorated with two concentric circles. Not stratified.

EARTHENWARE

4.   (48) Spindle whorl, buff clay.

6.   (12) Disc chipped from sherd of pink pottery.

12.   (3) Graffito on outside of bowl with cream clay and buff slip.

STONE

5.   (11) Bowl. Vertical rim with three grooves on outside. Green *pietra ollare* (Blake 1978, 161-162; Mannoni and Messiga 1980).

13.   (66) Grinding stone, 0.41 × 0.11 × 0.035 m, rounded at corners. Grey volcanic rock.

MOTHER OF PEARL

7.   (7) Counter or gaming piece.

ANTLER

8.   (64) Both tines are highly polished. Use unknown.

9.   (65) Similar. One tine is battered, apparently through use.

10.   (55) Point, length 90 mm, highly polished, with two incised bands.

GLASS

11.   (9) Described by the excavators as having 'black' elements in an opaque bluish matrix.

PROVENANCES:

Period IIIb: 6.
Period IV: 7.
Period V: 1, 2, 5, 11, 13.
Period VII: 4, 9.
Not stratified: 3, 10, 12.

(vi) TESSERAE

Frank Sear

(a) STONE

A great many tesserae were found, mainly in demolition layers later than the room with the mosaic (period VII) and in topsoil. The stone tesserae fall into two categories: (i) small black and white pieces, used for the background of the mosaic floor, and (ii) larger, well-cut tesserae from the centre motifs in the main design and border. The small back tesserae are basalt and the white ones limestone. All are somewhat irregular, varying in area from 15×12 mm to 8×8 mm and in depth from 10 to 30 mm. On the whole, the white tesserae are longer than the black. The large tesserae are of porphyry, verde antico and various other marbles. All have well-polished surfaces. They are regular in area, varying only a millimetre or two, the average being 28 mm square. The depth, however, varies between 12 and 20 mm. For a description of the mosaic floor itself, see above, Chapter 2, v.

(b) GLASS

About a hundred glass tesserae were found: thirty-nine were unstratified, six were single finds from various parts of the excavation, forty-four came from units associated with the robbing of the mausoleum. Apart from two white tesserae and three of 'black' glass, all are of varying shades of blue or green. Some of the pastel blue, turquoise and green tesserae are opaque; others, especially those that are medium blue and sea-green, are translucent. Many of the tesserae, notably the green and translucent turquoise ones, are bubbly and cracked. This characteristic, together with the large number of translucent tesserae and the particular range of colours, would indicate a rather late date for the mosaic to which they belonged.

Three fragments of plaster contain traces of the mosaic. The first has impressions only. In the holes can be seen black or very dark paint, probably part of a preliminary painting of the plaster, before the tesserae were attached. Similar traces of paint were found under the tesserae in the nymphaeum in Nero's Golden House (Lavagne 1970) and in Mausoleum M beneath Saint Peter's (Toynbee and Ward-Perkins 1956, 72-74).

In the second fragment, fifteen translucent turquoise tesserae survive. The glass is poor and the tesserae unevenly cut and laid. They vary in area from 3×8 mm to 6×10 mm and are set very closely together with very little plaster visible in the interstices. Behind the tesserae are traces of very pale turquoise paint, and in some of the holes where they have fallen out, red paint. In the third fragment, eleven tesserae survive, all translucent or opaque turquoise. They are roughly square and average 7 mm per side. The tesserae were pressed into a bed of white plaster 10 mm thick, behind which was a second layer 25 mm thick.

The fact that the tesserae are of glass, coupled with the type of plaster bed, indicate that the mosaic came from a wall or vault. As already indicated, the quality of the tesserae is perfectly consistent with the date proposed for the mausoleum on archaeological grounds (construction: period IIIc, fourth century AD; repairs and buttressing: period IV, fifth century). Nearly half the tesserae were found among debris from the mausoleum. It is likely, therefore, that the mosaic adorned the interior of this building.

(vii) WALL PLASTER

Numerous fragments of painted wall plaster were found, but none could be restored to make a recognisable design. Much of the material belongs to the following groups:

(a) Fragments from units attributed to periods IIIa and IIIb. These have a strong mortar base and a layer of plaster which varies in thickness up to 5 mm. The finely prepared surface is painted in purple, red and green with dark bands.

(b) Fragments from the highest filling in the collapsed catacomb of period IV. Again, the quality is good. The colours include green, yellow and purple.

(c) Fragments from debris associated with the demolition of the mausoleum and the ossuaries. The quality is poor. The paint is almost invariably applied directly to the mortar and the surface is rough. Some fragments are painted to imitate marble, others have architectural elements. There are light blue fragments and examples of bands decorated with white dots.

(viii) LAMPS (Figs 62-64)

(a) BAILEY TYPE R

Equates with Provoost 1970, type 5. A local product, which came into use in the mid- or late third century and lasted until the fifth century AD.

1.   (61) Two filling holes, crescentic thumb-plate and ribbed handle. Decorated with six rows of bosses. Inside base ring, letter R. Buff clay with orange-brown slip. MM1.4a. (Cf. Bailey 1980, 380 and Pl. 87, number Q1428.)

2.   (67) Broad ribbed handle. Four pairs of grooves extend upward from base. Decorated with four or five rows of bosses. Cream clay. T2.4, from the ledge of loculus VII.

3.   (70) Pinched handle. Decorated with four rows of bosses. Inside base ring, letters **PR** beneath cross. Buff clay. T2.3a. (Cf. Bailey 1980, 380 and 186, number Q1424.)

4.   (73) As above, but without mark. Buff clay with brown slip. T2.4, from ledge of loculus VII.

5.   (71) As above. Buff clay. T2.4.

7.   (69) As above. Buff clay. T2.4.

(b) BAILEY TYPE U

Equates with Provoost 1970, type 12, variant 2: 'catacomb' lamp. A local product of the fifth century, which may have continued for some time after *c.* 500.

6.   (68) Carinate body with almost vertical shoulder, flat top and pierced handle. On discus, rosette surrounded by bosses. Light brown clay. T2.4.

(c) MISCELLANEOUS

8.   (60) Vertical handle with single groove. Rim decorated with oblique grooves. Plain concave discus with groove at edge. Hard red clay. T2.3a.

9.   (10) Pierced, grooved handle. Cream clay. 5.5.

10.   (5) Pierced, grooved handle. Cream clay with brown mottled slip. I.1.2.

11.   (45) Concave discus decorated with animal running from left to right; at edge, ovules and pair of grooves. Buff clay with glossy reddish brown slip. North African. DDD1.9.

12.   (62) Discus has one filling hole and is decorated with palm frond. Cream clay, covered on outside with 'thick shiny green glaze'. 5.5a.

13.   (44) Discus with animal head and three concentric grooves at edge. Buff clay with red to dark brown slip. DDD1.9. (Cf. Perlzweig 1961, Pl. 3, number 65, which has biga and driver.)

NOT ILLUSTRATED

14.   (11) As 13, but with two grooves on shoulder. DDD1.9.

15.   (47) Plain concave discus with one filling hole and groove at edge. Buff clay with red slip. DDD1.9.

16.   (46) Cream clay with mottled orange-brown slip. (Cf. Perlzweig 1961, 81, number 99). DDD1.9.

17.   (6) As 13. 16.4.

18.   (53) Abraded fragment. Cream clay with orange slip. IK 1.4.

19.   (50) Plain discus with groove at edge. Cream clay. KK1.3.

20.   (72) Broneer type XXVIII, with perforated handle. T2.3b.

21.   (2) Saucer lamp with inturned rim and slightly pinched lip. 00 1.1.

22.   (13) Fragment. V 1.10.

PROVENANCES:

Period II:	1
Period IIIa:	11 (and 1 similar), 13 (and 1 similar), 14-16, 22.
Period IIIb:	9, 12.
Period IIIc:	2, 4, cf. 5 (2 examples), 6, 7, 19.
Period IV:	3, 8, 20.
Period V:	18.
Not stratified:	10, 21.

(ix) TERRACOTTA, BRICK AND TILE (Figs 69 and 70)

(a) TUBULAR TILES (Fig. 69)

These are approximately 0.20 m long and 55 mm in diameter, with sides 7 mm thick. The wall runs straight for

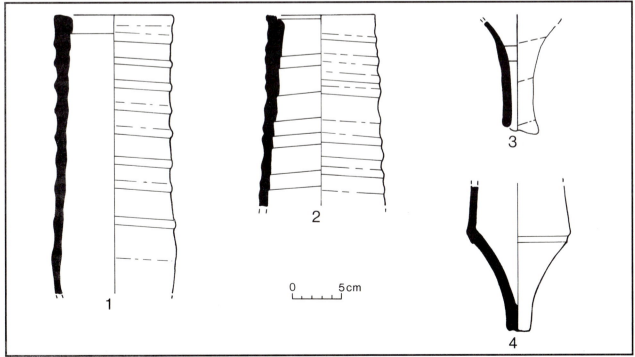

Fig. 69. Santa Rufina: tubular tiles

0.14 m, then curves inward to a pointed base, which may be open or closed. The turning marks are pronounced on the interior and exterior alike. The clay usually is cream or pink.

1.   (P344a) Open tubular fragment.
2.   (P344a) As above.
3.   (P344a) Open base.
4.   (P344b) Closed base.

    One hundred and thirty-five fragments were found. The greatest number came from the site of the mausoleum, which suggests that they formed part of its roof. Most of the remainder were found on the slope to the east of the mausoleum. For the use of earthenware tubes in the construction of vaults and domes, see Arslan (1965).

(b) OTHER OBJECTS (Fig. 70)

1.   (59) Possibly part of a sarcophagus with moulded decoration: woman seated on a dolphin, looking right. Coarse buff-grey clay.

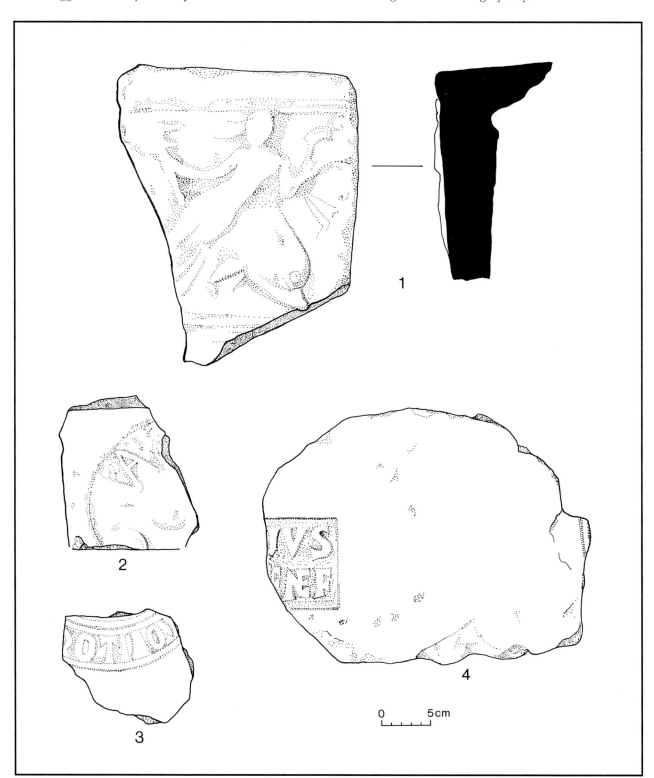

Fig. 70. Santa Rufina: terracotta, brick and tile

2. (96) Circular brick stamp:

    ...]A[..

    Coarse buff clay.

3. (63) Circular brick stamp:

    ...]OTI O[...

    Coarse buff clay.

4. (95) Rectangular brick stamp:

    ...]IVS [...
    ...]ENE F[...

    Buff clay.

5. Not illustrated. Tegula, 0.5 m long, 0.37 m wide at one end and 0.43 m wide at other end, with flanges 30 mm high. At narrower end, impressed semi-circle and ring of ten impressed circles, 30 mm across. Pink clay.

6. (100) Not illustrated. Tegula with dimensions as 5, although flanges are lower at narrow end. Found on floor of catacomb: evidently from one of the loculi.

PROVENANCES:

Period IIIc:	6.
Period IV:	1, 4.
Period VII:	3.
Not stratified:	2, 5.

(x) ETRUSCAN POTTERY (Figs 71 and 72)

This includes (a) bucchero, (b) painted, (c) coarse, and (d) internal slip ware.

(a) BUCCHERO

71.1 (P634) Bowl. Gritty light grey clay with dull, black burnished surfaces.

71.2 (P731) Shallow bowl. Gritty light grey clay with very dull, black burnished surfaces. (Cf. Murray-Threipland and Torelli 1970, 87, Fig. 2.6.)

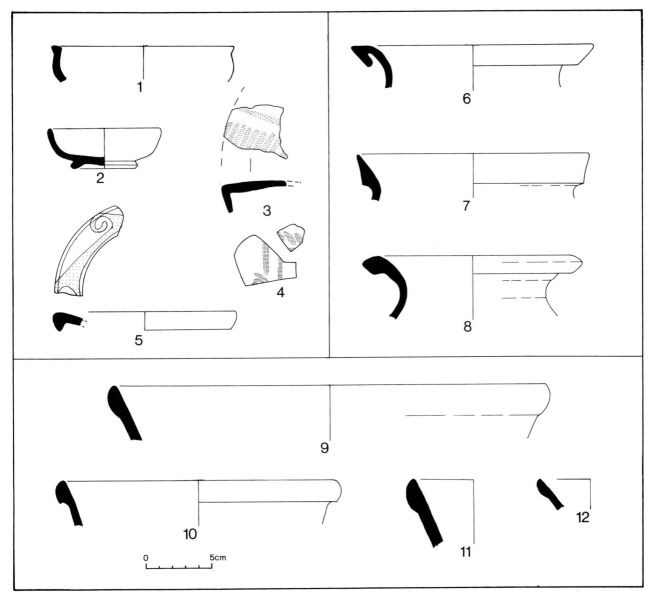

Fig. 71. Santa Rufina: Etruscan pottery

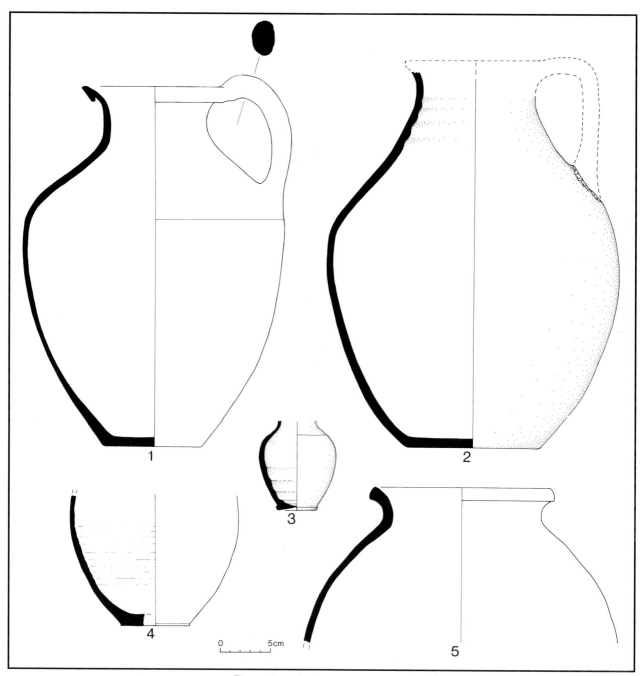

Fig. 72. Santa Rufina: Etruscan pottery

(b) PAINTED POTTERY

71.3   (P24) Lid. Fine light buff clay with thin brown and black slip on side and upper surface. Part of large fan palmette in matt black slip.

71.4   (P329 and P676) Two fragments. Light buff clay. Dull black exterior, decorated with part of palmette scroll. Prof. Trendall comments: 'the fragments probably come from a beaked *oinochoe* (shape vii) of the Phantom Group – see *EVP* (Beazley 1947) 205, where a list of these vases is given'. He suggests a date in the later fourth century BC.

71.5   (P74) Plate. Fine, light buff clay. On upper surface of rim, wave pattern in black to red slip. Under rim, horizontal band, also in black to red. One similar piece (P143) not illustrated. Prof. Trendall writes: 'These two fragments of star

plates showing the wave border are from the Genucilia group. For Genucilia plates, see Beazley *EVP* (1947), 175f – later fourth century BC'.

(c) COARSE POTTERY

The only forms are jugs and a juglet. The clay of the jugs is less well levigated than that of the juglet. It is gritty, with quartzite and black augite inclusions. The colour varies from cream to pink or buff. The juglet is cream. Numbers 7 and 8 have a smooth cream surface.

(i) **Jugs**

71.6   (P106) Rim with everted, strongly hooked lip and curving neck (2 examples).

71.7 (P107) Rim, collared, with pointed lip and curving neck.

71.8 (P454) Rim, flat-topped and bevelled outside, with deeply curved neck.

72.1 (P436) Jug. Rim hooked, though less markedly so than on 33.6. Neck merges gently with piriform body. Base flat. Oval-section handle rises from rim and is attached above maximum diameter, where there is a shallow groove.

72.2 (P2) Jug.

(ii) Juglet

72.3 Neck, body and base, with cordon at base of neck. Piriform body with pad base.

(d) INTERNAL SLIP WARE

71.9 (P109a) Jar. Coarse grey-brown clay with brown outer surface. On inside and top of rim, burnished yellowish slip. (Cf. Murray-Threipland and Torelli 1970, 116, Fig. 31.12.)

71.10 (P453) As above, but with slightly hooked almond rim (2 examples).

71.11 (P109) Jar, cf. 71.9 (4 examples).

71.12 (P104) Similar, but smaller (3 examples).

72.4 (P161) Base of jar. Coarse, grey-brown clay with patchy cream slip on interior and horizontal burnish marks. Some time after firing, base was perforated.

72.5 (P632) Upper part of large jar. Coarse, gritty grey-brown clay with light brown surfaces. On inside and top of rim, yellowish slip with roughly horizontal burnishing.

PROVENANCES:

Period I: 71.3, 71.4 (P676), cf. 71.5 (P143), 71.9, 71.11 (2 examples) and 71.12 (3 examples)
Period IIIa: Cf. 71.11
Period IIIc: 71.10 and cf. 72.4
Period IV: 71.10
Period V: 71.1, 71.2, 72.5
Period VII: 71.5 (P74)
Not stratified: 71.4 (P329)

(xi) BLACK SLIPPED POTTERY (Figs 73 and 74.1-15)

Parts of at least sixty-three diagnostic vessels were found. The clay varied considerably. Most pieces had orange clay, but others were light brown or pink. In general, the clay was smooth and well-levigated; several, however, had coarser clay. A few contained mica and were fired to a hard consistency. As far as the black 'glaze' is concerned, only one or two vessels were fired completely successfully, and very few had a uniform black finish. Most varied in colour from grey to brown, with some shading to orange. The surface was more often shiny than not, and frequently thin. Most vessels had a dull sheen, but some were quite glossy and others completely matt.

On only a few vessels did the workmanship reach a high standard. Many were badly fired, and several had turning marks or flaws on the surface. Indeed, some of the vessels were coarse enough to suggest that they were local copies of established products. Given the diversity of fabrics, it appeared that several centres of production supplied the site.

The forms comprise (i) plates, (ii) lids, (iii) bowls, (iv) jugs, (v) jars, and perhaps (vi) skyphoi. The commonest of these are bowls, examples with incurved (nine examples) or ribbon band rims (seven) being particularly frequent. Among the bases, the most frequent type of footring has a straight oblique interior and a bevelled exterior (73.6, 74.5, 74.9-11). Two specimens, however, have straight oblique sides (74.8, 74.14). Two others have pedestals (73.1, 73.4).

The small amount of decoration is confined to the interior of the vessel: two bowls have stamped rosettes, each consisting of a dot in a dotted circle (e.g. 74.11); one has a stamped palmette, for which no precise parallel was found (74.7); a few fragments have zones of rouletting (e.g. 74.9, 74.14); a bowl with an out-turned rim has two concentric grooves (73.19) and another bowl has a tiny central indentation encircled by a small shallow groove (74.13).

(a) PLATES

73.1 (P13) Plate with high pedestal foot and convex rim with overhang. Slender pedestal, flaring to broad foot with retrousals. Hollow base. Pale orange clay. Exterior and base reserved except for two retroussis and decorative band, 15 mm wide, in middle of wall. Thick, shiny black slip.
(Cf. Morel 1965, 51-52, number 65, and Morel 1963, 43-44, Form 81. In the former, Morel states that the form derives from Genucilia plates, adding that 'black glazed vessels of form 81 must have continued to be made during the course of the third century (or at least during the first half of that century)'. In the latter, he reports that form 81 occurs in tombs of the period c. 340-290 BC in southern Italy.)

73.12 (P213) Plate with incurving upturned rim. Exterior of rim slightly ridged. Light orange clay. Thick, glossy black slip on both surfaces. Three other examples.
(Cf. Lamboglia 1952, 146, form 5a, in Campana B ware, which according to Taylor's (1975, 148) revised chronology for Ventimiglia belongs to the first century BC.)

73.13 (P617) Plate with carinate wall and slightly concave out-turned rim. Coarse, poorly levigated reddish orange clay. Uneven, but quite thick and shiny black slip on interior; slip on exterior uneven, thinner greyish brown with slight sheen.

73.14 (P223) Plate or lid. Rounded rim with groove on interior. Poorly levigated light grey-brown clay. Thin slip with slight sheen on both surfaces.

74.2 (P658) Plate with horizontal offset rim. Irregular circle of rouletting near centre. Coarse, reddish orange clay with grey patches. Silvery black slip on both sides; quite thick on exterior and inner surface of rim, slightly thinner elsewhere on interior; moderate sheen.
(Cf. Lamboglia 1952, 168, form 6, in Campana A ware, late second and first centuries BC and

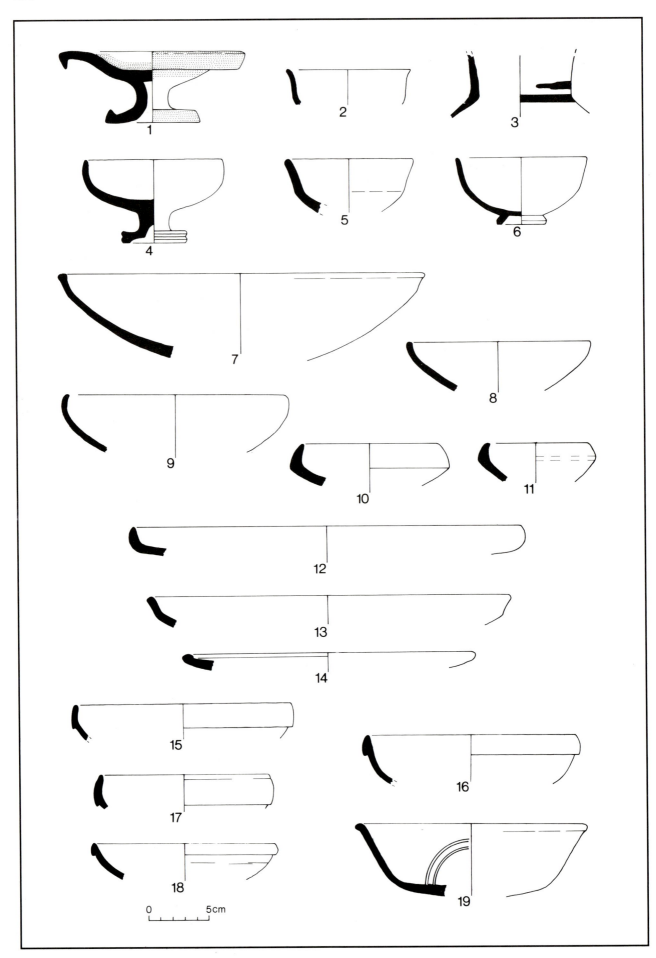

Fig. 73. Santa Rufina: black slipped pottery

Taylor 1975, D1a in type I fabric. The form did not appear at Cosa until the last quarter of the second century, or perhaps even later; it probably remained in use until c. 40-30 BC. In both cases, the rim edge is slightly different from our example, which may be a local version.)

74.14   (P256) Plate? Fragment of base. Footring has short oblique exterior and straight inner surface. Rouletting near centre. Coarse orange clay. On interior of vessel, slip is brown-black with slight sheen except where rouletted, which is reddish brown and matt. Exterior more shiny but uneven, varying from black, through dark brown to orange. Underside of base has brown slip with slight sheen.

(b) LID

74.4   (P729) Coarse grey-brown clay. Thin, dark grey-black slip with slight sheen on both surfaces. (Cf. Taylor 1975, 172, B52b in fabric Type III, Campana C, 'known at Cosa by c. 140 BC. It was in use, but rare, in the late second and first centuries'.)

(c) BOWLS

73.2   Bowl with thin flaring rim. Orange to light grey clay. Thin, somewhat uneven black slip on both surfaces, brownish on rim. (No close parallel, but see Duncan 1965, 146, form 13, number 52.)

73.4   (P267) Bowl with incurving rim and low pedestal foot, which flares at bottom, with slight retroussis. Deep groove round edge of base, underside of which is concave with central conical depression. Orange clay. Thick, glossy slip, olive green and brown on interior, black to olive green and brown (the dominant colour) on outside; edge of rim brown; splashes of slip on edge and underside of base. Poorly fired. (Cf. Morel 1965, number 263. He publishes one fragment of a pedestal base, but the description of the clay is comparable to our example; his base, however, has a ring round the pedestal and no retroussis. Also, Lamboglia 1952, form 4c, Campana A: 'vases of this kind are already noted in Greek ceramics at the end of the sixth and in the fifth centuries, with numerous variations'. Also Lake 1934-1935, type 48, with similar base but sharp rim, and Fabbricotti 1969, 59 and 130, Pl. XX, which is perhaps the closest parallel, although it lacks grooves on the base.)

73.5   (P523) Bowl with slightly out-turned, concave rim and carination, below which wall curves sharply inward. Slightly coarse, light orange clay, grey in places. Fairly thick, glossy black slip. (Cf. Morel 1965, 215, type 96a, third century BC.)

73.6   (P8) Bowl with plain rim, curved wall and small base with bevelled foot. Exterior slightly rilled. Rim distorted. Light orange clay. Fairly thick black slip with slight sheen. Underside of base reserved. Graffito on side, near centre: perhaps gamma and alpha in capitals. (No close parallels,

although Duncan 1965, 145, form 10, is similar. For a larger version, see Lake 1934-1935, type 17.)

73.7   (P605) Bowl with out-turned rim and carinate wall. Pinkish orange clay. Thin, matt grey-black slip, uneven on outside.

73.8   (P236) Bowl with slightly incurving rim and swelling lip. Slightly coarse, micaceous orange clay with grey patches. Fairly thick, glossy black slip. (Cf. Taylor 1975, form A22 in fabric Type I, Campana A: 'The unpainted bowl with incurved rim was known at Cosa in the first half of the second century, perhaps earlier. It continued in use during most of that century'. See also Lamboglia 1952, 176, form 27, also Campana A: 'beginning in the fourth century and in common use throughout the third and second centuries B.C.' Examples are cited from Enserune, Minturnae, Ampurias and Ventimiglia.)

73.9   (P82) Bowl with incurving rim. Fine orange clay. Uneven, glossy black slip, thinner and slightly brown on inside of rim. A common form: eight other examples. (Cf. Duncan 1965, 144, form 6; Lamboglia 1952, 176, form 27; Morel 1965, number 133, compared to Lamboglia's form 27b.)

73.10   (P728) Bowl with sharply carinate side and incurved rim. Pale orange clay. Exterior has thick, black, lustrous slip; slip on interior is thinner, with dull sheen. (Cf. Lamboglia 1952, 182, form 34b, Campana A: second century BC; Morel 1965, numbers 59, 192. Morel suggests that it may be necessary to revise Lamboglia's chronology, since the form may be of Etruscan origin. It is found in bucchero and impasto, for example, at Todi in a fourth-third century BC cemetery: Villa Giulia Museum, inventory number 2771, 9671. See also Taylor 1975, type D10b, in fabric Type I, Campana A, attributed to the period c. 130/120–70/60 BC.)

73.11   (P80) Bowl with carinate side and incurved rim. Coarse, pale orange clay. Slip is thick, black and lustrous on exterior, thinner, uneven and grey-brown to matt black on interior; both sides of rim are matt light brown. (Cf. 73.10.)

73.15   (P674) Bowl with broad ribbon-band rim; distinctive ridge at junction of rim and wall. Coarse orange clay. Slip uneven, matt dark brown on exterior, matt grey-black on inside, thin on rim. Poorly made. (Cf. Taylor 1975, 184, B13, etc., in Type IV clay, local: second century BC. See also Duncan 1965, 144, form 7, number 35, also with a ridge at the base of the rim and larger than our example.)

73.16   (P699) Bowl with incurved ribbon-band rim. Bright orange clay with lighter patches. Greenish black lustrous slip. (Cf. Duncan 1965, 144, form 7, number 37, mid-second century BC or later; Morel 1965, numbers 47, 202, probably third or early second century BC; Taylor 1975, 88 and 185, A31a.)

73.17   (P616) Bowl with broad ribbon-band rim and straightened lip. Very pale brown clay. Slip is brown shading to grey, with slight sheen on

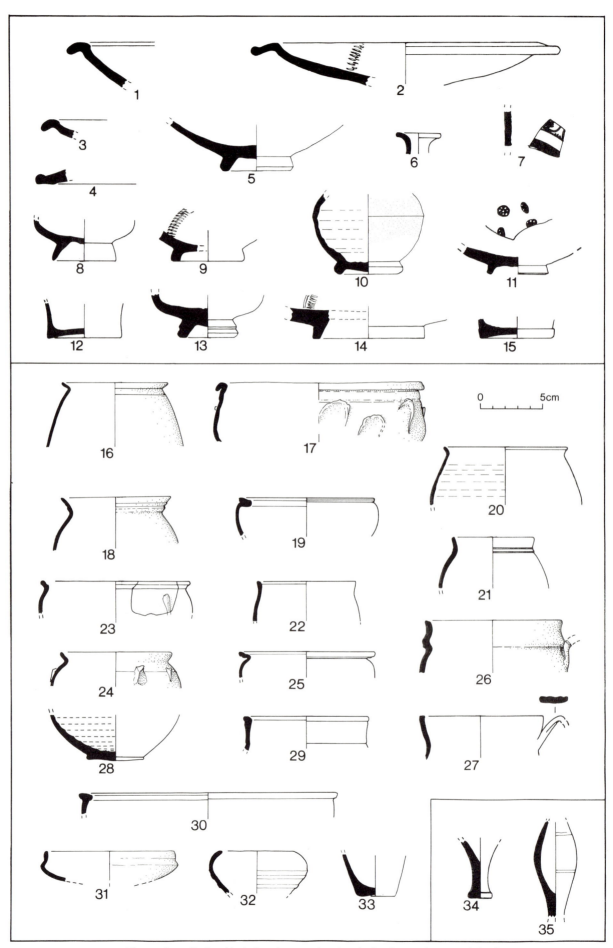

Fig. 74. Santa Rufina: black slipped pottery (1-15) and other Roman fine wares (16-35)

exterior, grey black with thin brown patches on inside.

(No good parallels, but cf. Duncan 1965, 144, form 7, and Taylor 1975, 184, 'bowl with ribbon-band rim' of Type IV clay, especially A28, which is probably a smaller version of our fragment.)

73.18 (P656) Bowl with small ribbon-band rim. Light orange-pink clay. Thick, lustrous, metallic grey slip, brown on rim.
(Cf. Morel 1965, numbers 47, 384.)

73.19 (P618) Bowl with out-turned rim; two concentric grooves on bottom of interior. Pale orange clay. Slip ranges from black, through chocolate to light brown and orange on outside, is mottled brown-black to chocolate on interior.
(Cf. Duncan 1965, 140, form 5, number 11, mid-second century BC; Taylor 1975, 157, A14, Type II clay.)

74.1 (P659) Bowl with horizontal recurving rim. Coarse, pale orange-brown clay with mica. Thin black slip with slight sheen on walls and shiny rim.
(Cf. Taylor 1975, 146, C16, etc., in Type I clay, 'the second half of the second century BC seems to represent the period of their popularity at Cosa'; Lamboglia 1952, 183, form 36, Campana A, 'a long-lived form most frequent in sites of the third century and above all the second and first centuries'.)

74.3 (P480) Bowl with short horizontal recurving rim. Coarse light brown clay. Fairly thin, matt grey slip. A variant of 74.1.

74.5 (P148) Bowl with ring-base and bevelled foot. Coarse orange to light brown clay. Slip is black on interior with slight sheen, matt grey-black to brown on outside; uneven, matt dark-brown slip on side of foot; underside reserved, with touches of slip.

74.8 (P732) Bowl with ring-base and raised foot. Smooth, pale orange clay. Slip is black shading to tan on both surfaces, dull on interior, shiny on exterior; side of foot similar to outer surface; underside of base reserved.
(Perhaps cf. Taylor 1975, 108, C9 and Pl. VII, although this is of Type IV, local clay; Morel 1965, number 236 is similar, but has a wider, taller base.)

74.9 (P725) Bowl with low ring-base and curved foot; circle of rouletting on bottom of interior. Very pale orange clay. Fairly thick, lustrous black slip on both surfaces; side of foot is matt black, shading to grey-brown, lustrous in patches; underside of base reserved, but with touch of slip.

74.11 (P75) Bowl with ring-base and bevelled foot. Bottom of interior stamped with rosette pattern consisting of one dot encircled by seven other dots, all in relief. Coarse, pale orange clay. Slip is lustrous grey-black, shading to light brown on both surfaces; foot incompletely covered and only locally lustrous; underside of base reserved, with small patch of slip.
(Cf. Taylor 1975, 131, D26a1, in Type I clay, Campana A; Morel 1965, 103, number 217.)

74.13 (P716) Bowl with ring-base and raised bevelled foot; lower part of foot grooved. On bottom of

interior, small central depression surrounded by concentric groove. Bright orange clay with pale patches and traces of mica. Thin, lustrous, silvery grey-black slip on both surfaces, shading to brown on outside and foot; underside of base has similar slip.
(Cf. Duncan 1965, 147, number 62.)

(d) JUGS

73.3 (P157) Jug or amphora; flaring neck with broad rim and upturned lip; faint ridge just below junction of rim and neck. Very pale orange clay with trace of mica. On upper rim surface, thick matt brown slip; thin, slightly lustrous black slip on inside of neck; exterior reserved, except for interrupted band of matt brown to black slip on neck and light matt brown band on lower part of rim.

74.6 (P434) Flaring neck with out-turned rim. Light orange clay. Thick slip, lustrous dark grey to black on both surfaces, thin and brownish on rim.
(A tiny fragment, but perhaps cf. Taylor 1975, 130, D21e.)

(e) JAR

74.10 (P243) Jar with ring-base, bevelled foot and carinate side. Coarse orange clay with mica. Part, only, of exterior wall with thin brown slip.
(Cf. Morel 1965, number 221.)

(f) SKYPHOI

74.12 (P612) Perhaps a skyphos; concave base and thin, flaring side. Fine, very pale orange clay. Reserved bands of lustrous black slip and small patch of brown on exterior.

74.15 (P611) Perhaps a skyphos; thick concave base with ribbed foot and curving side. Fine, very pale orange clay. Slip on exterior only, extending upwards from base: thick, lustrous black with dark brown patches; some accidental splashes.
(Cf. Morel 1965, number 520; although the base differs from our example, the clay is almost identical. See also Lamboglia 1952, 190, form 43a, Campana A: ' the longest-lived vase, most frequent in levels of the fourth and third centuries', although one fragment from Ventimiglia was found in Stratum IV, datable to the second century BC; Lake 1934-1935, types 34-36, 101.)

(g) DECORATED FRAGMENTS

74.7 (P72) Thin, flat fragment, probably from a plate with stamped palmettes. The complete decoration, it seems, was a concentric series of adjoining palmettes. Nearer the centre, two shallow concentric grooves. Coarse light orange clay. Fairly thick black slip with moderate sheen.

PROVENANCES:

Period I: 73.2, 73.4, 73.6, 73.9, 73.11
Period II: 73.15, 73.17 and cf. 73.6; 74.1, 74.2, 74.4, 74.9 and cf. 74.5
Period IIIa: 73.10, 73.13, 73.19 and cf. 73.8; 74.12, 74.15 and cf. 74.5
Period IIIb: 73.3 and cf. 73.5
Period IIIc: 73.7, 73.8, 73.12, 73.14, cf. 73.15-16; 74.5 (and 2 similar), 74.7, 74.14 (and 1 similar)
Period IVa: 73.5
Period V: 73.1, 73.6, 73.16; 74.3, 74.6, 74.10, cf. 74.5 and 74.9
Period VII: 74.11
Not stratified: 74.8

(xii) MISCELLANEOUS FINE WARES
(Figs 74.16-35 and 79.24-27)

These comprise: (i) colour-coated beakers, (ii) plain beakers, (iii) colour-coated bowls, (iv) plain bowls, (v) unguentaria, and (vi) one glazed fragment.

(a) COLOUR-COATED BEAKERS

74.16   (P42) Buff clay with darker slip inside and out, and irridescent orange inside (four examples). (Duncan 1965, form 1, c. AD 60-70).

74.18   Flaring out-turned rim with groove on inner side. Buff clay with slightly darker slip.

74.20   (P411) Short out-turned rim. Orange clay, with orange slip on both surfaces (two examples).

74.21   (P786) Flaring rim with two ridges on outside. Slightly granular brown clay with brown interior and grey exterior.

74.24   (P54) Buff clay with trace of darker slip and applied petals on outside (two examples).

74.33   (P149) Light brown clay with darker slip on outside (nine examples).

(b) PLAIN BEAKERS

74.22   (P58) Fine cream clay.
74.26   (P53) Light brown clay. (Duncan 1965, 141, form 7. Claudian/Neronian.)
74.27   (P767) Fine pink clay with buff exterior.
74.33   (P149) Light brown clay.

(c) COLOUR-COATED BOWLS

74.17   (P43) Light brown clay with darker slip on exterior; barbotine decoration (one other example).

74.19   (P392) Cream clay with orange slip.

74.23   (P769) Buff clay with orange slip on both surfaces; applied petals on outside.

74.25   (P374) Cream clay with brown slip on both surfaces.

74.28   (P126) Slightly gritty light brown clay with irridescent brown slip; roughcast (four other examples).

74.29   (P172) Light brown clay with brown slip.

79.24   (P50) Buff clay with red slip (three other examples)

79.25   (P6, P7) Buff clay with reddish brown slip on neck and upper part of body. (Duncan 1965, 157, form 37, c. AD 60-70.)

79.26   (P150) Buff clay with orange slip on both surfaces.

(d) PLAIN BOWLS

74.30   (P532) Slightly granular pinkish brown clay.
74.31   (P41) Fine cream clay.
74.32   (P372) Fine cream clay.

(e) UNGUENTARIA

74.34   (P570) Fairly hard pinkish brown clay with dark brown slip.

74.35   (P723) Fairly hard buff clay with dark brown slip.

(f) GLAZED

79.27   (P4) Fine buff clay with glaze on both surfaces, now cream and much worn, perhaps originally green and/or yellow; applied rosettes, each with four ribbons.

PROVENANCES:

Period IIIa: 74.16 (2), 74.17 (2), 74.18, 74.20 (2), 74.24 (2), 74.26, 74.27, 74.28 (4), 74.31, 74.33, 74.44 (2), 79.24 (2), 79.25 (2)
Period IIIb: 74.23, 74.33 (5), 74.29, cf. 79.24 and 79.26 (2)
Period IIIc: cf. 74.16 and 74.33
Period IV: 74.19, 74.25, 74.30, 74.32, 74.33, 74.35, 79.26 (2)
Period V: 74.22 and cf. 74.34
Not stratified: 74.21, 79.27, cf. 74.28, cf. 74.33-34

(xiii) TERRA SIGILLATA (Figs 75 and 76)

The terra sigillata falls into three groups: (i) Arretine, (ii) late Italic, and (iii) South Gaulish.

(a) ARRETINE

Plates:

75.1   (P39) Loeschke 1909, form 00, c. AD 0-25.
75.2   (P146) Goudineau 1968 type 15, c. AD 15 or later (one other example).
75.4   (P610) Loeschke 1909, form 5a, c. AD 0-25.
75.6   (P620) Possibly cf. 75.1.
76.11 (P606) Cf. Oswald and Price 1920, 23, Pl. XLII. Claudian?
76.15 (P542)

Bowls:

75.3   (P171) One other example.
75.5   (P158)

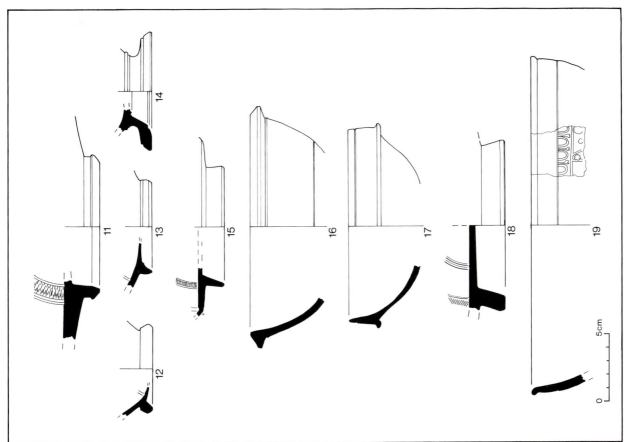

Fig. 76. Santa Rufina: terra sigillata

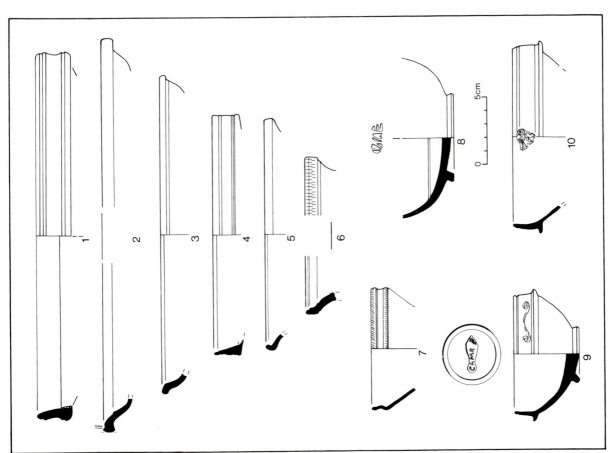

Fig. 75. Santa Rufina: terra sigillata

75.9   (P35) Stamp of CAMVR and part of 'oreille spirale' appliqué: Goudineau 1968, type 38, Claudian-Neronian. For stamp *in planta pedis*, Oxe and Comfort 1968, 397: variant of CAMVRIVS.

75.10   (P176) Cf. 75.9. Appliqué of putto playing double pipes (one other example).

76.12   (P821)

76.13   (P321)

76.14   (P609)

75.7   (P40) Loeschke 1909, form 8, c. AD 0-25.

(b) LATE ITALIC

75.8   (P34) The form resembles bowls from the Prima Porta kiln and the stamp is a variant of the commonest type. Claudian-Neronian.

76.16   (P36) Similar to 75.8 (one other example)

76.17   (P38) Goudineau 1968, type 38. Claudian-Neronian.

76.18   (P37)

(c) SOUTH GAULISH

76.19   Rim of bowl.

PROVENANCES:

Period IIIa: 75.1, cf. 75.3, 75.4, 75.6-10, 76.12-14, 76.16-18

Period IIIb: 75.2, 75.3, 75.5, 76.11

Period IVa: 76.15

Not stratified: 76.19

(xiv) AFRICAN RED SLIP WARE (Figs 77, 78 and 79.16-23)

The type-series and chronology are those of Hayes (1972, 1980).

77.1   (P677) Orange to buff clay with pale grey core and dull dark orange slip on both surfaces.

77.2   (P45) Hard pink clay with dark orange slip on both surfaces. On rim, appliqués from worn moulds: panther at rest, looking left towards three loops of draped ribbon; mask of bearded male, either Dionysus or satyr, crowned, looking right; stemmed cup(?). For a parallel from Santa Prisca, see Vermaseren and Van Essen 1965, 483, number 146, Fig. 400.1. Carandini *et al.* 1968, 62-63, Fig. 119 and Pl. LV, 776.

78.1   (P258) Hayes 8a, c. 80/90-160 + (two other examples).

78.2   (P257) Hayes 9a, c. 100-160.

78.3   (P819) Cf. Hayes 6b, mid- to end second century.

78.9   (P301)

78.10   (P816) Perhaps Hayes 52, probably mid- to late fourth century.

78.12   (P501) Hayes 67, c. 360-470.

79.16   (P547) Hayes 91a/b, late fourth to late fifth century.

79.18   (P813) Hayes 92, c. 510-540 (one other example).

79.23   (P814) Hayes 91, c. 600-650.

78.6   (P614) Hayes 6, mid- to end of second century.

78.7   (P177) As 78.6.

78.11   (P526) Hayes 61a, c. 325-380 (two other examples).

78.14   (P740) Possibly Hayes 50, c. 300-360 (two other examples).

78.15   (P613) Hayes 64, early to mid-fifth century.

79.17   (P77) Perhaps Hayes 61, late fourth to fifth century.

78.8   (P153) Dull slip and blackened exterior. Hayes 23b, mid-second to early third century.

78.4   (P540) Perhaps Hayes 182, c. 150-250?

78.5   (P808) Cf. 78.4.

78.13   (P538) Cf. 78.6. Decorated with stamped palm branches and groups of circles. Hayes 67, stamp style A(ii), c. 350-420.

79.22   (P138) Possibly Hayes 8 or 9, second century (four other examples).

79.20   (P385) Hayes 105, c. 570-660.

79.21   (P384) Cf. 79.20.

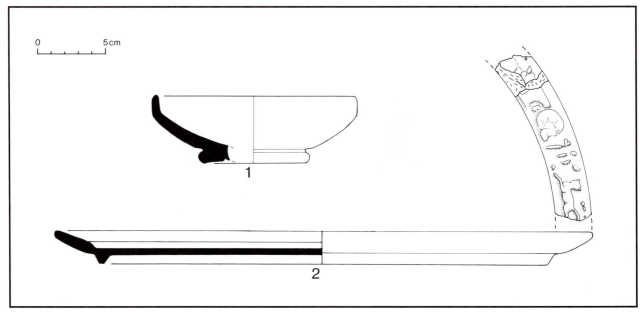

Fig. 77. Santa Rufina: African red slip ware

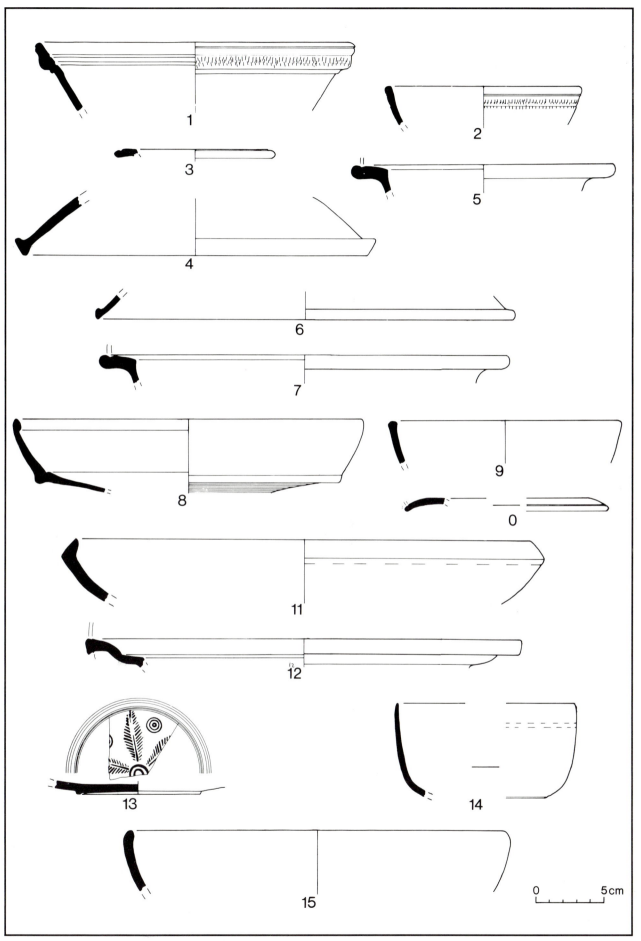

Fig. 78. Santa Rufina: African red slip ware

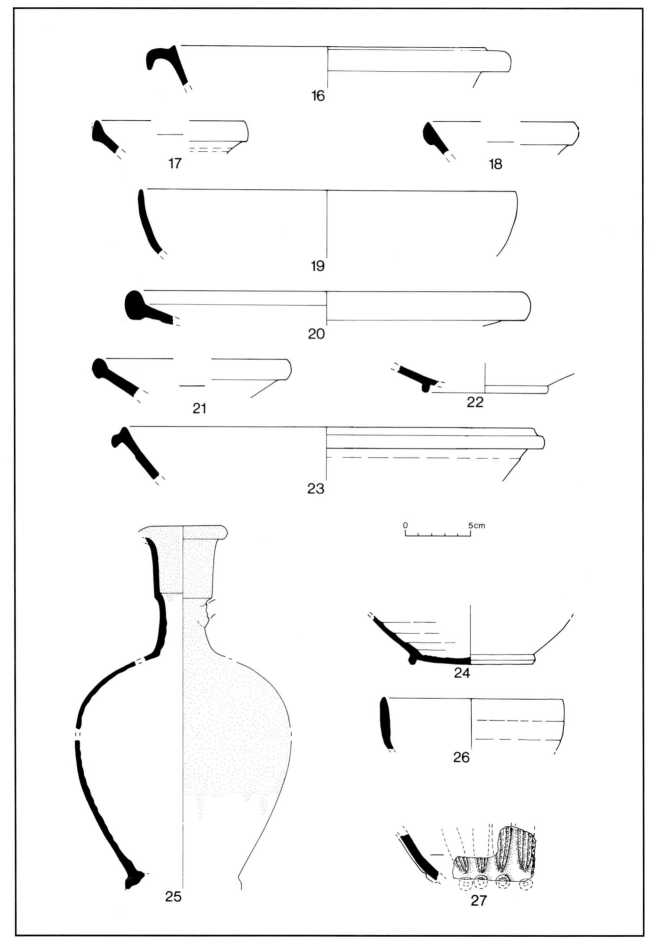

Fig. 79. Santa Rufina: African red slip ware (16-23) and other Roman fine wares (24-27)

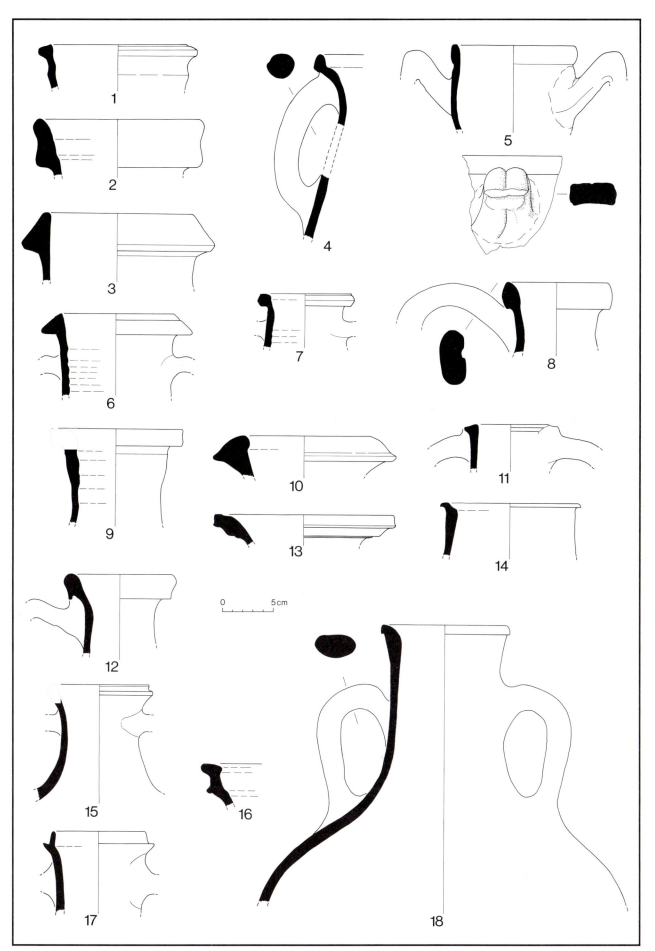

Fig. 80. Santa Rufina: Roman amphorae

PROVENANCES:

Period IIIb: 78.1, 78.2, 78.8, 79.22
Period IIIc: 78.6, 78.7, cf. 78.8, 78.9-10, cf.
                    79.22
Period IV: 77.1-2, 78.4, cf. 78.8, 78.11-13,
                    78.15, 79.16, 79.20-21
Period VII: 78.1, 79.14, 79.17, cf. 79.19
Not stratified: 78.3, 78.5, 78.18, 78.19, 78.23

(xv) ROMAN AMPHORAE (Fig. 80)

80.1   (P105) Orange clay.
80.2   (P327) Cream clay. (Cf. Carandini *et al.* 1968, 111 and Pl. XLIII, 572; Berti *et al.* 1970, Pl. XXXIII, 545.)
80.3   (P777) Reddish orange clay with small white inclusions. (Cf. Berti *et al.* 1970, Pl. XXXIII, 548.)
80.4   (P776) Light brown clay. (Cf. Carandini *et al.* 1968, 101, Pl. XXVIII, 463.)
80.5   (P66) Cream clay (one other example). (Cf. Berti *et al.* 1970, Pl. XXX, 528.)
80.6   (P601) Orange clay (three other examples).
80.7   (P288) Orange to red clay with white inclusions.
80.8   (P718) Well prepared cream to buff clay (two other examples). (Cf. Carandini and Panella 1977, 41, Pl. XXV, 165.)
80.9   (P778) Red clay with smooth cream to orange-brown slip on exterior of rim.
80.10   (P265) Brownish buff clay.
80.11   (P721) Red clay with micaceous inclusions, grey core and brown surfaces.
80.12   (P377) Orange clay (one other example). (Cf. Carthage I.2, 133, form 53 (= Fig. 40, number 71).)
80.13   (P783) Orange clay with white inclusions; cream slip outside.
80.14   (P774) Red clay with white inclusions and some mica (two other examples).
80.15   (P709) Red clay with white inclusions and some mica (one other example). (Cf. Neuru 1980, 202 and Pl. VII, 53; Whitehouse *et al.* 1982, 69 and Fig. 11, 148.)
80.16   (P586) Light orange clay with cream slip on outside. (Cf. Berti *et al.* 1970, 109 and Pl. XXXIV, 551.)
80.17   (P710) Cream to buff clay with yellow slip on outside (two other examples). (Cf. Neuru 1980, Pl. VII, 53; Whitehouse *et al.* 1982, 69 and Fig. 11, 150.)
80.18   (P779) Dark red clay with greyish brown exterior surface.

PROVENANCES:

Period I: 80.1, 80.5
Period IIIa: 80.2, 80.4, 80.16
Period IIIb: 80.6 (4), cf. 80.8 (2), 80.10, 80.18, and cf. 80.18
Period IV: 80.3, 80.12, 80.14
Period V: 80.13
Period VII: 80.7
Not stratified: 80.8, 80.11, 80.15, 80.17

(xvi) ROMAN POTTERY WITH A LIGHT SURFACE (Figs 81 and 82)

In most cases, the clay may be compared with fabric 5 at the Schola Praeconum: smooth, varying in colour from cream, through very pale brown to pink, and without large inclusions. The forms comprise: (i) jugs, (ii) bowls, and (iii) jars.

(a) JUGS

81.1   (P52) (Cf. Carandini and Panella 1977, 29, Pl. II, 64.)
81.2   (P580)
81.3   (P568) One other example.
81.4   (P217)
81.5   (P558)
81.6   (P689) (Cf. Carandini and Panella 1977, 62, Pl. XLII, 285.)
81.7   (P205) Pink clay with buff slip on outside.
81.8   (P156) Twelve other examples.
81.9   (P790)
81.10   (P266) Twelve other examples.
81.11   (P151) Buff clay with cream slip on outside and inside of rim (one other example). (Cf. Dyson 1976, 133, Fig. 51, 22 II 114.)
81.12   (P191) Fine pink clay.
81.13   (P173) One other example.
81.14   (P488) Pink clay with buff slip on outside.
81.15   (P419) Fine cream clay.
81.16   (P513)

(b) BOWLS

81.17   (P218) Pink clay with cream slip on outside (one other example).
81.18   (P376)
81.19   (P254) Pink clay, rather brittle.
81.20   (P801) Pink clay with cream surface.
81.21   (P583)
81.22   (P274)

(c) JARS

82.1   (P229) One other example.
82.2   (P233)
82.3   (P261)
82.4   (P391)
82.5   (P51) Coarse red clay with cream slip on outside and inside of rim.
82.6   (P557) (Cf. Dyson 1976, 165, Fig. 67, 26, 'kitchen' ware.)
82.7   (P563) (Cf. Dyson 1976, 132, Fig. 51, 108.)
82.8   (P95) One other example.
82.9   (P33)
82.10   (P788)
82.11   (P536)
82.12   (P367)
82.13   (P793) Pink clay with cream slip on outside and interior of rim.
82.14   (P743)

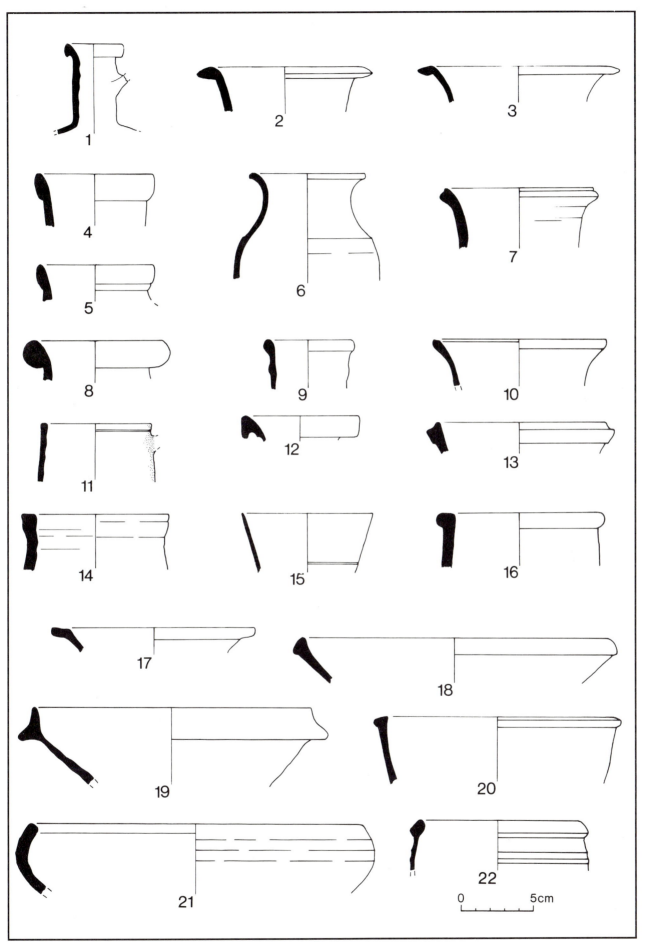

Fig. 81. Santa Rufina: Roman pottery with a light surface

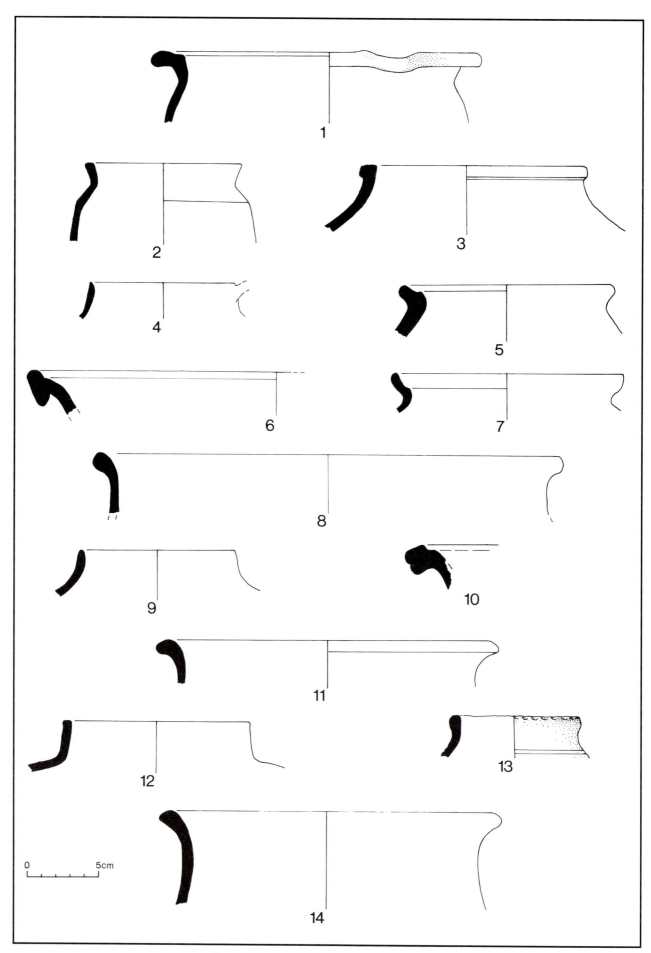

Fig. 82. Santa Rufina: Roman pottery with a light surface

PROVENANCES:

Period IIIa: 81.1, 81.5, 81.12, 82.5-7 and cf. 81.8
Period IIIb: 81.8, 81.11
Period IIIc: 81.2-4, 81.6-7, 81.10 (3), 81.13, 81.17 (2), 81.19, 81.21, 81.22, 82.1 (2), cf. 81.8 and cf. 81.11
Period IV: 81.3 (2), 81.18, 82.4
Period V: 81.15, 82.14
Period VI: 81.9, 82.9
Period VII: 82.12 and cf. 82.8
Not stratified: 81.14, 81.16, 81.20, 82.8, 82.11, 82.13

(xvii) ROMAN AND MEDIEVAL REDUCED WARES (Figs 83-87)

A large and varied group with coarse, rather gritty reduced clay. The surfaces vary in colour from red, through brown to dark grey. Many examples are comparable with fabrics 7-9 at the Schola Praeconum. The forms include: (i) casseroles, (ii) dishes, (iii) bowls, (iv) jars, and (v) lids.

(a) CASSEROLES

83.1   (P724) Collar rim, concave on the inside, slightly curved upright wall protruding internally to join rim. Marked carination at base of wall. Sagging base. Light brown clay, hard and with dark outer surface.

83.2   (P380) Almond rim, carinate shoulder and rounded base. Gritty light brown clay.

83.3   (P116) Carinate shoulder, vertical wall and sagging base. Decorated with notches on shoulder. Buff grey clay (two other examples).

83.4   (P735) Curved rim, slightly hooked at edge and vertical wall. Coarse red clay, blackened on outside (one other example).

83.5   (P463) Curved rim and vertical wall, decorated with notches. Coarse red clay with brown band on outside of rim (three other examples). (Cf. Carandini and Panella 1973, 190, Pl. XXXVII, 267-8; Carandini and Panella 1977, 28, Pl. X, 53.)

83.6   (P139) Slightly curved side, with groove on inside of rim. Clay as 45.5, blackened on outside (one other example).

83.7   (P690) Angular everted rim with groove on inner surface, curving side. Red clay, blackened on outside (three other examples). (Cf. Carandini and Panella 1973, 89, Pl. XXI, 104; Carandini and Panella 1977, 28, Pl. X, 54.)

83.8   (P642) Collar rim and curving wall. Grey-brown clay.

83.9   (P141) Rounded everted rim with groove on inside, carinate shoulder. Coarse red clay. (Cf. Carandini and Panella 1973, 190, Pl. XXXVII, 267-268.)

(b) DISHES

83.10   (P232) Simple rim with groove on inside, curving side and flat base. Coarse reddish-grey clay, fired fairly hard (one other example).

83.11   (P47) Everted rim, bevelled on outside and with groove on inner surface. Gritty red clay.

83.12   (P584) Curved everted rim with groove on inside. Greyish red clay.

83.13   (P211) Similar to 83.12.

83.14   (P295) Red clay. Rounded rim with groove on upper surface.

83.15   (P579) Coarse buff-grey clay, blackened on outside (one other example).

(c) BOWLS (Fig. 84)

84.1   (P154) Coarse, gritty clay, varying in colour from pink through brown to purple; overall effect is purplish (eight other examples).

84.2   (P766) Eleven other examples.

84.3   (P115) Eleven other examples.

84.4   Cf. 84.11.

84.5   Cf. 84.3.

84.8   (P102) Coarse pink clay with specks of mica. (Cf. Dyson 1976, Fig. 54.1-5; Whitehouse 1980a, 134, Fig. 4.26.)

84.9   (P496) Coarse reddish brown clay. (Cf. Whitehouse 1980a, 134, Fig. 3.17.)

84.10   (P789) Hard, pink to brown clay.

84.11   (P247) Coarse, gritty, light brown clay. (Cf. Whitehouse 1980a, 131, Fig. 3.9.)

84.12   (P683) Greyish brown clay (seven other examples).

84.13   (P764) Dark grey clay.

84.14   (P28) Gritty grey clay with pink surfaces. (Cf. Whitehouse 1980a, 131, Fig. 3.3.)

84.15   (P696) Gritty, light grey clay (two other examples).

84.16   (P641) Cf. 84.15.

84.17   (P667) Dark grey clay, blackened on outside.

84.18   (P637) Coarse, greyish brown clay.

84.19   (P625) Coarse, light brown clay (one other example).

(d) JARS (Figs 85 and 86)

(i) Almond rims

85.1   (P230) Five other examples.

85.2   (P749) (Cf. Dyson 1976, 97, Fig. 34.70.)

85.3   (P747) Cf. 85.2.

85.4   (P231) Cf. 85.2.

85.5   (P680) Cf. 85.2.

85.6   (P655) (Cf. Dyson 1976, 97, Fig. 34.69.)

85.7   (P552)

85.8   (P299)

85.9   (P176)

85.10   (P748)

85.11   (P598)

(ii) Out-turned rims

85.12   (P588) Four other examples. (Cf. Dyson 1976, 98, Fig. 35.75.)

85.13   (P679) (Cf. Dyson 1976, 126, Fig. 48.22.II.70.)

85.14   (P744)

85.15   (P252)

(iii) Rolled rim

85.16   (P121) Coarse purple clay (one other example).

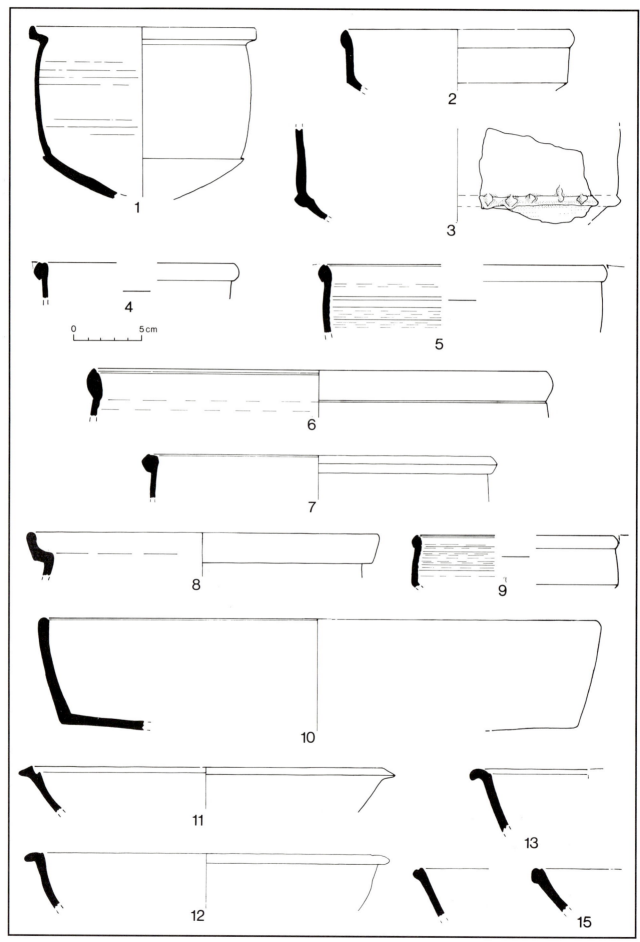

Fig. 83. Santa Rufina: Roman reduced ware

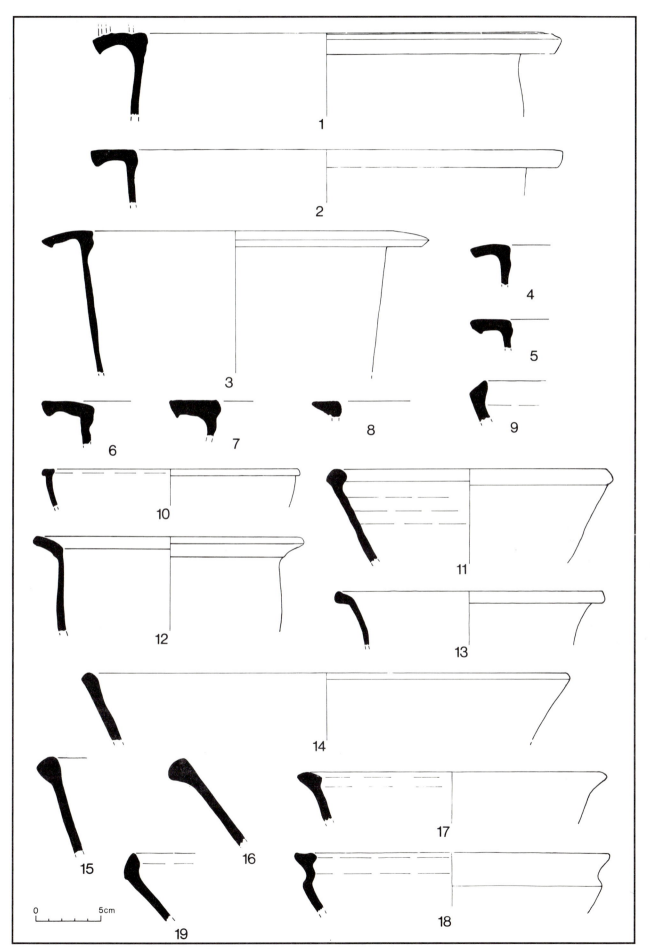

Fig. 84. Santa Rufina: Roman and medieval reduced ware

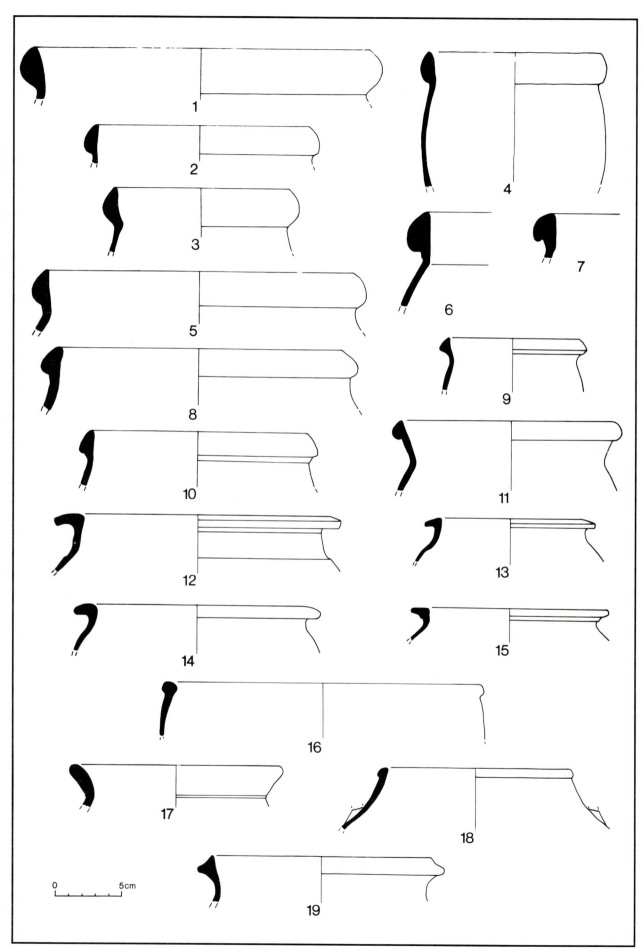

Fig. 85. Santa Rufina: Roman and medieval reduced ware

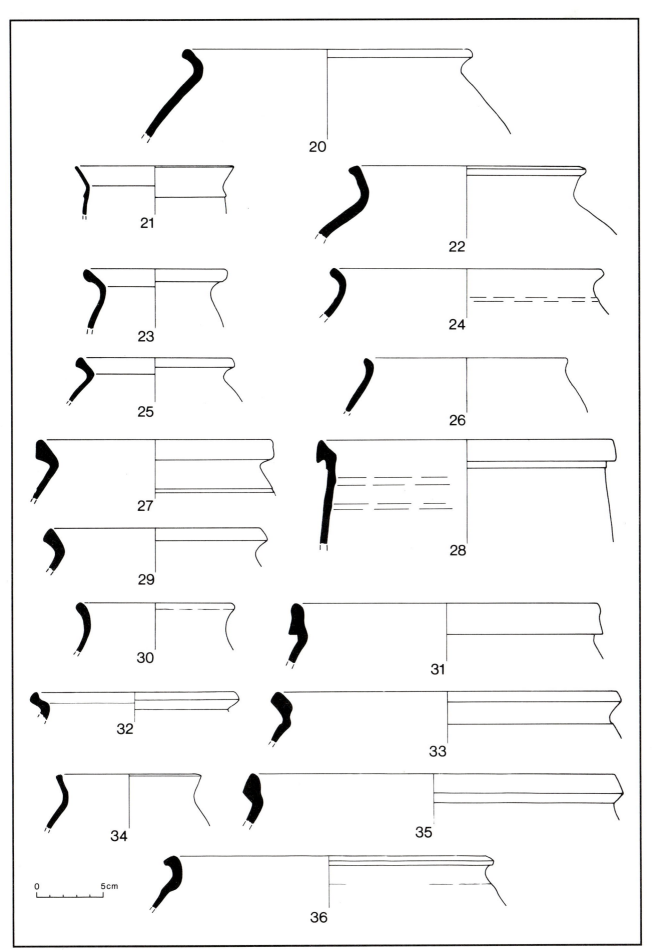

Fig. 86. Santa Rufina: Roman and medieval reduced ware

(iv) Everted rims

86.20 (P746) Four other examples.
86.21 (P758)
86.22 (P144) (Cf. Whitehouse *et al.* 1982, 67, Fig. 7.106.)
86.23 (P678)
86.25 (P756)
86.27 (P630) (Cf. Dyson 1976, 165, Fig. 67, FC 25; Whitehouse *et al.* 1982, 67, Fig. 7.99.)
86.29 (P751) Six other examples. (Cf. Dyson 1976, 165, Fig. 67, FC 27.)
86.32 (P521)
86.33 (P752) One other example. (Cf. Carandini and Panella 1973, 202, Pl.XLI, number 321.)

(v) S-shaped rims

86.24 (P745) Nine other examples.
86.26 (P90) Seven other examples.
86.30 (P416)
86.34 (P755)

(vi) Collar rims

86.28 (P669)
86.31 (P549)

(vii) Miscellaneous

86.17 (P759)
86.18 (P757)
86.19 (P569)
86.35 (P345)
86.36 (P684) (Cf. Whitehouse *et al.* 1982, 67, Fig. 7.91.)

(e) LIDS (Fig. 87)

These have coarse red or brown clay. They may be divided into seven categories:
(i)   with upward curving rims (87.2-4, 87.6, 87.9, 87.11, 87.16, 87.18)
(ii) with downward curving rims (87.1, 87.8, 87.10, 87.12-13, 87.17)
(iii) colour-coated (87.7)
(iv) internally burnished (87.5)
(v)   with hollow knob (87.19)
(vi) with external ridge (87.14)
(vii) with thickened rim (87.15)

87.1 (P780) One other example.
87.2 (P123) One other example.
87.3 (P122) Eighteen other examples.
87.4 (P215)
87.5 (P48) Greyish brown clay with light brown burnishing inside.
87.6 (P119)
87.7 (P49) Prima Porta fabric with brown slip above and under rim.
87.8 (P770) Red clay with blackened rim.
87.9 (P373)
87.10 (P546) Red clay with blackened rim.
87.11 (P567) Red clay with blackened rim (one other example).
87.12 (P297) One other example.
87.13 (P135) Coarse red clay with blackened rim.
87.14 (P761)
87.15 (P733)

87.16 (P763)
87.17 (P762)
87.18 (P530)
87.19 (P787)
87.20 (P760) Seven other examples.
87.21 (P686)
87.22 (P332) Three other examples.
87.23 (P785) Coarse red clay with band of brown on outside of rim (eight other examples).

PROVENANCES:

Period I: 87.1
Period II: 87.19-20, cf. 83.15, cf. 85.1
Period IIIa: 83.3 (3 examples), 83.4, 83.7, 83.11, 84.3 (4), 84.4, 84.5 (5), 84.6, 86.21, 86.25, 87.2 (2), 87.3 (8), 87.5 (2), 87.6, 87.14, 87.17, cf. 84.1, cf. 86.20 (2), 86.21, cf. 86.23
Period IIIb: 83.5, 84.1, 84.3, 85.3, 87.8, cf. 83.4, cf. 86.3, cf. 86.23 (2)
Period IIIc: 83.2, 83.6, 83.9, 83.10 (2), 83.12-15, 84.10, 84.11 (2), 84.12 (3), 84.15-16, 85.4-5, 85.7-9, 85.11, 86.22-23, 87.4, 87.11, 87.13, 87.16, cf. 83.5, cf. 84.2-3, cf. 84.19, cf. 85.1 (5), cf. 86.29, cf. 87.3 (7), cf. 87.20 (2), cf. 87.22
Period IV: 83.5 (2), 84.2, 87.9-11, 87.13, cf. 83.6, cf. 84.3 (3), cf. 86.26 (2), cf. 86.29, cf. 87.3, cf. 87.20, cf. 87.22-23
Period V: 83.8, 85.6, 86.29 (3), 86.32-33, 87.1, cf. 84.1-3, cf. 84.12, cf. 84.15, cf. 86.20 (3), cf. 86.24 (5), cf. 87.20 (2), cf. 87.23
Period VI: Cf. 87.3
Period VII: 83.1, 84.1 (2), 86.24, 86.26 (4), 86.30, 87.15, 87.18, 87.22, cf. 86.32-33, cf. 87.23 (2)
Not stratified: 83.7 (3), 84.1, 84.12 (3), 84.13-14, 84.18-19, 85.2, 85.10, 86.20 (2), 86.24 (3), 86.27, 87.18, 87.23, cf. 84.3, cf. 86.26, cf. 86.34, cf. 87.3, cf. 87.12. cf. 87.22

(xviii) MORTARIA (Fig. 88)

88.1 (P103) Very coarse, gritty, cream clay with remains of cream slip on outside and top of rim. (Cf. Murray-Threipland and Torelli 1970, 79, type D, 8-12, attributed to the late fifth or early fourth century BC.)
88.2 (P114) Well-prepared pinkish buff clay with pink and grey grits on inner surface. (Cf. Berti *et al.*. 1970, Pl. XXV, 453.)
88.3 (P537) Clay as 50.2 but without grits. (Cf. Berti *et al.* 1970, Pl. XX, 412.)
88.4 (P651) Coarse, creamy grey clay with cream slip.
88.5 (P771) Fairly fine buff to cream clay with few small brown grits on inner surface. Two impressed circles on outside of rim.
88.6 (P541) Coarse, gritty cream clay.
88.7 (P695) Coarse buff clay with cream surfaces.

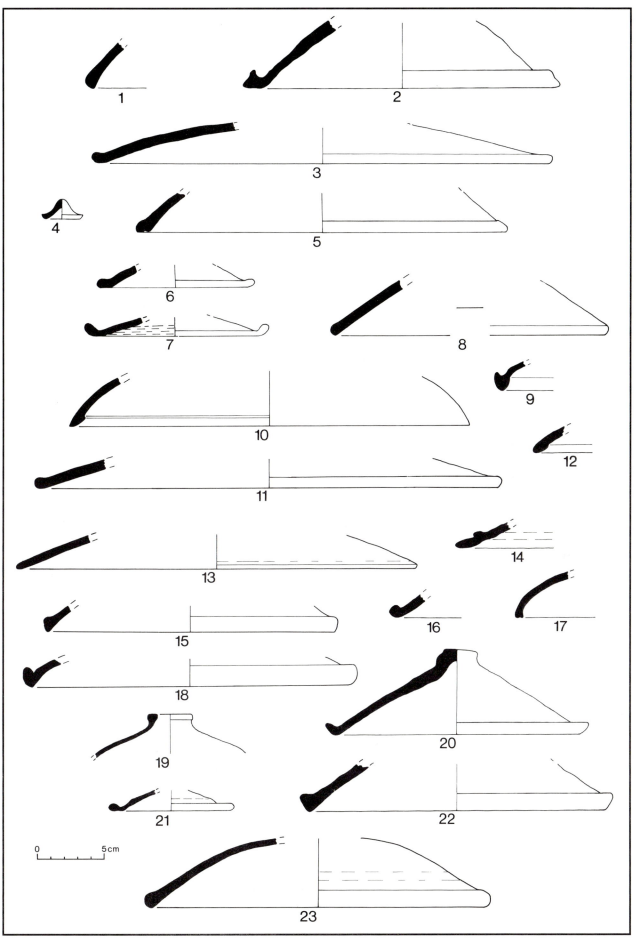

Fig. 87. Santa Rufina: Roman and medieval reduced ware

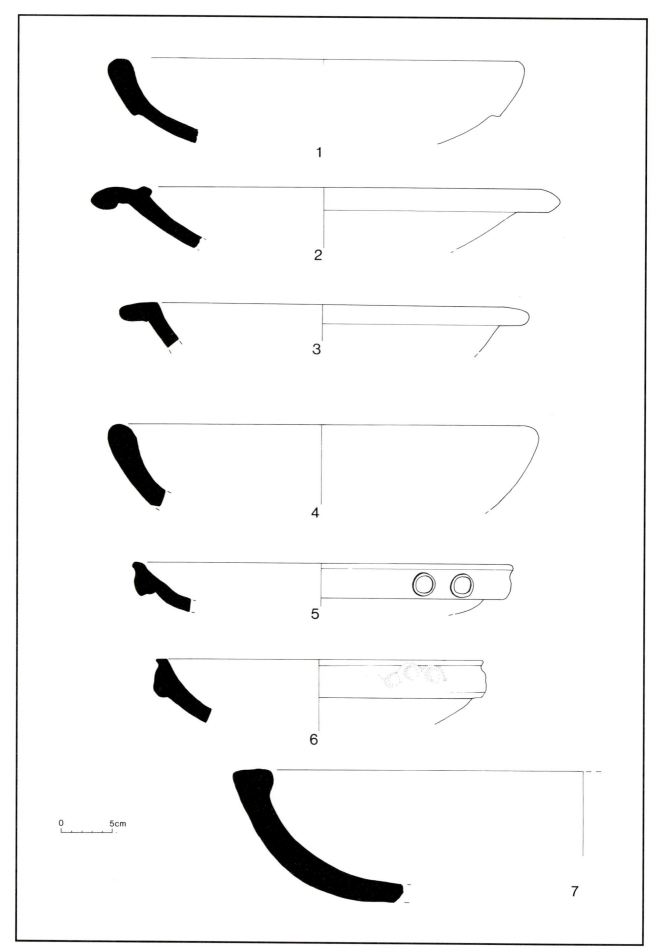

Fig. 88. Santa Rufina: mortaria

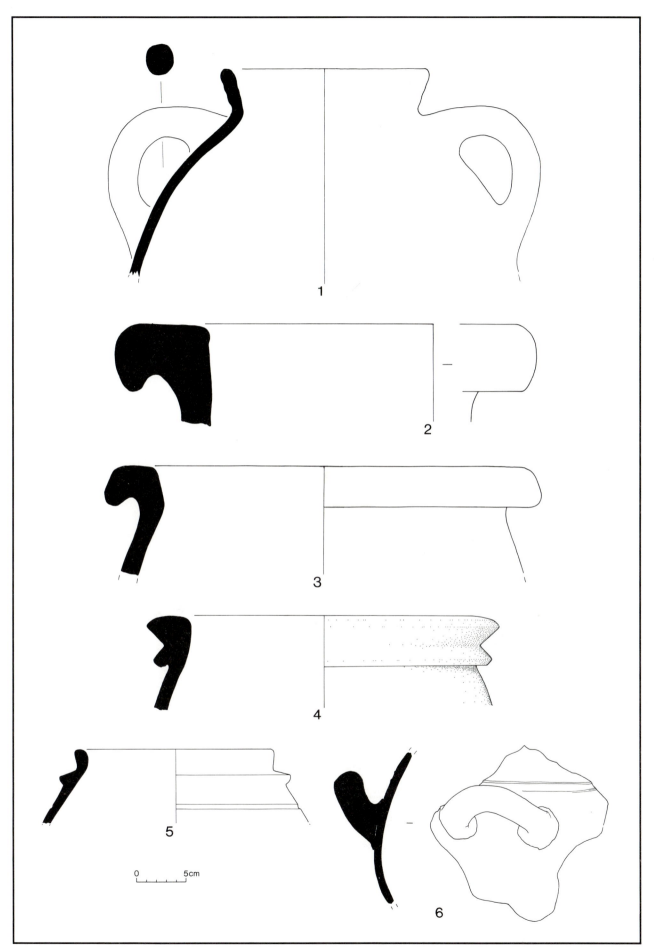

Fig. 89. Santa Rufina: jars

PROVENANCES:

Period I: 88.1
Period IIIa: 88.2
Period IIIc: 88.7
Period IV: 88.3, 88.6
Not stratified: 88.4-5.

(xix) JARS (Fig. 89)

89.1   (P781) Very coarse, gritty buff clay, with buff slip on outside and interior of rim.
89.2   (P681) Very coarse, gritty rust-coloured clay.
89.3   (P238) Gritty buff clay.
89.4   (P9) Coarse, gritty, greyish buff clay with smooth surfaces.
89.5   (P17) Well-prepared pink clay with cream slip on outside.
89.6   (P241) Coarse, gritty red clay with grey core and red burnish or slip on interior.

PROVENANCES:

Period I: 89.1
Period IIIa: 89.4-5, cf. 89.2
Period IIIc: 89.2
Not stratified: 89.3, 89.6

(xx) LATE ROMAN SLIP WARE (Fig. 90)

90.1   (P100) Fine buff clay with small black inclusions; on the rim, darker buff slip. (Cf. Whitehouse *et al.* 1982, 65, Fig. 5.45.)
90.2   (P503) Fairly fine buff clay with darker buff slip on outside and inner surface of rim.
90.3   (P718) Clay as 90.1; red slip on top of rim. (Cf., but not closely, Whitehouse *et al.* 1982, 65, Fig. 5.42.)
90.4   (P694) Buff clay with grey core and darker buff slip. Faint rouletted decoration.

PROVENANCES:

Period IV: 90.1, 90.4
Not stratified: 90.2-3

(xxi) OTHER ROMAN WARES (Fig. 91)

(a) POMPEIAN RED WARE

91.1   (P737) Reddish brown clay with quartzite inclusions; deep red burnished surface on inside, rim and top of outside; rest of outside is reddish brown (Bruckner type 2).

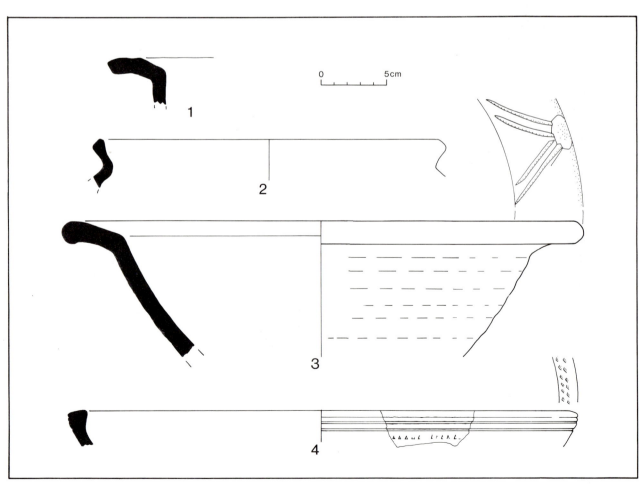

Fig. 90. Santa Rufina: late Roman slip ware

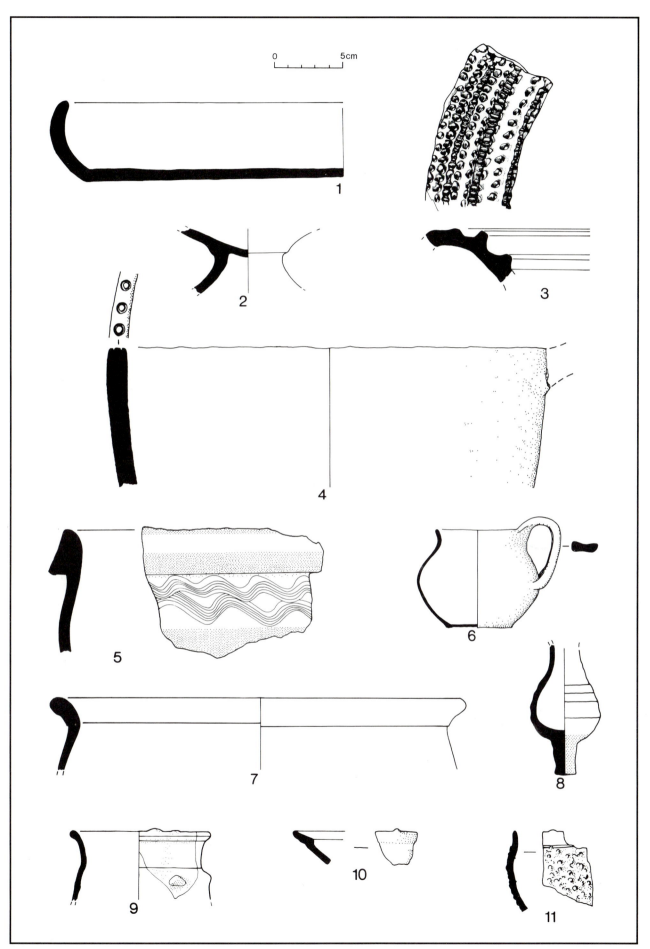

Fig. 91. Santa Rufina: other Roman wares

(b) LARGE BOWLS AND JAR

91.4   (P12) Very coarse buff clay with rough, gritty exterior. Trace of handle. Decorated on top of rim with impressed circles.

91.5   (P713) Red clay with bands of cream slip and incised wavy lines

91.7   (P646) Light brown clay.

(c) DECORATED BOWL

91.3   (P715) Brown clay.

(d) PLAIN COARSE WARE

91.2   (P124) Coarse red clay.

91.6   (P17) Light brown clay.

91.8   (P440) Coarse cream clay.

(e) GLAZED POTTERY

91.9   (P807) Fine, fairly hard putty-coloured clay. Dark apple-green glaze on both surfaces, with blobs of glaze on rim.

91.10   (P291) Clay as 91.9. Apple-green glaze on both surfaces, blob of glaze on rim.

91.11   (P78) Clay as 91.9. Decorated on outside with large grits, which give surface distinctly rough texture, and with fine white grits on interior. Dark apple-green glaze on outside and top of rim, which has blob of glaze; pale green glaze on inside.

PROVENANCES:

Period IIIa:	91.2-4, 91.8
Period IIIb:	91.1
Period Va:	91.7
Period VI:	91.10-11
Not stratified:	91.5-6, 91.9

(xxii) FORUM WARE (Fig. 92)

The Forum Ware ('*ceramica a vetrina pesante*') from Santa Rufina, comprising some 200 sherds, has the same characteristics as the Forum Ware from Rome, Santa Cornelia and other sites in the Roman Campagna. The clay is coarse and fairly hard, varying in colour from dark grey, through weak red to red; the usual colour is weak red, with pale red unglazed surfaces. The glaze, which may be blistered, is thick. Unblemished examples have a glossy surface, which ranges in colour from dark green to dark reddish brown. The fragments illustrated in Fig. 92 include two unusual forms (92.7 and 92.14). The collection may be divided into: (i) jugs, (ii) a bowl, (iii) handles, (iv) jars, (v) bases and (vi) decorated body sherds.

    The following offers merely a catalogue. A detailed discussion of Forum Ware and of sparse glaze ware (see below, section xxiii) is provided in the pottery section of the Santa Cornelia excavation report.

(a) JUGS

92.1   (P794) Upright rim and ovoid body. Closely applied petals run diagonally towards the spout, which juts out with two petals on either side.

92.2   (P22) Pinched spout (four other examples).

92.4   (P417) Slightly pinched spout.

92.6   (P25) Pinched spout (one other example).

92.9   (P797) Upright rim decorated with three incised lines. The handle springs just below the lip (five other examples).

92.10   (P86) Incurving rim and swelling body, with two applied petals at base of neck.

(b) BOWL

92.14   (P805) Hard grey clay. The glaze is olive green and thickly applied to the exterior and the interior of the rim.

(c) HANDLES

The handles are either flat or oval in section. They may be glazed on the upper surface only, or overall and are plain or decorated with applied petals. The decoration consists of either one or two vertical rows. There were nineteen examples.

92.12   (P798) Decorated with a single line of petals.

(d) JARS

92.3   (P806) Tall, flaring rim decorated with incised wavy lines.

92.7   (P799) An unusual form, with thickened rim, which is concave on the outside. One upright petal attached to body (one other example).

(e) BASES

Of eleven fragments, nine are flat and two have concentric rings, 2 mm deep, on the underside.

92.11   (P67) Thick green glaze on outside and thinner glaze underneath. Decoration stabbed, not applied.

92.15   (P309) Glazed outside and underneath, with streaks of glaze on inside.

(f) DECORATED BODY SHERDS

The petals are arranged in a variety of patterns: in vertical lines (as 92.5), randomly (92.8), in diagonal rows, and overall (92.1).

92.5   (P795) Petals applied in vertical rows (seven other examples).

92.8   (P67) Petals applied in rather haphazard diagonal rows (thirteen other examples).

92.13   (P796) Neck of jar or jug with combed decoration.

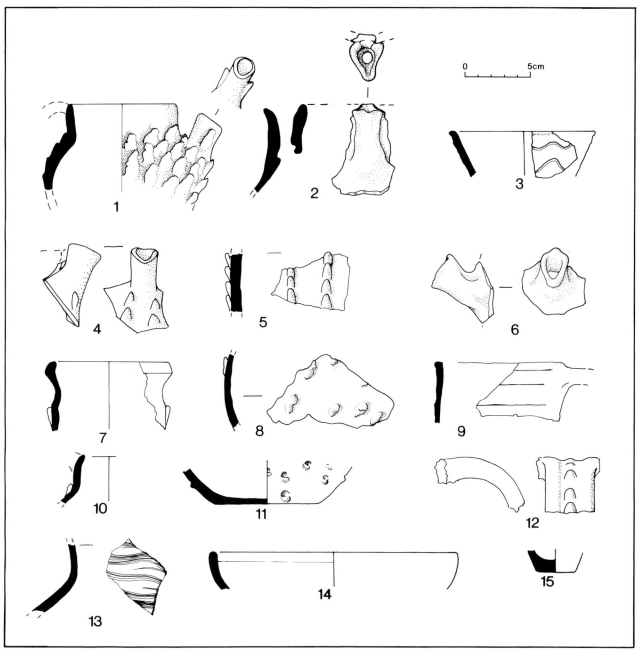

Fig. 92. Santa Rufina: Forum ware

PROVENANCES:

Period Va: 92.2, 92.3, 92.13, cf. 92.6
Period Vb: 92.1, 92.15
Not stratified: 92.4-12, 92.14.

(xxiii) POTTERY WITH SPARSE GLAZE (Fig. 93)

Again, with the exception of 93.1, which is an unusual form, the finds are typical of Rome and the Roman Campagna. Most vessels are of fairly hard, light red to reddish pink clay, usually thinly potted. The glaze, which occurs as spots, streaks and patches, is thin and green or greenish brown, with numerous 'pin holes'. The following forms occurred in a sample of 180 sherds: (i) jugs, (ii) small jugs and/or jars, (iii) bases, and (iv) handles.

(a) JUGS

93.1 (P693) Buff clay with splashes of yellow glaze on the rim and neck. The lip is rounded with a slight outward curve and bulge in the neck. Handle with kidney-shaped section springs just below the rim and attaches to the body at the shoulder. The fragment is too small to indicate whether the vessel had a spout or a second handle.

93.2 (P364) Splashes of yellow glaze on body, which splays outward from simple lip. Rills (characteristic of pottery with sparse glaze) on lower neck. Narrow strap handle (one other example).

93.3 (P804) Slightly pinched spout. Orange clay with trace of glaze (one other example).

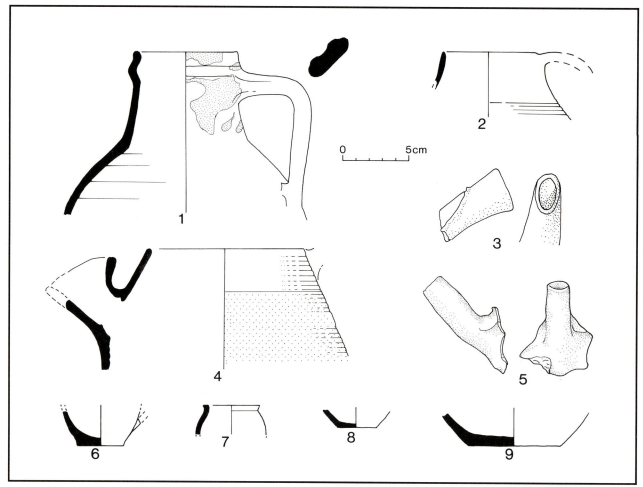

Fig. 93. Santa Rufina: pottery with sparse glaze

93.4   (P88) Greenish buff clay with yellow-green glaze on the body. The bulbous body curves outward from the base of the neck (eight other examples).

93.5   Long tubular spout, covered with drab greenish glaze.

(b) SMALL JUGS AND/OR JARS

93.6   (P823) Pink clay. Swelling body with attachment for handle; flat base. Thin glaze on outside and underneath, with spots on interior.

93.7   (P30) Grey clay. Short upright rim and swelling body, covered with thin glaze on outside and interior of rim.

93.8   (P701) Base with thin glaze on exterior and spots on inside.

(c) BASE

93.9   (P388) Flat base and swelling body. Thin glaze on outside and underneath.

(d) HANDLE

Twenty-two fragments, mostly flat or oval in section.

PROVENANCES:

Period Vb: 93.1, 93.5, 93.7
Period VI: 93.3, cf. 93.4
Not stratified: 93.2, 93.4, 93.6, 93.8-9.

(xxiv) MEDIEVAL POTTERY WITHOUT GLAZE (Figs 94 and 95)

As at other sites in the Roman Campagna – Santa Cornelia is typical – most of the medieval pottery without glaze falls into two groups: (i) with fine, well-prepared clay, usually fired in oxidizing conditions and ranging in colour from white, through very pale brown, to light red, and (ii) with coarse clay, fired in reducing conditions. The first group includes open forms, jars, jugs and all amphorae. The second group includes open forms and all cooking pots. Here, pots in the first group are described by colour; those in the second group are labelled 'reduced'. The south Etruria type-series appears in Whitehouse 1982.

(a) JARS (SOUTH ETRURIA, TYPE 8)

94.1   (P132) Simple, everted rim, bulbous body and flat base; missing handle. Reduced. One other example. (Cf. Whitehouse 1980a, 134, Fig. 4,33.)

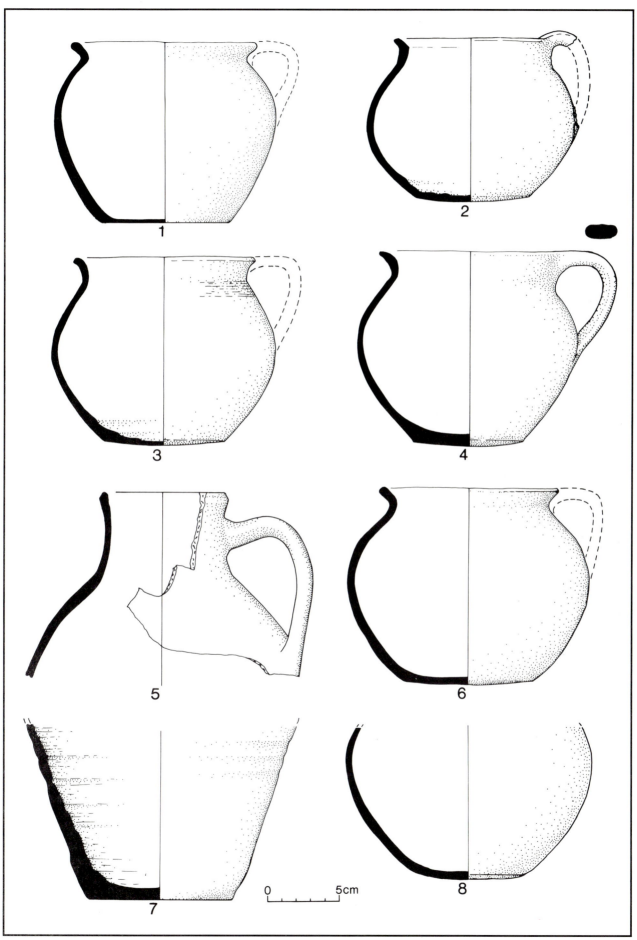

Fig. 94. Santa Rufina: medieval pottery without glaze

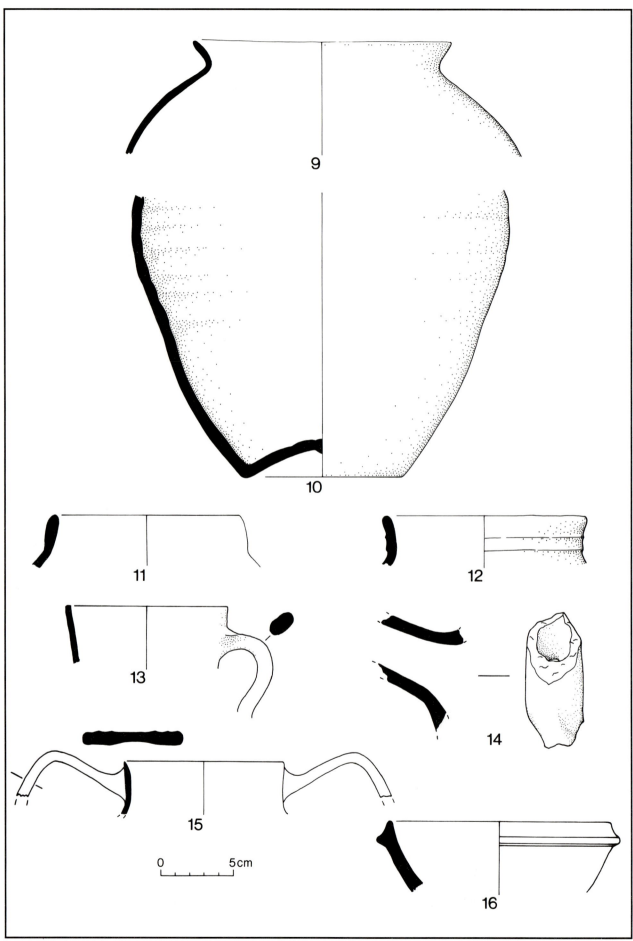

Fig. 95. Santa Rufina: medieval pottery without glaze

94.2   (P128) Everted rim with internal bevel, bulbous body and slightly sagging base; one strap handle. Reduced. (Cf. Whitehouse 1980a, 134, Fig. 4,35.)

94.3   (P131) Similar to 94.2, but without internal bevel. Reduced. Two other examples.

94.4   (P129) Everted rim, bulbous body and slightly sagging base; one strap handle. Four other examples.

94.6   Reduced. Four other examples. (Cf. Whitehouse 1980a, 134, Fig. 4,29.)

94.8   (P1) Similar to 94.3, with curving side and slightly sagging base. Reduced.

95.9   (P133) Everted rim and swelling body. Reduced.

95.11   Rim inclined inwards, swelling side. Reduced.

95.12   Reduced. (Perhaps cf. Whitehouse 1980a, 137, Fig. 6,60.)

(b) JUGS

94.5   (P127) Pointed rim with external bevel, flaring neck and swelling side; strap handle with median groove attached to rim and shoulder. Cream clay.

94.7   (P10) Coarse pink clay.

95.13   (P269) Flattened rim and flaring neck; oval-section handle attached to neck and shoulder. Cream clay.

(c) BOWL

95.16   (P422) Flange rim. Coarse buff-pink clay.

(d) AMPHORAE

95.10   Omphaloid base. Coarse pink clay. (Cf. Whitehouse 1980a, 139, Fig. 9,89, etc.; south Etruria, type 19.)

95.15   Globular amphora with broad strap handles; cf. 95.10.

(e) SPOUT

95.14   (P26) Reduced.

PROVENANCES:

Period V: 94.1 (2), 94.2, 94.3 (2), 94.4 (5), 94.6-8, 95.9-11, 95.13, 95.16, cf. 95.15 (2)
Period VII: 95.15 (17)
Not stratified: 95.12, 95.14

(xxv) LATE AND POST-MEDIEVAL GLAZED POTTERY (Fig. 96)

(a) PLAIN GREEN GLAZE

96.1   (P65) Rim and handle of carinate cup. Creamy pink clay with corroded apple-green glaze on both surfaces.

96.2   (P79) Rim of shallow bowl. Cream clay with yellowish green glaze on interior and outside of rim.

96.3   (P803) Cream clay.

(b) CERAMICA LAZIALE

96.4   (P83) Grey clay with greenish cream glaze on both surfaces; brown and green decoration.

96.5   (P89) Cream clay with cream glaze and decoration in brown, yellowish brown and grey-green on outside; colourless glaze on inside.

(c) POST-MEDIEVAL MAIOLICA

96.6,96.7 (P85) and 96.8.   Shallow bowls with wide flange rim inclined upwards towards edge, which is hooked. Fine cream clay with white enamel on both surfaces, but not under base. Decorated in blue, green and mustard yellow.

96.9   (P68) Bowl with white clay and white enamel on both surfaces, but not under base. Decorated with concentric circles of (from top to bottom) blue, yellow, blue (2), green, blue (3), yellow, blue (6), yellow and blue (2).

PROVENANCES:

Period VI: 96.2-4.
Not stratified: 96.1, 96.5-9.

(xxvi) MARBLE

Neil Christie

Most of the smaller fragments of marblework are now housed at the *Museo dell'Alto Medioevo*, Rome. I am grateful to dott.ssa Lidia Paroli for allowing access to the material. The location of many of the larger elements, such as column fragments, has not been traced. The following provides a brief catalogue of the surviving pieces.

(a) ARCHITECTURAL ELEMENTS

IV.8 1.3 (34) Section of Corinthian capital, 0.42 × 0.20 × 0.19 m, preserving three acanthus leaves with associated tendrils. Rough tooled on top. White marble.

PP 1.1c (28) Spiral fluted half colonette, 0.19 × 0.115 × 0.07 m, with flat, smooth back; side with nail hole. White marble with grey veins.

SQ 1.1 (23) Half fragment of small, early medieval(?) Ionic capital, 0.155 × 0.165 × 0.11 m. White marble.

055643 Small square moulded base, 0.17 × 0.17 × 0.11 m. Fine white marble.

CC 1.3, EEE 1.3 (three fragments), EXC 1.3, G.V 1.1, R 6 (38-44) (Fig. 97, 1a-d) A set of seven white marble fragments for open screen or frame (perhaps window featuring double-grooving on face and back with raised, upward-pointing knobs on side (outer face)); two junction fragments, forming swastika arrangement.

VV 1.1 (24) Triangular fragment, 0.165 × 0.115 × 0.04–0.06 m, white marble. Spirals on both preserved faces. From small, medieval(?) Ionic capital?

(b) MOULDED FRAGMENTS

OO 1.3 (30) White marble slab, 0.16 × 0.12 × 0.02 m, with painted brown stripes c. 10 mm broad, and rough incised marks.

EXC 1.3 (27) White marble fragment with grey streaks, 0.14 × 0.08 × 0.04 m. Moulded on one face with broad single-grooved edge c. 65 mm broad: on panel possible eye(?) motif, perhaps within grooved band; reverse face with probable flower motif within single-grooved band. Early medieval chancel screen?

IK 1.3 (13) Double-grooved fragment, 0.14 × 0.07 × 0.04 m. White marble.

JJJ 1.2 (31) Triangular moulded piece, 80 × 80 × 60 mm, perhaps from a lid.

JJ 1.4 (32) White marble piece, 95 × 100 × 12 mm, with single raised edge on side.

JJ 1.4 Grey-white marble with raised double-grooved moulding. 110 x 50 × 40 mm.

RR 1.1 Side element with double-grooved moulding, 80 × 65 × 35 mm.

YY 1.3 (30) Double-grooved fragment, 70–110 × 70 × 40 mm. White marble.

OO Ex 1.5 (22) Moulded pinkish-white marble piece with grey veins, 0.165 × 0.22 × 0.03 m. Part of panel with outer border framed by single-grooved band: within field of panel double-grooved rectangle with inward curving sides. Associated fragments: 798455 (115 × 45 × 20 mm); DDD 1.4, CCC 1.4 (×2), CCC 1.5.

XX S.1 1.2 (33) Deep, double-grooved fragment, 90 × 55 × 25 mm.

798455 Two small moulded fragments, one with arcade-like design.

798455 Two single-grooved fragments.

(c) RELIEF FRAGMENTS

OO RX 1.5 (21) White marble fragment of relief of deer's foot and shin, detached from any back panel; flat back and front. 190 × 25–55 × 25 mm.

QQ 1.2 (20) High relief fragment, 130 × 85 × 35 mm, likely knee portion related to deer relief (above).

OO/AA 1.2, YY 1.3 (25, 35) Two small pieces in shape of claw or wave, 45 × 30 × 9 mm and 50 × 30 × 9 mm. White marble with grey bands. Perhaps cut floor elements (see below).

DDD 1.6 (17) White marble. Incised scene depicting lion upon or standing upright facing a man, with its paw on the man's chest. Daniel in the lion's den?

798455 Fragment from sarcophagus with relief of man pulling on a chain: arm and upper leg of man shown with part of tunic. 140 × 95 × 60 mm. White marble.

(d) SHAPED FLOOR ELEMENTS – OPUS SECTILE

A quantity of small cut shapes – strips, squares, small tesserae, triangles – was also recovered. These presumably refer to an opus sectile floor, which, on the basis of the elements preserved, lacked any large elements (e.g.

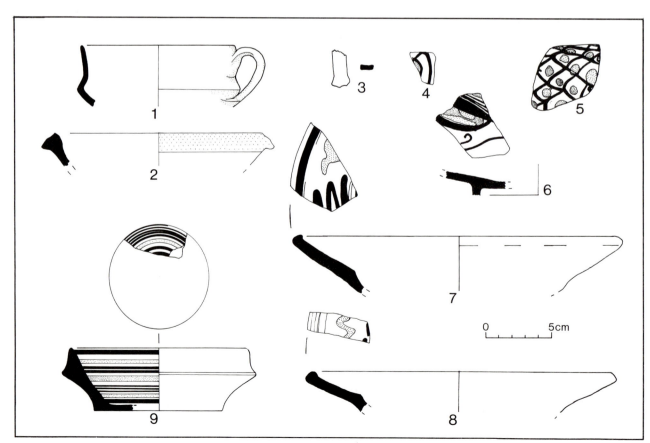

Fig. 96. Santa Rufina: late- and post-medieval glazed pottery

discs/roundels). Given the lack of material on the site dating from much after the eleventh century, it is hard to relate these pieces to a Cosmatesque floor; more probably they relate to an early medieval pavement. Where this was housed, however, must remain uncertain, since fragments were scattered quite widely over the site. A good range of marble types is present, which includes red and green porphyry and giallo antico. The quantity of porphyry is much less than that recovered at Santa Cornelia. The following list omits irregular fragments.

Strips – 70 mm wide: JJ 1.2; CD 1.4a.
   55 mm: JJ 1.2; CD 1.4a.
   46 mm: BB 1.3 (four examples); VI 1.4; XX/NN 1.1.
   49 mm: NN 1.6c.
   36 mm: EE 1.1; MM 1.1; OO EX 1.5; SS 1.1 (two examples); YY 1.3 (three examples).
   25 mm: LL 1.4; MM 1.2; SS 1.1; OO EX 1.1; PP 1.1d.
   20 mm: OO/AA 1.2 (two examples).
   12 mm: OO EX 1.3
    4 mm: OO/AA 1.2; OO EX 1.3 (four examples).

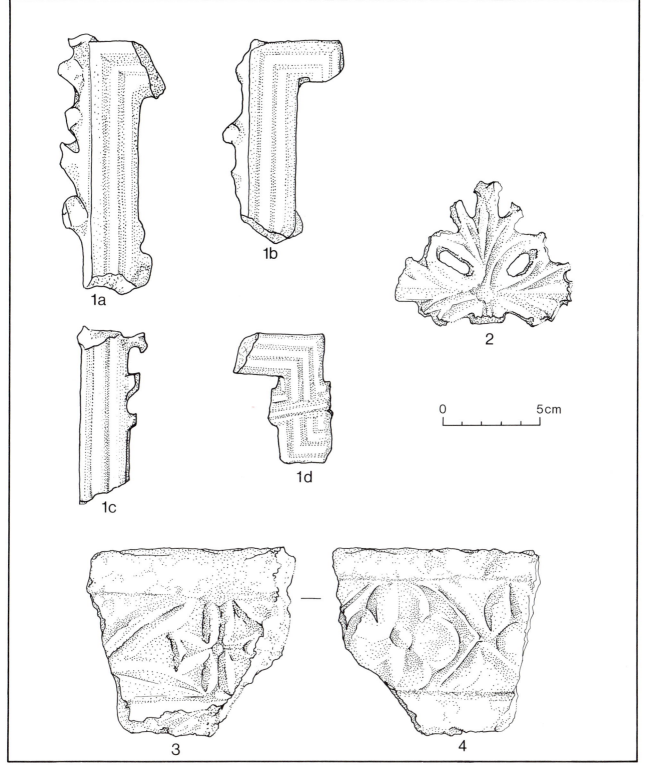

Fig. 97. Santa Rufina: marble screen fragments

Angled strips – DDD 1.3a (two examples).
Curved strip – KKK 1.1.
Squares – 70 × 70 mm: BB 1.3 (two examples); XX/NN
        1.1.
    40 × 40 mm: CD 1.4a; DDD 1.4; HHH 1.1 (two
        examples)
    30 × 30 mm: 8.1x pit (seven examples); PP 1.1d.
    1 × 1 (tesserae): 8.1a pit (nine examples); DDD 1.7.
Triangles – 120 mm base: CE 1.9; TT 1.1.
    90 mm: YY 1.3.
    70 mm: OO EX 1.1 (two examples); TT 1.1.
    40 mm: DDD 1.7; VI 1.4.
Circles – 30 mm radius: 10.1
Half-moon – BB 1.3; NN 1.6c.
Oval – OO EX 1.1.

'Beaked' – OO EX 1.1.
Crinkle-cut – CE 1.9.

Only one fragment featured more than one piece bedded
in mortar: YY 1.3. This, however, showed a poor
placement of a triangle near a square.

(xxvii) MOLLUSCS

Seven shells were retained: four oysters, one valve of
Auricula haliotis and one *Murex branderis*. Only one was
stratified: the *Auricula* was found beneath the floor of the
mosaic room (period Va).

(xxviii) INSCRIPTIONS

Joyce Reynolds

Of the inscribed stones found at Santa Rufina, number 1 is a fragment from the priestly *acta* of the Arval Brothers for a year within the first two decades of the second century AD, and probably AD 114. These *acta* were cut on monuments in the Brethren's sacred grove, described in much modern literature as the Vigna Ceccarelli, more recently as La Magliana, four miles outside Rome on the Via Portuensis [1]. In AD 382 when the grove was confiscated by the Emperor Gratian it appears to have been handed over to the Church; the available evidence suggests that Christian reuse of the stones of its pagan monuments followed, perhaps beginning in the last decade of the fourth and continuing in the fifth and sixth centuries. Fragments are found in Christian cemeteries of this period at Rome, and one or two, including the Santa Rufina piece, travelled further afield.

The presence of this item strongly suggests that a load of stone was brought out from Rome for use on the site, and that most of the inscriptions came in this. Only numbers 8 and 9 can be considered as at all likely to be of local origin.

(a) CLASSICAL TEXTS

1. Fragment of white marble, probably Luna (0.11 × 0.085 × 0.015 m), inscribed on one face in small capitals, designed freehand (lines 1 and 6, truncated, line 2, 0.013, lines 3-5, average 0.006, with stops in the form of a three-pointed thorn and an apex above O in line 4. Inventory number SR00 Ex.1.4. Published Reynolds 1969. (Photo: F. Sear.)

```
                                 ...]
          ...]ERV[...
          ...]MCOS III K[...
          ...]ALEXANDRVM stop IVLI[...
          ...]GILLO stop BITTIVS PRO[...
   (5)    ...]ATRIMIS stop ET stop MATR[...
             ...]RETTVL[...
      [...
```

Line 2, in larger letters than the rest, was a heading for what followed and contained a date. Line 5 preserves part of a formula describing children whose parents were both living, and points to an account of a religious ceremony from which we may identify the text as part of the Arval Acta. The formulae used in these were not altogether stereotyped so that any restoration can only be approximate; but what follows must be more or less what was written [2]. ? printed before a word indicates that an alternative word or phrase is possible:

```
                                                                    ...]
Line 1      ...adfu]eru[nt ?in collegio isdem qui VI k(alendas) easdem vac.]
Line 2 [      ?vacat      isde]m co(n)s(ulibus) III k[(alendas) easdem  v.]
Line 3 [in ?domo apud Ti. Iulium] Alexandrum Iuli[anum ?mag(istrum) Fratres Arvales
        ?ad consummandum sacrum Deae Diae cenauerunt et inter cenam Ti. Iulius Alexander]
Line 4 [Iulianus mag(ister) Q. Fuluius] Gillo Bittius Pro[culus ..c.70.. ture uino fecerunt]
Line 5 [ministrantibus pueris p]atrimis et matr[imis senatorum filis isdem q(ui) VI
        k(alendas) easdem et fruges libatas  ministrantibus kalatoribus pueri riciniati]
Line 6 [praetextati cum publicis ad aram] rettul[erunt ...
```

The festival concerned is that of the Dea Dia, in a year in which it was celebrated on 27, 29 and 30 May; i.e. in years with even numbers by modern counting. Two senators are named in lines 3 and 4. Q. Fulvius Gillo Bittius Proculus (*PIR* F.544) was an Arval by AD 101 but had died by 7 February 120, thus giving us an approximate *terminus post quem* and a certain *terminus ante quem*; Tib. Julius Alexander Iulianus (*PIR* I.142) was an Arval by AD 118. Letter forms and lay-out – especially the very long lines – show affinities between this piece and what is preserved of the records for AD 109-112 in Rome, and very strong links with those for 117 (we lack those for 112-116), but have few affinities with those of 101, 105 and 118; thus a date between 109 and 117 seems likely. The piece cannot belong to any of the years for which any part of the record survives, and so only 114 or 116 are open. Grillo was proconsul of Asia in 115/6 and might well not have been able to return to Rome in time for this ceremony in 116 [3]. When the text was first published it was thought that Alexander was present at the capture of Seleuceia in 116 and could certainly not have reached Rome in time, but it has recently been shown that this was not so [4]. 114, however, remains the more likely year.

NOTES

1. On recent French excavations, see Scheid and Broise 1980, 215f; Scheid 1981, 343f; Scheid 1990. For the texts the basic publication is Henzen 1874; fragments subsequently discovered are in Pasoli 1950; Ferrua 1961-1962, 116f; Panciera 1968, 315f; 1975-1976, 279f.
2. See Beard 1985, especially page 127f.
3. Cf. *IGRR* IV.172.
4. Halfmann 1979, number 53.

2. Fragment of marble without edges (0.125 × 0.175 × 0.017 m), inscribed on one face in Greek letters (line 1, 0.03, line 2, 0.02-0.025) of poor design, perhaps of the third century AD. Inventory number 797455.

```
                ...]
   ...]ων  vac. [...
   ...] v.  συνζ [...
   ...] vac. λ [...
   [...
```

Probably a tombstone. Line 2 suggests συνζήσας or συνζήσασα, or something similar, indicating that the survivor of a couple had erected it. The age of the deceased and the length of the marriage will have followed.

3. Fragment of marble without edges (0.14 × 0.105 × 0.022 m), inscribed on one face in poorly designed Latin lettering (0.034-0.041) of uncertain, but comparatively late, date. Not stratified.

```
               ...]
     ...bene]merent[i...
      [...
```

Most probably a tombstone, in which the deceased was described, very conventionally, as well-deserving. The word is used in both Christian and non-Christian funerary texts.

4. Piece without edges (0.115 × 0.10 × 0.015 m) inscribed between strongly marked guidelines. What survives of the letters (0.04) suggests a comparatively late date, but they are nevertheless quite well-cut. CCC 1.5.

```
            ...]
   ...]VII[...
   ...]STE[...
   [...
```

Line 1, V might be O.

5. Fragment of white marble without edges (0.023 × 0.042 × 0.021 m), inscribed on one face. oo Ex.1.3a.

```
            ...]
   ...]C[...
   [...
```

6. Fragment of white marble without edges (0.10 × 0.11 × 0.024 m), inscribed on one face. Not stratified.

```
           ...]
   ...]M[...
   [...
```

(b) POST-CLASSICAL TEXTS

7. Part of a circular brick stamp. Inventory number 797455. Not stratified.

```
   ...]QRIS OFSOFDO[...
```

Clearly identical with the text of *CIL* XV. 1.1850, interpreted as: *Of(ficina) s(ummae)*, *of(ficina) Dom(itiana) Victoris*, and attributed to the post-Diocletianic period. Bloch (1947, 183-184) suggests that the group to which it belongs is likely to be of Constantinianic date.

8. Upper left corner of a white marble panel (0.135 × 0.18 × 0.025 m), inscribed on one face in letters (line 1, 0.03-0.032, lines 2 and 3, 0.025) which are quite well designed with the use of a ruler and possibly a compass, and featuring serifs. SR00 Ex. 1.4.

```
Cross        vacat
Hic re[quiescit...
qui uix[it annos ..?..?et deposit- est]
sub die BN[...
[...
```

Line 3, B might be R; N might be M. If rightly read, the letters are perhaps from *B(e)neris*. The first dated instance of the formula *sub die* is put by Leclercq in Cabrol and Leclercq 1907-1953 III, col.799 to AD 400; it is rare in fifth century texts and only becomes common in those of the sixth. The lettering may also fit a sixth century date, although it could be as early as the fourth.

9. Ten fragments, all apparently from the same white marble panel, inscribed on one face in well-cut letters (Pl. 75a-d).
(a) Two adjoining fragments with the top edge surviving (0.15 × 0.095 × 0.022), the surface worn at the left side. Letters, 0.018. CC 1.3.

```
   ...]PICVLOEX[...
      ...]IT v.CV[...
 [...
```

Line 1, the word division must come between O and E; of the first surviving letter we have only part of an upper bowl, and we cannot exclude B or R. No likely name fits with this letter group, whether the reading is B, P or R; among nouns there are very few words of any kind to choose from if it is P, and none with obviously relevant sense (unless perhaps *spiculus, spiculum*), if it is B only *cubiculum*, but if R a greater range, of which *terriculum, periculum* could be relevant; *cubiculum* is used in the sense of 'oratory-cum-mortuary' by Paulinus of Nola, *Epistulae* 32.12, and of 'tomb' in *Liber Pontificalis*, i, 162, 232 (information from Dr S. Barnish); *periculum ex* with an account of the source of the danger (e.g. one encountered by the donors from some natural disaster, or from brigands, would provide the context in which a vow might be made that was now being paid, cf. b, line 1, on the lines of *liberationis periculum maris votum solvent, ILCV* 20e).
Line 2 appears to show a division, perhaps of phrases or even of sentences, between T and C; the traces of a serif at the end are consonant with a restoration *cum*.

(b) Upper right corner with top and right side surviving (0.175 × 0.155 × 0.028 m). Letters, 0.017-0.018; the final letter in line 2 is cut small and that of line 4 a little reduced. 00 Ex.1.5.

```
    ...]VEPERSO    vac.
   ...]S v. HVIC DONA vac.
  ...]SISPRAESEN    vac.
 ...]0 v. ET LIGURIA vac.
 [...
```

Line 1, *q]ue* is probable at the beginning; then either *per so[* ... or *perso[* ... , e.g. from *persona* or *persolvo*, the latter being particularly appropriate if a vow was being paid, e.g. *persolvit votum*, see (a), line 1.
Line 2, the vacant space after S may mark the end of a sentence or phrase but could have been used to emphasize the clearly important words which follow; *huic dona[tioni* is certain.
Line 3, the word division lies between S and P, the second word might be from the noun *praesentia* or the participle *praesens*, or indeed from the personal name *Praesens*; *ip]sis praesen[tibus* suggested by Dr Barnish or *praesen[tibus testibus* could be considered.
Line 4, the vacant space may indicate the end of a sentence but, again, could have been used to emphasize the words which follow; *Liguria* suggests a geographical reference, perhaps one linked to a preceding geographical term (cf. *Aemilia et Liguria* as an administrative district in the classical period), but I have been unable to find anything of the kind to restore here; alternatively it could be taken as a feminine personal name, the wife of the donor perhaps, in which case the first letter of the line would suggest that man and wife appeared in the ablative, not the nominative (although a nominative masculine name ending in *-o* is not impossible).

(c) Piece without edges (0.165 × 0.145 × 0.037-0.041 m), the surface damaged at the left side. Letters, 0.015-0.018. 00 Ex. 1.2.

```
               ...]
   ...]MVALE[...
    ...]SECONSILIOV[...
  ...]COPALISDEP[...
    ...]CTASR[...
  [...
```

Plate 75,a. Santa Rufina: inscription number 9, fragments a, e, f and g (*Museo dell'Alto Medioevo*, Rome)

Plate 75,b. Santa Rufina: inscription number 9, fragment b (*Museo dell'Alto Medioevo*, Rome)

Plate 75,c. Santa Rufina: inscription number 9, fragment c (*Museo dell'Alto Medioevo*, Rome)

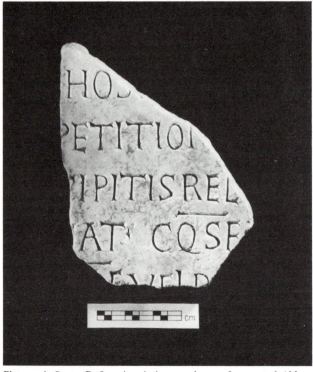

Plate 75,d. Santa Rufina: inscription number 9, fragment d (*Museo dell'Alto Medioevo*, Rome)

Line 1 the word division is presumably between Ṃ and V; M could be A; the next word may be part of the name *Valerius* or *Valeria*, cf. (e), line 1.

Line 2,]*s e consilio* (suggested by Dr Barnish),]*se* (whether for *se* or from e.g. *esse, donavisse*) are both technically possible; the final V might begin another noun (e.g. *vigilantia*), a personal name or perhaps *v[enerabilis*, a common title for a bishop.

Line 3, the first word division between S and D is certain; what follows might be *de p*[. . or *dep*[. .; the final letter could be R or B; Dr Barnish attractively conjectures *Vale[rius . .?. .]s e consilio V[. .?. . viri epis]copalis dep[osuit. . .*

Line 4, the word division is uncertain and the final letter could be P or B; Dr Barnish's proposal *ad san]ctas R[ufinam et Secundam* is very tempting – but *au]cta sp[e*, or the like, remains technically possible.

(d) Piece without edges (0.18 × 0.17 × 0.03 m). oo Ex.1.5.

```
                        ...]
        ...]HOS[...
        ...]PETITION[...
        ...]CIPITISREL[...
        ...]TAT stop vac. CQSF ?stop [...
   (5)  ...]ṢF̣ ?stop ṾẸLP[...
        [...
```

Superscript bars above CQSF in line 4 and]SF in line 5.

Line 3, the word division lies between S and R; the first word might be from a verb (second person plural), e.g. *sus]cipitis, per]cipitis*, or from an adjective (genitive singular), e.g. *an]cipitis, prae]cipitis*; the second is probably a noun, e.g. *rel[atio* or *rel[iquiae*. A *relatio* here would fit well with the *petitio* of line 2; another attractive possibility is something on the lines of *suscipitis reliquias*, with reference to the saints' relics.

Line 4, begins with a verb, and after the stop and space, gives an abbreviation; this does not seem to represent any of those common in classical Latin but is recorded with the resolution *c(um) q(ue) s(uscepta) f(uisset)* from two eighth century inscriptions by Cappelli 1912, 64, col.II (reference owed to Miss A. Duke). The traces of the stop conjectured after it are not certain.

Line 5, there was probably the same or a similar abbreviation at the beginning – the superscript bar clearly continued to left of the break; little survives of the S, however, and F might be E; at the end P might be R or B.

(e) Two adjoining fragments without edges (0.17 × 0.10 × 0.025 m). Letters, 0.015-0.018. oo Ex.1.4 and oo Ex.1.5.

```
                        ...]
        ...]LER[.2-3.]ẸXDE[...
        ...]RADEDIMVSS[...
        ...]PAROECIANOS[...
        [...
```

Line 1 perhaps begins with the name Valerius, Valeria, cf. (c), line 1, and could be followed by the title *ex defensor*, or, more simply, by some such phrase as *ex de[creto, ex de[bito, ex de[votione* (suggestions of Dr Barnish).

Line 2 suggests *sup]ra* or *inf]ra*.

Line 3, either *paroecia nostra* or *paroecianos* (but the adjective seems unattested at any likely date); for the spelling see below. *Paroecia* should refer to a suburbicarian diocese, possibly Santa Rufina itself (information owed to Dr Llewellyn).

(f) Two adjoining pieces without edges. CC 1.3 and oo Ex.1.3a.

```
                        ...]
        ...]Ṣ[...
        ...]ṬEṬỊ[...
        ...]C stop DI[...
        ...]CTO[...
        [...
```

A superscript bar covered an abbreviation ending with C in line 3.

Line 2, there is no doubt of the initial T, although very little of it survives; there was perhaps a verb ending]*t*, followed by *et* or *etiam*, or a verb ending]*tet* (cf.]*tat* in d, line 4).

Line 3, begins with an abbreviation in which several letters were cut between stops and under a bar which continued to left of the break. Line 4, *san]cto* is attractive, but e.g. *au]cto* not impossible, cf.(c) line 4.

(g) Piece without edges. oo Ex.1.3.

```
              ...]
    ...]AEPI[...
    ...]DVMVT[...
    [...
```

Line 1, there are too many possibilities for useful speculation, but *epi[scop-* is perhaps worth mentioning.

Line 2, perhaps a gerund or gerundive followed by *ut*, e.g. *statuen]dum ut [* . . .

The inscription must have occupied a sizeable panel of good marble. Its lettering was well-cut with shaped trenches and shading, and with pronounced, but not exaggerated serifs. Its letters were designed with the help of a ruler (probably also of a compass) and with monumental capitals of the classical period in mind (only G is influenced by cursives but it remains elegantly adapted to its surroundings). Its layout shows concern for lineation, but also for avoidance of the monotony which can result from a rigid calculation of letter-heights; that aim is also nicely shown at the line-ends of fragment (a), where words running over from one line to the next have been divided very correctly (with breaks after a vowel or between adjacent consonants) and the viewer's eye is provided with a satisfying conclusion in each line which also offers a satisfying effect down the whole right side; there the border is not so regular in width as with a printer's justification (line 1 is a little indented, line 2 a little outspaced, and here, as in line 4, the A which obtrudes, or, in line 4, might have obtruded, into the margin is reduced in size) but not untidy as with an unprofessionally produced manuscript. Within the text there are normally no word divisions, although occasional very small vacant spaces which may mark the ends of sentences or phrases, but could have been used for emphasis of specific words; stops – finely cut in the shape of thorns – appear to be used in proximity to abbreviations (perhaps one on either side of each) and abbreviations are certainly marked by well executed superscript bars. It seems to me that the designer has sought to modify the formality of the best classical inscriptions (and indeed of those of Pope Damasus) with practices based on the best freehand work of a fine manuscript; but, whether or not that view is accepted, it is clear that a careful and skilful artist/craftsman was employed. The panel could easily have been displayed in Rome itself, but was more probably meant for the site, since it mentions a *paroecia* or *paroeciani* (c, line 3).

The date has been variously assessed by those who have seen the photographs, between the late fourth and the sixth centuries AD. In the absence of a really modern manual of Latin epigraphy of the period all proposals are not only subjective but inadequately based; arguments may be adduced for an earlier rather than a later date from the parallels between the letter-forms and those illustrated by Gordon and Gordon 1958-1965, III (1965), number 335 of *c*. AD 380, number 345 of AD 395 and number 354 of AD 408-423, and those visible on the Probus diptych of 406 and the mosaic inscription of 422-432 in Santa Sabina, Rome (all suggested by Dr Barnish). The spelling of *paroecia* in (e), line 3 may provide a subsidiary pointer; this, apparently the original form used, is cited from the works of Augustine and Jerome and one passage of Sidonius Apollinaris, although in a second the manuscripts have the form *parochia* (*TLL*, *sub voce*), which came to prevail during the sixth century (Niermeyer 1976). I hope that it is not purely a spirit of compromise that inclines me to think that there is also a good parallel for the letters in the middle of the fifth century (Gordon and Gordon 1958-1965, III (1965), 174, of AD 441-445).

There can be no controversy, however, about the implication that those who commissioned a monument of such quality had high, even old-fashioned, standards and the money to indulge them. It would befit a pope – although not, of course, Damasus who favoured the distinctive Filocalian letter, which is markedly different from these – but the reference to *paroecia nostra* (or indeed to *paroeciani*) seems inappropriate to a pope. So, perhaps, it suggests a member of the senatorial aristocracy, with whom modern scholars are now linking the martyr cults (Dufourcq 1900, i, 311; Llewellyn 1971, 37; points and references owed to Dr Barnish). Dr Barnish has indicated the connections that can be made between the great family of the Turcii and the saints Rufina and Secunda; the inscription may name a Valerius or a Valeria and possibly a Liguria, and Valerius is a name which can be fitted into the Turcian family tree. It would, however, be more satisfactory to put the words *paroecia nostra* into the mouth of a bishop.

Leaving aside conjecture, the text certainly concerns a donation which (from a and b, line 1) could have been made in gratitude for survival from some peril; and the plural verb *dedimus* (e, line 2) may indicate several donors, conceivably a husband and wife. Dr Barnish observes that the reference to *petitio* and perhaps to *relatio*, could indicate a background of family dispute – as when their family disputed the decision of Valerius Pinianus and his wife, the younger Melania, to give all their estates to charity. Another possibility, suggested by Dr Brown, is that we associate the text with the canonical need for a bishop's inspection of houses and lands granted to the Church as oratories, monasteries, etc. to ensure that they were adequately endowed.

It is most unfortunate that what is obviously an important document is in a condition so fragmentary as to defy reconstruction.

* I am greatly indebted to advice from a number of scholars better acquainted than I with the period to which this text belongs, and well aware that, since their comments were not entirely compatible, my notes are unlikely to commend themselves to any of them. However, thanks are especially due to Dr S. Barnish, Dr T. Brown, Prof. R. Coleman, Miss A. Duke, Mrs N. Gray, Dr P. Llewellyn, Dr R. McKitterick, Dr C. Wickham, as also Dr L. Paroli of the *Museo dell'Alto Medioevo*, who measured and re-read the fragments deposited there.

CHAPTER FOUR. DISCUSSION

The purpose of this discussion is to compare briefly the sequence of events disclosed by the excavation with (a) the pattern of settlement in the Roman Campagna in classical times, and (b) the documentary evidence for the history of *Silva Candida* and its cardinal bishop, as described in Chapter One.

The excavations showed that Santa Rufina had been occupied (with perhaps one break) for more than a thousand years. The structural history of the site may be summarized as follows, with the reservation that the excavation consisted mainly of trenches and that even major buildings could have escaped detection if they lay just a short distance outside the excavated area:

PERIOD I. The site was first occupied between *c.* 400 and *c.* 100 BC. Cuniculi show that the area was drained, presumably for cultivation, and rubbish pits suggest that some form of dwelling, probably a farm, stood in the immediate vicinity.

PERIOD II. Occupation continued, and some time between *c.* 100 and *c.* 30 BC structures with tufo walls of *opus quadratum* were built.

PERIOD III. In IIIa, between *c.* 30 BC and *c.* AD 75, a tank and overflow channels were constructed on the highest part of the promontory, presumably to provide water for a garden or orchard. Other water works were built in IIIb, between *c.* 75 and *c.* 200; at the same time, the opening of a small-scale quarry suggests construction on the site. Between *c.* 200 and the fifth century, however, the function of Santa Rufina changed: agricultural activity ceased after IIIb, and in IIIc a cemetery, mausoleum and catacomb were constructed.

PERIOD IV. Between the fifth and the seventh centuries, part of the catacomb collapsed and was abandoned. The mausoleum, on the other hand, was repaired. The site continued to be occupied, or frequented, until at least the seventh century. A period of abandonment *may* have followed, but there is no positive evidence for this.

PERIOD V. In Va, which began in or after the second half of the eighth century, the site was transformed. The mausoleum (or what was left of it) was demolished. The rectangular room which included a fine mosaic was constructed, as was the walled enclosure with a yard. In Vb, which began in or after the first half of the tenth century, the yard was resurfaced.

PERIOD VI. In and after the late medieval period, the site was virtually abandoned. Thereafter, it was visited from time to time by persons seeking building materials or (presumably) treasure, and by those who grazed their flocks or grew their crops over the remains of the Roman and early medieval buildings.

In many respects, the development of Santa Rufina in periods I-IIIb is typical of agricultural sites of the republican and early imperial periods in the vicinity of Rome. As a well-drained site on a well-established route, it was occupied at a relatively early date (before *c.* 100 BC). We have next to no information about the size and character of the site in periods I and II, but such evidence as exists implies that the occupation was modest. Perhaps it approximated to the villa at Crocicchie, on the *Via Clodia*, fourteen kilometres north-west of Rome (Potter and Dunbabin 1979). If this is correct, Santa Rufina was one of hundreds – perhaps thousands – of minor sites in the Roman Campagna, where at the end of the first century AD 'the countryside was being farmed on a scale that was quite unprecedented', with two or three sites per square kilometre (Potter 1979a, 133-137).

In the late third, or more probably the early fourth century, the farm was abandoned, as were numerous other small establishments, as large centralized estates absorbed many of the smaller units (Potter 1979a, 138-146). Here, however, there was a special reason. The most prominent features of the site were now the cemetery, mausoleum and catacomb: clear indications that it had become a Christian burying-place. Indeed, the physical remains are consistent with the view that Santa Rufina was the burial place of Saints Rufina and Secunda, who were martyred during the joint reign of Valerian and Gallienus (AD 253-259).

The site continued to attract pilgrims until at least the seventh century, when it appeared in itineraries, such as the *Notitia portarum* (Valentini and Zucchetti 1942, 141). It is tempting to conjecture that the fragmentary inscription (number 9), probably of the mid-fifth century, which mentions a donation and perhaps the translation of relics, may refer to the removal of the relics of Rufina and Secunda from the catacomb, which by this time had collapsed, and their installation in the newly-restored mausoleum or in the church, the existence of which is implied in a document of 501.

The next activity revealed by the excavations consisted of the demolition of the mausoleum, and the construction of the room with the mosaic and the walled enclosure. These events seem to be reflected in an entry in the *Liber Pontificalis*, datable to the years 782-783, which records that Hadrian I '*Immo et basilicam SS Rufinae et Secundae quae ponitur in episcopio Silvae Candidae, quae ab olitana vetustate marcuerat, una cum baptisterio summo studio renovavit*'. At about the same time, a papal farm, or *domusculta*, was established in the vicinity. The farm, which was known as *Galeria*, may have consisted of two estates separated by other holdings, since the name is attached to two separate entities, one on the *Via Aurelia* [sic] *ab urbe Roma plus minus X ad Sanctam Rufinam* (*Liber Pontificalis* i, 502). It is not clear whether this was actually *at* Santa Rufina or somewhere in the neighbourhood. Regardless of the location and fate of the farm, subsequently the basilica received a donation from Leo IV (847-855) (*Liber Pontificalis* ii, 113), and was restored in 906 in the wake of damage inflicted by Moslem raiders.

The correlation of the site and the documents is not without problems. The room with the mosaic was identified as a church or chapel almost immediately after its discovery. This may be correct, but the evidence is inconclusive. There is no trace of an altar (and no break in the mosaic floor that corresponds with the likely position) and the wall that projects from the east end, which has been identified tentatively as part of an apse (cf. Potter 1979a, 151, Fig. 43), shows *no* trace of curvature (see Fig. 55).

While the identity of the room with the mosaic remains uncertain, it does seem likely that the walled enclosure, originally identified as a 'medieval village', in fact is either the *episcopium*, or one of the home farms of the *domusculta*. The evidence is too flimsy to support any conclusive argument, but the absence of fortifications suggest that the enclosure was *not* the *episcopium* which bishop Peter refortified in the 1020s.

By the eleventh century, the importance of the office of cardinal bishop of *Silva Candida* bore no relation whatsoever to the character of the site as revealed in these excavations. Santa Rufina had declined from a major cult centre to a minor rural shrine, and in the centuries that followed it was to lose even this modest status. Thus, in the pontificate of Callistus II (1119-1124), the diocese was merged with that of Porto, neither region (it seems) having the population or prestige to sustain its own prelate. The decline of Santa Rufina between the ninth and the twelfth centuries, at a time when its cardinal bishop was a powerful and prestigious figure at the papal court, sounds a salutary warning against assuming that the importance of an office accurately reflects the importance of its titular seat.

APPENDIX 1. Il Mosaico. Tipologia e Cronologia

Federico Guidobaldi

La cronologia proposta per le sequenze stratigrafiche di Santa Rufina suggerirebbe di collocare nell'VIII-IX secolo il pavimento musivo dell'ambiente maggiore del complesso. Si deve però osservare che gli elementi cronologici specifici sono pochi e, comunque, sono riferiti ad aree adiacenti a quelle realmente coperte dai resti pavimentati sopravvissuti: non mi risulta infatti che elementi archeologici riferibili alla stessa età siano stati ricavati da materiali trovati al disotto dello strato musivo (e

quindi 'sigillati' da esso), dopo la sua totale rimozione.

Sussiste dunque un ragionevole margine di dubbio sulla datazione proposta ed è quindi opportuno cercare conferme o confutazioni sulla base di altri criteri di analisi cronologica.

Esaminando la documentazione grafica (Fig. 55 e 56) e fotografica (Pl. 67-71) di scavo e servendoci della accuratissima descrizione dei resti superstiti, già a suo tempo redatta da Demetrios Michaelides (sopra, pp. 241-244), possiamo facilmente ricostruire lo schema disegnativo dell'intero pavimento che si compone di una cornice a filà di svastiche allacciate ed intercalate da rombi, in nero su fondo bianco [1], e di un campo centrale decorato in bianco su fondo nero da un reticolo a maglie quadrate in cui i punti di incrocio sono ruotati a formare svastiche, lasciando così all'interno un campo ottagonale sottolineato da una cornice interna, pure ottagonale [2].

I motivi risultano relativamente comuni e semiubiquitari specialmente se si considerano, come sembra più logico, scomponendone gli elementi disegnativi di base [3]: essi quindi non offrono possibilità di una precisa definizione cronologica pur se, almeno per il campo centrale le analogie con esempi tardoantichi e paleocristiani sono più precise e più frequenti di quelle con esempi più antichi [4]. In tal senso risultano particolarmente suggestivi anche i confronti con la scultura decorativa del VI secolo nella quale compaiono talvolta motivi identici a quello di Santa Rufina ereditati dal repertorio tradizionale specialmente nelle sue elaborazioni tardoantiche. Tra i numerosi esempi ne ricordo uno poco noto da Costantinopoli (Pl. 76a) ed un altro, ben noto, da Hermopolis Magna (Pl. 76b).

D'altronde il criterio di analisi, oggi largamente usato, che privilegia la ricerca delle analogie dei motivi in un ambito geografico praticamente illimitato può fornire solo occasionalmente risultati definitivi a fini strettamente cronologici.

Nel nostro caso, data la scarsa originalità dei motivi, le speranze di una positiva applicazione di tale criterio sono ancor minori e quindi sembra più logico rivolgersi ad altri elementi redazionali, che, nel nostro caso, sono certamente assai più connotanti, specialmente se esaminati in un ambito geografico circoscritto.

Le caratteristiche principali, e comunque specifiche, del nostro mosaico sono certamente la grossolanità della redazione, specialmente nel campo centrale, e la presenza di semplici motivi, interni ai campi ottagonali nel centro ed a quelli romboidali nella cornice, redatti a tessere assai grandi (2-3 cm di larghezza) e sempre di porfido rosso o verde o comunque di marmo e non di pietra (selce e palombino) come quelle tradizionali (da 1 cm circa) usate nel resto del tappeto musivo.

La trascuratezza della resa del disegno, tracciato, nel campo centrale, con larghe fasce piuttosto che con linee sottili e l'evidente difficoltà che il mosaicista

Plate 76. Scultura decorativa del VI secolo a) Costantinopoli, lapidario di Santa Sofia (A. Guiglia), b) Ashmounein (Hermopolis Magna) basilica (A. Guiglia)

incontro nel comporre le svastiche e, soprattutto, nel raccordarle al bordo, fanno pensare ad un intervento tardo cioè corrispondente ad un periodo di forte decadenza dell'arte musiva: per l'area romana il quarto secolo avanzato sembrerebbe il periodo più probabile anche se il pieno III secolo ed anche le epoche successive al IV non possono essere escluse.

L'uso di tessere porfiretiche e marmoree di grandi dimensioni è invece, come è stato altrove proposto [5], un particolare redazionale che viene introdotto a Roma nell'età tardoseveriana (Terme di Caracalla) ed in seguito entra sempre più decisamente come componente stilistica, oltre che tecnica, dei pavimenti musivi, subendo continue

evoluzioni e trasformandosi infine in una ben definita tipologia, unica erede del mosaico pavimentale tradizionale, che, appunto nell'area romana, scompare precocemente nel IV secolo o, al massimo, all'inizio del V [6]. Questa tipologia, che si arricchisce, sempre più nel tempo, di inserti marmorei geometrici recuperati probabilmente dall'*opus sectile* parietale (per questo è stata chiamata *sectile*-tessellato marmoreo), rinuncia gradualmente alla forma quadrata delle tessere [7] e, nel VI (e in parte del VII) secolo si presenta ormai come forma pavimentale 'marmorea' con intelaiatura a pannelli inquadrati da file di lastrine di marmo e compiture a semplici disegni nei quali i porfidi (talvolta anche il rosso antico o le ofiti) sono usati per i toni scuri ed i marmi bianchi o colorati (con prevalenza di giallo antico e pavonazzetto) sono usati indistintamente per i campi chiari.

L'evoluzione successiva, nell'VIII-IX secolo, corrisponde ad un sempre più accentuato ritorno all'*opus sectile* cioè ad una prevalenza degli elementi marmorei geometrici sulle tessere che diventano sempre più grandi e ritornano alla forma quadrata ma non più per imitare l'antico mosaico quanto per trasformarsi in elementi di intarsio e comporre scacchiere col contrasto cromatico delle tessere adiacenti.

Il mosaico di Santa Rufina, in cui coesistono la redazione tradizionale in bianco e nero e quella a tessere marmoree ancora quadrate di dimensioni grandi, ma non eccessive (sono solo il doppio di quelle di selce e palombino) non trova confronti nel periodo tardo in cui il mosaico bianco-nero non è testimoniato in alcun esempio [8] e quindi si può considerare del tutto fuori uso. Esso trova invece, proprio per la tecnica 'mista' riscontri tipologici con esempi databili al IV secolo semmai alla seconda metà del III.

Si tratta di casi poco frequenti (e poco noti), ma comunque, a mio parere, associabili come testimonianza di un periodo di transizione tra mosaico tradizionale e mosaico marmoreo nell'area romana. Mi riferisco soprattutto ad un pavimento ostiense inedito della *domus* Reg. IV, ins. IV, 7 (Pl. 77), che presenta una tecnica mista con uso di porfidi

Plate 77. Ostia, *domus* IV, 4, 7, particolare del mosaico del corridoio (F. Guidobaldi)

e motivi molto semplici; la datazione al secolo IV (senza escludere la fine del III) si ricava per analogia di struttura e pavimentazione con altre *domus* ostiensi [9].

A Roma la tecnica 'mista' è documentata nell'edificio sotto San Teodoro [10] ed in quello sotto Santa Cecilia in Trastevere [11] di epoca analoga e, quest'ultimo, con motivi centrali talvolta simili a quelli di Santa Rufina anche se redatti con marmi ma senza porfidi. Ad Ostia poi la coesistenza tra tessere minori di selce e palombino e tessere maggiori di marmo talvolta con porfidi è documentata sia in un unico pavimento [12] sia in pavimenti contemporanei di stanze diverse [13] e ci offre datazioni spesso ancora interne al III secolo per gli esempi più 'embrionali' di queste nuove sperimentazioni tecniche.

Concludendo dunque il pavimento di Santa Rufina sembrerebbe appartenere a tipologie redazionali tardoantiche dell'area romana collocabili sia nel III secolo avanzato che nel IV e potrebbe costituire un'ulteriore testimonianza della disgregazione dell'arte musiva pavimentale di tipo tradizionale che in questa zona, come abbiamo più volte ricordato, scomparve precocemente.

Certo, una datazione assai più tarda, cioè successiva all'inizio del VII secolo, non si può escludere del tutto poichè la totale assenza di confronti potrebbe essere casuale. Se così fosse, il pavimento di Santa Rufina sarebbe la testimonianza di una ripresa altomedievale, finora mai ravvisata, della tecnica musiva di età classica nell'area romana.

Questa ipotesi però potrebbe aver qualche consistenza solo se i dati di scavo avessero fornito più solide prove per una datazione altomedievale; allo stato attuale delle conoscenze preferiamo invece mantenere l'ipotesi 'medievale' solo in via del tutto subordinata ad una attribuzione al pieno IV secolo (senza escludere la fine del III o l'inizio del V secolo), più coerente con la redazione 'mista' a grandi e piccole tessere e con le incertezze della resa del disegno, che sembra mantenere una struttura ed una intelaiatura essenzialmente corretta e quindi 'antica'.

Se la datazione che abbiamo proposto come più probabile fosse quella vera si dovrebbe forse rivedere la datazione dell'aula e potrebbe aprirsi una possibilità di interpretazione di essa come parte di una villa o fattoria tardoantica che avrebbe costituito poi il nucleo dell'insediamento cristiano ospitando nell'aula stessa l'ambiente per il culto, come si è verificato d'altronde in numerosissimi altri casi proprio nell'area romana [14].

NOTES

1. Il motivo si trova in Balmelle *et al.* 1985, 81, numero 38, e, anche se è in redazione policroma anzichè in bianco e nero: l'esempio riferito è quello di Ippona pubblicato da Marec 1958, 59-60 e fig. 57a. Manca comunque un confronto per il motivo completo cioè con gli inserti a grosse tessere all'interno delle losanghe.

2. Lo schema di base più vicino al nostro (pur se con motivi interni assai diversi e variati) è quello del Museo di Brescia riportato in Balmelle *et al.* 1985, 255, numero 166b, e più recentemente ristudiato (Donderer 1986, 111, Taf. 38) e datato alla II metà del II secolo. Qualcosa di più prossimo, ma solo dal punto di vista geometrico, si può vedere sia in un mosaico di Sousse (Foucher 1960, numero 57.168, p. 73 e Pl. XXXVIa) ora perduto, in un altro di Ostia (Becatti 1961, numero 419, p. 222 e Tav. LX) datato alla fine III-inizio IV secolo, e in uno rinvenuto nelle catacombe dei Santi Pietro e Marcellino (Blake 1940, 123 e Tav. 33,3) circa dello stesso periodo; il motivo base è comunque decisamente comune e si incontra anche in Spagna (Blasquez 1982, da Toledo, numero 26, tam. 23; Blasquez e Mezquiriz 1985, da Liedena, numero 19, lam. 26; Garcia Guinea 1990, pavimento della stanza 22, Fig, A, p. 38, etc.) in Tripolitania (Aurigemma 1960, tavv. 54,b villa di Ain Zara, 62 villa di Gargaresc, 120 villa di Zliten) in Grecia (Asimakopoulou-Atzaka 1987, pin. 277, da *Klapsi* e 288 da *Axinos*); a Bolsena (Balland *et al.* 1971, 203, Fig. 84).

3. Sembra in effetti poco significativa la ricerca di un motivo identico o simile che può essere fruttuosa solo nei casi in cui si riscontra una netta limitazione geografica dell'insieme dei confronti. In ogni caso, a mio parere, la ricerca di analogia geometrica è uno strumento più debole della ricerca di analogia tecnica e stilistica e, in questo caso, dobbiamo dire che nessuno dei confronti che ho citati si avvicina al nostro da un punto di vista tecnico mentre dal punto di vista tecnico-stilistico qualche somiglianza per la redazione a tratto molto largo si può vedere nell'esempio di Klapsi, ma anche questo è lontano dal nostro perché non presenta l'uso di grandi tessere marmoree e porfiretiche.

4. Gli esempi citati (cfr. note 1 e 2) sono in effetti quasi tutti tardoantichi il che fa pensare, pur se con le dovute eccezioni, che il motivo non fosse diffuso che a partire dal III secolo.

5. Guidobaldi 1983; Guidobaldi e Guiglia Guidobaldi 1983, 198-261.

6. Mentre a Roma non sono individuabili esempi databili oltre il IV secolo tranne un esempio del Museo Nazionale Romano di provenienza privata e quindi dubbio almeno dal punto di vista della zona di origine, ma forse anche da quello dell'autenticità, che viene datato al V secolo senza escludere, in qualche caso (Parlasca) la fine del IV (Paribeni 1932, 88; Blake 1940, 101, Tav. 20, 5 e 7; Dorigo 1966, 253, nota 3 e Tavv. XXXVII e XXXVIII a colori; Parlasca 1969, vol. III, numero 2246, p. 154; Bianchi Bandinelli 1976, 426). È strano che nessuno finora abbia notato in questo mosaico la insolita forma e disposizione delle tessere che sono estremamente rade rispetto a tutti i mosaici a me noti ed anche come materiali sembrano di composizione piuttosto anomala. Alla seconda metà del IV secolo sono attribuiti i mosaici più tardi di Ostia, sempre però del tipo tradizionale cioè quelli della casa dei Dioscuri (Becatti 1961, numeri 214-218, pp. 114-122, tav. CCXXIII).

7. Soltanto nel IX secolo c'è un ritorno alle tessere quadrangolari di dimensioni anche notevoli (4-7 cm) spesso disposte a scacchiera con marmi vari usati per i toni chiari e porfidi (spesso indistintamente) usati per quelli scuri (Guidobaldi e Guiglia Guidobaldi 1983, 460-485). I contesti però sono in questi casi esclusivamente marmorei:

non si riscontra mai, infatti, l'uso associato di tessere tradizionali di materiali non marmorei come selce e palombino.

8. A partire dal V secolo (cfr. nota 6).

9. L'aula tricliniare absidata con pavimento in *opus sectile*, insieme alla muratura in opera listata, abbastanza trascurata, sono elementi sufficienti per ascrivere questa interessante *domus* alla serie messa in evidenza da Becatti (1948) e più recentemente da Pavolini (1986). L'edificio è praticamente quasi del tutto inedito: un cenno delle pavimentazioni in *opus sectile* con due illustrazioni si trova in Guidobaldi 1985, in particolare 206 e 208 (dove, però, per un errore tipografico, è indicato IV,IV,8 invece che IV,IV,7 come nelle figure) e Tavv. 12,2 e 13,2; la pianta ed un cenno al primitivo impianto severiano ed al rifacimento (con aggiunta di abside) nel IV secolo era però già in Becatti 1953, 153. Del tutto inediti sono invece i pavimenti musivi a tratti di mosaico tradizionale alternati a tratti con mosaico marmoreo a grandi tessere anche porfiretiche.

10. Guidobaldi e Guiglia Guidobaldi 1983, 217-224, figg. 61-63 e Tav. I a colore numero 5 (dopo p. 504). Il pavimento è attribuito alla metà del IV secolo.

11. Guidobaldi e Guiglia Guidobaldi 1983, 207-211, Figg. 56-57 e Tav. I a colore numero 4 (dopo p. 504). Il pavimento è attribuito all'inizio del IV secolo. È interessante sottolineare che in questo pavimento a semplice partizione geometrica sussistono, all'interno dei riquadri, anche motivi simili a quelli di Santa Rufina e vi compare anche una svastica ormai intesa probabilmente come eredità del passato.

12. È quello della *domus* Reg. IV, ins. IV, 7 già citata in precedenza (Pl. 77), nella quale le tessere grandi sono in porfidi (rosso o verde) africano, giallo antico, pavonazzetto, ecc., mentre le tessere piccole sono di selce e di palombino.

13. Tra i contesti decorativi che presentano le grandi tessere e le piccole tessere in pavimenti appartenenti alla stessa fase decorativa ricordiamo ad esempio: la *domus* di Amore e Psiche della fine III – prima metà IV secolo; la *domus* dei Dioscuri della seconda metà del IV secolo, che ha peraltro anche un pavimento (numero 218) in cui coesistono tessere piccole e grandi e materiali marmorei e non marmorei; l'edificio in via del Serapide della metà III sec.; le *stationes* delle corporazioni della fine del III secolo; le Terme Reg. IV, ins. IV, 8, della fine del III secolo; le Terme del filosofo della seconda metà del III secolo, etc. (cfr. Becatti 1953, rispettivamente alle pp. 27-29; 114-123; in particolare 119-122; 142; 64-85; 186-187 e 211-213).

14. Guidobaldi 1989.

PART III

San Liberato
A medieval church near Bracciano

by
N. Christie, S. Gibson and J. B. Ward-Perkins

with a contribution by
Joyce Reynolds

FOREWORD

On a visit to Rome in 1978, John Ward-Perkins entrusted David Whitehouse with two box-files of notes, drawings and photographs of San Liberato. The notes consisted of a manuscript draft of the introduction to this article, a revised typescript (prepared by David Whitehouse) of the Description up to and including part of section iv, after which it was in draft, and an unfinished manuscript of the Discussion. In preparing the material for publication, certain changes have been made to the Introduction, and the Description has undergone slight revision. In the Discussion, sections i and ii have been modified and extended, while I have added sections iii and iv, making use of Ward-Perkins' very schematic notes. I have also added the references. Appendices on both the Roman inscriptions and the fragments of early medieval sculpture preserved in the church are included.

Neil Christie (Rome, 1987)

INTRODUCTION

The small church of San Liberato, lying three kilometres north-north-west of Bracciano and thirty-eight kilometres north-west of Rome, occupies a magnificent site in a terraced clearing of the chestnut woods (the *Macchia della Fiora*) that cover the steep western slopes of the Bracciano crater. From here one gains extensive views over the lake, from Trevignano on the north shore to Anguillara at the south-east corner (Pl. 79). Bracciano itself, with its towering medieval castle, lies just out of sight to the right, while above and behind lie the villages of Manziana and Oriolo.

Until the construction of the country residence of the former owner, Count Sanminiatelli, on higher ground a short distance to the north-west, the church was the only building standing on the presumed site of the small Roman town of *Forum Clodii*. At this point, the line of the Roman *Via Clodia*, laid out in the early third century BC to give access to the newly-annexed territories of south-central Etruria, left the lakeside and climbed steeply to the higher ground that constitutes the watershed between the Tiber valley and the Mignone and its tributaries. Here, in a clearing of what at the time must have been

Plate 78. San Liberato: view of church from north-east (Gibson)

largely virgin forest, *Forum Clodii* was established to serve as the focal point for the scattered population of the area. Like most of the roadside settlements in the region, the town enjoyed a modest prosperity during the early Empire, but unlike most of them, it also appears to have survived as an urban entity throughout late Antiquity and the early Middle Ages. A number of inscriptions of the third and fourth centuries AD exist, while bishops are attested at *Forum Clodii* in 313 and 465 [1]. One may hazard the guess that urban life came to an end in or about the tenth century, a period which saw the virtual extinction of such open settlements throughout the area and the establishment in their place of the strongly-fortified centres of the later Middle Ages – including Bracciano, Trevignano and Anguillara. The inhabitants of *Forum Clodii* may have been absorbed by one or all of these sites [2].

The church of San Liberato, however, otherwise known with the dedication of Saint Marcianus, is not definitely attested until 1234, when a document establishing the boundary between Bracciano (*castrum Brachiani*) and Manziana (*castrum sancti Pupae*) refers to the *tenuta sancti Marciani* [3]. At what stage it actually acquired the relics of San Marciano is not known. Subsequently it is recorded with a triple dedication to the martyrs, Saints Marcus, Marcianus and Liberatus, when it lay in the hands of the Augustinian Fathers of Bracciano. A fresco within the church, dated to 1589, shows the Madonna and child flanked by the Saints Marcianus and Marcus. The Fathers were responsible for the transformation of San Liberato in the sixteenth century into the form in which we see it today, converting sections of an enlarged church complex to secular use [4]; such work was continued in the later nineteenth century when the church came into the possession of the Odescalchi family, who own the site today. The church has, however, never lost its function and is occasionally still used for services.

Although nothing of the visible structure is as early as the Roman period, it is not unreasonable to argue that the presence of an early medieval church in this location implies some form of continuity with the site's classical past. At the very least we should assume that when the church was built, there were ruinous Roman buildings in the vicinity to provide the materials for construction. It is, therefore, a building of some historical as well as purely architectural interest; and since its much-needed restoration in 1961 offered a uniquely favourable opportunity for studying its structural history, it seemed amply worthwhile to include it in the topographical and historical survey which the British School at Rome was then conducting in south Etruria [5].

In July 1963, one of the present authors, Miss Sheila Gibson, carried out the architectural survey on which this article is based. Concurrently, Miss Joyce Reynolds, Mr (now Prof.) Michael Mallett and other members of the British School were able to study the building, the many inscriptions that it contains and the other archaeological and documentary evidence for the site of *Forum Clodii* in classical and medieval times. An analysis of the early medieval sculpture is included in this article as an appendix. The main body of text offers an account of the church itself, its structural history and its chronology and local affinities. We wish to record our gratitude to colleagues at the British School; to the British Academy, which made Miss Gibson's visit possible; and above all to the late Count Samminiatelli, without whose enthusiasm, erudition and hospitality the project would never have taken shape.

DESCRIPTION

The church of San Liberato, as one sees it today (Pls 78-80), is an organism that evolved slowly over many centuries [6]. Excluding the recent restorations, which consisted entirely of the elimination of certain modern alterations and the consolidation of the ancient structure, the surviving building displays the work of at least four periods. These may be summarized as follows:

I. The original chapel, a simple rectangular building with a lean-to porch at the east end, and, quite possibly, an annular crypt at its west end.

II. The enlargement of the original chapel by the addition of an arcaded aisle along the north side and of a campanile at the south-west corner, and by the replacement of the earlier porch by a more substantial, arcaded structure.

III. The remodelling of the interior, including the building of the present apse and the construction (or restoration) of the annular crypt, the addition of an upper storey to the porch, and certain other additions or modifications along the north flank of the church.

IV. The construction of a range of rooms along the south flank of the church and a number of other alterations, of uncertain but probably quite recent date, converting all but the original chapel and the western extremity of the north aisle to secular use.

Before turning to a description of the building itself, it will be helpful at this point to describe briefly the types of masonry used in each phase of construction.

The first period builders made extensive use of massive tufo blocks, presumably drawn from the ruins of *Forum Clodii*, some still carefully squared, others damaged in reuse and somewhat irregular in shape. These are set in a thick bed of mortar and the interstices patched with smaller stones. As one would expect, the larger blocks tend to be employed in the footings and in the lower courses of the structure, with the more regularly shaped blocks set at the angles, or framing such features as doors and windows. In general the blocks were laid with one good face towards the outside, and the resulting irregularities of the inner face were made up in smaller work, which is apt to convey the misleading impression of a patchwork of many periods. In the upper parts of the walls (e.g. on the inner face of the facade wall, at bracket level) there are considerable stretches of small, roughly-coursed rubble, with occasional bricks, laid in the same thick mortar; the walls were capped with square blocks to provide a substantial seating for the roof.

The period II builders reused the earlier masonry wherever it was convenient, but they also introduced two new and distinctive techniques – smaller blocks of tufo (*tufelli*) laid in neat courses, and brickwork. To judge from the uniformity of its colour and texture,

Plate 79. San Liberato: view of church and Lake Bracciano from west (Gibson)

the tufo was freshly quarried rather than recut, and it was laid to form a facing of regular, neatly-joined courses, varying in height from 0.16 to 0.24 m. The core was of mortared rubble, and, as in period I, the outer face was the more carefully contrived. In places the inner face is a rougher version of the coursed work of the outer face, but more commonly it consists of a patchwork, distinguishable from that of period I by a far more liberal use of brick, by the rough squaring of many of the smaller, brick-sized chunks of tufo, and by a well-marked tendency for these materials to be laid in roughly horizontal courses. This masonry can be seen at its most characteristic in the outer face of the added north aisle (see below Fig. 104) and in the north wall of the chapel, immediately above the Period II arcades (below, Fig. 102).

The period II brickwork was laid in regular courses with abundant, greyish-white mortar. The five module height for the brickwork (= the height of five bricks with their mortar beds) was *c.* 0.28-0.3 m. The fragmentary nature of the brickwork should be an indication of the reuse of Roman brick, again from the nearby ruins. The campanile is predominantly brick-built and can be attributed to period II; at intervals in its face, however, there are single levelling courses of dark grey blocks of tufo (see below Pl. 84). This brickwork and the roughly contemporary tufo-faced rubblework noted above can most probably be equated with the work of two separate squads of workmen, one of which was responsible for the campanile, and the other for the north aisle.

The masonry of the third period is a mortared rubble, in which the mortar is in places used so liberally (as in the upper part of the facade and the exterior of the main apse) that it conveys the impression of a separate rendering. Such a rendering is in fact apparent on the period IV south wing, where the masonry, whenever visible, is correspondingly cruder in finish. The most characteristic feature of this fourth period work is the treatment of the heads of doors and windows as a flat arch or

Plate 80. San Liberato: view of church from south-west (Gibson)

brick laid to the distinctive pattern visible in Pl. 84 (below).

The church can be divided into four main structural components: the central chapel, the north wing, the campanile, and the porch. The following paragraphs provide a detailed description of each.

(i) THE CENTRAL CHAPEL

Despite many alterations of detail, the body of the chapel is still that of the original building (cf. Figs 98 and 99). This was a plain rectangular hall, of west–east orientation, measuring 13.35 (13.45) × 8.05 (8.30) m internally (the shape is slightly irregular) and standing just over 6 m high from the floor to the open timber roof. No trace survives of a possible apse contemporary with this church at its west end. The main entrance lay in the middle of the east wall, whence it was displaced about half a metre to the north by the builders of period II in order to position it directly opposite the central archway of the new porch.

The existing masonry of the lower part of the south wall substantially relates to that of the original building, and the blocked doorway located near the middle of this belongs either to this or to the following period. The lower part of the north wall appears to have been entirely rebuilt in period II, when three

arches were inserted to form an arcade between the original church and an added north aisle. The upper part, however, including two splayed windows, can be regarded as original. The present raised presbytery, the underlying annular crypt and the apse are all of period III, though it is plausible that the presbytery and crypt replaced equivalent features of an earlier date. To the first period probably also belong the three blocked windows (each 1.25 m high) of the east wall, the blocked window (c. 1.5 m high) near the east end of the south wall and the central window of the west wall. A number of elements relating to the internal fittings of the early church, which include the carved frame of the east door and fragments of the chancel screen, are described in Appendix 2.

The principal surviving alterations that can be definitely attributed to period II are the northward displacement of the main door, referred to above, and the insertion of the three arches of the north arcade. To achieve the latter it was necessary to dismantle piecemeal the entire period I wall except for a very short stretch at the two ends and a strip of masonry immediately below the roof. Evidently the underpinning of the upper wall was considered a less formidable task than the removal and replacement of the roof timbers. The bottom stones of the piers of the arcade project outward and are noticeably rougher than the stonework above, suggesting that when they were built the floor level was some 0.25-0.3 m higher than it is today.

Another feature attributable to period II is the window (1.25 m high) over the door in the middle of the south wall, which was either inserted or narrowed on this occasion (see below). This window may, however, have replaced a period I opening here. At the same time a great deal of the upper part of this wall was replaced in characteristic period II masonry, consisting largely of bricks and of tufo block courses. Period II also saw the blocking of the three windows of the east wall and the opening of the oculus (of 0.85 m diameter) in the gable above (Pl. 81).

In period III the presbytery and crypt were drastically remodelled, obliterating all but the scantiest traces of whatever had preceded them. The principal new feature was the insertion of an apse, of somewhat splayed semi-circular form, of diameter 4.55 m and internal depth 1.75 m. The squat proportions and eccentric position of this apse – well to the north of the central axis – were determined respectively by the existence of a large period I window in the middle of the west gable and by the correspondingly eccentric position of the period II doorway (Figs 98 and 100). The altar stood in front of the apse in the centre of the presbytery, 1.18 m above the floor level in the body of the church, access from which was by means of two flights of six steps, set up against the outer walls with a vertical wall face 4.8 m long between them (Fig. 100). The northern steps were 1.4 m wide, while those to the south measured

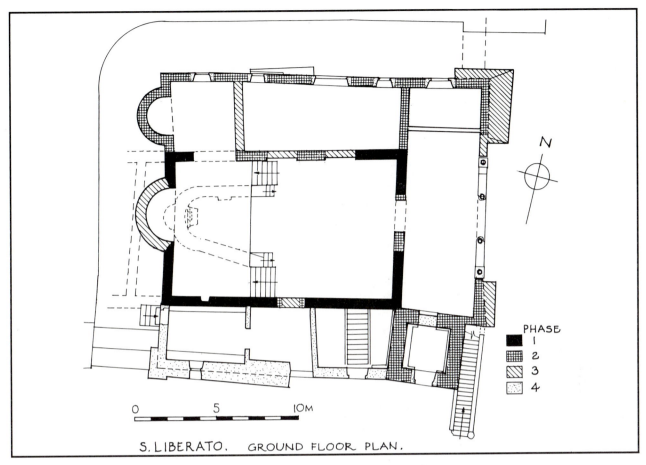

Fig. 98. San Liberato: ground floor plan (SG)

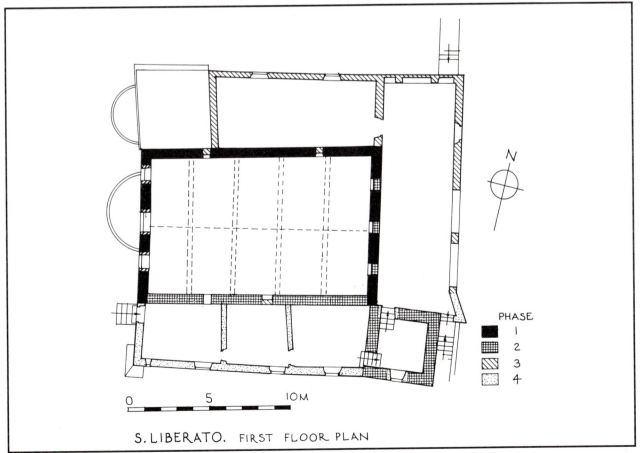

Fig. 99. San Liberato: first floor plan of church (SG)

Plate 81. San Liberato: church interior, east wall and entrance (Gibson)

1.8 m. Between the outer steps and the dividing wall, additional narrower steps (0.6 and 0.8 m wide) were present, leading down to the two entrances of a low, annular crypt. In both cases the steps on the northern side were narrowest, in part compensating for the discrepancy between the axis of the building and that between the entrance, altar and apse. The adjustment was completed within the apse itself whereby the reliquary chamber was positioned directly under the altar (Fig. 98).

As it now stands, the crypt is entirely of period III. The walls are of rough masonry with a crudely contrived barrel vault, the only tangible features being a shallow, rectangular recess in the south wall of the north corridor, which probably once contained a marble plaque or inscription, and the small reliquary chamber, which is little more than a semi-circular widening (c. 0.75 m deep) of the corridor at its farthest point. Opposite this, in the inner wall, can be seen the remains of the three small brick reliquary recesses presumably designed to hold the relics of the martyr-saints Marcus, Marcianus and Liberatus. The chamber itself has suffered greatly in recent times from the attentions of pious hands, crumbling the soft tufo in the belief that it possesses therapeutic qualities.

To provide head-room the floor had been cut down into the solid bedrock to a maximum exposed depth of 0.45 m, and it is here alone that one could hope to find any traces of an earlier crypt. There is in fact an oblique cut in the tufo bedding below the left-hand flight of stairs, on an alignment that suggests a possible association with the otherwise unexplained doorway in the middle of the south wall; in addition, a break, now blocked with masonry, exists in the otherwise continuous tufo at ground level towards the far end of the right-hand wall of the same corridor, just short of the present reliquary chamber. All these indications are consistent with the hypothesis of an earlier crypt of somewhat similar, annular form, but laid out symmetrically about the structural axis of the building and thus coinciding with the presumed original position of the altar. Traces of the other arm of such a crypt will have been destroyed by the construction of the north corridor of the period III crypt. Obviously this hypothesis cannot be tested without dismantling the existing presbytery floor; but that there was a raised presbytery (and therefore some form of crypt) in the earlier building seems to be established by the level of the period II floor in the adjoining north-west chapel, which may be presumed to have been continuous with that of the main presbytery. The steps up to this earlier presbytery must have lain in a different place to the present steps, since those on the north side partially block the central arch of the north arcade. We can rather suggest the former presence of a central flight between the two entrances to the crypt.

To period III must belong the mortared rubble blocking of the windows of the north and east walls,

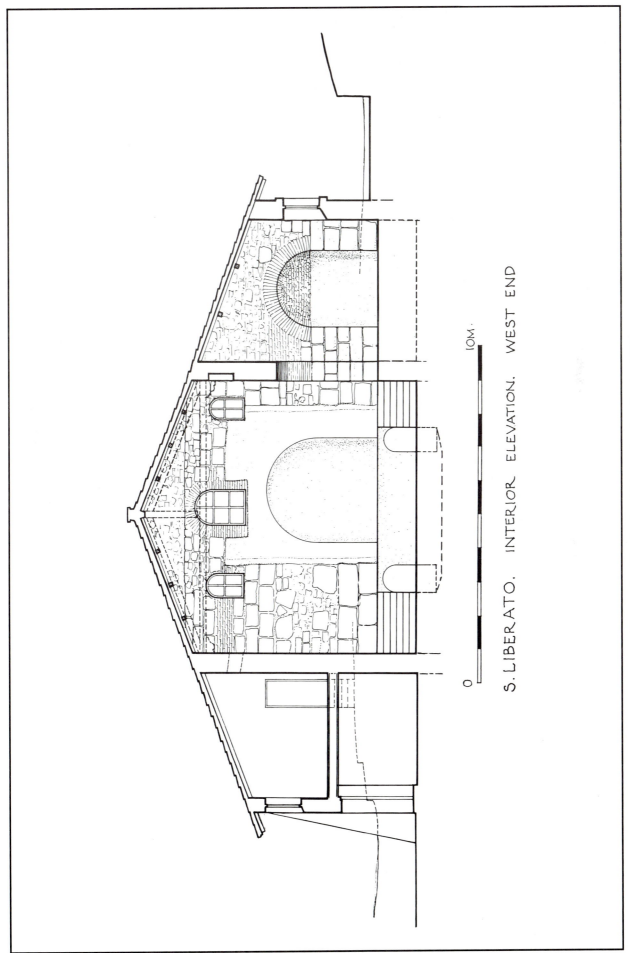

S. LIBERATO.   INTERIOR   ELEVATION.   WEST END

0   10M.

Fig. 100. San Liberato: church interior, elevation of west wall (SG)

and possibly those of the south wall; to this we can probably also add the blocking of the two eastern arches of the north arcade.

The alterations of period IV were almost all of a superficial character and were eliminated in the restorations of 1961. This work has restored the building to substantially the form which it had assumed in period III, except that the north, south and east walls have been stripped of all later accretions of plaster, exposing the masonry beneath. The two blocked windows have been partly opened so as to display the earlier structures. There are traces of period II painting on the plaster of the arcades of the central arch, consisting primarily of parallel red lines, perhaps imitating the fluting of a pilaster.

The analysis of the masonry of the central chapel is complicated by the considerable reuse of the massive period I tufo blocks in later periods, a reuse that was not accompanied by any appreciable change in the character of the mortar bedding. The difficulties are increased by the rather confusing appearance of the inner facing at all periods, particularly in period I, when the irregularities of the reused blocks were made up in smaller masonry in what in many cases have all the superficial appearance of later patches. On the other hand, whereas it is consequently often difficult to determine the exact date of any individual piece of walling, the broad chronological development set out schematically in Figs 98 and 99, seems to be relatively clear and consistent.

That the east wall is basically of period I seems to be securely established by the fact that the band of rubblework above the doorway and below the windows incorporates the brackets of the period I porch and, furthermore, that the windows themselves could never have functioned after the rebuilding of the porch in period II (cf. Fig. 101). Apart from the shifting of the door, it is only in the upper part, above the windows, that there is a great deal of later work. The gable certainly can be attributed to period II. Not only is this of different, and altogether more flimsy build, but the oculus, an integral part of the structure, was evidently added when the windows below it were blocked and was itself made redundant when the porch was reconstructed in period III. The slight eccentricity of the oculus within the gable is perhaps to be explained by the limitations of space and a wish to avoid unduly weakening the seating of the roof timbers.

In the north wall the only substantial element of doubt concerns the ends. In Fig. 102 the east end is shown as being of period I, since both the materials and the manner of their use closely resemble those of the adjoining east wall. On the other hand, the jamb of the arch looks very much as if it had been laid to this form rather than cut out of the existing wall, and it is possible, therefore, that it (and the corresponding jamb at the west end) was carefully rebuilt in period II, using the original materials. The narrow, splayed

windows are, however, clearly set in period I masonry (Pl. 82).

The surface of the south wall is so varied in detail as to suggest at first sight a patchwork of many periods; but once again close inspection reveals a broader pattern (Fig. 103). The lower part of the wall throughout its length and the whole wall at the east end should probably belong to period I: the lower part is built in large, reused tufo blocks patched with rubblework, while the upper part consists of a rubble masonry which towards the west end is noticeably coarser than that of the facade. If the feature high up near the east end is rightly identified as a blocked window, then this too is of this period, corresponding in build and in position to the window located in the opposite wall. Similarly, although one cannot fully exclude the possibility that the blocked doorway was inserted in period II, it seems far more likely that the very massive, irregularly shaped jambs are an original feature (Fig. 103). The upper part of the wall, except for patches of relatively recent date (perhaps connected with the addition of the south wing in period IV), is of typically period II masonry (compare the masonry work located immediately above the arches of the opposite wall). The rather curiously placed window near the west end, from its shape and build, suggests a period I date.

The west wall is still largely covered with sixteenth century plaster. The central window is, as it stands, a recent feature, though it occupies the position of one that was symmetrical with the gable and eccentric to the present apse, and therefore prior to the period III remodelling of the chancel (Fig. 100). The other two windows have been reopened on the evidence of the rather scanty traces of the early jambs. The reason for their curiously asymmetrical setting is not apparent. The gable, like that at the east end, is of flimsier construction than the wall beneath, with a 0.15 m internal offset. The nucleus is presumably of period II.

The present roof cannot be earlier than period III, involving the suppression of several of the earlier windows. The brick floor of the church is a relatively recent replacement. However, in 1837 Nibby described it as composed of various reused material, including part of an inscription to Germanicus. Sections of this flooring were discovered during the 1961 restorations within the church entrance and in the north-west chapel, although it was clear that this had been removed at many points [7].

(ii) THE NORTH WING

In period II the church was enlarged through the addition of an aisle extending the full length of the church north wall (14.75 m) and projecting northwards 4.3 m (4.7 m) (Fig. 98; Pl. 82). Beyond it, to the east, the outer wall was continuous with that of the period II porch. The structural sequence is clear

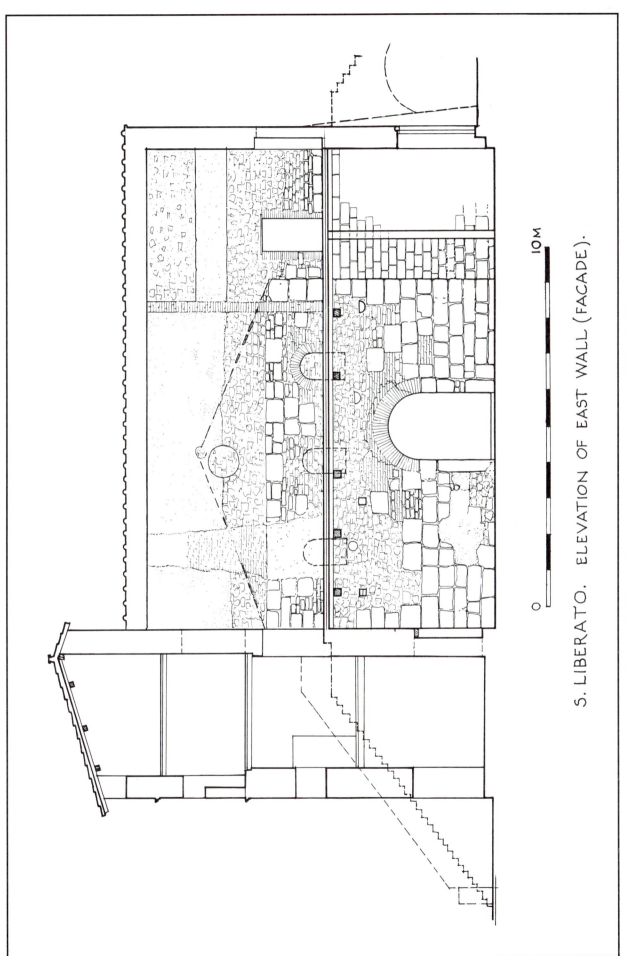

S. LIBERATO. ELEVATION OF EAST WALL (FACADE).

10M

Fig. 101. San Liberato: church exterior, elevation of church east wall (facade) (SG)

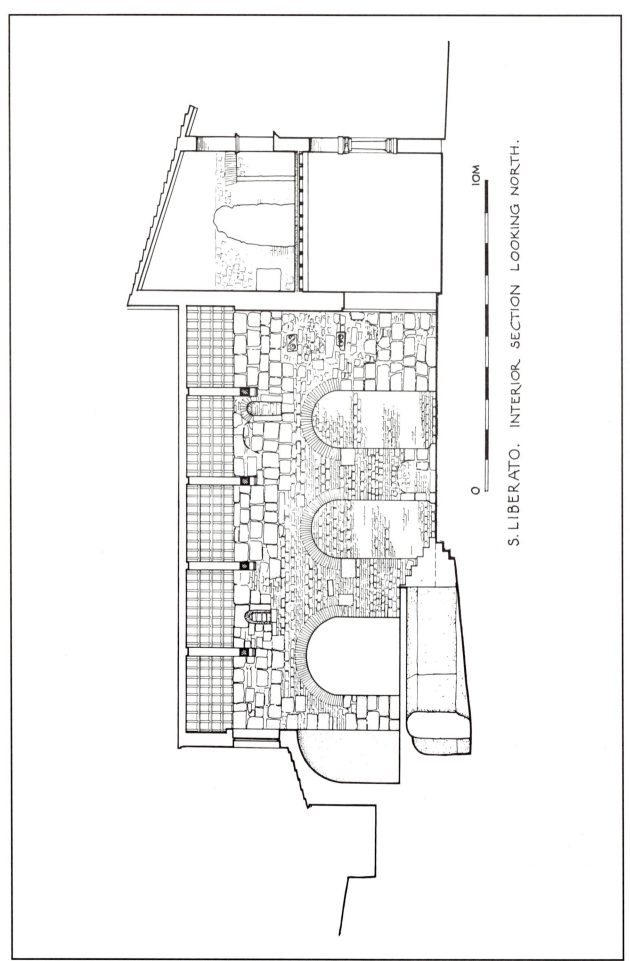

S. LIBERATO. INTERIOR SECTION LOOKING NORTH.

Fig. 102. San Liberato: church interior, elevation of north wall of nave (SG)

Plate 82. San Liberato: church interior, north wall/north arcade (Christie)

at both the north-east and the north-west corners of the early building, where in both cases the period II walls can be seen to have been built up against what were originally free-standing corners of typically massive period I masonry. At a later date, almost certainly in period III, the eastern two-thirds of the added aisle were cut off and the nave arcade blocked, leaving the western part a small chapel of *c*. 3.8 × 4.25 m internally, equipped with a western apse 3.3 m in diameter and accessible only from the church presbytery. This chapel is dedicated specifically to San Liberato [8]. The eastern part of the aisle was converted to secular use, with a second storey added above it. Subsequently, in period IV, the whole wing except for the chapel underwent various minor alterations.

The period II additions to the building are characterized externally by the liberal use of a distinctive facing of medium-sized tufo blocks, most probably quarried for the purpose and laid in courses which range from 0.17 to 0.24 m in height (Fig. 104). Along the outer north face this masonry is mostly rather worn and heavily patched and repointed, but inside the porch, where it has been protected from the weather, there are several stretches that are in excellent condition. At the west end, where the ground level rose rapidly westwards and to a lesser extent northwards, larger blocks were used for the

foundations and for the outer angle of the edifice. The masonry of the apse, which must always have been liberally plastered against the infiltration of water, is somewhat coarser in quality; its most distinctive feature is a corbel table immediately below the roof, consisting of twelve small corbels of very variable shape carrying a projecting course of large flat tiles (Fig. 105). Towards the middle of the north side there is what appears to have been a shallow, rectangular, decorative pilaster.

Internally, with the exception of the window in the north wall, which was added or replaced in period III, the north-west chapel is very much as it was when first built. The floor is continuous with that of the period III presbytery, but it is clear from the level of the painting in the apse that this floor replaced an earlier one at virtually the same level. As noted above, the 1961 restorations here revealed various fragments of marble (including white marble, porphyry and serpentine, and two pieces of an inscription) which must relate to the paving noted by Nibby in 1837. The work further revealed at a depth of *c*. 0.45 m below the floor level some fragments of human bone covered in quick-lime and a small box-like feature of 0.42 × 0.24 × 0.35 m containing additional bone and with further quick-lime around [9].

Only the east wall of the chapel is later, being a

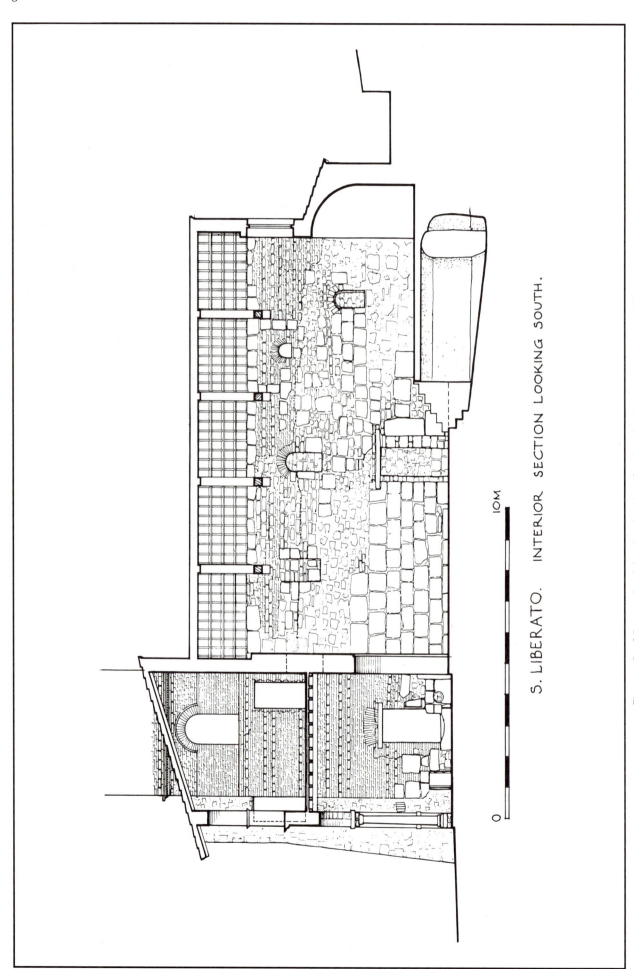

S. LIBERATO. INTERIOR SECTION LOOKING SOUTH.

10M

0

Fig. 103. San Liberato: church interior, elevation of south wall and campanile north face (SG)

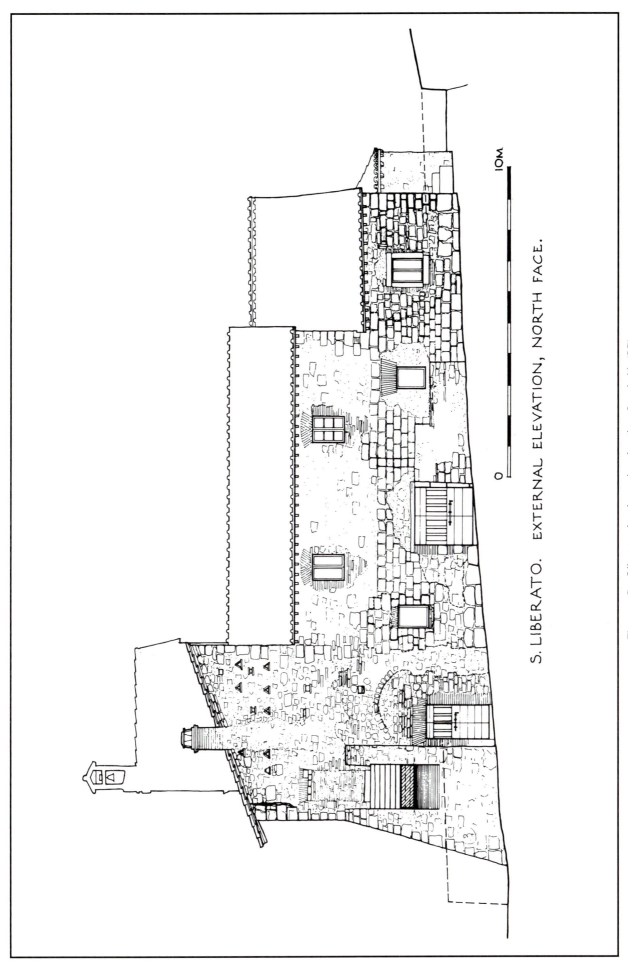

S. LIBERATO. EXTERNAL ELEVATION, NORTH FACE.

IOM

0

Fig. 104. San Liberato: church exterior, elevation of north side (SG)

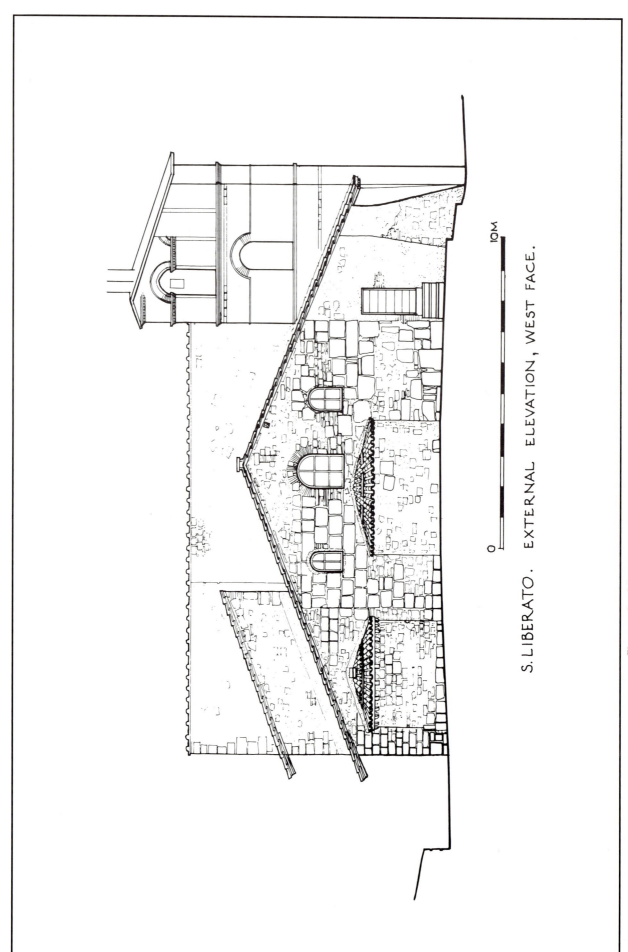

S. LIBERATO. EXTERNAL ELEVATION, WEST FACE.

Fig. 105. San Liberato: church exterior, elevation of west end with apses (SG)

roughly-built partition standing on a line that corresponds with the presumed front of the raised presbytery in period II. The relative levels of the floor and roof did not leave much room for the apse, which is consequently rather squat.

The plaster of the inner face of the apse is missing altogether from the semi-dome, but that of the drum is substantially preserved and features sufficient traces of painting to establish the main lines of its design (Pl. 83). The most distinctive feature is a dado of formal draperies, painted in black upon a white ground, with what appears to be sprays of reddish-brown foliage. Below it is set a band of white and above it a band of red and yellow stripes framing a rather broader black band, on which are traces of a simple white scroll. Above this is the lower part of what appears to have been a circular frame, or disc, painted in black, white and red on a yellow ground and seemingly occupying the rest of the drum and the whole of the semi-dome above it. This frame presumably contained the figure, or group of figures, which was the principal subject of the painting.

The period III alterations to this area were part of a larger scheme whereby the whole of the front of the building except for the narrow passage-way leading to the church was converted into a two-storey residence. The eastern part of the period II north aisle became a storeroom with a large door in the middle of the north wall; above this was added an upper storey accessible from the north end of the upper storey of the porch (cf. Figs 98 and 99). Except for the more westerly of the two ground-floor windows, which is of the following period, the windows and door are all presumably contemporary, as is also the broad, sloping buttress immediately to the west of the door, the top of which was cut away with the insertion of a window in period IV (Fig. 104).

The principal dating evidence lies in the character of the masonry, which is indistinguishable from that of the upper storey of the porch. The whole structure certainly predates the period IV repairs; and a rather tentative straight joint just below roof-level at the east end, where it joins the period III superstructure of the porch, does not necessarily represent any substantial lapse of time. It could equally well mark a distinction in building methods at the point where the builders were anxious to establish a good masonry quoin for what was to be the tallest free-standing corner of the added building. On the other hand, the three windows here attributed to period III are quite different in construction from those of the facade or of the north-west chapel. It is not impossible, therefore, that the upper storey was added at some date after the sixteenth century and before the nineteenth, and that a window was added to the hitherto unlit storeroom on the same occasion. On balance, however, the latter is perhaps the more likely reading of the structural evidence.

The arcade between nave and aisle has been

Plate 83. San Liberato: apse of north chapel (Christie)

discussed above. The differentiation in width between the western arch (2.6 m) and the other two (1.9 m) confirms that there was the same distinction between presbytery and nave as in the main body of the church. The removal of the blocking of the arcades of the north aisle during the 1961 restoration in fact revealed numerous small fragments of marble, including three fragments of inscriptions and a piece of interlace [10].

The character of the added period III masonry is clearly visible in Fig. 104. The window in the north wall of the north-west chapel has a framework of dressed stone slabs similar to those of the period III facade, as it was before the recent restoration. The period IV window set over the buttress, against the storeroom, features a flat arch of brick, which finds comparison with the window and door inserted into the lower part of the south face of the campanile (cf. Pl. 84). The other three windows of the north face have a wooden lintel capped by a rather rudimentary brick relieving arch. The stout wooden lintel of the doorway can probably be regarded as a replacement.

The east end of the church north aisle is discussed below.

(iii) THE CAMPANILE

The campanile stands at the south-east angle, corner to corner with the early chapel (Pl. 84). This is of virtual square plan, 4.5 × 4.4 m (internally 2.7 × 2.7 m), and it survives to a height of roughly 12.35 m. Its axis is markedly askew to that of the church; and although it seems most likely that its erection was part of the same general programme of enlargement and embellishment as the addition of the porch and of the north aisle, the actual construction undoubtedly took place independently, and certainly the lower part at least seems to have been standing when the porch was added. There is a slight overlap with the pre-existing masonry of the angle of the church, sufficient to ensure a weathertight inner corner to the porch, but in other respects the campanile was planned and built as a free-standing structure. At some later date the upper part of the tower fell or was demolished, and subsequent enlargements of the church complex as a whole have resulted in the concealment of some of its lower part. From the standing remains, however, the main lines of the bell-tower are nowhere in doubt.

Since construction of the campanile the ground level has been lowered by more than a metre both externally and on the side facing the porch, thus exposing its foundations. These consist of massive blocks of marble and squared tufo, undoubtedly derived from the ruins of the Roman town, and including several inscriptions and fragments of carving (Fig. 106; Pl. 80). Above the footings, the facing of the tower is almost entirely of coursed brick, periodically interspersed with single courses of small squared blocks of dark tufo *c*. 0.08-0.10 m high. The average height of five courses of brickwork (with mortar beds) is 0.28-0.3 m. There are traces in the horizontal jointing of the decorative scoring known as '*falsa cortina*'. About 3 m above the builders' ground level and thereafter at intervals of about 2 m there are square putlog holes, originally three to each face, marking the position of the scaffolding.

As was regular practice in Romanesque bell-towers of Latium the tower was divided into a series of ascending zones or storeys, each more elaborate than the one below. The lowest and tallest zone, rising to a height of nearly 7 m above the present ground level, was severely plain, the only access to it being a door on the north side, opening off the porch, and the only decoration provided by the pattern introduced by single tufo block courses. The second zone, 2.6 m high, is separated from the first by a simple moulding made up of two courses of bricks each of which projected slightly beyond the one beneath. This zone has a single, round-headed window in the middle of each of its four faces and is otherwise plain except for a course of bricks which projects to form a string course and a frame for the window arch. The two plain projecting courses of the crowning moulding are enriched by one of triangular bricks laid points outwards in a serrated pattern (Pl. 85).

The third zone, 2.7 m high, is considerably more elaborate. There are two windows in each face; the windows themselves are framed within shallow rectangular set-backs, making the piers between the windows look more slender than they are; the string course at the level of the springing of the window arches is enriched with a serrated course of triangular bricks; and between the two hood-moulds there is a patch of herringbone brickwork. The crowning moulding also appears to have been more elaborate than that of the previous zone, featuring the presence of an extra serrated course: however, at this point the tower has been broken off to accommodate a makeshift tiled sloping roof which truncates the windows on the south face (Fig. 107). The little gabled belfry at the north-east corner is contemporary with this roofing. We must assume that the tower was originally much taller (at least one additional storey), but that it had fallen (violent thunderstorms are frequent in the area and it may well have been struck by lightning) or else had become so unsafe that the period III builders found it necessary to truncate it to its present form. At this point or later the existing windows were blocked, doorways were cut through the upper part of the lowest zone, giving access to the added south wing, and a new doorway and window were opened in the south face (Pl. 84). The two last-named alterations can certainly be attributed to period IV.

The interior faces of the campanile closely resemble those of the visible exterior, with the courses of tufo blocks, for example, being continuous through the core and matching up on both faces.

The bricks used in the tower appear to have been taken from nearby ruinous Roman buildings and include roof-tiles, some of which retain their flanges. The principal irregularities in the coursing occur in the initial stages of the structure when the bricklayers were bothered by having to incorporate large, irregular blocks of stone and a doorway opening; the courses above the flat brick arch of the latter show slight undulations (Fig. 103). Above the first line of putlog holes the coursing becomes far more regular, and it is likely that the occasional courses of tufo blocks, which begin at this point, served a practical purpose as levelling courses. It is noticeable that they occur immediately below the decorative crowning mouldings of the first two zones, which in turn formed the seating for the window arches of the zone above.

The irregular nature of the footings on the south side can be seen clearly in Fig. 107. It is perhaps even clearer on the north face, where for a height of 1.1 m above the present pavement the footings of the north-east corner slope inwards, as if originally laid within a tapering trench (Fig. 103). A number of carved or inscribed stones were incorporated in these footings: on the south side can be seen a monumental keystone of white marble carved in relief with an ox-head, and a block of a marble architrave-and-frieze; on the north face we can note part of the bolster-like rolled ornament from the upper angle of a marble funerary monument; part of a marble inscription (*CIL* XI. 3309) used, right way up, as part of the jamb of the north door; and part of another marble block (*CIL* XI. 3312) used sideways as the angle block of the footings of the north-east corner. The wooden lintel of the doorway in the north face is inserted, and the whole of the left jamb is a later patch. The presence of a doorway here in period II is, however, securely attested by the remains of the brick relieving arch above the lintel. The set-back in the right jamb contained a reused marble slab, the fluting of which has left its impression in the mortar.

Plate 85. San Liberato: campanile, detail of upper levels of east face (Gibson)

Plate 84. San Liberato: campanile, from south-east (Christie)

(iv) THE PORCH

The porch in its original period II form was a single-storey structure occupying the angle between the facade of the early church and the newly-built campanile, and extending right across the eastern faces of both the nave and the added north aisle. The plan (Fig. 98) is markedly irregular, particularly where it abuts on the campanile, so much so in fact that, although there can be very little real difference in the dates of the two structures, one is tempted to regard the porch almost as an afterthought, added when the campanile was already complete. This is certainly consistent with the structural sequence at the point of junction. On the other hand, although the north wall of the porch was dismantled and rebuilt in period III (see below), there is good reason to believe that in period II it was continuous with that of the added north aisle. The discrepancies of plan may be no more than the structural phase of a building programme involving workmen trained in two very different traditions of craftsmanship.

The principal feature of the porch was the elegant facade, consisting of a tall columnar central arch flanked by two pairs of slightly smaller arched openings set on a low parapet (Fig. 106; Pl. 78). While the columns, bases and impost-slabs are classical *spolia*, the simple Ionic capitals can be regarded as contemporary medieval workmanship. The arches are turned partly in voussoir blocks of dressed tufo of the same quality as that of the period II walls and partly in brick, without any very consistent differentiation between the two materials. The outermost pair were presumably carried on masonry piers, now masked by later buttresses. The roof was probably a simple pent roof at roughly the height of the existing ceiling.

The plan is not symmetrical, but despite this the central arch fell well to the right of the axis of the early building and of the doorway leading into it; and in order to locate arch and door directly opposite each other in their proper relationship, it was necessary to relocate the door about half a metre to the right of its original position. The work was skilfully carried out, the original door-frame being retained and many of the large blocks of the period I facade reused to fill the resulting gap. In other respects the masonry of the period I facade is still substantially intact to the height of the present ceiling, and incorporated in this, 3.75 m above the present pavement level, are three projecting marble brackets and the stump of a fourth. These brackets are too low to have had anything to do with the roofing of the present porch, and in any case they are symmetrical about the axis of the period I building. The simplest explanation for these brackets is that they formed the supports for the timbers of an earlier, plainer version of the porch. To judge from the small size of these brackets, this was a simple structure (perhaps of timber) built across the front of the early church and set immediately below the three windows of the period I facade (Fig. 101).

Plate 86. San Liberato: porch, previous to the 1961 restorations, showing ninth century door jambs and lintel *in situ* (Ward-Perkins)

The porch underwent drastic modification in period III. The north wall, which must have been in poor condition, was entirely rebuilt and the two outer angles were heavily buttressed; the lateral arches of the arcade were closed and the ground floor divided into three small rooms, leaving only a narrow passage (*c.* 2 m wide) between the central arch and the door into the church; a handsome second storey was added, running the full width of the facade; and, to give access to the second storey, an arch was built at the north-east corner, carrying an open staircase to a doorway in the north wall (Fig. 104). Despite the makeshift character of the buttresses, the facade still had some architectural pretensions. On the ground floor, square, stone-framed windows were incorporated in the blocking of the lateral arches; above, at the south end of the long upper room, two large arches constituted a loggia with fine views down over the lake.

Finally, in period IV, the arches of the loggia were blocked, leaving only one small window (Pl. 86). The door at the north end of the upper room was closed and its place was taken by a new door at the extreme south-east corner. At the same time, doorways were cut through the masonry of the bell-tower to give direct access from the upper room to the first floor of the newly-built south wing.

With the exception of the actual columns and arches, there is now very little of the masonry of the outer facade that can be attributed to period II. That of the balustrades (which must always have had a somewhat makeshift appearance in order to accommodate the differing heights of the columns) is so patched and weathered externally that it might be of any date, but internally it shows regular courses of tufo blocks 0.24-0.25 m high. Everything above the arches appears to be of period III or later, even the

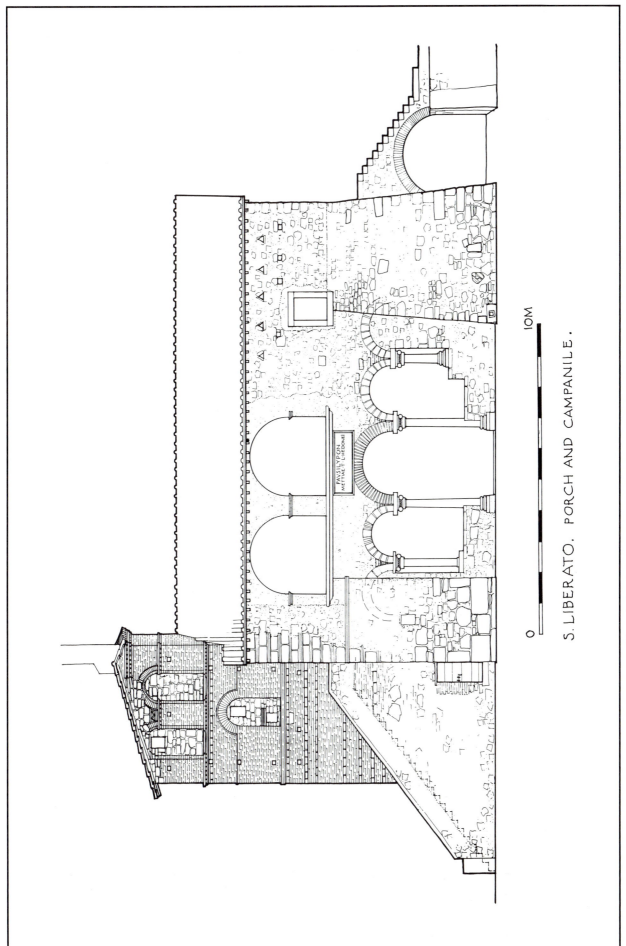

S. LIBERATO. PORCH AND CAMPANILE.

0 IOM

Fig. 106. San Liberato: porch and campanile, elevation of east faces (SG)

tufo voussoirs having been partially patched and replaced in brick. Most of the period IV accretions have now been removed, except for the angle about the south-east buttress, which is formed by masonry in *opus listatum* (alternate courses of tufa blocks and brick bands) and which projects at a slight angle to make room for a doorway between the outer corner and the campanile (see Pl. 84). The door lintel is a characteristic flat, brick arch. Though the lateral arches have been re-opened and one of the sixteenth century window frames inserted in the upper storey (above the north-east buttress), the facade appears much as it did in period III (Fig. 106).

Three of the four porch columns are reused classical pieces. The materials and heights are (from south to north): white Italian marble, 1.94 m; white Greek marble, 2.52 m; a cast of number 2; and white Greek marble, 1.22 m. The first stands on a marble slab, the other three on Attic column-bases, all of which appear to have come from the same building and are much too large for the columns. The Ionic capitals (number 3 is a cast) are of good medieval workmanship, copying classical models. Above each capital a marble slab serves as an impost block.

Built into the south buttress is a marble slab with the date 1816 and the initials (?) L.G.; and incorporated into the north buttress is a marble block with three letters of a Roman inscription (PRI . . . .). At the bottom left-hand corner of the north buttress there is a tufo block with a central square hole of what originally must have been its upper face; the mouth of the recess is rebated to take a lid. This can perhaps be interpreted as a container for a reliquary from one of the earlier churches.

For the south wall of the interior of the porch (the north wall of the tower) see Fig. 103. The present doorway, blocked in period IV, replaces an earlier one, of which the brick relieving arch survives and is an original feature. The height of the footings and their inward batter at the north-east angle of the bell-tower show that, when the latter was built, the ground level at this point was at least one metre higher than today.

The spring of the brick arch over the doorway in the facade of the early church survives on both sides of the door, justifying the restoration of this feature. It was, however, purely constructional, since the original carved jambs were replaced when the doorway was shifted and remained in place until recently. The scars are plainly visible in the masonry. Of the period I brackets, three whole brackets and the stump of a fourth survive *in situ*. They comprise (from south to north): a block of white marble dressed to bracket shape; a plain block of white Greek marble; the stump of a small white marble column; and part of a small column of grey granite flattened above.

The masonry added in period II at the north end of the east wall may be seen in Pl. 79; it extends into the adjoining room at the north-east corner of the building. The north wall of the porch is modern. The floor too appears modern, though Nibby noted here the use of slabs taken from a Roman road surface [11].

(v) THE SOUTH WING (Fig. 107)

This, as it stands, is a recent addition with no hint that it occupies the site of any earlier structure, unless the doorway in the south wall of the early church (see Fig. 103) led to some external feature now totally destroyed. Although the masonry of the south wing is indeterminate, the associated alterations to the campanile, giving access to the upper storey, include the insertion of a window of definite period IV form.

DISCUSSION

(i) THE PROBLEM OF CONTINUITY

In studying the significance of the buildings described above, one is naturally led to ask what their relationship was to those of the Roman town of *Forum Clodii*. In particular, is there any material confirmation of the continuity which the documentary evidence tends to suggest existed between the Roman and medieval periods?

To give a satisfactory answer to this question, one would need to have excavated not only the site of the church itself, but also the adjacent Roman remains. Certain facts, however, are already established, and these do materially limit the possibilities. One is the topographical relationship of the church to the main area of Roman settlement. Except for a piped water-supply leading from a spring in the woods that lie to the north, nothing of Roman (or any subsequent) date was found on the site of a new residential house, just uphill and north-west of the church. The *via Clodia* passed well to the south, following a line that corresponds closely with that of the present track along the edge of the woods, some 300 m away; this then ran uphill beyond the church towards Oriolo. In fact, the clearance of a stretch of this path uncovered a well-preserved section of paved Roman road. The intervening area is full of Roman debris, and cultivation has disclosed the remains of a substantial bath-building of the second or third century AD, only 300-400 m east of the campanile [12]. The church itself, however, clearly lay on the extreme north or north-west edge of the town.

This fact, coupled with the presence at a later date of the worship here of three martyrs, might give weight to the hypothesis that the church originated as a cemetery-chapel on the outskirts of *Forum Clodii*. This theory, however, can be immediately excluded. Although human remains have predictably been discovered at several points around the church, there is no trace whatsoever of the sort of crowded cemetery that is typical of the surroundings of an early

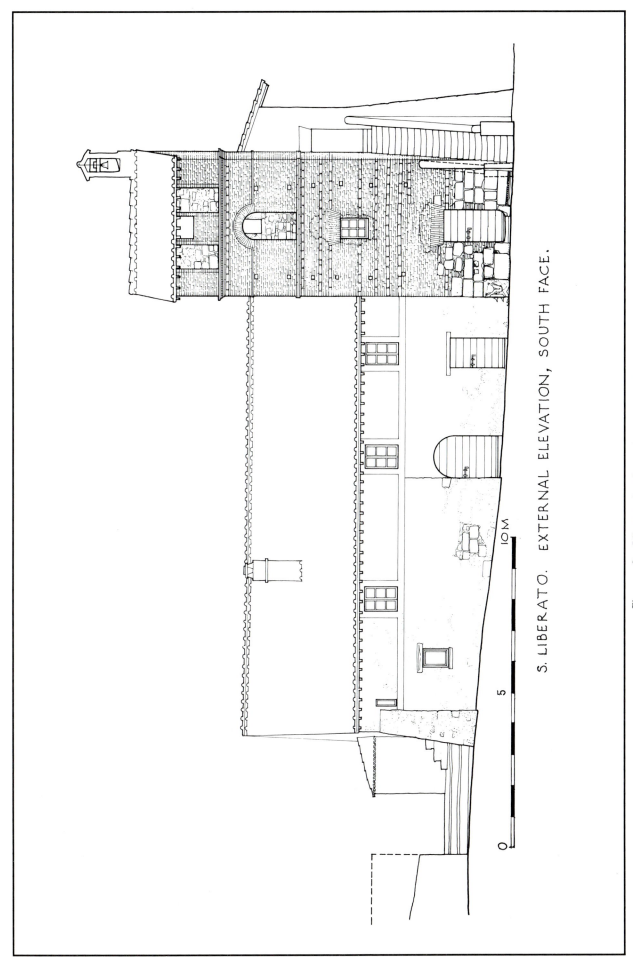

S. LIBERATO. EXTERNAL ELEVATION, SOUTH FACE.

Fig. 107. San Liberato: church exterior, south side (SG)

martyrium. It is inconceivable that evidence of such burials *ad martyres* should not have come to light in the one area that was systematically exposed during the 1961 restoration work, that is, just outside the apse, within a few metres of the focal point of the later church.

Here a small trench (Pl. 87) revealed the foundations of a Roman building in good second century AD brickwork. The orientation of this Roman construction matched that of the period I church; indeed, two of its walls appear to have served as foundations for the sides of the nave. At right angles to these lay a third wall, roughly parallel with the west flank of the church and lying 1.15-1.6 m from this. The springs of the arches in the inner (east) face of the third wall indicated that there was a corresponding fourth wall beneath the present chancel; and the fact that the exposed transverse wall was built against the longitudinal walls, which continued westwards, shows that this was just one room of a much larger complex. This structure will have extended some distance under the church, though not apparently under the eastern part, since the only traces of Roman construction identified here were of different masonry and lay on a slightly different alignment (see Fig. 98).

That the builders of the first church were aware of, and made use of, the remains of this pre-existing structure of imperial date is evident. For some uncertain reason, however, they did not use the transverse wall as a foundation for their west wall, which rests instead on a footing of rough boulders (Pl. 87). The outer walls, in contrast, were placed squarely on those of the Roman building, which thus determined both the width and orientation of its successor. Whether this was a matter of purely constructional convenience, or whether it represents some continuity of Christian association, real or imagined, with the earlier building, is impossible to say. One may perhaps be tempted to see the Roman walls as part of an early *domus ecclesiae* and to link this with the seat of the bishop of *Forum Clodii* recorded for 313; there is, however, nothing in the available evidence to support such an identification, other than the coincidence of location. Without excavation, one can do no more than state the terms of the problem.

(ii) THE FIRST CHURCH

With the construction of the small chapel which forms the nucleus of the present building we reach firmer ground. The main lines of this early church are clear enough and have been described in detail above. This was a simple rectangular hall, measuring 13.35 (13.45) × 8.05 (8.30) m internally and *c.* 7 m

Plate 87. San Liberato: Roman walls uncovered by trenches around the church apse (Daniels)

high from floor to roof, with the altar located at the west end and the main facade facing east. The only structural points which are in doubt, and which call for further comment, concern the nature of the roof and the porch, and the form of the chancel.

The existing roof timbers may well date back to period III, but can hardly be earlier. The positions that they occupy, slotted into the masonry of the side walls, makes nonsense of at least two of the earlier windows. The original roof was undoubtedly slightly higher and was carried on the levelling course of larger blocks which runs right round the building and is, despite later repairs, basically of period I. The fact that this levelling course is carried across the bases of the two gables (which are less substantially built and date from period II) might be taken to indicate that the building originally possessed a hipped roof, that is to say, a roof which sloped at the two ends as well as along the two sides. This is a possibility that cannot be excluded altogether, although there is at least one fact which renders it unlikely. The builders of period II, in their remodelling of the north wall as an arcade, went to a great deal of trouble to avoid displacing the existing roof; and in period II the roof was certainly of conventional gabled form. There is a strong likelihood, therefore, that it had always been so, and it is shown thus in the period I reconstruction (Fig. 108).

The evidence for the existence of a period I porch is drawn solely from the location of four brackets in the facade; but although any additional traces have been inevitably swept away by the more substantial period II structures, it is hard to see what purpose the brackets could have served other than to support a porch feature. This may have been built entirely in timber, with four uprights corresponding to the four brackets. Such a structure would offer an interesting local precedent for the monumental porches of the suceeding, Romanesque period, including that of San Liberato itself. Parallels for such a structure are lacking.

For the form of the original chancel we are dependent upon analogy, supplemented by such evidence as can be drawn from the *disjecta membra* of the early chancel fittings. There were no traces either above or below ground of an early apse (which would have lain some 0.85 m south of the central axis of the period III apse, and therefore might have been expected to leave some remains, at any rate at foundation level), nor could there have been room for an apse below the central window if the period I chancel were already raised above the level of the nave, as it certainly was in period II. On balance, one can argue that the chancel was in fact raised from the outset, and that there was no apse. This at least would suggest a function for the otherwise unexplained door in the middle of the south wall of the church, as giving access to an earlier version of the present sixteenth century annular crypt [13]. The evidence for this period I crypt is slight, however, and one should not

exclude the possibility that in the absence of this feature, the relics of Saint Marcianus were instead housed in a *confessio* beneath the main altar.

As regards the fittings, these comprise several fragments of screen panels of interlace design with related posts, two finely-carved interlace-decorated door jambs, and a number of elongated impost-capitals of a type that was widely diffused in the pre-Romanesque and early Romanesque architecture of central Italy. These elements are all discussed in more detail below (see Appendix 2).

There is much that is hypothetical about the schematic restoration of the chancel (*schola cantorum*) given in Fig. 108, but it is consistent with such evidence as survives. A raised western chancel of this type, with an annular crypt and a chancel screen, would have been a theoretical possibility at any date after the restoration of Saint Peter's undertaken by Pope Gregory the Great (590-604) in *c.* 590, although it would have a more plausible context after the close of the eighth century, when Saint Peter's became a powerful influence on the architecture of Rome and Latium [14]. The carving of the choir screens and the door jambs is hard to date with precision, but would appear to be in keeping with examples known from churches in Rome belonging to the first half of the ninth century – a date recommended, as noted, by the hypothesized period I annular crypt.

One should not forget in this context the isolated reference in the *Liber Pontificalis* to the donation by Leo IV (847-855) of cloth and curtains to an *ecclesia sancti Marciani* situated in the *domucella* of *Balnearola*. Although the location itself cannot be identified, the church dedication may be significant [15]. Why relics of Saint Marcianus came to be deposited there is uncertain, but it may be linked to the general movement of relics within Italy and the Carolingian Empire in the later eighth and ninth centuries. Leo IV does not claim to have built the church: perhaps it was a foundation by one of his predecessors such as Leo III, who had continued Hadrian I's policy of founding estates or *domuscultae* in the papal lands around Rome; in the manner of Hadrian's foundation of the *domusculta Capracorum*, relics of the saint may have been translated to the church which then formed the religious focus of the estate [16]. Although relics changed hands and multiplied at a fearful pace in this period, there is surprisingly no other reference to a church of Saint Marcianus.

We must of course be cautious in applying these data to the church of San Liberato. Nevertheless, it is difficult otherwise to explain the presence of the church: this quite clearly overlay the remains of what had once been a flourishing Roman centre, and can in no way be associated with a fortified or nucleated site in the immediate vicinity. Rather it must be assumed that either it marked an isolated (we lack data to show that anything of *Forum Clodii* still stood) cult centre which owed its survival to the possession of important relics, or that it was founded as part of an

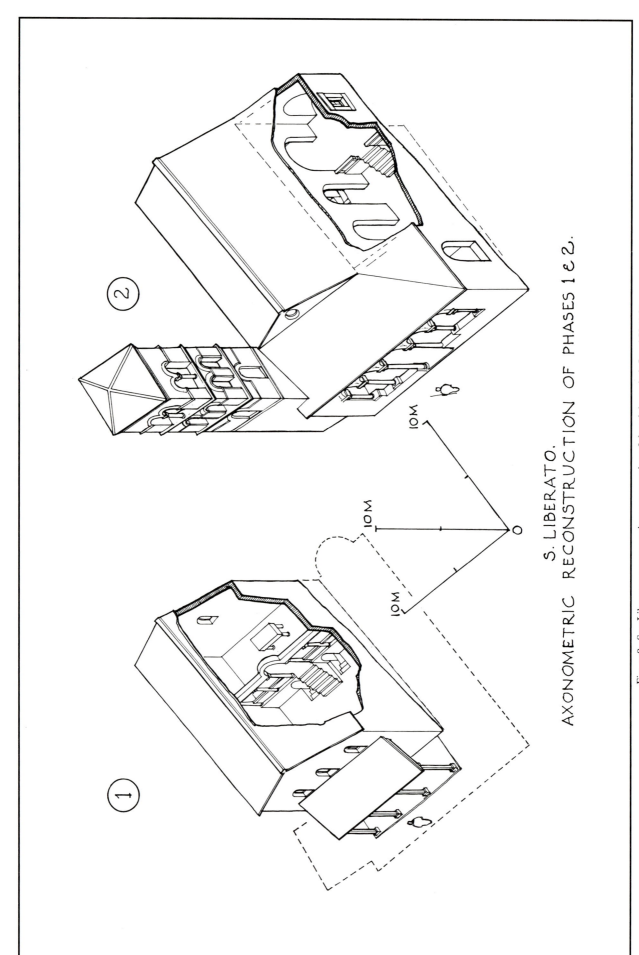

Fig. 108. San Liberato: axonometric reconstruction of church in periods I and II (SG)

estate similar to those founded by the popes between *c.* 750-815, and duly endowed with relics. Presumably the importance of these will have guaranteed the church's survival after the break-up of papal rule in the countryside around Rome. All this must necessarily remain supposition. What is certain, however, is that the construction of the first church at San Liberato belongs substantially to the ninth century.

(iii) THE REMODELLING OF THE CHURCH: PERIOD II

The key problem as regards the chronology of period II at San Liberato concerns the date of construction of the campanile. In order to attempt to define this, it is important to survey briefly the presumed typology of campanili in Rome and in Latium.

One of the earliest surviving bell-towers in Rome is that preceding the atrium of Santi Quattro Coronati [17]. Here we find a powerful construction, lacking divisions into different levels and built rather as a plain brick tower, pierced by windows only at its top where on each face occur arcades supported by three columns. Serafini regarded this as a medieval tower designed to defend the monastery and only subsequently converted into a campanile. Analysis of the brickwork of the church suggests that the tower was part of the building scheme undertaken by Leo IV (847-855) [18]. Comparable structures are lacking. Serafini considered the tower at Santa Sabina to be of ninth century date, although the tendency has been to post-date this to the tenth century. This is a predominantly brick-built structure featuring some tufo in its lowest courses and reusing three Augustan pilaster capitals higher up; in elevation it was pierced on all sides by '*bifore*' or double-windows divided by brick piers, though there does not appear to have been a clear division of the tower into individual zones [19].

Between the eleventh and twelfth centuries, however, the form of the bell-tower developed rapidly, with the design of the windows and of the various levels undergoing the principal changes; the vertical growth of these campanili (see, for example, that of Santa Maria in Cosmedin) was a natural stage in this sequence of elaboration. Unfortunately, we lack precisely dated examples: oddly enough, credit for the construction of a campanile was not readily publicized, and we rely basically on historical inferences and structural data for our understanding of the evolution of the bell-tower. Typical stages in this evolution can be given by two examples, the bell-towers of Santa Maria in Cappella and San Bartolomeo all'Isola.

The first of these, Santa Maria in Cappella, is generally dated to *c.* 1090, when the church was consecrated by Urban II (1088-1099). This brick-built campanile is set towards the facade of the church and rises above the roof for two storeys. The first level is marked by a moulding comprising at its base a projecting brick course, over which is set a serrated course of triangular bricks laid point-outward; above this run two additional projecting brick courses. This moulding is repeated on the second storey, and indeed is very closely comparable with the moulding on the gable of the church facade. The faces of both storeys feature pairs of tall round-headed windows, with a plain projecting string course hood moulding [20]. In the lower storey the windows are separated by a plain brick pier; this is repeated on the upper floor, though here the pier replaces an original single impost column. Similar campanili are visible at San Benedetto in Piscinula, San Lorenzo *de Piscibus*, and on a larger scale at San Lorenzo fuori le mura – these should belong to the late eleventh or early twelfth century; those of San Salvatore alle Coppelle and San Lorenzo in Lucina are more elaborately built and may therefore belong to the second half of the twelfth century [21].

Of later date is the campanile of San Bartolomeo all'Isola. The church itself was of Ottonian foundation (997), but underwent important restorations under Paschal II (1099-1118), and was again consecrated under Alexander II (1159-1181) in 1174 or 1179. The campanile most probably belongs to this later phase of restoration [22]. The brick-built tower comprises five levels, the lowest plain, the second featuring blind double-windows, the third open double-windows with central pier, the fourth with triple-windows with central piers, and the top storey also featuring triple-windows, but decorated with impost columns [23]. The zones are divided by elaborate cornices consisting of seven courses. The central feature is a series of white marble mensoles, between which lie decorative brickwork formed by upright bricks and bricks set as inverted V's; above and below run projecting brick courses, serrated triangular brickwork, and an additional brick course. Each level projects outward slightly more than the course below. The open windows are all set back with respect to the wall face. The window arches are framed by a single brick course, while a moulding runs round each zone at the level of the window arches composed of projecting brick, serrated brick, and projecting brick courses. The upper two levels also feature small mensoles at the springing of each window arch. Glazed bowls ('*bacini*') are present in the wall face above the piers and columns of the top three storeys. The roof, typical of Roman campanili, is tiled and pyramidical in form [24]. Comparable is the smaller campanile of Santa Rufina, also in Rome, though this lacks the glazed bowls (Pl. 88; cf. Pl. 84).

Despite the numerous factors hampering the formulation of an accurate typology, the above two examples serve to demonstrate the principal stages of the evolution of campanili in Rome between the later eleventh and early thirteenth centuries. Examination of the main features of the campanile at San Liberato

Plate 89. San Liberato: campanile of San Giorgio al Velabro, Rome (Christie)

Plate 88. San Liberato: campanile of Santa Rufina, Rome (Christie)

would suggest that its construction belongs earlier rather than later in this sequence: it lacks the use of mensoles in the cornices and of glazed bowls in the faces above the windows (admittedly a feature of the upper floors of bell-towers in Rome and San Liberato of course lacks at least one additional storey). Problematic, however, is the presence of the decorative brickwork between the window arches of the third storey: whereas the '*spina pesce*' brickwork or *opus spicatum* of the north-east face would appear to be an early feature – Serafini notes *opus spicatum* used as decorative levelling courses at Santa Maria della Cella, Viterbo, dated by him to the early ninth century [25] – the use of single bricks set in geometric patterns (principally zig-zag or inverted V's) is a feature common to the elaborate cornices of mid-twelfth century bell-towers in Rome [26].

It is difficult to draw significant data from the actual wall structure of the campanile. Bricks were clearly readily available from the nearby Roman ruins, and while it is possible that the tufo blocks were also reused, it is more likely that these were cut specifically for this work. The tufo blocks were employed more as levelling courses than as components of walling in *opus listatum*. In terms of size, both the tufo blocks and the five module height of the brickwork conform to figures prevalent in Rome during the twelfth century. Confirmation of this general twelfth century date is also obtained from the use of '*falsa cortina*' pointing, whereby the mortarbeds between the brick courses were marked by a horizontal line [27].

Taken as a whole, our evidence would suggest the construction of the San Liberato campanile in the first half of the twelfth century, perhaps contemporary with closely similar towers at Santa Maria del Carmine, Civita Castellana, and San Silvestro, Orte [28], and undoubtedly in response to developing fashions in Rome.

The new period II north wing was constructed in regular courses of tufo blocks *c.* 0.16-0.24 m high, material quite probably freshly-quarried. This does not correspond well with the *opus saracinescum* known in Rome in the thirteenth century which features courses solely of tufo blocks of dimensions 0.075-0.17 × 0.04-0.08 m; in twelfth century contexts, in contrast, tufo was used only in conjunction with brick in *opus listatum* [29]. More valid is a comparison with tufo-built structures in northern Latium (around Viterbo), where, in the period between *c.* 1000 and 1300, one can perceive a general transition from blocks *c.* 0.4 m high to those of *c.* 0.26-0.34 m [30]. At Santa Cornelia, however, the second church (eleventh-thirteenth century) contained tufo blocks 0.2-0.24 m high in both plain tufo walling and in *opus listatum*. This suggests that where natural sources of tufo were available, an active local tradition of building in stone was maintained, bearing little relation to developments elsewhere; it is quite possible, therefore, that local skilled builders were

called in to construct the north aisle and porch at San Liberato. The extensive use of brick in the campanile, on the other hand, suggests the hand of a group of builders skilled in a different medium, perhaps indeed hired from Rome.

Tufo blocks 0.24-0.25 m high are also visible on the internal face of the porch balustrades and can be associated with the period II work. The analysis of the structure of the porch shows clearly that this slightly post-dates the campanile, yet need not be much later than this or the north aisle. In Rome the addition of porches to church facades was in vogue throughout the twelfth and thirteenth centuries: at San Giorgio al Velabro (Pl. 89) an inscription records the donation of the porch in the early thirteenth century, consisting of four columns flanked by brick piers at each corner, resting on a low parapet; twelfth century porches of similar form can be noted at Santi Giovanni e Paolo (dated 1154-1159), San Giovanni a Porta Latina (dated *c.* 1191), San Crisogono and Santa Maria in Cosmedin [31]. Closer to San Liberato we can point to the presence of a porch at Santa Cornelia in *c.* 1040, remodelled in the mid-twelfth century [32].

The construction at San Liberato of three new elements – the campanile, the north aisle and the porch (cf. Fig. 108) – testify to significant attention being paid to what had been a relatively small ninth century chapel. This attention was presumably due to a revival in interest and thus in frequentation of the shrine of the martyr Saint Marcianus with a corresponding requirement for additional internal space (the north aisle) and for updating the existing structure (the addition of a bell-tower and, soon afterwards, a porch). These elements can probably all be placed in the first half of the twelfth century, a period of quite intense church building and restoration activity in Rome [33]. The absence of documentary evidence prevents speculation as regards the patron of these works.

(iv) THE PERIOD III AND IV ALTERATIONS (Fig. 109)

The sole fixed point on which we can assign the building activity of period III is the apse painting dated to 1589. This demonstrates that certainly by this time the church contained the relics of three martyrs, though the construction of a side chapel in period II may be an indication that the arrival of these additional relics in fact dates back to the twelfth century.

Within the main body of the church a series of modifications were carried out. Chief among these were the addition of an apse, the probable insertion of an annular crypt (or the remodelling of an earlier crypt) beneath a new presbytery, and a replastering of the walls. A peculiarity of these additions was the annular crypt, a type which had been current in

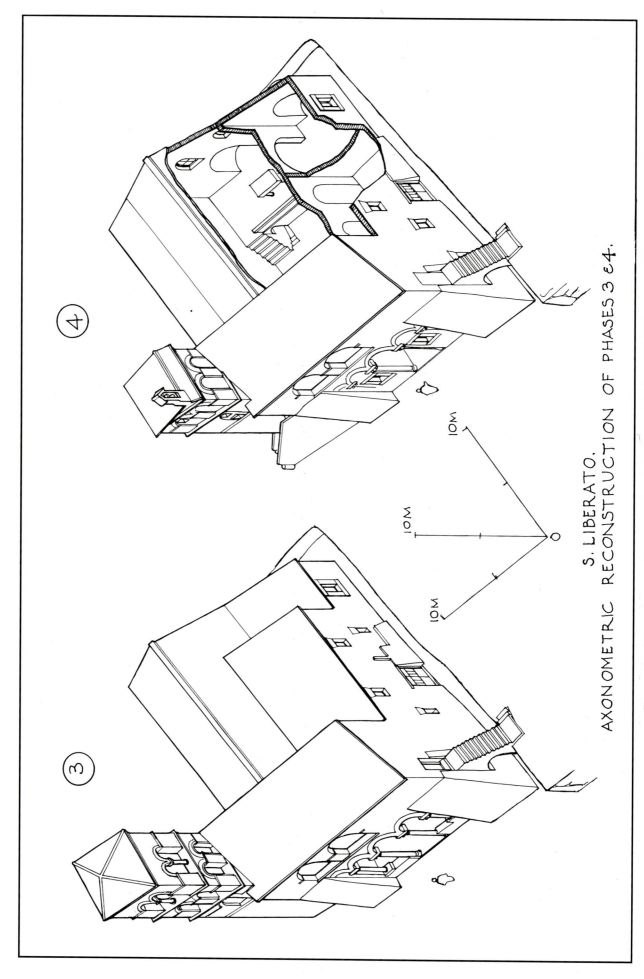

S. LIBERATO.
AXONOMETRIC RECONSTRUCTION OF PHASES 3 &4.

Fig. 109. San Liberato: axonometric reconstruction of church in periods III and IV (SG)

Rome between the seventh and ninth centuries, but which had died out soon after *c.* 900 [34] – hence giving rise to the hypothesis of a period I antecedent.

The modifications to the north flank and to the porch (the addition of a second storey) apparently formed part of a scheme converting sections of the enlarged edifice into residential quarters or storage rooms. Although we cannot be certain, these modifications can probably be associated with the transfer of ownership of San Liberato to the Augustinian friars of Santa Maria Novella, Bracciano, who may have used the church as a base for their apostolic missions. The community was already in existence in 1436 when the monastery was formally founded, and a charter of 1481 indicates that the church of San Marciano/Liberato was by then in their possession [35].

We do not know when the upper storeys of the campanile were demolished and the present belfry attached to the top of a sloping roof – however, the form of the belfry (campanile '*a vela*') is not out of place in a fourteenth to sixteenth century context. Our only guide is a plan of 1651 showing the lands held by the Duke of Bracciano bordering those of Santo Spirito: these depict a group of buildings including one which, while not recorded as a church, very closely resembles the appearance of San Liberato in that it exhibits a tower flanking the facade with a cropped, angled roof. If the identification is correct, the belltower was certainly reduced by the mid-seventeenth century [36].

The final period of building activity at San Liberato relates to further transformations of the edifice into a residential building. This consisted primarily of the construction of the south range, with access provided from this into the upper storey of the bell-tower, the blocking of the arcades of the porch, and the probable renovation of parts of the church structure. The church itself, however, was maintained as a religious, non-secular establishment. It seems probable that this final phase of construction belongs to the mid-nineteenth century, to the time when the church and its surrounding land passed from the hands of the Augustinian friars to those of the Odescalchi family. Some of these late accretions have been removed, in particular those obscuring the porch, and we must be grateful for the careful restorations which have helped clarify the complex, and important, structural evolution of the church of San Liberato.

NOTES

1. Inscriptions: *CIL* XI. 3303-3319 (pp. 502-505). Bishops: cf. Tomassetti 1913, 110.
2. Bracciano is first attested by name in 1234 as *castrum Brachiani* (Tomassetti 1913, 97-98); the same document names the *castrum S. Pupae*, identifiable with Manziana, west of San Liberato; further west lay Monterano, first named in 649 as a bishop's seat, and in the tenth century inserted into the diocese of Sutri (Tomassetti 1913, 117). A *castrum* is recorded at Anguillara Sabazia in 1020, though its origin, like that of Bracciano, should be much earlier (Tomassetti 1913, 77f). Trevignano is also first named in the thirteenth century (Tomassetti 1913, 214f).
3. See Tomassetti 1913, 97-98.
4. The saints Marcus and Marcianus were Egyptian martyrs, whose festival is celebrated on 4 October; Saint Liberatus was a Roman martyr, with a festival on 20 December: cf. Nibby 1837, 325; *Acta Sanctorum. Decembris*, Brussels 1940, 433-434 and 594. Augustinian friars: Tomassetti 1913, 110. They are recorded at Bracciano certainly by 1437, and we should assume their presence from at least the fourteenth century. On the origin of this and other mendicant orders, see Lawrence 1984, 192-220, especially 216-218.
5. Potter 1979a.
6. The church is briefly described in both Nibby 1837, 325-327 and Tomassetti 1913, 111.
7. Nibby 1837, 326, describes the floor as '*di frantumi tolti di quà e di là*'. The details regarding the restorations of 1961 are taken from notes made by Count Sanminiatelli.
8. Cf. Nibby 1837, 325-326, noting that while in documents the church is designated as San Marciano, '*il volgo*' di Bracciano prefer the name San Liberato.
9. See note 7 above.
10. Details regarding the clearance of the arches of the north aisle are taken from notes made by Count Samminiatelli.
11. Nibby 1837, 326, describing the porch flooring '*co'poliedri della antica via*'.
12. Roman finds from the Bracciano/*Forum Clodii* zone: Gamurrini *et al.* 1972, 297-306; Sommella Mura 1969, 22-23; Brunetti Nardi 1981, 38-41; some details also occur in Ashby 1927, 236-237 and Martinori 1930, 180-181. See also the series *Quaderni della Forum Clodii*.
13. Annular crypts were certainly in vogue in Rome between the seventh and ninth centuries as a result of the adoption of this crypt form beneath the altar at Saint Peter's: Toynbee and Ward Perkins 1956, 216f; Krautheimer 1977, 259-260; Magni 1979, 43, who describes the subsequent adoption of 'corridor crypts' and 'room crypts' or '*cryptes à salle*'.
14. See Krautheimer 1980, 85-87; Krautheimer 1937-1977, IV, 258-261.
15. *Liber Pontificalis*, ii, 130. Full reference: '*Fecit autem et in ecclesia sancti Marciani, quae sita est in domucella qui vocatur Balnearola, vestem de fundato I et vela spanisca II*'. Duchesne does not offer an identification of the site location: p. 139, note 58. Caraffa 1981, 176 number 234, however, records a document of 1374 of Gregory XI referring to a *monasterium S. Marciani de Domoculta O.S.B., Sutrinensis diocesis*, again without any site identification. My thanks to G. Ortolani for this reference.
16. *Domuscultae*: Krautheimer 1980, 110-111. On the movement of relics and ninth century church building see Krautheimer 1980, 112-114, 141-142.
17. Cf. Serafini 1927, 223-224; Spartà 1983, 34-35.
18. Bertelli *et al.* 1976-1977, 153-155, noting undulating brick courses, probably all *spolia*, of five module height *c.* 0.27-0.29 m, with bricks of 0.18-0.24 × 0.025-0.045 m.
19. Spartà 1983, 36; Serafini 1927, 94-96, comparing it with the now-lost campanile of San Clemente.
20. Serafini 1927, 96-97 with Pl. XI; Spartà 1983, 46, 50.
21. See individual references in Serafini 1927.

22. Cf. Avagnina *et al.* 1976-1977, 181-184.

23. Serafini 1927, 162-163, with Pl. XLV-XLVII.

24. Comparisons with San Bartolomeo include the campanili of Santa Cecilia, Santa Croce, Santi Giovanni e Paolo, San Giovanni a Porta Latina, Santa Maria in Cosmedin, Santa Maria in Monticelli, Santa Maria in Trastevere and Santa Prassede, all of which belong to the period *c.* 1140-1200; cf. entries in Avagnina *et al.* 1976-1977, and plates in Serafini 1927. Glazed bowls (*bacini*): Mazzucato 1976, though the author has here used Serafini's somewhat dubious dates for the bell-towers in order to date the glazed bowls; cf. Scerrato 1983.

25. Serafini 1927, 87-89, 92.

26. Cf. note 24 above; Serafini 1927, 92-93.

27. Avagnina *et al.* 1976-1977, 245, arguing that it was used chiefly in the first half of the twelfth century; Barclay Lloyd 1985, 233, 237-238.

28. Serafini 1927, 113-114, 176-177, with Pl. XXII and Pl. LVIII.

29. Barclay Lloyd 1985, 239-242; Avagnina *et al.* 1976-1977, 244.

30. Andrews 1978, 391-400, noting (p. 396) that the eleventh-twelfth century church of San Pietro, Tuscania, features long tufo blocks laid in courses 0.18-0.20 m high.

31. San Giorgio: Krautheimer 1937-1977, I, 248-249. For the other churches see individual references in Krautheimer 1937-1977; Krautheimer 1980, 167f.

32. See this volume, Santa Cornelia.

33. Krautheimer 1980, 161ff. A general comparison may be claimed with the church of Santa Maria in Vescovio, a church which arose in the ninth century over the area of Roman *Forum Novum* in the Sabina and which underwent similar structural changes in the twelfth century: see Tomei 1985.

34. See note 13 above.

35. See note 4 above on the friars. Documents relating to Santa Maria Novella are now stored in the Archivio dello Stato, Roma, in *Cassetta* 107 *Collezione Pergamene.* Document of Jan. 3, 1481: *Pergamene* 21, *Cassetta* 107. The church is further recorded in 1521 (*Pergamene* 26) and in 1780 (*Pergamene* 49) when the joint dedication to Marcianus and Liberatus occurs.

36. Plan in the Archivio dello Stato, Rome: *Disegni e Piante Collezion*e I *cartella* 10a number 113. The group of buildings, referred to as '*tre cassette*', is sited in the '*Prato nel territorio della Solfarata di S. Spirito*', either side of which are woods.

APPENDIX 1: The Roman Inscriptions

Joyce Reynolds

The following group of rather fragmentary inscriptions found at *Forum Clodii* is taken from the corpus of inscriptions of the town prepared in 1964 for the British School at Rome to publish with its survey of the church of San Liberato; as far as I can discover they are still unpublished. For recent publication of the more important texts from the site and neighbourhood see Gasperini (1978 and 1984), and Paci (1978).

It is a pleasure to record here the generous help given at the time by the Count and Countess Sanminiatelli. In particular, the Count provided many photographs of the inscriptions considered below.

In all instances, except where noted, the stones were inscribed on the face only.

RELIGIOUS DEDICATIONS

1. Upper left hand corner of a rough stone altar, moulded above (0.24 × 0.53 × 0.19 m); inscribed face in poor condition. Letters, too worn to date, 0.055.

```
Genio [...
Decemb[er? ...
[...
```

No secure identification of this Genius is possible; but the dedicant's name suggests that he was a slave, and slaves not infrequently dedicated to the Genius of their masters. See *PW*, VII, column 1161.

2. Piece of marble from a circular or semi-circular feature (not measured) carved on the face with a finely-cut *bucranion* above a garland, and an inscription above and to the right of the carving. Found in 1963 during digging a drain under the east wall of the campanile. Letters, probably Augustan – Julio-Claudian: line 1, 0.042; line 2, 0.04; trisceles stops between the words, resembling those of number 3.

```
Curtia Ç[...
vv.d(e) s(uo) [p(osuit)]
    vacat
```

Line 1, of the last letter only part of a curve survives, from C, G, O or Q; if it is right to associate this text with number 3 it should be C, and the initial either of the lady's *cognomen* or of the *praenomen* of her father or husband.

Given the shape and decoration of the piece this is likely to be a dedication to a deity, perhaps an altar or *puteal*. Curtii have not hitherto been attested on the site.

3. Three fragments from a marble base with a shallow depression on top (a, 0.29 × 0.31; b, 0.445 × 0.11 × 0.565; c, 0.18 × 0.16). Letters, probably Augustan – first century AD: 0.05; triangular stops between words, resembling those of number 2. *CIL* XI. 3319 (fragment 3a only).

```
a    ...]tia Ç[...
b    ...]o s(ua) p(ecunia) posit    sic
c    ...]T[...
```

Given the likelihood of an association between this text and number 2 it is reasonable to conjecture that this too was a dedication to a deity and by the same donor Curtia C[. . .

EMPERORS AND IMPERIAL FAMILIES

4a. Fragment of a white marble base (0.34 × 0.44 × 0.22) There is a hole at the back, near the top, for a cramp to attach the base to a wall. Letters, Augustan – first century AD: line 1, 0.095; line 2, 0.07; line 3, 0.06; very similar to those of 4b and of *CIL* XI. 3312 (see under number 4b).

```
                         ...]
      ...]ĪĪ f(ili-) v. [...
      ...]VVE[...
      ...]ẸR̥[...
      [...
```

Line 2 seems likely to give part of the title *princeps iuventutis* conferred on the heir or heirs of emperors from the reign of Augustus onwards. If the letters are rightly dated, the subject would be Gaius or Lucius Caesar, and it is a plausible conjecture that this base recorded the honours of Gaius Caesar which must have been part of the dedication to the imperial princes made by the IIviri of *Forum Clodii* in 5/4 BC; of this *CIL* XI. 3304-5 in honour of Lucius Caesar and Agrippa Postumus were copied in the seventeenth century but are now lost. A possible reconstruction of lines 1 and 2 would be:

```
[vacat C(aio) Caesari Augus]ṭị f(ilio) [vacat]
[pontif(ici) co(n)s(uli) desig(nato) principi
i]uue[ntutis]
```

Admittedly the letters in line 3 do not fit into the formulae of dedication in the other two texts; but some additional description of Gaius, the oldest and most distinguished of the three brothers, may have stood there.

It seems very likely that the following fragment should be considered with 4a:

4b. Fragment of a marble base (0.29 × 0.20 × *c*. 0.40). Letters, Augustan – first century AD: 0.055; see on 4a.

```
            ...]
   ...]Ḹị[...
   ...]uir v.[...
   [...
```

Line 1, E might be L and I part of any letter incorporating an initial upright stroke.
Given the similarity of lettering this could well be from the same base, and from the lines carrying the names of the IIviri responsible for the dedication; or, since the bases in honour of Lucius Caesar and M. Agrippa are both lost, from one or other of these. On either hypothesis a reconstruction on the following lines is possible:

```
[A(ulus) Octauius A(uli) f(ilius) Ligur]
[M(arcus) G]en[ucilius M(arci) f(ilius) Sabin(us)]
[vac.  II]uir(i) v.[  vacat       ]
```

For the abbreviation and layout in the last line see *CIL* XI. 3304-5 with the illustrations of the seventeenth century transcriptions in Paci 1978, Pl. 27.

5. Upper left corner of a white marble panel (0.32 × 0.30 × 0.013). Letters, probably second century: line 1, 0.10; line 2, 0.08.

```
Imp(erator - ) [Caesar- ...
Ne[rua- ...
[...
```

The spacing strongly suggests that the emperor was Trajan:

```
Imp(erator-) [Caes(ar-) diui Neruae f(ili-)]
Ne[rua- Traian- Aug(ust-)]
[...
```

6. Fragment from the top of a white marble panel (0.27 × 0.235 × 0.05). Letters, second century: line 1, 0.05; line 2, 0.04; line 3, 0.035; stops between words.

```
[vac.  Bruttiae Cris]pinae A[ugustae vac.]
[Imp. Caes. L.Aeli Aureli]Commọd[i Antonini Aug.]
[Pii  Felicis  Ger]ṃanici  Sar̥[matici maximi]
[...
```

Bruttia Crispina (*PIR*[2] B.170) married Commodus and became Augusta in AD 177. She is usually said to have been exiled in 182/183 and executed shortly afterwards (Cassius Dio, *Historia* LXXIII, 4.6), but the literary evidence is not quite clear, and the erasure of Commodus' name in line 2 here suggests that this panel was still in position when his memory was condemned in 192; there is a parallel at Thamugadi (*CIL* VIII. 2366, *ILS* 405). The two texts may perhaps be taken with *CIL* III. 12487, erected in Crispina's honour and dated 187, as throwing some doubt on the tradition concerning her fate.

7. Upper right corner of a moulded marble panel (0.40 × 0.38 × 0.10). Letters, second century: 0.095; resembling those of 6 quite closely.

```
... Aug]ustae
    ...]N[.]
    [...
```

A mid-second century empress is indicated, but without sufficient clue for her identification.

8. Fragment of a marble panel (0.19 × 0.18 × 0.09). Letters, second century: 0.04.

```
              ...]
       ...]ICỊ[...
   ...]Aug(usti-) PỊ[...
       ...] soṛ[or- ...
```

Line 2, of the last surviving letter there is only part of an upright.
Clearly a sister of an emperor is being honoured, perhaps a Cornificia, as suggested by line 1. If so, there are two possibilities, Annia Cornificia Faustina (*PIR*[2] A.708), sister of Marcus Aurelius, and Cornificia (*PIR*[2] C.1505), daughter of Marcus and sister of Commodus; the latter certainly survived into the reign of Caracalla, and if the text refers to her she may, like her sister Vibia Aurelia Sabina, have been honoured as *diui Severi soror* (*CIL* VIII. 3328, *ILS* 388) after Severus' self-adoption into the Antonine family.

9. Fragment of a marble panel with traces of moulding above (0.20 × 0.34 × 0.055). Letters, third century. Rustic capitals: 0.035.

```
   [Iuliae] Maeṣ[ae]
   [Aug]ustae au[iae]
   [domi]ni n(ostri) Imp(eratoris) C[aes(aris)]
   [M(arci) Au]ṛẹlii Sever[i Ale]-
   [xandri] Pị[i Fel(icis)]
 5 [Aug(usti)]ị v. [ .... ]
```

Line 1, Julia Maesa became Augusta in 218 on the accession of Heliogabalus and died in 223 shortly after the accession of her second grandson Alexander in 222. The inscription must therefore be dated 222/223 and was erected in connection with the opening of the new reign. For the erasure of her name, see on line 5.
Line 5, the right hand end of an erasure is visible although no letter can be read. Severus Alexander died in 235 and, although his memory was not formally condemned, his name was sometimes erased from inscriptions (cf. *ILS*

22 19) in an excess of loyalty to the usurper Maximinus who succeeded. His grandmother's name was presumably erased here at the same time (cf. *ILS* 484).

10a. Two adjoining fragments of a marble panel (together 0.10 × 0.28 × 0.07). Letters, probably third century: *c.* 0.035.

```
              ...]ĮĮ[...
          ]  vac.  [
      ...]trib(unicia) p[ot(estate)...
      ...]  v.   p(at-) p(atriae)[...
  ...Forocl]odi[ens-...
```

Too little survives for identification of the emperor. The monument was presumably recorded as erected by the town of *Forum Clodii*, perhaps *ordo et populus Foroclodiensium*.

On the basis of the letter forms the following fragment should probably be taken with 10a:

10b. Fragment of marble (0.15 × 0.13 × 0.04). Letters, probably third century: 0.03-0.04.

```
            ...]
    ...]VM[...
    ...]a ob I[...
    ...]DEIIC[...
    [...
```

Line 1, D might be P or R, E might be F, either upright could be L, C might be G.

11. Fragment of a marble panel, probably from the upper right hand corner (0.09 × 0.125 × 0.015). No edges survive, but a large ivy leaf emerging from an incised angle at the top right strongly suggests that this was a corner. Letters, probably third century: 0.025.

```
    ...]        leaf[
    ...] v.    P v. P[...
    ...] v.    QV[...
```

Line 1, if the second letter is a P then we have *p(at-) p(atriae)* and the text refers to an emperor.

12. Fragment, apparently from the top of a marble panel (0.18 × 0.14 × 0.045). Found among debris in an area probably occupied by baths. Letters, fourth century: 0.05.

```
    ...]*io piis f[elicibus...
    ...s]emper [Augustis...
        ...]IA[...
    [...
```

Line 1, a small part of the top of the first letter survives – it seems most likely to be S, but could also be B, C, D, G, O, P, Q, R; at the foot of the second I of *piis* the right hand serif has been extended and runs into the curve of the S; very little of the final surviving letter is preserved. Nevertheless it is clear that we have part of an imperial title for a group of emperors reigning jointly, with the end of the last name in the group at the beginning of line 1; Theodosius is the most likely, the last of a group of three emperors from AD 379 to 383.

SENATORS

13. (Pl. 90) Part of the left hand side of a marble base (0.35 × 0.42 × 0.21) inscribed on one face within a moulded panel (die, 0.22 × 0.42) from which an earlier inscription has been erased; the surface is very worn.

Plate 90. San Liberato: inscription number 13 (Ballance)

Letters, third century: 0.022; very poorly designed and so lightly cut that some are almost and others completely worn away.

```
                        ...]
       ... quaestori kandida-]
   to Aug(usti) [tr]ib(uno) [pl(ebis)..?..prae-]
   tori k(andidato) curat[ori ...
   iuridico per[...
5  legato leg[ionis ..?..        in]
   Germania [    ..?..        ?ornato]
   sacerdotiǫ [   ..?..        curatori]
   reip(ublicae) Cartag[iniensium ...
   XVuiro sacr[is faciundis ...
10 Pannoniae Inf[erioris ..?.. per No-]
   ricum et Retia[m ..?.. In-]
   ferioris et Su[perioris ...
   CIAIS[.. c.7 ..]IĮ[...
   [...
```

Lines 2, and 13 are uncertainly read; in line 7 the last letter might be C, G or Q, but the priesthood named must be a public priesthood of the Roman People reserved for Senators and if we read *sacerdoti* only the quindecemvirate, which appears in line 9 (see below), would fit, so that the alternative formula, using *sacerdotio*, is inevitable; the rest is passably clear.

The subject, although a senator of importance, is not identified. His extraordinary postings on the Danube (lines 10f) would be conceivable during the Marcomannic Wars of the reign of Marcus Aurelius, but it is hard to believe that in the second century *Forum Clodii* would honour anyone of this quality with a reused base so inadequately prepared and lettered by so incompetent a craftsman. Further, Camodeca (1974, 250f) has argued that the spelling *kandidatus* for *candidatus* (line 3) does not occur before the reign of Septimius Severus, and although his evidence is not, perhaps, sufficient to establish an absolute rule, it is suggestive; the spellings of geographical names in lines 8 and 11, and perhaps 13 (if there is a reference to *Hispania* here – see below), also point to the third century.

There were, of course, crises on the Danube frontier then to provide a good context for this career. The *terminus ante quem* is the cessation of military appointments for Senators under Gallienus.

The first appointment recorded here shows that the subject had imperial patronage (for the position of a plebeian *quaestor candidatus Augusti* from the time of Marcus see Cébeillac 1972), which continued at his candidature for the praetorship, ensured him two public priesthoods at a relatively early stage in his career, and unusual postings later. It is probable that his juridicate (line 4) was Italian and not provincial, since juridicates defined in a formula including *per* are common in Italy but comparatively rare in the provinces. In general outline, his career conforms reasonably well with the pattern for careers of third century *juridici* as tabulated by Christol in Panciera (1982, 159-162). Thus, as a praetorian he held a curatorship (perhaps of roads), the juridicate and command of a legion in one of the German provinces (VIII Augusta or XXII Primigenia in Upper Germany, I Minervia or XXX Ulpia in Lower Germany). Presumably it was as a praetorian that he received his first public priesthood (line 7), and it is very unfortunate that its name is lost; it was rare for a man to be a member of more than one of the four major priestly colleges and if this priesthood was in one of these, his subsequent quindecimvirate (line 9) would have put him in a very small and very distinguished category.

It is not quite clear when his appointments became consular in rank. A *curatela reipublicae* at African Carthage (lines 7 to 8) might well be a consular appointment, but was not necessarily so (in any case the city might perhaps have been Carthago Nova, Cartagena); and if the posting to Pannonia Inferior (line 10) was a regular governorship, that was normally a praetorian appointment until AD 214 but consular thereafter. It is clear that the conjunction of Noricum and Raetia (line 11) indicates some extraordinary appointment, and it is not excluded, on the evidence surviving, that this was simultaneous with his appointment in Pannonia Inferior. The subsequent tenure of office simultaneously in an upper and lower province (? the Pannonias, the Moesias, the Germanies) is a further abnormality, surely indicative of military crisis on the northern frontiers. In lines 12 and 13 it would be just possible to see a reference to Spain (?*provin/cia Is[pania . . .*) but it is too hazardous to be worth discussion.

* I am indebted for discussion of the text many years ago to the late Prof. John Morris, but must acknowledge that his final advice was to publish with virtually no proposals for restoration or commentary.

EQUESTRIANS

14. Fragment of marble (0.195 × 0.135 × 0.155) inscribed on the face (0.19 × 0.105). Letters, probably second century: line 1, truncated; line 2, 0.045; superscript bar above the figure in line 2 and trisceles on either side of it.

```
            ...]
 ...]NĮAĮ[...
 ...] ex V de[curiis
 [...
```

Line 1, perhaps from a name, e.g. Montanus.
Line 2, shows that the subject was on the panel of equestrian jurymen.

MUNICIPAL OR POSSIBLY SO

15. Fragment from the bottom of a marble panel (0.15 × 0.15 × 0.07). Letters, third or fourth century: 0.03.

```
              ...]
 ... Foroclodie]ṇsium   leaf
```

Probably from the end of an inscription recording honours decreed by the *ordo et populus Foroclodiensium*.

16. Two adjoining fragments from the bottom of a moulded marble panel (0.155 × 0.115 × 0.037). Letters, second-third century: line 1, 0.045; line 2, 0.035.

```
              ...]
  ...]ṂṂE[...
 ...p]raesta[ntissim- ...
```

Perhaps from honours paid to a patron as outstanding.

17. Lower right hand corner of a marble base (0.12 × 0.23 × 0.08) inscribed within a moulded panel (die, 0.065 × 0.17). Letters, probably third century: line 1, not measurable; line 2, 0.04; lines 3f, 0.02.

```
            ...]
   ...]ṃ
   ...]s
   ...]v.
   ...]io
   ...]ṭio
 5 ...]no
```

Probably an honorary inscription; the last word might be *patro]no*.

18. Part of a white marble block, cut down and reused as a cushion on one of the capitals of the portico of San Liberato (not measured); inscribed face is damaged. Letters, perhaps first century AD: line 1, truncated; line 2, 0.045-0.05.

```
            ...]
 ...]RǪ[...
 ...]ḥolo M(arco) Aemịḷịọ [..c.3..]ọṇo[..
```

Line 1 could come from the adjective *Foroclodiensis*.
Line 2 appears to give two names, probably in the dative or ablative case, possibly those of IIviri or of the officials of a *collegium*, used to date the text.

FUNERARY OR PROBABLY SO

19. Fragment from the bottom of a white marble panel (0.117 × 0.099 × 0.035) inscribed within an area defined by two incised lines. Letters, perhaps second century AD: 0.025.

```
            ...]
 ...] Diḷi[...
 ...]is fec[...
```

Line 1, probably from the name Dilius, not otherwise known here.
Line 2, perhaps ... *sibi et su]is fec[it]*, or a comparable formula.
The monument for which Dilius paid might have been public, but given the modest appearance of the panel seems more likely to have been funerary.

20. Two adjoining fragments of a marble panel (0.16 × 0.16 × 0.02) forming the right side of a triangular feature. Letters, probably third or fourth century: 0.03.

```
    ...]ṇo
...]ụrum
...]nius Ruius        sic
```

Probably funerary. The final word may have been intended for Rufus.

21. Fragment from the top of a marble panel (0.195 × 0.125 × 0.045) inscribed within a sunken panel, of which the upper right corner survives; there are traces of a second sunken area to the right, apparently containing sculpture. Letters, second-third century, showing the influence of cursives: line 1 (on the frame), 0.019; lines 2 and 3, 0.024; line 4, not measurable.

```
    [D(is)] v.   M(anibus) v.
      ...]ẹst(-)  uet(-)
      ...]castis
  ...uixit̯ annos ?]ṃ(enses) X̣Ị et
5   [dies ...
```

Line 2, this line should contain the name of the deceased or of the person responsible for the burial – *est* may be from a name like Modestus(a), *uet* from the name Vetus or possibly from the status tag, *veteranus*.
Line 3, probably from *castissimus*, suggesting that the subject was a woman and that the phrase *uxori castissimae* stood here.

22. Part of the lower right hand corner of a moulded marble altar cut in half vertically and reused as a funerary stele with inscription on one face (die, 0.185 × 0.31) from which an earlier inscription may have been erased; the top part was later broken away. A relief of a jug on the right face, indicative of the first use, has been chiselled flat, perhaps to facilitate the final reuse in the structure of the church. Letters, proably third century: line 1, 0.02; lines 2f, 0.025.

```
      ...]
  ano coniu
  gi beneme
  <neme>renti
  vacat
  q(ui) bixit anni[s]
5  XXV m(ensibus) II d(iebus) V
```

23. Upper right hand corner of a limestone panel (0.30 × 0.415 × 0.012). Found underneath the church portico. Letters, probably first century BC: 0.07; trisceles stops between words.

```
...]oda
...]sepulcri
...] et sibi
...]ụs
[...
```

Line 1, cf. Philoda(mus) in *ILLRP* 155a.

24. Fragment of marble, probably from the lower part of a base with simple moulding below (0.13 × 0.14 × 0.13). Letters, probably second century: truncated.

```
            ...]
...]ọ ụx[or...
```

Presumably a wife built the tomb for her husband; the first letter is probably the end of her name, one of the many, of Greek origin, which ended in -o (e.g. Theano).

25. Fragment of marble (0.16 × 0.20 × 0.85) probably from the lower part of a base. Letters, probably second century: 0.04.

```
          ...]
...]ENTQ[...
     v.
```

Line 1, from a formula such as *ex testamento*, or *in hoc monumento*.

UNASSIGNED FRAGMENTS

26. Fragment from the left side of a white marble base (0.21 × 0.36 × 0.25). Letters, fine capitals, perhaps first century AD: 0.115; trisceles stop after the first letter.

```
  [...
  L(uci-)Ị[...
  [...
```

27. Fragment of white marble (0.23 × 0.19 × 0.115). Letters, fine capitals, perhaps first century AD: 0.09.

```
  ...]
...]Ị[...
...]ỊV[...
  [...
```

28. Fragment of white marble (0.18 × 0.11 × 0.065). Letters, 0.07.

```
    ...]
...]VP̣[...
  [...
```

P might be R, and if so suggests the *cognomen* of A. Octavius Ligur, *duumvir* of *Forum Clodii* in 5 BC – see numbers 4a and b.

29. Fragment of a white marble panel cut down for reuse in a floor mosaic (0.08 × 0.065 × 0.035). Letters, second-third century, rustics, truncated.

```
        ...]
...]ỊAC[...
  [...
```

30. Fragment of white marble (0.21 × 0.18 × 0.07) inscribed below a moulding. Letters, showing some rustic influence, 0.055; stops between words.

```
...]A stop S vac. [...
  [...
```

Perhaps *s(eruus)* or *s(erua)*.

31. Fragment of white marble (0.22 × 0.32 × 0.22). Letters, truncated.

```
        ...]
...]ỊỊṢ[...
  [...
```

32. Fragment of white marble, not measured. Letters, capitals, perhaps second century AD.

```
        ...]
...]A[...
...]Ẹ[...
  [...
```

Line 2, E might be F.

APPENDIX 2: The Early Medieval Sculpture

Neil Christie

The following catalogue offers a brief summary of the various fragments of early medieval sculpture found within the church of San Liberato and provides a short discussion regarding the general date of these fittings. This catalogue can be considered as an addendum to the material described for the diocese of Sutri in *Corpus della Scultura Altomedievale VIII: Le Diocesi dell'Alto Lazio*. The format for describing the various pieces is that employed by the *Corpus*.

1 and 2 – DOOR JAMBS

Before 1961 preserved *in situ* in the church east door; now located against south wall of church, interior. Dimensions: (1) 2.05 × 0.22 × 0.49 m, with bottom 0.40 m a separate slab; (2) 2.06 × 0.20 × 0.49 m, with bottom 0.24 m a separate slab.

The two jambs feature a well-carved, balanced design composed of a single-grooved wicker band which describes a simple plait of eyelets joined by lozenges; the eyelets are arranged in pairs down the length of the jambs. The design is framed within a plain, flat border.

A number of parallels are available for this patterning (Verzone 1945, 181f): within Rome we can note pilasters or screen posts from Santa Maria in Cosmedin (Melucco Vaccaro 1974, 159, Pl. XVIV, number 117), Santi Quattro Coronati (Melucco Vaccaro 1974, 202, Pl. LX, number 167), Santa Maria in Aracoeli (Pani Ermini 1974, 88, Pl. XIV, number 37) and San Saba (Trinci Cecchelli 1976, 142-144, Pl. XLV, number 114b), while the design is also found on chancel screens at Santa Maria in Domnica (Melucco Vaccaro 1974, 173, Pl. LI, number 133-4) and from the so-called temple of Fortuna Virile (Melucco Vaccaro 1974, 230-231, Pl. LXX, number 221). Outside of Rome, chancel posts of this type can be noted for the church of San Pietro at Tuscania (Raspi Serra 1974, 275-276, Pl. CCLXIX, Fig. 446, number 391), the Bishop's residence, Civita Castellana (Raspi Serra 1974, 93, Pl. LXI, Fig. 111, number 95), Sant'Oreste al Soratte (Raspi Serra 1974, 111, Pl. LXXVIII, Fig. 138, number 121), the acropolis at Ferentino (Ramieri 1983, 85, 95-96, Pl. XXVIII and XXXIV, numbers 71, 82), and from Arezzo (Fatucchi 1977, 60-62, Pl. XXII, number 40).

The design appears to have been current from the later eighth century and for much of the ninth century. We should most probably see the example from San Liberato as early ninth century in date.

3 – FRAGMENT OF CHANCEL SCREEN POST (Pl. 91)

Located in church nave, against north wall. 0.62 × 0.21 × 0.10 m

This is the lower half of a post or pilaster, decorated with the same eyelet plait design as the door jambs described above (numbers 1 and 2), again with a plain border. The sides and reverse of the post are plain. A separate slab forms the base of the post.

Early ninth century.

Plate 91. San Liberato: chancel screen post, fragment number 3 (Ward-Perkins)

4 – FRAGMENT OF CHANCEL SCREEN POST

Church nave, against north wall. 0.74 × 0.275 × 0.13 m

This lower portion of a screen post is decorated by a double-grooved wicker band which describes a series of interwoven circles. This was a fairly common design type, in particular in the ninth century (see Verzone 1945, 178f.). Closely similar post fragments come from Santa Maria in Cosmedin (Melucco Vaccaro 1974, 159, Pl. XLV, number 118) and Santa Maria in Aracoeli (Pani Ermini 1974, 88-90, Pl. XIV, number 38a), and the design occurs on many plutei, including an example from San Giorgio in Velabro (Pani Ermini 1974, 75, Pl. V, numbers 14-15). Outside of Rome, we can cite examples from the churches of San Pietro and Santa Maria Maggiore at Tuscania (Raspi Serra 1974, 262, 275, Pl. CCLII, Fig. 423, number 370, and Pl. CCLXVIII, Fig. 445, number 390) and from the Duomo, Sutri (Raspi Serra 1974, 228-229, Pl. CCXVIII-CCXIX, Figs 356-358, numbers 305-307).

Ninth century.

Plate 92. San Liberato: pilaster, fragment number 5 (Ward-Perkins)

Plate 93. San Liberato: pilaster, fragment number 6 (Ward-Perkins)

5 – PILASTER OR POST FRAGMENT (Pl. 92)

Church nave, against north wall. 0.32 × 0.23 × 0.08 m

This is the central portion of a screen post, with the sides marked by a smooth raised border. Between these the decoration is formed by a shoot-like plain band which defines a rising series of circles terminating in spirals or volutes, set on alternate sides of the circles as one ascends. Within the circles – one whole example of which is preserved, along with the upper and lower part of two others – are depicted birds. The complete bird is of uncertain type, but features large, ungainly legs, and a chunky tail; in its beak it holds a bunch of grapes. The gaps between the border and the circles will have contained additional volutes.

A close comparison can be drawn with examples from Santa Maria in Aracoeli and San Stefano del Cacco (see Pani Ermini 1974, 90-91, Pl. XIV, number 39a). San Saba features a door jamb of similar but slightly more delicate workmanship, which is regarded as of late tenth century date (Trinci Cecchelli 1976, 153-154, Pl. LI, numbers 132 and 133).

Late eighth or early ninth century.

6 – PILASTER OR POST FRAGMENT (Pl. 93)

Church nave, against north wall. 0.33 × 0.22 × 0.16 m

This rough base fragment of a crudely carved screen post, features the head, shoulders and arms of a bearded man; the fragment has a raised, slightly rounded bottom moulding and a thinner border on the right side of the piece, which runs inwards as one ascends. The figure appears to wear a sleeved top and stands as if listening, with the left hand raised to the ear and the right arm crossed over the chest. The significance of this gesture is uncertain. The beard is only scantily represented, while incised lines beneath the nose may denote a moustache. The eyes are formed by an inset oval within a larger inset outline. The top of the head was not preserved.

There are no direct parallels to this piece. Figured reliefs in this period are somewhat rare, and the few examples known appear to depict hunters, in the tradition of Roman hunt sarcophagi (for example, in particular, San Saba (Trinci Cecchelli 1976, 112-113, Pl. XXIX, number 77) and Civita Castellana (Raspi Serra 1974, 64-67, Pl. XXXI, Fig. 55, number 43), or relate to biblical scenes. An example of a biblical scene is that of the Annunciation, depicted on a cornice from San Giorgio in Velabro (Melucco Vaccaro 1974, 81-84, Pl. IX, number 27), dated to the late tenth to eleventh century, though it may perhaps be slightly earlier in date. The treatment of the eyes on this piece bears some similarity to the figure at San Liberato. The crude style and the method of depicting the man's eyes may suggest a later ninth century date for our piece, although this must remain open to question.

Late ninth century (?).

7 – *FRAGMENT OF PLUTEUS(?)*

Present location uncertain. Dimensions uncertain.

This is a small, narrow, fragment, perhaps from a pluteus or chancel screen, which depicts the heads of two birds drinking from a vessel in the form of a volute krater, which rests on a cable moulding. The area below the moulding is plain. The vessel features volute handles at its mouth, while the body shape is defined by grooves, and the wide base shows both vertical and horizontal grooves. The birds, probably to be seen as two peacocks facing one another, have rounded heads, large eyes and neatly curved beaks.

A general comparison may be made with the *paliotto* from Santi Quattro Coronati featuring a complete drinking peacocks scene: in particular we can note the lines emphasizing the shape of the krater, the curved beaks of the birds, and the method of depicting their eyes (Melucco Vaccaro 1974, 189-190, Pl. LV, number 155), dated to 847-855. Similar panels come from San Giorgio in Velabro (Melucco Vaccaro 1974, 70-71, Pl. III, number 7) and the cathedral at Sutri (Raspi Serra 1974, 217-219, Pl. CCVI, Fig. 333, number 285), though unfortunately both are damaged and do not preserve the peacocks' heads or the vessel.

First half of the ninth century.

8 – *FRAGMENT OF PLUTEUS(?)*

Church nave, against north wall. 0.3 × 0.275 × 0.085 m.

The fragment forms the top right corner of a panel, marked by a plain, broad border; within the border is depicted the head and neck of a bird-like animal, most probably a griffin. The neck features feather-like decoration with a central spine; this stops at the head, which is plain, except for the large eye, curved beak, and pointed ears. Part of the body, also depicted with feather-like grooves, is preserved in the lower left corner.

We lack parallels to this piece. Elements of the decoration are, however, found elsewhere, as for example the method of depicting the feathers of the creature: a peacock tail of this type is known from Santi Giovanni e Paolo (Melucco Vaccaro 1974, 137-138, Pl. XXXVI, number 93b), while other examples show the use of 'buttons' along the length of the spine (for example, Santa Maria in Cosmedin (Melucco Vaccaro 1974, Pl. XLI, number 103), Sutri (Raspi Serra 1974, Pl. CCVI, Fig. 333, number 285), and Castel Sant'Elia (Raspi Serra 1974, Pl. CL, Fig. 163, number 144)). Griffins are a rare subject, and no clear examples exist in the area of Rome, unless we include the ferocious winged dog-like creatures depicted in plutei at Castel Sant'Elia (Raspi Serra 1974, 150-153, Pl. CXXVI, Fig. 206, number 176, Pl. CXXVIII, Fig. 208, number 178); to the north we can note a panel in the Museo Cristiano, Brescia of eighth-ninth century date (Panazza and Tagliaferri 1966, 120-121, Pl. XLV, Figs 145-146).

Ninth century(?).

9-17 – *FRAGMENTS OF ALTAR SCREEN(?)*
(Pl. 94)

Church nave, against north wall. Overall dimensions: *c.* 1.0 × 1.25 × 0.09 m. Largest fragment: 0.72 × 0.42 × 0.09 m.

Plate 94. San Liberato: altar screen, fragment numbers 9-17 (Christie)

Nine fragments of varied size belong to a screen, perhaps originally part of an altar front: its greater height with respect to its width may argue against a use as a chancel screen. The screen is divided into a series of (probably) six rectangular panels by means of a tight double-grooved band plait, featuring central 'buttons', which also runs round the edges of the screen. Outside of this is a plain cornice. The panels depict a variety of 'fantastic' beasts: best-preserved is the lower right panel containing a lion-like creature with a man's head running towards the right; the lower left panel shows a beast of similar form, although here the head is not preserved. The central panels are fragmentary: to the left, we can see only claws; on the right, clawed legs and the ends of two possible wings may denote an eagle – one wing features 'buttons' on the spine of its decoration (cf. number 8 above). The upper two panels are missing.

There are adequate parallels for the border decoration, chiefly from pilasters or screen posts, which can only be broadly dated to the later eighth and ninth centuries: San Giovanni in Laterano (Melucco Vaccaro 1974, 121, Pl. XXIX, number 73), Mercati Traiani (Pani Ermini 1974, Pl. XLVI, number 123, Pl. LVI-LVII, numbers 171-174, Pl. LIX, number 183, Pl. LXV, numbers 205-207), Castel Sant'Elia (ciborium fragments) (Raspi Serra 1974, Pl. CXXIII, Fig. 202-3, number 173). The division of the screen into distinct panels is found in a few instances in and around Rome (Kautzsch 1939, 21f), the best preserved being the pluteus from Santa Maria dell'Arco, Civita Castellana: the figures in this piece relate to a hunting scene, and it has been claimed that this represents an evolution from the open scenes depicted on sarcophagi to enclosed, segmented figurative schemes (Raspi Serra 1974, 79-80, Pl. XLVI, Fig. 80, number 67). An 'open' hunt scene occurs on the sarcophagus formerly in the porch of the cathedral of Civita Castellana (Raspi Serra 1974, 64-67, Pl. XXXI, Fig. 55, number 43). A 'fantastic' beast panel is known from San Saba, depicting unicorn, ibis and deer (Trinci Cecchelli 1976, 113-116, Pl. XXX, number

78), but we lack parallels for the San Liberato human-lion figures.

Second half of the eighth century(?).

DISCUSSION

The fragments are all carved on whitish-grey marble of medium-coarse grain. The fact that they had been mortared onto the face of the church north aisle wall precluded examination of their rear faces in order to observe whether they had been recarved from classical *spolia*. This does, however, appear to be true of the door jambs. Reuse of *spolia* can also be claimed for the series of impost capitals and corbels now housed within the church: twelve impost capitals are present (dimensions *c.* 0.53 × 0.25 × 0.18 m), all quite roughly worked, and six corbels (*c.* 0.20 × 0.13 × 0.1 m). Some of these elements may derive from the demolished upper storey of the bell-tower; alternatively, the corbels perhaps once decorated the exterior of the main apse (corbels are present on the north apse).

The fragments described above form only a small part of the fittings which would have originally adorned the first church at San Liberato. That the pieces actually originate from the church and were not elements brought to the site at some later date is attested by the fact that the door jambs (numbers 1 and 2) stood *in situ* until 1961 and framed the facade doorway (Pl. 86). The post (number 3) has identical eyelet decoration and is clearly a contemporary element. Fragments 3-6 all relate to such posts or pilasters and can probably be associated with a screen which formally separated the priest and clergy from the rest of the congregation. Fragments 7 and 8 may well relate to two panels of this screen, and the possibility that fragments 9-17 also formed a panel here should not be excluded. Such a screen would probably have run across the width of the raised presbytery, being accessible from the centre of the nave (cf. Fig. 108). An arrangement of this type – an iconostasis – is preserved in the church of San Leone, Leprignano (Capena), *c.* 30 km east of San Liberato: this features a central arched entrance, supported on low pilasters and flanked by small columns supporting an architrave carried over the chancel screens. Raspi Serra (1974, 154-156, Pl. CXXX-CXLIV, Figs 210-235, numbers 180-197) dates this to the pontificate of Nicholas I (858-867).

Fragments 9-17, however, form a somewhat tall and narrow screen, and may in fact relate to a panel which originally decorated the church altar. Against this can be set the fact that the screen contains an unusual series of figured reliefs, of dubious Christian significance, which may seem out of place for the face of an altar. The presence of so many figured fragments, depicting both humans and animals (whether real or fantastic) is notable: in this context, the relative absence of such representations in Rome may perhaps denote that this was a somewhat 'rural' tradition, marking a fusion between Roman and local styles. We can note in this respect the two plutei from Castel Sant'Elia which clearly combine both elements (see fragment 8, above).

Dating of the various fragments is problematic given that many of the designs found in sculpture of this type had a relatively long currency, covering the later eighth and ninth centuries and in some cases extending into the tenth century. Frequently dates are assigned to pieces chiefly on the basis of the building history of the church to which they belonged, often leading to 'fixed' dates being proffered for certain design types. However, through consideration of the extensive evidence now provided by the various volumes of the *Corpus*, it is possible to offer at least a broad date for many of the pieces found at San Liberato. In general these appear to belong to the ninth century, and we may perhaps tie this down more closely to the first half of that century. Problems remain, however, as regards elements such as the proposed altar screen (fragments 9-17). Whilst it is likely that these pieces too belong to this same period, we could also regard them as part of the original fittings of the church and the insertion of the hypothetical iconostasis as a somewhat later development. This ninth century date accords well with all the additional data regarding the first phase of the small chapel of San Liberato.

PART IV

Three South Etrurian churches
An overview

by
Neil Christie

The south Etruria survey offered a detailed and complex panorama of human settlement from the earliest to modern times. It raised as many questions as it had answered and prompted a gathering volume of newly-oriented archaeological research. Field survey has become now an integral part of Italian archaeology, frequently, but not always, in conjunction with site excavation. Such work has amassed a huge body of data, whose analysis has had a major impact in many fields. In particular, interest in early medieval settlement has increased markedly in recent years, to the extent that many projects are now geared chiefly (but not exclusively) towards elucidating the 'darker' centuries of Italian history – the San Vincenzo al Volturno project in Molise merits mention in this respect, combining excavation with field survey. Yet experiences and failures on the ground have shown that field survey on its own often produces scanty results for the early medieval centuries, and that only an integrated historico-archaeological approach can hope to yield a more complete picture of this period [1]. Survey and archive work are basically non-destructive tools; and, as more data accumulate, methods for collecting and understanding them can be refined. However, surface finds can only be broadly classified into periods, and, in addition, early medieval material is rare and hard to identify. Excavation remains vital, for careful excavation of selected sites will more often than not provide invaluable stratigraphic contexts tying down artifacts to more closely datable periods. As this chronology is refined, so our survey data become better defined. Likewise, even where documentation for a 'site' exists, this is often concerned with one given period and rarely produces any detailed insights into its social and economic character. Survey may provide information about the size of a site and its general chronology, but often only excavation will provide fuller information regarding factors such as origins, abandonment, population, architecture, material culture, and trade.

Any study of early medieval settlement patterns necessarily revolves around the Church, whose role in this period was extremely important, and which is dominant in the documentary sources. The institution of the Church and its possessions had become a vital force in society, and its material presence in the form of a house of worship was the focus of many settlements. Devout Christians in all walks of life contributed to the Church and its buildings to guarantee their own salvation. Money and pride were poured into churches: significantly, excavations have shown that despite declining building standards after c. 500-550, whereby private housing very often reverted to timber or dry stone construction or cannibalized and patched up old Roman buildings, churches continued to be built in stone and were finely decorated – albeit at a much reduced scale from fourth and fifth century examples [2]. For example, in the sixth century, the town of Luni (in modern Liguria) featured rough timber-built houses over the former Forum, while to its west the cathedral church of Santa Maria was renovated and embellished with a fine floral mosaic [3]. Churches were at the same time a reflection of the vitality of the Church itself and of the community in which they lay: a prosperous phase could see major remodelling or expansion; an impoverished phase a crude patching of dilapidated structures. The factors that might affect the status and material condition of a church were varied: clerical strength and weakness, economic growth or decline, periods of peace or war, rise or fall in pilgrim traffic, a transfer of population to a new centre or to a defensive location, etc. In effect a church helps us understand the community or landscape in which it lay. Sometimes the picture is distorted, proffering a false image (for instance, a church may well persist on a site long after the settlement it once served has been abandoned), but the more comprehensive the archaeological and historical research the more readily such distortions will be revealed.

Each of the three churches examined in this volume offers significant historical, architectural and archaeological data for refining our current picture of early medieval and medieval settlement. In two cases excavation revealed the complex structural sequences; in the other a detailed architectural survey filled in the gaps in the site's minimal historical record. We can here draw together the main results of each study, present some overall conclusions, and outline some remaining problems related to these sites and to the period of the sixth-twelfth centuries in Italy.

The churches themselves formed the natural focus of study, but by the very nature of their function can be difficult to interpret. As is most evident in the standing example of San Liberato, the wall fabrics demonstrate a remarkable history, providing a patchwork of different structural phases relating to partial repairs, major remodellings, changes in function, and so on. Each event testifies to the persistence in use and continuous maintenance of the building. Although no single structural alteration can be closely dated, a relatively clear, if broad, chronology can be put forward, demonstrating an eighth-ninth century chapel, twelfth-thirteenth century remodelling and additions, and fourteenth-fifteenth century alterations: in practice, however, we cannot say how long each phase took to complete and whether a series of alterations relates to a single moment or to an extended work programme. This analysis is relatively easy when the structure remains as intact and as 'legible' as that at San Liberato. Where little more than the foundations survive, however, as at Santa Cornelia, the story is necessarily more difficult to unravel, and while the principal structural phases may be discerned (e.g. addition of belltower, construction of second church, addition of porch, etc.), the amalgam of activities above ground is largely lost to us (e.g. reroofing, remodelling to accommodate the monastery, alterations to belltower, internal decorative works).

Continuous changes to a church's fabric are often destructive to the archaeological record: rebuilding of a structure disturbs or even destroys levels associated with earlier phases, leading to a mixing of finds and the displacement of crucial contexts. In such instances, only broad, and rarely fixed, dates can be offered. The level of disturbance is likely to be proportional to the longevity of a structure and its functions. In the case of Santa Cornelia the density of graves to the south of the church and the overall uniformity in burial practice throughout the church's lifetime meant that the task of dividing graves into distinct phases was extremely arduous. Here finds were mixed by reburial (the insertion of new graves or the reuse of old graves), by the construction of the second church, and later of the monastic complex: these factors, along with the constant digging and redigging of the cloister garth, resulted in a collection of poorly stratified artifacts covering the tenth to fourteenth centuries. Similarly, in many instances graves lay right alongside the church, removing traces of its foundation trenches as well as elements such as scaffolding points. At San Liberato excavation beyond the apse showed a mass of graves gathered around the outer wall hoping to be near the martyr's relics. Given the lack of graves associated with the building housing a mosaic at Santa Rufina, however, we should be cautious in interpreting the building as a chapel.

Associated artifactual data are, for the most part, rare. Churches are non-domestic structures and therefore lack the assemblage of material usually recovered from domestic settlement debris: cooking, eating and industrial activities all went on elsewhere. Items such as liturgical vessels were of course used, but were often of prized metal and thus rarely discarded within the church. Fittings such as carved choir screens, ambos and door frames were, as at Santa Cornelia and San Liberato, often made redundant and replaced at later dates, and occasionally incorporated into later foundations or walls (although not always in walls contemporary with their period of replacement) or indeed reused or recarved in their former location. However, small finds such as pottery and coins are exceptional, and it is extremely fortunate if sherds, either from vessels broken by workmen on the site, or contained in debris mixed in with mortar, etc. to provide a floor make-up, are found in useful contexts.

In the case of Santa Cornelia the church complex can be related to various structures within an enclosure wall. These provided sizeable quantities of domestic debris, thus offering a more closely definable archaeological setting. At Santa Rufina, by contrast, many features, particularly the 'chapel', could not be coherently related to each other, given

that excavation here was largely by trenches: for instance, we cannot be certain if the enclosure wall and associated settlement traces to the north belonged to the chapel phase, nor can we properly define the character of the Roman period holding. For San Liberato there is the potential for excavation to clarify the context in which the church is situated, although modern activities may have damaged much of the immediate area.

One of the most important aspects which could still be examined at San Liberato involves the question of continuity from Roman to early medieval. As noted above, much current field research in Italy is geared to the transitional period c. 400-1000, pin-pointing the breakup of the old 'open' or 'dispersed' pattern of settlement and the movement to upland or nucleated units (incastellamento). It is evident that these processes of change varied greatly in time and nature both regionally and intraregionally: there is no monocausal explanation for the process as a whole, although the 'later' stages of incastellamento (eleventh-twelfth centuries) conform to a broadly similar pattern of nucleation [4]. In some areas the switch from dispersed to nucleated comes late, perhaps only in the eleventh century (as the Ager Veientanus) or the twelfth (as in parts of Liguria and Emilia-Romagna). Elsewhere, in more 'exposed' locations, as for instance on known military borders (such as that between Byzantine and Longobard provinces in the later sixth–later eighth centuries), the abandonment of open sites would appear to come sooner rather than later [5]. We will return to this problem shortly. However, even when the transfer from open to nucleated site appears demonstrably late, there remain major difficulties in proving through structural and material traces the actual maintenance or continuity of human activity on open sites between c. 600 and 800. Even in a scrupulously detailed excavation, such as at Monte Gelato near Nepi, although there are clear enough signs that the late Roman church 'continued' and one or more rooms remained in use, propped up by posts, there is nothing to date this 'continuity'[6].

At San Liberato, limited trenching behind the apse revealed that the church sides directly overlay Roman foundation walls. It is not possible to state at present whether this represents direct continuity (that is continuous use of the site from the late Roman period to the later eighth century), or abandonment in the fifth century and reoccupation in the later eighth century. Careful excavation of the site might reveal whether a settlement survived at Forum Clodii between c. 500 and 800.

Santa Cornelia and, perhaps, Santa Rufina comprise early medieval cult buildings with associated structures in proximity to, but not directly overlying, Roman period remains. Both evidently reused Roman masonry and other materials in their construction, much of which was presumably culled locally. This implies ruinous buildings in the vicinity (as is most apparent at Santa Rufina), but does not negate the possibility of some degree of continuous settlement. Certainly for Santa Cornelia the *Liber Pontificalis* notes that Hadrian I combined new and existing estates to create his *domusculta* and these must have included estate buildings. Where these lay is not known, but the archaeological evidence does at least seem to show that farming in the area (though not settlement) had preceded the construction of the papal estate. Beneath the south-east corner complex the clay surface and the subsequent vine plantation (phase 1d) may attest agricultural activity going on close by in the later eighth century, when the area was cleared to make way for the new estate centre. Given that material associated with this clearance relates to phase 2a and the period *c.* 775, it offers a suggestion at least of farming already going on in the vicinity at the time of the *domusculta*'s foundation. In effect, the *domusculta Capracorum* does not represent *re*settlement of the countryside, but simply continued use, or rather a reorganization of an existing farming system. Significant may also be the few sherds of fifth-sixth century date and the high number of stamped tiles of the later fifth century – the latter, however, may have come as *spolia* from Rome, or from a more nearby source.

At Santa Rufina farming/agricultural activity in the excavated area ceased by *c.* AD 200. This was replaced by a religious complex, comprising cemetery, mausoleum and catacomb dating from the mid- to late third century (phase IIIc). In the case of the mausoleum there were signs (on the basis of coin evidence) of maintenance and/or frequentation at least into the seventh century (phase IV). It is plausible to argue from these data that the site and mausoleum persisted into phase V when secure chronological evidence in the form of Forum Ware re-emerges. Future re-examination of the small finds may well discern elements relating to the postulated gap 650-800.

For the present, however, the ceramic gap remains here, as at most sites in Italy, despite the attempts of various excavations to address this problem. In Molise, for example, the San Vincenzo al Volturno project has demonstrated how at San Vincenzo itself the late Roman *villa rustica*, comprising a tower and a small church founded in the early fifth century, had fallen into disuse by the mid-sixth century, with the population perhaps moving to an upland, defensible site: burials, however, continued to be made near the former church into the seventh century. The monastery was founded in the early eighth century prompting a revival of settlement close by. Some settlement may have persisted here throughout the seventh century but there were no artifactual data to show this [7].

In south Etruria, south of Lake Bracciano and not far from San Liberato, important excavations have occurred at 'Le Mura di Santo Stefano' (Anguillara): here survive the splendid remains of a three storey second century AD villa tower structure, which, in the fifth century may have undergone defensive remodelling whereby the lower storey windows were blocked up and a ditch cut around the building. Even before this, however, a small apsed church was built *c.* 100 m distant around which developed a small cemetery. This church was later restored, an event dated to the early ninth century by Forum Ware and sculptural fragments. The prominent survival of the tower-building could indicate a continued habitational role between these two events, even if physical evidence for this is lacking [8].

Lastly, important data have come from the excavations at Mola di Monte Gelato in the *Ager Faliscus* south-east of Nepi. Previously it was assumed that this site conformed to the sequence (postulated for much of the *Ager Faliscus*) of late Roman villa, followed by sixth-seventh century abandonment, and later nucleation on a nearby promontory. However, a quite different sequence has emerged: the Roman villa, only partially investigated, was at least partly still in use in the fifth century when a small apsed church was inserted, following the villa orientation and close to the road. Despite a lack of finds, the excavators contend that there was no obvious break in the stratigraphy (i.e. no level of abandonment or destruction) between this phase (3) and the rebuilding of the church in the early ninth century (phase 4a) – again offering an indication of 'continuity'. Indeed in one room north of the church, probably in the sixth century, posts were inserted alongside one wall to support it, while the adjoining corridor featured a wooden partition and a number of hearths. The buildings as a whole were clearly in a state of decline, but someone was there to utilize at least a limited area. Whether the church too was decaying is unclear. Two sixth century coins also show continued activity up to *c.* 550 at least. Significant may be the fact that phase 4a, which saw the rebuilding of the church, also saw the demolition of the late Roman structures, burying most of the walls: no new domestic structures were built (though a pottery kiln was set up) and if people continued living there they must have been in an area not yet excavated [9].

These examples serve to show the elusiveness of proof of continuity. The problem relates not solely to rural settlements but extends also to urban sites where documents securely argue for continuity of population. Here too churches often represent our sole physical trace of human activity: palaeochristian structures were maintained and repaired; old Roman temples (as, for example, the Pantheon in Rome) were converted to Christian worship; occasionally between *c.* 600 and 800 new churches were built, but were generally tiny affairs. Although money and technical expertise were scarce, clearly people were still around to build and maintain such structures [10].

We cannot reject, therefore, the possibility that at

each of the three church sites investigated in this volume there was continuity of settlement/land use. What is certain, however, is that the later eighth and early ninth century for each marked a notable resurgence in activity. This coincides neatly with the Carolingian renaissance which, in Italy, had its greatest expression in Rome in the period *c.* 775-855 [11]. The extinction of the Longobard kingdom in 774, the consolidation of papal territorial claims, and close connections with the Carolingian rulers, released the popes from a sizeable financial burden and prompted an energetic programme of restoration (extending principally to churches, city walls and aqueducts) and building (concentrated mainly on churches from *c.* 815). This programme clearly extended into the Roman countryside, where a number of churches furnish evidence for construction, restoration or embellishment (particularly in the form of chancel screens and *opus sectile* flooring). To a large degree, these were all expressions of church and papal power, seeking to establish dominance in both town and country: the *domuscultae*, notably *Capracorum*, were a statement of papal strength; while building at Santa Rufina was a statement of individual episcopal opulence [12]. San Liberato may be a small cousin to these sites, but nonetheless its construction denotes a significant investment of funds, with relics an integral part of its success and survival.

As a showpiece, Santa Cornelia/*Capracorum* was lavishly endowed with Roman *spolia*, including marblework, comprising columns, capitals, screens and flooring (a large proportion of which being prized red and green porphyry), and sanctified with the bodies of four pope-saints. Constructed in large, well-selected tufa blockwork, both church and baptistery were intended to impress.

Our documentation for Santa Rufina likewise points to the rich embellishment of a site which housed the important relics of saints Rufina and Secunda; again, according to the literary evidence, the site comprised a church with baptistery and related *domusculta*. We must, however, be cautious in accepting fully the attribution by the excavators of the mosaic and its associated room to this late eighth century phase. Serious doubts are expressed regarding the dating of the mosaic, on stylistic and typological grounds, in an early medieval context, given the total lack of parallels or even vaguely comparable floors in Rome in this epoch. *Opus sectile* floors, of moderate quality, were by then becoming the norm: instead, a fourth or fifth century date may best suit the Santa Rufina tesselated mosaic. It is difficult, if we accept this proposed chronology, to reconcile wholly the art historical and archaeological data. However, it can be noted that Forum Ware sherds were not found under the mosaic floor or in its make-up, but were recovered primarily from the trench of the reinforcement or 'jacket' (B1) of wall B. Given that wall B had been maintained, or at least

was still clearly visible in period III when it formed part of the Roman cemetery enclosure, it is possible that B1 marks a much later repair. Indeed, the sections reveal no major temporal gap between the cutting of the various graves in the area and the laying of the mosaic. If these arguments are accepted, a connection may tentatively be placed between the abandonment of the catacomb sometime in the fifth century and the construction of the 'room with mosaic', perhaps as a cult house designed to hold the relics from the now ruinous catacomb. The documented existence of a bishopric at *Silva Candida* in 501 and the fragmentary (mid-fifth century?) inscription number 9 which refers to a *paroecia* may be relevant in this discussion. Coins and Forum Ware would then indicate continued use of the room and other adjoining structures into the seventh and eighth centuries; while the lack of elements relating to chancel screens or other such church furniture from the excavation (except, perhaps, fragment 27, EXC 1.3) may show that the cult building existed elsewhere on the site.

These arguments are all problematic. However, it is important to stress that mis-readings of the archaeological data are always possible: at Santa Cornelia, for instance, contamination of previously assumed 'sealed' or 'secure' levels was high, making a coherent ceramic analysis of the monastic sequence arduous at best. Poor excavation techniques or erroneous evaluation of structural sequences are constant companions in archaeology and it is always salutary to give heed to these factors. Consequently, although it is enticing to locate the Santa Rufina mosaic in the milieu of the later eighth-ninth century Carolingian renaissance and to regard it as an unique expression of the revival of Roman tesselated paving, we must be aware that it suits much better a fifth or sixth century context [13].

Outside of possible revivals in the artistic and cultural sphere, the Carolingian connections may have prompted economic revival in Italy. There was certainly traffic, notably pilgrims, between Carolingian Francia and Italy, and given the known trading contacts between Francia and the Baltic and with Britain and Spain, we should not doubt some movement to and from Italy. Marblework and relics went north of the Alps, while architects may well have come south. Simultaneously, trade contacts from the eastern Mediterranean became stronger, as is most evident in the rise of Venice [14]. The developments in terms of the ceramic traditions and distributions during this period have been described and discussed by Patterson (see above), who points out the possibility of there having been a Carolingian stimulus for the production of Forum Ware.

The construction of the south-east corner complex at Santa Cornelia, well-dated by Forum Ware, coincided with the erection of a perimeter wall. As argued above, while this lacks evident defensive features (towers, outer ditch), its thickness and general solidity imply a certain defensive potential. Likewise the inclusion of structures within and backing onto the wall (room 6; south-east complex) represents a nucleation of the estate into a compact shell. This phenomenon may be repeated at Santa Rufina, where construction of a walled enclosure, identified to the north of the 'chapel', was also dated by Forum Ware. What area this enclosed was unclear, but presumably it included the cult building. For each site, the unstable relations with the Roman nobility, and later the threat from Arab warbands are useful causative agents; we should not forget of course that workmen from various *domuscultae*, including *Capracorum*, aided in building the Leonine walls at Rome in *c.* 846 against the Moslems. Nevertheless, these perimeter walls were a fairly nominal defence; Santa Rufina we know suffered damage from Arab raids.

Significantly this site nucleation coincides with a radical transformation of settlement in the northern half of south Etruria, the *Ager Faliscus*, where Forum Ware helps document an early phase of occupation on promontories and other defensive sites (e.g. Castel Porciano, Mazzano) which later developed into medieval *castelli* and villages. This process is impossible to date with precision, though in some cases it may relate to the first half of the eighth century and the conflict between Rome, the Longobard king Liutprand and the duchy of Spoleto; in others it may relate to the break-up of papal territorial control and the rise of the nobility [15]. However, re-examination of the Forum Ware from such sites may yet show later ninth or even tenth century initial, datable occupation, as opposed to activity of the late eighth-early ninth century. Indeed, as the work at Monte Gelato has shown, 'open' sites could continue into the tenth or eleventh century. Only later did the process known as *incastellamento* or *accentramento* really develop. Its mechanics, causes and permutations are still a matter of great debate, but it basically comprised the nucleation (often enforced) of population on to new defensive sites or the nucleation of existing sites – creating thereby the typical pattern of medieval settlement, which only in the past century has been reversed [16].

The apparent early nucleation in the *Ager Faliscus* may reflect a relatively widespread shift of sites in the Early Middle Ages (sixth-ninth centuries) to hilltop locations in the face of military insecurity. In the proximity of a large city, such as Rome, this process was arrested, as may be witnessed in the open sites of the *Ager Veientanus*. In the tenth and early eleventh centuries, however, nucleation spread, transforming the countryside, and in place of farms like Santa Cornelia emerged villages like Isola Farnese, Formello and Sacrofano [17]. At Santa Cornelia the south-east corner complex, the estate working area, was out of use by *c.* 950, and the church alone seems to have been left by the early 1000s. Had the estate workers by then all been drawn away to nearby

Formello (first recorded in 1026) or Isola Farnese (989), leaving Santa Cornelia an isolated parish church? At Santa Rufina bishop Peter refortified the *episcopium* in the 1020s – was this an attempt to sustain the site or an act of nucleation? The settlement, if any, around San Liberato, will have dispersed to defended lakeside townships like Trevignano, although the church itself was maintained.

Many former papal lands had fallen into the hands of the various noble families who dominated Rome from *c.* 850-1050; the *territorium* of the *domusculta Capracorum* had certainly been broken up, and other estates suffered a like fate [18]. Within this period there had been a revival in monasticism, encouraged by the reforms at Cluny as elsewhere. The monastery of Saint Cornelius appears at a relatively late phase in this movement, making use of the generosity of a local noble landowner. The monks were no doubt grateful to shield themselves from the turmoil in and around Rome in the eleventh and twelfth centuries as the popes strove to maintain papal authority and independence from both noble and imperial interference – a struggle largely won by the end of the twelfth century [19]. Over this period the papacy established itself in western Christendom as a powerful and rich international institution, and along the way, pontiffs and cardinals began to amass fortunes. The new-found wealth of the church prompted a second revival of Rome, on a more opulent scale than that of the first half of the ninth century. Between the twelfth and late thirteenth centuries large numbers of churches were built, rebuilt or redecorated [20]. The effects extended well into the countryside and are clearly reflected in phases of structural extensions and improvement, and of internal embellishment (e.g. belltowers, and Cosmati work) at both San Liberato and Santa Cornelia. The excavated structures at Santa Rufina, by contrast, appear to have missed out in this prosperity and continued to decline, despite the attested importance of its cardinal bishop.

By 1308 Rome's latest renaissance was over: the pope moved to Avignon, and the fourteenth century marked a decline in the city's fortunes: pilgrims still came but the revenue generated by the papal bureaucracy had gone, leaving little for building activity within the city and even less outside [21]. With the pope's transfer, the position of the bishop of *Silva Candida* was seriously undermined and Santa Rufina suffered accordingly. In the case of Santa Cornelia a decline is evident even from the mid-thirteenth century, and by *c.* 1300 the monastery's Roman owners could no longer afford to maintain the site – the church perhaps lingered on but eventually lost out to Formello; San Liberato persisted, but had never been much more than a small parish church and was therefore easier to maintain.

In 1963 John Ward-Perkins wrote that: 'In Italy medieval archaeology is still in its infancy and, quite apart from its historical implications, the excavation (at Santa Cornelia) breaks what is, archaeologically speaking, fresh ground' [22]. Much more ground has been broken since then and medieval archaeology in Italy has certainly grown in stature. The three south Etrurian churches presented here were important elements in the promotion of this new branch of archaeology. Although published many years after their initial investigation, this has the advantage that their results can now be integrated into a greatly increased and ever-growing body of data for the period *c.* 700-1400, and it can be argued that they have far more significance now than they would have had back in the 1960s, when they seemed fascinating but very isolated phenomena. However, these churches remain but small pieces in a large historico-archaeological jigsaw, whose general outline appears to be relatively clear but whose details are only slowly being discerned. It is hoped that this volume will stimulate more research into this exciting field of study.

NOTES

1. South Etruria survey: Ward-Perkins 1972; Potter 1979a; 1979b. San Vincenzo: Hodges and Mitchell 1985; Hodges 1988. Field survey and the early medieval epoch: Noyé 1988.

2. Churches in a late antique/early medieval context: Ward-Perkins 1983; 1984, 51-84; Delogu 1988. Contemporary urban decline: Brogiolo 1987.

3. Luni: Ward-Perkins 1981. Cathedral of Santa Maria: Lusuardi Siena 1985-1987.

4. Cf. in general Noyé 1988, especially 411-535.

5. See the contributions in Settia and Comba 1984.

6. See below, with note 9.

7. Hodges and Mitchell 1985; Hodges 1988.

8. Whitehouse 1982; revised report by Blagg *et al.* forthcoming. My thanks to Dr Richard Hodges for allowing me access to this report.

9. Potter and King 1988; Marazzi, Potter and King 1989.

10. See note 2.

11. Cf. Krautheimer 1980, 109-142; Delogu 1988, 37-38.

12. Wickham 1978a, 175-177; Potter and King 1988, 307-308. Christie, this volume; Llewellyn, this volume.

13. I am grateful to John Mitchell of the University of East Anglia, Dr Katherine Dunbabin of MacMaster University, Prof. X. Barral I Altet, Université de Rennes II and Dott. Federico Guidobaldi of C.N.R., Rome, for their comments regarding the Santa Rufina mosaic. In particular I must thank Dott. Guidobaldi for agreeing at a late stage to provide an appendix on this.

14. Carolingian trade: Hodges and Whitehouse 1983, 102-122. Ravennate marblework: Pierpaoli 1986, 214-215; *Codex Carolinus*, 81. Relic trade: Geary 1978. San Vincenzo: Hodges 1985, 2, 27. We can also note the abbey of Farfa's imperial links: McClendon 1987, 71, 116-117.

15. Christie 1987, 458-461.

16. Toubert 1973a; Wickham 1978b; 1979, 87-92; 1985; 1988a.

17. Wickham 1978b, 375; cf. Ward-Perkins 1972, 878.

18. Partner 1966, 75-78; Wickham 1979, 80-82.

19. Krautheimer 1980, 143-160.

20. Cf. Krautheimer 1980, 161-202.

21. Krautheimer 1980, 228.

22. Ward-Perkins 1963, 39.

BIBLIOGRAPHY

ABBREVIATIONS USED IN TEXT

CIL	see *Corpus Inscriptionum Latinarum*
CNI	see *Corpus Nummorum Italicorum*
CVA	see *Corpus Vasorum Antiquorum*
IGUR	see Moretti 1968-1979
ILCV	see Diehl 1925-1931
ILLRP	see Degrassi 1957-1963
ILS	see Dessau 1892
MNR I/3.	see Giuliano 1982
MNR I/7.1,2.	see Giuliano 1984
MNR I/8.1,2.	see Giuliano 1985
PIR	see *Prosopographia Imperii Romani*
PW	see Pauly 1893-
TLL	see *Thesaurus Linguae Latinae*

PRIMARY SOURCES

Acta Sanctorum quotquot toto orbe coluntur, Acta Sanctorum Decembris, Brussels, Société des Bollandistes 1940.

Aldhelm of Malmesbury, *De Virginitate, Monumenta Germaniae Historica, Auctorum Antiquissimorum* 15, edited by R. Ehwald, Berlin, Weidmann 1919.

Cassiodori Senatoris Variae, Monumenta Germaniae Historica, Auctores Antiquissimi 12, edited by T. Mommsen, Berlin, Weidmann 1894.

Chronicon Farfense di Gregorio di Catino, edited by U. Balzani (*Fatti per la Storia d'Italia* 33-34), Rome, Istituto Storico Italiano 1903.

Codex Carolinus, edited by W. Gundlach, in *Monumenta Germaniae Historica, Merowingici et Karolini Aevi vol. 1, Epistolarum* iii, 469-657, Berlin, Weidmann 1892.

Collectionis bullarum sacro sanctae basilicae Vaticanae I, Rome 1747.

Collezioni di Disegni e Piante, Rome, Archivio dello Stato.

Columella, *De re rustica*, translated by H. Ash, E. Forster, E. Heffner, Loeb edition, London, Heinemann 1941-1955.

Dio, Cassio, *Historia*, translated by E. Cary, Loeb edition, London, Heinemann 1914-1927.

Gregory the Great, *Gregorii I Papae Registrum Epistolarum*, edited by P. Ewald, L.M. Hartmann, *Monumenta Germaniae Historica, Epistolarum* I and II, Berlin, Weidmann 1891, 1899.

Leges 3, Concilia 2: Concilia Aevi Karolini, Monumenta Germaniae Historica, edited by A. Werminghoff, Hanoun-Lipsiae, Hahnia 1906.

Liber Pontificalis, edited by L. Duchesne, Paris, Ernest Thorin 1886-1892.

Martyrologium Hieronymianum, edited by J.B. de Rossi and L. Duchesne, Brussels, Polleunis et Ceuterick no date.

Monumenta Germaniae Historica, Scriptores 2, edited by G. Pertz 1895.

Odilo, *Translatio S. Sebastiani, Monumenta Germaniae Historica, Scriptores* 15 (i).

Passio S. Caeciliae, Bibliotheca Hagiographica Latina Antiquae et Mediae Aetatis 1495, Brussels, Société des Bollandistes 1898-1911.

Passio S. Calisti, Bibliotheca Hagiographica Latina Antiquae et Mediae Aetatis 1523, Brussels, Société des Bollandistes 1898-1911.

Passio SS. Marcellini et Petri, Bibliotheca Hagiographica Latina Antiquae et Mediae Aetatis 5230, Brussels, Société des Bollandistes 1898-1911.

Passio SS. Marii, Marthae et Audifacis, Bibliotheca Hagiographica Latina Antiquae et Mediae Aetatis 5543, Brussels, Société des Bollandistes 1898-1911.

Passio SS. Rufinae et Secundae, Bibliotheca Hagiographica Latina Antiquae et Mediae Aetatis 7539, Brussels, Société des Bollandistes 1898-1911.

Paul the Deacon, *Historia Langobardorum*, edited by L. Bethmann and G. Waitz, *Monumenta Germaniae Historica, Scriptores rerum Langobardicarum et Italicarum saec. VI-IX*, 12-187, Hanover, Hahniani 1878.

Paulinus of Nola, *Epistulae*, edited by G. van Hartel, *Sancti Pontii Meropii Paulini Nolani opera* (Corpus Scriptorum Ecclesiasticorum Latinorum XXIX-XXX), Vindobonae, Tempsky 1894.

Pergamene dei Agostiani di Santa Maria Novella, Bracciano, Rome, Archivio dello Stato.

Pergamene del Monasterio di SS. Cosma e Damiano in Mica Aurea, Rome, Archivio dello Stato.

Pliny, *Naturalis Historia*, translated by H. Rackham, Loeb edition, London, Heinemann 1938-1950.

Procopius, *De Bello Gothico*, edited by J. Maury, *Opera* ii, revised edition, Leipzig, Teubner 1963.

Servius, Maurus Honoratus, *De Aeneid*, in *Vergil Aeneis II, mit dem commentar des Servius*, edited by E. Diehl (Leleine texte 80), Bonn 1911.

Valerii Maximi, Factorum et dictorum memorabilium libri novem, Lipsiae, Teubner 1888.

Vitae Hludowici Imperatoris, Monumenta Germaniae Historica, Scriptores 2.

William of Malmesbury, *History of the Kings of England*, edited by W. Stubbs, Rolls Series 90, London, HMSO 1887.

SECONDARY SOURCES

Agosti, G., Farinella, V., Gallo, D., and Tedeschi Grisanti, G. 1984: Visibilità e reimpiego: 'A Roma anche i morti e le loro urne camminano'. Proceedings of the *Colloquio sul reimpiego dei sarcofagi romani nel medioevo (Pisa 1982)* (Marburg, Lahn) 155-170.

Alfonsi Mattei, G., Camilli, L., Pavolini, C., Taglietti, F. and Zara, G. 1974: Contributo allo studio dei bolli laterizi del Museo Nazionale Romano. *Rendiconti dell'Accademia dei Lincei* 28, 295-348.

Andreae, B. 1980: *Die antiken Sarkophagereliefs, I.2. Die Sarkophage mit Darstellungen aus dem Menschenleben: die römischen Jagdsarkophage* (Berlin, Mann).

Andrews, D. 1978: Medieval masonry in northern Lazio: its development and uses for dating. In Blake, H., Potter, T.W. and Whitehouse, D.B. (eds), *Papers in Italian archaeology I: the Lancaster conference* (Oxford, British Archaeological Reports S41) 391-422.

Andrews, D. 1982: Ceramiche dall'archeologia di superficie in Lazio. In *Atti XI Convegno Internazionale della Ceramica, Albisola 1978* (Albisola, Centro Ligure per la Storia della Ceramica) 109-120.

Annis, M.B. forthcoming: Ceramica altomedievale a vetrina pesante e ceramica medievale a vetrina sparsa proveniente dallo scavo di San Sisto Vecchio in Roma: analisi tecnologici e proposte interpretative. In Paroli, L. (ed.), *La ceramica invetriata tardo antica e altomedievale – Italia* (Atti del seminario di studio (Siena-Pontignano 23-24 febbraio 1990)).

Arslan, E.A. 1965: Osservazioni sull'impiego e la diffusione delle volte sottili in tubi fittili. *Bollettino d'Arte* 50, 45-62.

Arthur, P. and Whitehouse, D.B. 1983: Appunti sulla produzione laterizia nell'Italia centro-meridionale tra il VI e XII secolo. *Archeologia Medievale* 10, 525-537.

Arthur, P. and Williams, D. 1981: Pannonische glasierte Keramik. In Anderson, A.C. and Anderson, A.S. (eds), *Roman pottery research in Britain and north west Europe* (Oxford, British Archaeological Reports S123 (ii)) 481-510.

Ashby, T. 1927: *The Roman campagna in classical times* (London, E. Benn Ltd).

Asimakopoulou-Atzaka, P. 1987: *Sintagma ton paleochristianikon psephidoton dapedon tes Ellados, II, Peloponnesos – Sterea Ellada (Byzantina Mnemeia* 7) (Thessalonika).

Aurigemma, S. 1960: *Tripolitania. I. I monumenti d'arte decorativa. I, i mosaici* (Rome, Poligrafico dello Stato).

Auvray, L. (ed.) 1890: *Les regestres de Gregoire IX. Recueil des bulles de ce pape (Bibliothèque de l'École Française d'Athènes et de Rome)* (Paris, Fontemoing).

Avagnina, M.E., Garibaldi, V. and Salterini, C. 1976-1977: Strutture murarie degli edifici religiosi di Roma nel XII secolo. *Rivista dell'Istituto Nazionale d'Archeologia e dell'Arte* 23-24, 173-255.

Bailey, D.M. 1980: *A catalogue of the lamps in the British Museum, volume 2* (London, British Museum).

Balbi de Caro, S. 1983: I ripostigli monetali di età medioevale e moderna del Museo Nazionale Romano di Roma. Note critiche e programmi di edizione. *Bollettino di Numismatica* 1, 11-23.

Balland, A., Barbet, A., Gros, P and Hallier, G. 1971: *Fouilles de l'École Française de Rome a Bolsena (Poggio Moscini). II Les architectures (Mélanges de l'École Française de Rome Supplement* 6) (Paris, De Boccard).

Balmelle, C., Blanchard-Lemee, M., Christophe, J., Darmon, J-P., Guimier-Sorbets, A-M., Lavagne, H., Prudhomme, R. and Stern, H. 1985: *Le décor géométrique de la mosaïque romaine* (Paris, Picard).

Baratte, F. and Metzger, C. 1985: *Musée du Louvre: catalogue des sarcophages en pierre d'époques romaine et paléochretienne* (Paris, Éditions de la Réunion des Musées Nationaux).

Barclay Lloyd, J.E. 1985: Masonry techniques in medieval Rome, c. 1080-c. 1300. *Papers of the British School at Rome* 53, 225-277.

Barnish, S. 1983: *The fall of Boethius: a study in the relations between late Roman senator and barbarian* (Oxford, unpublished D.Phil. thesis).

Bass, G.F. and van Doorninck, F.H. 1982: *Yassi Ada, I. A seventh century Byzantine shipwreck* (Texas, A and M University Press).

Beard, M. 1985: Writing and ritual. A study of diversity and expansion in the Arval Acta. *Papers of the British School at Rome* 53, 114-162.

Beazley, J.D. 1947: *Etruscan Vase Painting* (Oxford, Clarendon Press).

Becatti, G. 1948: Case ostiensi del tardo impero. *Bollettino d'Arte* 33, 101-128, 197-224.

Becatti, G. 1961: *Scavi di Ostia IV. Mosaici e pavimenti marmorei* (Rome, Poligrafico dello Stato).

Bertelli, G., Guidobaldi, A.G. and Spagnoletti, P. 1976-1977: Strutture murarie degli edifici religiosi di Roma dal VI al IX secolo. *Rivista dell'Istituto Nazionale d'Archeologia e Storia dell'Arte* 23-24, 95-172.

Berti, F., Carandini, A., Fabbricotti, E., Gasparri, C., Giannelli, M., Moriconi, M.P., Palma, B., Panella, C., Picozzi, M.G., Ricci, A., Tatti, M., and Istituto di Paleontologia Umana 1970: Ostia II. Le terme del nuotatore. Scavo dell'ambiente I. *Studi Miscellanei* 16 (Rome, De Luca Editore).

Bertolini, O. 1947: Roma di fronte a Bisanzio e ai Longobardi. *Storia di Roma* 9 (Bologna, Cappelli Editore).

Bertolini, O. 1952: La ricomparsa della sede episcopale di 'Tres Tabernae' nella seconda metà del sec. VIII e l'istituzione delle domuscultae. *Archivio della Reale Società Romana di Storia Patria* 75, 103-109.

Bianchi Bandinelli, R. 1976: *Roma. La fine dell'arte antica* (second edition) (Milan, Rizzoli).

Biddle, M. 1965: Excavations at Winchester, 1964. *The Antiquaries Journal* 45, 230-264.

Blagg, T.F.C. 1978: Bell-founding in Italy: archaeology and history. In Blake, H., Potter, T.W. and Whitehouse, D.B. (eds), *Papers in Italian archaeology I: the Lancaster conference* (Oxford, British Archaeological Reports S41) 423-434.

Blagg, T.F.C., van der Noort, R., Luttrell, A. and Whitehouse, D. (eds) forthcoming: *Excavations at Le Mura di S. Stefano, Anguillara.*

Blake, H. 1978: Ceramiche romane e medievali e pietra ollare. In Ward-Perkins, B., Blake, H., Nepoti, S., Castelletti, L., Barker, G., Wheeler, A. and Mannoni, T., Scavi nella Torre Civica di Pavia 141-170. *Archeologia Medievale* 5, 77-272.

Blake, H. 1981a: La ceramica medioevale di Assisi. In Guaitini, G. (ed.), *Ceramiche medioevali dell'Umbria: Assisi, Orvieto, Todi* (Florence, Nuova Guaraldi Ed.) 15-33.

Blake, H. 1981b: Ceramica paleo-italiana. *Faenza* 67, 20-54.

Blake, H. 1983: Sepolture. *Archeologia Medievale* 10, 175-197.

Blake, M.E. 1940: Mosaics of the late Empire in Rome and vicinity. *Memoirs of the American Academy in Rome* 17, 81-130.

Blanchard, M., Cristophe, J., Darmon, J.P., Lavagne, H. and Prudhomme, R. 1973: *Repertoire graphique du décor géométrique dans la mosaïque antique, (Bulletin de l'association internationale pour l'étude de la mosaïque antique* 1) (Paris, AIEMA).

Blasquez, J.M. 1982: *Corpus de mosaicos de España V* (Madrid, CSIC).

Blasquez, J.M. and Mezquiriz, M.A. 1985: *Corpus de mosaicos de España VII* (Madrid, CSIC).

Bloch, H. 1947: *I bolli laterizi e la storia edilizia romana (Contributi all'archeologia e alla storia romana)* (Rome, Il Comune di Roma).

Bloch, H. 1948: Supplement to volume XV, 1 of the *CIL* including complete indices to the Roman brick-stamps. *Supplementary Papers of the American School of Classical Studies in Rome* 1, 1-86.

Bond, F. 1908: *Fonts and font covers* (London, Frowde).

Bonifay, M., Paroli, L. and Picon, M. 1986: Ceramiche a vetrina pesante scoperte a Roma e a Marsiglia. *Archeologia Medievale* 13, 79-95.

Borbein, A.H. 1968: *Campanareliefs. Typologische und*

stilkritische Untersuchungen (*Mitteilungen des Deutschen Arch-äologischen Instituts, Römische Abteilung Erganzungsheft* 14) (Heidelberg, Kerle).

Bossi, G. 1915: I Crescenzi. Contributo alla storia di Roma e dintorni dal 900 al 1012. *Dissertazione del Pontifica Accademia Romana di Archeologia, serie 2* 12, 111-170.

Bovini, G., Brandenberg, H. and Deichmann, I. 1967: *Repertorium der christlich-antiken Sarkophage. I: Rom und Ostia* (Wiesbaden, Steiner).

Broccoli, U. (ed.) 1981: *Corpus della scultura altomedievale. VII: la diocesi di Roma, V: il suburbio, 1* (Spoleto, Centro di Studi sull'Alto Medioevo).

Brogiolo, G.P. 1987: A proposito dell'organizzazione urbana nell'alto medioevo. *Archeologia Medievale* 14, 27-46.

Brogiolo, G.P. and Gelichi, S. 1986: La ceramica grezza medievale nella pianura padana. In *La ceramica medievale nel mediterraneo occidentale* (Florence, All'Insegna del Giglio) 310-315.

Broise, H. and Scheid, J. 1987: *Recherches archéologiques à La Magliana. Le balneum des Frères Arvales* (Rome, École Française de Rome/Soprintendenza Archeologica di Roma).

Brooke, C. and Swaan, W. 1974: *The monastic world, 1000-1300* (London, Elek).

Brothwell, D. 1981: *Digging up bones* (Oxford, Oxford University Press).

Brown, P. 1981: *The cult of saints; its rise and function in Latin Christianity* (Chicago, SCM Press Ltd).

Brown, T.S. 1984: *Gentlemen and officers. Imperial administration and aristocratic power in Byzantine Italy A.D. 554-800* (London, British School at Rome).

Brunetti Nardi, G. (ed.) 1981: *Repertorio degli scavi e delle scopertearcheologichenell'EtruriameridionaleIII1971-1975*(Rome, Centro Nazionale delle Ricerche).

Bruun, P. 1963: Symboles, signes et monogrammes. In Zilliacus, H. (ed.), *Acta Instituti Romae Finlandiae* 1.2: *Sylloge Inscriptionum Christianorum Veterorum Musei Vaticani* (Helsinki, Helsingfors) 73-166.

Bullough, D. 1983: Burial, community and belief in the early medieval West. In Wormald, P. (ed.), *Ideal and reality in Frankish and Anglo-Saxon society* (*Studies presented to J.M. Wallace-Hadrill*) (Oxford, Blackwell) 177-201.

Cabrol, F. and Leclercq, H. 1907-1953: *Dictionnaire d'archéologie chrétienne et de liturgie* (Paris, Letouzey and Ane).

Cain, H. 1985: *Römische Marmorkandelaber* (Mainz, Philipp von Zabern).

Calza, G. (ed.) 1953: *Scavi di Ostia I. Topografia generale* (Rome, Poligrafico dello Stato).

Calza, R., Bonnano, M. and Messineo, G. 1977: *Antichità di Villa Doria Pamphilj* (Rome, De Luca Editore).

Cameron, A. 1976: *Circus factions. Blues and greens at Rome and Byzantium* (Oxford, Clarendon Press).

Cameron, F., Clark, G., Jackson, R.P., Johns, C., Philpot, S., Potter, T.W., Shepherd, J., Stone, M., and Whitehouse, D.B. 1984: Il castello di Ponte Nepesino e il confine settentrionale del Ducato di Roma. *Archeologia Medievale* 9, 63-147.

Camilli, L. and Taglietti, F. 1979: Nuovo contributo allo studio dei bolli laterizi del Museo Nazionale Romano. *Rendiconti dell'Accademia dei Lincei* 34, 187-222.

Camodeca, G. 1974: La carriera di L. Publilius Probatus e un inesistente proconsole d'Africa A. Volateios. *Atti della Accademia di Scienze Morali e Politiche della Società Nazionale di Scienze, Lettere ed Arti di Napoli* 85, 250-268.

Cappelli, A. 1912: *Dizionario di abbreviature latine ed italiane usate nelle carte e codici del medio evo* (Milan, Hoepli).

Capobianchi, V. 1895: Appunti per servire all'ordinamento delle monete coniate dal Senato Romano dal 1184 al 1439, *Archivio della Reale Società Romana di Storia Patria* 18, 75-124.

Capobianchi, V. 1896: Il denaro pavese e il suo corso in Italia nel XII secolo. *Rivista Italiana di Numismatica* 9, 21-60.

Caraffa, F. (ed.) 1981: *Monasticon Italiae I. Roma e Lazio* (Centro Storico Benedettino Italiano) (Cesena, Badia di S. Maria del Monte).

Caraffa, F. 1988: Il monachesimo nel Lazio dalle origini al Concilio di Trento. *Lunario Romano* 18, 3-23.

Carandini, A., Fabbricotti, E., Gasparri, C., Gasparri Tatti, M., Giannelli, M., Moriconi, M.P., Palma, B., Panella, C., Polia, M., Ricci, A. and Istituto di Paleontologia Umana 1968: Ostia I. Le terme del nuotatore. Scavo dell'ambiente IV. *Studi Miscellanei* 13 (Rome, De Luca Editore).

Carandini, A. and Panella, C. (eds) 1973: Ostia III, parte prima. Le terme del nuotatore. Scavi degli ambienti III, VI, VII. *Studi Miscellanei* 21 (Rome, De Luca Editore).

Carandini, A. and Panella, C. (eds) 1977: Ostia IV. Le terme del nuotatore. Scavo dell'ambiente XVI e dell'area XXV. *Studi Miscellanei* 23 (Rome, De Luca Editore).

Carson, R.A.C. and Kent, J.P.C. 1960: *Bronze Roman imperial coinage of the later empire AD 346-498* (*Late Roman bronze coinage* II) (London, Spink and Son).

Cébeillac, M. 1972: *Les 'quaestores principis et candidati' aux Ier et IIeme siècles de l'Empire* (Centri studi e documentazione sull'Italia Romana, monografia a supplemento degli Atti 4) (Cisalpino, Goliardica).

Cecchelli, C. 1935: Note sulle famiglie romane tra il IX e il XII secolo, II: la famiglia di Giovanni XIII e le prime fortune dei Crescenzi. *Archivio della Reale Società Romana di Storia Patria* 58, 72-97.

Ceramica invetriata 1985: *La ceramica invetriata tardoromano e altomedievale* (Como, New Press).

Christie, N. 1987: Forum Ware, the Duchy of Rome, and incastellamento: problems in interpretation. *Archeologia Medievale* 14, 451-466.

Christol, M. 1974: La carrière de Q. Cerellius Apollinaris, préfet des vigiles de Caracalla. In *Mélanges d'histoire ancienne offerts à W. Seston* (*Publications de la Sorbonne, Études* 9) (Paris, de Boccard) 119-126.

Cipolla, C. 1975: *Le avventure della lira* (Bologna) (first edition 1958).

Cipriano, M.T., Paroli, L., Patterson, H., Saguì, L. and Whitehouse, D. forthcoming: La documentazione ceramica dell'Italia centromeridionale nell'alto medioevo: quadri regionale e contesti campione. In *IV congresso de ceramica medieval do mediterraneo occidental. Lisbon, 16-22 november 1987*.

Coccia, S. and Nardi, S. forthcoming: Monte della Tolfa e la Valle del Mignone. In Paroli, L. (ed.), *La ceramica invetriata tardo antica e altomedievale – Italia* (Atti del seminario di studio (Siena-Pontignano 23-24 febbraio 1990)).

Coccia, S. and Paroli, L. forthcoming: La basilica cristiana di Pianabella (Ostia Antica): L'architettura, l'insediamento e l'ambiente naturale. *Archeologia Laziale* 11.

Conant, K. 1959: *Carolingian and Romanesque architecture, 800 to 1200* (Harmondsworth, Penguin).

Corpus Inscriptionum Latinarum 1898- (Berlin, George Reimer/De Gruyter).

Corpus Nummorum Italicorum 1910-1943 (Rome/Milan, Accademia dei Lincei/Forni).

Corpus Vasorum Antiquorum 1930- (Milan/Rome, Bestetti/Libreria dello Stato).

Corswandt, I. 1982: *Oscilla. Untersuchungen zu einer römischen Reliefgattung* (Berlin, Diss).

Cortonesi, A. 1986: Fornaci e calcare a Roma e nel Lazio nel basso medioevo. In *Scritti in onore di Filippo Caraffa* (*Biblioteca di Latium* 2) (Anagni, Istituto di Storia e di Arte del Lazio Meridionale) 277-307.

Coutts, C. and Mithen, S. 1985: The late Roman and early medieval cemeteries at San Vincenzo al Volturno. In Hodges, R. and Mitchell, J. (eds), *San Vincenzo al Volturno. The archaeology, art and territory of an early medieval monastery* (Oxford, British Archaeological Reports S252) 61-81.

Cozzo, G. 1936: La corporazione dei figuli ed i bolli doliari. *Memorie dell'Accademia dei Lincei* 5, 233-366.

Crowfoot, G. and Harden, D. 1931: Early Byzantine and later glass lamps. *Journal of Egyptian Archaeology* 17, 196-208.

Cubberley, A.L., Lloyd, J.A. and Roberts, P. 1988: Testi and clibani: the baking covers of classical Italy. *Papers of the British School at Rome* 56, 98-119.

Daniel, N. 1975: *The Arabs and medieval Europe* (London, Longman).

Davidson, G.R. 1952: *Corinth – Results of excavations conducted by the American School of Classical Studies. XII The minor objects* (Princeton, The American School).

Degrassi, A. (ed.) 1957-1963: *Inscriptiones Latinae Liberae Rei Publicae* (Florence, La Nuova Italia).

Delogu, P. 1988: The rebirth of Rome in the 8th and 9th centuries. In Hodges, R. and Hobley, B. (eds), *The rebirth of towns in the west, AD 700-1050* (London, CBA research report number 68) 32-42.

De Marinis, G. 1977: *Topografia storica della Val d'Elsa in periodo etrusco* (Florence).

De Rossi, G. 1980: Cloche avec description dédicatoire du VIII e IXs. trouvée a Canino. *Revue de l'Art Chrétienne* 40, 1-9.

De Rossi, G., Di Domenico, P. and Quilici L. 1968: La via Aurelia da Roma a Civitavecchia. In *La Via Aurelia da Roma a Forum Aurelii* (*Quaderni dell'istituto di topografia antica della Università di Roma* 4) (Rome).

Dessau, H. 1892: *Inscriptiones Latinae Selectae* (Berlin, Weidemann).

Diehl, E. 1925-1931: *Inscriptiones Latinae Christianae Veteres* (Berlin, Weidemann).

Donderer, M. 1986: *Die Chronologie der römischen Mosaiken in Venetien und Istrien bis zur Zeit des Antonine* (*Archäologischen Forschungen des Deutschen Archäologischen Instituts* 15) (Berlin, Mann).

Dorigo, W. 1966: *Pittura tardo romana* (Milan, Feltrinelli).

Dufourcq, A. 1900: *Études sur les Gesta Martyrum Romaines* (*Bibliothèque de l'École Française d'Athènes et de Rome* 83) (Paris, Fontemoing).

Duhr, J. 1934: Le Pape Marin 1er (882-884) était-il évêque ou archdiacre lors de son élection? *Recherche de Science Religeuse* 24, 200-206.

Duncan, G.C. 1964: A Roman pottery near Sutri. *Papers of the British School at Rome* 32, 38-88.

Duncan, G.C. 1965: Roman Republican pottery from the vicinity of Sutri. *Papers of the British School at Rome* 33, 134-176.

Dwyer, E. 1981: Pompeian Oscilla collections. *Mitteilungen des Deutschen Archäologischen Instituts, Römische Abteilung* 88, 247-306.

Dyson, S.L. 1976: *Cosa. The utilitarian pottery* (*Memoirs of the American Academy in Rome*, 33) (Rome, American Academy).

Eschapasse, M. 1963: *L'architecture Benedectine en Europe* (Paris, Édition des Deux Mondes).

Fabbricotti, E. 1969: Ritrovamenti archeologici sotto la chiesa della Visitazione di Santa Maria in Camuccia. *Res Tudertinae* 10 (Todi).

Fabre, P. and Duchesne, L. 1910: *Étude sur le Liber Censuum de l'Église Romaine* (*Bibliothèque de l'École Française d'Athènes et de Rome*) (Paris, Thorin).

Farioli, R.O. 1966: Sarcofagi paleocristiani 'ad alberi'. *XIII corso di cultura sull'arte Ravennate e Bizantina*, 353-390.

Fatucchi, A. 1977: *Corpus della scultura altomedievale. IX: la diocesi di Arezzo* (Spoleto, Centro Italiano di Studi sull'Alto Medioevo).

Fedele, P. 1898: Carte del monasterio dei SS. Cosma e Damiano in Mica Aurea. *Archivio della Reale Società Romana di Storia Patria* 21, 459-534.

Fedele, P. 1899: Carte del monasterio dei SS. Cosma e Damiano in Mica Aurea. *Archivio della Reale Società Romana di Storia Patria* 22, 35-107, 383-447.

Felici, S. 1972: *L'Abbazia di Farneta in Val di Chiana* (Arezzo, Tipografia Sociale).

Ferrari, G. 1957: *Early Roman monasteries* (*Studi di Antichità Cristiana* 23) (Vatican City, Pontificio Istituto di Archeologia Cristiana).

Ferrua, A. 1961-1962: Nuovi frammenti degli Atti degli Arvali. *Bullettino della Commissione Archeologica Comunale di Roma* 78, 116-129.

Fiorilla, S. 1986: Bolli e iscrizioni su laterizi altomedievali del territorio lombardo. *Archivio Storico Lombardo* 112, 321-415.

Fittschen, K. and Zanker, P. 1983: *Katalog der römischen Porträts in den Capitolinischen Museen und der anderen kommunalen Sammlungen der Stadt Rom. Band III: Kaiserinnen- und prinzessinnen Bildnisse Frauenporträts* (Mainz, Philipp von Zabern).

Foucher, L. 1960: *Inventaire des mosaïques. Sousse* (Tunis, Imprimerie Officielle).

Frayn, J. 1978: Home baking in Roman Italy. *Antiquity* 52, 28-33.

Gai, S. 1986: La 'Berretta del Prete' sulla via Appia Antica: indagini archeologiche preliminari sull'insediamento medievale 1984. *Archeologia Medievale* 13, 365-404.

Galinie, H., Kemp, R., Lorans, E., Mabire La Caille, C., Randoin, B. and Watkinson, B. 1982: Fouilles archéologiques à Tours 1982. Rapport préliminaire. *Bulletin de la Société Archéologique de Touraine* 40, 153-199.

Gamurrini, G.F., Cozza, A., Pasqui, A. and Mengarelli, R. 1972: *Forma Italiae II. Documenti I. Carta archeologica d'Italia (1881-1897): materiale per l'Etruria e la Sabina* (Florence, Olschki).

Garcea, F. and Williams, D. 1987: Appunti sulla produzione e circolazione delle lucerne nel Napoletano tra VII e VIII secolo. *Archeologia Medievale* 14, 537-546.

Gracia Guinea, M.A. 1990: *Guia de la villa romana de Quintamilla de la Cueza* (Palencia).

Gasbarri, C. 1978: Le 'domuscultae' di Papa Zaccaria. *Lunario Romano* 8 ('Fatti e figure del Lazio medievale'), 219-228.

Gasperini, L. 1978: Nuova dedica onoraria di Forum

Clodii. *Miscellanea Greca e Romana* 6 (Rome, Istituto Italiano di Storia Antica) 439-458.

Gasperini, L. 1984: Nuova dedica onoraria di Forum Clodii. *Archeologia Classica* 36, 361-374.

Gatti, G. 1909: Tegole fittili col bollo di Innocenzo II. *Bullettino della Commissione Archeologica Comunale di Roma* 37, 107-112.

Gatto, L. 1962: Mainardo vescovo di Silva Candida e abate di Pomposa. *Rivista di Storia della Chiesa in Italia* 16, 201-248.

Geary, P.J. 1978: *Furta Sacra. Thefts of relics in the central Middle Ages* (Princeton, Princeton University Press).

Geertman, H. 1975: *More Veterum. Il Liber Pontificalis e gli edifici ecclesiastici di Roma nella tarda antichità e nell'alto medio evo* (Groningen, H.D. Tjeenk Willink).

Gelichi, S. 1986: Studi sulla ceramica medievale riminese. 2. Il complesso dell'ex Hotel Commercio. *Archeologia Medievale* 13, 117-172.

Gibbs, S.L. 1976: *Greek and Roman sundials* (New Haven/London, Yale University Press).

Gibson, S. and Ward-Perkins, B. 1979: The surviving remains of the Leonine wall. *Papers of the British School at Rome* 47, 30-57.

Gibson, S. and Ward-Perkins, B. 1983: The surviving remains of the Leonine wall. Part II: the Passetto. *Papers of the British School at Rome* 51, 222-239.

Gilbert, B. and McKern, T. 1973: A method for ageing the os pubis. *American Journal of Physical Anthropology* 38, 31-38.

Gismondi, I. 1953: Materiali, tecniche e sistemi costruttivi nell'edilizia ostiense. In Calza, G. (ed.), *Scavi di Ostia I. Topografia generale* (Rome, Poligrafico dello Stato) 181-211.

Giuliano, A. (ed.) 1982: *Museo Nazionale Romano. Le sculture. I. 3. Giardino del chiostro* (Rome, De Luca Editore).

Giuliano, A. (ed.) 1984: *Museo Nazionale Romano. Le sculture. I.7. Giardino dei cinquecento. Parte 1, 2* (Rome, De Luca Editore).

Giuliano, A. (ed.) 1985: *Museo Nazionale Romano. Le sculture. I.8. Aule delle Terme. Parte 1, 2* (Rome, De Luca Editore).

Glass, D. 1980: *Studies on Cosmatesque pavements* (Oxford, British Archaeological Reports S82).

Gordon, A.E and Gordon, J. 1958-1965: *Album of dated Latin inscriptions* (Berkeley, University of California Press).

Goudineau, C. 1968: *La céramique aretine lisse* (*Mélanges d'archéologie et d'histoire* 6) (Paris, de Boccard).

Grierson, P. 1957: Mint output in the 10th century. *The Economic History Review* 9, 462-466.

Grierson, P. 1976: *Monnaies du Moyen Age* (Fribourg, Office du Livre).

Grilletto, R. and Lambert, C. 1989: Le sepolture e il cimitero della chiesa abbaziale della Novalesa. *Archeologia Medievale* 16, 329-356.

Guidobaldi, F. 1983: Mosaici con tessere porfiretiche a Roma tra III e IV secolo. In Farioli Campanati, R. (ed.), *Atti del III colloquio internazionale sul mosaico antico, Ravenna 6-10 settembre 1980)* (Ravenna, Edizioni del Girasole) 491-503.

Guidobaldi, F. 1985: Pavimenti in *opus sectile* di Roma e dell'area romana. In Pensabene, P. (ed.), Marmi antichi. Problemi d'impiego, di restauro e d'identificazione. *Studi Miscellanei* 26 (Rome, De Luca Editore) 171-233.

Guidobaldi, F. 1989: L'inserimento delle chiese titolari di Roma nel tessuto urbano preesistente: osservazioni ed implicazioni. In *'Quaeritur inventus colitur'. Studi in onore di p. U. Fasola O.S.B. (Studi di Antichità Cristiana* 40) (Vatican City, Pontificio Istituto di Archeologia Cristiana) 383-396.

Guidobaldi, F. and Guiglia Guidobaldi A.G. 1983: *Pavimenti marmorei di Roma dal IV al IX secolo (Studi di Antichità Cristiana* 36) (Vatican City, Pontificio Istituto di Archeologia Cristiana).

Halfmann, H. 1979: *Die Senatoren aus dem östlichen Teil des Imperiums Romanum* (Gottingen, Vandenhoeck and Ruprecht).

Hamilton, B. 1962: Monastic revival in tenth century Rome. *Studia Monastica* 4, 35-68.

Hartmann, L.M. 1889: *Untersuchungen zur Geschichte der byzantinischen Verwaltung in Italien, 540-750* (Leipzig, S. Hirzel).

Hayes, J.W. 1968: A seventh century pottery group. In Harrison, R.M. and Fıratlı, N., Excavations at Sarachane in Istanbul: fifth preliminary report, 203-216. *Dumbarton Oaks Papers* 22, 195-216.

Hayes, J.W. 1972: *Late Roman pottery* (London, British School at Rome).

Hayes, J.W. 1980: *Supplement to late Roman pottery* (London, British School at Rome).

Hayes, J.W. forthcoming: *Sarachne II*.

Heilmeyer, W. 1970: *Korinthische Normalkapitelle* (*Mitteilungen des Deutschen Archäologischen Instituts, Römische Abteilung, Ergunzungsheft* 16) (Heidelberg, F.H. Kerle).

Heitz, C. 1980: *L'architecture religieuse carolingienne. Les formes et leurs fonctions* (Paris, Picard).

Henzen, W. 1874: *Acta Fratrum Arvalium quae supersunt* (Berlin, George Reiner).

Herklotz, I. 1985: *'Sepulcra' e 'monumenta' del Medioevo (Collana di Studi di Storia dell'Arte)* (Rome, Rari Nantes).

Hermann, K. 1973: *Das Tuskulaner Papstum (1012-1046)* (Stuttgart, A. Hiersemann).

Herrmann, J. 1974: *The schematic composite capital: a study of architectural decoration at Rome in the later Empire* (New York).

Hodges, R. 1985: Excavations at San Vincenzo al Volturno: a regional and international centre from AD 400-1100. In Hodges, R. and Mitchell, J. (eds), *San Vincenzo al Volturno. The archaeology, art and territory of an early medieval monastery* (Oxford, British Archaeological Reports S252) 1-35.

Hodges, R. 1988: The San Vincenzo project: a preliminary review of the excavations and surveys at San Vincenzo al Volturno and in its terra. In Noyé, G. (ed), *Castrum II. Structure de l'habitat et occupation du sol dans les pays méditerranéens: les méthodes et l'apport de l'archéologie extensive (Collection de l'École Française de Rome* 105, *Publications de la Casa de Velázquez, serie archéologie, fasc.* 9) (Rome-Madrid, École Française de Rome/Casa de Velázquez) 421-431.

Hodges, R. and Mitchell, J. (eds) 1985: *San Vincenzo al Volturno. The archaeology, art and territory of an early medieval monastery* (Oxford, British Archaeological Reports S252).

Hodges, R. and Patterson, H. 1986: San Vincenzo al Volturno and the origins of the medieval pottery industry in Italy. In *La ceramica medievale nel Mediterraneo occidentale* (Florence, All'Insegna del Giglio) 13-26.

Hodges, R. and Whitehouse, D.B. 1983: *Mohammed, Charlemagne and the origins of Europe* (London, Duckworth).

Horn, W. and Born, E. 1979: *The plan of St. Gall (I-III)* (Berkeley, University of California Press).

Huls, R. 1977: *Kardinale, Klerus und Kirchen Roms 1049-1130 (Bibliothek des Deutschen Historischen Instituts Rom* 48) (Tübingen, Max Niemeyer Verlag).

Isings, C. 1957: *Roman glass from dated finds (Archeologia Traiectina)* (Groningen-Djakarta, Walters).

Johns, J., Ward-Perkins, B., Lamarque, W., Beddoe, M. and Ward-Perkins, J. 1973: Excavations at Tuscania, 1973: report on the finds from six selected pits. *Papers of the British School at Rome* 41, 45-154.

Jones, G.D.B. 1980: Il Tavoliere romano: l'agricoltura romana attraverso l'aerofotografia e lo scavo. *Archeologia Classica* 32, 85-107.

Jones, P. 1965: L'Italia agraria nell'alto medioevo: problemi di cronologia e di continuità. *Settimane di studio del centro Italiano di studi sull'alto medioevo* 13, 57-92, and 225-248 (discussion).

Journel, P. 1977: *Le culte des saints dans les basiliques du Lateran et du Vatican au douzième siècle (Collection de l'École Française de Rome 26)* (Rome, Ecole Française de Rome).

Kahane, A., Murray-Threipland, L. and Ward-Perkins J.B. 1968: The Ager Veientanus north and east of Veii. *Papers of the British School at Rome* 36, 1-218.

Kajanto, I. 1963: Onomastic studies in the early Christian inscriptions of Rome and Carthage. In Zilliacus, H. (ed.), *Acta Instituti Romani Finlandiae* 1.2: *Sylloge Inscriptionum Christianorum Veterorum Musei Vaticani* (Helsinki, Helsingfors) 1-141.

Kautzsch, R. 1936: *Kapitellstudien. Studien zu spätantiken Kunstgeschichte* (Berlin, De Gruyter).

Kautzsch, R. 1939: Die römische Schmuckkunst in Stein von 6 bis zum 10 Jahrhundert. *Römisches Jahrbuch für Kunstgeschichte* 3, 3-73.

Keay, S. 1984: *Late Roman amphorae in the western Mediterranean. A typology and economic study: the Catalan evidence* (Oxford, British Archaeological Reports S196).

Kehr, P.F. 1901-1902: *Papsturkunden in Italien. Reiseberichte zur Italia Pontificia* III (*Acta Romanorum Pontificium* 3) (Vatican City, Biblioteca Apostolica Vaticana).

Kelly, J.N.D. 1986: *The Oxford dictionary of saints* (Oxford, Oxford University Press).

Kirsch, J. 1924: *Le memorie dei martiri sulle vie Aurelia e Cornelia (Studi e Testi 38)* (Vatican City, Pontificio Istituto di Archeologia Cristiana).

Koch, G. 1975: *Die antiken Sarkophagreliefs. 6. Die mythologischen Sarkophage: Meleager* (Berlin, Mann).

Krautheimer, R. 1937-1977: *Corpus Basilicarum Christianarum Romae* (Vatican City, Pontificio Istituto di Archeologia Cristiana).

Krautheimer, R. 1942: The Carolingian revival of early Christian architecture. *The Art Bulletin*, 24 (1), 1-38.

Krautheimer, R. 1980: *Rome. Profile of a city, 312-1308* (Princeton, Princeton University Press).

Kuttner, S. 1945: 'Cardinalis': the history of a canonical concept. *Traditio* 3, 129-214.

Lake, A.K. 1934-1935: Campania Supellex. The pottery deposit at Minturnae. *Bollettino dell'Associazione Internazionale di Studi Mediterranei* 5 (4-5), 97-136.

Lamboglia, N. 1952: Per una classificazione preliminare della ceramica campana. *Atti del I Congresso Internazionale di Studi Liguri*, 139-206.

Lavagne, H. 1970: La nymphée au Polypheme de la Domus Aurea. *Mélanges de l'École Française de Rome* 82, 673-721.

Lawrence, C.H. 1984: *Medieval monasticism. Forms of religious life in western Europe in the Middle Ages* (London/New York, Longman).

Leciejewicz, L., Tabaczyńska, E. and Tabaczyński, S. 1977: *Torcello. Scavi 1961-62, (Istituto Nazionale d'Archeologia e Storia dell'Arte, Monografie III)* (Rome, Istituto Nazionale d'Archeologia e Storia dell'Arte).

Leon, C. 1971: *Die Bauornamentik des Trajansforum* (Vienna/Cologne/Graz, Bohlaus).

Leotardi, P.B. 1979: *Marmi di cava rinvenuti ad Ostia e considerazioni sul commercio dei marmi in età romana (Scavi di Ostia 10)* (Rome, Istituto Poligrafico e Zecca dello Stato).

Llewellyn, P. 1971: *Rome in the Dark Ages* (London, Faber and Faber).

Llewellyn, P. 1976: The Roman Church during the Laurentian Schism: priests and senators. *Church History* 45, 417-427.

Llewellyn, P. 1977: The Roman clergy during the Laurentian Schism (498-506): a preliminary analysis. *Ancient Society* 8, 245-275.

Llewellyn, P. 1979: La première développement du Collège des Cardinaux. *Recherches de Science Religeuse* 67, 31-44.

Llewellyn, P. 1986: The popes and the constitution in the eighth century. *English Historical Review* 100, 42-67.

Loeschke, S. 1909: Keramische Funde in Haltern. *Mitteilungen der Altertumskommission für Westfalen* 5, 101-322.

Lovejoy, C., Meindl, R., Pryzbeck, T. and Mensforth, R. 1985: Chronological metamorphosis of the auricular surface of the ilium: a new method for the determination of adult skeletal age at death. *American Journal of Physical Anthropology* 68, 15-28.

Lucchi, L. 1984: Viterbo e i centri abbaziali del Lazio: primi risultati di un'indagine sui sarcofagi romani reimpiegati. Proceedings of the *Colloquio sul reimpiego dei sarcofagi romani nel medioevo (Pisa 1982)* (Marburg, Lahn) 171-185.

Lusuardi Siena, S. 1985-1987: Luni paleocristiana e altomedievale nelle vicende della sua cattedrale. *Quaderni del Centro di Studi Lunensi* 10-12 (*Atti del convegno studi lunensi e prospettive sull'occidente Romano*), 289-320.

Luttrell, A. 1976: La campagna a nord di Roma: archeologia e storia medievale. *Atti del colloquio internazionale di archeologia medievale (1974, Palermo)* 123-126.

Maccarrone, M. 1974: La reologia del primato romano del sec. XI. In *Atti della quinta settimane internazionale di studio. V. Le istituzioni ecclesiastiche della 'Societas Christiana' dei secoli XI-XII: papato, cardinalato ed episcopato, Mendola 26-31 agosto 1971* (Milan, Università Cattolica del S. Cuore/Vita e Pensiero) 21-122.

Maetzke, G. 1974: Vasi medioevali dal centro di Firenze. In Manselli, R. and Arnaldi, G. (eds), *Studi sul medioevo cristiano offerti a Raffaello Morghen I* (Rome, Istituto Storico Italiano per il Medio Evo) 475-498.

Maetzke, G. 1978: Contributi per la conoscenza della ceramica medievale delle Marche. *Rivista di Studi Marchigiani* 1 (1), 85-117.

Magni, M. 1979: Crypts de haut Moyen Age en Italie: problèmes de typologie du IXe jusqu'au début du XIe siècle. *Cahiers Archéologiques* 28, 41-85.

Mallett, D. and Whitehouse, D. 1967: Castel Porciano: an abandoned medieval village of the Roman Campagna. *Papers of the British School at Rome* 35, 113-146.

Manacorda, D. (ed.) 1984: *Archeologia urbana a Roma: il progetto della Crypta Balbi 2. Un 'mondezzaro' del XVIII secolo. Lo scavo dell'ambiente 63 del conservatorio di S. Caterina della Rosa* (Florence, All'Insegna del Giglio).

Manacorda, D. (ed.) 1985: *Archeologia urbana a Roma: il progetto della Crypta Balbi. 3. Il giardino del conservatorio di S. Caterina della Rosa* (Florence, All'Insegna del Giglio).

Manacorda, D., Paroli, L., Molinari, A., Ricci, M. and Romei D. 1986: La ceramica medioevale di Roma nella stratigrafia della Crypta Balbi. In *La ceramica medievale nel Mediterraneo occidentale* (Florence, All'Insegna del Giglio) 511-544.

Mann, J. 1988: The organisation of *Frumentarii*. *Zeitschrift für Papyrologie und Epigraphik* 74, 149-150.

Mannoni, T. 1965: Il 'testo' e la sua diffusione nella Liguria di Levante. *Bollettino Liguistico per la Storia e la Cultura Regionale* 17, 49-64.

Mannoni, T. and Messiga, B. 1980: La produzione e la diffusione dei recipienti di pietra ollare nell'alto medioevo. In *Atti del 6 Congresso Internazionale di Studi sull'Alto Medio Evo (Milan 1978)* (Spoleto, Centro Italiano di Studi sull'Alto Medioevo) 501-522.

Mansi, J.D. 1759: *Sacrorum Conciliorum Nova et Amplissima Collectio* 9.

Mara, M. 1964a: *Contributo allo studio della 'Passio Anthimi'* (Rome, Edizioni dell'Ateneo).

Mara, M. 1964b: *I Martiri della via Salaria (Verba seniorum, collana di testi e studi patristici*, N.S. 4) (Rome, Editrice Studium).

Marazzi, F. 1985: Le 'domuscultae' papali della campagna romana: un problema storico, topografico ed archeologico dell'alto medioevo laziale. *Romana Gens (Bollettino del Associazione Archeologica Romana)* 2(3), 13-18.

Marazzi, F., Potter, T.W. and King, A. 1989: Mola di Monte Gelato (Mazzano Romano-VT): notizie preliminari sulle campagne di scavo 1986-1988 e considerazioni sulle origini dell'incastellamento in Etruria meridionale alla luce di nuovi dati archeologici. *Archeologia Medievale* 16, 103-119.

Marchei, M. and Marvasi, L. 1976: Alcuni reperti archeologici nel giardino comunale di Formello (Roma). *Archeologia Classica* 28, 273-279.

Marec, E. 1958: *Monuments chrétiens d'Hippone, ville épiscopale de Saint Augustin* (Paris, Arts et Métiers Graphiques).

Margarini, C. (ed.) 1670: *Bullarum casinese* II (Todi).

Marini, G. 1805: *Papiri diplomatici* (Rome, Propaganda Fide).

Martin, J-M. 1986: Le monete d'argento nell'Italia meridionale del XII sec. secondo i documenti d'archivio. *Bollettino di Numismatica* 6-7, 85-96.

Martindale, J.R. (ed.) 1980: *Prosopography of the Later Roman Empire Vol. II, A.D. 395-527* (Cambridge, Cambridge University Press).

Martinori, E. 1930: *Via Cassia (antica e moderna)* (Rome, SAPE).

Mattingley, H. and Sydenham, E. 1923-: *Roman Imperial coinage* (London, Spink and Sons Ltd.).

Matz, F. 1968a: *Die antiken Sarkophagreliefs IV Die Dionysischen Sarkophage I* (Berlin, Mann).

Matz, F. 1968b: *Die antiken Sarkophagreliefs IV Die Dionysischen Sarkophage II* (Berlin, Mann).

Matz, F. 1969: *Die antiken Sarkophagreliefs IV Die Dionysischen Sarkophage III* (Berlin, Mann).

Matz, F. 1975: *Die antiken Sarkophagreliefs IV Die Dionysischen Sarkophage IV* (Berlin, Mann).

Mazzucato, O. 1972: *La ceramica a vetrina pesante* (Rome, Consiglio Nazionale delle Ricerche).

Mazzucato, O. 1976: *La ceramica laziale dei secoli XI-XIII* (Rome, Consiglio Nazionale delle Ricerche).

McCann, A. 1978: *Roman sarcophagi in the Metropolitan museum of art* (New York, Metropolitan Museum of Art).

McClendon, C.B. 1980: The revival of *opus sectile* pavements in Rome and the vicinity in the Carolingian period. *Papers of the British School at Rome* 48, 157-165.

McClendon, C.B. 1987: *The imperial abbey of Farfa. Architectural currents of the early Middle Ages (Yale Publications in the History of Art*, 36) (New Haven-London, Yale University Press).

McClendon, C.B. and Whitehouse, D.B. 1982: La badia di Farfa, Fara in Sabina (Rieti). Terza nota preliminare. *Archeologia Medievale* 9, 323-330.

McKern, T. and Stewart, T. 1957: Skeletal age changes in young American males, analysed from the standpoint of age identification. *Technical report EP-45. Environment protection research division Quartermaster Research and Development Center, U.S. Army Natick, Mass.*

Meindl, R., Lovejoy, C., Mensforth R. and Walker, R. 1985: A revised method of age determination using the *os pubis*, with a review and tests of accuracy and other current methods of pubic symphyseal ageing. *American Journal of Physical Anthropology* 68, 29-45.

Meischner, J. 1964: *Das Frauenporträt der Severerzeit* (Berlin, Universität Berlin).

Melucco Vaccaro, A. 1974: *Corpus della scultura altomedievale. VII: la diocesi di Roma. Tomo III: la II regione ecclesiastica* (Spoleto, Centro di Studi sull'Alto Medioevo).

Meneghini, R. and Staffa, A.R. 1985: Ceramica a vetrina pesante da nuovi scavi in Roma. *Archeologia Medievale* 12, 643-665.

Mercando, L. 1970: Matelica (Macerata). Rinvenimenti di età gallica e di età medievale. *Notizie degli Scavi ser. VIII* 24, 394-435.

Messineo, G., Petracca, L. and Vigna, L.M. 1984: Fornaci romane in località Ospedaletto Annunziata (Circ. XX). *Bullettino del Commissione Archeologica Comunale di Roma* 89, 192-196.

Meyer, W. 1976: *Il Castel Grande di Bellinzona: rapporto sugli scavi e sull'indagine muraria del 1967* (Olten, Walter-Verlag).

Migne, J.-P. 1844-1888: *Patrologia Latina* (Paris, Migne/ Garnier/ Vrayet).

Mitchell, J. 1985: The painted decoration of the early medieval monastery. In Hodges, R. and Mitchell, J. (eds), *San Vincenzo al Volturno. The archaeology, art and territory of an early medieval monastery* (Oxford, British Archaeological Reports S252) 125-176.

Morel, J.P. 1963: Notes sur la céramique Etrusco-Campanienne. Vases à vernis noir de Sardeigne et d'Arezzo. *Mélanges d'Archéologie et d'Histoire* 75, 1-58.

Morel, J.P. 1965: *Céramique à vernis noir du Forum romain et du Palatin (Mélanges d'Archéologie et d'Histoire, Supplement* 3) (Paris, De Boccard).

Moreland, J. 1985: A monastic workshop and glass production at San Vincenzo al Volturno, Molise, Italy. In Hodges, R. and Mitchell, J. (eds), *San Vincenzo al Volturno. The archaeology, art and territory of an early medieval monastery* (Oxford, British Archaeological Reports S252) 37-60.

Moretti, L. 1968-1979: *Inscriptiones Graecae Urbis Romae* (Rome, Bardi/L'Erma).

Morgan, C.H. 1942: *The Byzantine pottery. Corinth XI* (Cambridge, Mass., Harvard University Press).

Motta, R. and Ungaro, L. 1986: Le diocesi intorno a Roma: il caso di Silva Candida. *Atti del Congresso Nazionale di Archeologia Cristiana (Pesaro-Ancona 1983)* 6 (Florence, Nuova Italia Editrice) 325-336.

Murray-Threipland, L. 1963: Excavations by the north-west gate of Veii, 1957-58: Part II: the pottery. *Papers of the British School at Rome* 31, 33-73.

Murray-Threipland, L. and Torelli, M. 1970: A semi-subterranean Etruscan building in the Casale Pian Roseto (Veii) area. *Papers of the British School at Rome* 38, 62-121.

Nardini, F. 1647: *L'antico Veio* (Rome).

Neuru, L. 1980: Late Roman pottery: a fifth century deposit from Carthage. *Antiquités Africaines* 16, 195-211.

Nibby, A. 1837: *Analisi storico-topografico-antiquaria della carta de'dintorni di Roma*, I (Rome, Tip. Belle Arti).

Niermeyer, J.F. 1976: *Mediae latinitatis lexicon minus* (Leiden, Brill).

Nilgen, U. 1974: Die grosse Reliquieninschrift von S. Prassede: eine quellenkritische Untersuchung zur Zeno-Kapelle. *Römische Quartalinscrift* 69, 7-29.

Nordberg, H. 1963: Éléments paiens dans les tituli chrétiens de Rome. In Zilliacus, H. (ed.), *Acta Instituti Romani Finlandiae* 1.2: *Sylloge Inscriptionum Christianorum Veterorum Musei Vaticani* (Helsinki, Helsingfors) 211-219.

Noyé, G. (ed.) 1988: *Structures de l'habitat et occupation du sol dans les pays Méditerranéens: les méthodes et l'apport de l'archéologie extensive* (Collection de l'École Française de Rome 105 – Publications de la Casa de Velázquez, serie archeologie fasc. IX) (Rome/Madrid, L'École Française de Rome/Casa de Velázquez).

Oliver-Smith, P. and Widrig, W. 1981: Roma. Loc. Tor Bella Monaca. Villa rustica romana. Relazione sulle campagne di scavo 1976 e 1977 nell'agro romano. *Notizie degli Scavi di Antichità serie 8*, 35, 99-114.

Osborne, J. 1983: The tomb of Alfanus in S. Maria in Cosmedin, Rome, and its place in the tradition of Roman funerary monuments. *Papers of the British School at Rome* 51, 240-247.

Oswald, F. and Price, T.D. 1920: *Terra sigillata* (London, Longmans, Green and Co.).

Oxe, A. and Comfort, H. 1968: *Corpus Vasorum Arretinorum* III (Bonn, R. Habelt Verlag).

Paci, G. 1978: Senatori e cavalieri nelle iscrizioni di Forum Clodii. In Gasperini, L. (ed.), *Scritti storico-epigrafici in memoria di Marcello Zambelli* (Rome, Centro Editoriale Internazionale) 261-314.

Palumbo, P. 1942: *Lo schisma del MCXXX* (*Miscellanea della Reale Deputazione Romana di Storia Patria*) (Rome, Reale Deputazione Romana di Storia Patria).

Panazza, G. and Tagliaferri, A. 1966: *Corpus della scultura altomedievale. III: la diocesi di Brescia* (Spoleto, Centro Italiano di Studi sull'Alto Medioevo).

Panciera, S. 1968: Due novità epigrafiche Romane. *Atti dell'Accademia Nazionale dei Lincei (Rendiconti)* 23, 315-340 + plates.

Panciera, S. 1975-1976: Un frammento degli Acta Arvalium ed altre novità epigrafiche romane. *Rendiconti della Pontificia Accademia di Archeologia a Roma* 48, 279-308.

Pani Ermini, L. 1974: *Corpus della scultura altomedievale. VII: la diocesi di Roma. Tomo I: la IV regione ecclesiastica* (Spoleto, Centro Italiano di Studi sull'Alto Medioevo).

Paoletti, M. 1987: Nuovi dati sul territorio pisano e sull'acroma con bolli a crudo: a proposito della mostra 'Terre e paduli: reperti documenti e immagini per la storia di Coltano' (Pisa, gennaio 1986). *Archeologia Medievale* 14, 467-478.

Paribeni, R. 1932: *Le terme di Diocleziano ed il Museo Nazionale Romano* (Rome, Poligrafico dello Stato).

Parlasca, K. 1969: In Helbig, W. *Führer durch die öffentlichen Sammlungen klassischer Altertümer in Rom* (fourth edition) (Tübingen, E. Wasmuth).

Paroli, L. 1985: Reperti residui di età medievale. In

Manacorda, D. (ed.), *Archeologia urbana a Roma: il progetto della Crypta Balbi. 3. Il giardino del Conservatorio di S. Caterina della Rosa* (Florence, All'Insegna del Giglio) 173-244.

Paroli, L. 1986a: Ceramica a vetrina pesante e a macchia. In Manacorda, D., Paroli, L., Molinari, A., Ricci, M. and Romei, D. La ceramica medioevale di Roma nella stratigrafia della Crypta Balbi, 516-520. In *La ceramica medievale nel Mediterraneo occidentale* (Florence, All'Insegna del Giglio) 511-544.

Paroli, L. 1986b: In Bonifay, M., Paroli, L. and Picon, M. Ceramiche a vetrina pesante scoperte a Roma e a Marsiglia: risultati delle prime analisi fisico-chimiche, 79-85, 91-92. *Archeologia Medievale* 13, 79-96.

Paroli, L. 1990: Ceramica a vetrina pesante altomedievale (Forum Ware) e medievale (Sparse Glazed). Altre invetriate tardo-antiche e altomedievali. In Saguì, L. and Paroli, L. (eds), *Archeologia urbana a Roma: il progetto della Crypta Balbi 5: l'esedra della Crypta Balbi nel medioevo sec. XI-XV ** (Florence, All'Insegna del Giglio) 314-356.

Paroli, L. forthcoming a: In Cipriano, M.T., Paroli, L., Patterson, H.L., Saguì, L. and Whitehouse, D. La documentazione ceramica dell'Italia centromeridionale nell'alto medioevo: quadri regionale e contesti campione. In *IV Congresso de ceramica medieval do Mediterraneo occidental. Lisbon, 16-22 November 1987*.

Paroli, L. (ed.) forthcoming b: *La ceramica invetriata tardo antica e altomedievale – Italia* (Atti del seminario di studio (Siena-Pontignano 23-24 febbraio 1990)).

Partner, P. 1966: Notes on the lands of the Roman church in the early Middle Ages. *Papers of the British School at Rome* 34, 68-78.

Partner, P. 1972: *The lands of St Peter* (London, Methuen).

Pasoli, A. 1950: *Acta Fratrum Arvalium quae post annum MDCCCLXXIV reperta sunt* (*Studi e ricerche* 7) (Bologna, C. Zuffi).

Patterson, H. 1985: The late Roman and early medieval pottery from Molise. In Hodges, R. and Mitchell, J. (eds), *San Vincenzo al Volturno. The archaeology, art and territory of an early medieval monastery* (Oxford, British Archaeological Reports S252) 83-110.

Patterson, H. 1989: *The later Roman and early medieval to medieval pottery from San Vincenzo al Volturno, Molise: production and distribution in central and southern Italy, AD 400-1100* (Sheffield, unpublished Ph.D. thesis).

Patterson, H. forthcoming a: The medieval pottery. In Blagg, T., Luttrell, A., van der Noort, R. and Whitehouse, D. (eds), *The excavations at Le Mura di Santo Stefano, near Anguillara, Sabazia*.

Patterson, H. forthcoming b: The Forum Ware and sparse glazed ware from sites in the Roman campagna. In Paroli, L. (ed.), *La ceramica invetriata tardo antica e altomedievale – Italia* (Atti del seminario di studio (Siena-Pontignano 23-24 febbraio 1990)).

Patterson, H. forthcoming c: The *ceramica a vetrina pesante* from the excavations of Otranto, Puglia. In Paroli, L. (ed.), *La ceramica invetriata tardo antico e alto medievale* (Atti del seminario di studio (Siena-Pontignano 23-24 febbraio 1990)).

Patterson, H. and Whitehouse, D. forthcoming a: The medieval pottery from Otranto. In Michaelides, D. and Wilkinson, D. (eds), *Otranto: the excavations of the British School at Rome, 1978-79*.

Patterson, H. and Whitehouse, D. forthcoming b: Otranto. In Cipriano, M.T., Paroli, L., Patterson, H., Saguì, L. and Whitehouse, D. La documentazione ceramica dell'Italia centromeridionale nell'alto medioevo: quadri regionale e contesti campione. In *IV congresso de ceramica medieval do Mediterraneo occidental. Lisbon, 16-22 November 1987.*

Pauly, A. 1893-: *Real-Encyclopadie der classischen Altertumswissenschaft,* edited by G. Wissowa (Stuttgart, Metzlersche).

Pavolini, C. 1986: L'edilizia commerciale e l'edilizia abitativa nel contesto di Ostia tardoantica. In Giardina, A. (ed.), *Società romana e impero tardoantico II- Roma: politica, economia, paesaggio urbano* (Bari, Editori Laterza) 239-297, 460-474.

Peacock, D.P.S. 1977: *Pottery and early commerce* (London, Academic Press).

Peacock, D.P.S. 1982: *Pottery in the Roman world: an ethnoarchaeological approach* (London, Longman).

Peacock, D.P.S. 1984: The amphorae: typology and chronology. In Fulford, M.G. and Peacock, D.P.S. *Excavations at Carthage: the British mission. I. The Avenue du Président Habib Bourquiba, Salammbo. 2. The pottery and other ceramic objects from the site* (Sheffield, Department of Prehistory and Archaeology) 116-140.

Pearse, L. 1975: A forgotten altar of the *collegium fabrum tignariorum* of Rome. *Epigraphica* 37 (1-2), 100-123.

Pensabene, P. 1972: *Scavi di Ostia VII: I capitelli* (Rome, Poligrafico e Zecca dello Stato).

Pensabene, P. 1989: Reimpiego dei marmi antichi nelle chiese altomedievale a Roma. In Borghini, G. (ed.), *Marmi antichi* (Rome, De Luca) 55-64.

Perkins, P. forthcoming: The Roman pottery. In Blagg, T., Luttrell, A., van der Noort, R. and Whitehouse, D. (eds), *The excavations at Le Mura di Santo Stefano, near Anguillara, Sabazia.*

Perlzweig, J. 1961: *The Athenian Agora, VII* (Princeton, American School of Classical Studies).

Pesce, G. 1957: *Sarcofagi romani di Sardegna* (Rome, L'Erma di Bretschneider).

Petracca, L. and Vigna, L.M. 1985: Via Veientana – Località Ospedaletto Annunziata (Circ. XX). *Bullettino della Commissione Archeologica Comunale di Roma* 90 (1), 175-177.

Pfeiffer, G.J., Van Buren, A.W. and Armstrong, H.H. 1905: Stamps on bricks and tiles from the Aurelian wall at Rome. *Supplementary Papers of the American School of Classical Studies in Rome* 1, 1-86.

Pierpaoli, M. 1986: *Storia di Ravenna* (Ravenna, Longo Editore).

Poey d'Avant, F. 1862: *Monnaies feodales de France, III* (Paris, Bureau de la Revue Numismatique Française).

Potter, T.W. 1972: Excavations in the medieval centre of Mazzano Romano. *Papers of the British School at Rome* 40, 135-145.

Potter, T.W. 1979a: *The changing landscape of south Etruria* (London, Paul Elek).

Potter, T.W. 1979b: Population hiatus and continuity: the case of the south Etruria survey. In Blake, H., Potter, T.W. and Whitehouse, D.B. (eds), *Papers in Italian archaeology I: the Lancaster conference* (Oxford, British Archaeological Reports S41) 99-116.

Potter, T.W. and Dunbabin, K.M. 1979: A Roman villa at Crocicchie, Via Clodia. *Papers of the British School at Rome* 47, 19-26.

Potter, T.W. and King, A. 1988: Scavi a Mola di Monte Gelato presso Mazzano Romano, Etruria meridionale. Primo rapporto preliminare. *Archeologia Medievale* 15, 253-311.

Prosopographia Imperii Romani 1897-1898 (Berlin, George Reimer) (second edition 1953- (Berlin, De Gruyter)).

Provoost, A. 1970: Les lampes à recipient allonge trouvées dans les catacombes romaines. Essai de classification typologique. *Bulletin de l'Institut Historique Belge de Rome* 41, 17-56.

Ramieri, A.M. (ed.) 1983: *Corpus della scultura altomedievale. II: la diocesi di Ferentino* (Spoleto, Centro Italiano di Studi sull'Alto Medioevo).

Rasmussen, T. 1979: *Bucchero pottery from southern Etruria (Cambridge Classical Studies)* (Cambridge, Cambridge University Press).

Raspi Serra, J. 1972: *La Tuscia romana* (Rome, Banco di Santo Spirito/ERI, Edizioni RAI).

Raspi Serra, J. 1974: *Corpus della scultura altomedievale. VIII: le diocesi dell'alto Lazio* (Spoleto, Centro Italiano di Studi sull'Alto Medioevo).

Rathje, W.L. 1975: The last tango in Mayapan: a tentative trajectory or production-distribution systems. In Sabloff, J.A. and Lamberg-Karlovsky, C.C. (eds), *Ancient Civilization and Trade* (Albuquerque, University of New Mexico Press) 409-448.

Reece, R. 1982: A collection of coins from the centre of Rome. *Papers of the British School at Rome* 50, 116-145.

Reekmans, L. 1964: *La tombe du Pape Corneille et sa région cemeteriale* (Vatican City, Pontificio Istituto di Archeologia Cristiana).

Respighi, A. 1956: *Galeria* (Rome, Istituto di Studi Romani).

Reynolds, J. 1962: Q. Cerellius Apollinaris, Praefectus Vigilum in AD 212. *Papers of the British School at Rome* 30, 31-32.

Reynolds, J. 1969: A new fragment of the Arval Acta. *Papers of the British School at Rome* 37, 158-160.

Ricci, M. 1986: La ceramica da fuoco. In Manacorda, D., Paroli, L., Molinari, A., Ricci, M. and Romei, D. La ceramica medioevale di Roma nella stratigrafia della Crypta Balbi, 516-520. In *La ceramica medievale nel Mediterraneo occidentale* (Florence, All'Insegna del Giglio) 511-544.

Rodwell, W. 1976: The archaeological investigation of Hadstock church, Essex: an interim report. *The Antiquaries Journal* 56 (i), 55-74.

Romei, D. 1986: Ceramica acroma depurata. In Manacorda, D., Paroli, L., Molinari, A., Ricci, M. and Romei, D. La ceramica medioevale di Roma nella stratigrafia della Crypta Balbi, 523-529. In *La ceramica medievale nel Mediterraneo occidentale* (Florence, All'Insegna del Giglio) 511-544.

Rossi, P. 1986: *Civita Castellana e le chiese medioevali del suo territorio (Collana di Studi di Storia dell'Arte, VII)* (Rome, Edizioni Rari Nantes).

Sacchi Lodispoto, G. 1987: Le cattedrali della diocesi suburbicaria di Porto e S. Rufina. *Lunario Romano* 17, 47-63.

Saguì, L. and Paroli, L. (eds) 1990: *Archeologia urbana a Roma: il progetto della Crypta Balbi 5: l'esedra della Crypta Balbi nel medioevo sec. XI-XV ** (Florence, All'Insegna del Giglio).

Salmi, M. 1961: *Chiese romaniche della Toscana* (Milan, Electa).

Santifaller, L. 1940: Saggio di un elenco dei funzionari, impiegati e scrittori della Cancelleria Pontificia dall'inizio all'anno 1099. *Bullettino dell'Istituto Storico Italiano per il Medio Evo* 56.

Scerrato, U. 1983: Arte Islamica in Italia. In *Arte Islamica in Italia: i bacini delle chiese pisane (Roma, Palazzo Brancaccio)* (Pisa, Pacini Editore) 7-14.

Scheid, J. 1981: Un nouveau fragment des actes des arvales de l'année 186/7. *Zeitschrift für Papyrologie und Epigraphik* 43, 343-352.

Scheid, J. 1990: *Le collège des frères arvales* (Rome, L'Erma di Bretschneider).

Scheid, J. and Broise, H. 1980: Deux nouveaux fragments des actes des frères arvales de l'année 38 ap. J.C. *Mélanges de l'École Française de Rome. Antiquité* 92 (1), 215-248.

Schiaparelli, L. (ed.) 1901: Le carte antiche dell'archivio capitolare di S. Pietro in Vaticano. *Archivio della Reale Società Romana di Storia Patria* 24, 393-496.

Schiaparelli, L. (ed.) 1902: Le carte antiche dell'archivio capitolare di S. Pietro in Vaticano. *Archivio della Reale Società Romana di Storia Patria* 25, 273-354.

Schneider, F. 1924: *Die Entstehung von Burg und Landgemeinde in Italien* (Berlin, Rothschild).

Schuring, J.M. 1986: The Roman, early medieval and medieval coarse kitchen wares from the San Sisto Vecchio in Rome; continuity and break in tradition. *BABesch* 61, 158-207.

Schuring, J.M. 1987: Supplementary note to 'The Roman, early medieval and medieval coarse kitchen wares from the San Sisto Vecchio in Rome': the distribution of the fabrics. *BABesch* 62, 109-129.

Sefton, D.S. 1980: *The pontificate of Hadrian I (772-795): papal theory and political reality in the reign of Charlemagne* (Michigan State University Ph.D. thesis, 1975) (Michigan, University Microfilms International).

Serafini, A. 1927: *Torri campanarie di Roma e del Lazio nel medioevo* (Rome, Società Romana di Storia Patria).

Settia, A. and Comba, R. (eds) 1984: *Castelli: storia e archeologia* (Turin, Archeologia Medievale/Comune di Cuneo/Regione Piemonte).

Sichtermann, H. 1966: *Späte Endymion Sarkophage. Methodisches zur Interpretation (Deutsche Beitrage zur Altertumswissenschaft* 19) (Baden-Baden, Bruno Grimm).

Sichtermann, H. and Koch, G. 1975: *Griechische Mythen auf römischen Sarkophage* (Tübingen, E. Wasmuth).

Skelton, J. 1988: *Papyrologia florentina, XVII. Greek ostraka in the Ashmolean Museum* (Oxford, Oxford University Press).

Sommella Mura, A. (ed.) 1969: *Repertorio degli scavi e delle scoperte archeologiche nell'Etruria meridionale I 1939-1965* (Rome, Centro Nazionale delle Ricerche).

Sparkes, B.A. 1962: The Greek kitchen. *Journal of Hellenistic Studies* 82, 121-137.

Spartà, S. 1983: *I campanili di Roma* (Rome, Newton Compton).

Spufford, P. 1986: *Handbook of medieval exchange (Royal Historical Society Guides and Handbooks,* 13) (London, Royal Historical Society).

Steinby, M. 1973: I bolli laterizi. In Pelliccioni, G. *Le nuove scoperte sulle origini del Battistero Lateranense (Memorie della Pontificia Accademia Romana di Archeologia* 12 (1)) 115-225.

Steinby, M. 1973-1974: Le tegole antiche di S. Maria Maggiore. *Rendiconti del Pontificia Accademia di Archeologia* 46, 101-133.

Steinby, M. 1974: I bolli laterizi e i criteri tecnici nella datazione delle cortine laterizie romane. *Miscellanea Arqueologica* 2, 389-405.

Steinby, M. 1977: La cronologia delle figline doliari urbane dalla fine dell'età repubblicana fino all'inizio del III secolo. *Bullettino della Commissione Archeologica Comunale di Roma* 84, 7-132.

Steinby 1977-1978: Lateres Signati Ostienses, I-II. *Acta Instituti Romani Finlandiae* 7 (1-2).

Steinby, M. 1978: Ziegelstempel von Rom und Umgebung. *Real Encyclopadie, Suppl. XV*, coll. 1489-1531.

Steinby, M. 1981a: La diffusione dell'opus doliare urbano. In Giardina, A. and Schiavone, A. (eds), *Merci, mercati e scambi nel Mediterraneo (Società romana e produzione schiavistica* II) (Bari, Editori Laterza) 237-245.

Steinby, M. 1981b: I bolli laterizi dell'area sacra di Largo Argentina. In Coarelli, F., Kajanto, I., Nyberg, U. and Steinby, M. *L'area sacra di Largo Argentina I* (Rome, Comune di Roma) 298-332.

Steinby, M. 1986: L'industria laterizia di Roma nel tardo Impero. In Giardina, A. (ed.), *Roma: politica economia paesaggio urbano (Società romana e impero tardo-antico* II) (Bari, Editori Laterza) 99-164, 438-446.

Steinby, M. 1987: Indici complementari ai bolli doliari urbani (CIL XV, 1). *Acta Instituti Romani Finlandiae* 11.

Stone, M. 1984: I laterizi. In Cameron, F., Clark, G., Jackson, R.P.J., Johns, C.M., Philpot, S., Potter, T.W., Shepherd, J.D., Stone, M.J. and Whitehouse, D.B. Il castello di Ponte Nepesino e il confine settentrionale del Ducato di Roma, 108-121. *Archeologia Medievale* 11, 63-147.

Stoppioni, M.L. 1984: Ariminum, area Rastelli Standa, 1961. Materiali III. In Delbianco, P. (ed.), *Culture figurative e materiali tra Emilia e Marche. Studi in memoria di Mario Zuffa* (Rimini, Maggioli) 351-378.

Strong, D.E. 1953: Late Hadrianic architectural ornament in Rome. *Papers of the British School at Rome* 21, 118-151.

Strong, D.E. and Ward-Perkins, J.B. 1962: The temple of Castor in the Roman Forum. *Papers of the British School at Rome* 30, 1-30.

Stuveras, H. 1969: *Le putto dans l'art romain (Collection Latomus* 99) (Brussels, Universa).

Tatton-Brown, A. 1984: The glass. In Hurst, H.R. and Roskams, S. *Excavations at Carthage: the British mission. I. The Avenue du Président Habib Bourguiba, Salammbo. 1. The site and finds other than pottery* (Sheffield, Department of Prehistory and Archaeology) 194-212.

Taylor, D.M. 1975: *Cosa. Black glaze pottery (Memoirs of the American Academy in Rome* 25) (Rome, American Academy).

Testini, P. 1975: *Ricerche archeologiche all'Isola Sacra* (Rome, Istituto Nazionale di Archeologia e Storia d'Arte).

Thesaurus Linguae Latinae 1900- (Lepizig, Teubner).

Thomas, C. 1971: *The early Christian archaeology of north Britain* (Oxford, Oxford University Press).

Thomas, C. 1981: *Christianity in Roman Britain to A.D. 500* (London, Batsford).

Thurston, H. and Attwater, D. (eds) 1956: *Butler's lives of the saints* (London) (reprinted 1981).

Tomassetti, G. 1882: Della Campagna romana nel medio evo: Via Cassia e Via Clodia. *Archivio della Reale Società Romana di Storia Patria* 5, 67-156.

Tomassetti, G. 1913: *La Campagna romana. Antica, medioevale e moderna. III. Via Cassia e Clodia, Flaminia e Tiberina, Labicana e Praenestina* (Rome, E. Loescher) (new edition edited by L. Chiumenti and F. Bilancia (Florence, Olschki), 1979).

Tosti-Croce, M.R. (ed.) 1985: *La Sabina medievale* (Milan, Amilcare Pizzi Editore).

Toubert, P. 1973a: *Les structures du Latium médiéval (Bibliothèque de l'École Française d'Athènes et de Rome* 221) (Rome, L'École Française de Rome).

Toubert, P. 1973b: Une des premières vérifications de la loi de Gresham: la circolazione monetaire dans l'état pontifical vers 1200. *Revue Numismatique* 6s, 15, 180-189.

Toynbee, J.M.C. and Ward Perkins, J.B. 1956: *The shrine of Saint Peter and the Vatican excavations* (London, Longmans).

Travaini, L. 1980: *Grottaferrata (Roma) 1951 (Ripostigli monetali in Italia – Schede anagrafiche)* (Milan).

Travaini, L. 1981: La riforma monetaria di Ruggero II e la circolazione minuta in Italia meridionale tra X e XI secolo. *Rivista Italiana Numismatica* 83, 133-153.

Travaini, L. 1988: Mint organisation in Italy between XII and XIV centuries: a survey. In Mayhew, N. and Spufford, P. (eds), *Later medieval mints: organisation, administration and techniques (8th Oxford symposium on coin and monetary history)* (Oxford, British Archaeological Reports S389) 39-60.

Travaini, L. forthcoming: La moneta milanese tra X e XII secolo. *XI Congresso Internazionale di Studi sull'Alto Medioevo* (Spoleto, Centro Italiano di Studi sull'Alto Medioevo).

Trifone, B. 1908: Le carte del monastero di San Paolo di Roma dal secolo XI al XV. *Archivio della Reale Società Romana di Storia Patria* 31, 267-313.

Trinci Cecchelli, M. 1976: *Corpus della scultura altomedievale. VII: la diocesi di Roma. Tomo IV: la I regione ecclesiastica* (Spoleto, Centro Italiano di Studi sull'Alto Medioevo).

Turcan, R. 1958: Dionysus Dimorphos. Une illustration de la théologie de Bacchus dans l'art funeraire. *Mélanges d'Archéologie et d'Histoire* 70, 243-293.

Turcan, R. 1966: *Les sarcophages romains à representations Dionysiaques (Bibliothèque de l'École Française d'Athénes et de Rome 210)* (Paris, De Boccard).

Tusa, V. 1957: *I sarcofagi romani in Sicilia* (Palermo, Accademia dei Scienze, Lettere e Arti).

Ubelaker, D. 1978: *Human skeletal remains* (Washington, Taraxacum).

Ugolini, P. 1957: *Un paese della campagna romana, Formello. Storia ed economia agraria* (Rome, Baldazzi).

Ullmann, W. 1972: *A short history of the papacy in the Middle Ages* (London, Methuen).

Valentini, R. and Zucchetti, G. 1942: *Codice topografico della città di Roma*, II (*Fonti per la storia d'Italia* 88) (Rome, Istituto Storico Italiano).

Valentini, R. and Zucchetti, G. 1946: *Codice topografico della città di Roma*, III (*Fonti per la storia d'Italia* 90) (Rome, Istituto Storico Italiano).

Valenziani, R.S. and Volpe, R. 1980: Tentativo di ricostruzione di una sistemazione agricola di età repubblicana nei dintorni di Roma. *Archeologia Classica* 32, 206-215.

Van der Werff, J. 1978: Amphores de tradition punique à Uzita. *BABesch* 52-53, 171-200.

Vannini, G. 1974: Stratigrafia e reperti ceramici dal 'Castrum' di Ascianello. *Archeologia Medievale* 1, 91-110.

Vasina, A. 1978: Aspetti e problemi di storia plebana nelle Marche. In *Le pievi nelle Marche (Fonti e Studi* 4) (Fano, Edizioni 'Studia Picena') 11-60.

Vermaseren, M. and Van Essen, C. 1965: *The excavation in the Mithraeum of the church of Santa Prisca in Rome* (Leiden, E.J. Brill).

Verrando, G. 1981: Note di topografia martiriale della via Aurelia. *Rivista di Archeologia Cristiana* 57, 255-282.

Verrando, G. and Liberio, F. 1981: Osservazioni e rettifiche di carattere storico-agiografico. *Rivista di Storia della Chiesa in Italia* 35, 91-125.

Verzone, P. 1945: *L'arte preromanica in Liguria* (Turin, A. Viglongo and Co.).

Violante, C. 1977: Pievi e parrocchie nell'Italia centro-settentrionale durante i secoli XI e XII. In *Atti della sesta settimana internazionale di studio. Le istituzioni ecclesiastiche della 'societas christiana' nei secoli XI e XII. Diocesi, pievi e parrocchie* (Milan, Università Cattolica del S. Cuore/Vita e Pensiero) 643-799.

Von Falkenhausen, V. 1986: La circolazione monetaria nell'Italia meridionale e nella Sicilia in epoca normanna secondo la documentazione d'archivio. *Bollettino di Numismatica* 6-7, 53-79.

Von Hessen, O. 1978: *Il cimitero altomedievale di Pettinara, Casale Lozzi (Nocera Umbra)* (Florence, La Nuova Italia).

Ward-Perkins, B. 1981: Two Byzantine houses at Luni. *Papers of the British School at Rome* 49, 91-98.

Ward-Perkins, B. 1983: La città altomedievale. *Archeologia Medievale* 10, 111-124.

Ward-Perkins, B. 1984: *From classical antiquity to the Middle Ages. Urban public building in northern and central Italy, A.D. 300-850* (Oxford, Oxford University Press).

Ward-Perkins, J.B. 1962: Etruscan towns, Roman roads and medieval villages: the historical geography of southern Etruria. *Geographical Journal* 128, 389-405.

Ward-Perkins, J.B. 1963: Contribution to: The British Schools Abroad, 1962. *Antiquity* 37, 37-39.

Ward-Perkins, J.B. 1964: Contribution to: British Archaeology Abroad, 1963. *Antiquity* 38, 8-9.

Ward-Perkins, J.B. 1965: Contribution to: The British Schools Abroad, 1964. *Antiquity* 39, 35-36.

Ward-Perkins, J.B. 1966: Contribution to: The British Schools Abroad, 1965. *Antiquity* 40, 89-90.

Ward-Perkins, J.B. 1968: Contribution to: The British Schools Abroad, 1967. *Antiquity* 42, 89-91.

Ward-Perkins, J.B. 1972: Central authority and patterns of rural settlement. In Ucko, P.J., Tringham, R. and Dimbleby, G.W. (eds), *Man, settlement and urbanism* (London, Duckworth) 867-882.

Wegner, M. 1939: *Die Herrscherbildnisse in antoninischer Zeit.* (Berlin, Mann).

White, K.D. 1970: *Roman farming* (London, Thames and Hudson).

Whitehouse, D.B. 1965: Forum Ware: a distinctive type of early medieval glazed ware from the Roman Campagna. *Medieval Archaeology* 9, 55-63.

Whitehouse, D.B. 1978: The medieval pottery of Rome. In Blake, H., Potter, T.W. and Whitehouse, D.B. (eds), *Papers in Italian archaeology I. The Lancaster conference* (Oxford, British Archaeological Reports S41) 475-493.

Whitehouse, D.B. 1980a: The medieval pottery from S. Cornelia. *Papers of the British School at Rome* 48, 125-156.

Whitehouse, D.B. 1980b: Forum Ware again. *Medieval Ceramics* 4, 13-16.

Whitehouse, D.B. 1981: Nuovi elementi per la datazione della ceramica a vetrina pesante. *Archeologia Medievale* 8, 583-587.

Whitehouse, D.B. 1982: Medieval pottery from South Etruria. In Andrews, D., Osborne, J. and Whitehouse, D.B. *Medieval Lazio. Papers in Italian archaeology III* (Oxford, British Archaeological Reports S125) 299-344.

Whitehouse, D.B. 1985: Farfa Abbey: the eighth and ninth centuries. *Arte Medievale* 2, 245-256.

Whitehouse, D.B., Barker, G., Reece, R. and Reese, D. 1982: The Schola Praeconum I. *Papers of the British School at Rome* 50, 53-101.

Whitehouse, D.B., Costantini, L., Guidobaldi, F., Passi, S., Pensabene, P., Pratt, S., Reece, R. and Reese, D. 1985: The Schola Praeconum II. *Papers of the British School at Rome* 53, 163-210.

Wickham, C.J. 1978a: Historical and topographical notes on medieval South Etruria (Part i). *Papers of the British School at Rome* 46, 132-179.

Wickham, C.J. 1978b: Historical aspects of medieval South Etruria. In Blake, H., Potter, T.W. and Whitehouse, D.B. (eds), *Papers in Italian archaeology I. The Lancaster conference* (Oxford, British Archaeological Reports S41) 373-390.

Wickham, C.J. 1979: Historical and topographical notes on early medieval South Etruria (Part ii). *Papers of the British School at Rome* 47, 66-95.

Wickham, C.J. 1985: *Il problema dell'incastellamento nell'Italia centrale. L'esempio di San Vincenzo al Volturno* (Florence, All'Insegna del Giglio).

Wickham, C.J. 1988a: L'incastellamento ed i suoi destini undici anni dopo il *Latium* di P. Toubert. In Noyé, G. (ed.), *Castrum II. Structures de l'habitat et occupation du sol dans les pays Méditerranéens: les méthodes et l'apport de l'archéologie extensive* (*Collection de l'École Française de Rome* 105 – *Publications de la Casa de Velázquez, serie archeologie* fasc. IX) (Rome/Madrid, L'École Française de Rome/Casa de Velázquez) 411-420.

Wickham, C.J. 1988b: L'Italia e l'alto medioevo. *Archeologia Medievale* 15, 105-124.

Widrig, W. 1980: Two sites on the ancient Via Gabina. In Painter, K. (ed.), *Roman villas in Italy: recent excavations and research* (*British Museum Occasional Paper* 24) 119-140.

Wilpert, G. 1936: *I sarcofagi cristiani antichi* (Rome PADA).

Wilson-Jones, M. 1989: Designing the Roman Corinthian order. *Journal of Roman Archaeology* 2, 35-69.

Wroth, W. 1908: *Imperial Byzantine coins in the British Museum*, II (London, British Museum).

Yegul, F.K. 1986: *Sardis 3: the bath-gymnasium complex at Sardis* (Cambridge, Mass., Harvard University Press).

Young, C. 1979: The processing of Roman tile. In McWhirr, A. *Roman brick and tile. Studies in manufacture, distribution and use in the western empire* (Oxford, British Archaeological Reports S68) 401-403.

Zimmermann, H. 1969: *Regesta Imperii II, Sachsische Zeit. Papstregestern 911-1024* (Vienna, Hermann Bohlaus).

INDEX